Living Signs of Law

Volume 1

Series Editors

Anne Wagner, Lille University, Lille, France

Sarah Marusek, University of Hawai'i Hilo, Hilo, USA

The series *Living Signs of Law* aims to delve into the diverse and innovative work within the field of law, specifically focusing on areas such as legal semiotics, hermeneutics, pragmatism, deconstructionism, interpretation, and history. It recognizes law as a complex system of signs that is constantly evolving and can have varying orientations, sometimes working independently and at other times conflicting with one another. *Living Signs of Law* seeks to explore how different perspectives on legal truth and legal culture can emerge within this dynamic and tension-filled system.

The concept of law as "living signs" highlights its capacity to adapt to social changes while also creating alternative trajectories or means of change for more contemporary visions. However, certain lines of resistance may arise, hindering the process of change and resulting in inertia or slow transformation. These tensions within the system of legal signs reflect its non-homogeneous nature, influenced by internal and external forces that shape and divide it. The series aims to examine these forces and adjustment variables, providing a realistic and semiotically grounded understanding of the reality expressed through laws, statutes, decisions, and other legal activities.

By exploring various trajectories and analyzing their relationships, the series seeks to reveal lines of evolutionary resistance or transformation within the field of law. It welcomes proposals that focus on semiotics or related theories and models of analysis, as well as topics such as rhetoric, political and legal discourse history, philosophy, pragmatics, sociolinguistics, deconstruction, and other types of semiotic analyses. *Living Signs of Law* aims to shed light on the dynamic nature of law and its diverse manifestations, providing a comprehensive exploration of legal signs, justice, hermeneutics, pragmatism, deconstructionism, interpretation, and history within the field of law, as well as examining the role of communication and representation in these processes.

Stephen Dersley

Thought Collectives and Cultural Change

Applying Ludwik Fleck's Theory of Thought Collectives to the Study of Cultural Transformations

Springer

Stephen Dersley
Adam Mickiewicz University in Poznań
Poznań, Poland

ISSN 2948-2410 ISSN 2948-2429 (electronic)
Living Signs of Law
ISBN 978-3-031-97430-4 ISBN 978-3-031-97431-1 (eBook)
https://doi.org/10.1007/978-3-031-97431-1

This Springer imprint is published by the registered company Springer Nature Switzerland AG
The registered company address is: Gewerbestrasse 11, 6330 Cham, Switzerland

For Aneta, Ezra, Nathan, and my parents

Preface

To begin, let me put my cards on the table: this book was shaped by a long-standing preoccupation with Kant, whose thought has remained a source of both stimulation and obsession—and no small degree of frustration—for over three decades. His ideas have lingered in the back of my mind since the early 1990s, surfacing again and again in unexpected ways. I have often told myself I am finished with Kant, only to find myself drawn back in once more. Rather than offer a sustained reading of the *Critiques*—a task still beyond me—here I approach Kant from the edges, primarily through *The Conflict of the Faculties*, in an effort to trace the specific institutional and social factors that shaped his thought. This sheds light on how his abstract, universal epistemology was deeply bound up with questions of status, authority, and the control of cultural production.

I first encountered Ludwik Fleck's texts in 2007, and they have fascinated me ever since. Fleck's writing has a peculiar quality: it provokes thought in ways that are difficult to articulate. His concepts have helped me peel back layers of culture, uncovering perspectives I would never have reached on my own. Yet each time I return to his texts, I feel as though I have only scratched the surface. Paradoxically, his works are neither dazzling nor particularly well written, yet they possess an undeniable brilliance.

For a long time, I read Fleck without consulting scholarly interpretations. This had its advantages: I internalized his ideas on my own terms, grappling directly with his texts. However, when I eventually began writing about Fleck in an academic context, I often discovered that my hard-won interpretations were not as original as I had imagined—a humbling experience that persists to this day. Over time, I realized that striving for an original interpretation of Fleck's work is far less interesting than truly embracing his method: applying his concepts to the world and seeing what they uncover.

This book, therefore, is an experiment undertaken in the spirit of Fleck. It applies his ideas to the study of culture, for I am no natural scientist. Writing about Fleck also obliges me to give some indication of the influences that have shaped my own thought style. When I studied philosophy in the early 1990s, I was drawn to the edges—to poets and novelists I regarded as profound thinkers, such as Blake and

Joyce. At different points, I found myself absorbed in philosophers who engaged literature in distinct ways, including Derrida, Nietzsche, and Deleuze and Guattari. As my interests evolved, I turned increasingly to history, and then to Darwin, Dawkins, and Pinker, which gradually led me toward the scientific method and figures such as Descartes, Bacon, Galileo, and Copernicus. At one point, I tried to explain these shifting preoccupations to Professor Andrzej Klawiter at Adam Mickiewicz University in Poznań, who recognized my underlying concern with the social context of thought. He invited me to join his seminar and suggested I explore the work of Ludwik Fleck. I began writing, but life—as it often does—got in the way.

In 2015, I had the privilege of meeting Professor Przemysław Rotengruber, whose encouragement led me to begin writing a PhD thesis within the Faculty of Anthropology and Cultural Studies at AMU. Throughout the process, I attended seminars in the Faculty of Philosophy and greatly benefited from feedback, but it was Professor Karolina Cern whose support proved genuinely invaluable. The initial version of this book was written between 2017 and 2023 and defended as a doctoral thesis in December 2023. Revising the manuscript throughout 2024–2025 has been a rewarding, humbling, and exhausting journey. As Bruno Latour so rightly observed, engaging seriously with Fleck's theory entails committing to a process of constant rectification. When applied, Fleck's comparative epistemology is a truly open framework that compels you to keep digging and revising.

This work is intended for readers who are drawn to the edges—those who enjoy stepping beyond disciplinary boundaries to discover fresh ways of understanding familiar texts and concepts. At its core, the book is about thought: about how people have come to think in particular ways, what has shaped the thoughts transmitted across time to us, and how we, in turn, receive and reframe those thoughts in our own cultural context.

There have been many theories about what shapes our thinking—*Geist*, economic relations, Will, the unconscious, power, discourse, the media, posthuman intelligences from the future, and so on. Fleck's theory keeps many of these in the frame but shifts the focus to a more immediate suspect: our thoughts are shaped by other people, by the numerous collectives we belong to. These thought collectives train us, teach us, and ultimately shape how we perceive and think about the world. They form the cognitive frameworks and thought styles through which we interpret reality.

This work may strike some readers as overly detailed, while others might find it treads familiar ground or ventures too superficially into certain topics. At times, it strays far out of its depth—just as Fleck himself did. I have done my best to tell the story as thoughtfully and clearly as I can. Any omissions, oversights, or missteps are mine alone.

Poznań, Poland
May 2025

Stephen Dersley

Acknowledgments

I am deeply grateful to Professor Przemysław Rotengruber for his insightful guidance, for his exceptional patience, and for granting me the freedom to explore my ideas with remarkable independence.

My heartfelt thanks go to Professor Andrzej Klawiter, whose encouragement many years ago introduced me to the fascinating work of Ludwik Fleck.

I am greatly indebted to Professor Andrzej W. Nowak, whose push toward a more radical approach and timely guidance were instrumental in shaping my perspective.

I would also like to thank Professor Agnieszka Jelewska and Dr. Michał Krawczak for encouraging me to engage with cutting-edge theory.

I extend my sincere thanks to the reviewers of this work in its PhD form—Professor Krzysztof Abriszewski, Professor Dorota Brzozowska, and Professor Tomasz Michaluk—whose constructive feedback significantly contributed to refining this book.

Above all, I would like to express my deepest gratitude to Professor Karolina Cern. Her invaluable guidance and steadfast encouragement have been an unwavering source of support throughout the writing of this book.

Competing Interests The author has no competing interests to declare that are relevant to the content of this manuscript.

Contents

Chapter 1
Introduction

Abstract This chapter lays the groundwork for rethinking cultural transformation by juxtaposing Plato's vision of cultural control in the *Laws* with the historical reality of Europe's dynamic and often revolutionary change. Plato's imagined polity of Magnesia is presented as a model of cultural stasis: artistic innovation is outlawed, tradition codified by law, and philosophy institutionalized as a supervisory authority. Yet the long arc of European history—from Greek tragedy to the Enlightenment—reveals how culture escapes such constraints through the circulation of ideas, technological change, institutional reordering, and epistemic conflict.

In response to this complexity, the chapter introduces the study's central aim: to develop a more flexible framework for analysing cultural change. It critically engages with established models—Marxian determinism, Kuhnian paradigms, Foucauldian discourse analysis—arguing that each isolates particular determinants while neglecting the interplay between epistemic, institutional, and material forces. Beyond these models, it also challenges entrenched interpretive frameworks—such as the 'myth to logos' paradigm, the Socratic caesura, and the Enlightenment/Counter-Enlightenment dichotomy—that continue to shape scholarship through disciplinary inheritance and conceptual rigidity.

In place of these reductive schemes, the chapter turns to Ludwik Fleck's theory of thought collectives and thought styles. While not fully developed into a model of cultural transformation, Fleck's account of cognition as a historically situated and socially embedded process gestures toward one. Building on this foundation, the chapter outlines the analytical approach developed in this study—drawing also on Bourdieu, Laclau and Mouffe, and Foucault—as a means of analysing how thought and culture are mutually shaped.

1.1 Plato's *Laws*, or How to Stop Cultural Change

In Plato's *Laws*, the Athenian Stranger presents Egypt as a commendable example of a society where cultural production and education are strictly regulated by law:

S. Dersley, *Thought Collectives and Cultural Change*, Living Signs of Law 1,
https://doi.org/10.1007/978-3-031-97431-1_1

> Painters and others who represented postures and that sort of thing were not allowed to make innovations or think up things different from the ancestral. And they are still not allowed to—not in these things; or in music altogether. If you look into this you will find that for ten thousand years—not 'so to speak' but really ten thousand years—the paintings and sculptures have been in no way more beautiful or more ugly than those that are being made with the very same skill, by their craftsmen now. (656e)[1]

Egypt is a country whose culture does not change; its painters, musicians, and other artists endlessly repeat the same forms. This cultural immutability is implicitly contrasted with the Athenian pursuit of novelty, where even the once-sanctified chorus is now considered old-fashioned—a tendency that, according to the Stranger, has led to moral decay and political instability (657b). The Stranger notes that in Egypt, 'it was possible to be firm about such things, and mandate in law (*nomōi*) songs which are by nature correct' (657a). Thus, Egypt serves as a precedent for regulating artistic production by law to prevent the corruption that—the Stranger suggests—inevitably follows from cultural change.

This critique of cultural change becomes sharper in the Athenian Stranger's description of Athenian society's descent into *theatrokratia* (700a–701c). According to the Stranger's account, in the past, the Athenians, like the Egyptians, had strictly regulated music, treating it as an essential component of moral education. Specific forms of song were tied to particular instruments, and any deviation was prohibited by law (*mousikēs nomos*). Audiences of all ages and levels of education—whether children, the mob, or the educated (*hoi pepaideumenoi*)—were expected to listen in silence, under the threat of corporal punishment. However, this disciplined cultural order unravelled when poets began to pander to popular tastes, abandoning traditional forms and laws. This *anomou amousias* ('unmusical lawlessness') introduced pleasure as the primary criterion of artistic value, making the masses believe themselves competent judges (*hikanoi kritai*). What followed was a 'wretched theatocracy' (*itamē theatrokratia*), where the unchecked pursuit of novelty and pleasure led to the erosion of civic virtue. The Stranger laments that this loss of respect for authority and tradition bred a dangerous fearlessness, ultimately giving rise to disobedience, disrespect, shamelessness, and moral decay. In this analysis, the collapse of musical and cultural discipline is identified as a direct cause of the political instability and ethical decline that the Stranger attributes to Athens' love of freedom.

Plato's *Laws* develops a broader argument that the combined arts of the lawgiver (*nomothetēs*) and the statesman (*politikos*)—applied with firmness—can maintain societal stability by preventing artistic innovation and cultural change. In Magnesia, the colony envisioned in the dialogue, this approach would ensure that education, cultural production, and modes of thought remain firmly aligned with tradition. The result would be a self-contained, agrarian society, insulated from the volatility that accompanies the pursuit of novelty. Its geographical isolation and landlocked character symbolise its rejection of the imperial ambitions and cultural experimentation of Athens, whose *thalassocracy* and openness to change had fostered both brilliance and instability. As the Stranger explains in Laws 704b–705b, maritime life encourages injustice, arrogance and instability by exposing citizens to foreign customs and

[1] Plato (1980, p. 37).

pleasures. Magnesia, by contrast, is to be landlocked and free from harbours in order to preserve civic order and cultural permanence. Magnesia, by contrast, is imagined as the anti-Athens: a society designed for peace, permanence and harmony, secured through unwavering adherence to ancestral laws.[2]

Yet far from achieving the cultural stasis he idealized, Greek culture—and the cultures it inspired—became engines of innovation and change. European culture, for instance, driven by its incessant transfers of hegemony, imperial expansion, and the demands of extractive-colonial projects, managed to throw off top-down control and trigger global transformations. Europe, as a result, came to self-reflexively view itself as being on a progressive historical trajectory and as a powerful transmitter of the best possible change.

This contrast between Plato's vision of control, hierarchy, and aristocratic order and the realities of cultural dynamism raises a set of questions that frame the present study. How are such wide-reaching shifts in cultural values and practices to be understood? What kinds of mechanisms or conditions make them possible, and how should we interpret their origins and effects?

These questions inform this study's dissatisfaction with existing frameworks for analysing revolutionary cultural change—here defined as the intricate mesh of epistemic, discursive, economic, scientific, technological, informational, and institutional developments that culminate in foundational shifts. While each of these dimensions has been foregrounded in influential models—Marxian economic determinism, Kuhn's paradigms, and Foucauldian discourse analysis—they tend to amplify one determinant at the expense of others. Equally, they often rely on entrenched binary categories that obscure the complexity of cultural transformation. The following sections will outline the need for a more flexible and interdisciplinary approach.

1.2 Single Determinant Models

This study contends that single-determinant models—such as Marx's economic determinism, Kuhn's paradigm shifts, and Foucault's discourse analysis—provide valuable insights but ultimately oversimplify cultural transformation by amplifying certain determinants while minimizing or excluding others. These models are considered more thoroughly in subsequent chapters, yet a brief orientation here is useful.

1.2.1 Marxian Economic Determinism

In 1859, Karl Marx famously introduced the distinction between the 'economic foundation' and the 'superstructure' of social, political, legal and intellectual life: 'The changes in the economic foundation lead sooner or later to the transformation

[2] Munn (2012), Laks (2022).

of the whole immense superstructure'.[3] This binary framework—which came to be codified as the classic base-superstructure model—prioritizes changes in the material forces of production, treating transformations in the superstructure (the cultural and political sphere[4]) as secondary, derivative and delayed.

This model amplifies the role of economic development while diminishing the capacity of intellectual communication to contribute to revolutionary cultural change. It aligns with the binary logic of *The German Ideology* (1846), where material activity and behaviour are primary, and mental production—'as expressed in the language of politics, laws, morality, religion, metaphysics etc. of a people'—is secondary.[5] On one side, there is life, physical matter, and productive activity; on the other, consciousness of that life, matter and activity.

Before the division of labour, thinking and mental intercourse were, in Marx and Engels' terms, interwoven with real life as a 'direct efflux'. But once class society emerged, mental labour and production became monopolized by the ruling class, subordinated to its economic interests.[6] Within this framework, revolutionary cultural change—such as the dissemination of revolutionary ideas—is only possible if there has first been a transformation in the economic base that produces a new class (e.g. the bourgeoisie, the proletariat).

Perhaps the most famous application of the base-superstructure model is Boris Hessen's *The Social and Economic Roots of Newton's "Principia"* (1931). Contra the 'great man' narratives, Hessen draws directly on *The German Ideology* and the *Critique of Political Economy* to argue that scientific discoveries are driven by transformations in the material productive forces. 'With the change of the economic foundation', he repeats, 'the entire immense superstructure is also transformed'.[7]

In his analysis, Newton's *Principia* is presented as a response to practical problems arising from the needs of merchant capital and manufacture. The study of the movement of bodies answered to mining, pumping and water transport; trajectories and resistance derived from ballistics and artillery; optics was shaped by the needs of marine navigation. Newton's science is thus embedded in a broader cultural process through which bourgeois knowledge production, emerging outside feudal institutions, reshaped the superstructure in alignment with the interests of merchant capital.

Hessen's work—a foundational statement of 'Classical Marxist Historiography'—helped initiate externalist accounts of science. It sheds valuable light on forces neglected by internalist accounts. Yet it has also been criticized for its historical simplifications and rigid determinism.[8]

---

[3] Marx (1987, p. 263).

[4] Cohen (1978), Eagleton (2011).

[5] Marx and Engels (2011, p. 14).

[6] Marx and Engels (2011, pp. 39-41).

[7] Hessen (2009, p. 42).

[8] Freudenthal and McLaughlin (2009).

First, Hessen reduces the turbulent complexity of seventeenth-century English history—encompassing the Civil War, Cromwell's Protectorate, the Stuart Restoration, and the Glorious Revolution—to the formula: 'The English Revolution of 1649–1688 was a bourgeois revolution'.[9] As a result, Newton's *Principia* (1687), Boyle's earlier work, and the practices of the Royal Society are positioned as superstructural expressions of transformations in the base—specifically, the rise of merchant capital and the emergence of a new bourgeoisie.

However, as J. A. Downie notes (2005), drawing on E. P. Thompson's work,[10] the real beneficiaries of the 1688 Settlement were the landed gentry, not the bourgeoisie. While the merchant and professional classes were growing in wealth and influence, they had not yet achieved cultural or political hegemony. The landed gentry, whose power was rooted in landownership and inherited privilege, continued to dominate.

In this respect, Hessen anticipates Habermas's later imposition of a rigid Marxian schema—one that assumes England must have become a bourgeois state by the late seventeenth century.[11] In both cases, dynamic social configurations are compressed to fit the determinist narrative of dialectical materialism. Such reductionism occludes patterns of cross-class cooperation (e.g. between aristocrats and artisans), discursive conflict within classes, and even intergenerational contestation.

Second, the base-superstructure model downplays the potential of intellectual or institutional innovation to transform social practices—especially those with commercial relevance. Hessen reduces universities to reactionary feudal strongholds: 'In the 15th to the 17th centuries the universities were the scientific centres of feudalism. They were not only the bearers of feudal traditions, but the active defenders of those traditions'.[12] Yet this neglects the role of institutions such as the Italian universities in the production and circulation of anatomical knowledge. Competitive teaching, new print formats, and the commercial book market—epitomized by the 1543 publication of Vesalius' *De humani corporis fabrica*—made the university a critical site of innovation with real cultural effects.

Hessen's framework also struggles to accommodate intellectual figures who fall outside its class-based categories. His account draws a linear line from Bacon to Toland and Overton, but falters when faced with Hobbes. Hessen claims Hobbes's 'geometric' and 'esoteric' materialism aligned with the aristocracy and elite culture. Yet, as Chap. 11 will show, Hobbes was denounced across the political spectrum: by Cambridge Platonists, Nonconformist Protestants, experimentalists in the Royal Society, and the dominant institutions of the Church, the universities, and the law. Hobbes's rejection by nearly every segment of the elite exposes the limits of Hessen's explanatory model.

---

[9] Hessen (2009, p. 63).

[10] Thompson (1993, p. 27).

[11] Downie 2005, p. 64).

[12] Hessen (2009, p. 53).

Even Lenin's revolutionary practice complicates the rigid application of the base-superstructure model. While Hessen concludes that only the framework of Marx, Engels and Lenin can explain the historical development of science,[13] Lenin's own position departs from strict economic determinism.

Marxian economism, which reduces all social and political phenomena to economic causes and dismisses the role of ideas, culture and agency, was subjected to profound critique by both Weber and Gramsci. However, Lenin's rejection of its restrictions offers a particularly striking contrast. While the role of the intelligentsia in contributing to revolutionary change remains a controversial issue within the Marxist tradition, Lenin's conception of the Party as a *vanguard*—a group of theoreticians, propagandists, agitators, and organisers tasked with educating workers and instigating revolutionary change[14]—explicitly countered the determinism of prevailing Marxist economism. In Lenin's diagnosis, political consciousness had to come 'from without' the economic struggle.

Hence, in what is arguably the most significant modification of orthodox economism, Lenin insisted that mental labour and education were not merely by-products of economic transformation but vital catalysts for political action.

1.2.2 Kuhnian Paradigm Shifts

Thomas S. Kuhn's theory of paradigm shifts originated in his analysis of *The Copernican Revolution* (1957), which sought to account for how Copernicus' technical rejection of Ptolemaic astronomy ultimately led to a complete transformation of the European worldview. From the outset, Kuhn's investigations stressed that scientific revolutions are, first, deeply embedded in cultural change and, second, capable of triggering far-reaching cultural transformations.

While implicitly opposing the Popperian focus on the epistemic innovations of bold scientific geniuses, and while reframing science as a collective-institutional practice grounded in consensus, Kuhn's framework remains predominantly focused on perceptual-epistemic factors—those that undermine consensus and catalyse innovation. A new paradigm is seen as emerging chiefly due to an intolerable accumulation of anomalies and the loss of predictive capacity. Although Kuhn acknowledges the cultural and psychological importance of paradigms, he devotes only cursory attention to the role of broader social developments, technological innovations, or economic imperatives in driving paradigm shifts.

For example, he briefly notes that the Protestant Reformation and the 'general ferment' facilitated Copernicus' innovation; that voyages and exploration created a demand for better maps and star charts (implicitly recognizing economic determinants); and that Copernicus became involved in calendar reform to meet a pressing

[13] Hessen (2009, p. 82).

[14] Lenin (1961, pp. 421–423).

social need for precise dating. Yet in a book of nearly three hundred pages, these socio-economic determinants receive only two or three pages of discussion.[15]

Kuhn likewise overlooks the explosion in print and publishing that transformed Europe during Copernicus' lifetime—an upheaval that facilitated the spread of Luther's Reformation and is reflected in the shift from the privately circulated manuscript of *Commentariolus* (1509–1514) to the printed *De revolutionibus orbium coelestium* (1543), published by a German Protestant in Wittenberg.[16] He also fails to consider the potential influence of Copernicus' years at the Universities of Bologna and Padua on his astronomical work. The University of Padua, in particular, was renowned for its tolerance, humanist curricula, and stimulating teaching methods.

One of the central arguments of this study is that educational institutions can exert a tangible influence on epistemic and cultural innovation. The extent to which such institutions suppress, constrain, allow, or encourage the development of new thought styles directly shapes the contours of broader cultural change. I would argue that Copernicus' years studying medicine at Padua (1501–1503) were a significant determinant of the bold hypotheses he later set out in the *Commentariolus*.

In *The Structure of Scientific Revolutions*, Kuhn claims that paradigms direct scientists' attention and shape their problem choices: a paradigm defines the problems to be solved.[17] Yet science is not simply a theoretical problem-solving activity; it is a networked, collective practice[18] involving interaction with material agency,[19] and one ultimately driven by socio-economic imperatives beyond science itself. Kuhn's account, by focusing almost exclusively on perceptual-conceptual structures, effectively seals off laboratories, universities, disciplines, and scientists from the socio-economic conditions in which they operate. Like Ernst Mach's histories of science, Kuhn's narrative offers a fundamentally internal perspective—an image of science untouched by industrial or military entanglements.

But the scientists populating Kuhn's *Structure* lived in societies shaped by various stages of capitalist development, and the emergence of new disciplines—such as chemistry and thermodynamics around 1800—cannot be separated from the needs of the Industrial Revolution. Scientific paradigms do not merely pose problems; they are also shaped by societies seeking solutions to material challenges. In this light, capitalist modes of production—Marx's economic base—must be considered external determinants of paradigm change. They fund laboratories, shape research agendas, and underwrite university departments that respond to urgent social and economic demands. Kuhn's emphasis on internal epistemic factors limits his framework's capacity to address the material conditions under which paradigms emerge, thrive, and transform scientific thought.

[15] Kuhn (1957, pp. 124–126).

[16] Dersley (2015a, b).

[17] Kuhn (1962, pp. 25–27).

[18] Latour (2008).

[19] Pickering (1995).

1.2.3 Foucauldian Discourse Analysis

When Foucault turns to the problem of change and transformation in *The Archaeology of Knowledge* (1969), he contrasts the history of ideas with 'the archaeological description of change'.[20] The former seeks continuity, linear causality, homogenous processes, and cumulative evolution; the latter emphasizes discontinuity, rupture, breaks, and the emergence of new formations. Where the history of ideas views change as a container—constructing historical periods by articulating 'the abstract unity of change and event'[21]—archaeology disarticulates this linear unity to identify systems of transformation.

New discourses and discursive formations emerge, as 'positivities', through differentiation, interrelation, and dispersion, which give rise to new rules of enunciation and formation. For Foucault, Marx's critique of political economy exemplifies this: it constitutes a new discourse that emerged through differentiation from Ricardian political economy. Marx employed many of the same concepts as classical political economy (e.g., surplus value, falling rate of profit), but redefined 'the conditions in which the discourse of economists takes place', thereby creating a new discursive practice.[22] This shift from political economy to critique—whether framed as change, transformation, or rupture—marks the emergence of something new in the discursive field.

Foucault's framework robustly accounts for discursive transformation, but ambiguity arises when it is applied to phenomena he defines as external to discourse: non-discursive practices and events. For example, Foucault links the emergence of the Analysis of Wealth as a seventeenth-century discursive formation with a range of non-discursive practices—'the circulation of goods, monetary manipulations and their effects, the system of protecting trade and manufactures, [and] fluctuations in the quantity of metal coined'.[23] While these are acknowledged, he does not clearly articulate how they interact with or influence discursive practices.

Foucauldian discourse circa 1969 is narrowly defined: it is constituted by statements—relations between statements, the rules for enunciation, and the structural conditions that make a discursive practice possible. Ultimately, this model traps itself in a binary framework: phenomena not constituted by statements (e.g., monetary manipulations, economic systems) are defined as non-discursive. Yet cultures clearly assign meaning to such phenomena: money is embedded in symbolic systems; decimal numerals, as part of broader numerical regimes, encode and constrain monetary values.

Thus, in Foucault's archaeological framework, discourse is shaped by changes in meaning systems and social practices that, by definition, lie beyond the discursive sphere. In *The Archaeology of Knowledge*, the relationship between discursive and

---

[20] Foucault (1989, p. 183).

[21] Foucault (1989, p. 195).

[22] Foucault (1989, pp. 194–195).

[23] Foucault (1989, p. 193).

non-discursive practices remains unresolved. Foucault's remarks on the Analysis of Wealth suggest that discourse—much like Marx's superstructure—registers a delayed response to transformations in the non-discursive field. However, he does not explore whether discursive practices might themselves instigate changes in non-discursive domains, such as monetary manipulation.

Similar ambiguities arise in Foucault's claim that the French Revolution is not 'an event exterior to discourse' but a 'complex, articulated, describable group of transformations' that established new discursive formations.[24] This framing appears to place the Revolution's vast cultural ramifications wholly within the discursive field. Yet the binary distinction between discursive and non-discursive complicates this view. If the Revolution was constructed discursively—through statements, texts, systems of knowledge—then, in Foucault's terms, it must also have been shaped by extra-discursive forces and semiotic regimes. For instance, economic pressures such as crop failures and rising bread prices, and demographic factors like population growth, undoubtedly influenced the Revolution, even before they were registered in texts. Foucault offers little insight into how discursive formations respond to, or integrate, such external factors.

These ambiguities persist in his later genealogical method. The archaeological approach gestures at non-discursive practices while positioning them as inaccessible. At the same time, it often treats discourse as an all-encompassing cultural system that constitutes subjects and their positions. The genealogical method shifts focus to the exterior of discourse, locating power as a productive network that permeates the social body.[25] Power constitutes discourse as an effect, positioning subjects through relations of force. In this framework, power—rather than non-discursive practices—emerges as the singular, overarching determinant of discourse and knowledge. This entails a shift from analysing statements and meaning relations to mapping 'relations of war and battle'.

The transition to genealogy may thus be read as a reformulation of the base-superstructure model. In *Truth and Power*, Foucault explicitly refers to the state as 'superstructural in relation to a whole series of power networks that invest the body, sexuality, the family, kinship, knowledge, technology, and so forth'.[26] What was once framed as a binary between non-discursive and discursive becomes a new dichotomy: power versus its effects.

A more detailed examination of Foucauldian discourse follows in Chap. 5; here, it will suffice to argue that the archaeological method is too general and ambiguous to account adequately for cultural change. The genealogical method inherits its core conceptual assumptions, amplifying the constitutive role of discourse while rendering the subject a passive effect of discourse and power. The communicative agency of groups and individuals is downplayed; little attention is paid to how, at the local level, agents accrue and wield power by generating new discourses.

---

[24] Foucault (1989, p. 195)

[25] *Truth and Power*, in Foucault (1980).

[26] Foucault (1980).

This critique aligns with Edward Said's observation that Foucault's focus on rules and the suppression of agency impedes his capacity to explain historical change. Said argued that individual wills and actions must be considered if one is to grasp transformations in discourse.[27] From a Fleckian perspective, however, the focus shifts from individual to collective will and action: how and why do specific groups begin articulating new discourses at particular historical junctures?

1.2.4 Fleck's 'Open Epistemology'[28]

This is not to suggest that the Marxian, Kuhnian, and Foucauldian frameworks do not shed valuable light on aspects of cultural change, or that their frameworks are 'incorrect' and should be abandoned. These models have undeniable explanatory power when applied to transformations in the socio-cultural field. However, by amplifying certain determinants, they exclude, downplay, or distort others. This study argues that Fleck's theory of thought collectives and thought styles is robust and flexible enough to address aspects of cultural change that elude these frameworks, while also integrating conceptual tools from them to enhance its explanatory power.

Fleck's theory posits that all perception and cognition are socially determined. This determination arises through the interaction of 'thought collectives and passive elements', where a community draws on an existing fund of knowledge to apply conventions in the process of perception and cognition.[29] While conventions may be arbitrary (e.g., using inches or centimetres), their application is socially determined (imperial vs. metric systems), and they reveal non-arbitrary relations in the world (a horse is taller than a cat regardless of the unit).

When a thought collective develops a new system of measurement or a method for testing the world, this transformation is shaped by multiple determinants, including: the existing fund of knowledge (*proto-ideas* and conventions), contributions of *strong individuals*, social and political needs (*intellectual unrest*, *collective mood*), technological developments, and communication between thought collectives (*the circulation of ideas*). Fleck's concepts function as levers that pry open these fields of determination, allowing for more detailed analysis.

Certain overlaps with other frameworks can be identified. For instance, the existing fund of knowledge (*Wissensbestand*)[30] parallels Foucauldian discourse, intellectual unrest[31] resonates with Marxian ideological conflict, and Fleck's thought

27 Said (2003, p. 23).
28 Borck (2004).
29 Fleck (1979, pp. 40, 10, 48).
30 Fleck (1979, p. 38).
31 Fleck (1986b, pp. 74–75).

styles share similarities with Kuhn's paradigms as collective epistemic frameworks.[32] However, Fleck's theory distinguishes itself by focusing on *cognition* as a social activity. While Marxism reduces cognition to a (mostly 'false') reflection of underlying processes, and Foucauldian discourse buries the subject within institutional and bureaucratic infrastructures, treating discourses as autonomous supra-individual entities, Fleck's theory emphasizes that all perceptions, theories, ideologies, and discourses are the products of cognizers. Without ongoing acts of cognition, books are merely paper with marks, and universities are merely brick and mortar.

Thus, while Vesalius—Fleck's example—can be assigned to a privileged professional social class, and while the discursive-institutional influences of the Universities of Bologna and Padua are clearly evident in his practices, as are the impact of printing innovations and the development of social networks associated with the publishing trade, Fleck's theory necessitates viewing all these factors in terms of their impact on collective cognition. What factors led Vesalius to perceive, represent, and describe the human body in a particular way, and what allowed his students and the reading public to accept and adopt this new mode of cognition?

The key elements of Fleck's theory, analysed in detail in Chaps. 2, 3, and 4, demonstrate its flexibility in accounting for cultural change by considering economic, technological, discursive, and epistemic determinants. Through the application of concepts such as thought collectives, thought styles, intellectual unrest, and the circulation of ideas, Fleck's framework enables the continuous exploration of heterogeneous layers and factors, offering a uniquely broad explanatory power.

Leszek Nowak's idealizational theory of science provides a useful criterion for assessing the explanatory power of Fleck's concepts. Nowak defines explanatory power as 'the proportion of facts explained by the theory to the facts in a given domain'.[33] While this study adopts a less quantitative approach, it emphasizes the importance of reconsidering established facts to uncover new, provisional facts. If Fleck's theory allows the reconstruction of cultural facts that are overlooked or suppressed by other frameworks, it may be said to demonstrate a clear advantage in terms of explanatory power.

This issue also opens up a reflexive complexity, as Fleck's theory posits that facts have a genesis and development: they are not static entities awaiting discovery but are generated through interactions between a thought style, the existing fund of knowledge, and the cognized.[34] Researchers must navigate the twin dangers of uncritically inheriting concepts from their research material or anachronistically projecting contemporary frameworks back into the past. Fleck's notion of comparative epistemology offers a critical tool here, enabling researchers to reflexively compare past and emergent thought styles while acknowledging their own cognitive entanglements.

[32] Fleck (1979, pp. 38–42).

[33] Nowak (2012, p. 38).

[34] Fleck (1979, pp. 10, 38).

Hegel's history of philosophy exemplifies the risks of maximal projections, where past thought is appropriated entirely for present purposes. Fleck's approach, by contrast, advocates more curious and sensitive projections, using contemporary concepts to explore the complex heterogeneity of cultural phenomena. Comparative epistemology thus becomes crucial: while researchers cannot escape their own thought styles, they can use them reflexively to illuminate differences and emergent trends in past representations.

Ultimately, this study's claim is modest but straightforward: if Fleck's theory sheds light on aspects of facts—constructed or reconstructed—that are obscured by other frameworks, it can be said to possess a unique explanatory power. This power lies in its capacity to facilitate open-ended, iterative exploration, continuously rectifying and expanding our understanding of heterogeneous determinants. This flexibility underscores its value as a tool for understanding cultural change.

1.3 Entrenched Frameworks and Categories

Beyond theoretical models, the study of cultural change is also hampered by deeply embedded interpretive frameworks. These frameworks—solidified through layers of scholarly discourse and institutionalisation—tend to rearticulate inherited binary categories. Their rigid grip on disciplines and publishing conventions inhibits the emergence of alternative perspectives and often obscures more complex or multidimensional accounts of transformation. Examples include the 'from myth to logos' paradigm, the 'Socratic caesura', and the Enlightenment/Counter-Enlightenment dichotomy.

1.3.1 'From Myth to Logos'

The 'from myth to logos' paradigm constructs a transformation in Ancient Greece between the seventh and fourth centuries BC, commonly described as a shift from the Homeric and Hesiodic poetic worldview to the increasingly abstract and generalising thought of the Milesians, culminating in the rational frameworks associated with Socrates, Plato, and Aristotle. Developed explicitly in the nineteenth and twentieth centuries, this binary mirrored phases of European self-reflection, particularly during the Renaissance and Enlightenment, when transformations linked to modernity—such as secularisation and the rise of science—were retrojected onto Antiquity. In German scholarship especially, Ancient Greece was invoked to construct a differentiated national identity, aligning Hellenic thought with ideals such as *paideia* and *Bildung*.

Hegel's *Lectures on the History of Philosophy* (1806–1831) represent the culmination of this conceptual strategy. For Hegel, Greek philosophy marked a radical discontinuity: the emergence of thought reflecting on itself, as distinct from the sensuous imagery of myth and religion. In opposition to Creuzer's view of mythology as containing a continuum of rationality, Hegel's schema reinforced philosophy's claim to primacy while marginalising other forms of cultural production.

This framing of early Greek thought as a clean break persisted into modern scholarship. Figures such as William Nestle and Jonathan Barnes replicated Plato's dichotomies, hailing Milesian cosmology as the 'birth of rationality' and dismissing Hesiod's *Theogony* as a collection of 'unargued fables'. Yet such triumphalist accounts often fail to reflect on the strategic context of Plato's distinctions, which emerged in the aftermath of the Peloponnesian War and served to reassert Athenian cultural dominance.

Several major studies have challenged this narrative. Cornford (1912) and Jaeger (1947) drew attention to the theological dimensions of early Greek cosmology. Havelock (1963) interpreted Plato's quarrel with poetry as reflecting a generational conflict between oral and literate cultures. Vernant (1988) situated rational discourse within the competitive *agon* of the *polis*, while Lloyd (1979) examined the emergence of rational demonstration across varied social spheres. More recently, André Laks (2018), drawing on Weber's model of rationalisation, stressed the heterogeneity of early Greek thought and the importance of incremental epistemic mutation rather than absolute rupture. Such works resist the reductive myth-to-logos framework by illuminating the multiplicity of socio-cultural factors that shaped epistemic developments.

1.3.2 The Socratic Caesura

The 'Socratic caesura' is André Laks' term (2018) for the notion that Socrates' way of thinking constituted a rupture—a moment of radical discontinuity—in the history of philosophy and Western thought more broadly. This caesura was most explicitly articulated in Plato's *Apology*, where Socrates is portrayed as a uniquely civic-minded philosopher, standing in stark opposition to the naturalist and sophist caricature of him presented in Aristophanes' satire and in the charges brought against him at his trial. However, Plato's portrayal of Socrates as the first thinker to centre philosophy on everyday practices in the *polis* was inseparable from the marginalization and exclusion of alternative intellectual traditions.

The heterogeneous itinerant wise men whose impact is tangible across the field of cultural production—in Herodotus' and Thucydides' histories, in the plays of Sophocles and Euripides, in political rhetoric and legal argumentation—were homogenized as teachers of rhetoric and dismissed as sophists who charged for their services. Other practices—such as the trial-and-error reasoning of Hippocratic medicine or the materialist accounts of Democritean natural science—were similarly downgraded and excluded from true knowledge by stringent epistemic criteria and legalistic disciplinary demarcations.

Reinforced by Xenophon, Aristotle, and later Cicero, the caesura solidified Socrates' image as a moral philosopher uniquely devoted to civic virtue. This narrative resonated with Renaissance and early Enlightenment thinkers, particularly Shaftesbury, who saw in Xenophon's and Cicero's Socrates an archetype of philosophical rationality and integrity. By the late eighteenth century, scholars at German universities increasingly focused on Socrates as a quintessential Greek philosopher, reimagining the caesura through a nationalistic lens. It came to symbolise the foundation of philosophy's autonomy and societal authority, with the institutional power of the German University central to promoting philosophy as a discipline distinct from other modes of knowledge production.

Even Nietzsche—who turned his guns on the pious reverence for German classical studies and philology, and who cast Socrates as the nemesis of tragedy and the Dionysian spirit—could not entirely escape the grip of the Socratic caesura. In *The Birth of Tragedy* (1872), Nietzsche's binary opposition between the Dionysian and the Apollonian framed Socratic rationalism as the apotheosis of the Apollonian drive for order, clarity, and individuation. This framework imposed a reductive reading that flattened the immense complexity of Euripides' engagement with Athenian society during the Peloponnesian War, reducing it to a single, cataclysmic turning point: the destruction of tragedy under the corrosive influence of Socratic rationalism (§11–15).[35]

The Socratic caesura grounds Nietzsche's later anti-Christian philosophy of culture, where the Dionysian–Apollonian binary evolves into an overarching sickness-versus-health framework. In this reframing, decadence, decline, asceticism, and reason become symptoms of cultural sickness, while instinct, vitality, joy, and life-affirming impulses are celebrated as signs of health. Within this schema, Socrates becomes not only the destroyer of Greek tragedy but also the root of Western moral decadence, paving the way for Christianity's ascetic ideal and its life-denying ethos. Nietzsche thus casts Socrates as the harbinger of a cultural trajectory that sacrifices instinct and vitality on the altar of rationality and moral absolutism.

The portrayal of Socrates as an absolute discontinuity in Greek philosophy, Western thought, and European culture rests on a largely uncritical acceptance of the discursive strategies employed by ancient thinkers—particularly Plato and Cicero—who pursued specific agendas and engaged in discursive struggles shaped by their respective cultural contexts.

1.3.3 The Enlightenment/Counter-Enlightenment Dichotomy

The ascent of the philosophy faculty in the German university system—from a subordinate position in the thirteenth century to its short-lived dominance under the Humboldtian model—was shaped by complex economic, social, cultural, and institutional transformations. These developments generated significant conflict in the 1790s, exemplified in key texts such as Wöllner's *Edict on Religion* (1788), Kant's

[35] Nietzsche (1999, pp. 55–75).

Religion within the Bounds of Mere Reason (1793), Wöllner's *Royal Proclamation Against Kant* (1794), and Kant's *The Conflict of the Faculties* (1794–1798). At the core of these struggles lay competing visions of authority—over religious teaching, public discourse, and the structure of the university itself. For Kant, the issue was ultimately freedom of thought: 'The constraint which deprives people of the freedom to communicate their thoughts in public also removes their freedom of thought'. [36]

In much of the scholarly literature, this conflict has been interpreted through what one historian has called 'the classic Enlightenment/Counter-Enlightenment dichotomy'.[37] This framework casts Frederick the Great, Zedlitz, and Kant as champions of progress and rationality, while portraying Frederick William II and Wöllner as defenders of censorship, orthodoxy, and reaction. This interpretive schema shaped works by Friedrich Paulsen (1902), Paul Schwartz (1925), and Mary J. Gregor (1979), and it continues to influence textbook accounts and popular narratives.

A more nuanced approach—developed by Epstein (1966), Whaley (1981), Blanning (1981), Schmidt (1996), Laursen (1996), and Sauter (2009)—rejects this binary. These scholars highlight the complexity of the German *Aufklärung* and expose its fractures, contradictions, and contextual limits. Epstein's *Genesis of German Conservatism*, for instance, reconstructs the social field of the late eighteenth century to reveal ambivalent and cross-cutting allegiances. Support for the *Aufklärung* came not only from liberal professors and monarchs like Frederick II, but also from groups such as impoverished students and liberal pastors. Conversely, resistance came from multiple quarters—peasants, guild masters, military officers, and segments of the aristocracy.[38]

Whaley and Blanning stress the distinctive character of the German Enlightenment, noting that its universities did not simply import English or French ideas, but selectively adapted them to fit local traditions. Cameralism, for example, aligned Enlightenment ideals with a vision of state service and bureaucratic rationality, linking intellectual reform to the training of administrators and military officers.[39]

Schmidt's volume *What is Enlightenment?* (1996) and his Introduction emphasize the diversity of the Enlightenment debate in the German public sphere of the 1780s and 1790s. One of the volume's more revealing essays, Laursen's *The Subversive Kant*, underscores the degree to which the controversy between Kant and Wöllner was shaped by rival communicative strategies within the educated elite, rather than by a simple opposition between liberal and conservative camps. Laursen explores how both sides employed the rhetoric of *Aufklärung* to serve competing ends.[40]

[36] Kant (1970, p. 247).

[37] Sauter (2009, p. 7).

[38] Epstein (1966).

[39] Whaley (1981), Blanning (1981).

[40] Laursen (1996).

Sauter builds on this insight by identifying two intersecting antagonisms: one between elites and the wider population, and another between rival elite factions. What was at stake, he argues, was not simply whether the Enlightenment should occur, but who had the authority to define, regulate, and disseminate its principles. Wöllner's *Edict on Religion*, for example, did not reject *Aufklärung* outright but condemned certain pastors for spreading errors 'under the much abused banner of Aufklärung'. The contest, then, was over control—of interpretation, dissemination, and institutional authority.[41]

Sauter's reading of *The Conflict of the Faculties* also challenges the assumption that Kant was defending an unqualified freedom of thought. While his earlier 1784 essay on Enlightenment appeared to demand public freedom of expression for all scholars (*Gelehrten*), by 1794–1798 Kant was retreating from that stance. His later position sought to defend only the limited autonomy of the philosophy faculty within the university, or of those scholars in the higher faculties who were acting in a philosophical capacity.[42] This was a pragmatic response to the shifting political climate—the tightening of censorship, the radicalization of the French Revolution, and the broader European fear of intellectual subversion.

Proponents of the Enlightenment/Counter-Enlightenment dichotomy often frame intellectual history as a struggle between two opposed worldviews.[43] The scholars discussed above, by contrast, reconstruct the communicative networks within the educated elite and reveal the ideological and institutional diversity that shaped eighteenth-century public life.

1.3.4 Fleck's Theory: 'Always in the Very Midst'

The 'from myth to logos' paradigm, the 'Socratic caesura', and the Enlightenment/Counter-Enlightenment dichotomy all explain cultural change through overly simplistic binary frameworks: an epistemic rupture within Greek communities, a before-and-after discontinuity centred on a single Athenian figure, or a Manichean struggle between two opposed intellectual camps. By contrast, the alternative approaches discussed above point to a more complex array of interacting determinants and processes, constructing a multidimensional image of socio-cultural transformation. While authors such as Vernant, Buxton, and Sauter have explicitly rejected these binary models, to my knowledge no alternative theoretical framework has been proposed that can be flexibly applied across diverse examples of cultural change.

---

[41] Sauter (2009).

[42] Laursen (1996).

[43] Steven Pinker's *Enlightenment Now* (2018), especially Chap. 3, and 20–23, is an example of a popular re-enactment of this dichotomy. For a more scholarly reiteration, see Graeme Garrard's *Counter Enlightenments. From the eighteenth century to the present* (2006).

Fleck's theory offers such a framework. It suggests that deep socio-cultural change occurs when a new thought style develops within an existing thought collective, eventually giving rise—through differentiation—to new collectives. Applying Fleck's model allows us to trace (while reflexively acknowledging the sedimented layers of construction and reconstruction) the gradual emergence and mutation of thought styles at specific historical moments.

In Chap. 6, for instance, I argue that the Socratic thought style emerged from within an oligarchic thought collective that opposed Athenian *dēmokratia* between 432 and 403 BC. Similarly, the Platonic thought style can be seen as shaped by the trauma of the Peloponnesian War and the oligarchic coup of 404 BC, shifting focus from the control of the *polis* to the regulation of education and cultural production. Neither style is reducible to the figures of Socrates or Plato. The texts of Aristophanes, Plato, and Xenophon portray Socrates interacting with various groups—past and present, sympathetic and hostile—while also participating in inter-group antagonisms over social practices. These texts engage with other genres, target distinct audiences, and articulate precisely calibrated provocations within a field of cultural production[44] prestructured by tradition, consensus, and orthodoxy.

Given the collective nature of such processes, I argue that Fleck's theory of thought collectives and thought styles provides a uniquely apt framework for exploring cultural change. Unlike models based on binary ruptures, Fleck's theory posits that new thought styles emerge gradually, modifying the inherited fund of knowledge and perception within specific local contexts. As Latour stresses, with Fleck, a new way of seeing does not arise from a leap across an epistemic abyss—as in Kuhn's paradigm shifts—but through a chain of continuous experience, becoming clearer 'through an indefinite number of intermediary stations'.[45] As Fleck puts it, 'Wherever and whenever we touch on something, we are always in the very midst and never at the beginning of cognition'.[46]

Of particular importance is Fleck's idea that communication within and between thought collectives—the circulation of ideas[47]—can provoke transformations within a thought style. His example of the concept of 'race' illustrates this process: originally developed in the natural sciences, the concept was radically reconfigured when taken up by political theorists and propagandists, producing new, often disastrous, perceptions of human beings across the social field. Similar transformations occurred in Ancient Greece and during the German Aufklärung, as concepts migrated between fields of knowledge production, giving rise to new thought styles.

For instance, Anaximander applied political ideas of justice to nature, conceiving it as a self-regulating equilibrium.[48] Plato's *Republic*, as explored in Chap. 6, redirected innovations from Athenian law—such as weighing arguments and passing

---

[44] Bourdieu (1993).

[45] Latour (2008, pp. 11–14).

[46] Fleck (1986a, p. 48).

[47] Fleck (1986c, p. 87).

[48] Vlastos (1947).

judgment—into philosophy, transferring these practices from the evaluation of individual citizens to entire fields of cultural production. Shaftesbury's 'philosophy of politeness', another example, inspired the German ideal of *Bildung*.[49] While Shaftesbury's ideas of self-formation reflected English individualism and circulated via entrepreneurial publications beyond university control, *Bildung*, as developed within German philosophy faculties, became a tool of state-sponsored character formation (see Chap. 10). These examples show how thought collectives such as the Milesians, Athenian oligarchs, English Whigs, and German professors shaped new thought styles through cross-disciplinary repurposing.

One might be tempted to claim that Fleck's theory 'fits the phenomena' or provides an 'accurate' account of cultural change. But such a claim risks methodological overreach and confirmation bias. This study takes a different, more experimental approach, drawing on Fleck's exploratory attitude. Its aim is to assess whether his theory, applied to specific cultural phenomena, can shed new light on processes of transformation.

Following Kuhn's 1976 *Foreword* to the English translation of Fleck's *Genesis and Development of a Scientific Fact*, [50] there was a tendency in works from the fields of philosophy of science and science and technology studies to acknowledge Fleck's thought—perhaps positioning him as an oddball precursor of Kuhnian relativism, constructivism, and the sociology of scientific knowledge—but then to question his contemporary relevance,[51] switch to another theoretical model,[52] or provide only superficial readings of his contributions, 'in passing'. [53] In recent years, there have been admirable attempts to free Fleck's thought from this 'precursor of Kuhn' model and to appreciate his unique and still-relevant contributions.[54] Beyond such theoretical re-evaluations, another trend has also emerged: the application of Fleck's theoretical tools to a wide range of phenomena, such as the development of scientific practice in seventeenth-century England,[55] scientific imagery,[56] and archaeological communities.[57]

This study follows both trajectories. Part One reconsiders Fleck's theory in the socio-cultural context in which it arose, assesses its distinctive contributions, and extracts a working model applicable to diverse cultural phenomena. Part Two applies this model to historically recognized episodes of cultural transformation, aiming to illuminate overlooked aspects and dynamics.

---

49 Horlacher (2017).

50 Kuhn (1976).

51 Harwood (1986).

52 Shapin and Schaffer (1985).

53 See, for example, Hacking (1999, pp. 70–71), Fuller (2006, p. 28).

54 For example, Latour (2008), Binney (2023), Condé and Jarnicki (2023).

55 Afeltowicz and Sojak (2015).

56 Mößner (2016).

57 Milosavljevic (2020).

1.4 Necessary Supplements to Fleck's Theory

The justification for supplementing Fleck's concepts is presented in depth in Chap. 5; the following comments are therefore cursory and preliminary. Fleck's theory, while robust, remains skeletal and requires supplementation with additional conceptual tools for in-depth analyses of cultural change. This approach has been successfully employed in studies such as Afeltowicz and Sojak's *Arystokraci i rzemieślnicy* [*Aristocrats and Craftsmen*] (2015), which combined Fleck's concept of thought style with White's network theory and Bourdieu's habitus to examine the synergy between aristocrats and craftsmen in seventeenth-century English science. Similarly, Milosavljević (2020) supplemented Fleck's ideas with Latour's actor-network theory to analyse Serbian archaeological communities as dynamic knowledge networks.

This study also broadens Fleck's framework by integrating concepts of social and cultural practices, cultural production, and discourse, in order to situate thought collectives and styles within broader cultural environments. Fleck's primary focus was epistemological—on how external factors shape perception and cognition—but his theory is enriched by tools that address the contexts in which such processes unfold.

One such tool is the concept of **social practice** as a set of purposeful activities shaped by normative beliefs, evaluative hierarchies, and social need.[58] These include practices such as reciting Homer's *Iliad*, which offered young Greek men models for sacrifice, speech, and negotiation, or the analytic practices exemplified in Plato's *Gorgias*, *Phaedrus*, and *Sophist*, which defined and distinguished between different arts, ways of speaking, and social roles. Just as Homeric models served practical purposes, the Socratic-Platonic thought style's emphasis on making distinctions can be understood as responding to emerging social needs—such as clarifying roles, allocating status, and evaluating new forms of knowledge and activity.

Drawing on Pierre Bourdieu's analytical model (1993), this study adopts a broad understanding of **cultural production**. Texts—whether 'religious', 'poetic', 'philosophical', or 'scientific'—are treated as cultural artefacts shaped by specific contexts, conditions, and social relations. While Bourdieu's *The Field of Cultural Production* centres on nineteenth- and twentieth-century literary and artistic forms, his concept of fields (economic, political, cultural, scientific, philosophical) offers a valuable framework for analysing the production, circulation, and consumption of texts. The central works considered in this study—*Republic*, *Tusculan Disputations*, *Fabrica*, *Leviathan*, *The Conflict of the Faculties*, and *Lectures on the History of Philosophy*—are examined as instances of cultural production, allowing their contextual determinants to be drawn out.

Fleck's concepts of thought collectives and styles effectively map intra-group interaction and the emergence of shared cognitive frameworks, especially within laboratory contexts. However, they lack a developed account of how collectives

[58] Kmita (1991, pp. 78–82).

articulate positions within institutions and define themselves in relation to other groups. To address this, I draw on Foucault's claim that subjects produce knowledge—scientific or otherwise—about objects discursively constructed from **institutionalized subject positions**. For instance, late eighteenth- and early nineteenth-century German professors writing on Reason, Ancient Greece, or *Volk* frequently carried the authority of the Prussian or German state into their work, often unconsciously.

This study also incorporates Laclau and Mouffe's concept of discourse as **articulatory practices grounded in antagonism**,[59] in which collective identities are constructed through opposition. From this perspective, thought styles emerge as institutionally shaped ways of seeing, thinking, and writing, intrinsically bound to social struggles and discursive contests.

In summary, while Fleck's theory effectively outlines the broad dynamics of cultural change, these supplementary tools permit a richer investigation of external determinants—modes of cultural production, institutional factors—and the antagonistic articulation of thought styles. Together, they provide a comprehensive framework for understanding how thought styles evolve, interact, and contest one another, shaping the transformations at the heart of cultural change.

1.5 Research Framework, Methodology and Outline

1.5.1 Research Framework

This study rests on two primary hypotheses:

1. Fleck's theory of thought collectives and thought styles sheds light on aspects of revolutionary cultural change that elude other theoretical frameworks (e.g., Marx, Kuhn, Foucault).
2. Fleck's concepts offer a means to both avoid and critically analyse entrenched binary frameworks and categories frequently used in accounts of cultural change.

To test these hypotheses, Fleck's supplemented theory is applied to two interrelated processes of cultural transformation:

- the emergence of philosophy as a distinct cultural practice in ancient Athens and its later reception and transformation in Roman thought, and
- the liberation of European thought from theological control between the seventeenth and early nineteenth centuries.

These examples are not merely illustrative but interlinked—especially in Hegel's philosophy, where *Bildung* is treated as a modern outgrowth of Greek *paideia*. Across both cases, the study explores the recurring claim of philosophical thought

[59] Laclau and Mouffe (1985).

styles to supervise and regulate other modes of cultural production. Rather than treating philosophical systems as isolated or internally coherent wholes, it reconstructs them as historically embedded forms of cultural production shaped by discursive antagonism and institutional positioning.

1.5.2 Methodological Orientation

While Fleck's theory provides the conceptual backbone of this study, its epistemological scope must be expanded in order to account for the broader social and institutional determinants of cultural change. Chapter 5 develops this expansion in detail, but the general orientation is already clear: Fleck's theory is supplemented with analytic tools drawn from Bourdieu (fields and cultural production), Ernesto Laclau and Chantal Mouffe (discursive struggle and articulatory practices), and Michel Foucault (discursive practices and institutional subject-positions). These conceptual resources allow thought styles to be situated within cultural contexts.

The study adopts an interdisciplinary and reflexive approach, drawing on scholarship from philosophy, the sociology of knowledge, classical studies, discourse analysis, and various branches of historical research—including ancient, early modern, intellectual, medical, media, and institutional history. At each stage, the study attempts to engage critically with influential interpretations and scholarly narratives, scrutinizing them for reductive assumptions, implicit binaries, or unexamined historiographical projections. This critical stance is not confined to theoretical literature; it extends also to classical and early modern source texts, which are treated both as cultural products and as interventions in ongoing struggles over meaning, legitimacy, and authority.

The method combines close analysis of key texts—including Plato's *Republic* and *Laws*, Cicero's *Tusculan Disputations*, Vesalius's *Fabrica*, Hobbes's *Leviathan*, Kant's *The Conflict of the Faculties*, and Hegel's *Lectures on the History of Philosophy*—with a reconstruction of the discursive and institutional conditions in which these texts were produced, circulated, and received. The aim is not to produce a comprehensive intellectual history, but to trace the emergence and transformation of thought styles across different contexts, illuminating the role of collective cognition and discursive conflict in shaping cultural shifts.

1.5.3 Outline

1.5.3.1 Chapters 2–5: Theory and Methodology

This section lays the theoretical and methodological groundwork for the study. It reconstructs Ludwik Fleck's concepts of thought collectives and thought styles within their intellectual, historical, and sociological contexts, clarifying their distinctiveness and explaining how they diverge from better-known models such as those of Kuhn or Foucault. Fleck's theory is then supplemented with tools from Bourdieu (cultural production and social fields), Laclau and Mouffe (discursive antagonism and articulatory practices), and Foucault (institutionalized subject positions), enabling a more robust engagement with the external conditions that shape cognition. A flexible, multi-layered methodological approach is developed that integrates discourse analysis, institutional critique, and historical reconstruction.

1.5.3.2 Chapters 6–10: Application

The second part applies the theoretical framework to selected case studies of cultural transformation. Beginning with the emergence of philosophy in fifth- and fourth-century Athens, the analysis explores how philosophical thought styles differentiated themselves from rival practices such as sophistry, medicine, and tragic poetry. It then traces the transmission and rearticulation of the Socratic caesura through Roman and early modern contexts, before examining how Hegel reimagined *Bildung* as a synthesis of Greek *paideia* within the institutional setting of the German university. The final case study explores Enlightenment and post-Enlightenment debates over the autonomy of philosophy in relation to the state, censorship, and religious authority. Each study highlights the explanatory reach of Fleck's framework while showing how thought styles were shaped by complex interplays between discourse, power, and institutions—including, in the modern period, contests over philosophical autonomy, state censorship, and the regulation of public reason.

1.5.3.3 Conclusions

The concluding chapter synthesizes key findings, reflects on the utility of Fleck's framework, contrasts rival models of cognitive authority, and situates Fleck within overlooked intellectual traditions.

References

Afeltowicz Ł, Sojak R (2015) Arystokraci i rzemieślnicy. Synergia stylów badawczych. Wydawnictwo Naukowe Uniwersytetu Mikołaja Kopernika, Torun

Binney N (2023) Ludwik Fleck's reasonable relativism about science. Synthese 201:40. https://doi.org/10.1007/s11229-022-04018-w

Blanning T (1981) The enlightenment in Catholic Germany. In: Porter R, Teich M (eds) The enlightenment in national context. CUP, Cambridge, pp 106–117

Borck C (2004) Message in a bottle from 'the crisis of reality': on Ludwik Fleck's interventions for an open epistemology. Stud Hist Philosophy Biol Biomed Sci 35(3):447–464

Bourdieu P (1993) The field of cultural production. Columbia University Press, New York

Cohen G (1978) Karl Marx's theory of history a defence. Princeton University Press, Princeton
Condé ML, Jarnicki P (2023) Ludwik Fleck: thought style and thought collective in the historiography of science. In: Condé ML, Salomon M (eds) Handbook for the historiography of science. Historiographies of science. Springer, Cham. https://doi.org/10.1007/978-3-031-27510-4_5
Cornford FM (1912) From religion to philosophy: a study in the origins of western speculation. E. Arnold, London
Dersley S (2015a) The Copernican hypotheses Part 1. J Appl Cult Stud 1
Dersley S (2015b) The Copernican hypotheses part 2. J Appl Cult Stud 1
Downie JA (2005) Public and private: the myth of the bourgeois public sphere. In: Wall C (ed) A concise companion to the restoration and the eighteenth century. Blackwell, Oxford, pp 58–79
Eagleton T (2011) Why Marx was right. Yale University Press, New Haven
Epstein K (1966) The Genesis of German conservatism. Princeton University Press, Princeton
Fleck L (1979) Genesis and development of a scientific fact [1935]. The University of Chicago Press, Chicago
Fleck L (1986a) On the Crisis of 'Reality' [1929]. In: Cognition and Fact. Boston Studies in the Philosophy of Science, vol 87. Springer, Dordrecht. https://doi.org/10.1007/978-94-009-4498-5_3
Fleck L (1986b) Scientific observation and perception in General [1935]. In: Cognition and Fact. Boston studies in the philosophy of science, vol 87. Springer, Dordrecht. https://doi.org/10.1007/978-94-009-4498-5_4
Fleck L (1986c) The problem of epistemology [1936]. In: Cognition and fact. Boston studies in the philosophy of science, vol 87. Springer, Dordrecht. https://doi.org/10.1007/978-94-009-4498-5_5
Foucault M (1980) Truth and power. In: Gordon C (ed) Power/knowledge. Selected interviews and other writings 1972–1977. Harvester Press, Hemel Hempstead, pp 109–133
Foucault M (1989) The archaeology of knowledge [1969] (trans: Sheridan Smith AM) Routledge, London
Freudenthal G, McLaughlin P (2009) Classical marxist historiography of science: the Hessen-Grossmann-Thesis. In: Freudenthal G, McLaughlin P (eds) The social and economic roots of the scientific revolution. Boston studies in the philosophy of science, vol 278. Springer, Dordrecht. https://doi.org/10.1007/978-1-4020-9604-4_1
Fuller S (2006) The philosophy of science and technology studies. Routledge, New York and London
Garrard G (2006) Counter-enlightenments from the eighteenth century to the present. Routledge, Abingdon
Gregor MJ (1979) Translator's introduction. In: Kant I (ed) The conflict of the faculties (pp. vii–xxxiv). Anaris Books, New York
Hacking I (1999) The social construction of what? Harvard University Press, Cambridge, MA
Harwood J (1986) Ludwik Fleck and the sociology of knowledge. Soc Stud Sci 16(1):173–187. https://doi.org/10.1177/030631286016001009
Havelock EA (1963) Preface to Plato. Harvard University Press, Cambridge
Hessen B (2009) The social and economic roots of newton's principia. In: Freudenthal G, McLaughlin P (eds) The social and economic roots of the scientific revolution, pp. 41–101. Boston Studies in the Philosophy of Science, vol. 278. Springer, Dordrecht
Horlacher R (2017) The educated subject and the German concept of building. Routledge, New York and London
Jaeger W (1947) The theology of the Early Greek philosophers. Oxford University Press, London
Kant I (1970) What is orientation in thinking. In: Reiss H (ed) Kant's political writings. CUP, Cambridge, pp 237–249
Kmita J (1991) Essays on the theory of social cognition. PWN, Warsaw
Kuhn TS (1957) The Copernican revolution. Harvard University Press, Massachussetts
Kuhn TS (1962) The structure of scientific revolutions. University of Chicago Press, Chicago and London

Kuhn TS (1976) Foreword to genesis and development of a scientific fact. In: Trenn TJ, Merton RK (eds) Fleck L Genesis and development of a scientific fact. Chicago, pp vii–xi
Laclau E, Mouffe C (1985) Hegemony and socialist strategy. Verso, London and New York
Laks A (2018) The concept of presocratic philosophy: its origin, development, and significance. Princeton University Press
Laks A (2022) Plato's second republic: an essay on the laws. Princeton University Press, Princeton
Latour B (2008) A textbook case revisited. knowledge as mode of existence. In: Hackett EJ, Amsterdamska O, Lynch M, Wajcman J (eds) The handbook of science and technology studies. The MIT Press, Cambridge, MA, pp 83–112
Laursen JC (1996) The subversive Kant: the vocabulary of "Public" and "Publicity". In: Schmidt J (ed) What is enlightenment? University of California Press, Berkeley, pp 253–269
Lenin V (1961) Collected works volume 5. Foreign Languages Publishing House, Moscow
Lloyd GE (1979) Magic, reason and experience: studies in the origin and development of Greek Science. CUP, Cambridge
Marx K (1987) A contribution to the critique of political economy (1859). In: Marx K, Engels F (eds) Collected works volume 29 (pp. 257–389). International Publishers, New York
Marx K, Engels F (2011) The German ideology. Martino Publishing, Bristol
Milosavljevic M (2020) How archaeological communities think: re-thinking Ludwik Fleck's concept of the thought-collective according to the case of Serbian archaeology. In: Julia Roberts J, Sheppard K, Hansson U, Trigg JR (eds) Communities and knowledge production in archaeology. Manchester University Press, Manchester, pp 14–33
Mößner N (2016) Scientific images as circulating ideas: an application of Ludwik Fleck's theory of thought styles. J Gen Philos Sci 47:307–329
Munn M (2012) Eros and the laws in historical context. In: Recco G, Sanday E (eds) Plato's laws: force and truth in politics. Indiana University Press, Bloomington, pp 31–47
Nietzsche F (1999) The birth of tragedy and other writings (trans: Speirs R). CUP, Cambridge
Nowak L (2012) On the hidden unity of social and natural sciences. In: Brzechczyn K, Paprzycka K (eds) Thinking about provincialism in thinking (Poznań studies in the philosophy of the sciences and the humanities, vol. 100). Rodopi, Amsterdam and New York, pp 15–50
Paulsen F (1902) Immanuel Kant, his life and doctrine (trans: Creighton JE, Lefevre AC). Scribner, London
Pickering A (1995) The mangle of practice. University of Chicago Press, Chicago and London
Pinker S (2018) Enlightenment now. Viking, New York
Plato (1980) The laws of Plato (trans: Pangle TL). The University of Chicago Press, Chicago and London
Said EW (2003) Orientalism. Penguin, London
Sauter MJ (2009) Visions of the enlightenment: the Edict on Religion of 1788 and the politics of the public sphere in eighteenth-century Prussia. Brill, Boston
Schmidt J (1996) Introduction. In: What is enlightenment. University of California Press, Berkeley, pp 1–44
Schwartz P (1925) Der erste Kulturkampf in Preußen um Kirche und Schule. Weidmannsche Buchhandlung, Berlin
Shapin S, Schaffer S (1985) Leviathan and the Air-pump: Hobbes, Boyle, and the experimental life. Princeton University Press, Princeton, N.J.
Thompson EP (1993) Customs in common. Penguin, London
Vernant JP (1988) Myth and society in ancient Greece. Zone Books, New York
Vlastos G (1947) Equality and justice in early Greek cosmologies. Class Philol 42(3):156–178
Whaley J (1981) The Protestant Enlightenment in Germany. In: Porter R, Teich M (eds) The enlightenment in national context. CUP, Cambridge, pp 106–117

Chapter 2
Fleck's Theory in Context

Abstract This chapter contextualizes Ludwik Fleck's epistemology, emphasizing his commitment to democratic values and collaborative knowledge production, and contrasting his inclusive vision of science with elitist models of knowledge control. It examines Fleck's critique of Kurt Riezler's neo-Kantianism and his alignment with Niels Bohr's interactive framework, which inspired Fleck's rejection of representational cognition and the notion of absolute reality. Extending Bohr's insights beyond quantum physics, Fleck developed a socially interactive model of cognition. His marginalization in interwar Lwów informed his rejection of prevailing thought styles and reinforced his commitment to collective, historically grounded modes of knowing.

The chapter then assesses Fleck's relationship to the so-called Polish School of Philosophy of Medicine—a category whose coherence is itself debated. Drawing on Ilana Löwy's work and more recent scholarship, it examines how figures such as Biegański and Kramsztyk articulated a patient-centred, holistic epistemology that emerged under conditions of political subjugation and professional exclusion. Fleck drew on this milieu—particularly its emphasis on therapy, specificity, and reflexivity—while remaining at its margins due to his position as a Jewish intellectual.

Finally, in response to Thomas Schnelle's interpretation, the chapter reconsiders Fleck's critique of the Lwów School, especially his rejection of Twardowski's emphasis on objectivity and the ideal of the neutral university instructor. In contrast to nationalist and universalist abstractions, Fleck emphasized the situated, collective, and evolving nature of cognition. His epistemology, shaped by marginalization, implicitly challenges the exclusionary structures of the interwar Polish university and advances a reflexive, open-ended model of knowledge.

S. Dersley, *Thought Collectives and Cultural Change*, Living Signs of Law 1,
https://doi.org/10.1007/978-3-031-97431-1_2

2.1 Positioning Fleck's Thought

2.1.1 The Democratic Origins of Scientific Thinking

From 1929 to 1960, Fleck's texts consistently championed 'democratic values' and the 'communal style of thinking'.[1] This was not merely a rhetorical gesture: Fleck argued that democracy and the natural sciences were deeply interconnected. In *On the crisis of 'Reality'* (1929) he suggests that the style of thinking typical of the natural sciences emerged from skilled labour and children's play:

> It was to be found among the artisans, the seamen, the barber-surgeons (*Wundärzte*), the leather-workers and saddlers, the gardeners and probably also among children playing. Wherever serious or playful work was done by many (*von vielen*), where common or opposite interests met repeatedly, this uniquely democratic way of thinking was indispensable (*war diese einzige demokratische Denkart unentbehrlich*). (Fleck 1986b, 50)

Fleck maintains that the way of thinking of the natural sciences (*die naturwissenschaftliche Denkart*) has retained this democratic character: 'it rejects the privilege of divine origin and seeks to be accessible and useful to everybody'.[2]

Fleck's polemical characterization places the practical knowledge produced by the natural sciences in opposition to the theoretical-philosophical explanations of astrology—a Great Science (*eine große Wissenschaft*) that exerted its influence over 'almost every branch of knowledge', and on 'political-economic and personal life'.[3] The democratic thought style of the natural sciences is said to have 'replaced' (*abgelöst*) that of astrology.

Based on Fleck's explicit framing, the following extrapolation would appear reasonable: the thought style of the natural sciences emerged through bottom-up processes—through the collaborative and competitive knowledge production involved in specialized trades and crafts, and from the trial-and-error methods used in practical problem-solving and games. This thought style can be described as democratic due to its origin and purpose: it emerged from the everyday knowledge practices of the *demos*—widely disseminated and accessible—and, unlike systems claiming divine authority and exerting elite, top-down control, it aims to be accessible and useful to the people.

This positive valorization of practical knowledge, explicitly linked to skilled labour and children's play, positions Fleck's social epistemology in direct opposition to elitist, anti-social, and institutionalized philosophies. For instance, in contrast to the oligarchic thought style represented in Plato's works, such as *Charmides* and *Republic*, whose protagonists sought to control the *technē* and material production of the metics (*metoikoi*) and regulate the forms of cultural production

---

[1] Fleck (1929, 1986b, p. 55); Fleck (1986g, p. 156).

[2] Fleck (1929, 1986b, p. 50).

[3] Fleck (1929, 1986b, p. 50).

consumed by the *dēmos*, thereby constructing a hierarchical epistemology that excluded skilled manual work from the exalted realm of true knowledge and real science (*epistēmē*), Fleck's thought style moves in the opposite direction. He argues that the experimental approach inherent in skilled manual labour—which develops spontaneously when democratic, collaborative, and competitive knowledge practices are allowed to flourish—is, in fact, the very foundation of scientific thinking.

Apparently aware that his framing edges towards a somewhat rose-tinted conception of both democracy and the natural sciences, Fleck adds a cautious qualification:

> Yet we have learned from experience that every democracy contains its little untruths (*jede Demokratie ihre kleinen Lügen hat*), since what is wanted is an impressive, majestic government not just a useful and wise one. This is why there are medals, titles, flags and presidents. Therefore the natural sciences have their own natural philosophy and their *Weltanschauung*. (Fleck 1986b, 50)

Fleck's subsequent paragraphs, which focus on the disparity between official theory and living practice—between how democracy and the natural sciences function in reality and how we would like them to function—suggest that Fleck believes the natural sciences *would be* democratic if they were true to their origin and essential purpose. Yet the lure of prestige introduces a quiet distortion: the natural sciences accommodate their own 'little untruths'—their natural philosophy and *Weltanschauung*—that prevent them from being fully accessible and beneficial to all.

These passages place Fleck in opposition to both his immediate political environment and the scientific community. Firstly, as a resident of the then-Polish Lwów, in 1929 Fleck was living under Józef Piłsudski's Sanation (*Sanacja*) government, an autocratic regime that had taken power through the May 1926 Coup, significantly curtailing parliamentary democracy. Fleck's biting observation—'what is wanted is an impressive, majestic government not just a useful and wise one. This is why there are medals, titles, flags and presidents'—can be read as a sarcastic critique of the militaristic pomp that characterized Piłsudski's presidency.

Secondly, in 1929, Fleck occupied 'an extremely marginal position' in relation to renowned academic and research institutions. After losing his position at Lwów University in 1923, most likely due to the antisemitic policies and campaigns prevalent at the university during the early 1920s, he made a living as a bacteriologist and serologist in a hospital laboratory.[4] Nevertheless, despite his position of peripheral and professional obscurity, *On the Crisis of 'Reality'* was published in the prestigious German journal *Naturwissenschaften* as *Zur Krise der "Wirklichkeit"* and credited to 'Von Ludwik Fleck, Lemberg'.[5] Cornelius Borck describes it as 'the response of an almost unknown Polish microbiologist' to a paper published the previous year by the German philosopher and high-ranking diplomat Kurt Riezler.[6]

---

[4] Freudenthal and Löwy (1988, pp. 636–637).

[5] Fleck (1929, p. 425).

[6] Borck (2004, p. 449); Riezler (1928).

The designation of Fleck's place of residence as 'Lemberg' situates his text at the former periphery of the German-speaking world, in the 'shatterzone' created by the collapse of the Habsburg Empire.[7] The city of Lemberg (German)/ Lwów (Polish)/ Львів–L'viv (Ukrainian)/ Львов–Lvov (Russian)/ לעמבעריק–Lemberik (Yiddish) was a highly contested, multiethnic city of great symbolic significance, claimed, fought over, and ruled by various regimes throughout Fleck's lifetime. Control of the city shifted repeatedly: it was Lemberg under Habsburg rule from 1772 to 1914; Львов (Lvov) under Russian occupation in 1914–1915 during the early stages of WWI, which saw an intense Russification campaign[8]; Lemberg once more from 1915 to 1918, after Austria-Hungary regained control; briefly L'viv in November 1918 under the West Ukrainian People's Republic; and Lwów from 1919 to 1939, when it became 'a center and a prize of Polish nationalism' in the *Kresy*,[9] the Eastern Borderlands of the Second Polish Republic.

Fleck would witness his hometown become Львов under Soviet occupation in 1939, then Lemberg again in 1941 under Nazi occupation, as the city became a focal point in the 'bloodlands'—a region ravaged by mass deportation, enslavement, death pits, genocide, and ethnic cleansing, caught between the alliance and eventual confrontation of the Soviet Union and Nazi Germany.[10] This shifting geopolitical landscape, with its cycles of conquest and oppression, shaped Fleck's peripheral position both geographically and professionally.

In the 1920s and 1930s, Fleck's marginality was cemented through antisemitic exclusion from academic institutions and the constraints of working in a hospital laboratory. Yet this marginalization prefigured an even darker trajectory during the Holocaust, where his scientific practice was literally ghettoized. Initially, Fleck developed a typhus vaccine to save lives in the ghetto, using the urine of typhoid sufferers to aid his fellow inhabitants. This effort was later appropriated by the Nazis, who forced him to produce the vaccine on a larger scale—first in a factory in Lwów, even as his family and community were annihilated in the Janowska concentration camp just outside the city, and later under conditions of enslaved scientific labour at Auschwitz and Buchenwald. These experiences testify to levels of exploitation and peripheralization that resist full articulation in language: while we have the term 'ghettoized', no word adequately captures the situation of a scientist and philosopher compelled to conduct his work in extermination camps.[11]

---

[7] Bartov and Weitz (2013).

[8] Mick (2016, pp. 27–30).

[9] Amar (2015, p. 3).

[10] Snyder (2010).

[11] On the horrors of the Lwów Ghetto and the Janowska camp, see Friedman F (1945) [in Polish] and Friedman P (1980) [in English]. For an account of Fleck's scientific research conducted whilst in the Lwów Ghetto, see Ciesielska (2020). On Fleck's experiences at Auschwitz and Buchenwald, see e.g. Grzybowski and Ciesielska (2014) and Löwy (2020). For an account of the tragic fate of Lvov-Warsaw philosophers during World War II and the Holocaust, including Fleck, see Pakszys (2019).

Returning to 1929, Fleck's response to Riezler can be treated—quite literally—as a communication from the marginalized periphery to the prestigious centre, from a laboratory worker struggling to support his family in one of the poorest cities in Europe[12] to a man who, on the one hand, was the *Kurator* and professor of philosophy at Frankfurt University, rubbing shoulders with the likes of Leo Strauss and Martin Heidegger and responsible for hiring Max Horkheimer, and on the other hand, had served as speechwriter to the Kaiser, adviser to the Chancellor, and representative of the Weimar Republic's Foreign Office.[13]

2.1.2 Fleck vs. Riezler

A few aspects and features of Riezler's 1928 paper evidently prompted Fleck's response. First, as Wayne C. Thompson makes clear, Riezler focused on various kinds of crises throughout his diplomatic and academic work: World War I, the revolutions in Russia and Germany, the multifaceted crises facing the Weimar Republic, and the threat to the University posed by the spread of National Socialism among students.[14] Additionally, as Borck shows, Riezler's paper *On the Crisis of Reality* was 'deeply embedded in a rich debate on a crisis in the sciences with widely acknowledged consequences for the traditional concept of reality'.[15] Throughout the 1920s, German scholars in fields such as psychology, biology, medicine, and philosophy published numerous articles addressing what they perceived as an epistemological crisis arising from developments in physics and the increasing fragmentation of the sciences into ever more specialized fields.

This epistemological crisis was of crucial importance for Fleck's thought—not only in terms of the issues at stake but also, we can suppose, due to his growing interest in collective cognition and the fact that this crisis was widely recognized in

[12] Norman Davies drew on statistics to state that in 1887 'Galicia could fairly claim to be the poorest province of Europe' (2005, p. 106). Christoph Mick emphasizes the devastating impact that World War I had on the economic situation of L'viv (2016, p. 98). In her analysis of ethnic tensions and student life at Lwów University, Ewa Bukowska-Marczak highlights unemployment and poverty as key factors that not only contributed to conflict but were also exploited for its purposes: '[...] in the interwar period, Lwów was a city where poverty reigned' (2019, p. 23).

[13] Thompson (1980, ix, pp. 211–216). This passage from Thompson's Preface (ix) attempts to convey Riezler's centrality: 'Few Americans were aware of Riezler's German past or of his anti-Hitler resistance activity while in the United States. Few suspected that this eminent scholar of Parmenides and Thucydides, Michelangelo and Goethe had, at the age of twenty-five, attracted the attention of the German kaiser, for whom he wrote speeches, and had become a political adviser to Chancellor Theobald von Bethmann Hollweg. Few knew that he had advised Bethmann Hollweg on the dangers and prospects of war in July 1914, had helped place Lenin into power in 1917, had guided Germany's diplomatic mission in Moscow in 1918, had helped arrange peace with the United States in November 1918, and had helped create the Weimar Republic'.

[14] Thompson (1980). For a perspective on the broader cultural 'craving for crises' in Weimar Germany, which Riezler's focus might reflect, see Forman (2011, pp. 144–156).

[15] Borck (2004, p. 450).

the scholarly community. Krzysztof Szlachcic points out that the perception of crisis was not unique to German-speaking philosophers, such as the Vienna Circle: '[…] there was a widely expressed belief in Lviv regarding the necessity to rethink many fundamental issues of epistemology in light of the results being obtained at that time'.[16] While this belief became more evident in writings of the Lwów philosophers from the 1930s—Szlachcic gives the examples of Kazimierz Ajdukiewicz and Roman Ingarden—it is telling that in 1929 Fleck chose to bypass the community of Polish philosophers and insert his new ideas into the debate taking place in the German intellectual community.

Riezler's paper was likely of particular interest to Fleck because it went beyond the widely recognized crisis in epistemology to suggest the crisis lies in the nature of reality itself. The problem diagnosed by Riezler can be summarized as follows: if it is assumed that scientific knowledge represents absolute reality, what happens to this knowledge when science reveals that absolute reality is itself disordered and unpredictable?

As Borck points out, Riezler's epistemology is fundamentally neo-Kantian, anchored in a 'triple-layer model of reality'.[17] The first layer of reality consists of sensation; the second is that of representation (ranging from perception in space and time to scientific laws); and the third is the absolute reality that exists independently of any subjective sensation or representation.[18] For centuries, the scientific worldview had assumed that this absolute reality was lawfully ordered and coherent, and that science could sift through the apparent chaos of sensation to uncover general and immutable laws reflecting this underlying order. The role of science, within this framework, was to bring the second reality as close as possible to absolute reality, with the ultimate aim of fusing scientific knowledge with reality itself.[19]

In Riezler's account, this progressive scientific worldview (*die wissenschaftliche Weltanschauung*) has been shaken by developments in physics,[20] and the unity of science has fractured into multiple second realities with divergent and conflicting logical structures. Crucially, Riezler's framework suggests that absolute reality is also 'entangled' (*verstrickt*) in this crisis.[21] He argues that physics, through its use

[16] Szlachcic (2006, p. 27).

[17] Borck (2004, p. 452).

[18] Riezler (1928, pp. 705–706).

[19] Riezler (1928, p. 705): 'Je mehr wir von diesen Gesetzeli und ihrem Zusammenhang entdeckendesto mehr nähert sich das Provisorium der zweiten Wirklichkeit der absoluten dritten um am Ende der Wissenschaft ganz und gar in ihr aufzugehen'.

[20] Riezler (1928, p. 706): 'Und doch hat gerade die Entwicklung der erfolgreichsten Forschung, der physikalischen, diesen Glauben ins Wanken gebracht'.

[21] Riezler (1928, pp. 706–707): 'Diese Erwartung wurde nicht erfüllt. Die Einzelwissenschaften konvergierten nicht, sondern divergierten; sie entwickelten ihre Begriffssysteme in verschiedener Richtung. Hierdurch gingen diese Begriffssysteme der Möglichkeit eines gemeinsamen Bezuges auf eine und dieselbe dritte Wirklichkeit verlustig. Nun trat an Stelle der Ergänzung zu einer Totalität der Widerstreit. Das einheitliche Provisorium einer zweiten Wirklichkeit zerfiel in mehrere zweite Wirklichkeiten, verschiedener und einander widersprechender logischer Struktur. Hierdurch wurde die dritte Wirklichkeit in eine eigenartige Problematik verstrickt.'

of mathematical symbolism, has gone beyond intuition—sacrificing the ordering principle of the intuitive world—to adopt a conceptual framework that reveals absolute reality as disordered and unpredictable.[22] The foundational concepts underpinning the scientific worldview—matter, causality, and Euclidean space—have been undermined and cast into doubt.

Riezler proposes three possible implications of this entanglement. The first is that the large-scale order science discovers in absolute reality is actually grounded in small-scale chaos. In other words, order exists in reality, but it emerges from disorder or unknown order (*Unordnung oder unbekannten Ordnung*).[23] The second possibility is that the order science perceives in reality is a distortion: our understanding acts as a mirror, but the images of order it reflects are distortions arising from the mistaken assumption that the mirror is being held up to the flawless order of absolute reality.[24] The third possibility is that science employs multiple mirrors (conceptual frameworks), and inconsistencies or distortions arise when an inadequate or inappropriate framework is applied to a particular aspect of reality (e.g., geometry cannot capture the life of a beetle).[25]

Riezler refuses to abandon the belief in absolute reality, ultimately concluding that it must be reconceived. Instead of adhering to a worldview based on the assumption that absolute reality is static, ordered, complete, and flawless, he proposes a new worldview—one in which absolute reality is assumed to be dynamic and incomplete, where order continually emerges from disorder: its order is not a being, but a becoming (*Ihre Ordnung ist keine seiende, sondern eine werdende*).[26]

Fleck's response focuses on three elements of Riezler's paper: (1) the neo-Kantian epistemology, (2) the belief in absolute reality, and (3) the crisis of the scientific worldview.

(1) **Neo-Kantian epistemology**. Fleck rejected Riezler's distinction between first and second realities.[27] Instead of a model in which science starts from sensory data (the first reality), proceeds to construct coherent representations in the form of laws (the second reality), and ultimately aims to correspond with the third, absolute reality, Fleck proposes an alternative. He insists on a model in which sensory interaction with what is cognized is always already socially and culturally conditioned: 'every new cognitive activity depends on the previously accumulated store of knowledge. [...] Wherever and whenever we touch on something, we are always in

[22] Riezler (1928, p. 707): 'Diesem Streben opferte die Physik Stück für Stück das Ordnungsgestütze unserer anschaulichen Welt, ergriff die von der Mathematik gegebenen Möglichkeiten, über die Anschauung hinaus zu anderen Ordnungsgerüsten fortzuschreiten'.

[23] Riezler (1928, p. 706).

[24] Riezler (1928, pp. 708–709) 'Was wir fassen, ist ein Spiegelbild; der Spiegel ist unser Verstand. Wir wissen nicht, inwieweit dieser Spiegel getreu und inwieweit er ungetreu ist. Er kann getreu sein, kann aber auch bis zur Unkenntlichkeit verzeichnen. [...] So wurden wir verffihrt, mit der Vorstellung einer absoluten Wirldichkeit die einer lfickenlosen Ordnung zu verbinden.'

[25] Riezler (1928, p. 711).

[26] Riezler (1928, p. 712).

[27] Borck (2004, p. 452).

the midst and never at the beginning of cognition'.[28] Sensations, according to Fleck, are not presented to the understanding as pure or neutral building blocks; rather, what one sees is what one has been taught to see.

In the first pages of his essay, Fleck repeatedly emphasizes the role of education in instilling 'ready-made dispositions': students must learn to see. Thus, rather than Kantian subjects disinterestedly constructing objects from the sensory manifold, Fleck argues that what is given and sensed is already shaped by an intellect formed through culture. Hence, epistemology must 'be brought into a social and cultural historical context'.[29]

(2) **Absolute reality**. Following his explicit rejection of Riezler's model of reality, Fleck introduces his own model of multiple realities, in which each act of cognition and each interaction with what is cognized generates a reality:

> Thus every thinking individual, being a member of some society, has his own reality in which and according to which he lives. Everybody has even many, sometimes contradictory, realities: the reality of everyday life, a professional, a religious, a political, and a small scientific reality. And secretly he has a superstitiously fateful personal reality that renders the actual I exceptional.
>
> Each cognition, each system of cognitions, each entry into the social realm has its own corresponding reality. This is the only correct position.[30]

This is one of the passages that, in the 1980s and 1990s, led to claims that 'Fleck abandons the claim to any reality independent of the subject'[31] and to descriptions of Fleck's epistemology as 'constructivist and relativist'.[32] *On the Crisis of 'Reality'* is regarded as his most radically relativist text, primarily due to its conception of reality but also because of the explicitly political thrust of the paper.[33] However, as the scholarly literature has increasingly recognized,[34] the simplistic portrayal of Fleck as a relativist who denies the existence of a reality independent of the subject can only be upheld by ignoring key aspects of his thought as well as his explicit

[28] Fleck (1986b, p. 48).

[29] Fleck (1986b, p. 48).

[30] Fleck (1986b, p. 49; 1929, p. 426): 'Jedes denkende Individuum hat also als Mitglied irgendeiner Gesellschaft seine eigene Wirklichkeit, in der und nach der es lebt. Jeder Mensch besitzt sogar viele, zum Teil einander widersprechende Wirklichkeiten: die Wirklichkeit des alltäglichen Lebens, eine berufliche, eine religiöse, eine politische und eine kleine wissenschaftliche Wirklichkeit. Und verborgen eine abergläubisch-schicksalsvolle, das eigene Ich zur Ausnahme machende, persönliche Wirklichkeit.

Jedem Erkennen, jedem Erkenntnissystem, jedem sozialen Beziehungseingehen entspricht eine eigene Wirklichkeit. Dies ist der einzig gerechte Standpunkt.'

[31] Schnelle (1986b, p. 242).

[32] Löwy (1990b, p. 224).

[33] See e.g. Zittel (2010, p. 187).

[34] Borck (2004), Zittel (2010), Condé and Jarnicki (2023), Binney (2023).

statements (e.g., his denial of relativism in response to accusations from both Izydora Dąmbska and Tadeusz Bilikiewicz[35]).

Yet even in *On the Crisis of 'Reality'*, when Fleck is at his most radical, there are clear indicators that his theoretical stance should not be understood as straightforwardly relativist. As Zittel points out, Fleck concludes this passage by shifting to the meta-level: 'This is the only correct position (*Dies ist der einzig gerechte Standpunkt*)'. Zittel further observes that Fleck does not provide any epistemological justification for this claim; the use of the German word *Gerecht* suggests only a normative or political judgment.[36]

Six years later, in 1935–36, Fleck will attempt to clarify this meta-level position through his proposed science of 'comparative epistemology'. *On the Crisis of 'Reality'*, being Fleck's first attempt at outlining a general epistemology, presents ideas, positions, and accounts that are refined and expressed with greater clarity in his mid-1930s writings. For instance, the use of Vesalius and the example of the emergence of a new thought style that first appears in *Crisis* are reworked in *Scientific Observation and Perception in General* (1935)[37]—discussed in detail in Chap. 4. Similarly, Fleck's account of how the multiple realities generated by individual cognition become shared and constrained realities will be more thoroughly developed over the next 6 years.

Nevertheless, the core component of Fleck's epistemology is clearly articulated here in 1929, in opposition to Riezler's neo-Kantian conception of reality:

> *For cognition is neither passive contemplation nor acquisition of the only possible insight into something given. It is an active, live interrelationship, a reshaping and being reshaped, in short, an act of creation.* Neither the 'subject' nor the 'object' receive a reality of their own; all existence is based upon interaction and is relative. [emphasis in the original][38]

For Fleck, cognition is interactive rather than representational. Ways of knowing—whether everyday or scientific—do not hold up a mirror to absolute reality; instead, they create multiple, different realities. At the most basic level, reality is defined as what is created when the 'individual' or 'human being' interacts with 'the cognized' using socially conditioned ways of knowing. Fleck uses the example of a schizophrenic's cognition to illustrate that these individual realities, though shaped by language, can nevertheless be ephemeral, insignificant, and inaccessible to others.

However, in the very next paragraph, Fleck indicates two critical points: (1) there are realities that transcend the individual, and (2) the cognized is independent of the individual:

---

[35] Fleck (1938, 1990, p. 268); For Fleck's insistence that he is not a relativist, see Seidel (2011, p. 224).

[36] Zittel (2010, p. 188).

[37] Fleck (1986c).

[38] Fleck (1986b, p. 48; 1929, p. 426): '*Denn Erkennen ist weder passive Kontemplation, noch Erwerb einzig möglicher Einsicht ins fertig Gegebene. Es ist ein tätiges, lebendiges Beziehungseingehen, ein Umformen und Umgeformtwerden, kurz, ein Schaffen.* Weder dem "Subjekt"noch dem "Objekt"kommt selbstständige Realität zu; jede Existenz beruht auf Wechselwirkung und ist relativ'.

> However, there exist realities with style that are founded upon serious, continual work by large groups and great mean, in the spirit of which people live (or for the sake of which they die). They develop, flourish, endure, waste away – leading their own lives, such as forms of government or social arrangements. The relative independence of the cognized from the individual is well illustrated in the fact that different individuals frequently make the same discovery or invention simultaneously but independently from one another. Cognitions are formed by human beings, but also conversely they form their human beings. It would be simply foolish to ask here what is 'cause' and what 'effect'.[39]

Fleck's argument suggests that *existence* is relative, with each of us continually producing our own realities through individual acts of cognition. At the same time, we inhabit less arbitrary, shared realities that are made accessible and meaningful through language. Furthermore, we can participate in supra-individual, highly stylized realities that transcend individual cognition and persist across generations.

It is at this point in *On the Crisis of 'Reality'* that Fleck invokes the accessible, democratic style of thinking characteristic of the natural sciences, which, as discussed earlier, emerged from manual work and children's play. The natural sciences interact with 'the cognized' (*das Erkannte*). Since reality is defined as the socially conditioned interaction between the cognizer and the cognized, it makes no sense to conceive of any reality outside of cognition or to attempt to bring knowledge closer to an ideal reality that exists prior to such interaction:

> We approach the ideal, 'absolute' reality not even asymptotically since it changes incessantly, renews itself and moves away from us at the same pace as we are advancing. [...] The striving to know, to gain knowledge of the absolute is based upon a strange misunderstanding: is it not the same as if one wanted to open up a pristine jungle, without changing its condition?[40]

Fleck's polemical response to Riezler is, as Zittel notes,[41] fundamentally political. When Fleck compares the natural philosophy and *Weltanschauung* of the natural sciences to the distorted trappings of democracy ('medals, titles, flags and presidents'), he suggests that what Riezler takes to be the scientific worldview—an 'awkward metaphysics' fixated on absolute reality—is, in fact, a distortion of the democratic natural sciences. For Fleck, this fixation obstructs progress and must give way to a new style of thinking: 'A new, up-to-date reality will be created'.[42]

---

[39] Fleck (1986b, p. 50).

[40] Fleck (1986b, p. 55; 1929, p. 429): 'Wir nähern uns der idealen "absoluten"Wirklichkeit nicht einmal asymptotisch, denn unaufhörlich ändert und erneuert sie sich und entfernt sich in gleichem Maße von uns, wie wir vorwärts schreiten [...] Das Streben nach dem Erkennen des Absoluten beruht auf einem sonderbaren Missverständnis: Ist es nicht dasselbe, als wollte man einen jungfräulichen Dschungel erschließen, ohne seinen jungfräulichen Zustand zu verändern?'

[41] Zittel (2010).

[42] Fleck (1986b, p. 57; 1929, p. 430): Fleck's polemical invocation at the end of his paper: 'Man wird anders zum Leben erziehen, Leben und Kunst anders gestalten. Man wird eine neue, zeitgemäße Wirklichkeit schaffen. Wozu plumpe Metaphysik, wenn die Physik von morgen jede Phantasie überflügeln wird?' Man lasse freie Bahn der Arbeit von Fachleuten und halte im eigenen Denken freien Platz für die Zukunft!.

(3) **Crisis in the Scientific Worldview**. For Fleck, there was *no crisis*. Or rather, what Riezler presents as a crisis—the unity of science fracturing into divergent and contradictory individual sciences, the problematizing of key scientific concepts, and the discovery of small-scale disorder and unpredictability—are developments that Fleck welcomes or even celebrates.

2.1.3 Fleck's Alignment with Bohr

Riezler's 1928 paper, primarily a response to Niels Bohr's *The Quantum Postulate and the Recent Development of Atomic Theory* published earlier that year in *Naturwissenschaften*, identified the new physics as the primary culprit behind the crisis in epistemology and reality. In contrast to Riezler, Fleck aligned himself deeply with Bohr. Scholars have suggested that Fleck drew on Bohr's work as one of several influences shaping his epistemology,[43] engaging with it selectively and somewhat instrumentally to illustrate his own considerations,[44] while relying on a relatively narrow set of sources,[45] and using Bohr's text to expand his focus beyond the 'medical way of thinking' to a general epistemology applicable to all sciences and styles of thought.[46] However, Fleck's engagement with Bohr's text—though undoubtedly more intuitive than in-depth—went far beyond instrumental use; it involved deep epistemological concerns, and Bohr's framework—which emphasized interaction and problematized the subject-object distinction—was an abiding touchstone in Fleck's theorizing (for instance, he cited Bohr again in *Scientific Observation and Perception in General*—a key text from his peak years (1935–1936)[47]—and later in 1947 in *To Look, To See, To Know*[48]).

The emphasis on interaction linked Fleck's emerging conception of thought styles to Bohr's insights into quantum mechanics, particularly the interplay between observer and phenomenon. At the same time, Fleck signaled, implicitly but publicly—in a prestigious German journal—that his alignment with Bohr could be read as an act of opposition to the thought styles prevalent in Vienna and Lwów.

Fleck's alignment with Bohr signaled his rejection of any thought style that claimed scientific concepts or theories represented objective reality, in the sense of a reality independent of observers. Hence, this alignment implicitly challenged the thought styles that held sway at the University of Vienna and at Kazimierz University in Lwów, which wielded great cognitive authority and cultural capital. By explicitly aligning with Bohr against Riezler, who bemoaned the fragmentation of science,

[43] Löwy (1990b, pp. 223–224).

[44] Sady (2000, p. 19).

[45] Hedfors (2007, pp. 74–75).

[46] Zittel (2010, p. 188).

[47] Fleck (1986c, p. 66).

[48] Fleck (1986e, p. 142).

Fleck also implicitly staked out his position in opposition to the Vienna Circle's pursuit of a unified science and neutral knowledge—articulated precisely in 1929—which contrasted sharply with his emerging, 'relativist' theory of thought styles. Similarly, while Fleck did not explicitly oppose Twardowski or the Lwów school, his embrace of Bohr's interactional model—along with its emphasis on uncertainty and the logic of complementarity—set him at odds with Twardowski's enduring concern for objective truth.[49]

Mauro L. Conde and Paweł Jarnicki rightly situate Fleck's engagement with Bohr in the context of his opposition to the Vienna Circle, particularly their physics-based epistemology.[50] However, their emphasis on Fleck's 'biological model' as an alternative to the 'model of physics' is somewhat misleading. I would argue that in 1929 Fleck had not yet developed his biological model, which took shape in the mid-1930s; rather, his engagement with Bohr's quantum postulate marked a more fundamental positioning. By publicly aligning himself with the most radical thought style in Europe—physicists who were just embarking on the 'Second Quantum Revolution' and considering a critical break from classical physics—while implicitly opposing others, Fleck positioned himself within a broader epistemological debate about science, observation, and knowledge. This deeper alignment, grounded in shared epistemological concerns, especially the centrality of interaction, will be explored in the following paragraphs.

In *On the Crisis of 'Reality'*, Fleck highlights a passage from the non-technical, accessible introductory section of Bohr's paper that discusses the non-negligible influence of observation on atomic phenomena:

> Now the quantum postulate implies that any observation of atomic phenomena will involve an interaction with the agency of observation not to be neglected. Accordingly, an independent reality in the ordinary physical sense can neither be ascribed to the phenomena nor to the agencies of observation. After all, the concept of observation is in so far arbitrary as it depends upon which objects are included in the system to be observed.[51]

Bohr goes on to clarify that his argument applies specifically to quantum-level phenomena rather than to all physical systems:

> Just as the relativity theory has taught us that the convenience of distinguishing sharply between space and time rests solely on the smallness of the velocities ordinarily met with compared to the velocity of light, we learn from the quantum theory that the appropriateness of our usual causal space-time description depends entirely upon the small value of the quantum of action as compared to the actions involved in ordinary sense perceptions.[52]

Fleck responds to Bohr's position in a way that suggests he saw Bohr's focus on small-scale non-negligibility as a limiting factor. When Fleck expands on Bohr's account of the observer's influence, he insists that Bohr's insights can be applied universally, arguing that the entanglement of observer and observed is an inevitable

[49] Twardowski (1900, 1933), Schnelle (1986b, p. 238).

[50] Condé and Jarnicki (2023, p. 94).

[51] Bohr (1928, p. 580); Fleck (1929, p. 428).

[52] Bohr (1928, p. 580).

condition of all observation, not just at the quantum level. To emphasize this point, Fleck extends the discussion to the temporal scale of centuries, where the cumulative impact of prolonged observation and treatment becomes undeniable:

> This statement applies to all observations of any phenomenon whatever, but the mutual relationship with the means of observation is relatively negligible in most cases. Yet, if the 'treatment' of the phenomena, with whatever instruments, goes on over centuries, will the effect not become significant? To observe, to cognize, is always to probe and thus literally to reshape/transform the object of knowledge (*Beobachten, Erkennen, ist immer ein Abtasten, also wörtlich Umformen des Erkenntnisgegenstandes*).[53]

This move to a broader temporal scale—though compelling—was not strictly necessary to make the essential point. Since Fleck had already argued that cognition creates realities through interaction with the cognized, it follows that observation—whether at the quantum level or the scale of galaxies—interactively creates and reshapes the objects of knowledge.

Bohr's later reflections resonate with this interpretation, as he himself acknowledged the applicability of quantum theoretical insights beyond physics:

> In this respect, quantum theory presents us with a novel situation in physical science, but attention was called to the very close analogy with the situation as regards analysis and synthesis of experience, which we meet in many other fields of human knowledge and interest. As is well known, many of the difficulties in psychology originate in the different placing of the separation lines between object and subject in the analysis of various aspects of psychical experience.[54]

Thus, Bohr provided Fleck with a key conceptual tool for his rejection of neo-Kantian epistemology and metaphysics: the dynamic and unavoidable entanglement between the cognizer and the cognized—the interaction that Fleck will later argue is the essential requirement for there to be any knowledge at all.

In this way, Fleck entered the debate on the side of the most cutting-edge challengers to classical physics—Bohr and Werner Heisenberg—who had not only rejected Newtonian absolute space and time, as Einstein had done, but were also questioning the remaining classical commitments that Einstein upheld. Central to Einstein's realism, as articulated in his essay *Physics and Reality* (1936), was the belief that scientific theories and concepts represented an objective reality independent of human perception and that nature itself was governed by deterministic causal laws.[55]

In the concluding paragraph of the 1928 essay, which Riezler responds to and Fleck cites in support of his position, Bohr presents a striking argument. He implicitly addresses Einstein's criticisms of quantum theory, explaining why quantum theory must build upon Einstein's insights while rejecting classical assumptions. Bohr argues for overcoming visualizations and language rooted in ordinary

---

[53] Fleck (1986b, p. 53; 1929, p. 428). Translation slightly modified.

[54] Bohr (1949, p. 224).

[55] Einstein (1936, p. 374) described quantum theory as 'an incomplete representation of real things,' cautioning that its statistical nature, while successful in explaining phenomena, might mislead efforts to find a uniform basis for physics.

perception and suggests that complementarity transcends the duality of subject and object:

> Already the formulation of the relativity argument implies essentially the union of the spacetime co-ordination and the demand of causality characterising the classical theories. In the adaptation of the relativity requirement to the quantum postulate we must therefore be prepared to meet with a renunciation as to visualisation in the ordinary sense going still further than in the formulation of the quantum laws considered here. Indeed, we find ourselves here on the very path taken by Einstein of adapting our modes of perception borrowed from the sensations to the gradually deepening knowledge of the laws of Nature. The hindrances met with on this path originate above all in the fact that, so to say, every word in the language refers to our ordinary perception. In the quantum theory we meet this difficulty at once in the question of the inevitability of the feature of irrationality characterising the quantum postulate. I hope, however, that the idea of complementarity is suited to characterise the situation, which bears a deep-going analogy to the general difficulty in the formation of human ideas, inherent in the distinction between subject and object.

Bohr's complex argument contends that Einstein's innovation had not left classical causality intact but had, in fact, fundamentally altered it by embedding it within the spacetime framework. Quantum theory, Bohr argued, demanded an even deeper departure from classical assumptions. Relativity intertwines causality and spacetime, requiring causal determinacy to be understood within a framework where spatial and temporal coordinates—and even simultaneity—are relative to the motion of observers. Here, Bohr presents complementarity as just another conceptual tool that, like Einstein's theories, helps us transcend common-sense perceptions and the limitations of language and ideas, such as the subject-object distinction. By framing complementarity as consistent with Einstein's approach, Bohr positions it as a natural extension rather than a radical break.[56]

However, the idea of complementarity, as Einstein and others soon came to realize, reflected a profound shift in scientific thinking. In Abraham Pais's reconstruction of the interactions between Heisenberg and Bohr from 1925 to 1928, two distinct approaches emerged within this new thought style. Heisenberg questioned the continued use of the concepts of classical physics (e.g., waves, particles), advocating that they be abandoned 'to a certain extent',[57] while Bohr insisted on continuity: the interpretations of quantum mechanics still relied on classical concepts (e.g., position, momentum), and the modes of detection and observation were described

[56] Bohr returned to the issue of language again in 1949 'Meanwhile, the discussion of the epistemological problems in atomic physics attracted as much attention as ever and, in commenting on Einstein's views as regards the incompleteness of the quantum-mechanical mode of description, I entered more directly on questions of terminology. In this connection I warned especially against phrases, often found in the physical literature, such as "disturbing of phenomena by observation" or "creating physical attributes to atomic objects by measurements." Such phrases, which may serve to remind of the apparent paradoxes in quantum theory, are at the same time apt to cause confusion, since words like "phenomena" and "observations," just as "attributes" and "measurements," are used in a way hardly compatible with common language and practical definition' (Bohr 1949).

[57] Pais (1991, p. 310).

in classical terms.[58] For Bohr, classical concepts and the concepts of quantum mechanics did not provide a singular or definitive description but rather revealed different aspects of the phenomena, showing that no single concept could exhaustively capture the full nature of physical reality.

This approach—foregrounding the need to probe phenomena from different perspectives—can be interpreted as a rejection of the notion of a single, correct way of looking at things: a master discourse that presumes unity and totality in scientific understanding. While this represents a significant extrapolation from Bohr's precise and careful scientific language, his complementarity framework implicitly acknowledges the limits of any single conceptual framework and opens up new avenues for insight. In this way, Bohr's approach to the examination of physical phenomena aligns closely with Fleck's insistence on the coexistence, overlap, and interaction of multiple thought styles as a fundamental feature of scientific knowledge production. Both thinkers challenge the assumption of a universal, unmediated access to reality, emphasizing instead that knowledge arises through specific, situated perspectives that interact with the objects of inquiry.

Thus far, the attempt to position Fleck's thought has relied on extrapolating internal signals within his texts, but at a certain point, it becomes necessary to step outside his work and situate it within the broader cultural and intellectual field, relating his thought to other schools and discourses. As Sady observes, Fleck explicitly acknowledges few intellectual debts or influences. The two most rigorously researched efforts to locate Fleck's thought—Thomas Schnelle's analysis of Fleck's relationship to the philosophy of Lwów and Ilana Löwy's positioning of his work within the Polish School of the Philosophy of Medicine—both emphasize that Fleck makes no direct mention of these philosophers or schools in his texts. While these connections are evident, they remain implicit, suggesting that Fleck's mode of referencing may have been, at least in part, shaped by the peripheral position he occupied in Polish society. Considering Schnelle's and Löwy's approaches will help illuminate this context and clarify Fleck's intellectual alignments.

2.2 External Positioning 1—The Polish School of Philosophy of Medicine

In 1947, Władysław Szumowski (1875–1954) situated Ludwik Fleck within the discipline and tradition he outlined in the first part of his *Filozofia Medycyny*, writing: 'Dr. Ludwik Fleck (b. 1896) made a creative contribution to the philosophy of medicine in Lwów'.[59]

By 1947, Szumowski was being denounced and attacked by the communist authorities as a reactionary 'enemy of materialism', his works dismissed as

[58] Pais (1991, p. 314).

[59] Szumowski (2007, p. 68).

'pseudoscientific' and 'idealistic propaganda', while his poor health, stemming from his imprisonment in Sachsenhausen concentration camp in 1939–1940, was used as the ostensible reason to force him into a 'starvation retirement' in 1948.[60] However, in the interwar period Szumowski had been an influential figure: in 1920 he became the first professor of the history of medicine at the Jagiellonian University in Kraków, and as Director of the Department of Higher Education in the Ministry of Religious Affairs and Public Education, he was responsible for founding departments of the history and philosophy of medicine in five of Poland's newly regained universities.

Importantly, Szumowski had studied philosophy under Twardowski in Lwów before World War I. Along with Władysław Tatarkiewicz, he belonged to the generation of scholars shaped by Twardowski's programme—one that sought to define and disseminate a distinctly Polish philosophy through academic institutions, scholarly journals, and inexpensive educational brochures produced by university publishing houses in the interwar period.

One of Twardowski's aims in establishing 'the School of philosophy' at Lwów University was to define a distinct and original national philosophy. The premise was simple: just as there existed English, French, and German philosophies, so too should there be a Polish philosophy, with textbooks authored by Polish scholars.[61] While Twardowski postulated that philosophy should be separated from worldview[62] and insisted that as an institution the University requires 'unconditional intellectual independence',[63] he was a deeply patriotic Pole[64] who viewed Lwów University as a cultural good that should primarily serve the interests of the Polish nation.[65] Thus, Szumowski's *Philosophy of Medicine* (1947), which placed particular emphasis on the groundbreaking contributions of Polish philosopher-physicians, should be viewed—alongside Tatarkiewicz's *Zarys dziejów filozofii w Polsce* (An Outline of the History of Philosophy in Poland) (1948)—as attempts to continue Twardowski's program in the hostile environment of post-war Poland. Tatarkieiwcz suffered a similar fate to Szumowski: according to Jan Woleński, he was labelled a bourgeois philosopher and banned from teaching in 1948.[66]

Szumowski, in his survey of the evolution of medical thought—which ranges from Ancient Greece, through the Renaissance and Enlightenment with contributions from Italy, England, France, and Germany, and culminates in contemporary Poland—places particular emphasis on the achievements of Polish physicians, professors, and philosophers who focused their thought on medical matters.

[60] Śródka and Gryglewski (2007, p. 8).

[61] Woleński (2019, pp. 20–21).

[62] Woleński (2019, p. 22).

[63] Twardowski (1933).

[64] Twardowski (1919).

[65] Twardowski (1908).

[66] Woleński (2019, pp. 29–30) identifies Tatarkiewicz as fulfilling Twardowski's program (2019, p. 21).

Szumowski's approach is primarily geographical rather than strictly chronological, as demonstrated by Fleck's inclusion in a section structured around philosophers and publications from specific cities—Kraków, Poznań, Łódź, Warsaw, Vilno, and Lwów. Within the Lwów section, Fleck is situated between discussions of a philosopher and a doctor from the same city. After mentioning that Fleck published in both Polish and German, Szumowski characterized his contribution as follows:

> ...the author insightfully and originally demonstrates that in science, systems of facts and hypotheses sometimes contain so many subjective components and acquire such particular characteristics that one can occasionally speak of a specific thought style, and, in some complex issues—dependent, for example, on specialization and thus on a group of specialists—even of a thought collective. Such a collective is exemplified by the relationship between the Wassermann reaction and the presence of syphilitic infection. Fleck later expanded these views to encompass the entire history of medicine, shedding original light on it.[67]

Interestingly, despite this positive evaluation, Fleck and his concepts of thought collectives and thought styles were omitted from the shortened 1948 edition of *Filozofia Medycyny. Sprawozdania, rozważania* (*The Philosophy of Medicine: Reports and Reflections*). Even so, the work highlighted many key philosopher-physicians later singled out in Ilana Löwy's invaluable 1990 study, including Władysław Biegański, Edmund Biernacki, and Zygmunt Kramsztyk. Fleck's exclusion cannot be attributed solely to considerations of space, as Szumowski still devoted several paragraphs to himself and his colleague Adam Wrzosek—appointed head of the department of higher education in the Ministry of Education immediately after Poland regained independence, professor of the history of medicine at the University of Poznań in the 1920s and 1930s, and a central figure in steering the 'institutionalization of Polish philosophy of medicine' toward a more Catholic and Christian nationalist orientation.[68]

Fleck's omission from Tatarkiewicz's *Outline of the History of Philosophy in Poland* is understandable, as when he covers the twentieth century, Tatarkiewicz prioritizes mainstream philosophy, particularly the Warsaw logicians. Fleck's removal from the shorter version of Szumowski's book is more perplexing; however, the political circumstances may provide a basis for a possible explanation. Andrzej Śródka and Ryszard Gryglewski describe the publication context as fraught: in 1948, the deepening Stalinization of Poland brought intense scrutiny to historical

[67] Szumowski (2007, p. 68): 'W pracach tych autor w sposób wnikliwy i oryginalny wykazuje, że w nauce układy faktów i hipotez mają w sobie czasem tyle składników subiektywnych i nabierają pewnych cech tak szczególnych, że można mówić niekiedy o swoistym stylu myślowym, a w niektórych złożonych zagadnieniach, zależnych na przykład od specjalizacji, a więc niejako od zbiorowiska specjalistów—nawet o kolektywie myślowym. Takim kolektywem jest na przykład stosunek reakcji Wassermanna do obecności zakażenia syfilitycznego. Poglądy te autor rozszerzył później na całą historię medycyny, na którą rzucił w ten sposób oryginalne światło'.

[68] Szumowski (1948, pp. 10–15) For more on Wrzosek's activity and publications, see Löwy (1990b), and for more details of his nationalist and racist texts, see Löwy (2000, pp. 299–300).

and philosophical works.[69] Fleck's open epistemology—with its emphasis on the inevitable multiplicity of thought styles and their relative, contextualized truths—may have been seen as ideologically incompatible with the rigid dogmatism of Stalinist orthodoxy.

Significantly, Fleck did not publish any papers on epistemology between 1947 and 1960, despite—or perhaps even because of his—holding secure positions as a bacteriologist at the Maria Curie-Skłodowska University in Lublin (1945–1952) and later as a director at a state institute in Warsaw until his emigration in 1957. During this period, his research output shifted almost entirely to medical topics, particularly immunology and the study of leukergy—a phenomenon related to white blood cell responses in infections and inflammatory processes.[70]

Before turning to Löwy's 1990 reinstatement of Fleck within 'the Polish Philosophy of Medicine,' it will prove useful to first consider how Szumowski and Wrzosek originally conceived and defined the Polish philosophy of medicine during 1918–1921—a transformative period marked by Poland's struggle to regain independence, the fight to establish its borders, and Twardowski's tenure as Rector of the University of Lwów (1918–1919).

2.2.1 *Wrzosek in 1918*

Adam Wrzosek's essay *Udział medycyny polskiej w kulturze powszechnej ze szczególnym uwzględnieniem czasów porozbiorowych* (The Contribution of Polish Medicine to Universal Culture with Particular Emphasis on the Post-Partition Era), published immediately after Poland regained its independence in November 1918, emphasizes the philosophical underpinnings of medical practice in Poland, particularly through the works of figures like Tytus Chałubiński. Wrzosek portrays Chałubiński as a distinguished physician and pioneer of medical philosophy, credited with advancing the logic of medicine and initiating a uniquely Polish intellectual tradition in the field. According to Wrzosek, Chałubiński's approach—blending practical medical insights with broader philosophical inquiry—exemplifies the Polish effort to integrate intellectual depth with practical application.

Wrzosek emphasizes the pivotal role of Polish universities, particularly the University of Kraków, in shaping Polish medical and scientific thought. Founded in 1364, the University served as a vital bridge connecting Poland to the intellectual currents of Western Europe. In his view, the University fostered scholarly exchanges and produced influential figures like Józef Dietl. Despite the political and social challenges of the partition periods, Wrzosek argues that these institutions provided

[69] Śródka and Gryglewski (2007, p. 13). Woleński (2019, p. 30) also identifies 1948 as the onset of 'the ideological offensive of Marxism and administrative restrictions' that intensified in 1951–1952.

[70] For an excellent recent study that devotes serious attention to Fleck's scientific work and raises awareness of this underexplored side of his thought, while also including an exhaustive bibliography of his publications, see Ciesielska and Jarnicki (2021).

a strong foundation for advancing medical education and research within Poland and beyond.

Polish nationalism is a subtle yet persistent theme in Wrzosek's narrative. He laments the limited international recognition of Polish scholars, attributing this to the lack of independent statehood and the dominance of foreign powers during the partitions. As he notes:

> The working conditions of Polish scholars during the partition periods were difficult. And yet, they did what they could. There was no lack of their presence in any field of scientific endeavor. A significant number of them worked in the medical sciences. And if, despite the very unfavorable conditions, they contributed to the progress of science and need not feel ashamed of their scientific output—admittedly modest, yet not without essential value—then we may all the more confidently hope that, in an independent Poland, this output will be a hundredfold richer, for Poles have never lacked ability. They have only often lacked their own workshops for work.[71]

The achievements of figures like Jędrzej Śniadecki, Józef Dietl, and Tytus Chałubiński are framed as examples of Polish resilience and intellectual vigour. For Wrzosek, the 'workshops' Polish scholars lacked during the partitions—institutions where they could fully realize their abilities—emphasize the crucial role of universities in an independent Poland. His conclusion expresses hope that these institutions would enable Polish scholars to make far greater contributions to global culture and science, affirming Poland's capacity to contribute to international intellectual and scientific progress.

2.2.2 *Szumowski in 1921*

In a 1921 paper in an issue of *Przegląd Filozoficzny* dedicated to commemorating the twenty-fifth anniversary of Twardowski's teaching activity, Szumowski discussed the importance of the philosophy of medicine as a university subject. He considered the philosophy of medicine integral to understanding the medical sciences as a coherent whole rather than as a set of disconnected subjects. As he defined it: '[...] The philosophy of medicine generalizes and unites the results of the individual medical sciences [...]; it examines, from the standpoint of logic, epistemology, and psychology, the methods of medical thinking and, from the standpoint of ethics, the ways of medical conduct'.[72]

---

[71] Wrzosek (1918, p. 319) 'Trudne były warunki pracy uczonych polskich w czasach porozbiorowych. A jednak robili, co mogli. Nie brak ich było na żadnem polu pracy naukowej. Liczny szereg ich pracował w dziedzinie nauk medycznych. A jeżeli, mimo bardzo niekorzystnych warunków, przyczynili się do postępu nauki i nie potrzebują się wstydzić swego, wprawdzie skromnego, lecz nie bez wartości istotnej plonu naukowego, to tem bardziej tuszyć sobie możemy, że w niepodległej Polsce plon ten będzie stokroć obfitszy, albowiem nigdy Polakom na zdolnościach nie zbywało. Brakowało im tylko często własnych warsztatów pracy'.

[72] Szumowski (1921, p. 290) 'Filozofja medycyny uogólnia i łączy wyniki nauk lekarskich poszczególnych, z szerokim uwzględnieniem biologii; daje pogląd na całość medycyny: jej rozwój,

Szumowski believed that the philosophy of medicine could address the fragmented nature of medical education, helping students form a comprehensive understanding of medical practice. He also regarded it as a means to foster clear thinking and ethical reasoning, especially in areas touching upon moral and social issues such as those related to sexual behavior. In his words, '[...] The physician's influence upon youth in matters of sexual conduct is enormous. [...]'[73] and '[...] A physician easily becomes [...] a center from which a certain thought and way of conduct radiate. It is therefore necessary to ensure that the physician's views are truly at the level of contemporary science and that his advice promotes health both somatically and spiritually'.[74]

Beyond the confines of the university, Szumowski saw philosophical approaches to medicine as essential for confronting various pseudoscientific doctrines and dubious practices that had infiltrated medical thought. He maintained that philosophical training could help preserve the integrity of the profession and ensure that physicians were not swayed by misleading ideas.

Furthermore, Szumowski connected the philosophy of medicine to a broader Polish intellectual tradition. He acknowledged the significant role that Polish universities and thinkers played in shaping this field, describing it as '[...] the crowning of fifty years of activity by an entire school [...] which I have termed the Polish philosophical-medical school [...]',[75] and emphasizing that '[...] we may be proud that we now possess in Poland [...] a scholarly current that is our own, original, and indigenous intellectual achievement'.[76] In this context, the philosophy of medicine aligned with wider Polish Catholic aspirations to influence ethical and social norms, especially in times of perceived moral and social upheaval.

Lastly, Szumowski expressed concern about overly materialistic tendencies in medical thought. He argued that an approach grounded in philosophical reflection could prevent an excessive reduction of human phenomena to mere physical

---

podstawy, wartość, granice, metody, błędy; bada, ze stanowiska logiki, teorii poznania i psychologii—metody myślenia oraz ze stanowiska etyki—sposoby postępowania lekarskiego'.

[73] Szumowski (1921, p. 286) 'Wpływ lekarza na młodzież w zakresie spraw seksualnych jest olbrzymi. Postulat więc wychowania fizycznego i wychowania moralnego naszej młodzieży wymaga, aby przede wszystkim wychowawcom nie zbywało na właściwym wykształceniu'.

[74] Szumowski (1921, p. 286) 'Warto też w ogóle przypomnieć o roli lekarzy w społeczeństwie, jako jedynych nieraz pionierów oświaty, zwłaszcza na prowincji, i krzewicieli pewnych idei. Lekarz bardzo łatwo staje się na prowincji ośrodkiem, skąd promieniuje pewna myśl i pewien sposób postępowania. Trzeba więc starać się o to, ażeby poglądy lekarza stały rzeczywiście na poziomie współczesnej nauki i żeby jego rady szerzyły zdrowie zarówno pod względem somatycznym, jak i duchowym'.

[75] Szumowski (1921, p. 282) 'Ostateczna sankcja, udzielona terminowi "filozofia medycyny" [...] jest zresztą tylko uwieńczeniem pięćdziesięcioletniej działalności całej szkoły, którą nazwałem polską szkołą filozoficzno-medyczną (Tytus Chałubiński, Henryk Hoyer sen., Zygmunt Kramsztyk, Henryk Nusbaum, Edmund Biernacki, Władysław Biegański i in.), a nie stworzeniem nowej dziedziny nauki'.

[76] Szumowski (1921, p. 294) 'Możemy być z tego dumni, że mamy teraz w Polsce nie tylko w piśmiennictwie lekarskim polskim, ale i w organizacji szkolnictwa lekarskiego polskiego kierunek naukowy, który jest naszym własnym, oryginalnym, rodzimym dorobkiem naukowym'.

processes.[77] It could be argued that this anti-materialist perspective resonated with the intellectual environment of the Lwów school, which emphasized logical and systematic thinking to counter one-sided materialist views.

As we have seen, in *Filozofia Medycyny* in 1947, Szumowski situated Ludwik Fleck within the broader philosophical tradition, noting Fleck's 'creative contribution to the philosophy of medicine in Lwów (*Twórczo w dziedzinie filozofii medycyny wystąpił we Lwowie dr Ludwik Fleck*)'.[78] However, he stopped short of explicitly identifying Fleck as Polish or aligning him with the 'Polish philosophical-medical school (*polska szkoła filozoficzno-medyczna*)' that he had defined in 1921[79] to emphasize an original and distinctly Polish intellectual tradition. Szumowski's careful phrasing is particularly telling, given the emphasis in *Filozofia Medycyny* on Poland's indigenous contributions to the field. His acknowledgment that Fleck published in both Polish and German is also significant, perhaps indicating a reluctance to fully integrate Fleck into the Polish intellectual tradition. Szumowski may have been acknowledging the complexities of national identity in interwar Lwów, where Polish, Jewish, and Ukrainian cultures intersected, as well as the broader implications of Fleck's multilingual scholarship, which sought to transcend narrowly national frameworks.

2.2.3 Löwy's 1990 Reconstruction of 'the Polish School of Philosophy of Medicine'

Löwy characterizes 'the Polish School of Philosophy of Medicine' as a tradition formed from a position of marginality and exclusion. The main publications associated with the Polish School appeared between 1874 and 1908—a period during which, due to the partitions by Prussia, Russia, and Austria (1772–1918), there was no independent Polish state, and Poland had been erased from the political map of Europe. Under the Prussian and Russian partitions, Poland's higher education system was subjected to forms of imperial subjugation that could be described as colonization, since they involved deliberate attempts to suppress the Polish language, Polish cultural production, and Polish educational institutions. For instance, the

[77] Interestingly, Szumowski treats the discovery of the electron as an argument against materialism: 'The final blow to materialism was dealt by modern physical chemistry, which demonstrated that the atom is entirely composed of electrons, i.e., certain immaterial forces. Thus, so-called matter, in its ultimate structure, can be reduced to a system of electrons, from which it would follow that materialism is less aligned with the truth than some form of dynamism.' This positions Szumowski as a precursor to the appropriation of quantum mechanics by religious writers in the late 1920s, as outlined by Robert P. Crease and Alfred Scharff Goldhaber in *The Quantum Moment* (2014), Chap. 7.

[78] Szumowski (2007, p. 68).

[79] Szumowski (1921, p. 282).

russification of Warsaw University following the Uprising of 1863–1864 transformed the institution into a tool of imperial power.[80]

Polish scholars have identified intent behind these policies: 'The Russians effectively suppressed the major centers of knowledge at the Russified university. The authorities' policy aimed at lowering the university's standards. There was a lack of infrastructure, and funding for the University was severely curtailed, which negatively affected the quality of education'.[81] This suppression aligns with Jürgen Osterhammel's classifications of colonial expansion. Russia employed two distinct forms of domination: 'border colonization'—conducted primarily in the East through its expansion into undeveloped Asian territories for resource extraction and settlement—and 'Empire-building wars of conquest'—conducted in the West, as it annexed and controlled more developed states and territories, subjugating existing institutions and repurposing them to serve imperial needs.[82]

In light of Zofia Hałęza's recent research, it becomes clear that the intellectual life of partitioned Poland was more complex than the impression of uniform subjugation and exclusion conveyed in Löwy's 1990 account. While imperial domination undoubtedly shaped conditions for Polish scholars, Hałęza demonstrates that responses to these constraints varied regionally, producing divergent intellectual trajectories. For instance, although Russian authorities closed the Warsaw Main School in 1869 and established the Imperial University of Warsaw in 1870, clandestine initiatives such as the 'Flying University' exemplified resistance to imperial policy. Meanwhile, the previously Germanized universities in Lwów and Kraków underwent a process of Polonization in the mid-nineteenth century, reflecting efforts by Polish elites to assert cultural hegemony in the absence of political autonomy. These developments show how intellectual activity across the three partitions was shaped by different administrative regimes: Warsaw, under Russian control, became a centre for positivism, while Galicia and the Prussian partition developed stronger traditions in the historical sciences and political thought. Hałęza's observations suggest that Polish intellectual life persisted not only in defiance of imperial constraints, but also through regionally specific adaptations to them.[83]

Löwy's 1990 study identified a pattern of systemic marginalization she described as a 'brain drain': Polish students with the means sought education abroad, particularly in German and Austrian universities. Upon graduating, they faced a difficult choice: remain abroad and pursue careers in well-supported scientific environments or return to Poland, where such infrastructure simply did not exist. Those who returned encountered a lack of laboratory facilities and institutional support, working instead under grim public health conditions in occupied Poland. Here, extreme

[80] Löwy (1990a, p. 14). Chałubiński was fired from Warsaw University in 1874, during the Russification process.

[81] Polak et al. (2015, p. 100).

[82] Osterhammel (2009, pp. 5–9).

[83] Hałęza (2021, pp. 113–114).

poverty was pervasive, and the occupying powers showed little interest in addressing the plight of the population.[84]

Figures such as Tytus Chałubiński (1820–1889), Edmund Biernacki (1866–1908), Władysław Biegański (1857–1917), and Zygmunt Kramsztyk (1848–1920) exemplify the tension between staying abroad to build prestigious careers and returning to Poland, where they often faced significant challenges, limited opportunities, and professional frustration. Despite these obstacles, they were first and foremost practicing physicians, dedicating their days to consulting patients and writing in what little free time they could find.

Many of those who returned were motivated by a profound sense of social responsibility. Biegański, for instance, worked in a provincial hospital while also engaging in social work alongside his medical practice. He authored major works on ethics, logic, and methodology despite his demanding workload. As Hałęza observes, Biegański worked 'not only as a doctor but also as a philosopher, publicist, social activist, and philanthropist. He worked not only in a hospital but also ran a private practice and served as a railway and factory doctor'.[85] Similarly, Kramsztyk, an ophthalmologist, embodied this sense of duty by dedicating himself to improving public health infrastructure in Warsaw. He played a pivotal role in advocating for the construction of a modern hospital on the outskirts of the city, actively raising funds, and ensuring the facility was equipped to serve the city's poor with dignity and high standards of care.[86]

Their demanding day-to-day work shaped both the form and substance of their intellectual contributions. While their writing was imbued with urgency and conviction, it often bore the imprint of lives lived under pressure, with little time for the careful editing or polish characteristic of university-based scholarship. Nevertheless, these texts were directed not toward academic prestige but toward improving medicine and serving society—engaging fellow physicians and scholars working under occupation and in hardship. They reflected the marginal position of their authors, yet remained intellectually ambitious and socially engaged. Kramsztyk's journal, *Krytyka Lekarska* (Medical Critique), which he owned and edited from 1897 to 1908, stands as a material expression of this collective ethos. It provided a forum for critical reflection, historical insight, and medical discourse, sustained by intellectual labour and civic commitment rather than institutional support. In this sense, *Krytyka Lekarska* exemplifies the resilience of a thought collective working for the public good, beyond the auspices—and the constraints—of the university.

The shared concerns, topics, and positions articulated by Chałubiński, Biernacki, Biegański, and Kramsztyk enabled Löwy to assign their writings to a coherent thought style that developed over decades. Arguing that Fleck's thought did not emerge from a vacuum, Löwy demonstrates that many elements of the School's

[84] Löwy (1990a, pp. 3–5).

[85] Hałęza (2021, p.107).

[86] Polak et al. (2015, pp. 101–102).

thought provided the foundation for his first forays into epistemology.[87] The following sections revisit her 1990 reconstruction—now somewhat neglected—to extend and refine her analysis, bringing to the fore dimensions of Fleck's epistemology that have since received closer attention.

2.2.3.1 Epistemology Grounded in a Patient-Oriented Approach

In Löwy's reconstruction, closely based on the source texts, the Polish School's thought is characterized by a holistic, patient-oriented approach and therapy-centered theories.[88] In contrast to German and French microbiology and bacteriology, which were discursively framed as laboratory-based, disease-centered, and universalist, Chałubiński proposed focusing on symptoms ('disease moments') and treating each patient as a unique case.[89]

Building on this, Biernacki examined the gap between the science of diseases and the art of healing, concluding that while pathology can formulate general laws, this was not possible with medicine, since 'each patient has his own illness' and a disease is influenced by 'the specific biological constitution of the patient'.[90] He also emphasized the critical role of psychological factors in shaping the course of illness, arguing that the doctor's influence and ability to assure recovery play a piv-

---

[87] Löwy (1990a, pp. 215–216).

[88] Löwy (1990a, pp. 19, 71).

[89] Such a detailed investigation lies beyond the scope of this study, but Fleck's theory of thought styles and the interactive production of facts could offer a productive framework for analysing how Polish physician-philosophers developed their patient-centred approach through a strategic, differential identification articulated against the laboratory-based models institutionalized in scientific centres such as Paris and Berlin from the 1830s onwards. These Polish thinkers can, in fact, be regarded as early precursors of the Foucauldian critique which exposed how the institutionalised clinical gaze positioned the patient as a resource for the production of medical knowledge—and thereby as an object of control: 'in the hospital, one is dealing with individuals who happen to be suffering from one disease or another; [...] in the clinic, on the other hand, one is dealing with diseases that happen to be afflicting this or that patient' (Foucault 1973, pp. 70–71). While Foucault foregrounded the hospital as the locus of medical objectification, *The Laboratory Revolution in Medicine* (ed. Cunningham and Williams, 1992) redirects attention to the rise of laboratory-based epistemologies, showing how epidemiology and experimental physiology became institutionalized in France and Germany and came to dominate nineteenth-century medicine. Lenoir attributes this development to the Prussian 'discourse of practical interest', while Kremer and Weindling trace its materialisation in state-sponsored institute-building, where theoretical models of disease were translated into bricks, mortar, and curricula. See Lenoir 1992; Kremer 1992; Weindling 1992; and Gradmann's invaluable 2009 account of how Koch's laboratory-based bacteriology literally generated—from a cognitive perspective—new disease entities: 'the investigation of traumatic infections produced a number of completely new and experimentally generated diseases' (Gradmann 2009, pp. 60–61). In contrast, excluded from such resources, the Polish physician-philosophers articulated a holistic, civic-minded, patient-oriented epistemology aimed at improving conditions deliberately degraded by occupying powers—a full century before Foucault's diagnosis of clinical power.

[90] Löwy (1990a, p. 43).

otal role in therapeutic success. For Biernacki, fostering trust and addressing individual needs were integral to the art of healing, as they complemented biological and psychological understanding.[91]

Biegański critiqued German academic medicine for reducing patients to mere material for scientific investigations, leading to unethical experiments and neglecting therapy the central aim. He argued that medicine must refocus on treating patients as whole beings, emphasizing that the physician must address not only the disease but also the patient's overall condition. Effective therapy, he stressed, depends as much on the psychological bond between physician and patient as on scientific knowledge. He also warned against the 'scientific fanaticism' that subordinated human life to abstract scientific pursuits, proclaiming that 'salus aegroti suprema lex medicorum' (the well-being of the patient is the supreme law of physicians).[92]

Kramsztyk introduced a reflexive turn to the Polish School's approach. He cautioned against the uncritical reliance on schematic textbook representations of disease, which are 'synthesized from individual cases' and shaped by contemporary assumptions. Instead, he advocated for a focus on 'real-life pathological states' and 'precise descriptions of concrete clinical cases'. However, he also warned that observation is never entirely neutral, stating, 'The investigator is never completely passive. His mind is not a blank sheet but contains many general ideas and pieces of information that are unconsciously transferred to the observed facts'.[93] This reflexivity deepened the epistemological dimension already evident in the work of Biernacki and Biegański. While they emphasized the factors shaping how a disease develops in a particular individual, Kramsztyk shifted the focus to the factors influencing the physician's perception of the patient's disease. By adding this layer of critical awareness, Kramsztyk enriched the Polish School's ongoing interrogation of the epistemological foundations of medical knowledge, building on and reorienting the insights of his predecessors.

Fleck's 1927 *Some Specific Features of the Medical Way of Thinking*[94] reflects and formalizes many of the principles articulated by previous Polish physician-philosophers. His emphasis on the dynamic and atypical nature of medical phenomena, the abstraction of individual cases into broader types, and the divergence between theoretical constructs and clinical realities aligns closely with the patient-oriented and increasingly reflexive approach championed by Chałubiński, Biernacki, Biegański, and Kramsztyk. Fleck's work demonstrates how this way of thinking developed into a more systematic critique of the universalist, disease-centered approach, while maintaining its focus on the individuality and complexity of clinical cases.

---

91 Biernacki (1899).

92 Löwy (1990a, p. 110).

93 Löwy (1990a, p. 127).

94 Fleck (1986a).

As Löwy observes,[95] Fleck's 1927 study marked his first explicit engagement with epistemological questions. Initially presented as a lecture and later published, the work advocated for a holistic approach to pathological phenomena, rejecting reductionist explanations such as the idea that infectious diseases have a single etiological cause. For Fleck, diseases were highly complex phenomena, shaped by multifactorial interactions between microorganisms and their hosts, which defied simplistic classifications. His central argument is that this complexity defines 'the medical way of thinking' and distinguishes it from other modes of thought: unlike the natural sciences, which focus on typical, systematic, and universal phenomena, medical practitioners study 'atypical, abnormal, and morbid phenomena' and rely on fictions, intuition, statistical observation, and hypothesis construction.[96] To rephrase this in Fleck's later terminology, the medical thought style—its attitudes, assumptions, and techniques—is fundamentally shaped by what it interacts with.

Löwy's 1990 interpretation, strongly influenced by Kuhnian relativism and constructivist readings of science, emphasized the active, constructivist elements of Fleck's model of cognition and his references to incommensurability (*niewspółmierność*). However, this approach downplayed Fleck's insistence on the interactionist component of cognition, as well as the porous nature of thought styles—dimensions that have been more fully explored in recent scholarship.[97] I would argue that Fleck's interactionist model of cognition—which, as we have seen, was articulated in 1929's *On the Crisis of 'Reality'*, in opposition to Riezler and in support of Bohr—emerged from the patient-oriented approach developed by Polish physician-philosophers.

2.2.3.2 Critiquing the Concept of Facts

Kramsztyk's divergence from the positivist conception of facts marks an important step in the evolution of epistemological thought in the philosophy of medicine, one that appears to have paved the way for Ludwik Fleck's more radical reinterpretation (bearing in mind that Fleck does not explicitly reference Kramsztyk, so this connection remains an inference). Like other Polish philosophers of medicine, including Biegański and Trzebiński, Kramsztyk critiqued the ideal of the unbiased observer, emphasizing that 'Man does not see new facts with the unprejudiced eyes of a newborn child, but he perceives them with the eyes of his mind which contains many bits of information, theories, and pre-conceived ideas'.[98]

He also argued that observers tend to notice phenomena consistent with their prior knowledge and might even perceive non-existent phenomena if these align

[95] Löwy (1990a, pp. 216–217).

[96] Fleck (1986a, pp. 39–40).

[97] Condé and Jarnicki (2023), Binney (2023).

[98] Löwy (1990a, pp. 127, 221). Kramsztyk (1899c, p. 70): 'Bo człowiek nie patrzy na fakt nowy nieuprzedzonemi, nowonarodzonemi oczyma, ale patrzy i postrzega umysłem, który ma liczne wiadomości, teorye i uprzedzenia i świat widzi w barwie tych swoich teoryi i uprzedzeń'.

with their preconceived views. In *Fakt Kliniczny*, Kramsztyk's critique of science as an institutionalized practice goes as far as to suggest that medical education itself can obstruct the perception of new facts. In a passage that seems to anticipate Fleck's assertion that the training of specialized thought styles constrains what scientists are able to perceive, Kramsztyk writes:

> People are usually dependent on what their masters have turned their attention to, not only in their judgments but also in the use of their senses. To see something that has not been noticed before and to show it to others, one must be able to look at the world through one's own eyes. One must possess independence of mind, a very rare quality and the basic feature of genius.[99]

Nevertheless, despite these significant contributions to the critique of the unbiased observer and the institutional constraints on perception, Kramsztyk ultimately stopped short of challenging the foundational assumption of positivism: that facts exist independently in nature, awaiting discovery. This duality—acknowledging the profound influence of preconceptions while preserving the notion of facts as preexisting entities—marks the point at which Kramsztyk's critique came to a halt.

It is precisely this boundary that Fleck would cross, advancing the more radical view that facts are not discovered but produced through the processes and interactions of scientific cognition. In Chap. 3, I will argue that his critique of Ernst Mach's conventionalist epistemology played a pivotal role in shaping this conception. It is worth noting that Biegański engaged deeply with Mach's ideas, which indicates that the Polish physician-philosophers were not detached from major philosophical debates of their time but participated in them—albeit from a marginal position. Though often overlooked in broader intellectual histories, their writings fostered a milieu in which critical engagement with figures like Mach and Poincaré was possible. It was within this largely unacknowledged context that Fleck's epistemology could emerge—by drawing on, synthesising, and ultimately exceeding the debates sustained by this peripheral but critical and responsive collective.

2.2.3.3 The Critique of Institutionalized Science

The 'Polish School of Philosophy of Medicine' engaged not only with the theoretical dimensions of medical knowledge but also with the practical and moral issues arising from its application, thereby constructing a peripheral counter discourse that was distinct from and challenged the dominant, laboratory-based framework disseminated from German and French centres.

Biernacki's *Istota i granice wiedzy lekarskiej* (*The Essence and the Limits of Medical Knowledge*) (1888) presented a critique of institutionalized medicine that focused on the epistemological limits of medical science. Drawing a distinction between 'knowing' and 'recognizing' diseases, Biernacki argued that the essence of diseases remained elusive despite diagnostic advances. He contended that therapy

[99] Löwy (1990a, p. 157), Kramsztyk (1899c, p. 69).

developed historically apart from scientific understanding: 'Medicine is a strange branch of science indeed, which, we could say, has developed backwards'.[100] His scepticism of therapeutic claims bordered on therapeutic nihilism, as he asserted that the patient's recovery often relied on nature's own processes, with the doctor's primary role reduced to moral reassurance: 'The only real help provided by the doctor to the patient is his personal influence [...] the assurance of improvement, or the assurance that the patient will recover'.[101] Highlighting the disjunction between medical science and practice, Biernacki contrasted medicine's shortcomings with the clear progress seen in fields like physics and chemistry, where 'aniline inks and the dyestuffs industry have followed the studies on properties of certain carbon compounds; steam machines have followed the studies of steam properties; telegraph and telephone systems have followed the studies on electric current, etc.'[102] In this way, he cast therapy as a historically contingent art, rather than a straightforward application of scientific breakthroughs.

Biegański's critique of medical science combined an ambitious vision for the rationalization of therapy with a nation-oriented critique of Poland's scientific culture. Unlike Kramsztyk, who revalorized and embraced the status of healing as an art, Biegański attempted to ground therapy on a firm logical basis. Löwy summarizes his position: 'Therapy should become a rational and deductive science based on formalized logical assumptions and on the achievements of the theoretical medical sciences. It should enjoy the same prestige as the other natural sciences'.[103]

However, Biegański also expressed deep frustration with Poland's lack of a robust scientific tradition: 'Science has always been an imported commodity for us; what we created arose for centuries under the influence of echoes reaching us from the West... And, notably, we were an echo that was always late'.[104] For Biegański, Poland's failure to cultivate a distinctive intellectual tradition stifled scientific productivity. He called upon younger physicians to develop 'our own thought,' linking national renewal to a synthesis of therapy and science.

Kramsztyk's critique of established medical science focused on the irreducibility of medicine to pure science, emphasizing the vital role of practical skill and moral engagement in the craft of healing. Describing medicine as 'the most difficult craft of all',[105] he condemned the overemphasis on theoretical knowledge in medical education, which left physicians ill-equipped for the realities of patient care.

Kramsztyk's *O Cytatach* (On Citations) (1882) presented a sharp critique of the norms underpinning institutionalized science, particularly the prioritization of referencing other works over substantive engagement with nature. He denounces

[100] Löwy (1990a, p. 52).

[101] Löwy (1990a, p. 62).

[102] Löwy (1990a, p. 51).

[103] Löwy (1990a, p. 77).

[104] Cited in Hałęza (2021, p. 114).

[105] Löwy (1990a, p. 148), Kramsztyk (1899b, p. 121): 'Rzemiosło najtrudniejsze, bo przedmiot jego jest stokroć bardziej od innych zawiłym i wiele badań i namysłu nieraz musi łożyć lekarz, zanim obmyśli i postanowi sposób swego działania'.

citation as 'an expression of intellectual dependency (*uczucie zależności umysłowej*)',[106] arguing that the relentless focus on cataloguing prior works reduces scientific inquiry to an imitative exercise. Kramsztyk argues that this citation-obsessed culture not only stifles creativity but perpetuates systemic inertia within institutional science and subordinates researchers to the role of soldiers in 'an army where only the commanders act independently'.[107] The imposition of these norms extends into academic practices such as doctoral examinations, where the failure to include certain references is criticized more severely than the substantive content of the work itself.

For Kramsztyk, this imbalance not only inhibits scientific development but also erodes the intellectual joy and autonomy of researchers. He insists that true scientific knowledge must emerge from direct engagement with nature—the 'sole subject of science and its principal teacher'.[108] Borrowed knowledge, no matter how extensive, remains foreign to the researcher's mind until it is thoroughly assimilated and rediscovered. Yet this rediscovery requires a rare 'independence of mind'[109]—a quality undermined by a system that elevates conformity and citation over originality and critical thought.

The critiques of Biernacki, Biegański, and Kramsztyk, articulated during the partition era, thus created a counter-discourse to the hegemonic, prestigious Western laboratory-based focus on disease entities. The prestige generated by 'the School', particularly through Kramsztyk's valorization of therapy, enhanced the cultural capital of medical thought, elevating its status and setting the stage for the institutionalization of the Polish philosophy of medicine after 1918—a process that increasingly came to be influenced by nationalistic elements.

2.2.3.4 The 'Polish' School of Philosophy of Medicine?

In a 2006 polemical article, Stefan Zamecki critiqued Ryszard Gryglewski's use of the term 'Polish School of Philosophy of Medicine', raising points that can also be applied to Ilana Löwy's 1990 reconstruction. Zamecki's argument focuses on the issue of conceptual precision, particularly with the terms 'Polish' and 'school'. He questioned the appropriateness of describing 'the School' as 'Polish', given the historical context of the partition era, when Poland was divided among Prussia, Russia, and Austria.

While he acknowledged that the label 'Polish' may be justified to distinguish these thinkers from foreign intellectual traditions—especially given their emotional

[106] Kramsztyk (1899a, p. 15).

[107] Kramsztyk (1899a, p. 15): 'Cała naukowa rzesza robi wtedy wrażenie armii, w której dowódcy tylko są samodzielni i mają wyłączne prawo myślenia, a przeważna część pracowników za ich kierunkiem, za ich niejako idzie rozkazem'.

[108] Kramsztyk (1899a, p. 13).

[109] Kramsztyk (1899c, p. 69).

and cultural ties to Polish identity—he warned that it risks obscuring the diverse political and institutional conditions under which they operated. As for the term 'school', Zamecki highlighted its connotations of coherence, shared methodology, and a unified intellectual tradition, which he argued do not adequately capture the varied and independent contributions of figures like Kramsztyk, Biegański, and Nusbaum. He called for greater analytical rigour in defining these terms to avoid misrepresenting the intellectual legacy of the so-called 'Polish School'.[110]

Hałęza builds on Zamecki's critique, agreeing that the phrase 'Polish School of Philosophy of Medicine' is conventional and insufficiently defined. However, she defends the use of 'Polish' as a patriotic marker, reflecting the cultural identity of these thinkers during the partition era. While sharing Zamecki's concerns about conceptual clarity, she is more willing to accept the term as a practical—if imperfect—descriptor for a historically situated intellectual phenomenon.[111]

The passage from Biegański that Hałęza cites (also quotes more extensively above)—'Science has always been an imported commodity for us; what we created arose for centuries under the influence of echoes reaching us from the West'—employs the rhetorical strategy of addressing a Polish audience directly. The original Polish text uses phrases such as *nam brak* ('we lack'), *u nas* ('among us'), and *dobiegającego do nas* ('reaching us') to evoke a sense of collective identity and shared responsibility. This emphatic appeal to Polish identity in Biegański's argument justifies describing his contribution to the discourse as 'Polish' and aimed at constructing a distinctly Polish strand of medical discourse.

Yet what 'Polish' means in this context—particularly when applied to figures socially categorised as Jewish—demands closer scrutiny. Matters become more complex when we turn to figures like Kramsztyk and Fleck, both of whom occupied ambiguous positions within Polish society, shaped by varying forms of assimilation and exclusion.

Kramsztyk embodied the tensions inherent in the term 'Polish' at the turn of the twentieth century. His family, deeply influenced by the Haskala movement, embraced assimilation as a pathway to integration: adopting Polish names, educating their children in Polish schools, and immersing themselves in Polish culture. Kramsztyk exemplified this commitment not only through his medical writings but also through his deep engagement with Polish literature.[112] In 1907, he published an interpretation of Adam Mickiewicz's *Pan Tadeusz* that portrayed the Jewish musician Jankiel as central to the epic's themes of Polish–Jewish friendship. Yet this reinterpretation was ridiculed in the Polish press, a rejection that reflected the broader antisemitism he faced. Around the same time, the Warsaw Medical Society refused to admit Jewish members, prompting Kramsztyk to resign in protest and establish the Society for Social Medicine.[113] These experiences—of profound cul-

---

[110] Zamecki (2006, p. 27).

[111] Hałęza (2021, p. 111).

[112] Polak et al. (2015).

[113] Löwy (1990a, p. 132).

tural commitment met with systemic exclusion—complicate any straightforward use of the term 'Polish School of Philosophy of Medicine'.

Although Kramsztyk came from an assimilationist milieu, his philosophical writings and the journal *Krytyka Lekarska*(1897–1908) coincided with the growing rejection of assimilationist aspirations within a resurgent and increasingly intolerant Polish nationalist movement. The changing political climate in which he worked can be traced most clearly in the ideological consolidation of Roman Dmowski.

In *Myśli nowoczesnego Polaka* (*Thoughts of a Modern Pole*, 1903), Dmowski sought to forge a new Polish national subjectivity. Rather than defining the nation in biological or racial terms, he envisaged Poland as a civilisational and moral subject capable of reconstituting itself as a culturally homogeneous Catholic nation-state. This political body, he argued, should only seek to assimilate elements that could be entirely absorbed. At this point in his writing, Dmowski's stance remained ambivalent: he did not entirely reject the possibility that a small number of Jews who felt Polish could be assimilated.[114] However, he regarded large-scale assimilation as both improbable and harmful—for Poland and for Jews. As he wrote:

> They possess too distinct, too crystallized an individuality, shaped over thousands of years of civilized life, to be assimilated in larger numbers by a nation as young as ours, still forming its national character. Rather, they are more likely to assimilate our majority spiritually, and to some extent even physically. On the other hand, the characteristics of this race, which has never lived the life of societies like ours, have accumulated and solidified over time with traits distinct and foreign to our moral system and, ultimately, harmful to our society. The blending with a larger number of such an element would destroy us, replacing the young, creative principles on which we are building our future with disintegrative elements.[115]

Krzysztof Kosiński's monumental analysis of Dmowski's œuvre identifies the year 1905 as a critical turning point.[116] Following the failed Russian Revolution, which Dmowski interpreted as revealing the dangers of Jewish political activism and interests incompatible with Polish nationalism, his rhetoric shifted dramatically.

In *Separatyzm Żydów* (*Jewish Separatism*, 1909)—published 1 year after Kramsztyk ceased publication of *Krytyka Lekarska*—Dmowski claimed that Jewish assimilation had grown increasingly superficial, resulting in the rise of a distinct intelligentsia whose aspirations diverged from those of Polish society. He accused such intellectuals of abandoning Polishness in favour of a 'Jewish national banner' and insisted that any notion of dual allegiance was illusory: individuals had to choose between being Polish or Jewish. According to Dmowski:

> Assimilation undoubtedly exists, although opinions may vary regarding its scope and intrinsic value. However, assimilation can no longer be a programmatic solution to the Jewish question as a whole. The majority of Jews are already moving, and will continue to move, in the opposite direction.[117]

---

[114] Kosiński (2022, pp. 420–421).

[115] Dmowski (1933, p. 86).

[116] Kosiński (2022, p. 397).

[117] Dmowski (1909, p. 29).

Dmowski was, of course, no marginal figure. As chief ideologue of the National Democracy (*Endecja*) movement and co-founder of the National League, he served as one of Poland's delegates to the Paris Peace Conference in 1919. The *Endecja* movement, whose members were known as *Endeks*, promoted a culturally exclusive vision of Polish identity, rejecting the possibility of Jewish integration. Jews were cast as a fundamental threat to national cohesion and to the cultural and economic fabric of Polish society.[118]

Dmowski's pre-war writings exemplify the increasingly exclusionary nationalism that confronted Kramsztyk and other Jewish intellectuals, in stark contrast to their aspirations for integration. His arguments against assimilation and his calls for the structural exclusion of Jews from the Polish national body long predated Poland's regaining of independence in 1918. They thereby laid the ideological groundwork for the institutional barriers and cultural hostility that intensified during the interwar period. In the years when Kramsztyk was still publishing *Krytyka Lekarska*, Dmowski's language had already shifted towards a register of purity, struggle, and defence: the Polish nation, he argued, must be 'cleansed' of alien elements, and its intelligentsia must 'wake up' to the Jewish question. This rhetorical hardening foreshadowed the economic boycotts, discriminatory legislation, and campaigns of intimidation in Polish universities that would form the broader social backdrop to Fleck's development of his theory.

While Kramsztyk confronted these pressures as a Warsaw-based intellectual, Fleck lived through the fluid and volatile political circumstances of Eastern Galicia in the years 1914–1939, during which Polish identification was anything but straightforward for an individual categorized or self-defined as Jewish. As Timothy Snyder and Alexander Prusin have shown, the collapse of imperial structures and the emergence of competing national projects placed Galician Jews—especially in Lwów—under acute pressure to navigate multiple, and often conflicting, allegiances.[119] Some continued to pursue integration into Polish culture; others remained loyal to the Austro-Hungarian order. When the Ukrainian independence movement seized L'viv in 1918 and entered into armed conflict with the Poles, segments of the Jewish community declared neutrality—a position recognized by the Ukrainian leadership but denounced by the Polish elite and press as a betrayal, confirming, in their eyes, longstanding suspicions that Jews could not be trusted as members of the Polish nation. Still others turned toward socialist or communist internationalism, while some embraced Zionism.

The social structure of Galicia—marked by deep ethno-religious stratification and the Jewish intelligentsia's relative prominence in the professions—provoked mounting resentment from both Polish and Ukrainian nationalist movements, which increasingly viewed Jews as economic rivals or political obstacles. By 1918, as Prusin argues, the Polish *Endeks* had begun to articulate de-Judaization (*odżydzenie*) as a cardinal political goal, asserting that Jewish influence must be purged from the

---

[118] Modras (1994), Rudnicki (2008).

[119] Snyder (2003), Prusin (2005).

economic and cultural life of the future Polish state.[120] In this fraught environment, marked by violent nationalist struggle, state-building efforts, and episodic antisemitic violence, identifications were politically charged and often perilous. While Fleck's education, language, and early career suggest an alignment with Polish scientific culture, this should not be mistaken for an uncomplicated or stable national identification. His path—like that of many Galician Jews—unfolded within a matrix of assimilationist aspiration, systemic exclusion, and strategic alignment, where the category 'Polish' was not simply inherited but actively negotiated under duress.

The consequences of this intensifying climate of exclusion were soon felt by Fleck himself. After Fleck obtained his doctoral degree in 1922 from the Jan Kazimierz University in Lwów and beginning work as an assistant to the typhus specialist Rudolf Weigl, he soon lost his position at the university in 1923. The details surrounding this event remain scarce, and scholarly accounts offer divergent explanations. Schäfer and Schnelle's vague 1980 reference attributes it to the 'politically and economically tense situation in Poland, and particularly in the city of Lwów'.[121] In contrast, Löwy presents a more explicit but still tentative suggestion: '[...] because of personal conflicts with faculty members, or perhaps due to the antisemitism that prevailed at Lwow during this period, or both, he was obliged to leave the university in 1923'.[122]

However, historical reconstructions allow us to see that Fleck's dismissal from the Jan Kazimierz University in 1923 coincided with a surge in nationalist activities in Lwów, targeting Jewish students and academics. In March 1922, the first Congress of Młodzież Wszechpolska (All Polish Youth) had formalized nationalist efforts across Polish universities, advocating for a *numerus clausus* to limit the admission of Jewish students to match their proportion of the national population. This movement intensified in Lwów, where Jewish students constituted 42.5% of the student body at Jan Kazimierz University, sparking demands for strict quotas. By the start of the 1922–1923 academic year, rallies and memoranda amplified these calls, culminating in a February 1923 resolution restricting Jewish admissions to 11% of total students. Such campaigns, accompanied by exclusionary resolutions and rising tensions on campus, created a hostile environment for Jewish academics and scientists like Fleck, compounding personal and professional challenges in ways that intersected with broader patterns of antisemitism in interwar Poland.[123]

As a citizen identifiable as Jewish and thus assigned to the 'minority nation' under the Second Polish Republic, Fleck's experiences of antisemitic policies were shaped by the shifting political landscape. During Piłsudski's presidency (1926–1935), systemic antisemitism was relatively less pronounced compared to the preceding years of postwar parliamentary democracy (1918–1926) or the

[120] Prusin (2005, p. 7).

[121] Schafer and Schnelle (1980, pp. X–XI), also Zittel and Schmaltz (2007, pp. 24–5).

[122] Löwy (1990a, p. 215).

[123] Biedrzycka (2012, p. 188), Rudnicki (2008, p. 248), Ciesielska (2022, p. 23).

semi-authoritarian regime that emerged after Piłsudski's death (1935–1939).[124] In his 1950 *Życiorys* [biographical sketch], Fleck provided key details about this period, stating: 'In 1935, I was dismissed as part of the then-current actions of the Sanation authorities, and until 1939, I supported myself through private practice'.[125] This dismissal involved his removal from the laboratory at the Health Insurance Fund. In 1937, he was also expelled from the Związek Lekarzy Państwa Polskiego (ZLPP) [Association of Physicians of the Polish State] following the introduction of the *aryjski paragraf* (Aryan paragraph). This statute restricted ZLPP membership to 'a doctor, a citizen of the Republic of Poland, a Christian by birth'—effectively formalizing Fleck's exclusion.[126,127]

---

[124] Ciesielska (2022, p. 9).

[125] Fleck (2007, p. 315): 'W roku 1935 zostałem zredukowany w ramach ówczesnej akcji władz sanacyjnych i do roku 1939 utrzymywałem się z praktyki prywatnej'.

[126] Ciesielska and Jarnicki (2021, pp. 47–48).

[127] The question of antisemitism's impact on Fleck's professional life is complex and sensitive, and exceeds the scope of this chapter. Early reluctance to engage with this topic reflects the fraught nature of invoking antisemitism as an explanatory factor in the 1980s, before the fall of communism. Schäfer and Schnelle's vague reference to the 'politically and economically tense situation in Poland, and particularly in the city of Lwów' in their 1980 work exemplifies this hesitance. *Cognition and Fact* (CaF) (1986a), published five years after the *Kolloquium Ludwik Fleck* in Hamburg (13–16 September 1981), similarly avoids direct discussion. At the time of the *Kolloquium*, Solidarność (Solidarity) was at the height of its popularity, amidst severe food shortages and political unrest. Shortly after, martial law was declared in Poland on 13 December 1981 to suppress Solidarity and prevent broader civil unrest. Martial law, lasting until 22 July 1983, saw Solidarity outlawed, its leaders—including Lech Wałęsa—imprisoned, and many activists subjected to brutal repression. Among them was the philosopher Leszek Nowak, a critic of the regime and member of the Solidarity movement, who faced detention and surveillance. These repressive circumstances no doubt overshadowed the contributions of Polish participants and help explain the reluctance in *CaF* to engage with systemic factors like antisemitism, reflecting broader sociopolitical constraints of the time.

For instance, Bogusław Wolniewicz's essay *Ludwik Fleck and Polish Philosophy* (1986) attributed the neglect of Fleck's ideas by the Lwów-Warsaw school to epistemological and ideological incompatibilities. Wolniewicz argued that the school's liberal-rationalist ideology, grounded in faith in human rationality and the power of discourse to achieve mutual understanding, fundamentally conflicted with Fleck's insistence that differences in thought styles could preclude genuine agreement. By characterising the Lwów–Warsaw school's ideology as liberal-rationalist and positioning Fleck's thought in opposition to it, Wolniewicz offered a philosophically framed account of Fleck's marginality that effectively displaced any consideration of systemic factors—such as antisemitism. While this is not to suggest that the Lwów–Warsaw school excluded Fleck for antisemitic reasons, the conspicuous absence of any reference to antisemitism in Wolniewicz's contextualization is notable, especially given that between 1981 and 1986 he was free to critique liberal-rationalist ideology but probably not free to openly broach the topic of antisemitism—a topic still fraught under Poland's communist regime, which was itself not free of antisemitic episodes and tendencies.

Similarly, Władysław Markiewicz's essay *Lwów as Cultural and Intellectual Background of the Genesis of Fleck's Ideas* (1986) presented a somewhat idyllic portrayal of interwar Lwów as a centre of 'intensive cultural diffusion.' Markiewicz suggested that, under Austrian rule before World War I, the Jewish community's participation in a 'social contract' among national groups may have contributed to Fleck's intellectual development. He argued that this arrangement, which

In this complex and controversial context, situating Fleck within 'the Polish School of Philosophy of Medicine' is far from straightforward. Szumowski and Löwy identify this 'Polish School' as having emerged from a period of exclusion and marginalization during the partitions of Poland (1874–1918), when philosophy became a space for addressing the frustrations of a constrained intellectual environment. Paradoxically, as the school gained institutional footing—through university departments and the international recognition of the Lwów school—Fleck himself faced exclusion. As Löwy observes:

> Fleck was in all likelihood rejected by the professional Polish historians of medicine of his time; his numerous publications on this subject notwithstanding, he was never given the opportunity to teach history or philosophy of medicine.[…] This lack of recognition of Fleck by Polish historians and philosophers of medicine can perhaps be explained on the basis of personal conflicts, or perhaps by the growing nationalist-Catholic orientation of *Archives*, or by both.[128]

Fleck's position within the Polish School was paradoxical: he was excluded from its institutional core and remained peripheral to the dominant nationalist-Catholic intellectual currents of his time. This dual exclusion did not simply sideline him; it profoundly influenced his intellectual trajectory. His decision to submit *On the Crisis of 'Reality'* to a German journal, to write *Genesis and Development of a Scientific Fact* in German, and his reflexive epistemology and strategically oblique critiques all reflect a thought style forged on the margins—one that was never entirely 'at home'.

Eva Hedfors' often valid criticisms of Fleck—for his 'sparse knowledge of history and lack of philosophical rigour',[129] his highly selective use of few sources, and her more debatable assertions, such as that he was 'a marginalized professional out

---

recognized cultural and intellectual achievements across communities, probably shaped Fleck's 'neutral' and 'tolerant' intellectual outlook (1986, 227–228). However, Markiewicz failed to address the broader decline in interethnic relations after 1918, when systemic antisemitism became more entrenched. While he acknowledged geopolitical tensions between Poles and Ukrainians, describing the Polish–Ukrainian War (1918–1919) as 'an armed struggle between Poles and Ukrainians concerning where the city belonged geo-politically, both claiming it,' and noting that this led to a 'considerable escalation' of national differences (1986, 228), he omitted any discussion of the worsening position of Jewish residents, particularly the discrimination they faced in interwar Poland. This omission ultimately results in an idealized depiction of the city's multicultural environment, which only hints at the deeper social and political tensions that shaped Fleck's early life, particularly the challenges he likely encountered as a Jewish intellectual. Markiewicz's portrayal may reflect the broader constraints of the academic and political context of 1981–1986, where such tensions were often underexplored or avoided.

In contrast, Löwy's 1990 study addressed the issue directly, explicitly acknowledging the role of antisemitism in shaping Fleck's career and intellectual development (1990, 2015). The issue resurfaced with renewed urgency following Hedfors's controversial 2008 paper on Fleck's conduct at Buchenwald, which provoked significant debate (see Hedfors 2008; Amsterdamska et al. 2008). More recent scholarship, such as Ciesielska and Jarnicki (2021), has been still more forthright in foregrounding antisemitism as a key factor in Fleck's professional trajectory.

[128] Löwy (1990a, p. 223).

[129] Hedfors (2007, p. 72).

of touch with his time and his science',[130] or that his views were rejected by his contemporaries rather than overlooked[131]—often seem to border on outright hostility to Fleck and his thought style.[132] Her sense of 'puzzlement' on encountering *Genesis and Development of a Scientific Fact* for the first time[133] can perhaps itself be read as an expression of the master discourse of secure academic privilege seeking to recontain the challenge posed by Fleck's marginalized and 'strange' way of thinking.

Fleck's exclusion shaped his perspective, making it acutely sensitive to the instability of knowledge, the fluidity of cultural boundaries, and the pressures of marginality. Writing from a multiethnic and politically fractured city during a period of profound social upheaval, Fleck developed an epistemology that implicitly—and occasionally explicitly—critically interrogates the power structures, assumptions, and exclusions underlying scientific thought. His rejection by the institutionalized Polish School was not simply an act of alienation but a formative experience that sharpened his focus on the contingent, constructed, and interactive nature of knowledge.

In this light, Fleck's work emerges not merely as a product of scientific insight but as a deeply situated intellectual response to the conditions of his exclusion. His epistemology reflects the vantage point of an outsider: a perspective that interrogates established frameworks precisely because it arises from a position at the margins. The often-cited limitations of Fleck's texts—his superficial knowledge of certain philosophers and schools of thought, sparse citations, frequent contradictions and ambiguities, and the unfinished or rushed nature of his writing—can themselves be understood as consequences of his marginalization, shaped by the constraints of working in his spare time without institutional support. Like the earlier generation of Polish physician-philosophers—writing after days filled with medical and civic labour—Fleck produced texts shaped as much by pressure as by conviction. Yet these very constraints imbue his work with extraordinary power: his texts were not blunted by peer review or softened by timid deference to authority figures in the scientific-academic community.

---

[130] Hedfors (2006, p. 157).

[131] Hedfors (2007, p. 68).

[132] With regard to the hostility towards Fleck, Eva Hedfors' article *Medical Science in the Light of the Holocaust: Departing from a Post-war Paper by Ludwik Fleck* (2006) raised provocative and controversial questions about his conduct during his imprisonment in Nazi concentration camps—most notably, allegations of complicity in medical practices performed under conditions of extreme duress. Her interpretation prompted a strongly worded rebuttal from Cornelius Borck, Ilana Löwy, Thomas Schnelle, and Claus Zittel in *Medical Science in the Light of a Flawed Study of the Holocaust* (2008). These authors criticized Hedfors' approach for lacking historical and contextual sensitivity, particularly her failure to acknowledge the coercion and moral ambiguity inherent to Fleck's situation. The controversy reflects broader tensions surrounding the ethical evaluation of individuals acting under conditions of extreme constraint and invites reflection on how such experiences may have shaped Fleck's epistemological outlook. For a more recent account of Fleck's time at Buchenwald, see Löwy (2020).

[133] Hedfors (2006, p. 132).

2.3 External Positioning 2—Opposition to the Lwów School

2.3.1 Schnelle's Positioning of Fleck in Relation to the Lwów School

In *Ludwik Fleck and the Influence of the Philosophy of Lwów* (1986), Thomas Schnelle argued that Fleck's thought implicitly responded to questions posed by 'three philosophers of Lwów': Kazimierz Twardowski (1866–1938), Kazimierz Ajdukiewicz (1890–1963), and Leon Chwistek (1884–1944), concerning the foundations of reality, knowledge, and truth. A thorough engagement with Schnelle's analysis falls beyond the scope and aims of this work. Here, I limit myself to highlighting key aspects of Schnelle's positioning of Fleck's thought in relation to Twardowski and proposing additional ways Fleck's polemical *On the Crisis of 'Reality'* can be seen as engaging with positions articulated by Twardowski in a highly complex and contested discursive field.

Schnelle's reading of Twardowski's essays from 1894–1900 traces how his representational model of cognition led to a restricted definition of truth. This Brentano-inspired framework is fraught with epistemological ambiguities: the subject's psychic activity is directed toward 'an object, which is assumed to be independent of thought', yet the phenomenological approach entails that such an object, as a thing-in-itself, 'remains of no interest to the psychically active subject: the subject is unable to grasp it, or whatever influence it might have'.[134] This Kantian dilemma, concerning the gap between representation and reality, raises a crucial question: if it is impossible to determine whether the subject's representations correspond to a reality independent of the subject, how can judgments claim objective truth? Are not all truths necessarily subjective and therefore relative? According to Schnelle, Twardowski resists both relative truths and ontological relativism. Judgments, he argues, are absolutely true (or false) for the individual making them, but never relatively true. The consequence, however, is that Twardowski 'must abandon the attempt to determine for more than one individual subject the truth value of such judgments as claim to be valid. Scientific knowledge can therefore never be described as "true" or "false": the challenge of the objectivity of statements thus becomes the problem of their singularity'.[135]

In Schnelle's reconstruction, Twardowski partially resolves this dilemma between 1912 and 1921 by distinguishing between individual and scientific knowledge. While true knowledge is attainable for the individual subject, scientific knowledge—relying on intersubjective interpretation and abstraction—cannot itself be true. Instead, it strives for objectivity through intersubjective consensus, while fully acknowledging its inherent limitations. In *On the Dignity of the University* (1933),

[134] Schnelle (1986b, p. 237).

[135] Schnelle (1986b, p. 238). For relevant passages from Twardowski's *O tak zwanych prawdach względnych* (*On Relative Truths*), see Twardowski (1900, pp. 20–25 [Polish]; 1999a, pp. 167–169 [English]).

Twardowski emphasizes that the pursuit of objective knowledge remains central to the mission of science and the University, but—given the limitations he had acknowledged in previous decades—we can surmise that this has to be understood as the pursuit of an ideal.

Fleck's response to Twardowski, as presented by Schnelle, centres on rejecting the correspondence model of cognition and 'the claim to any reality independent of the subject'. According to Schnelle's account:

(a) Fleck's model of cognition is constitutive—super-subjective collectives actively create reality through the social activity of cognition.[136]
(b) Truth is redefined as agreement with a specific thought style.[137]

Schnelle's interpretation of Fleck's epistemology can be described as constructivist rather than interactionist. While Schnelle's description of Fleck's active linkages—conventions constructed by thought collectives—is insightful, and his emphasis on the productive role of misunderstandings is particularly valuable, his treatment of Fleck's passive elements is more problematic. Schnelle attributes the resistance and constraints encountered in cognition to the 'interplay of actively posited presumptions', rather than recognizing the non-arbitrary resistance encountered through interaction with the cognized. In other words, Schnelle reduces resistance to conceptual relations—that is, conceptual *interplay* rather than perceptual-cognitive *interaction*, overlooking Fleck's emphasis on how conventions engage with external, non-arbitrary elements. This tension will be explored in greater detail in the next chapter.

The broader implications of Fleck's rejection of the correspondence model extend beyond Schnelle's analysis. As I suggested previously, Fleck's 1929 critique of Riezler's neo-Kantian model of reality can also be interpreted as an implicit critique of Twardowski's attempts to preserve objective knowledge. This critique was further developed—somewhat more explicitly—in a public exchange with Twardowski's student and assistant, Izydora Dąmbska, which clarified the tensions between Fleck's open epistemology and the Lwów school's emphasis on unbiased objective knowledge.[138]

2.3.2 The Unbiased University Instructor and Normal People

In a speech delivered on November 21, 1932, at Jan Kazimierz University in Lwów, in response to being awarded an honorary doctorate by Poznań University, Twardowski declared:

[136] Schnelle (1986b, p. 239).
[137] Schnelle (1986b, p. 242).
[138] Dąmbska (1937), Fleck (1938).

> A University instructor is first and foremost a servant of objective truth, its exponent and promulgator among the young and within society. It is a service that is both noble and highly commendable, yet one that simultaneously requires not only the appropriate intellectual qualifications and suitably specialized erudition, but great fortitude and strength of character as well. Whoever enlists under the banner of science, must renounce all that might cause him to swerve from the path indicated by this banner. Thus, he must first of all work very hard to eliminate all biases that might obstruct the path to objective knowledge, biases that have their source in traditions, customs, influences of the surrounding milieu, and personal preferences or aversions.[139]

In 1937, in the pages of *Przegląd Filozoficzny*, Izydora Dąmbska engaged critically with Fleck's *Zagadnienie teorii poznania* (*The Problem of Epistemology*),[140] published in the same journal the previous year. Addressing Fleck's notion of thought styles and the limits of intersubjective understanding, she proposed the existence of a universal thought style rooted in shared human experiences:

> [...] generally, normal people, under given conditions of perception, tend to accept the same statements. [...] It appears that, regardless of the specific thought style one may possess—be it philosophical, mystical, scientific, or another—there exists a universal thought style that nearly everyone is capable of comprehending. The most inspired prophet, poet, or mystic, under certain life circumstances, discovers a common language with the sober natural scientist and aligns with the same style of thought. In what circumstances does this occur? In those wherein individuals, fully awake, must earnestly contend with the realities of life. This shared, universal human thought style is one that compels individuals to rely upon observational judgments.[141]

Twardowski's vision of eliminating biases and pursuing objective knowledge serves as a foundation for Dąmbska's later notion of a universal thought style rooted in shared human experience. For Twardowski, this neutrality requires intellectual discipline and the renunciation of personal preferences, supported by the university's role in fostering civilized dispute resolution and aiming at objective knowledge. For Dąmbska, neutrality emerges when individuals are compelled by life's realities to

---

[139] Twardowski (1999b, p. 282), (1933, section 11): 'Nauczyciel uniwersytecki jest przedewszystkiem sługą prawdy objektywnej, przedstawicielem jej i głosicielem wśród młodzieży i społeczeństwa. Służba to szczytna i niezmiernie zaszczytna, ale zarazem wymagająca nietylko odpowiednich kwalifikacyj intelektualnych i stosownej wiedzy fachowej, lecz także wielkiego hartu ducha i silnego charakteru. Kto się zaciąga pod sztandar nauki, musi się wyrzec wszystkiego, co mogłoby go zepchnąć z drogi, sztandarem tym wskazywanej. Musi więc przedewszystkiem usilnie pracować nad wyrzeczeniem się wszelkich uprzedzeń, które mogą mu zagrodzić drogę, wiodącą ku wiedzy objektywnej, a które mają swe źródło w tradycyach, w zwyczajach, we wpływach otoczenia, w osobistych zamiłowaniach i wstrętach'.

[140] Fleck (1986d).

[141] Dąmbska (1937): '[...] na ogół ludzie normalni w danych warunkach spostrzegania, skłonni są uznawać takie same twierdzenia. [...] Otóż wydaje się, że jakimkolwiek bądź stylem myślowym ktoś się odznacza: filozoficznym, mistycznym, przyrodniczym czy innym jakimś jeszcze, jeden styl myślowy gotów jest każdy prawie zrozumieć. Najbardziej natchniony prorok, poeta czy mistyk w pewnych sytuacjach życiowych odnajduje wspólny język z trzeźwym przyrodnikiem i do jednego należą z nim stylu. W których to sytuacjach? W tych, w których nie śpią i na serio z warunkami życiowymi liczyć się muszą. Ten wspólny ogólnoludzki styl myślowy, to styl, w którym się człowiek do sądów spostrzeżeniowych ucieka'.

rely on observational judgments. Both thinkers affirm the possibility of intersubjective agreement, whether through institutional structures that promote rational discourse or through practical engagement with the world.

This shared ideal of objectivity and neutrality is precisely what Fleck critiques. In his response to Dąmbska, he challenges the construct of the 'normal observer' and argues that universal agreement does not arise naturally but rather depends on specific conditions of training or artificially controlled environments. As Fleck notes, 'Experience shows that untrained individuals often make widely differing judgments under the same conditions.' He adds, 'To achieve agreement, one must either specially train individuals or create highly artificial, laboratory-like conditions of perception', emphasizing that in the latter case, judgments are shaped by predetermined paths, leaving no room for full responsibility or authorship.[142]

Fleck challenges the assumption that agreement among observers is a natural or straightforward outcome, emphasizing instead the sociological and methodological processes that shape perception and understanding. Extrapolating from Fleck's argument and his 1936 essay, a universal thought style appears impossible: a thought style, by definition, distinguishes itself by standing apart from others.[143] Rather than leading to consensus, thought styles—in the process of interaction—fragment, branch off, and evolve through misunderstandings and distortions as concepts circulate between thought collectives.

2.3.3 Nations, National Minorities and the Polish Universities

Twardowski's ideal of the unbiased university instructor was immensely problematic, for the simple reason that in the interwar years, Polish universities were far from unbiased institutions. Nowhere was this tension more apparent than at Jan Kazimierz University in Lwów. Situated in a multiethnic city at the intersection of Polish, Ukrainian, and Jewish communities, the university was both a symbol of Polish cultural ascendancy and a site of bitter contestation. At its best, the university functioned as a bastion of Polish national identity while accommodating the region's ethnic diversity with sensitivity and tolerance; at its worst, it became entangled in segregationist policies and institutionalized forms of marginalization.

These included attempts to formalize such divisions through changes to laws, statutes, and university regulations—most notoriously, the *numerus clausus* (a quota limiting Jewish student admissions), *numerus nullus* (a complete exclusion of Jewish students), and the introduction of ghetto benches (*ławka gettowa*), which physically separated Jewish students in lecture halls. Such measures were actively championed by nationalist student organizations through protests, petitions, and lobbying, with support from the nationalist press and broader societal forces.

[142] Fleck (1938). For a rigorous analysis of the Dąmbska-Fleck dispute, see Szlachcic (2006).

[143] For a discussion of the concept of 'style', see Afeltowicz and Sojak (2015, pp. 29–33).

However, these pressures met resistance from many faculty members and student groups who opposed the institutionalization of such discriminatory practices.[144]

The political climate in Lwów made such policies deeply divisive, exacerbating tensions between Polish faculty and students and the city's Ukrainian and Jewish populations. In this fraught environment of nationalism and exclusion, Twardowski's vision of the University as a space of objectivity and neutrality—where conflicts are best resolved through scientific methods[145]—was profoundly idealistic. While he opposed exclusionary practices within lecture halls and faculty meetings, his principled refusal to publicly condemn such policies—for instance, in his 1933 public speech *On the Dignity of the University*—reflected a stance of apolitical detachment that smacks of passivity in the face of an extremely volatile situation, where violence was commonplace in universities, particularly during the 1930s.

2.3.3.1 Polonization and the Suppression of Minority Education

The exclusionary practices of the interwar period should be situated within the broader historical trajectory of Polish universities, where national identity and academic institutions were deeply intertwined. Earlier, we saw how, at the moment Poland regained its political independence, Wrzosek defined the universities as specifically Polish institutions, and Szumowski constructed a distinct Polish philosophical-medical school (*polska szkoła filozoficzno-medyczna*).

On the one hand, the nationalistic thrust of Wrzosek and Szumowski's texts is entirely understandable. First, the Polish state had been removed from maps of Europe between 1795 and 1918, subjugated and subjected to official Germanization and Russification programs, which included the capture and deliberate suppression of its once-independent universities in the Prussian and Russian partitions. Second, during the years 1918–1921, which saw the publication of these texts, the new Polish state was embattled, with contested borders and wars with the Czechs, the West Ukrainian People's Republic, and the Soviet Union. Reconstructing the universities in Kraków, Poznań, Warsaw, Vilnius, and Lwów as specifically *Polish* universities was an essential strategic component of reestablishing Poland as a strong and stable state in the midst of the extremely volatile and chaotic Central and Eastern Europe of this time.

On the other hand, however, the assertion of Polish cultural hegemony through defining universities and scientific disciplines as specifically Polish was bound up with the suppression of other cultural practices and institutions. The clearest example of this is the Polish state's outlawing of the Ukrainian University in L'viv:

> In 1919 all Ukrainian-language chairs in L'viv University were abolished. The government broke its promise to create a Ukrainian university and tried to suppress the private Ukrainian university, where former Ukrainian professors and lecturers from the main university were

[144] Rudnicki (2008), Bukowska-Marczak (2019).

[145] Twardowski (1999b, p. 281 [English translation]), (1933, section 9 [original Polish]).

teaching. In the aftermath of the wave of repressions following the attack on Piłsudski and Grabowski, the Polish authorities closed down the private Ukrainian university, forcing it underground. According to Ukrainian sources, in 1922/1923 the university had 1,500 students and 54 professors and lecturers.[146]

Back in 1908, Twardowski had argued against the Ukrainian (Ruthenian[147]) demands that the University of Lwów/L'viv become '*utrakwistyczny*' (utraquist)—a bilingual and bicultural institution that would be shared between the Polish and Ukrainian populations. In 1908, when Lemberg/Lwów/L'viv was still under Habsburg control within the Austrian partition of Poland, Twardowski stated that '[…] the University of Lwów is a Polish university, not a Ruthenian one or even a Polish-Ruthenian (utraquist) one'.[148] His detailed account of the how the university became Polish, first through fait accompli, then by legal recognition by the Austrian government in 1882, emphasizes the active role of Poles and passivity of the Ukrainians, rather than Austria favouring the Polish elites and the 'Habsburg pro-Polish turn' in the 1860s–1870s.[149] Twardowski wrote:

> This Polonization of the University of Lwów was accomplished in an entirely legal and peaceful manner, as stipulated by the imperial decree of 4 July 1871. Thanks to this decree, Poles, having an open path to university chairs, eagerly took advantage of the opportunity, without in any way hindering the Ruthenians from doing likewise. Had the Ruthenians at that time followed the example set by the Poles, they might have secured for their language a position in the University of Lwów equal to that attained by the Polish language; they might even have truly transformed the university into a Ruthenian one, just as the Poles had Polonized it. However, the Ruthenians did not, at that time, avail themselves of the rights afforded to them equally with the Poles, and thus, by the force of circumstance, the University of Lwów became Polish.[150]

For Twardowski, making the University of Lwów utraquist—bilingual and bicultural—was against 'the interests of the Polish nation'. He explicitly defined universities as national institutions:

> Every nation rightly sees in its universities the strongest bulwarks and the brightest centres of national education, and universities, by shaping the nation's elite and preparing their students for civic service, cannot neglect the national elements within their activity. Universities can only fulfil their mission if they remain in close connection with the entire intellectual life of the nation, influencing that life while simultaneously basing their own

[146] Mick (2016, p. 215).

[147] Twardowski's use of 'ruski' (Ruthenian) rather than 'Ukrainian' reflects not only the linguistic conventions of the time but also a refusal to acknowledge the emerging Ukrainian national identity: 'In the 1890s the Ruthenian national movement started to use the term Ukrainian, initially in the composite form "Ruthenian-Ukrainian" and later as a stand-alone term. The new name emphasized the commonality of the Ruthenians with the Ukrainian-speaking population in the western provinces of the Russian Empire' (Mick 2016, p. 11). Twardowski's choice aligns with broader Polish efforts to downplay Ukrainian nationalism and reinforce Polish cultural hegemony, particularly in contested spaces such as Lwów University.

[148] Twardowski (1908, pp. 4–5): '[…] uniwersytet lwowski jest uniwersytet polskim, a nie ruskim lub przynajmniej polsko-ruskim (utrakwistycznym)'.

[149] Amar (2015, p. 28).

[150] Twardowksi (1908, p. 12).

> development upon it. A university that could not perceive itself as the driving force of the nation's intellectual life would lose the vital, life-giving warmth and light; it would become an alien entity in the life of the nation, stripped of its essence.[151]

Twardowski argued that the Polish character of the University of Lwów must be safeguarded through carefully crafted legislation, which he saw as essential to addressing the ongoing Polish-Ruthenian (Ukrainian) tensions. While he believed that the ultimate resolution lay in the establishment of a separate Ruthenian (Ukrainian) university, he contended that legal provisions were necessary in the interim to accommodate Ruthenian (Ukrainian) demands without compromising Polish interests or stability.

Twardowski served as Rector of the University of Lwów during the turbulent years of 1918–1919, a period marked by deepening interethnic tensions and political upheaval. The idea of establishing a legally separate Ukrainian university was ultimately abandoned amidst the toxic relationships that developed in the aftermath of the conflict. Following the Ukrainian attempt to capture L'viv in November 1918 and the Polish-Ukrainian War (1918–1919), as well as a wave of assassination attempts, the Polish authorities enacted strict measures to consolidate their control over state institutions. These included a mandate requiring all state employees to swear an oath of allegiance to the Polish state. In 1919, the Polish government removed all Ukrainian teachers and chairs from the University of Lwów, restricting access to higher education exclusively to citizens of Poland or its Allies. The following year, the authorities escalated these measures by banning all courses taught in Ukrainian. In response to these restrictions, the Таємний український університет/ Tajny Uniwersytet Ukraiński/ Underground Ukrainian University was founded in July 1921. It operated covertly to preserve Ukrainian higher education and protect cultural identity in the face of repression.[152] The Underground Ukrainian University ultimately closed in June 1925 due to a lack of official recognition and support, coupled with the Polish government's rejection of proposals to reestablish Ukrainian-language education.[153]

In the interwar period, the Jan Kazimierz University in Lwów occupied a position that was both geographically and metaphorically peripheral to the core of European knowledge production. Yet, as an institution, it played a pivotal role in bolstering the newly independent Polish state, particularly through its involvement

[151] Twardowski (1908, p. 27) 'Każdy naród upatruje słusznie w swych uniwersytetach najsilniejsze ostoje i najjaśniejsze ogniska oświaty narodowej, a uniwersytety, kształcąc kwiat narodu i przygotowując swych uczniów do służby obywatelskiej, nie mogą pomijać w swej działalności pierwiastków narodowych. Uniwersytety mogą zadanie swe spełniać tylko wtedy, jeżeli pozostają w ścisłej łączności z całym życiem umysłowym narodu, na życie to oddziaływając i w zamian na niem rozwój swój opierając. Uniwersytet, któryby nie mógł czuć się dźwignią życia umysłowego narodu, straciłby ożywcze promienie ciepła i światła, stałby się czynnikiem w życiu narodu obcym, pozbawionym'.

[152] For a chronological record of the Battle of Lwów, institutional directives issued by the governing bodies of the University of Lwów, and the details of the Undergound Ukrainian University, see Biedrzycka (2012).

[153] Biedrzycka (2012, p. 289), Encyclopedia of Ukraine (1993).

in the 'Polonization' campaigns following the Polish victory in the Polish-Ukrainian War (1918–1919).[154] These campaigns were designed to assert Polish national identity in the *Kresy,* or eastern Borderlands—historically contested and ethnically diverse regions. As Alexander V. Prusin, a historian of Eastern European and modern Jewish history born in L'viv, observed in his account of borderland violence: 'The "Polonization" campaign in the Kresy (the Polish term for the eastern provinces in Volhynia, Belorussia, and southern Lithuania) and in Galicia translated into a drastic reduction of Ukrainian schools; they dwindled dramatically from 1,050 in 1919 to 433 in 1922, and the remaining schools eventually became bilingual. The Ukrainian chair at the University of Lwów was closed and the attendance of Ukrainian students was restricted'.[155]

2.3.3.2 The Rise of Antisemitism and Jewish Exclusion in Higher Education

The prominence of Jews in certain professions and academic settings became a focal point of National Democrat (*Endecja*) propaganda in the interwar period. This propaganda framed Jewish achievements and participation as a threat to Polish society, fostering resentment among the Polish population. Before World War I, a significant portion of the Galician Jewish intelligentsia resided in Lemberg/Lwów, where Jews constituted 70% of the legal profession and about 60% of all doctors in the city.[156] At Jan Kazimierz University in Lwów, Jewish students constituted 56% of the student body in 1922–1923, a figure that *Endecja* leaders used to stoke fears of the so-called '"Jewification" of the Polish intelligentsia'.[157] This fear was amplified by accusations of preferential treatment for Jews in academic and professional opportunities, and even cultural grievances, such as the perception of a double standard in medical education due to the Jewish religious prohibition against interfering with Jewish corpses. This controversy was far more than a logistical dispute; it became a flashpoint for antisemitic agitation, with demands such as 'Christian corpses for the Christians!' used to justify the exclusion of Jewish students from medical training and to bolster broader exclusionary and segregationist policies.[158]

---

[154] In 1924, the Polish government enacted *Lex Grabski* (the Grabski Law), which sought to assimilate national minorities by reorganizing minority-language education. The law mandated the replacement of minority-language schools with bilingual ones, where Polish was prioritized, as part of a broader campaign to promote national integration in the *Kresy* region. Dz.U. 1924 nr 79 poz. 766, *Ustawa z dnia 31 lipca 1924 r. zawierająca niektóre postanowienia o organizacji szkolnictwa* [Journal of Laws 1924, No. 79, item 766, Act of 31 July 1924 containing certain provisions on the organisation of the education system].

[155] Prusin (2013, p. 366).

[156] Bukowska-Marczak (2019, p. 21).

[157] Ciesielska (2022, p. 23).

[158] Aleksiun (2012). See also Ciesielska (2022, pp. 27–32).

These anxieties and grievances were underpinned by broader debates about minority policy in interwar Poland. Two key concepts dominated Polish discourse: national-ethnic assimilation (*asymilacja narodowa*) and state-oriented assimilation (*asymilacja państwowa*). National-ethnic assimilation sought the linguistic, cultural, and sometimes religious Polonization of minorities, while state assimilation permitted some degree of ethnic identity but required submission to the Polish state. National assimilation dominated state policies in the early 1920s and resurged with greater intensity in the late 1930s. By the mid-1930s, state-led assimilation was increasingly regarded as a precursor to full national-ethnic integration.[159] These shifting frameworks informed exclusionary policies such as the introduction of the *numerus clausus* and later the *numerus nullus*, reflecting a vision of the nation-state that sought to marginalize certain ethnic groups.

This vision of legally enforced cultural homogeneity was part of a broader ideological conflict about Poland's identity. Józef Piłsudski and the Polish Socialist Party envisioned a pluralist federation where the Polish majority would lead a multiethnic state, echoing the inclusive traditions of the Polish-Lithuanian Commonwealth. In contrast, Roman Dmowski and the National Democrats sought to transform Poland into a unitary national state, where minorities would either be assimilated or excluded.[160] Although *Endecja* never held power directly, Dmowski's nationalist ideology heavily influenced the political atmosphere, marginalizing Piłsudski's more inclusive and pluralist vision. The media played a crucial role in amplifying Dmowski's ideas, shaping public discourse and reinforcing the dominance of his nationalist agenda.[161]

Lwów was the first city to limit the number of Jewish students in higher education, with concerns about the 'Jewification' of universities being voiced as early as October 1922.[162] The politicization of higher education and professions revealed a deeper cultural and ideological struggle. *Endecja's* promotion of the *Żydokomuna* stereotype—equating Jews with communism—further marginalized Jewish communities by portraying them as threats not only to Polish national identity but also to its Catholic foundations. As Polish nationalism became increasingly intertwined with religious and cultural exclusivity, Jewish participation in public life was depicted as an existential threat, fuelling policies and practices that systematically eroded Jewish access to education and employment.

The introduction of 'ghetto benches' (*ławki gettowe*) in Polish universities was a segregationist policy that targeted Jewish students. Beginning in the mid-1930s and officially instituted in 1937 following a conference of university rectors, these measures required Jewish students to sit in segregated sections, often on the left side of lecture halls. While the violence associated with these policies was widespread across institutions, it was particularly acute in Lwów, where Jewish students faced

[159] Amar (2015, p. 40).

[160] Amar (2015, p. 40).

[161] Modras (1994, p. 57).

[162] Ciesielska (2022, pp. 27–31).

physical attacks and systemic discrimination. By 1937, 'days without Jews' were organized at Lwów's universities, escalating into campaigns for a *numerus nullus* to completely bar Jewish students. These measures not only alienated Jewish students but also reinforced a culture of nationalist violence, with antisemitic groups justifying their actions as a defence of Polish Christian values.[163]

2.3.3.3 Principles in Tension: Twardowski's Public and Private Responses

Kazimierz Twardowski's approach to contentious issues such as the establishment of a Ukrainian University, the *numerus clausus*, and the Brześć affair exemplifies the tensions arising from his deep Polish patriotism, his principled apolitical stance, and his belief in the neutrality of academic institutions. His diaries, his conduct in lecture halls, his treatment of individual Ukrainian and Jewish students, and his popularity among them demonstrate his opposition to the violence associated with nationalistic agitation and the exclusionary policies that marginalized minority groups within the university.[164] At the same time, Twardowski clearly believed that Polish cultural hegemony should remain unchallenged, and his tolerance and fair treatment of individuals operated within this broader framework. Moreover, his commitment to defining the University as a space free from political interference constrained him from taking public stances on issues that, we might suppose, demanded a response from a figure in his position.

Twardowski's responses to Ukrainian demands reflect the evolution of his perspective over time. While he advocated for a separate Ukrainian university in 1908, in the 1920s he opposed establishing such an institution in Lwów, arguing instead that it should be located in Warsaw. By 1927, he dismissed Ukrainian demands as 'purely political in nature' rather than based on genuine educational needs. His diary recounts a conversation with the British consul, who shared his view and praised Poles as 'bearers of culture' in the region.[165]

Twardowski's engagement with the *numerus clausus* reveals his ambivalence and a distinctly 'legalistic' (*legalistyczny*) approach. He criticized the Faculty of Philosophy's unilateral implementation of the *numerus clausus* without ministerial approval, calling it a 'technical absurdity' and a breach of academic protocol. Yet, his critiques during Faculty Council meetings were procedural, focusing on ministerial oversight and cautioning against the political ramifications of such policies in ethnically diverse regions. His diary entries expose discomfort with the policy's consequences for departments that had not adopted it:

> 18.09.1925. The enrollment results for the Faculty of Humanities over the first two days were disastrous in terms of nationality, as the majority of new students are Jews and Ruthenians. Since, apart from the Faculty of Theology, the Faculty of Humanities is the

[163] Rudnicki (2008, pp. 258–261), Ciesielska (2022, pp. 32–34).

[164] Ivanyk (2017), Woleński (2019, p. 29).

[165] Brożek and Jadacki (2023, p. 88).

only one that has not implemented *numerus clausus*, students rejected by the Faculties of Law, Medicine, and Science are flocking to the Faculty of Humanities.[166]

Despite this discomfort, Twardowski consistently opposed anti-Jewish actions within the university:

7.03.1928. This morning, when I arrived at the university for my lecture, a group of students standing at the entrance tried to prevent Jewish students from attending the lecture. However, I quickly dealt with the situation, and the Jewish students were able to attend my lecture freely. It proceeded without interruption, with the usual number of listeners.[167]

His broader condemnation of student nationalism, which he termed '*pajdocracy*' (student dominance), revealed his frustration with the increasing politicization of academic life. However, his legalistic focus on institutional propriety rather than taking explicit stances against discrimination and bigotry reflects a cautious approach that bordered on detachment.

Twardowski's response to the Brześć affair (1930–1931)—the arrest and alleged mistreatment of opposition politicians by the Piłsudski regime—further illustrates his reluctance to engage in political controversies. Although he privately acknowledged the severity of these events, he declined to sign public protests, unlike many of his colleagues. He argued that professors should avoid partisan conflicts and actions that could deepen political divisions. His reflections, recorded in his diary, suggest an awareness of the potential impact of collective academic protest but also scepticism about its efficacy. This hesitation is particularly evident in the context of his 1933 speech *On the Dignity of the University*:

27.07.1933. I originally intended to publish this speech at my own expense, including explanatory notes to provide concrete examples for the general statements made therein. For instance, regarding the sentence in section 15 about the breakdown of solidarity among lecturers, I would have noted actions such as collecting signatures for the "Brześć protest" or the formation of the Society for Academic Culture. [...] However, when the University of Poznań agreed to publish my speech, the planned notes—which would have given the publication a political and polemical character—had to be omitted. Nevertheless, I do not rule out publishing a second edition with these notes, though it would undoubtedly invite criticism from various sides.[168]

---

[166] Brożek and Jadacki (2023, p. 84): '18.09.1925. Wpisy na Wydział Humanistyczny dały w swoich pierwszych dwóch dniach wynik pod względem narodowym fatalny, gdyż ogromną przewagę wykazują wśród nowo wstępujących studentów Żydzi i Rusini. Ponieważ Wydział Humanistyczny prócz Teologicznego jeden nie zaprowadził u siebie *numerus clausus*, więc studenci nieprzyjęci na Wydziałach Prawniczym, Lekarskim i Matematyczno-Przyrodniczym walą na Wydział Humanistyczny'.

[167] Brożek and Jadacki (2023, p. 91): '7.03.1928. Dzisiaj rano, gdy przybyłem na uniwerek na wykład, grupa studentów u wejścia stojących usiłowała nie dopuścić studentów żydowskich na wykład. Ale rychło poradziłem sobie z nimi i Żydzi mogli na mój wykład swobodnie wejść. Odbył się on bez przeszkód i przy normalnej liczbie słuchaczy'.

[168] Brożek and Jadacki (2023, p. 115) '27.07.1933. Pierwotnie zamierzałem przemówienie to wydać własnym nakładem i zaopatrzeć je w uwagi objaśniające, które by podawały podkład konkretny dla wypowiadanych tam twierdzeń ogólnych. I tak byłbym np. do zdania ustępu 15-ego, w którym mówię o rozbijaniu solidarności wśród docentów jednego i tego samego uniwersytetu, dodał uwagę, że takim rozbijaniem było m.in. zbieranie podpisów pod „protest brzeski" albo

This reluctance to frame the Brześć affair in moral terms leads Anna Brożek and Jacek Jadacki, the sympathetic authors of *Kazimierz Twardowski: Filozof ze Lwowa*, to conclude: 'It is interesting that Twardowski regarded the "torture of imprisoned deputies in Brześć" in political and party terms rather than moral ones'.[169]

2.3.3.4 Fleck's Critique of the Lwów School

In contrast to Twardowski's aspirations for a neutral, apolitical ideal of knowledge, Fleck's epistemology emphasizes the inherently collective and socially conditioned nature of cognition. Schnelle's constructivist interpretation of Fleck, which positioned him against Twardowski's representational model—an approach ultimately aimed at rejecting relative truth while salvaging objective knowledge as an ideal—can be revised and extended through an interactionist lens. Such a revision can cast Fleck's critique as a broader rejection of the social-epistemological claims advanced by Twardowski and Dąmbska within a volatile, dynamic, and contested field of cultural production.

Jan Woleński's accounts emphasize the pluralistic and tolerant ethos cultivated under Twardowski's mentorship at Lwów University after 1918. This intellectual community included Ukrainian and Jewish students, reflecting a degree of inclusivity that counterbalanced the exclusionary practices prevailing in the broader sociopolitical context.[170] Nevertheless, the philosophers who later gained international recognition as members of the Lwów-Warsaw School (LWS)—particularly through their interactions with the Vienna Circle in the 1930s—have been consistently framed within a distinctly Polish intellectual narrative. These framings celebrate the School as part of a 'Polish philosophical renaissance', describing its members as 'Polish philosophers' or 'Polish logicians', thereby subsuming its pluralistic character under the rubric of Polish national identity.[171]

I would suggest that Fleck's implicit challenge to notions of nation and national identity lies at the heart of his exclusion and marginalization. His concepts of thought collectives and thought styles imply that categories such as 'Polish school', 'Polish university', or even 'Polish nation' were not expressions of any essential or metaphysical identity, but historically contingent products of specific epistemic formations—a position that cut deeply against entrenched Polish Romantic and

utworzenie Towarzystwa Kultury Akademickiej. […] Gdy jednak oświadczył chęć i gotowość wydania mego przemówienia Uniwersytet Poznański, zamierzone uwagi, które by były nadały publikacji charakter polityczny, i to polemiczny w zakresie faktów i poglądów wysoce—przynajmniej po części—aktualnych, musiały oczywiście odpaść. Nie wykluczam jednak, że zdobędę się kiedyś na drugie wydanie tego przemówienia—a wtedy wydam je wraz z uwagami objaśniającymi, choć ściągnie to na mnie gromy z różnych, także przeciwnych sobie stron'.

[169] Brożek and Jadacki (2023, p. 115).

[170] Woleński (2011, p. 76).

[171] Smith (1989, p. 32); Woleński and Lapointe (2009,13); Woleński (2019, p. 32).

nationalist visions of the nation,[172] from Mickiewicz's messianism to Dmowski's ethno-political exclusivism. These identifications were sustained amd propagated through specific thought styles and their interactions with rival collectives and alternative affiliations. While Twardowski championed independence from party-political influence, he simultaneously subordinated universities to Polish national interests. In this sense, his thought was shaped by the nationalist categories that emerged with particular intensity in Eastern Galicia during the late nineteenth century, such as the promotion of Polish identity among sections of the elite at the expense of competing identities, including Ruthenian (later Ukrainian) and Jewish.[173]

Fleck's rejection of Dąmbska's insistence on a universal thought style or unbiased observer strikes at the assumption that philosophers can isolate themselves within university walls and detach their reflections from the sociopolitical currents shaping society at large. This book suggests that whenever philosophers claim to pursue pure thought—thinking about thinking without empirical taint—they may be most entangled in asserting cultural domination. Perhaps the Lwów-Warsaw School's increasing focus on logic and abstraction, in a realm of expertise inaccessible to the many—'the artisans, the seamen, the barber-surgeons (*Wundärzte*), the leather-workers and saddlers, the gardeners [...] children playing',[174] whom Fleck credits with developing the natural sciences—was bound up with a suppression of alternative ways of thinking.

2.4 Conclusion

This chapter has situated Ludwik Fleck's epistemology within its historical and intellectual contexts, showing how his marginal position in interwar Lemberg/Lwów/L'viv shaped his critique of elitist science and its claims to objectivity and neutrality. By examining the interplay between Fleck's working life, his engagement with broader intellectual currents, the contributions of 'the Polish School of Philosophy of Medicine', and the Lwów School, the chapter sheds light on the complexity of his thought and the unique position he occupied in a specific intellectual milieu.

Fleck's critique of objectivity and neutrality is inseparable from the socio-political realities he faced, including systemic antisemitism and nationalist

[172] See Walicki (1982), especially Part Three on Polish National and Religious Messianism.

[173] On the weakness of Polish identification among the peasants in Galicia in the mid-nineteenth century, see Davies (2005, Chap. 1); on the first half of the nineteenth century, see Kargol (2017); on the Galician peasants' loyalty to the Hapsburg emperor rather than the Polish nationalists, see Kieniewicz (1969, pp. 203–209) and Clark (2023). For a detailed study of efforts to instil a sense of Polish identity among Galician peasants, see Stauter-Halsted (2001), especially Part II The Construction of a Peasant Pole.

[174] Fleck (1986b, p. 50).

academic policies. His focus on the collective, socially mediated nature of knowledge formation built on the patient-oriented approaches of Polish physician-philosophers while extending their critique into a broader epistemological framework. This emphasis on specificities and shared thought styles enabled Fleck to challenge both neo-Kantian notions of absolute reality and the persistent pursuit of purely objective knowledge increasingly at odds with scientific developments.

Far from endorsing unchecked relativism, Fleck's epistemology sheds light on the constraints imposed by collective thought styles, positioning cognition as an interactive process shaped by historical, cultural, and institutional contexts. In reconstructing Fleck's relationship to the 'Polish School of Philosophy of Medicine' and the Lwów School, this chapter has portrayed him as a thinker who consistently crossed disciplinary boundaries. Rather than treating sciences, disciplines, traditions, and institutions as distinct and isolated domains, Fleck's work reveals their interconnectedness and their influence on collective life. By addressing the socio-political dimensions of knowledge, Fleck's epistemology provides a way to understand knowledge production as both deeply embedded in historical contexts and a trigger for broader cultural transformation.

Having outlined the context of Fleck's thought, the next chapter turns to his distinctive contributions to epistemology, focusing on how his engagement with relational and collective dimensions of cognition attempted to contribute to debates on the nature of knowledge and its constraints.

References

Afeltowicz Ł, Sojak R (2015) Arystokraci i rzemieślnicy. Synergia stylów badawczych. Wydawnictwo Naukowe Uniwersytetu Mikołaja Kopernika, Torun

Aleksiun N (2012) Jewish students and Christian corpses in interwar Poland: Playing with the language of blood libel. Jewish Hist 26(4):327–342. https://doi.org/10.1007/s10835-012-9163-5

Amar TC (2015) The paradox of Ukrainian Lviv: A Borderland City between Stalinists, Nazis, and Nationalists. Cornell University Press, New York

Amsterdamska O, Bonah C, Borck C, Fehr J, Hagner M, Klingberg M, Löwy I, Schlünder M, Schmaltz F, Schnelle T, Tammen A, Weindling P, Zittel C (2008) Medical science in the light of a flawed study of the Holocaust: a comment on Eva Hedfors' paper on Ludwik Fleck. Soc Stud Sci 38(6):937–952. https://doi.org/10.1177/0306312708098609

Bartov O, Weitz ED (eds) (2013) Shatterzone of empires: coexistence and violence in the German, Habsburg, Russian, and Ottoman Borderlands. Indiana University Press

Biedrzycka A (2012) Kalendarium Lwowa 1918–1939. Universitas, Kraków

Biernacki E (1899) Istota i granice wiedzy lekarskiej. Drukarnia Granowskiego i Sikorskiego, Warszawa

Binney N (2023) Ludwik Fleck's reasonable relativism about science. Synthese 201:40. https://doi.org/10.1007/s11229-022-04018-w

Bohr, N (1928) Discussions with Einstein on epistemological problems in atomic physics. In: Schilpp PA (ed) Albert Einstein: Philosopher–Scientist. The library of living philosophers. Open Court, Minnesota, pp 200–241

Bohr N (1949) The quantum postulate and the recent development of atomic theory. Nature 121:580–590, 14 April 1928. https://doi.org/10.1038/121580a0

Borck C (2004) Message in a bottle from 'the crisis of reality': on Ludwik Fleck's interventions for an open epistemology. Stud Hist Philos Biol Biomed Sci 35(3):447–464

Brożek A, Jadacki J (2023) Kazimierz Twardowski: filozof ze Lwowa. Życie. Warszawa

Bukowska-Marczak E (2019) Przyjaciele, koledzy, wrogowie? Relacje pomiędzy polskimi, żydowskimi i ukraińskimi studentami Uniwersytetu Jana Kazimierza we Lwowie w okresie międzywojennym (1918–1939). Wydawnictwo Neriton, Warszawa

Ciesielska M (2020) Wybrane badania naukowe prowadzone przez żydowskich mikrobiologów w getcie warszawskim i lwowskim. In: Bartuś A (ed) Pola wolności. Wydawnictwo WSB, Oświęcim-Poznań

Ciesielska M (2022) The Doctors of the Warsaw Ghetto (trans. Krzychylkiewicz A). Academic Studies Press, Boston

Ciesielska M, Jarnicki P (2021) Ludwik Fleck mikrobiolog i filozof. Oficyna Wydawnicza Politechniki Warszawskiej, Warszawa

Clark C (2023) Revolutionary spring: fighting for a new world 1848–1849. Allen Lane

Condé ML, Jarnicki P (2023) Ludwik fleck: thought style and thought collective in the historiography of science. In: Condé ML, Salomon M (eds) Handbook for the historiography of science. Historiographies of science. Springer, Cham. https://doi.org/10.1007/978-3-031-27510-4_5

Crease RP, Scharff Goldhaber A (2014) The quantum moment: how Planck, Bohr, Einstein, and Heisenberg taught us to love uncertainty. W. W. Norton & Company, New York

Cunningham A, Williams P (1992) Introduction. In: Cunningham A, Williams P (eds) The laboratory revolution in medicine. CUP, Cambridge

Dąmbska I (1937) Czy intersubiektywne podobieństwo wrażeń zmysłowych jest niezbędnym założeniem nauk przyrodniczych? Przegląd Filozoficzny *3*:288–294. Retrieved from https://sady.up.krakow.pl/fleck.dambska.htm

Davies N (2005) God's playground: a history of Poland (Vol. II: 1795 to the present). Columbia University Press, New York

Dmowski R (1909) Kwestya Żydowska. I. Separatyzm Żydów i jego źródła. Nakładem „Gazety Warszawskiej", Warszawa

Dmowski R (1933). Myśli nowoczesnego Polaka (fourth ed.). Skład Główny "Gazeta Warszawska", Warszawa. (Original work published 1903). Retrieved from Cyfrowa Biblioteka Myśli Narodowej: https://cbmn.pl/uploads/ebooks/Roman%20Dmowski%20-%20Myśli%20nowoczesnego%20Polaka.pdf

Einstein A (1936) Physics and reality (trans: Piccard J). J Franklin Inst 221:348–382

Encyclopedia of Ukraine (1993) Lviv Underground Ukrainian University. Retrieved [20.12.2024], from https://bit.ly/UndergroundUniversity

Fleck L (1929) Zur Krise der "Wirklichkeit". Naturwissenschaften 17:425–430. https://doi.org/10.1007/BF01513488

Fleck L (1938) W sprawie artykułu p. Izydory Dąmbskiej w Przeglądzie Filozoficznym (Rocz. 40, zesz. III). Retrieved from https://sady.up.krakow.pl/fleck.dambska.htm

Fleck L (1986a) Some specific features of the medical way of thinking [1927]. In: Cognition and fact. Boston studies in the philosophy of science, vol 87. Springer, Dordrecht. https://doi.org/10.1007/978-94-009-4498-5_2

Fleck L (1986b) On the Crisis of 'Reality' [1929]. In: Cognition and Fact. Boston studies in the philosophy of science, vol 87. Springer, Dordrecht. https://doi.org/10.1007/978-94-009-4498-5_3

Fleck L (1986c) Scientific observation and perception in general [1935]. In: Cognition and fact. Boston studies in the philosophy of science, vol 87. Springer, Dordrecht. https://doi.org/10.1007/978-94-009-4498-5_4

Fleck L (1986d) The problem of epistemology [1936]. In: Cognition and fact. Boston studies in the philosophy of science, vol 87. Springer, Dordrecht. https://doi.org/10.1007/978-94-009-4498-5_5

Fleck, L (1986e) To look, to see, to know [1947]. In: Cognition and fact. Boston studies in the philosophy of science, vol 87. Springer, Dordrecht. https://doi.org/10.1007/978-94-009-4498-5_7

Fleck L (1986g) Crisis in science. In: Cognition and fact. Boston studies in the philosophy of science, vol 87. Springer, Dordrecht. https://doi.org/10.1007/978-94-009-4498-5_8
Fleck L (1990) Texts of Ludwik Fleck and Tadeusz Bilikiewicz. In: The Polish School of Philosophy of Medicine. Philosophy and Medicine, vol 37. Springer, Dordrecht. https://doi.org/10.1007/978-94-009-2135-1_13
Fleck L (2007) Życiorys [1950]. In: Werner S, Zittel C, Schmaltz F (eds) Style myślowe i fakty: artykuły i świadectwa. Wydawn. Instytutu Filozofii i Socjologii PAN, Warszawa
Forman P (2011) Weimar culture, causality, and quantum theory, 1918–27: Adaptation by German physicists and mathematicians to a hostile intellectual environment. In: Carson C, Kojevnikov A, Trischler H (eds) Weimar culture and quantum mechanics: selected papers by Paul Forman and contemporary perspectives on the Forman thesis. Imperial College Press, pp 85–203
Foucault M (1973) The Birth of the clinic: an archaeology of medical perception [1963] (trans: Sheridan AM). Tavistock Publications, London
Freudenthal G, Löwy I (1988) Ludwik Fleck's roles in society: a case study using Joseph Ben David's paradigm for the sociology of science. Soc Stud Sci 18(4):625–651
Friedman F (1945) Zagłada Żydów lwowskich. Wydawnictwa Centralnej Żydowskiej Komisji Historycznej przy Centralnym Komitecie Żydów Polskich Nr 4, Łódź
Friedman P (1980) The destruction of the Jews of Lwów, 1941–1944. In: Friedman AJ (ed) Roads to extinction: essays on the Holocaust (pp. 244–321). The Jewish Publication Society of America and the Conference on Jewish Social Studies, Inc
Gradmann C (2009) Laboratory disease: Robert Koch's medical bacteriology (trans: Forster E). Johns Hopkins University Press, Baltimore
Grzybowski, A, Ciesielska, M (2014) Lesser known aspects of Ludwik Fleck's (1896–1961) heroic life during World War II. J Med Biogr, 0(0), 1–7. doi:https://doi.org/10.1177/0967772014532893
Hałęza Z (2021) Od sztuki lekarskiej do nowej logiki medycyny. Władysława Biegańskiego poszukiwania teoretycznych podstaw leczenia. Piotrkowskie Zeszyty Historyczne 22(2):101–127. https://doi.org/10.25951/4431
Hedfors E (2006) The reading of Ludwik Fleck: questions of sources and impetus. Soc Epistemol J Knowl Cult Policy 20(2):131–161. https://doi.org/10.1080/02691720600784477
Hedfors E (2007) Fleck in context. Persp Sci 15(1):82–102
Hedfors E (2008) Medical science in the light of the Holocaust: departing from a post-war paper by Ludwik Fleck. Soc Studi Sci 38(2):259–283. https://doi.org/10.1177/0306312707082959
Ivanyk S (2017) The Lvov-Warsaw School as a multicultural phenomenon. Ukrainian aspect. In: Brożek A, Stadler F, Woleński J (eds) The significance of the Lvov-Warsaw School in the European Culture. Vienna Circle Institute Yearbook, vol 21. Springer, Cham. https://doi.org/10.1007/978-3-319-52869-4_3
Kargol T (2017) Świadomość chłopów w Galicji w pierwszej połowie XIX wieku. Zarys problemu. Prace Historyczne 144(2):401–411. https://doi.org/10.4467/20844069PH.17.022.6265
Kieniewicz S (1969) The Emancipation of the polish peasantry. University of Chicago Press, Chicago
Kosiński K (2022) Bunt duszy polskiej: O twórczości politycznej i literackiej Romana Dmowskiego (z lat 1893–1934). Instytut Dziedzictwa Myśli Narodowej & Neriton, Warszawa
Kramsztyk Z (1899a) O Cytatach [1882] In: Szkice krytyczne z zakresu medycyny. Skład Główny w Księgarni E. Wendego i Spółki; Druk W. L. Anczyca i Spółki. Warszawa; Kraków
Kramsztyk Z (1899b) Czy medycyna jest nauką, czy sztuką? [1895] In: Szkice krytyczne z zakresu medycyny. Skład Główny w Księgarni E. Wendego i Spółki; Druk W. L. Anczyca i Spółki. Warszawa; Kraków
Kramsztyk Z (1899c) Fakt Kliniczny [1898]. In: Szkice krytyczne z zakresu medycyny. Skład Główny w Księgarni E. Wendego i Spółki; Druk W. L. Anczyca i Spółki. Warszawa; Kraków
Kremer RL (1992) Building institutes for physiology in Prussia, 1836–1846: contexts, interests and rhetoric. In: Cunningham A, Williams P (eds) The laboratory revolution in medicine. CUP, Cambridge

Lenoir T (1992) Laboratories, medicine and public life in Germany, 1830–1849: ideological roots of the institutional revolution. In: Cunningham A, Williams P (eds) The laboratory revolution in medicine. CUP, Cambridge
Löwy I (1990a) The Polish School of philosophy of medicine. Philosophy and medicine, vol 37. Springer, Dordrecht. https://doi.org/10.1007/978-94-009-2135-1_12
Löwy I (1990b) Medical Critique [Krytyka Lekarska]: a journal of medicine and philosophy - 1897-1907. J Med Philosophy 15(6):653–674. https://doi.org/10.1093/jmp/15.6.653
Löwy I (2000) The Polish School of philosophy of medicine: lessons from the past. In: Tymieniecka AT, Zalewski Z (eds) Life the human being between life and death. Analecta Husserliana, vol 64. Springer, Dordrecht. https://doi.org/10.1007/978-94-017-2081-6_27
Löwy I (2020) Typhus in Buchenwald: can the story be told? Ethics Progr 11(1):4–19. https://doi.org/10.14746/eip.2020.1.1
Markiewicz W (1986) Lwów as cultural and intellectual background of the genesis of Fleck's ideas. In: Cognition and fact. Boston studies in the philosophy of science, vol 87. Springer, Dordrecht. https://doi.org/10.1007/978-94-009-4498-5_12
Mick C (2016) Lemberg, Lwów, L'viv, 1914–1947: violence and ethnicity in a contested city. Purdue University Press, https://doi.org/10.2307/j.ctv15wxrkr
Modras R (1994) The catholic press in Interwar Poland on the 'Jewish question': metaphor and the developing rhetoric of exclusion. East Eur Jewish Aff 24(1):49–70. https://doi.org/10.1080/13501679408577764
Osterhammel J (2009) Colonialism (trans: Frisch SL). Markus Wiener Publishers, Princeton
Pais A (1991) Niels Bohr's Times, in physics, philosophy, and polity. Clarendon, Oxford
Pakszys E (2019) The victims and the survivors: the Lvov-Warsaw School and the holocaust. In: Drabarek A, Woleński J, Radzki M (eds) Interdisciplinary investigations into the Lvov-Warsaw School. History of analytic philosophy. Palgrave Macmillan, Cham. https://doi.org/10.1007/978-3-030-24486-6_3
Polak A, Grzybowski A, Sak J (2015) Zygmunt Kramsztyk - patriota, działacz społeczny, filozof medycyny i lekarz. Archiwum Historii i Filozofii Medycyny 78(1):96–108
Prusin AV (2005) Nationalizing a Borderland. War, ethnicity, and Anti-Jewish violence in East Galicia, 1914–1920. University of Alabama Press
Prusin AV (2013) A "Zone of Violence": the anti-Jewish Pogroms in Eastern Galicia in 1914–1915 and 1941. In: Bartov O, Weitz ED (eds) Shatterzone of empires: coexistence and violence in the German, Habsburg, Russian, and Ottoman borderlands (pp. 362–377). Indiana University Press
Riezler K (1928) Die Krise der "Wirklichkeit". Naturwissenschaften 16, 705–712 (1928). https://doi.org/10.1007/BF01505707
Rudnicki S (2008) From 'Numerus Clausus' to 'Numerus Nullus'. In: Polonsky A (ed) Jews and the emerging Polish State (Polin Volume Two). Liverpool University Press
Sady W (2000) Fleck O społecznej naturze poznania. Prószyński i S-ka, Warszawa
Schafer L, Schnelle T (1980) Einleitung. In: Ludwik Fleck, Entstehung und Entwicklung einer wissenschaftlichen Tatsache. Suhrkamp, Frankfurt a.M, pp vii–xlix
Schnelle T (1986a) Microbiology and philosophy of science, Lwów and the German Holocaust: stations of a life — Ludwik Fleck 1896–1961. In: Cognition and fact. Boston studies in the philosophy of science, vol 87. Springer, Dordrecht. https://doi.org/10.1007/978-94-009-4498-5_1
Schnelle T (1986b) Ludwik Fleck and the Influence of the Philosophy of Lwów. In: Cognition and fact. Boston studies in the philosophy of science, vol 87. Springer, Dordrecht. https://doi.org/10.1007/978-94-009-4498-5_13
Seidel M (2011) Relativism or relationism? A Mannheimian interpretation of Fleck's claims about relativism. J Gen Philos Sci / Zeitschrift für Allgemeine Wissenschaftstheorie 42(2):219–240
Smith B (1989) Kasimir Twardowski: an essay on the borderlines of ontology, psychology and logic. In: The Vienna Circle and the Lvov-Warsaw School. Nijhoff International Philosophy Series, vol 38. Springer, Dordrecht. https://doi.org/10.1007/978-94-009-2829-9_15
Snyder T (2003) The reconstruction of nations: Poland, Ukraine, Lithuania, Belarus, 1569–1999. Yale University Press, New Haven

Snyder T (2010) Bloodlands: Europe between Hitler and Stalin. Basic Books, New York
Śródka A, Gryglewski R (2007) Władysław Szumowski—życie i twórczość filozoficzno-medyczna. In: Szumowski W, Filozofia Medycyny (eds) Wydawnictwo Marek Derewiecki, Kęty, pp 3–15.
Stauter-Halsted K (2001) The Nation in the village: the genesis of peasant national identity in Austrian Poland, 1848–1914. Cornell University Press, Ithaca and London
Szlachcic K (2006) Konwencje, style myslenia i relatywizm. Kilka uwag o sporze I. Dambska—L. Fleck. Studia Philosophica Wratislaviensia vol. I, fasc. 1 (2006)
Szumowski W (1921) Filozoficzny rozwój medycyny jako przedmiot uniwersytetu. Przegląd Filozoficzny 23:278–294.
Szumowski W (1948) Filozofia Medycyny. Sprawozdania, rozważania. Gebethner and Wolff, Kraków
Szumowski W (2007) Filozofia Medycyny. Wydawnictwo Marek Derewiecki, Kęty
Tatarkiewicz W (1948) Zarys dziejów filozofii w Polsce. Polska Akademia Umiejętności, Kraków
Thompson WC (1980) In the eye of the storm: Kurt Riezler and the Crises of Modern Germany. University of Iowa Press, Iowa City
Twardowski K (1900) O tak zwanych prawdach względnych. nakł. Senatu Uniwersytetu Lwowskiego, Lwów
Twardowski K (1908) W sprawie Uniwersytetu Lwowskiego: głos Towarzystwa. owarzystwo Nauczycieli Szkół Wyższych, Lwów
Twardowski K (1919) O patryotyzmie. Biblioteka Macierzy Polskiej, Lwów
Twardowski K (1933) O dostojeństwie uniwersytetu. Uniwersytet Poznański, Poznan
Twardowski K (1999a) On so-called relative truths (1900). In: Brandl JL, Woleński J (eds) On actions, products and other topics in philosophy (trans: annot. A. Szylewicz). Rodopi. (Polish Analytical Philosophy, Vol. 1). pp 147–170
Twardowski, K (1999b) On the dignity of the university (1933). In: Brandl JL, Woleński J (eds) On actions, products and other topics in philosophy (trans: and annot. A. Szylewicz). Rodopi. (Polish Analytical Philosophy, Vol. 1) pp. 147–170)
Walicki A (1982) Philosophy and romantic nationalism: the case of Poland. Clarendon Press, Oxford
Weindling P (1992) Scientific elites and laboratory organisation in *fin de siècle* Paris and Berlin: the Pasteur Institute and Robert Koch's Institute for infectious diseases compared. In: Cunningham A, Williams P (eds) The laboratory revolution in medicine. CUP, Cambridge
Woleński J (2011) Jews in polish philosophy. Shofar: an Interdiscip J Jewish Stud 29(3):68–82 https://doi.org/10.1353/sho.2011.0083
Woleński J (2019) Lvov-Warsaw School: historical and sociological comments. In: Drabarek A, Woleński J, Radzki M (eds) Interdisciplinary investigations into the Lvov-Warsaw School. History of analytic philosophy. Palgrave Macmillan, Cham. https://doi.org/10.1007/978-3-030-24486-6_2
Woleński J, Lapointe S (2009) Introduction. In: Lapointe S, Wolénski J, Marion M, Miskiewicz W (eds) The golden age of polish philosophy. Logic, epistemology, and the unity of science, vol 16. Springer, Dordrecht. https://doi.org/10.1007/978-90-481-2401-5_1
Wolniewicz B (1986) Ludwik Fleck and Polish Philosophy. In: Cognition and fact. Boston studies in the philosophy of science, vol 87. Springer, Dordrecht. https://doi.org/10.1007/978-94-009-4498-5_11
Wrzosek A (1918) Udział medycyny polskiej w kulturze powszechnej ze szczególnym uwzględnieniem czasów porozbiorowych. In: Koneczny F (ed) Polska w kulturze powszechnej: Część II. Szczegółowa. Polskie Spółki Oszczędności i Pożyczek. Kraków
Zamecki S (2006) Kilka uwag na temat tzw. Polskiej szkoły filozofii medycyny. Medycyna Nowożytna 13(1–2):25–33
Zittel C (2010) The politics of cognition: genesis and development of Ludwik Fleck's 'Comparative Epistemology'. In: Epple M, Zittel C (eds) Science as cultural practice: Vol. I: cultures and

politics of research from the early modern period to the age of extremes (pp. 183–200). De Gruyter (A), Berlin. https://doi.org/10.1524/9783050087092.183
Zittel C, Schmaltz F (2007) Wstęp. In: Fleck L (2007) Style myślowe i fakty: artykuły i świadectwa. Warszawa: Wydawn. Instytutu Filozofii i Socjologii PAN. Werner S, Zittel C Schmaltz F (eds)

Chapter 3
Fleck's Thought: Internal Positioning

Abstract This chapter situates Ludwik Fleck's references to Lucien Lévy-Bruhl and Ernst Mach to clarify the distinctiveness of his proposed 'comparative epistemology'. It examines Fleck's engagement with Lévy-Bruhl's sociological anthropology and Mach's conventionalist history of science, showing how he draws on both traditions while departing from each in critical respects. Against Lévy-Bruhl, Fleck highlights the positivist assumptions underpinning the claim that scientific thought yields purely objective concepts. Against Mach, he critiques the internalist and biologically grounded account of scientific development for neglecting socio-cultural determinants.

Fleck's discussion of scientific facts does not stem from systematic engagement with Mach's epistemology, but from a critical reading that exposes implicit assumptions about perception and facticity. Reconsidering Jerzy Giedymin's insightful critique, the chapter contends that Fleck, despite mischaracterizing aspects of Machian thought, successfully identifies a blind spot in Mach's conception of historical development.

Central to this reappraisal is Fleck's notion of 'passive elements' in cognition—relational constraints that emerge from interaction with what is cognized. Rather than reintroducing objective reality 'through the back door', these elements function as a check on arbitrary constructivism, anchoring cognition in resistance. Recent scholarship has revisited this neglected component of Fleck's theory, emphasizing its relevance to epistemological models grounded in interaction and evolutionary adaptation. In light of these contributions, the chapter affirms Fleck's continuing importance to debates on the historical, social, and cognitive constitution of scientific facts.

S. Dersley, *Thought Collectives and Cultural Change*, Living Signs of Law 1,
https://doi.org/10.1007/978-3-031-97431-1_3

3.1 Transcendental Determination

Since Thomas Kuhn's 1976 *Foreword*, a distinct line of Fleck scholarship has situated his thought within the post-Kantian tradition: his thought styles are said to shape individuals' perception and thinking in much the same way that Kantian categories equip the subject prior to experience.[1]

For instance, Wojciech Sady traces Fleck's theory of thought styles back to Immanuel Kant's forms of intuition and categories of the understanding: 'the cognitive *a priori*' which transcendentally determines the subject's experience and knowledge.[2] This positioning is justified both by Fleck's explicit references to Kant and his engagement with post-Kantian thought, particularly Émile Durkheim's sociological critique of the Kantian categories and Ernst Mach's critique of the Kantian 'thing-in-itself'.

According to Sady, Fleck's thought is Kantian in that it posits the cognitive *a priori* as actively shaping experience, but non-Kantian in that the cognitive *a priori* is in turn posited as being shaped by social groups. Thus, while for Kant the cognitive *a priori* constitutes an innate, immutable, and universal framework that all human subjects apply to experience, for Fleck it is acquired from a socially determined collective and is therefore subject to change.

In *Genesis and Development of a Scientific Fact* (1935), Fleck refers to Kant on two occasions. In Chap. 2, Fleck uses the examples of Columbus and Kant to demonstrate the 'tenacity of viewpoints'. When a conception permeates a thought collective to such a degree that its contradiction becomes unimaginable, it becomes a viewpoint (*Anschauung*). It was such a viewpoint that led people to argue against Columbus: the absolute meaning attached to the concepts 'up' and 'down' made it impossible for them to conceive of the world as round. In turn, Kant's 'unknowable substratum of "things in themselves"' is treated as symptomatic of a tenacious viewpoint that uses the concepts of 'reality, truth and existence' in an absolute sense. Fleck suggests that the problems caused by these viewpoints disappear when a relativistic frame is adopted.[3]

Kant is thus invoked to represent an epistemology grounded in the assumptions of an absolutist metaphysics. Although Kant's thought denies unmediated access to reality—or the world beyond experience, as represented by the 'thing-in-itself'—Kantian epistemology is still identified as based on the metaphysical assumption of an absolute, Newtonian reality independent of human cognition. However, Fleck, due to his interactional conception of cognition and specific relativist stance, as outlined in *On the Crisis of 'Reality'* (1929), views this assumption as having been thoroughly undermined by subsequent thought styles and scientific developments.

---

[1] Kuhn (1976, p. xi).

[2] Sady (2000, 2021).

[3] Fleck (1979, pp. 27–28).

The second reference to Kant appears when Fleck, drawing on French sociology, emphasizes the role of the collective in shaping individual thought, quoting Wilhelm Jerusalem extensively. Jerusalem translated and edited Lucien Lévy-Bruhl's *Les fonctions mentales dans les sociétés inférieures* (1910) as *Das Denken der Naturvölker* (1921), a work of key importance for Fleck. In addition to his efforts to disseminate William James' pragmatism, Durkheim's sociology, and Lévy-Bruhl's sociological-ethnology to the German public, Jerusalem also made pioneering contributions to the sociology of knowledge. His *Die Soziologie des Erkennens* (1909) [*The Sociology of Cognition*], which received a 'sympathetic analysis from Durkheim,'[4] and *Die soziologische Bedingtheit des Denkens und der Denkformen* (1924) [*The Sociological Conditioning of Thinking and Thought Patterns*[5]] were influential works. Fleck quotes a passage from the latter essay:

> Kant's firm belief in a timeless, completely immutable logical structure of our reason, a belief that has since become the common heritage of all who adopt an a priori point of view and is maintained with great tenacity also by the latest representatives of this direction of thinking, has not only failed to be confirmed by the results of modern ethnology but proved to be definitely erroneous.[6]

Hence, according to Jerusalem—following Durkheim and Lévy-Bruhl—the mutability of the categories that determine human cognition is demonstrated by the empirical evidence supplied by ethnology and philology.

Fleck's two brief references to Kant are thus embedded within his critique of the sociological extension of Kantian categories, particularly in response to ethnological evidence. Fleck first characterizes Kant as a representative of an absolutist metaphysical tradition, characterizing his rigid categorization of knowledge as fixed and universal. Then, through his engagement with Jerusalem's texts, Fleck further identifies Kant as an advocate of an immutable and universalist epistemology—one that, in Fleck's view, fails to account for the socially and historically contingent nature of knowledge formation.

Hartmut von Sass also traces Fleck's thought back to Kant, situating him within the transcendentalist tradition. However, von Sass argues that Fleck's transcendentalism is more 'humble': while Kant claims to have uncovered the 'culturally and historically invariant' epistemic apparatus with which 'we' are all equipped, Fleck rejects this universalism in favour of a 'situated' transcendentalism; the transcendental determinants of cognition are 'embedded in concrete cultural environments, contexts, practices, or conceptual schemes'.[7]

---

[4] Uebel (2012).

[5] The title given in F. Bradley and T.J. Trenn's translation of *Genesis and Development of a Scientific Fact*. (1979). Daniel R. Huebner translates this essay title as 'The Sociological Determination of Thought and of the Forms of Thought'—Huebner (2013, p. 447).

[6] Fleck (1979, p. 47).

[7] von Sass (2016, p. 74).

Of course, Fleck was not the first to arrive at such a 'situated' transcendentalism. In *The Elementary Forms of Religious Life* (1912), Durkheim had posited that space and time are socially-determined collective representations, and that the categories of thought have a social origin and are thus subject to change: '[...] the categories of human thought are never fixed in a definite form. They are made, unmade and remade incessantly; they vary according to time and place'.[8]

Thomas Schnelle suggested that Fleck only had a superficial knowledge of the European sociological school, but that drawing on the ideas of Durkheim and Lévy-Bruhl helped him develop a position that could answer the questions collectively posed—but individually answered—by the philosophers of 'the Lwów school': Twardowski, Ajdukiewicz and Chwistek. These questions centered on 'the "what" and the "how" of the factors determining reality'.[9]

However, regardless of the depth of Fleck's knowledge of French sociology, in *Genesis and Development of a Scientific Fact* Fleck explicitly refers to Durkheim and his notion that collective and social structures are imposed on the individual.[10] Fleck's situated transcendentalism posits that cognition is not merely a dual relationship between subject and object, but requires the inclusion of a third element: 'the existing fund of knowledge' (*Wissensbestand*).[11] This socially and historically determined fund of knowledge, which can be viewed as a modification of the Kantian cognitive *a priori,* can be understood—at least in part—as analogous to Durkheim's social structures.

In Fleck's theory the communication of concepts between different thought styles necessarily involves an element of transformation (discussed in more detail in Chap. 4), hence when Fleck, a Polish microbiologist, appropriated concepts from the French sociological school, in order to stake out an epistemology in opposition to the philosophers of the Lwów school and the Vienna Circle,[12] innovation was inevitable. However, Fleck's adoption of Durkheim's social structures as determinants of thought, in the form of the 'existing fund of knowledge' is not particularly transformative, since it is fully consistent with the sociological critique of Kantian epistemology. Fleck's major innovation occurs elsewhere.

---

[8] Durkheim (2001, p. 16).

[9] Schnelle (1986, p. 233).

[10] Fleck (1979, p. 46). When Fleck writes 'Durkheim speaks expressly of the force exerted on the individual by social structures both as objective specific facts and as controlled behavior', he appears to be referring, via Jerusalem's introduction to Lévy Bruhl's *Primitive Mentality* (1922), see footnote 23, Fleck (1979, p. 46), to the passage in *The Elementary Forms of Religious Life* where Durkheim describes the categories as 'the common ground where all minds meet': 'When we try to rebel against it, to free ourselves of some of these essential notions, we run into sharp resistance. So not only are these categories independent of us, they impose themselves on us', Durkheim (2001, p. 15).

[11] Fleck (1979, p. 38).

[12] Schnelle (1986), Fleck (1979, p. 50).

3.2 Fleck's Critique of the French Sociological School

According to Fleck, while the representatives of sociology (Durkheim, Lévy-Bruhl, Gumplowicz and Jerusalem) correctly identify collective ideas as determinants of cognition, they also have a 'pious reverence for scientific facts'.[13]

Fleck bases this move on his reading of Lévy-Bruhl's *Les fonctions mentales dans les sociétés inférieures* (1910, translated as *How Natives Think,* 1926).[14] After identifying Lévy-Bruhl as a student of Durkheim, Fleck cites passages from Lévy-Bruhl's *Author's Introduction* which question the notion that the human mind is a permanent, unchanging entity.

In the introduction to *How Natives Think*, Lévy-Bruhl suggests that the contributions of Durkheim and his collaborators will lead to 'a theory of knowledge [...] founded upon the comparative method'.[15] Lévy-Bruhl traces the postulate of the comparative method back to Auguste Comte, who is identified as recommending that the 'higher mental functions' should be studied from the social perspective, rather than the individual perspective, employing the sociological method in a positive science.[16]

However, according to Lévy-Bruhl, E. B. Tylor and 'the English school of anthropology' took the comparative method further than Comte's postulate, in order to 'study mental phenomena in different types of human societies'.[17] Yet these anthropologists made a fundamental mistake: on encountering consistent similarities in the societies they studied—'the same institutions; the same religious or magical ceremonies; the same beliefs and customs relating to birth and death [...]',[18] they assumed that these similarities could be explained 'in one way only'—by positing that the human mind is universal. Lévy-Bruhl argues that this assumption functions as an unquestioned axiom, which in turn underpins the English school's hypothesis of animism.

In Lévy-Bruhl's reading of Frazer's *Golden Bough*, the hypothesis of animism is posited to explain the apparent uniformity of beliefs and practices in disparate societies. Hence 'the primitive' is said to treat the representations of dreams as real, which leads to a belief in a double existence populated with bodies alongside immaterial souls and phantoms, entailing that natural phenomena are attributed with causal agency. This 'primitive' philosophy is put forward as the *probable* explanation for customs such as destroying a dead man's weapons and placing coins or grain in the mouths of dead people. For Lévy-Bruhl, the hypothesis of animism and the notion of a uniform 'primitive' philosophy are inevitable consequences of

---

[13] Fleck (1979, pp. 46–47).

[14] Fleck refers to the German translation, *Das Denken der Naturvölker*, translated by Wilhelm Jerusalem. 2d ed. Vienna and Liepzig: Braumüller, 1926.

[15] Lévy-Bruhl (1966, p. 4).

[16] Lévy-Bruhl (1966, p. 5).

[17] Lévy-Bruhl (1966, p. 6).

[18] Lévy-Bruhl (1966, p. 7).

assuming the universality of the human mind. In his assessment, the hypothesis of animism proved to be a hindrance that prevented the English school of anthropology from becoming a 'positive science of the higher mental functions'.[19]

Lévy-Bruhl's counter-argument first focuses on the probable nature of the reasoning employed by Frazer (and by extension the English school of anthropology). The hypothesis of animism is only one possible explanation for the apparent uniformity in the accumulated data, as evident in Frazer's tentative language ('*may* have sprung [...] *probably* later'). For Lévy-Bruhl, such probable reasoning is extremely 'risky'.[20]

Second, Lévy-Bruhl homes in on the fact that the phenomena analysed by the English school—'institutions, beliefs, practices'—are fundamentally social in nature and thus concern 'collective representations'. This is the critical point: the hypothesis of animism and the axiom of the universal nature of the human mind are based on a conception of the human mind that treats the mind as an individual entity, *a priori* equipped with a 'primitive' philosophy, prior to any social experience. Drawing on Durkheim's sociology, Lévy-Bruhl asserts that collective representations are subject to social laws, that all minds are 'socialized', and asserts (as cited in Fleck (1935a, 46)): 'The idea of an individual human mind absolutely free from all experience is, then, as fanciful as that of man prior to social life. It does not correspond with anything that we can grasp and verify, and the hypotheses implying it could but be arbitrary'.[21]

For Lévy-Bruhl, mentality is determined by the type of society, meaning that different societies will have different mentalities. Up to this point, Lévy-Bruhl's sociological account of human thought is largely compatible with Fleck's theory of thought styles. Fleck appears to have drawn significantly from Lévy-Bruhl's work, especially regarding the comments on a theory of knowledge grounded in a comparative method.

Lévy-Bruhl and Fleck part company, however, over the difference between the 'primitive' mentality and 'our' mentality. Drawing on the work of Durkheim and Mauss, Lévy-Bruhl defines the 'primitive' mentality as 'prelogical and mystical', governed by the law of participation, rather than the law of non-contradiction.[22] According to Lévy-Bruhl, in its most 'primitive' form, this mentality does not employ collective representations, as these require the object to be perceived as distinct from the subject. Participation, instead, demands 'collective mental states of extreme emotional intensity', realized through rituals and totemism.[23]

Collective representations emerge only as social relations develop; as these relations evolve, individuals become conscious of themselves as members of a group, fostering both a sense of belonging and antagonism toward outsiders. As a

[19] Lévy-Bruhl (1966, p. 9).

[20] Lévy-Bruhl (1966, pp. 11-13).

[21] Lévy-Bruhl (1966, p. 14).

[22] Lévy-Bruhl (1966, p. 323).

[23] Lévy-Bruhl (1966, p. 324).

consequence, the 'mystical symbiosis' weakens, and participation is no longer directly experienced. Ancestor worship and myths then emerge as collective representations that provide access to the lost symbiosis. For Lévy-Bruhl, these collective representations are not aimed at logical understanding or explanation, but rather at realizing emotional communion.[24] Thus the 'primitive' mentality is defined as being 'differently oriented' to 'our' mentality.

At this point, Lévy-Bruhl addresses an issue that will become of paramount importance for Fleck: Given that 'our' mentality is governed by different laws and serves entirely different purposes, how can 'we' possibly understand the 'primitive' mentality? For example, when we translate a Māori myth into our language, for Lévy-Bruhl the 'very translation is a betrayal', and we cannot help but impose 'our customary habits of thought' in our sentence constructions.[25] Though Lévy-Bruhl does not explicitly associate the cognitive shift involved in the transition from oral myths to their written reconstruction, he comes close when he argues that for the 'primitive' the words of myths are realities, and the focus is on emotional, mystic communion; while 'what we call a myth is but the inanimate corpse which remains after the vital spark has fled'.[26] Lévy-Bruhl concludes that understanding such myths is at best deeply problematic, and at worst impossible. He warns against any explanations which seek to reduce myths to 'psychological and intellectual activity similar to our own'.[27]

Lévy-Bruhl's account of how the 'primitive' mentality evolves into 'our' mentality is as follows: certain individuals in the social group become responsible for mediating participation (e.g. a medicine man), and those families and people not involved in this mediation become 'represented in a more impartial and objective way', which leads to a distinction between the sacred and the profane.[28] Once mystic perception begins to lose its hold on the mind, nature is viewed with 'less-prejudiced eyes', concepts develop, experience becomes an authority, and the law of non-contradiction supplants the law of participation. While the law of participation holds sway, nothing is impossible or absurd, but when experience is trusted and concepts begin to classify nature, the previous mystical connections come to be seen as contradictory.[29]

The transition from the prelogical mentality to the logical mentality is gradual, with Lévy-Bruhl suggesting that the emerging 'abstract and general concepts' contain elements that are 'vestiges of an earlier stage'.[30] In fact, Lévy-Bruhl acknowledges that these vestiges are never permanently eliminated: 'our mental activity is

---

[24] Lévy-Bruhl (1966, pp. 324–330).

[25] Lévy-Bruhl (1966, pp. 330–331).

[26] Lévy-Bruhl (1966, p. 332). The notion that words have the status of things in some thought collectives is one that Fleck will propose in *The Problem of Epistemology* (1986d, p. 94)).

[27] Lévy-Bruhl (1966, p. 333).

[28] Lévy-Bruhl (1966, pp. 335–336).

[29] Lévy-Bruhl (1966, pp. 335–350).

[30] Lévy-Bruhl (1966, pp. 340–341).

both rational and irrational. The prelogical and the mystic are co-existent with the logical'.[31]

Fleck seizes on this notion that logical mentality, as defined by Lévy-Bruhl, is impartial, free from prejudice, and objective:

> Lévy-Bruhl believes that scientific thought yields concepts which "solely express objective features and conditions of beings and phenomena." But he would find it difficult to define the meaning of "objective features" and "perception proper." Moreover, the attraction of attention by objective properties alleged to occur "ipso facto" is psychologically impossible. The perception of scientifically accepted properties (assuming Levy-Bruhl considers these "objective") must first be learned. It does not occur ipso facto and, indeed, the ability to perceive scientifically is only slowly acquired and learned. Its prime manifestation is discovery. This occurs in a complex, socially conditioned way, which resembles the origin of other ideas of the collective.[32]

This reading of Lévy-Bruhl enables Fleck to incorporate many tenets of French-Durkheimian sociology while simultaneously highlighting its blindness to the implications of its own assumptions. Without directly analysing or even referencing Durkheim's *Les Règles de la Méthode Sociologique (The Rules of Sociological Method)* (1919),[33] in which Durkheim outlines his conception of social facts, Fleck uses a plausible reading of Lévy-Bruhl to portray the French sociologists as believing that their perceptions and way of thinking—finally free from absurd mythical ideas and religious modes of thought—can finally lay claim to the status of objective, impartial and true knowledge.[34] In doing so, Fleck implicitly charges French sociology with being inconsistent with its own principles: it identifies the social and historical determination of other thought-styles, yet assumes its own thought is 'purely theoretical' and free from such influences.

---

[31] Lévy-Bruhl (1966, p. 347).

[32] Fleck (1979, p. 48).

[33] Durkheim (2013, pp. 20–23) Durkheim's conception of social facts shares significant parallels with Fleck's thought style, particularly in the emphasis on collective frameworks shaping individual cognition and behaviour. Durkheim defines social facts as 'ways of acting, thinking and feeling which possess the remarkable property of existing outside the consciousness of the individual' and are 'invested with a coercive power by virtue of which they exercise control over him'. Durkheim provides examples, such as the language one speaks, the monetary systems one uses, or the conventions of dress, to illustrate how social facts constrain individuals, even when conformity is not directly enforced but arises from implicit societal pressures. These insights prefigure Fleck's notion of thought style as a collectively shared and constraining mode of cognition, shaping what can be perceived, thought, or expressed within a given thought collective.

[34] Fleck (1979, pp. 47–51).

3.3 Fleck on Conventionalism

One of Fleck's most remarkable qualities as a thinker was his ability to draw on different intellectual traditions and play them off against each other to construct new theoretical positions. This strategy was deployed in an open, dialogical manner and stands as a prime example of positive, constructive critique. When viewed through the lens of his own theory, it becomes clear that Fleck actively combined and critically engaged with the existing fund of knowledge (*Wissensbestand*) to develop unique conceptual tools capable of addressing the complexities of both scientific practice and thought.

In observing this interplay, Sady notes that Fleck drew on some fundamental tenets of conventionalism to counter the blind spots of sociology, while simultaneously using sociology to challenge the claims of conventionalism:

> From the conventionalists he adopted the stance that reality can be described in a variety of ways, which cannot be reduced to each other. However – and here Fleck rejects the thesis of Poincaré or Duhem, through appealing to the sociology of knowledge – we are not free to choose between theoretical systems. Social factors [...] not only determine which religious or legal doctrine prevails; they also determine the choice of scientific theory.[35]

Just as Schnelle suggested that Fleck had only cursory knowledge of French sociology, Jerzy Giedymin questioned whether Fleck had 'first-hand familiarity' with the writings of Mach, to whom Fleck refers on a few occasions, treating him as a representative of conventionalism. Giedymin goes as far as to argue that, like many thinkers of his generation, Fleck's understanding of the conventionalist philosophy was 'mistaken', and that a key component of his own theory, namely the distinction between the active and passive elements of a thought style, was actually an essential component of the conventionalist philosophy.[36]

Since Fleck makes only makes a few superficial references to Poincaré in his writings,[37] and does not mention Duhem at all, in this section I will focus on how Fleck explicitly positions his thought with regard to Mach's analysis of science. Fleck's first reference to conventionalism appears in Chap. 1 of *Genesis and Development of a Scientific Fact*, where he suggests that the various concepts of syphilis which emerged in history (the carnal scourge, the empirical-therapeutic concept based on treatment with mercury, and the various experimental-pathological concepts) were all grounded in observation (and possibly experimentation), entailing none of them 'can simply be declared wrong'.[38]

Since syphilis can be described in a variety of ways, it seems that it is 'a matter of free choice' which concept is chosen, but once such a choice is made, the associations which then ensue are necessary. So, for instance, if the concept of carnal scourge were 'chosen' and applied to syphilis, this concept would necessarily

---

[35] Sady (2000, p. 37).

[36] Giedymin (1986, pp. 185–1866).

[37] Fleck (1979, p. 59, 61).

[38] Fleck (1979, p. 8).

include other similar afflictions, such as gonorrhoea and soft chancre; while the concept of a scourge inflicted by a supernatural deity would entail that any ideas involving rational treatment were precluded. Fleck frames this notion of choice as typifying the position of Mach and his followers—a position which Fleck simply identifies as that of conventionalism:

> In this respect a certain amount of latitude appears to exist. It is only after the choice has been made that the associations produced by it are seen as necessary. As is well known, this is a viewpoint held by the conventionalists. [...] From this formal point of view, therefore, there are some associations which are open to choice, that is, free associations [*freie Koppelungen*], and others that are constrained. Those who recognize economy of thought as the intention to choose from among the active free associations are guided by the theory of Mach.[39]

In characterizing Mach's historical-philosophical analysis of science as straightforwardly 'conventionalist', Fleck fails to engage with Mach's unique critical engagement with and contribution to conventionalist thought. Instead, Fleck's image of Mach is constructed and deployed as a punchbag against which he can set out his own position. Thus Fleck implies that in Mach's 'conventionalism' the initial choice between various concepts (i.e. carnal scourge or experimental-pathological) is made with complete freedom, from a purely formal standpoint. Necessity or determinism only emerges once the initial choice has been made.

Fleck attacks (this characterization of) conventionalism by invoking cultural-historical determinism, and simultaneously introducing his concept of 'a thought style':

> First, the adherents of all these formal points of view pay far too little, if any, attention to the cultural-historical dependence [*die kulturhistorische Bedingtheit*] of such an alleged epistemological choice – the alleged convention [*der angeblichen Konvention*]. Sixteenth-century physicians were by no means at liberty to replace the mystical-ethical concept of syphilis with one based upon natural science and pathogenesis. A stylistic bond exists between many, if not all, concepts of a period, based on their mutual influence. We can therefore speak of a thought style which determines the formulation of every concept.[40]

Thus, Fleck's characterization of Mach's conventionalism clearly constructs Mach's thought as positing that scientific concepts are entirely arbitrary conventions, and that they are freely chosen from a formal point of view—without historical or cultural determinants.[41] Fleck's concept of 'a thought style' is conceived of in contrast to this image of conventionalism: rather than being able to choose concepts freely, sixteenth-century physicians were bound by a historically and culturally determined style of thinking.[42]

---

[39] Fleck (1979, pp. 8–9).

[40] Fleck (1979, p. 9).

[41] Giedymin (1986, p. 185).

[42] The only other significant reference to Mach appears in the context of language, where Fleck, discussing his concept of pre-ideas or proto-ideas, rejects Mach's conception of cognition as depending on the adaptation of thoughts to some 'arbitrary external facts as revealed to an average person' —Fleck (1979, p. 37). Following Erich von Hornbostel, Fleck proposes that originally

According to Giedymin, Fleck's error lies in interpreting the conventionalists as claiming that (1) 'conventions depend only on the free choice or the whims of the individual scientist and are unaffected by experiential, socio-historical or biological circumstances', when in fact no conventionalists made such a claim. Giedymin then suggests that (2) Fleck suppresses a component of conventionalist (and Machian) thought, which he then incorporates into his own epistemology, namely the distinction between the 'active' (subjective) elements of knowledge and the 'passive' (objective) elements.[43]

The next sections will address these two arguments put forward by Giedymin, focusing on the writings of Mach.

3.4 Free Choice in Mach's Conventionalism

The work in which Mach perhaps most clearly addresses the issues of choice and convention is *Principles of the Theory of Heat* (1896). As in his earlier work, *The Science of Mechanics* (1883), Mach borrowed and applied concepts from evolutionary theory to examine the development of scientific ideas and apparatus. His primary concern was optimizing scientific practice, as reflected in his notion of scientific economy.[44] Mach also saw education in the history of science as essential for developing the potential of practicing scientists.

According to Mach, historical studies reveal that current scientific thinking is contingent and transient: past conceptions were developed in response to specific problems and for particular purposes, and when new problems arise, existing conceptions are abandoned so that new ones can be developed. Awareness of this process of 'mutations, development and decay' helps scientists to subject their 'own unconsciously formed views' to criticism, and thus to adapt and transform their thinking.[45]

Mach's *Principles of the Theory of Heat* is a survey which traces the parallel development of conceptions of heat and measuring apparatus. Heat is treated as a unique problem: for Mach, the sensations of experience are the primary and ultimate sources of scientific knowledge, his 'epistemic base'.[46] Yet the phenomena of heat can only be directly accessed by the sense of touch, which provides variable sensations (e.g. they are affected by antecedent states, so a cellar feels cool in summer but warm in winter, even though a thermometer indicates the thermal state is the same throughout the year). In order to attain more accurate measurements of the

---

words were not names for objects, but were rather mental equivalents of experiences, and thus had a magical meaning.

[43] Giedymin (1986, p. 186).

[44] Pojman (2019).

[45] Mach (1900, p. 5).

[46] Cohen (1970, p. 131).

thermal states of bodies, which are assumed to produce the sensations of heat, indirect means have to be employed—involving the sense of sight and comparisons of various substances, the volumes of which increase or decrease in relation to the sensation of heat.

Mach credits Galileo with the invention of the thermometer, as he used changes in the volume of air in a glass bulb to register thermal states. In the early development of thermometry, the scale used to register thermal states was 'mostly quite arbitrary' until the freezing and boiling points of water were adopted as the fundamental points of the scale. Mach credits Halley with being the first to recommend mercury as a thermometric substance, owing to its constancy when measuring the boiling point of water.[47]

Crucially for Mach, the use of volume as a measure of thermal states—although reliable and useful—remained arbitrary:

> The stronger the thermal sensation, the greater the volume of the thermoscopic substance. Hence again, by analogy, the following arbitrary definition may be set up: *Those thermal states are to be regarded as the more intense in which bodies produce in the thermoscope greater augmentations of volume*.[48] [emphasis in the original translation]

Then the adoption of mercury as a universally accepted thermoscopic substance is described as involving a 'further arbitrary choice'.[49] However, even this system, dependent on names for points on the scale like 'the melting point of butter', was still inconvenient, and thus another, more convenient convention was adopted: that of using numbers to designate thermoscopic marks on thermometers. With these conventions in place, greater precision was attained, but this only led to the detection of further problems (e.g. the expansion of glass in mercury thermometers). Hence, for Mach, science is always 'unfinished'.

In Mach's account, an arbitrary convention is adopted as a solution to a problem initially arising in direct relation to sensation. This conventional solution then generates subsequent problems, the solutions to which, in turn, generate further problems, and so on. The problem is that scientists and philosophers are often unaware—or forget—that their scales and measures are conventions, let alone arbitrary ones, due to the human tendency to 'hypostatise their abstract ideas':[50]

> It is remarkable how long a period elapsed before it definitely dawned upon inquirers that the designation of thermal states by numbers rests on a convention. Thermal states exist in nature, but the conception of temperature exists only by virtue of our arbitrary definition, which might very well have taken another form. Yet until very recently inquirers in this field appear more or less unconsciously to have sought after a natural measure of temperature, a real temperature, a sort of Platonic Idea of temperature, of which the temperatures read from the thermometric scales were only the imperfect and inexact expression.[51]

[47] Mach (1900, pp. 7–16).

[48] Mach (1900, p. 47).

[49] Mach (1900, p. 49).

[50] Mach (1900, p. 56).

[51] Mach (1900, pp. 53–54).

In Mach's complex and amorphous epistemology, sensations are real, and, being the elements of nature, they are not arbitrary. However, humans have a tendency to attribute reality to arbitrary measures of these sensations. For instance, we feel hot or cold thermal states, which, in Mach's terms, means we feel something real; yet our arbitrary measure of these sensations—temperature—is hypostatized as an independent reality that causes them.

Conventions are arbitrary because there were—and are—viable alternatives. Mach provides examples such as using gas volume instead of liquid volume, or colour and thermal radiation instead of volume.[52] However, although Mach defines conventions as arbitrary, he acknowledges that scientists do not have complete freedom in choosing which conventions to adopt. Conventions are determined by how problems are conceived, the existing state of knowledge, and the currently existing set of conventions. The *Principles of the Theory of Heat* highlights how scientists were constrained in their thinking; for example, William Thomson's unwillingness to abandon the assumption that the quantity of heat (as a substance—caloric) remained constant—despite the fact that Mayer, Joule, and Helmholtz had 'clarified' the issue—is used to demonstrate how difficult it can be for scientists to adapt their thinking to new ideas.[53]

However, the ultimate reason why conventions are not completely arbitrary in Mach's account of science is that they are grounded in sensation. If a scientist chooses a measure or conception that is not derived from and applied to sensation, their science strays into metaphysics. Cohen explains:

> Indeed, knowledge is always provisional, in Mach's understanding, but nevertheless it is constructed upon an indubitable and elementary base – indubitable, that is, in the sense of being unavoidable, not in any sense of being unalterable. All conceptions which fail to relate ideas to that base are thereby suspect; their meaning is ultimately unclear, for they might be conjectures about phenomena which as yet are misapprehended, or whose apprehensions are mis-formulated, or they might be pseudo-intelligible assertions which, upon scrutiny, lose meaning, and thus lose all possible experiential reference. And such pseudo-intelligibility is the mark of metaphysics.[54]

Since for Mach, as an 'evolutionary empiricist',[55] science is fundamentally a human adaptation to the environment, scientific theories that are riddled with metaphysical assumptions and speculations lack biological efficiency or utility. Hence the strong normative drive in Mach's account of science: he is not content merely to describe the practice of science; he has firm views on the role that science should play in society and how it should be conducted. Regarding the latter, rather than speculate or seek final explanations, Mach argues that science should focus solely on describing experience, employing an extremely cautious method.[56] Hence, while

[52] Mach (1900, pp. 51–72, 133–137).

[53] Mach (1900, p. 218).

[54] Cohen (1970, p. 129).

[55] Banks (2003, p. 75).

[56] Cohen (1970, pp. 129–139).

conventions are arbitrary, choices between them are narrowed and restricted by the demands of descriptive efficiency and socio-biological utility.

In *Principles of the Theory of Heat*, Mach provides examples of scientists who stray into metaphysical speculation. For instance, in addition to stating the facts, Dalton also introduced the hypothetical notion that the particles of different gases exert pressure on one another, a hypothesis Mach dismissed as one that 'can never be made the subject of experimental verification' and led to unnecessary controversy.[57] Mach's famous rejection of the atomic hypothesis can be seen as the repudiation of an inadmissible convention: since three-dimensional atoms were not accessible to sensation in the nineteenth century (even indirectly, through apparatus), Mach classed them as metaphysical concepts projected into or behind the phenomena. Instead of hypothesizing atoms, the nineteenth-century scientist should have used the available apparatus and conventions (a galvanometer, thermometers, scales) to observe the facts of energy (which Mach considered to be accessible to sensation).[58]

The discussion above supports Giedymin's contention that Fleck's characterization of Mach's conventionalism—namely that it allowed completely free choice of concepts—is indeed a mischaracterization.

However, Fleck's charge that conventionalism 'pays too little, if any, attention to the cultural-historical dependence of such an alleged epistemological choice',[59] is more justifiable. Mach's historical survey of conceptions of heat is conducted from a position that is firmly entrenched within the conceptual interior of science. Following Paul Forman, this approach can be described as an 'intellectualist-internalist history',[60] a perspective that focuses on the internal logic and conceptual progress of science while largely overlooking external cultural or socio-economic influences. After an analysis of the sensations of heat, Mach tracks the conceptual responses of individual scientists to the problems encountered in the phenomena and conceptual problems bequeathed by other scientists. While his work includes detailed descriptions of apparatus and experiments, there is little mention of the socio-technological demands involved in such scientific practice.

In other words, Mach's descriptions do not address this process from the perspective of the external socio-economic environment. For example, there is no acknowledgment of the fact that from the sixteenth century onwards the modes of production in European societies required ever more precise conceptions of heat, and that scientific concepts, apparatus and institutions evolved in response to this demand, as inextricable, instrumental components of the Industrial Revolution.

Neither does Mach address the fact that science benefited from the study of technologies that had been invented to meet the demands of industry—the fact that Carnot's 1825 reflections on idealized heat engines were based on existing but

[57] Mach (1900, p. 26).

[58] Banks (2003, p. 181, 227).

[59] Fleck (1979, p. 9).

[60] Forman (1971, p. 90).

poorly understood steam engines is a case in point.[61] When viewed from a perspective that traces the development of scientific concepts in their socio-economic environment, the theory of thermodynamics has to be seen as a solution to the problems posed by nineteenth-century industry.

McKenzie Wark reframes Boris Hessen's influential externalist thesis—particularly its emphasis on the relationship between thermodynamics and industrial capitalism[62]—by succinctly illustrating the interplay between scientific development and industrial demands:

> Industrialization runs on carbon. Demand for carbon in the form of coal meant that miners dug deeper and deeper. Pumping water out of deep mines becomes an acute problem, and so the first application of steam power was for pumping water out of mines. Out of the practical problem of designing steam-driven pumps arises the abstract principles of thermodynamics as a science.[63]

While Mach acknowledges the steam engine—stating that 'Heat is capable of great performances of work. The best example of this is the steam engine'[64]— he neglects to address a fundamental question: *why* is such work required? Mach's treatment of thermodynamics ultimately neglects the socio-economic pressures that shape scientific development and drive technological innovation.

From Fleck's perspective, socio-economic and cultural forces do more than simply shape the focus and preoccupations of science by presenting problems to be solved; they are integral to the very development of scientific concepts and methods. Fleck's theory demonstrates that attempts to produce a 'pure' description of scientific progress fail to capture essential aspects of the phenomena. Any comprehensive account of scientific development must consider the socio-economic contexts that give rise to and shape scientific practices.

3.5 The Role Assigned to Culture and History in Mach's Conventionalism

In *History and Root of the Principle of the Conservation of Energy* (1872), Mach acknowledges the role of custom and history as determinants of cognition. In Chapter III, *Mechanical Physics*, Mach questions the prevailing 'mechanical conceptions of nature', by examining the modern notion that heat is motion (rather than a substance) to show that the conceptual scheme used to ground this position cannot also account for the (comparable) phenomena of electricity.

---

[61] 'Notwithstanding the work of all kinds done by steam-engines, notwithstanding the satisfactory condition to which they have been brought to-day, their theory is very little understood, and the attempts to improve them are still directed almost by chance'— Carnot (1943, p. 19).

[62] Hessen (2009).

[63] Wark (2015).

[64] Mach (1900, p. 200).

While the conclusion that *heat is motion* is based on the observation that *heat vanishes in proportion to the amount of work that is performed*, the same argument is not used, following the observation of the work performed by electricity in a Leyden jar, to conclude that electricity is motion. Mach writes: 'What, now, is the reason of this difference of view in our treatment of heat and electricity? The reason is purely historical, wholly conventional, and what is still more important, is wholly indifferent'.[65] According to Mach, electricity and other 'physical things', such as water, are conceived as substances because they are measured with scales; in other words it is a practice that is 'purely historical, accidental and conventional'.[66]

Ultimately, for Mach the way that scientists think about scientific phenomena is 'quite irrelevant'—it is entirely admissible for a scientist to think of heat as a substance, if they consider this substance to be the energy of heat, rather than the quantity of heat. It soon becomes apparent that, at its core, this issue is epistemological:

> One thing we maintain, and that is, that in the investigation of nature, we have to deal only with knowledge of the connexion of appearances with one another. What we represent to ourselves behind the appearances exists *only* in our understanding, (*Was wir hinter den Erscheinungen uns vorstellen, existirt eben nur in unserm Verstände*) and has for us only the value of a *memoria technica* or formula, whose form, because it is arbitrary and irrelevant, varies very easily with the standpoint of our culture.[67]

Here, Mach acknowledges that culture shapes the ontological conceptions involved in scientific cognition. Yet—and this is crucial for Fleck's critique of Mach's conventionalism—Mach then insists that scientists' conceptions of what the phenomena of physics are *in themselves*, or 'behind the appearances', have no bearing on the facts: 'This way of presentation does not alter the facts in the least *(Diese Vorstellungsweise ändert nichts an den Thatsachen)*'.[68]

At the same time, however, Mach concedes that these modes of conception/presentation (*Vorstellungsweise*) can in fact influence the direction of scientific inquiry: 'But if this way of presentation is so limited and inflexible that it no longer allows us to follow the many-sidedness of phenomena, it should not be used any more as a formula and will begin to be a hindrance (*hinderlich*) to us in the knowledge of phenomena'.[69] For Mach, the mechanical conception of physics is just such a limited and inflexible framework.

At the heart of his questioning of the conception of heat as motion lies the conviction that the pictorial image of molecules or atoms in motion that prevails in the mechanical conception is inherited from a metaphysics that assumes there is such a thing as absolute space for such atoms to move about in. As Eric C. Banks explains: 'This "metaphysical" error arose by assuming those atoms were already embedded

---

[65] Mach (1911, p. 44).

[66] Mach (1911, p. 46).

[67] Mach (1911, p. 49).

[68] Mach (1911, p. 49).

[69] Mach (1911, p. 49).

in 3-space, rather than letting space arise from their physical interactions'.[70] Mach's historical accounts were aimed precisely at exposing how such metaphysical assumptions had—and will continue to have—detrimental effects on the development of science.

Thus, to summarize and clarify, Mach's account seems to assert the following: (a) scientific conceptions of what lies behind physical phenomena (i.e., ontological conceptions of heat, electricity, etc.) are culturally determined and thus arbitrary; and (b) while these conceptions do not alter the facts themselves, (c) they can nevertheless hinder the investigation of phenomena, and prevent a fact being 'known on all its sides'.[71]

At this point, several questions arise. Firstly, if modes of conceiving what lies behind the phenomena can hinder the investigation of the phenomena—and Mach argues that the pictorial image of molecules and atoms in motion in three-dimensional space hinders the investigation of connections and combinations of phenomena—then why do such conceptions not have any bearing on the facts involved in such investigations, if only in terms of the selection of the phenomena to be investigated and thus the facts to be established? Secondly, what exactly is Mach's conception of scientific facts? How does Mach distinguish between facts and phenomena, if at all?

Towards the end of Chapter III, Mach comments on scientific theories in general and presents his economic model of science. He begins by suggesting that facts and phenomena are equivalent: 'If all the individual facts—all the individual phenomena (*alle einzelnen Thatsachen, alle einzelnen Erscheinungen*), knowledge of which we desire—were immediately accessible to us, a science would never have arisen'.[72] The first function of science is, then, to organize these facts economically, for instance. through the use of formulas and laws. The second function is explanatory: complicated facts are reduced to simple facts. However, the simplest facts, Mach notes, are 'unintelligible in themselves', meaning they cannot be resolved into, or reduced to, simpler ones, such as the fact that 'one mass imparts and acceleration to another'.

When Mach provides further elaboration on these simple facts, culture and history once again make their appearance as determining factors: 'What facts one will allow to rank as fundamental facts, at which one rests, depends on custom and on history'.[73] He gives the example of Newtonian gravitation as a 'common unintelligibility'—such fundamental facts are introduced as uncommon unintelligibilities, which initially 'disturb' the community of investigators, but then they become assimilated to the point where they no longer disturb anybody.

It is clear from these passages that Mach acknowledges culture plays a key role in determining which fundamental scientific facts are adopted and assimilated by

[70] Banks (2003, p. 33).

[71] Mach (1911, p. 58).

[72] Mach (1911, p. 54).

[73] Mach (1911, p. 56).

the scientific community, but there is no consideration of why a culture would be persuaded to abandon its fundamental facts in favour of new ones, nor is there a clear definition of facts—complex or simple—beyond their description as ultimate unintelligibilities and their contrast with hypotheses (since for Mach the epistemic base of facts is the senses, hypotheses that are grounded in the senses can be tested and become facts, while hypotheses impervious to such testing—like the mechanical molecular theory—are simply 'an evil').

In his reading of these passages, Cohen concludes that the 'culture-bound contingency of the empirical base compels Mach to transcend his own positivist reconstructions! [...] Mach saw that a theory of history must supplement epistemology, and perhaps even complete it'. Cohen's insightful final assessment is that while Mach mastered the European history of the ideas of nature, he did not explore the philosophical analysis of historical knowledge in any depth.[74]

When constructing his theory of thought styles through a critique of Mach's 'conventionalism', Fleck brings the constraints exerted by cultural and historical determinants to the fore. Regardless of the depth of his knowledge of the conventionalist tradition or Mach's writings, and contrary to Giedymin's charge of complete mischaracterization in this regard, in my view Fleck locates and exploits a weakness in Mach's epistemology and historical method. Fleck's call for a comparative epistemology can be viewed, at least in part, as an attempt to add a cultural-historical dimension to the Mach's conventionalist account of the history of science.

3.6 Facts in Mach's Epistemology

As mentioned, Giedymin argues that, in addition to mischaracterizing and suppressing elements of Mach's 'conventionalist' thought, Fleck also incorporates the conventionalist distinction between active and passive elements into his own epistemology. My contention is that while he does indeed draw on elements of Mach's epistemology, Fleck also problematizes the position that facts occupy in this aspect of Mach's thought. Before dealing with Fleck's conception of the active and passive elements, it is necessary to focus on how Fleck responds to Mach's ambiguous conception of facts.

In Chap. 2 of *Genesis and Development of a Scientific Fact*, Fleck rejects a notion he attributes to Mach, namely that cognition depends 'on the adaptation of thoughts to some arbitrary external facts as revealed to an average person'.[75] In a footnote, Fleck refers to a page of Mach's *Science of Mechanics* (1883) where Mach rejects Kant and Schopenhauer's innatist explanations of causality in favour of a more

[74] Cohen (1970, pp. 135–136).

[75] Fleck (1979, p. 27).

'common-sense' explanation, i.e. that: 'The ideas of cause and effect originally sprang from an endeavour to reproduce facts in thought.[76]

Fleck's rejection of this explanation is tied up with his conception of his proto-ideas, which I explore more thoroughly in Chap. 4. However, at this point it is important to emphasize that while for Mach the sensations of experience are distinct from thought, for Fleck, under the influence of Hornbostel, experience and cognition can be equivalent, especially when words have magical meanings.

In the Introduction to *Science of Mechanics*, Mach presents facts as emerging through the search for uniformity and regularity within the variety of nature, the flux of sensation, and the multiplicity of experience. Once humans began to conceive of nature as being unitary, they sought to identify elements that consistently remained the same in natural phenomena:

> By this means, on the one hand, the most economical and briefest description and communication are rendered possible; and on the other, when once a person has acquired the skill of recognising these permanent elements throughout the greatest range and variety of phenomena, of seeing them in the same, this ability leads to a *comprehensive, compact, consistent and facile conception of the facts* (*Erfassung der Thatsachen*).[77] [emphasis in the original translation]

When the elements of phenomena are recognised as being the same, despite their varied combinations, they are thereby explained (*erklärt*); in other words, they are no longer perplexing. Mach asserts: 'It is a process of adaptation of thoughts to facts (*ein Anpassungsprocess der Gedanken an die Thatsachen*) with which we are here concerned'.[78] The economical role of science is thus to classify and communicate these facts, conserving intellectual energy in the process.

These passages suggest that, for Mach, facts are regularities observed in experience, and are recognized as such. However, it remains unclear whether facts are constituted in the act of recognition, or whether there are pure, experiential facts which are constituted prior to recognition. Mach's oft-repeated description of thoughts adapting to fact supports the conclusion that for Mach facts are given in experience, prior to the operations of conscious thought.

The issue of when facts are constituted in the epistemological process is further complicated by Mach's notion that cognition can be 'instinctive'. In Chap. 1, when describing Stevinus' investigations of the inclined plane, Mach employs the terms '*purely instinctive* cognition (*ganz instinctive Erkenntniss*)' and 'instinctive knowledge' to describe the origin and chief resource of science: the experience that individuals gather throughout their lifetime. Mach explicitly describes this knowledge as arising from observations that precede comprehension and analysis:

> Everything which we observe in nature imprints itself uncomprehended and unanalysed in our percepts and ideas, which, then, in their turn, mimic the processes of nature in their most general and most striking features. In these accumulated experiences we possess a

[76] Mach (1893, p. 484).

[77] Mach (1893, p. 5).

[78] Mach (1893, p. 6).

treasure-store which is ever close at hand and of which only the smallest portion is embodied in clear articulate thought.[79]

Mach suggests that this treasure-store of instinctive knowledge, which seems to us to be free of subjectivity, becomes the source of scientific knowledge, forming the basis for assumptions, as much as—if not more than—direct observation of nature. Later, he proposes that instinctive knowledge exerts such authority on scientific thinking that—because its source is now forgotten—it comes to be treated as existing *a priori*.[80] Thus, scientific facts tend to be formed and deduced predominantly from the contents of accumulated instinctive knowledge, rather than from fresh experience of the natural world.

Another passage crucial for Mach's conception of facts appears in Chapter IV, in section IV entitled *The Economy of Science* (which is also the section to which Fleck refers). Mach begins the section by returning to the schema of reproduction (or replication—*Nachbildung*): 'It is the object of science to replace, or *save*, experiences, by the reproduction and anticipation of facts in thought'.[81] Again, the obvious implication is that these facts are given prior to their reproduction. After highlighting the roles of memory and writing in the economical, communicative function of science, Mach returns to the issue of facts in paragraphs that shed light on his epistemological convictions (and which are worth quoting extensively):

In the reproduction of facts in thought, we never reproduce the facts in full, but only that side of them which is important to us, moved to this directly or indirectly by a practical interest (*aus einem praktischen Interesse*). Our reproductions are invariably abstractions. Here again is an economical tendency.[82]

Thus, between facts being given in experience and their partial reproduction in thought, an element of practical utility intervenes: the partial reproduction is determined by our present needs.[83] Mach then describes the process of reproduction as one of abstraction:

Nature is composed of sensations as its elements. Primitive man, however, first picks out certain compounds of these elements, those namely that are relatively permanent and of greater importance to him. The first and oldest words are names of "things." Even here, there is an abstractive process, an abstraction from the surroundings of the things, and from the continual small changes which these compound sensations undergo, which being practically unimportant are not noticed. No inalterable thing exists. The thing is an abstraction, the name a symbol, for a compound of elements from whose changes we abstract. The reason we assign a single word to a whole compound is that we need to suggest all the constituent sensations at once. When, later, we come to remark the changeableness, we cannot at the same time hold fast to the idea of the thing's permanence, unless we have recourse to the conception of a thing-in-itself, or other such like absurdity. Sensations are not signs of things; but, on the contrary, a thing is a thought-symbol for a compound sensation of rela-

[79] Mach (1893, p. 28).

[80] Mach (1893, p. 83).

[81] Mach (1893, p. 481).

[82] Mach (1893, p. 482).

[83] Banks (2003, p. 130).

> tive fixedness. Properly speaking the world is not composed of "things" as its elements, but of colors, tones, pressures, spaces, times, in short what we ordinarily call individual sensations.[84]

Mach portrays experience as a flux of compound sensations, which are treated as equivalent to the elements of nature. Famously, for Mach the Kantian 'thing-in-itself' is an erroneous and pernicious conception, since 'things' are abstractions drawn from and imposed on these continually changing sensations. The natural world does not consist of objects and things: it consists of sensations (elements) in combinations and functional relationships. We organize this flux by isolating and abstracting things—as thought-symbols—and naming them.

Mach's evolutionary stance allows him to assert that this tendency to abstraction has become an instinctive inheritance: beneath our ideas of cause and effect we have 'a sense of causality' that was not acquired individually, but 'perfected in the development of the race.[85]

The evolutionary dimension of Mach's epistemology further complicates the status of facts. For instance, his conviction that reflex movements are examples of memory embodied outside the organs of consciousness, and his notion that the sense-organs were developed by evolutionary processes to do 'part of the psychical work and hand over the completed result to consciousness',[86] are part of a biological conception of knowledge. In this framework, reflex movements and sense-organs are adaptations to facts in the environment; they constitute a form of biological memory that extends 'beyond the individual'. Hence, in addition to being accumulated by the individual, instinctive knowledge is also hereditary, since it is developed at the level of the 'race.[87] In this conception, such instinctive knowledge must in some sense be knowledge of facts, i.e. regularities encountered in sensation.

This biological conception of knowledge marks a key difference between Mach's brand of conventionalism and the sociology of knowledge. While Durkheim's social structures (and Fleck's thought styles) replace Kant's categories as the cognitive *a priori*, with Mach the cognitive *a priori* is biologically determined:

> [...] what is *a priori* to an individual organism was *a posteriori* to its ancestors; not only does the *a priori* pre-form experience, but the *a priori* is itself formed from experience. It was simultaneously the contradiction and confirmation of Kantian epistemology. In as much as Kant used the *a priori* to explain how knowledge is possible, Mach uses the knowledge of the new sciences to explain how an *a priori* is possible.[88]

Hence a deeper level of determination is posited: the very possibility of culture emerging—which in Mach's account involves social combination and

[84] Mach (1893, pp. 482–483).

[85] Mach (1893, p. 485).

[86] Mach (1959, pp. 71, 73).

[87] Mach (1893, p. 1).

[88] Pojman (2019).

collaboration, communication, a division of labour, a certain amount of leisure, and writing[89]—depends on the biological development of cognition.

From this evolutionary-empiricist standpoint, combined with Mach's emphasis on abstraction, the following account of facts can be extrapolated: human beings, equipped with instinctive knowledge and embodied memory inherited through evolution, are able to perceive regularities and similarities in sensory experience. This enables them to abstract 'things' from this flux, in accordance with their biological and social needs; such abstraction eventually leads to the recognition of things, the observation of facts in experience, and their partial reproduction in thought—again in accordance with wants. In turn, this reproduction leads to the naming of things, a burden being placed on memory, the invention of writing, and finally to the classifications, corrections and communication of science. In such a model, all facts would be constituted cognitively, with varying degrees of precision and abstraction—ranging from dimly-sensed repetitions all the way to the fundamental facts of a culture's science.

However, this interpretation risks overlooking Mach's repeated insistence that facts are *reproduced* in thought or ideas. In *Knowledge and Error* (1905) Mach explicitly states: 'The goal of the ordinary imagination is the conceptual completion and perfection of a partially observed fact (*einer teilweise beobachteten Tatsache*)'.[90] He elaborates:

> The representation in thought of facts or the adaption of thought to fact, enables the thinker mentally to complete partially observed facts, insofar as completion is determined by the observed part. Their determination consists in the mutual dependence of factual features, so that thought has to aim at these.[91]

The implication here seems to be that there are facts *in nature*—waiting to be observed, and that human beings only partially observe such facts through sensation, in accordance with their needs, and then these facts are made more complete by the operations of thought and the imagination. Mach assigns science the role of improving the 'crude (*vulgäre*)' adaptation of thought to facts found in 'ordinary thinking' and 'incipient scientific thought'. Thus, on this reading, Mach's view of cognition is almost Baconian: in its ordinary state, when completely determined by practical utility, human cognition constructs a very limited picture of the facts of nature, but through the cautious development of improved conceptions and measurements science can present a fuller picture.

It is this notion—that facts exist independently in nature, waiting to be discovered—that Fleck fundamentally rejects. For Fleck, all facts are constituted interactively in the process and practices of cognition; they have a genesis and a development, as the products of evolving, socially-determined thought styles.

[89] Mach (1926, pp. 56–62).

[90] Mach (1926, p. 2).

[91] Mach (1926, p. 2).

3.7 The Active and Passive Elements of Cognition in Fleck's Theory

We can now finally address Giedymin's assertion that, in addition to mischaracterizing and suppressing elements of Mach's thought, Fleck also draws on the conventionalist distinction between active (subjective) and passive (objective) elements when constructing his own epistemology.[92]

Fleck's distinction between the active and passive elements of knowledge (*aktiven und passiven Koppelungen*—sometimes translated as 'relations', 'associations' 'linkages' or 'couplings') is problematic and somewhat controversial. It is introduced in Chap. 1 of *Genesis and Development of a Scientific Fact*, immediately after his criticism of Mach's conventionalism.

First, in a passage that is strikingly similar to Kuhn's historical image of science and his conception of paradigms, Fleck argues that the development of ideas is governed by 'historical laws', which is evident from the fact that theories tend to pass through a period of agreement, followed by a period focused on exceptions.[93] This law-driven, historical determination of scientific development is said to restrict choice, and thus serves as another argument against conventionalism (or at least Fleck's somewhat mischaracterized depiction of this thought style).

Fleck then asserts that: '[…] there are always other connections (*Zusammenhänge*) which are also to be found in the content of knowledge that are not explicable in terms either of psychology (both individual and collective) or of history. For this very reason these seem to be "real," "objective," and "true" relations'.[94] He defines such connections as 'passive associations' (*die passiven Zusammenhänge*). In contrast to active associations, which are clearly 'subjective' constructions (such as the concept of syphilis as a carnal scourge), passive associations *seem* to be 'real' or 'objective' (e.g. the curative effect of mercury).

Giedymin suggests that this distinction was borrowed from Heinrich Hertz's mechanics, though Fleck makes no explicit reference to Hertz's writings. According to Giedymin, this attribution is plausible because '*Koppelungen*' is not a commonly used expression, but it was employed in Hertz's *Die prinzipien der mechanik in neuem zusammenhange dargestellt* [The Principles of Mechanics] (1894) to describe the actions of forces between systems. Poincaré later analysed Hertz's contributions to mechanics, from a conventionalist perspective in *Les idées de Hertz sur la mécanique* (1897), part of which was included in Poincaré's *La Science et l'Hypothèse* (1902). This book was eventually translated into German as *Wissenschaft und Hypothese* (1928). Giedymin concludes that Fleck could have encountered the concept of '*Koppelungen*' either directly in Hertz's *Principles* or through Lindemann's annotations to the German translation of Poincaré.[95]

---

[92] Giedymin (1986, p. 186).

[93] Fleck (1979, p. 9).

[94] Fleck (1979, p. 10).

[95] Giedymin (1986, p. 213).

Hertz introduces the concept of coupling when describing *Systems acted on by Forces*:

> **450. Definition.** Two material systems are said to be directly coupled (*gekoppelt*) when one or more coordinates of the one are always equal to one or more coordinates of the other. Two systems will be simply said to be coupled when their coordinates can be so chosen that the systems become directly coupled. Coupled systems which are not directly coupled are said to be indirectly coupled.
>
> **451. Corollary 1.** The coupling of two systems is a relation between them which is independent of our choice, and in particular independent of the choice of coordinates. But whether an existing coupling is direct or indirect does depend on the choice of coordinates, and is thus a question for our arbitrary determination.[96]

The key point for Fleck's epistemology is that Hertz: (a) defines a coupling as a relation between two systems that is not determined by our choice of measure (coordinates), meaning that it is not an arbitrary convention, but is rather determined by something inherent in the relation; and (b) while the existence of the coupling is not arbitrary, the determination of whether it is direct or indirect is, since this is based on our chosen system of measurement, or coordinates.

For Giedymin, this conception aligns with Poincaré's conventionalism, since Poincaré treats Hertz's arbitrarily determined 'connections' as analogous to the multiplicity of models and unlimited explanations that conventionalism suggests can account for mechanical systems.[97] However, Giedymin's reading suppresses Poincaré's critique of Hertz's yearnings for the truth, which I would argue can be detected in **451. Corollary 1** above. Poincaré identifies this tendency in Hertz's concern that the 'impregnable principles of mechanics' can be revised in response to falsifying experiments. For Poincaré, such principles, though initially derived from experiment, are now purely definitional—and therefore conventional.[98]

Fleck's engagement with Hertz's notion of coupling allows him to reframe both objective reality and the presumed objectivity of scientific knowledge. The passive elements or linkages are shaped by nature—by what is cognized; they are what is encountered when a thought collective applies its active concepts, conventions, and perceptual apparatus in the interactive process of cognition.

Fleck offers the following definition: 'The constrained results correspond to passive linkages and constitute that which is experienced as objective reality'.[99] While the measures employed by science are arbitrary, certain elements within the results—and their consequences—are not. Once specific active linkages (e.g., measurement or classification systems) are applied, the passive linkages, as Schnelle and Cohen observe,[100] prevent scientists from freely fabricating reality. For instance, the use of alcohol in the preparation of extracts is an arbitrary, active element—

96 Hertz (1899, p. 183).

97 Giedymin (1986, p. 213).

98 Poincaré (1905, pp. 117–118).

99 Fleck (1979, p. 40).

100 Cohen and Schnelle (1986, p. xxx).

other substances could serve the same purpose—yet the utility of alcohol in this process is not arbitrary. Similarly, assigning the number 16 to the atomic weight of oxygen is arbitrary, but the subsequent derivation of hydrogen's atomic weight as 1.008, relative to oxygen, is on the one hand arbitrary in terms of numerical assignment, but on the other, it is an inevitable, passive consequence determined by the relationship being measured.

Alongside his repeated insistence that cognition is interactional, Fleck's concept of passive elements is a key component that prevents his epistemology from sliding into unfettered relativism or radical constructivism.

However, Fleck's admittedly rather sketchy introduction of active and passive elements into his epistemology was poorly received for decades, particularly by theorists inclined towards relativism, constructivism, and the sociology of knowledge. For instance, in his 1976 Foreword, Kuhn described Fleck's distinction between active and passive elements of knowledge as 'unenlightening', and suggested it was borrowed from psychology.[101] Missing the conventionalist origins of this distinction aligns with Kuhn's broader, and somewhat puzzling, neglect of conventionalist philosophy of science, even when addressing the issue of scientific choice.[102]

This negative characterization of Fleck's passive elements was continued by Jonathan Harwood, in 1986, who described it as follows:

> Possibly novel in their day, active and passive are little more than a sociological reformulation of the concepts 'subjective' and 'objective'. That is, active or subjective connections are characteristic of narrowly institutionalized (thus contentious) knowledge-claims. Broadly institutionalized (thus unexceptionable) knowledge-claims embody passive or objective connections.[103]

Although Harwood refers to a perfectly adequate passage in Cohen and Schnelle's 1986 Introduction that addresses this point, he treats Fleck's passive elements as nothing more than subjective active elements that have become objective through institutionalization. In other words, for Harwood, resistance to the scientific thought collective's knowledge comes solely from the consensus and authority of social conditioning, rather than from anything discovered in nature (what is cognized). Combined with Harwood's Wittgensteinian reading of Fleck, this failure to recognize that Fleck's passive elements anchor cognition to external determinants led to Fleck's dismissal as a historical curiosity—pioneering and original in his time, but with little relevance to contemporary investigations.[104]

The treatment of Fleck as a pioneer who had to be acknowledged but ultimately replaced by a Wittgensteinian framework is most clearly exemplified in Shapin and Schaffer's *Leviathan and the Air-Pump: Hobbes, Boyle, and the Experimental Life* (1985). In their analysis of the socio-political determinants underlying Boyle and

---

[101] Kuhn (1976, p. xi).

[102] Kuhn (1977).

[103] Harwood (1986, p. 184).

[104] Harwood (1986, p. 184).

Hobbes' epistemological and methodological conflict, their reliance on Wittgenstein's concepts of language games and forms of life is telling: it bypasses the possibilities offered by Fleck's interactive model of cognition—in which his conception of passive elements is crucial—in favour of focusing on the internal mechanics of social construction. By arguing that Boyle's experimental method primarily functioned as a means of polite dispute resolution in the aftermath of the English Civil War,[105] Shapin and Schaffer downplay another crucial objective of the seventeenth-century experimental method: understanding, mastering, and exploiting *Nature*.

While Fleck criticized Mach for overlooking the social determinants of scientific concepts and conventions, Shapin and Schaffer go to the opposite extreme, overemphasizing the social determinants while neglecting the central question in Boyle and Hobbes' debate: what did Boyle's air-pump reveal to the community of natural philosophers about *Nature*, if anything? Fleck's concept of passive elements prevents *Nature* from being reduced to a purely social construct, and his model can be adapted to investigate how various thought styles interacted with this *Nature* (meeting resistance; encountering passive elements) through their concepts, methods, and apparatus (active elements). Fleck's model also allows for studying how thought collectives interacted with each other and externalized cognition in scientific instruments.

In contrast to Kuhn and Harwood, Sady (2000) situated Fleck's thought within a rich tradition, tracing his distinction of active and passive elements back to Poincaré's conventionalism. Sady compares Fleck's active elements to Poincaré's conception of 'principles' as arbitrary, disguised definitions, with the difference being that Fleck does not view these definitions as freely chosen. Although Sady suspects that Fleck's distinction may bring '"objective reality" in through the back door',[106] he ultimately finds Fleck's notion of passive elements promising, since it contains the seeds of a demarcation criterion. For instance, in Chap. 4 of *Genesis and Development of a Scientific Fact*, Fleck argues that myth contains few passive elements and has little concern for them, while science is characterized by its search for and incorporation of a maximum number of passive elements.[107] Nonetheless, Sady concludes that Fleck's distinction between active and passive elements, while promising, was not fully developed and thus lacks clarity.[108]

[105] Shapin and Schaffer (1985, pp. 72–76).

[106] Sady (2000, p. 61).

[107] A possible application of this distinction could be to compare how natural phenomena are described in the texts of Homer and Aristotle. For instance, Homer's portrayal of animals, such as the swift, 'immortal horses' of Achilles in the *Iliad* (Book 16), shows little concern for precise naturalistic details, being primarily driven by mythic and symbolic needs, and thus full of active elements. In contrast, Aristotle's *On the Parts of Animals* offers systematic observations of animals, focusing on their anatomy, behaviour, and biological processes, reflecting an effort to incorporate as many passive elements as possible. Aristotle's approach could thus represent a shift towards a more 'scientific' thought style.

[108] Sady (2021).

From textual analysis it can be concluded that Giedymin was right to trace Fleck's couplings back to Hertz and conventionalism, and the fact that Hertz and certain contributions to conventionalist thought are not acknowledged as sources or influences on his concept of active and passive linkages does amount to a degree of neglect or scholarly sloppiness on Fleck's part. Furthermore, Sady's assessment of this component of Fleck's thought as unclear and underdeveloped is fair and accurate.

Nevertheless, in my view, it is possible—and indeed necessary—to reconstruct and clarify this element of Fleck's epistemology. Recent contributions from Mauro L. Condé and Paweł Jarnicki,[109] and Nicholas Binney,[110] have emphasized this aspect of Fleck's theoretical framework.

Condé and Jarnicki reject the Kuhnian interpretation of Fleck which overemphasizes the active side of Fleck's epistemology, focusing on social and historical elements involved in the production of knowledge at the expense of the passive component, which they recover through focusing on the biological and evolutionary threads in Fleck's writing. The passive connections are what allow scientists to actually interact with nature: 'Scientific knowledge is not constituted as a static "representation" of nature, as postulated by traditional epistemology, but is formed in "interaction" with nature, which is analogous to evolutionary dynamics'.[111]

In turn, Binney's focus on Fleck's passive element of knowledge uses the concept of resistance. Binney frames the active element of knowledge as a 'self-imposed constraint' that allows researchers to encounter another form of constraint: the passive element of knowledge that resists their will. The active element preconditions what scientists find in nature, but the passive element is beyond their control: sometimes the passive element conflicts with the active element and forces scientists to adjust the active elements (or even to abandon the model or hypotheses). Binney provides a detailed analysis of how this happened with the Wassermann reaction in Fleck's account, concluding:

> No matter how unexpected it was, no matter how much they would have preferred to believe something else, it was a fact that the Wassermann reaction was not immunologically specific. Even though this fact was generated by the serologists' thought style, and could not exist without it, it still undermined the very tenets that had brought it into existence. The serologists' thought style suffered the same fate as Victor Frankenstein—each being destroyed by what they created. [112]

[109] Condé and Jarnicki (2023)

[110] Binney (2023).

[111] Condé and Jarnicki (2023, pp. 93–97, quote on p. 97). I would suggest that Fleck's use of evolutionary terminology in the 1930s stems from his encounter with Mach's evolutionary-empiricism and his biological conception of knowledge. It is notable that Condé and Jarnicki make no mention of Mach in their insightful text.

[112] Binney (2023, p. 40). Another example of resistance that springs to mind is Kepler's reluctance to give up circular planetary orbits and being forced by the data to struggle with noncircular orbits, 'straining and gnashing … [his] teeth'. Martens (2000, p. 88).

Just as Mach's epistemic base of sensation, when combined with the biologized, species-specific *a priori*, prevents his epistemology from sliding into solipsism, Fleck's passive elements prevent his epistemology from drifting off into arbitrary constructivism and complete relativism. His passive elements anchor cognition in a dynamic relationship with what is cognized. Nature changes, continually, and so does knowledge. Fleck's conception of the active and passive elements of knowledge are key components that enable Fleck to get beyond what Latour describes as the 'teleportation scheme' obsessed with bridging the gap between subject and object towards 'a continuous scheme' in which facts, knowledge and truth are constantly emerging: 'successive rectification and revision are not peripheral but are the substantial part of the knowledge acquisition pathways'.[113]

Additionally, it is through the conception of active and passive couplings that Fleck's innovations with regard to the sociology of knowledge and conventionalism really come into sharp relief.

For Fleck—developing insights drawn from the sociology of knowledge—the active elements of cognition are determined by the complex operations of thought collectives and the existing fund of knowledge of a particular culture and society at a specific point in history, hence scientists are far more restricted than certain conventionalists[114] would allow when it comes to choosing between scientific conventions (theories, concepts, hypotheses, scales, measures, apparatus). At the same time, if it is granted that science is more focused on incorporating the passive elements of cognition into its fund of knowledge than other thought styles are (in more everyday language: it strives to be more 'objective'), for Fleck—following on from the contributions of conventionalism—science still cannot escape the fact that the active elements of its cognition are necessarily conventional and are thus constructed from arbitrary components; therefore, science (including the sociology of knowledge) can never lay claim to establishing completely objective facts.

Scientific facts are constituted through cognition, in the complex couplings of active and passive elements. In this process, socially-determined conventions are actively applied by scientists, who—trained in a specific thought style—seek out certain phenomena and interpret them in a particular way. While Fleck's passive elements function similarly to Mach's concept of sensation, in that they form the ultimate basis of knowledge and prevent scientific conventions from being completely arbitrary, the key difference lies in Fleck's epistemology. For Fleck, thought collectives determine what scientists can look for, perceive, and ultimately discover in the phenomena. Thus, the thought collective shapes which passive elements are detected, observed, and incorporated into the accepted facts.

In Mach's view, scientists correct and refine facts that are already present in ordinary experience and recognized through thought. Fleck, however, offers a contrasting image of science: it is a fundamentally creative practice, one that—by being open to new passive elements and flexible enough to discard outdated active

[113] Latour (2007, p. 14).

[114] For example, Ajdukiewicz's radical conventionalism. See Jedynak (1993, p. 304).

elements and adopt new ones—has the potential to continually discover and construct new facts.

3.8 Conclusion

Fleck's self-positioning within a network of intellectual traditions—ranging from Kant and post-Kantian philosophy to Durkheim's French sociological school, and from Machian to Poincaréan strands of conventionalism—demonstrates an evolving, dialogical approach to epistemology. By placing 'situated transcendentalism' in dialogue with Kant's innate cognitive a priori, Fleck retains the Kantian emphasis on the formative role of conceptual frameworks in experience while rejecting their universality and immutability in favor of a socially and historically contingent account. This reorientation becomes sharper through his engagement with Durkheim, Lévy-Bruhl, and Jerusalem, whose work illustrates how collective representations and social structures shape—and reshape—fundamental categories of thought.

Fleck's critical engagement with Mach's 'conventionalism' insists that scientific concepts are never freely chosen; they remain constrained by culturally inherited assumptions and by the inherent resistance of the phenomena they attempt to capture. By integrating a sociology of knowledge perspective with an acute sensitivity to active and passive elements of cognition, Fleck transcends the relativism that might otherwise accompany such a socially situated epistemology. In his account, historical and collective determinants guide not only the development of knowledge but also the constitution of 'facts' themselves, through processes of selection, measurement, classification, and conceptual adjustment.

Fleck's arguments demonstrate that his comparative epistemology must account for nature's resistance, which imposes constraints on the pathways of investigation. Science emerges as a fundamentally creative yet disciplined practice, but it is also a cultural phenomenon, shaped by—and shaping—the broader dynamics of historical and social transformation. These insights into the interplay between cultural change and knowledge formation offer a framework for rethinking the evolution of thought styles, a theme explored in greater depth in the chapters that follow.

References

Banks EC (2003) Ernst Mach's world elements. Springer, Dordrecht

Binney N (2023) Ludwik Fleck's reasonable relativism about science. *Synthese* 201:40. https://doi.org/10.1007/s11229-022-04018-w

Carnot S (1943) Reflections on the motive power of heat (trans: Thurston RH). Waverly Press, Baltimore

Cohen RS (1970) Ernst mach: physics, perception and the philosophy of science. In: Cohen R, Seeger ER (eds) Ernst Mach: physicist and philosopher. Reidel, Dordrecht, pp 126–164

Cohen RS, Schnelle T (1986) Introduction. In: Cognition and Fact. Boston studies in the philosophy of science, vol 87. Springer, Dordrecht

Condé ML, Jarnicki P (2023) Ludwik Fleck: thought style and thought collective in the historiography of science. In: Condé, M.L., Salomon, M. (eds) Handbook for the historiography of science. Historiographies of science. Springer, Cham. https://doi.org/10.1007/978-3-031-27510-4_5

Durkheim É (2001) The elementary forms of religious life (trans: Cosman C). Oxford University Press, Oxford

Durkheim É (2013) The rules of sociological method, 2nd edn. (trans: Halls WD). Palgrave Macmillan, Houndmills

Fleck L (1979) Genesis and development of a scientific fact [1935]. The University of Chicago Press, Chicago.

Forman P (1971) Weimar culture, causality, and quantum theory, 1918–1927: adaptation by German physicists and mathematicians to a hostile intellectual environment. In: Russell N, Kuhn TS (eds) Historical studies in the physical sciences, vol 3. University of California Press, Berkeley, pp 1–115

Giedymin J (1986) Polish philosophy in the inter-war period and Ludwik Fleck's theory of thought-styles and thought-collectives. In: Cognition and fact. Boston studies in the philosophy of science, vol 87. Springer, Dordrecht. https://doi.org/10.1007/978-94-009-4498-5_10

Harwood J (1986) Ludwik Fleck and the sociology of knowledge. Soc Stud Sci 16(1):173–187

Hertz H (1899) The principles of mechanics (trans: Jones DE). Macmillan, London

Hessen B (2009) The social and economic roots of Newton's Principia. In: Freudenthal G McLaughlin P (eds) The social and economic roots of the scientific revolution, pp. 41–101. Boston Studies in the Philosophy of Science 278. Springer, Dordrecht

Huebner DR (2013) Wilhelm Jerusalem's sociology of knowledge in the dialogue of ideas. J Class Sociol:430–459

Jedynak A (1993) Conventionalism in Ajdukiewicz. In: Wolenski J, Poli R, Coniglione F (eds) Polish scientific philosophy: the Lvov-Warsaw School. Rodopi, Amsterdam, pp 299–312

Kuhn TS (1976) Foreword to genesis and development of a scientific fact. In: Trenn TJ, Merton RK (eds) Fleck, L. Genesis and development of a scientific fact. Chicago, vii–xi

Kuhn TS (1977) Objectivity, value judgment, and theory choice. In: The Essential Tension. Chicago Press

Latour B (2007) A textbook case revisited: knowledge as mode of existence. In: Hackett EJ, Lynch M, Wajcman J, Amsterdamska O (eds) The handbook of science and technology studies. MIT Press, Cambridge

Lévy-Bruhl L (1966) How natives think (trans: Clare LA). Washington Square Press, New York

Mach E (1893) Science of mechanics (trans: McCormack TJ). Open Court, Chicago

Mach E (1900) Principles of the theory of heat (trans: Jourdain PEB, Heath AED). Reidel, Dordrecht

Mach E (1872 [1911]) History and root of the principle of the conservation of energy (trans: Jourdain PEB). The Open Court Publishing Company, Chicago

Mach E (1926) Knowledge and error (trans: McCormack TJD). Reidel, Dordrecht

Mach E (1959) The analysis of sensations (trans: Williams CM, Waterlow S). Dover, New York

Martens R (2000) Kepler's philosophy and the new astronomy. Princeton University Press, Princeton

Poincaré H (1905) Science and hypothesis. Walter Scott, New York

Pojman P (2019) Ernst Mach. In: Zalta EN (ed) The Stanford Encyclopedia of Philosophy (Spring 2019 Edition)

Sady W (2000) Fleck O społecznej naturze poznania. Prószyński i S-ka, Warszawa

Sady W (2021) Ludwik Fleck. In: Zalta EN, Nodelman U (eds) The Stanford Encyclopedia of Philosophy (Fall 2023 Edition)

Schnelle T (1986) Ludwik Fleck and the influence of the philosophy of Lwów. In: Cognition and fact. Boston studies in the philosophy of science, vol 87. Springer, Dordrecht. https://doi.org/10.1007/978-94-009-4498-5_13

Shapin S, Schaffer S (1985) Leviathan and the Air-pump: Hobbes, Boyle, and the experimental life. Princeton University Press, Princeton

Uebel T (2012) But is it sociology of knowledge? Wilhelm Jerusalem's "sociology of cognition" in context. Studies in East European Thought. Origins Soc Theor Knowl 64(1/2):5–37

von Sass H (2016) For your eyes only: transcendental pragmatism in Ludwik Fleck. Transversal: Int J Historiogr Sci, no. 1 (December). https://doi.org/10.24117/2526-2270.2016.i1.09

Wark M (2015) Molecular red. Verso, London

Chapter 4
A Fleckian Framework for the Study of Cultural Change

Abstract This chapter constructs a theoretical model for understanding cultural change by revisiting and extending Ludwik Fleck's key concepts of thought collectives and thought styles. Rejecting single determinant models of transformation, it emphasizes Fleck's account of socially conditioned perception and comparative epistemology, which foregrounds the interactive, collective nature of knowledge formation. Through a systematic analysis of Fleck's writings from 1929 to 1936, the chapter traces the development of key notions—including intellectual unrest, collective mood, and the circulation of ideas—from an initial emphasis on individual creativity toward a more sophisticated account of collective cognition.

The chapter argues that Fleck's framework must be revised when extended to broader socio-cultural categories such as class, race, and nation, highlighting how collective identities are discursively constructed. It also clarifies key differences between Fleck's thought styles and Kuhn's paradigms, particularly the distortions and transformations that occur when knowledge circulates across group boundaries. Fleck's notion of intellectual unrest is shown to provide a fruitful means for analysing external determinants of change—including the Vesalian turn to dissection, the role of print technology, and the institutional formations of early modern universities.

By exploring how such external and internal pressures destabilize established epistemic configurations, the chapter demonstrates how knowledge circulation between thought collectives can trigger reconfigurations of a thought style. Through these historical case studies, Fleck's comparative epistemology is extended beyond the confines of science to encompass broader processes of cultural transformation.

4.1 Key Definitions

Since subsequent chapters of this thesis will apply Fleck's key concepts to assess how well his theory accounts for the emergence of new and culturally transformative ideas, it is necessary to first isolate and examine Fleck's concepts. Given the non-systematic and scattered nature of Fleck's approach to comparative

S. Dersley, *Thought Collectives and Cultural Change*, Living Signs of Law 1,
https://doi.org/10.1007/978-3-031-97431-1_4

epistemology, a coherent and workable methodology must be extracted from his writings. This will allow for a clear comparison of the explanatory advantages they offer over alternative models, such as Kuhn's paradigms. Additionally, this methodology will help identify complementary tools, such as discourse analysis, which, I will argue, are necessary to fully integrate into the application of Fleck's theory.

With this in mind, the present chapter will analyse two of Ludwik Fleck's propositions and explore their implications. The first underpins his theory of thought styles and thought collectives, while the second is a programmatic, normative recommendation drawn from this theory:

1. All perception and cognition are socially conditioned;[1]
2. Epistemology should be a comparative science.[2]

Fleck defines a *thought-collective* (*Denkkolletiv*) as 'a community of persons mutually exchanging ideas or maintaining intellectual interaction'; it is also defined as the 'carrier' of a thought-style.[3]

In turn, a *thought-style* (*Denkstil*) is defined as: '[…] the result of the theoretical and practical education of the given individual; in passing from teacher to pupil, it is a certain traditional value which is subjected to specific historical development and specific sociological law'.[4]

A *thought-style* is also defined as: '[the readiness for] *directed perception, with corresponding mental and objective assimilation of what has been so perceived*'. Fleck also states that a thought style is characterized by: 'the problems of interest to the thought collective'; 'the judgment which the thought collective considers evident'; the 'methods which it applies as a means of cognition', and the 'technical and literary style characteristic of the given system of knowledge'.[5]

4.2 Three Levels of Thought-styles and Collectives

Fleck presented his concept of the thought collective in 1935–1936, in *Genesis and Development of a Scientific Fact* (1935), *Scientific Observation and Perception in General* (1935), and *The Problem of Epistemology* (1936). Three components of this concept can be highlighted.

---

[1] Fleck (1986b, p. 49) (1979, p. 38).

[2] Fleck (1986d, p. 98).

[3] Fleck (1979, p. 39, 102).

[4] Fleck (1979, p. 66). On previous uses of the term *Denkstil* by Mannheim (1925) and Carnap (1928), and 'style de pensée' by Koyré (1930), and the suggestion that Fleck may have picked up the term during his stay in Vienna in 1927, see Condé and Jarnicki (2023, 87, footnote 10).

[5] Fleck (1979, p. 99).

4.2.1 Specialized Science

In *Genesis and Development of a Scientific Fact*, Fleck asserts that 'Sixteenth-century physicians were by no means at liberty to replace the mystical-ethical concept of syphilis with one based upon natural science and pathogenesis. A stylistic bond exists between many, if not all, concepts of a period, based on their mutual influence'.[6] Thus, for Fleck, the cultural context determines the perceptions, concepts, and modes of thinking available to such specialists.

When syphilis was first recognised in the late fifteenth century, European culture was dominated by a 'sociopsychological attitude' that attributed agency to a (potentially vengeful) God (and other entities or people wielding supernatural powers). This attitude was thoroughly 'entrenched' at a 'deep psychological' level within the culture, and it was only after it gave way to a more empirical mindset that agency could be attributed to microscopic disease entities. A bacteriologist could only look through a microscope and 'see' a spirochaete bacterium if such a tool and the concept of microscopic disease entities had been developed in the techno-scientific culture, and if the bacteriologist had been previously trained to identify certain shapes with such entities, that is, had the necessary directed 'readiness'[7] to perceive them.

In the case of diphtheria bacilli, Fleck traces how the specialist perception of these bacilli over a period of 33 years (1900 to 1933), to demonstrate how perception and the readiness to see evolves, and to question the notion of timeless and reliable observations. After the discovery of the bacterium in 1884, at around 1900 specialists described its shape as that of 'spaced fingers, fingers of two superposed hands, letter V, *accent circonflexe*, *palisades*'.[8] By 1925, the specialists had abandoned such comparisons in their accounts, due to the blurring and chaos that resulted from such analysis, and because they now saw the specific form of the bacterium 'directly'.[9] Comparisons were then only used to train new members of the collective to recognize the shape of the bacilli. Fleck also asserts that this evolution in perception was accompanied by a 'parallel' evolution in concepts, which determined what could be considered 'true diphtheria' and what could be classed as 'pseudo-diphtheria':

> This evolution of notions causes that, at present, the meaning of the words 'diphtheria bacillus' and 'pseudo-diphtheria bacillus' differ from that in 1900. Hence it is impossible to understand 'in the modern way' the sentences dating back to 1900, even the authors them-

---

[6] Fleck (1979, p. 9)

[7] Fleck (1986d, p. 61).

[8] Fleck (1986d, p. 71).

[9] Latour (2008, p. 13) emphasizes the radical nature of Fleck's approach, which redefines 'direct perception' as a skill acquired through experience within a thought style. Unlike Kantian or Kuhnian models that treat perception as filtered through categories, Fleck integrates time and collective practice into the genesis of facts, demonstrating that perception becomes 'direct' only after it is trained and developed. This shift allows Fleck to view the social and practical elements of science as integral and positive, rather than as distortions or limitations.

> selves would lose the ability to have such an understanding of their one-time utterances which they had at that time.[10]

In this example, the perceptions and concepts of one specialist thought collective evolved with such rapidity that the concepts of the thought style of 1900—if isolated from their subsequent, gradual evolution—could not have been translated into those of 1935. Hence a specialist thought style is not just inaccessible to contemporaneous non-specialists belonging to other thought collectives but, over time, it also becomes incomprehensible even to the specialist thought collective itself.

This leads us to another key issue: the problem of understanding and communication between thought collectives and across time. While the Kuhn of 1962, at the time of *The Structure of Scientific Revolutions*, described paradigms as incommensurable, entailing that the representatives of different viewpoints are unable to completely understand each other unless there is 'a revolutionary transformation of vision',[11] Fleck's position is more one of degree: understanding and communication between thought collectives are inhibited by the combined effects of temporal distance and the distance resulting from specialization. As a concept develops over time, it becomes progressively more difficult to grasp it as a thought collective in the remote past might have understood it—hence the need for a historical and comparative approach to epistemology.[12]

Consequently, in contrast to Kuhn's rigid, psychological gestalt-switch image of incommensurability from 1962, Fleck's focus on the distance between thought collectives is more flexible and dynamic: if the distance caused by time or specialization is not too great, concepts *can* be communicated between thought collectives, but they are inevitably transformed and transformative in the process:

> As a rule communication is only possible within one collective while within kindred collectives it is feasible only with some complexity: the inter-group exchange of ideas is always connected with a more or less marked modification of the ideas. When passing from one group to another, words change their meaning, the ideas obtain a different style colouring, the sentences receive another meaning, the opinions a new value. If the groups are considerably distant from each other, the exchange of thoughts can be completely impossible, and transformation of a thought consists, in such a case, in its complete destruction.[13]

Fleck's model of comparative epistemology thus ultimately hinges on the notion of communicability or incommunicability, rather than incommensurability.[14] Two

[10] Fleck (1986d, p. 72).

[11] Kuhn (1962, p. 103, 112).

[12] Fleck (1986d, p. 98).

[13] Fleck (1986d, p. 85).

[14] Fleck scholarship has evolved through varying emphases. For example, Schnelle (1986b, p. 241) insightfully highlighted the productive role of 'misunderstandings' in communication between thought collectives. Löwy (1990, pp. 218–219), by contrast, focused on the 'incommensurable' perspectives of distinct thought collectives, drawing on Fleck's use of the term *niewspółmierność* in his 1927 essay *O niektórych swoistych cechach myślenia lekarskiego*. More recently, Condé and Jarnicki (2023, p. 91) introduced the intriguing concept of 'porosity', describing how 'this circulation of ideas and practices—not only within a thought style but also between different thought

thought styles can be compared in terms of the degree to which their concepts communicate recognizable content—whether perceptions, meanings, or values. Importantly, the transformation that occurs when concepts are communicated between kindred specialists can itself become an object of comparison.

In this way, Fleck's focus on communication is closer to Kuhn's later reformulation of incommensurability as 'semantic incommensurability', which posits the non-translatability of concepts. For example, Kuhn argued that the term 'phlogiston' as used by Joseph Priestley cannot be translated into modern chemical vocabulary since no modern equivalent exists. To understand Priestley's writings, one has to learn his language. Yet—crucially for Kuhn—non-translatability did not entail non-comparability.[15]

4.2.2 *General Fields of Knowledge*

While science can be sub-divided into numerous thought collectives and thought styles, Fleck uses comparative text analysis to demonstrate that there are broader groupings. The 'philosophers' Henri Bergson and James Clerk Maxwell might both discuss 'motion' in their texts, but their concepts are fundamentally incompatible:

> The two men would be unable to communicate with each other as regards motion: Bergson looks for the 'absolute', and believes that the ideal of cognition is the experience from 'the inside'. Maxwell looks for relations to and connections with the surroundings, and his basis of cognition is a relativism. [...] It becomes apparent that words have different meanings for both philosophers. At bottom, almost all words have different meanings for them: it is not as if the word of one of them meant a thing that the other would give a different name, but a thing to which one of them gave a certain name does not exist at all for the other one. That is why it is impossible to translate exactly the utterances of one of them into the language of the other one. Bergson's motion, the motion in itself, absolute motion, does not exist at all for Maxwell; there exists no word to express it, nor is there a need for it [...].[16]

And yet, while the concepts employed by these philosophers are defined as untranslatable, their thought-styles have actually more in common than the thought style of the eighteenth-century mystic Swedenborg: 'Swedenborg's moon is different from Maxwell's moon'. Fleck suggests that Swedenborg's concepts were comprehensible and consistent for his thought collective, that is, among people trained to think in this specific tradition of Lutheran mysticism.

In conclusion, Fleck outlines broad fields of knowledge that can be identified with certain clear thought styles:

> Thus, one should speak about a different philosophical, scientific and mystical thought-style. Each of these styles has passed through specific historical evolution, and each occu-

styles (both past and contemporary)—gives porosity to the thought style'. See also Sady (2021) on incommensurability.

[15] Kuhn (1982), Carrier (2004).

[16] Fleck (1986d, p. 83).

pies a specific place in the mental life of mankind. We have quite a few such thought-collectives which act as carriers of more or less distinct thought styles. They are produced by separate forms of collective thinking, e.g. certain disciplines such as physics, philology, economics, or the knowledge of some practical professions such as craft, commerce, or next the knowledge of religious, ethnographic, political and other communities, the philosophical systems of definite schools, the so-called common-sense philosophy of life, etc.[17]

Thus, while broadly defined communities (religious, political) can be identified as general thought collectives carrying less distinct thought styles, these can be divided into increasingly specific sub-collectives and sub-sub-collectives, with ever more distinct thought styles. For example: Protestants → Lutherans → Lutheran Pietists → Swedenborgians → late eighteenth-century English Swedenborgians. At each point, members of these sub-collectives will belong to many overlapping thought collectives. For instance, minimal research reveals that the congregations of the Swedenborgian Church of the New Jerusalem in London, Bristol, and Birmingham were associated with Methodist backgrounds and the traditions of English political radicalism.[18]

4.2.3 General Thought Collectives

As is evident from Fleck's references to professions, communities, and common sense in the above quotation, some thought collectives operate on a more general, everyday level. Fleck specifies the minimal requirement: 'A thought collective exists wherever two or more people are actually exchanging thoughts.[19] Moreover, each individual belongs to numerous thought collectives:

As a research worker he is part of that community with which he works. He may give rise to ideas and developments, often unconsciously, which soon become independent and frequently turn against their originator. As a member of a political party, a social class, a nation, or even a race, he belongs to other collectives. If he should chance to enter some other society, he soon becomes one of its members and obeys its rules.[20]

According to these definitions, thought collectives can range from two clearly identifiable people who exchange thoughts—unaware of the fact that they have created a temporary and nameless collective—all the way up to a social class constituted by an amorphous mass of individuals who are widely recognised as forming a social group and who—to varying degrees—may be aware of themselves as constituting such a group and may consciously identify with it.

When he classifies social classes, nations, and races as examples of general thought collectives, Fleck does not provide a clear account of the ontological status

[17] Fleck (1986d, p. 84).

[18] Thompson (1963), Rix (2007).

[19] Fleck (1979, p. 44).

[20] Fleck (1979, p. 45).

of such entities, or of how they come into existence. In other words, his writings do not explicitly distinguish the mechanisms by which thought collectives *can be* identified, or by which they *are* constructed. In the case of specific thought collectives, it can be presumed that communities are identified and constructed by political theorists, historians, sociologists, or anthropologists as research objects—for example, Marx and Engels' *bourgeoisie* of *The Communist Manifesto*, or Malinowski's 'natives' of Mailu and Melanesia. Alternatively, groups might self-identify as collectives or movements, such as the Italian Futurists, or the Black Panthers. However, the case of general thought collectives is more ambiguous.

Thaddeus J. Trenn, in his *Descriptive Analysis*, observes that the general collectives of social class, nation, and race do not necessarily align with Fleck's (previously mentioned) functional definition—*a community of persons mutually exchanging ideas or maintaining intellectual interaction*—since such large collectives are rarely defined by the fact that they actively exchange ideas. Trenn argues:

> Fleck does not seem clearly to distinguish between the thought style as a latent dispositional state giving an enduring character to thought collectives, and thought style as an active expression of a thought collective. He does point out that long-lived thought collectives tend to have permanent thought styles, but this is somewhat of a truism.[21]

While it has to be acknowledged that Fleck's conception of nations as thought collectives with stable and unique thought styles wanders into the realms of truism or even stereotype, it also has to be acknowledged that such stereotypes and *constructs of nations as thought collectives* do circulate in society and, furthermore, have been brought into play in the history of philosophy and science.

A case in point is the account of the Enlightenment *philosophes* overcoming national prejudice and provincial relativism—which depicts early eighteenth century France as being under the sway of Cartesian celestial vortices and irrationally rejecting Newtonian mechanics for the simple reason that it was the product of a protestant Englishman, until Voltaire persuaded his countrymen to abandon their national prejudice and use the light of Reason to accept the truth of Newtonian physics. Thus, Voltaire's *Fourteenth Letter on Descartes and Newton* (1733) can be read as addressing the relativism that arises due to scientific thought collectives being influenced by national and religious prejudice:

> A Frenchman arriving in London finds changes in philosophy as in other matters. He left a universe that was filled; he discovers the void; in Paris, they imagine a universe composed of vortices of subtle matter; in London none of this; we think it is the pressure of the moon that causes the fluctuation of the tides; the English believe that the ocean gravitates toward the moon [...] In Paris, the earth is shaped like a melon; in London, it is flattened at both ends. Light, for a Cartesian, exists in the air; for a Newtonian, it comes from the sun in six minutes and a half.[22]

At the same time, this letter can also be read as deploying *the construct of national thought collectives* discursively. In *The Newton Wars and the Beginning of the*

---

[21] Trenn (1979, p. 158).

[22] Voltaire (2007, p. 47).

Enlightenment (2008), J.B. Shanks subjects the historiography of the Enlightenment to 'a Foucault-inspired revisionist historical analysis', to suggest that Voltaire downplayed French engagement with Newtonian natural philosophy prior to 1728 and used strategies of 'self-fashioning' to overplay the conflict between the French and English scientific communities. According to Shanks, this strategy enabled Voltaire to construct the image of himself as the first French Newtonian *philosophe*; and this image then became a founding element of his Enlightenment mythology.[23]

However, Mordechai Feingold, being suspicious of Shanks' discursive approach, argues that Shanks himself downplays the extent of French opposition to Newton. In particular, Feingold takes issue with Shanks' assertion that 'France absorbed Newton's science immediately and in substantial, if idiosyncratic, ways from as early as 1690'. For Feingold, Shanks' '"France" can at best stand for a handful of people', namely a few members of the Académie des Sciences.[24]

This is a clear example of the difference between a specific thought collective (members of the Académie des Sciences in 1690) and a general thought collective (France as an intellectual community 1690–1726). The specific collective is constructed as an object on the basis of identifiable individuals, whereas the general collective is constructed as an abstract generalization (which can perhaps be traced back to interactive cognition which perceived patterns and regularity in the cognized). If carefully applied, Fleck's concept of thought collective is flexible enough to grasp and analyse both kinds of thought collective.

From the perspective of Fleck's comparative epistemology, Voltaire's *Letters Concerning the English Nation* constitute an example of complex communication between the learned communities of London and Paris, and apart from communicating conceptual content or ideas, the letters also construct and consciously attempt to communicate a national thought style, through descriptions of the attitudes and mentality of 'the English' (characterized, for example, by tolerance, intellectual freedom, economic pragmatism, and practical empiricism)—implicitly contrasted with the thought style of 'the French' (which the reader can deduce as being provincial, backwards, intellectually uncritical etc.). The extent to which the *Letters* played a key role in the disseminating the Newtonian resolution of the Copernican Revolution in France, and contributed to the ultimate rejection of the Cartesian solution, is an issue that could be effectively explored through Fleckian comparative epistemology. Such an analysis would consider source texts, historical data, and discourse analysis of historiography.[25]

Perhaps the closest Fleck comes to supporting his conception of nations or class as thought collectives is his notion of 'authorless' content—ideas and understandings which circulated in society but 'for which no original, primary components can

[23] Shanks (2008, p. 31).

[24] Feingold (2010, p. 186).

[25] Another famous example of a national thought style being posited to account for certain tendencies in thought and science can be found in Pierre Duhem's *The Aim and Structure of Physical Theory* (1914). See in particular Chapter IV. 4. *Ampleness of Mind and the English Mind*. Duhem (1954, p. 63 et seq.).

be found'.[26] Though Fleck uses this concept to describe information that has been popularized, propagandized, and circulated among the population at large, it also applies to popular conceptions of social groups and identities: it is not possible to pinpoint the creator of terms like 'the ruling class' or 'the English'. However, in Fleck's texts there is no indication of how such authorless conceptions of groups become treated as real, existing entities.

As was mentioned in Chap. 1, Fleck's conception of general thought collectives requires clarification or even correction. All thought collectives, whether specific or general, have to be regarded as the constructs of thought collectives. No general thought collective can be posited as existing 'in-itself' outside of the cognitive interaction between the cognizer, the cognized, and the general fund of knowledge. Concepts of general groups, like class, nations and race, can be viewed as constructs that were originally produced by thought collectives in their interactive cognition of society, but which now circulate as authorless content in the general fund of knowledge.

Thus, I argue that Fleck's theory lacks a concept that explains how groups and group identities are constructed, circulated, and identified. For reasons which will be presented in more detail in Sect. 4.5, it is argued that Laclau and Mouffe's theory of discourse (1985)—which was developed through performing crucial modifications of Foucault's theory of discourse—can be used to clarify or correct Fleck's conception of thought collectives. From this perspective, Fleck's thought collectives can be conceived as discursively constructed collective identities and objects of knowledge; thought styles can be viewed as sharing many functional properties with articulatory practices; and the existing fund of knowledge can be treated as overlapping with the field of discursivity.

Supplementing Fleck's theory with concepts from Laclau and Mouffe's discourse theory is particularly useful when focusing on the interaction between thought collectives, and especially when one thought style transmits its depictions of other thought styles. In the subsequent chapters, this applies in particular to Plato's antagonistic representations of poetry and 'the sophists' (Chap. 6), as well as to the depictions of Hobbes and Spinoza as 'atheists' and 'Epicureans' by theologians, university philosophers, and natural philosophers in seventeenth and eighteenth centuries (Chap. 10).

When applied to key instances of cultural change, Fleck's concept of thought styles and thought collectives has the necessary robustness and flexibility to cope with layers of interaction, the complexity of reconstructions based on reconstructions based on reconstructions, etc.—but only if the notions of discourse and intertextuality are borne in mind: while some thought collectives can be identified with concrete epistemic communities associated with specific individuals and distinct practices (e.g., Socrates' circle, the Stoa, Cicero's network), some thought collectives have been transmitted as less tangible constructs (e.g., 'the Presocratics') or

[26] Fleck (1986d, p. 88).

their transmission is inseparable from antagonistic characterizations of practices and the discursive suppression of their texts (e.g., the sophists).

4.3 Characteristics Shared by All Thought Collectives

4.3.1 Esoteric and Exoteric Circles

Fleck defines all 'thought communities'—whether a church community, a trade union, or scientific circle—as sharing certain 'structural characteristics',[27] one of which is that such communities consist of esoteric and exoteric circles. As the name suggests, the esoteric circle is the inner circle of the initiated, professionals, and experts, while the exoteric is the outer circle of followers, believers, semi-professionals, and non-specialists. In scientific thought collectives, initiation into the esoteric circle follows years of training, whereas in other thought collectives (religious, political) there may be other initiation procedures. The relationship between the esoteric and exoteric can vary: it can be democratic and open, which for Fleck means that the elite panders to the masses, as in the case of modern science, or it can be dogmatic and secretive, as in the case of religious thought collectives.

In addition to such social distance, the esoteric circle of a thought collective has to communicate across various spatial and temporal distances: if people are indoctrinated into a belief system as children, they are likely to remain lifelong believers; news of the latest fashions must be quickly disseminated to followers.[28]

As Sady points out, this component of Fleck's theory has great explanatory power, as it accounts for how an individual can belong to multiple thought collectives that may seem to be in conflict with each other at the cognitive level, or which even appear mutually exclusive.[29] According to Fleck, it is easier for a physician (a member of an esoteric circle) to also be a devout Christian (a member of the exoteric outer circle) than it is for a physician to be a chemist. This is because these thought styles do not influence each other and cause psychological contradiction (or 'cognitive dissonance', in contemporary terminology). In contrast, being an esoteric expert in two closely-related thought styles could cause in interference, resulting in the incapacitation of thought:

> If thought styles are very different, their isolation can be preserved even in one and the same person. But if they are related, such isolation is difficult. The conflict between closely allied thought styles makes their coexistence within the individual impossible and sentences the person involved either to lack of productivity or to the creation of a special style on the borderline of the field.[30]

---

[27] Fleck (1979, p. 108).

[28] Fleck (1979, pp. 105–107).

[29] Sady (2000, p. 49).

[30] Fleck (1979, p. 110).

This conception of mutually incompatible thought styles coexisting within an individual—due to the distance between the thought styles and the individual's position in the esoteric/exoteric circles—accounts for the contradiction between the radical astronomical hypotheses found in Copernicus's *Commentariolus* and the conservative Aristotelian physics found in his *De Revolutionibus*. Kuhn consistently stressed this contradiction to support his model of gradual paradigm shifts.[31] As a mathematical astronomer, Copernicus was clearly a member of an esoteric circle; however, in terms of his cosmology and physics, he occupied an exoteric position.[32]

Similarly, Fleck's framework sheds light on how the ancient Milesian School could offer demythologized accounts of nature that were simultaneously underpinned by the religious conception of Moira (Destiny), as F. M. Cornford contends.[33] Fleck's concepts can account for this apparent contradiction: the Milesian School were the esoteric representatives of a new thought style, yet they had likely been raised within the exoteric circles of a local religious thought collective.

4.3.2 *Collective Mood*

Trenn's reference to a 'latent dispositional state', in the passage cited above, signals another key element of Fleck's theory: the assertion that all thought collectives are bound together by a 'collective mood':

> The force which maintains the collective and unites its members is derived from the community of the *collective mood*. This mood produces the readiness for an identically directed perception, evaluation and use for what is perceived, i.e. a common thought-style. At the same time it is the source of that feeling of the intra-group mental solidarity mentioned before, of that specific comradeship which produces the '*comrade*', '*countryman*', '*coreligionist*', '*colleague*' etc. Something contrary is the feeling of hostility to the '*stranger*', to a man who worships foreign gods, uses foreign words devoid of the charm felt within the collective.[34]

From this and other passages,[35] it is clear that, for Fleck, collective mood is prior to directed perception; it produces the readiness for it. Collective feeling or mood functions as a kind of non-rational glue that binds the collective. According to Fleck, in scientific thought collectives this mood is 'expressed as a common *reverence* for an ideal—the ideal of objective truth, clarity, and accuracy'.[36] Here, Fleck applies the type of analysis familiar from sociological studies of religion—such as those of

---

[31] Kuhn (1957, p. 148).

[32] This framework only partially accounts for Newton's occult writings, which were written in parallel with the *Principia*: both genres could be classed as esoteric, though very distant in many senses.

[33] Cornford (1912).

[34] Fleck (1986d, p. 101).

[35] Fleck (1979, p. 142).

[36] Fleck (1979, p. 142).

Durkheim and Lévy-Bruhl—to science itself. He compares the reverence that scientific thought collectives have for the ideal of objective truth with emotional phenomena commonly associated with religious thought collectives: the ideal of objective truth is described as a 'belief', scientists are said to devote themselves to science, which has a 'tradition' and indulges in 'hero worship'.[37]

This reverence is bound up with the affective weight carried by the terms employed by a thought collective. The terminology of a particular thought-style takes on a 'sacramental power':

> It is a fundamental matter that the technical term expresses, within the relevant thought collective, something more than what corresponds to its logical definition: it possesses a certain specific power, being not only a name, but also a slogan or a symbol; it possesses something I would give the name of a specific thought charm. One can easily convince oneself of this by substituting for the technical term, a description with the same meaning, but without that specific sacramental power, without that charm: 'king' is something more than 'person in authority'; 'master' is something more than 'man who has mastered a certain skill'; 'element' is something more than the 'component brick' etc.[38]

Thus, in Fleck's view, the practice of science is maintained and animated by factors that are not reducible to logic—by conduct that cannot be classed as any more rational than that of other thought collectives.

It can be surmised that when studying the emergence of a new thought style, the application of Fleck's theory would involve tracking the development and use of terms to which collectives attach a high degree of ritualized affect—such as 'hypothesis' and 'observation' in the natural philosophy concerned with the Copernican turn, or 'experience' in British empiricist discourse.

4.4 Changes in Thought Styles

Hans Jorg Rheinberger argued that Fleck does not have 'a very convincing response' to the question of how major changes in a thought style arise.[39] In a similar vein, Sady suggested that a clear account of how a scientific thought collective undergoes a revolutionary transformation of its thought style is lacking in Fleck's writing.[40] It has to be acknowledged that Fleck's conception of change is certainly not as clear-cut or straightforward as Kuhn's conception of paradigms shifts. However, it is possible to demonstrate that in the years 1929 to 1936 Fleck made concerted efforts to develop and improve his account of changes in thought style, and to make it more capable of elucidating complex phenomena.[41] I would argue that Fleck's efforts in

[37] Fleck (1979, p. 142).

[38] Fleck (1986d, pp. 99-100).

[39] Rheinberger (2010, p. 31).

[40] Sady (2000, p. 69).

[41] This would be an example of the 'rectification' described by Latour (2008, 13): For Fleck 'successive rectification and revision are not peripheral but are the substantial part of the knowledge

this direction can also be continued, and therefore that it is possible to reconstruct Fleck's dispersed account and present a clarified model.

4.4.1 Strong Individuals and Acts of Creation

In *On the Crisis of 'Reality'* (1929), his first foray into general epistemology, analysed in detail in Chap. 2, Fleck tackles a major conceptual problem arising from his theory. If scientific thought is socially conditioned—that is, if 'the social realm' conditions what the individual perceives and cognizes, through educating the individual in the traditions of a community's style of thought[42]—then how does a new style of thinking emerge? If individuals can only think as their community has trained them, how can they begin to think in new ways?

In response, Fleck submits that some 'strong' and 'creative' individuals can exert a great influence on the thought collective, to the extent that their style becomes *the* style of the collective:

> If the individual was strong enough, and his qualities were not only those of a pioneer but those of a leader, then his style became universally accepted into the body of science. In this way the scientific style and recognized scientific practices became codeterminant agents in the formation of scientific reality.[43]

Fleck then enumerates factors that can affect this individual agency—namely 'conventionality, tact and intuition'. He suggests that research requires 'moderation': a balance must be struck between 'consistency', which can lead to one-sidedness if excessive, and 'criticism', which can result in sterility if overemphasized.

While Fleck's conclusions may not be explicitly detailed, it is plausible to infer from his account that normal research—anticipating Kuhn's depiction of conservative, normal science—requires a delicate equilibrium between individual creativity and the dogmas of the inherited thought style.

In order to account for the emergence of new modes of thinking in science, such as Vesalius's revolutionary contribution to anatomy, Fleck invokes the power of individual creativity. He explicitly frames the appearance of a new science, or a new style of thinking within a science, as a problem:

> In great creative moments, however, the newly emerging science is simply an artistic creation that one can only admire and never 'prove' and determine 'objectively'. For there never existed nor exists a scientific demand for fundamental changes because each moment already has a superabundance of fundamental content. [...] I am thinking, for instance, of Vesalius' idea to dispense with a completely elaborated, a hundred percent consistent, highly respected science, and consistently build a new one from confused, unstable, change-

acquisition pathways'.

[42] Fleck (1986b, p. 49).

[43] Fleck (1986b, p. 51).

> able, intertwined masses of flesh, such as the scholars of that time would have considered beneath their dignity even to touch.[44]

According to this account, Vesalius's challenge to Galenic anatomy did not arise from 'a scientific demand'—that is, a need that was recognized in the community of physicians—since the existing knowledge and practice were considered fully sufficient and consistent, at least for the dominant scientific thought collective.

Thus, Vesalius is cast as a heroic individual who battles both the accepted knowledge of 'the mighty scientists' and his own 'ingrained veneration for Galen and tradition'.[45] Fleck even goes as far as to assert that Vesalius's contribution to anatomy had far-reaching social significance—the battle for democratic values discussed in more detail in Chap. 2. In *On the Crisis of 'Reality'*, Fleck offers no explanation for this revolutionary change other than individual creativity. Though he warns that we must not be oblivious to the social-historical elements of science, he does not mention any contextual factors that may have triggered or contributed to Vesalius's innovation. Nor does he consider that Vesalius might have responded to a demand for more accurate and effective anatomical knowledge, either from within the community of physicians or wider society.

4.4.2 Intellectual Unrest

Fleck returns to the example of Vesalius in *Scientific Observation and Perception in General* (1935). After elaborating on the concepts of thought style and thought collective, Fleck turns to the issue of changes within a thought style. This time, rather than presenting Vesalius as creating a new style single-handedly, Fleck focuses on one of his precursors: 'Berengar', though without providing any contextual detail.

'Berengar' refers to the surgeon and physician Jacopo Berengario da Carpi (c. 1460–c. 1530), also known as Giacomo Berengario da Carpi, Jacobus Berengarius Carpensis, and Carpus. The classical scholars of pre-Vesalian anatomy, Ludwig Choulant and L. R. Lind, refer to him as 'Berengario'.[46,47]

According to Choulant's 1852 study, Berengario was a doctor and a teacher who claimed to have dissected hundreds of bodies and 'was the author of the first illustrations made from nature'.[48] Lind describes him as 'the best philological anatomist of the pre-Vesalians',[49] due to his comprehensive assessment of Greek, Latin, and

[44] Fleck (1986b, p. 53).

[45] Fleck (1986b, pp. 53–54).

[46] Choulant (1920, p. 136); Lind (1975).

[47] Berengario's illustrations for *A Short History of Anatomy* (*Isagogae breves*, 1522) can be viewed on the National Library of Medicine's *Historical Anatomies on the Web* collection, accessed 27 December 2024, https://www.nlm.nih.gov/exhibition/historicalanatomies/berengario_home.html.

[48] Choulant (1920, pp. 136–137).

[49] Lind (1975, p. 161).

Arabic anatomical terminology. Lind also recounts some of Berengario's case histories, which suggest that he was particularly focused on, and regarded as an expert on, the uterus:

> He publicly dissected a young and beautiful pregnant woman who had been hanged at Bologna; for four days before her execution she had had intercourse and he found intact sperm in her matrix, proving that it opened in coition. [...] In one instance he attended a woman with a large tumor in her uterus [...] and mentions the fact that he dissected many non-pregnant female cadavers.[50]

In Fleck's essay, Berengario is first used as an example of a thought style that is alien to 'us', due to the use of metaphors and symbols in his descriptions. We can find support for Fleck's characterization in Berengario's metaphorical description of the heart:

> For the dignity of the heart prevails over other parts since it is the chief of all the members and is called the sun of the microcosm because it illuminates the other members with its spirit. The heart has an especial heat. It certainly beats and has motion as if it were a living creature'.[51]

Secondly, for Fleck, Berengario is an example of an individual caught up in the *intellectual unrest* that must precede any change in a thought style:

> One cannot, simply and immediately, see something new and different. First the entire thinking style must be changed, the entire intellectual mood must be unsettled, and the brute force of the directed mental readiness must cease. A specific intellectual unrest must arise and change the moods of the thought-collective, which is the necessary condition for creating simultaneously the possibility and necessity of seeing something new and different.[52]

Fleck asserts that Berengario's opposition to the Galenic thought style was not based on anatomical details but was rather a matter of principle, although Fleck provides no further details on this point. For Fleck, this period of intellectual unrest is one of contradictions. For example, some individuals acknowledged that the innovators were correct on the anatomical details, but still sided with Galen, due to his ancient authority:

> This intellectual unrest of the society of anatomists in the period preceding the new epoch is reflected in individuals: this is perfectly visualized by Vesalius's precursor Berengar, who is full of contradictions, ever retreating and terrified by his own discoveries. [...] Were it not for this period of unrest, Vesalius would have failed to find people who would listen to him: it would have been impossible to attune the society, i.e. to create a new intellectual mood which would enable new forms to be seen.[53]

According to this account, then, the emergence of a new thought style has to be preceded by the appearance of a new intellectual mood, and a new intellectual mood arises from intellectual unrest, characterized by a 'dissimilarity of views' and 'a tendency to change'. Fleck's notion of 'intellectual unrest', thus conceived, has

---

[50] Lind (1975, p. 162).

[51] Carpi [Berengario] (1959, p. 95).

[52] Fleck (1979, pp. 74–75).

[53] Fleck (1979, p. 75).

some similarities with Kuhn's conception of science during periods of crisis. There is a significant difference, however.

According to Kuhn's 1962 conception, a period of crisis arises when scientists begin to recognize that the quantitative data gleaned from observation contradict the expectations dictated by the prevailing paradigm. The dominant paradigm determines what constitutes an anomaly. Kuhn asserts: 'Anomaly appears only against the background provided by the paradigm'.[54] During a period of crisis, a new paradigm emerges which can better account for these anomalies; once the new paradigm is accepted, a period of normal science follows, until the accumulation of anomalies becomes intolerable once again.

In contrast, the accounts of 'exceptions' or 'contradictory views' that appear in Fleck's texts are not entirely consistent. On the one hand, in *Genesis and Development of a Scientific Fact*, Fleck asserts that 'observations contradicting a view are "explained" and smoothed over by conciliators', and even that experts deliberately conceal 'exceptions' (*das Verschweigen einer »Ausnahme«*) from the public.[55] Here, the similarity with Kuhn's conception of anomalies is evident. On the other hand, Fleck also stresses the role that suppression plays in perception, cognition, and observation: 'To recognize a certain relation, many another relation must be misunderstood, denied, or overlooked'.[56] In other words, a thought style determines *what cannot be seen* as much as it determines *what can be seen*.

To make Fleck's account more consistent, it can be suggested that a thought style entails varying degrees of conscious resistance, ranging from entirely unconscious suppression of incompatible phenomena to deliberately concealed phenomena that are consciously recognized as incompatible with the prevailing 'system of opinion' or scientific theory. In this context, scientific thought styles are characterized as fulfilling psychological needs: 'logical conformity within a system at any costs', or 'wishful thinking'.[57] However, the question remains: how do scientists come to observe an exception [*Ausnahme*], i.e. phenomena incompatible with their thought style?

In *Scientific Perception and Observation in General*, Fleck suggests that for a scientist to see something new, the existing thought style has to collapse into chaos, contradiction, and intellectual unrest. Only then can a new thought style begin to emerge, allowing new observations to be made:

> [...] there arises a certain intellectual unrest and a tendency towards changes: a chaos of contradictory, alternate pictures. The picture, fixed up to now, disintegrates into blots which arrange themselves into different, contradictory shapes. [...] It depends on the intensity of feeling of the investigator whether the fact, whether the new shape will appear to him within this chaos as a symbolic vivid vision, or else as a weak hint of a resistance which inhibits the free, almost discretional choice between alternate pictures. [...] It is necessary to create

[54] Kuhn (1962, p. 65).

[55] Fleck (1979, pp. 30–31).

[56] Fleck (1979, p. 30).

[57] Fleck (1979, pp. 31–32).

directional interests, and to destroy inimical interests. One has to create another mental readiness and to educate people to live in it.[58]

Therefore, external shocks and intellectual unrest weaken or remove the resistance that prevents scientists from observing exceptions and phenomena incompatible with the logical system of their thought style. Consequently, the need to explain such phenomena away or conceal them from the public arises primarily during periods of intellectual unrest and chaos, when competing systems exist or during transitions between thought style.

As in *On the Crisis of 'Reality'*, in *Scientific Perception and Observation in General*, individual agency is credited with playing a crucial role in such periods: it is the individual's intensity of feeling that determines whether the new thought style will arrive as a vivid vision or a gradual weakening of resistance.

However, Fleck's account lacks an explanation of the factors that contribute to a shift in intellectual mood and unrest. In a footnote to his description of how a fact arises in *Genesis and Development of a Scientific Fact*, Fleck adds that 'great transformations in thought style, that is, important discoveries, often occur during periods of general social confusion',[59] citing the Early Renaissance and the years after World War I as such periods. Once again, Fleck does not explore factors that lead to periods of 'general social confusion'; perhaps he deemed such an account unnecessary.

If Fleck's somewhat vague concepts of 'intellectual mood' and 'intellectual unrest' are to be adduced as factors that can account for changes in thought styles, then it is necessary to supplement the analysis of source texts—Fleck's default research technique when considering distant thought styles and collectives—with principled reference to historical and historiographical studies. Such studies obviously must be treated with caution, since the historical facts they refer to have been constructed and filtered through the layered interaction of temporally distant thought styles, and are deployed within discourses that have distinct purposes and agendas. However, keeping Fleck's epistemology in mind, it is still possible to identify some passive elements that form the basis of historical facts, and to reflexively consider the complex interactions occurring between thought collectives and within thought styles.

When Fleck's concepts are applied to Vesalius's innovations, there are many facts and factors that can be associated with the intellectual mood and unrest of that period, which can be posited as determinants of the changes in thought style that evidently occurred during Vesalius's lifetime. Potential determinants can be explored through exploration of the following topics: (a) the return to dissection, (b) printing innovations, and (c) the University of Padua. The next sections will illustrate how Fleck's account of Vesalius can be updated in the light of scholarship focused on these areas.

---

[58] Fleck (1986c, pp. 76–77).

[59] Fleck (1979, p. 177).

4.4.2.1 The Return to Dissection

In his provocative book *The Anatomical Renaissance* (1997), Andrew Cunningham challenged the progressivist image of Vesalius as the heroic innovator who single-handedly rejected the ancient authority of Aristotle and Galen and launched 'modern, scientific, anatomy'.[60] Thus Cunningham's argument cuts against Fleck's first account of Vesalius, as the strong individual who dispensed with 'a completely elaborated, a hundred percent consistent, highly respected science' and built 'a new one'.[61] To contest such conceptions of the Vesalian moment as a revolutionary discontinuity, Cunningham puts forward the counter thesis that Vesalius's project actually aimed to revive Galenic anatomy in a more pristine and accurate form. By comparing Galen's *On Anatomical Procedures* with the structure of Vesalius's *Tabulae* and *Fabrica*, Cunningham argues that Vesalius loyally followed Galen's dissection procedures, functional divisions, and bodily systems.

While Vesalius famously detailed over three hundred of Galen's errors in *Fabrica* and engaged in public controversies with Galenist loyalists over discrepancies between Galen's texts and what could be observed from dissection, Cunningham asserts that Vesalius's aim was to show that Galen's errors resulted from his reliance on animal dissection and vivisection rather than human dissection, which Galen was unable to perform.[62] In other words, Galen was not truly Galenic in his practice.[63]

On this reading, Vesalius's contributions to anatomy can only be considered revolutionary insofar as they involved the adoption of certain *practices* associated with dissection, pedagogical methods, and text production techniques. His theoretical innovations were restricted to his rejection of textual authority and his methodology focused on identifying 'errors'; they did not extend to a critical overhaul of guiding principles.

Vesalius's innovations in dissection practices emerged amid widespread developments that had begun two hundred years before the publication of the *Fabrica* in 1543. Several key developments in dissection practices preceded Vesalius:

- **1315**: Mondino de' Luizi (also known as Mundinus) introduced human dissection into the curriculum at the University of Bologna.
- **1340 and 1465**: Annual dissections were established in the statutes of Montpellier University (1340) and the University of Padua (1465).[64]
- **1522**: As mentioned earlier, Berengario produced detailed anatomical descriptions and illustrations based on human dissection in *Isagogae breves* (*A Short History of Anatomy*).

---

[60] Cunningham (1997).

[61] Fleck (1986b, p. 53).

[62] On factors preventing Galen from performing human dissection, see Nutton (2020, p. 21).

[63] Cunningham (1997, chapter 4).

[64] Siraisi (1990, pp. 86–88).

- **1536**: Vesalius's Paris teacher, Johann Guinter, published a cutting-edge text-book on Galenic anatomy that referenced dissections. Vesalius highly regarded this work; he revised and published it to accompany his 1538–1539 lectures.[65]

Nancy G. Siraisi suggests that this newfound appreciation of dissection was inspired by a renewed focus on the works of Galen. However, she also concludes that such dissections were primarily performed for instruction purposes rather than for investigating the body.[66] Vivian Nutton situates Vesalius within the university movement of 'new Galenism': he was trained as a Galenist, edited Galen's texts for publication, and was generally accepted by his peers because they saw his work as 'a continuation of the empirical and experimental methodology that Galen had advocated but been unable to put into practice'.[67]

The university movement of new Galenism can be situated within the broader specialist movement of 'medical humanism', which in turn can be located within the broader movement of 'Latin humanism'. Though Nutton recently cautioned that the study of Latin humanism has been neglected in favour of scholarship focused on the Hellenist revival, and stresses that the term 'medical humanism' is still problematic and imprecise,[68] some key 'facts' have been constructed that indicate extensive changes were taking place in European society. One significant development was the rediscovery of lost medical texts (e.g., Celsus's *De medicina*) and the printing of Galen's Greek texts (e.g., the Aldine edition of Galen in 1525), which shed new light on aspects of ancient medicine, such as Alexandrian dissection and Galen's Platonism, previously unavailable to or suppressed by medieval or Islamic authors.

The awareness that Greek manuscripts were incomplete and inaccurate had significant consequences: scholars began searching for Greek manuscripts, there was renewed focus on accuracy and comparison, and it was recognized that Latin translations, in particular the 1490 edition of the Latin *Opera omnia Galeni*, had to be revised, leading to the boom in Latin translations of Galen and Hippocrates in the 1520s. Crucially, in 1526, Erasmus published his 'versions of three small Galenic treatises that appealed to a non-medical audience'.[69] The printing revolution and the demand for Latin translations were key factors that made the latest medical knowledge accessible to physicians and practitioners who lacked the competence to read Greek. As Nutton notes: 'it continued to be through the medium of Latin translation that most physicians were enabled to participate in intellectual discussions about Galen and their ancient heritage. Latin versions of classical texts sold more widely [...]'.[70]

The transmission of knowledge from the esoteric thought collective focused on Greek and Latin manuscripts to the broader exoteric thought collective—those who

65 Nutton (2018, p. 46).

66 Siraisi (1990, pp. 86–90).

67 Nutton (2012, p. 417).

68 Nutton (2021).

69 Nutton (2021, p. 3).

70 Nutton (2021, p. 4).

required this knowledge for more practical purposes—occurred thanks to networks of translators, editors, and printers, as well as commercial networks that stored, distributed, and sold books at fairs and shops throughout Europe.[71] Thus, Vesalius's innovations were made within an already innovative thought style (new Galenism) that was part of a broader revolution in the transmission and consumption of knowledge (medical humanism, Latin humanism). This broader revolution was itself indicative of revolutionary transformations in the modes of economic and cultural production.

According to Cunningham, during this period of innovation and revolutionary transformations, Vesalius's originality lay in his insistence that Galenic anatomy had to return to human dissection in order to resume investigation of the human body and, crucially, correct Galen's 'errors' where necessary. Vesalius framed this project as a return to Hellenistic practices (but obviously not to the legendary Alexandrian practice of human vivisection).[72]

As Vesalius stressed in *Fabrica* and *The China Root Epistle* (1546), Galen's errors were due to the fact that he had dissected monkeys and ungulates, rather than humans. Hence, Vesalius could claim to be vindicating the 'Ancients' and rooting out Galen's later 'misrepresentations'.[73] This emphasis on human dissection as a resumption of ancient practices was inseparable from Vesalius's most disruptive methodological reversal—his reallocation of authority from Galen to the human body. Cunningham succinctly captures the new attitude toward anatomical authority: 'The body is a better text than Galen, and where Galen differs from the text of the body, then Galen must be ignored'.[74,75]

This displacement of authority brought Vesalius into direct conflict with older representatives of the Galenic thought style, such as Professor Matthaeus Curtius at the University of Bologna and his former teacher Jacobus Sylvius (Jacques Dubois). In the public dispute between Sylvius and Vesalius, two main issues were at stake: whether Galen dissected humans, and whether Galen made errors. In *The China Root Epistle*, Vesalius went into great detail to demonstrate that Galen 'did not teach the fabric of the human body', but instead based his account on the study of apes.

[71] Nuovo (2013).

[72] Longrigg (2003, pp. 179–190); Nutton (2013, pp. 133–134).

[73] Vesalius (2015, p. 144).

[74] Cunningham (1997).

[75] Vesalius (2015, p. 114): 'When Galen cut up his monkeys and saw that they differed from the description of the ancients, who trained themselves on human dissections, he did not scruple to state that they had not seen that fiber of the lung and who knows what else. I should therefore be thought more impious if I had not vindicated those Ancients with a true description of the human fabric. If because of the powerful devotion to Galen under which I labor and my special regard for him I were to leave his opinions everywhere undisturbed contrary to the testimony of my eyes and the truth of the matter, I should be willing to have my generation wander in confusion like all the ages that have followed Galen, and let his misrepresentation of the Greeks go undetected'.

Regarding errors, Vesalius explicitly argued that anatomists should trust their own eyes rather than 'the authority of Galen'.[76]

In one of his responses, Sylvius seems to acknowledge the discrepancies between Galen's description of the human body and contemporary observations, because he argues that the incongruities must be due to changes that had occurred in the human body over the centuries, caused by 'variations in airs, waters and places over time'.[77] Through this ingenious adjustment, Galen's infallibility could be maintained despite the contradictory evidence provided by contemporary dissection.

The points to be stressed here are, first, that the change in the thought style of European anatomists occurred precisely and explicitly in a dispute over authority. Second, repositioning the body as the primary, authoritative text redirected the anatomists' thought style, allowing new information and images to enter the field of investigation.

Textual and diagrammatic evidence can be adduced to show how Vesalius gradually came to free himself from the hold of Galen's textual authority. For instance, Bataille et al.[78] analysed Vesalius's illustrations and applied his dissection procedure to the *rete mirabile* in sheep to track Vesalius's growing scepticism with regard to Galen's descriptions. In 1538, in the *Tabulae Anatomicae, Tabula III*, Vesalius simply followed Galen and drew the *rete mirabile* at the base of the human brain. In the *Fabrica* (1543), Vesalius corrected this error by denying the existence of the *rete mirabile* in humans. He had observed this network of vessels in sheep and oxen but not humans, leading him to reproduce Galenic drawings accompanied by sceptical comments.[79] In 1546, Vesalius made his criticism of Galen on this point more explicit, describing his statements on 'the reticular plexus' as 'absurd'.[80]

At the same time, however, while Vesalius was able to reject Galen's authority when it came to specific anatomical features of the human body, his fundamental loyalty to Galen's structural divisions, assumptions concerning function, and dissection procedures continued to direct his perception. In Fleckian terms, the guiding assumptions of the Platonic-Galenic thought style still determined Vesalius's 'readiness' to perceive certain anatomical elements and *not* perceive others. Thus, as Cunningham highlights, Vesalius, following Mundinus, maintained the Platonic-Galenic three-venter division of the human body, which assigned significance to the diaphragm as a border between the middle and lower venters. In terms of anatomical *function*, Vesalius also adhered to Galenic assumptions regarding the three independent bodily systems (brain and nerves, heart and arteries, liver and veins).[81]

In both the *Tabulae* and *Fabrica*, Vesalius followed Galen in treating the heart, lungs, and trachea as one system—a set of organs united in the function of

---

[76] Vesalius (2015, p. 70).

[77] Cunningham (1997).

[78] Bataille et al. (2007).

[79] Bataille et al. (2007, pp. 766–767).

[80] Vesalius (2015, p. 121).

[81] Nutton (2013).

respiration; and in presenting the veins and arteries as separate systems—the former transporting blood, the latter—*aer* or spirit.[82] Galen's influence even determined how Vesalius perceived and depicted the lungs: as surrounding the heart in Book 6, Fig 6 of the *Fabrica*.[83] This influence extends beyond the visual representation of perception into textual description: Vesalius's definition of the pulmonary vein as the structure that brings air from the lungs to the left ventricle (*Fabrica* Book 6, Plate 90) can be described as thoroughly Galenic.

Moreover, Vesalius externalized Galenic assumptions about anatomical *structure* in his texts and public rituals. Galen's somewhat impractical general dissection sequence, as outlined in *On Anatomical Procedures*—proceeding from the skeleton-muscles, to the nerves-veins-arteries, and then the internal organs,[84] was faithfully replicated in the structure of Vesalius's *Fabrica* (Book 1: The Bones and Cartilages; Book 2: The Ligaments and Muscles; Book 3: The Veins and Arteries; Book 4: The Nerves, etc.) and was re-enacted in the procedure Vesalius followed in his public dissections.

According to Fleck's framework, scientists can only perceive something 'new' if their thought style becomes 'unsettled'—whether through communication with other thought styles, or due to a change in intellectual mood and intellectual unrest. When applied to more detailed and critical historical accounts of Vesalius's contributions, Fleck's framework justifies two main conclusions. First, the thought style of professional anatomists underwent significant fracturing and transformation between 1538 and 1546, due to Vesalius's public downgrading of Galen's textual authority, which allowed new passive elements to be perceived and acknowledged (i.e. the 'fact' that the *rete mirabile*, the plexus of arteries and veins present in sheep, was not present in apes and humans).

Second, however, Cunningham's reframing suggests that despite heated disputes over authority and practices, the thought style carried by university-based anatomists—which can be provisionally designated as 'medical humanism'[85]—remained fundamentally unified and Galenic in the 1540s. Even Vesalius and his students—the stakeholders most committed to trusting their own eyes, those who reclaimed the practices of Alexandrian anatomy to position their project and practices in opposition to the older generation's new Galenism—still saw the human body through the invisible lens provided by the Platonic-Galenic strand of ancient anatomy. These inherited, unquestioned assumptions concerning bodily systems and functions actively directed the thought collective's perception of the human body, inhibited the perception of alternative content, and were externalized in the structures of printed materials and embodied in ritualized procedures.

This cursory analysis of scholarship focused on the history of anatomy shows that Vesalius cannot be straightforwardly depicted as single-handedly transforming

[82] Cunningham (1997).

[83] Vesalius (1973, p. 181).

[84] Galen (1999).

[85] Cunningham (1997, p. 88); Nutton (2021).

the prevailing thought style, nor as simply abandoning the conservative thought collective centred around the University of Paris for the innovative thought collective at the University of Padua. In other words, the progressivist narrative framing can only be maintained if certain key details are overlooked (for instance, the innovations of new Galenism, Vesalius's Galenic representation and description of the heart), or if it is possible to demonstrate that Vesalius questioned the Platonic-Galenic principles underlying his own approach to the study of anatomy. However, the scholarly consensus from Barcia Goyannes (1994), through Cunningham (1997), to Nutton (2018) and (2021), leans towards the position that the Vesalian Revolution, despite the vitriolic anti-Galenic rhetoric of *The China Root Epistle*, remained fundamentally Galenic.

In contrast to the contemporaneous Copernican Revolution, which proceeded from an esoteric critique of fundamental assumptions (1509–1514, 1543) and took centuries to be accepted and implemented in practice, the Vesalian Revolution sprang from the intersection of innovative practices and technologies in 1538–1546 and was almost immediately accepted. Several factors contributed to the swift dissemination and acceptance of Vesalius's innovations: the public nature of his dissections, the involvement of the student body, the public pamphlet wars, and institutional support. Combined with Vesalius's exceptional talents, determination, and forceful personality, these factors ensured the rapid transmission of his ideas from esoteric to exoteric circles. The acceptance of Vesalius's innovations is reflected in book sales—especially of the *Epitome*—a condensed version of the *Fabrica*,[86] in student expectations at Padua and Bologna in subsequent decades,[87] and in the construction of sixteenth and seventeenth-century anatomy theatres, for example at Padua and Leiden.[88]

However, the fact that the Vesalian Revolution left the core assumptions of Galenic anatomy intact and was limited by its singular focus on human anatomy is reflected in subsequent developments. The next major breakthroughs came through a revival of Aristotelian anatomy, institutionalized by Hieronymus Fabricius at Padua and continued by his pupil William Harvey in England. Fabricius's discovery of the *ostiola* (valves) in human veins (1603) and Harvey's discovery of the circulation of the blood (1628) were reached as a result of a return to Aristotelian comparative anatomy and a refocusing on 'the Animal' rather than 'the human fabric' (as reflected in the title of Harvey's *Exercitatio Anatomica de Motu Cordis et Sanguinis in Animalibus*).

From this perspective, Vesalius's project was limited to the description of structure, and lacked an account of action and purpose.[89] Harvey's extensive vivisection of numerous animals (dogs, eels, pigeons, frogs), and his experiments on living humans (*De motu cordis*, Chap. 13), were driven by his conviction that dissection

[86] Duffin and Wolfe (2014).

[87] Klestinec (2004).

[88] Persaud et al. (2014, p. 90).

[89] Cunningham (1997, chapter 6).

alone was insufficient. He argued: 'it is proper to more closely consider the matter and to study the motion of the heart and arteries not only in man, but in all animals that have hearts, to investigate and discern the truth by frequent appeals to vivisection and careful observation'.[90]

The fact that Harvey refers to Galen throughout his text—for instance, to refute his conception of the connection between the heart and lungs, and to reject his functional account of the liver, veins, and arteries—indicates that Galenic assumptions were still firmly in place 85 years after Vesalius's *Fabrica*. However, Harvey's critique of Galen's functional assumptions from an Aristotelian perspective entailed that Aristotelian assumptions, such as the heart as the foundation and source of growth, remained unchallenged. For example, Hippocratic-Aristotelian *pneuma* can be detected in Harvey's statement that arterial blood is 'impregnated with spirits'.[91]

The persistence of 'animals spirits' in Descartes' natural philosophy (1632) and Thomas Willis's neurology (1660–1672)[92] can be explained with Fleck's concept of proto-ideas: the ancient concept of *pneuma* was transmitted through the Vesalian Revolution, the Aristotelian revival, Cartesian natural philosophy, and English empiricism, as spirits/animal spirits. In other words, this proto-idea escaped critical analysis until the discoveries of 'oxygenated blood' and 'nerve impulses' emerged from later developments in 'the existing fund of knowledge'.[93]

If Fleck's account of Vesalius is to be updated in light of the above reflections, the change that occurred in the anatomists' thought style in the 1530s and 1540s has to recognized as partial: a revolution in method, cultural production, and pedagogical practices, but not in the basic assumptions of Galenic anatomy. Cunningham persuasively argues that these assumptions can be traced from Galen back to Plato's *Timaeus*, where the focus is on the human body as the dwelling place of the immortal and immaterial soul, rather than on the animated soul of the universal animal explored in Aristotle's comparative project.[94]

The emergence of modern anatomy, therefore, involved competition between rival thought styles—new Galenism, Vesalian Galenism, and Fabrician Aristotelianism—that defined themselves antagonistically and differentially, returning to ancient thought styles (Platonic-Galenic, Alexandrian, Aristotelian) and adopting their core assumptions in ways that served their respective scientific projects.

[90] Harvey (2017).

[91] Harvey (2017).

[92] Caron (2015).

[93] Fleck (1979, p. 38).

[94] Cunningham (1997, chapter 1).

4.4.2.2 Printing Innovations

The combination of graphic illustrations with textual descriptions was an innovation that both Berengario and Vesalius incorporated into their anatomical works. This cutting-edge print format was based on two techniques that were first developed—in the European context at least[95]—in the fifteenth century: woodcut printing (c. 1400) and movable type (c. 1450). Woodcut techniques were significantly developed by the artists Albrecht Dürer and Titian in the first decades of the sixteenth century. It was soon recognised that woodcut and movable type could make a perfect combination:

> Because the printing of movable type, like the woodcut, is a relief process, once the printing press and movable type were invented in the mid-fifteenth century, woodcuts provided the ideal means for illustrating early printed books. The woodblocks could be placed alongside the type in the flatbed press and printed at the same time.[96]

Vesalius utilized these techniques in his first published anatomical illustrations, the *Tabulae Anatomicae Sex*, produced in Venice in 1538, which consisted of six large sheets with drawings and explanatory captions. According to Vesalius himself, the sheets were produced in response to student demand for materials they could reference during lectures.[97] The sheets thus came to function as pedagogical tools: Vesalius could refer to them while simultaneously lecturing and dissecting—a practice which was itself a key innovation. Students, in turn, could refer to them before, during, and after lectures: 'The possibility of obtaining such essential material beforehand was a new development that further stresses Vesalius's novelty and his conviction of the unity between what was heard or read and what was seen'.[98]

As is often the case when new technology is introduced into an established educational setting, Vesalius's use of illustrations is reported to have been a source of inter-generational conflict:

> [...] many of the leading physicians of the day were actively opposed to the illustration of the printed word on the grounds that this had not been done in classical times and would degrade scholarship. Technical incapacity and the lack of development in standards of reproduction gave support to such opposition, but it was now to become apparent that if not the professors, at least the students quickly became aware of the value and power of graphic anatomical demonstration.[99]

This passage highlights a key feature of the intellectual unrest indicated in historical and biographical accounts: antagonism between the younger generation of students,

---

[95] Metal movable type appeared in China and Korea at least two centuries before Gutenberg's invention of the printing press. On the history of print in China: *Knowledge and Text Production in an Age of Print: China, 900–1400* Chia and De Weerdt (2011), and in Korea: *Engraving Virtue: The Printing History of a Premodern Korean Moral Primer* (Oh 2013).

[96] Thompson (2003).

[97] Saunders and O'Malley (1950, p. 16).

[98] Nutton (2018, p. 45).

[99] Saunders and O'Malley (1950, p. 16).

who responded to Vesalius's hands-on approach and encouragement of close-up participation, and the older generation of professors, who sought to maintain their authority over anatomical knowledge, control over the curriculum, and distance from their students. Cynthia Klestinec, in her essay on sixteenth-century anatomy theatres, suggests this conflict was part of university life for decades: in 1540, students at the University of Bologna sided with Vesalius against Matheaus Curtius in the conflict over Galen's errors and authority. Later, in the 1590s, students at the University of Padua complained about Fabricius's organ-focused demonstrations because they were 'focused not on the technical skills of dissection or the dissection of the whole body but on the philosophical principles that the anatomical parts reflected'.[100]

The figure of Vesalius came to symbolize the challenge posed by the younger generation, a perception shaped not only by the accounts of his students but also by his own polemicizing and self-representation. This contributed to the tendency to position Vesalius as a decisive turning point in the history of science. One of the most iconic images of Vesalius is the title page of the *Fabrica*, where he is depicted conducting a dissection, surrounded by a throng of students, while the 'greybeards have been relegated to the back'.[101] This carefully curated image—constructed by Vesalius, propagated by his students and contemporaries, and later reconstructed in historical narratives—has become emblematic of a tectonic cultural and cognitive shift.

Thus, we are presented with the image of Vesalius willing 'to get his hands dirty' in the ritual of dissection, symbolically breaking class barriers by uniting the intellectual role of the Lector with the manual labour of the Sector, a role previously performed by lower-class barber-surgeons.[102] We also have the image of Vesalius as the entrepreneur immersed in the grubby world of commerce, overseeing the production of his book, investing his own money to ensure he got exactly what he wanted, berating the printer, and making staggeringly detailed corrections.[103] Then there is the image of dexterity and practicality conveyed through Vesalius's emphasis on the importance of the hand, as 'the instrument of instruments'.[104] All these elements accumulate to create and transmit the image of a cultural icon representing a revolution in both mentality and practice—an individual who embodies the shift from the speculative theorizing of the older generation to the practical, hands-on knowledge of the younger generation.

These images of Vesalius and his revolutionary practices were transmitted by the cutting-edge print technologies that had been adopted in Northern Italy, particularly in Venice, where book production reached 'a genuinely industrial scale'.[105] These

[100] Klestinec (2004, p. 378).
[101] Cunningham (1997, chapter 4).
[102] Ghosh (2015).
[103] Nutton (2012).
[104] Cunningham (1997).
[105] Nuovo (2013, p. 2).

technologies, along with the mercantile practices associated with them, breached the walls of the universities and changed their function. During the Lutheran revolt and in its aftermath, this disruptive mode of cultural production had facilitated textual transmission that circumvented and challenged the control of the Church authorities.

Vesalius's use of printed sheets within the university and his publication of the *Fabrica* exploited a new potential afforded by this mode of cultural production: knowledge produced within the university could now be transmitted quickly and directly to other universities, but also into society at large. Thus, universities could take on a new function in addition to that of producing professional clergy, teachers, lawyers, and physicians: when connected with the commercial networks outside the university walls, they could also become centres of knowledge production and dissemination. Vesalius's embrace of commerce, print technologies, and disruptive pedagogical and communicative practices can thus be positioned within a broader revolution in knowledge production and consumption that was undermining authority and transforming the institutions of medieval-feudal society.

The classic Marxist account presents the Renaissance and the scientific revolution as a heroic struggle between the 'burgher' class and the feudal system.[106] From this macro-level perspective, Vesalius's innovations have to be viewed as superstructural interventions and situated within a wider struggle between the merchant class and the feudal nobility for control over the institutions of power: the state, the Church, the universities (or the ISAs—ideological state apparatuses).[107] Within this framework, this struggle would be further reduced to social relations and positions determined by productive forces and control over competing modes of production.

However, even a cursory close-up analysis of the city-states in Renaissance Italy reveals a more nuanced picture. Unlike territorial states such as England or France, where the hierarchical divisions of feudal society were more clearly defined and stable, in the case of the Italian city-states it is often impossible to draw distinct lines between the merchant class and the ruling nobility, particularly in Northern Italy. Here, merchants and bankers had come to control the machinery of the state and church institutions, and in the case of the Medici even the papacy itself—hence the use of terms such as 'mercantile oligarchy' and 'mercantile nobility' when describing Venice.[108]

Furthermore, the power of these ruling classes cannot be attributed to a single mode of production. While Lombardy and Milan's wealth was derived from agriculture and livestock, Florence was powered by the wool trade, artisans, and banking, whereas Venice owed its power to maritime trade and the production and trade of arms.[109] Thus, the complex power struggles and fluid social relations in the region—set against the backdrop of the fierce rivalry between Northern Italian city-states,

[106] Marx and Engels (1987, p. 474).

[107] Althusser (2014).

[108] Brown (2000).

[109] Braudel (2019).

the invasions by foreign powers between 1494 and 1559, and the reverberations of the Lutheran revolt— make the concept of class conflict, and the designation of a singular 'burgher/bourgeois class', somewhat limited in its explanatory power.

Peter Burke's historiographical synthesis of the scholarship on Renaissance Venice frames the Venetian publishing industry as just one component of a broader 'regime of information and communication' founded on Venice's unique position as a commercial port, a centre of a maritime empire, and a crossroads between East and West. Burke identifies the presence of foreigners and subcultures as critical factors which led to the rise of Venice as a cosmopolitan publishing centre: movable type came to Venice via the diaspora of German printers, and Venice was 'the principal gateway through which the ideas of the German reformation reached Italy'.[110] Venice also emerged as a hub for publishing in ancient Greek, Hebrew, Spanish, Slavonic, and Croat, and for producing translations of Arabic books.

Due to its maritime supremacy, Venice was also the source of printed information about the Americas, the East (e.g. Marco Polo), Persia, and the ascendant Ottoman Empire. According to Burke, this polyglot publishing and the trade and circulation of economic and political information were grounded in the unique nature of the Venetian Republic: rather than a feudal-agrarian state, it was a 'mercantile state' that was dependent on the powerful merchant network that had steadily gained influence since the fifteenth century.[111]

Since the category of bourgeois social class fails to capture the complexity of the phenomena determining the social and cultural changes that occurred in the Venetian Republic during the 1530s and 1540s, the concept of *commercial networks* can serve as a more effective research tool. As deployed by Angela Nuovo in *The Book Trade in the Italian Renaissance* (2013), the term 'commercial networks' denotes the transnational system of book commissioning, production, distribution and sales that emerged in Northern Italy, and particularly in Venice, where mercantile culture and practices thrived largely free from the constraints of state or church interference.

The appearance of 'bookmen' and the development of the Venetian book trade were encouraged by several key factors: anti-monopolistic legislation, the absence of a guild, a privilege system that protected small businesses, and the avoidance of prepublication censorship. These favourable conditions attracted migrants from across Italy and brought skilled entrepreneurs and technicians from Germany and France to Venice.[112] By the 1530s, Venice had become the centre for a transnational and cosmopolitan network of agents, commissioners, printers, and booksellers— forming the infrastructure through which the Republic of Letters disseminated its humanist content.

The merchants involved in the book trade have tended to be overlooked in historical accounts because 'they were not inclined to self-representation' and because their 'their production of books might make them seem to resemble too closely

---

[110] Burke (2000, p. 396).

[111] Burke (2000, pp. 306–404).

[112] Nuovo (2013, pp. 1–5).

professions that were considered "mechanical" (that is, involving manual labour) in the Renaissance'.[113] Thus, the glamorous superstructural innovations of Latin humanism, medical humanism, etc., were grounded in a more anonymous infrastructural transformation and collaboration closer to the messy economic base.

In a later study, Nuovo infers from dedications, papal privileges, counterfeit copies, and even dowries, to reconstruct the networks of printers, scholars, manuscript collectors, bibliophiles, editors, and students involved in huge publishing projects in the years preceding Vesalius's *Fabrica*, such as Aldus Manutius' edition of Aristotle's works. Publishers like Manutius, whose great and well-documented erudition compensated for his involvement in merchant practices, were keenly attuned to public demand. They responded with innovations, such as *enchiridia*—portable volumes of classic texts 'designed for easy readability, printed in a new typeface, the italic, which Aldus thought more intimate and pleasing to the eye'.[114]

In Fleckian terms, the commercial networks involved in book production and trading consisted of individuals who belonged to intersecting and overlapping specialist thought collectives (merchants, technicians, artists, scholars). However, these networks themselves created an interface between the esoteric thought collectives of specialized scholarly communities and the exoteric thought collective of the increasingly literate general public. The communication of Vesalius's innovative practice-oriented thought style to both specialists and the more general epistemic community was thus made possible by an innovative mode of production—one that emerged from an established, flourishing mercantile culture. This process operated through complex collaboration and communication at every stage, from commissioning to sales and consumption.

Though Vesalius stamped his personality on the *Fabrica*, and by all accounts micro-managed the artists, block-cutters, and printer involved in its production, often remotely, the publication and distribution of this huge 700-page book was very much a collaborative effort. It relied on the complex commercial and communication networks that had formed across in Europe by 1543, as well as cooperation among representatives of distinct but aligned thought styles—anatomists, physicians, natural philosophers, humanist scholars, and artists. For example, Jan van Calcar, a pupil of Titian, is credited with drawing the skeletons and dissections in Vesalius's *Tabulae* and *Fabrica*.[115]

It is significant that after having the *Tabulae* printed in Venice in 1538, Vesalius chose Johannes Oporinus, a Swiss publisher based in the Protestant city of Basel, to publish his *Fabrica*. This decision required the transport of the woodcuts from Venice—where they were produced—across the Alps to Basel, and involved extensive back-and-forth correspondence as Vesalius sought to supervise the printing remotely.

113 Nuovo (2013, p. 4).

114 Nuovo (2018, p. 28).

115 Nuovo (2018, p. 45).

Although Venice had been Europe's leading printing centre in the fifteenth century, by the sixteenth century, other cities—such as Paris and Basel—were beginning to eclipse it. Basel, in particular, became renowned for its production of illustrated books, largely due to the works of Johann Froben (1460–1527), whose publications included the *Opera* of Galen. Oporinus, a trained classicist who had taught Greek at the University of Basel before entering the book trade, developed a reputation as a meticulous, innovative, and daring printer—he was even imprisoned for publishing the first Latin edition of the *Koran*.[116]

Thus, the circumstances surrounding the production of Vesalius's *Fabrica* reflect key factors that contributed to the intellectual unrest of the time: intense competition in technological and cultural production, a highly developed and collaborative communication infrastructure operating largely beyond the control of state and church, and transnational networks connecting geographically remote and culturally diverse individuals and communities—who were nonetheless united by a shared commitment to innovative knowledge production..

4.4.2.3 The University of Padua

As discussed above, the heroic narrative of Vesalius abandoning the Galenic thought collective in Paris to join a more empirically-oriented thought collective in Padua, thereby single-handedly creating the new thought style of modern anatomy and observation-based science, can only be maintained by overlooking key aspects of Vesalius's practices, including textual features, assumptions, and production circumstances. If the Vesalian Revolution is characterized primarily as a revolution in scientific and pedagogical practices, facilitated by a revolution in the mode of cultural production—as argued above—the role of the University of Padua should be investigated from this perspective. Specifically, how did the University of Padua facilitate Vesalius's return to dissection and his challenge to the authority of Galen's texts?

Nancy Siraisi, in *Medieval and Renaissance Medicine* (1990), identified some key institutional features of the University of Padua which contributed to its rise as a major centre disseminating innovative ideas and practices in the fifteenth and sixteenth centuries. A crucial factor was Padua's close association with the University of Bologna, which—along with Paris and Montpellier—had been a leading centre of academic medical education from the thirteenth through to the sixteenth century. Padua and Bologna were connected not only through the constant circulation of medical faculty (which continued during Vesalius's time, as seen in his controversial demonstrations at Bologna during Curtius's lectures in 1540), but also through shared organizational characteristics that influenced the composition of the student population and the type of instruction provided.

[116] Saunders and O'Malley (1950, pp. 21–22).

Firstly, regarding the former factor, the University of Bologna had originally formed from two separate guilds or corporations: a professorially-controlled doctoral college reserved for Bolognese citizens, and a student-controlled *universitas* open to students from all Italian regions and other countries. These 'aliens' self-organized to form over twenty 'nations' on the basis of 'ethnic and geographical origin the Franks, Picards, Provençals, Alemanns (Germans), Angles, Spaniards, and others', which eventually consolidated into two main corporate bodies – those from north of the Alps and those from the south.[117] The Bologna model was 'transplanted' to other cities, including Padua, Pisa, Prague, Cracow, and Heidelberg.[118]

Following the rise of the German universities in the fourteenth and fifteenth centuries, Bologna and Padua began to attract significant numbers of students from German-speaking regions. Students would begin their studies in the philosophy and medical faculties of German universities before crossing the Alps to complete their medical training in northern Italy. By the fifteenth century, 30-40% of the degrees awarded at Padua went to students from northern Europe. As a result of this open policy, by the fifteenth century Padua became home to the largest community of medical students in Europe.[119]

Secondly, Bologna and Padua can be distinguished from Paris in terms of the style and content of the teaching, as well as the control exercised over it. The theology faculty dominated the University of Paris, resulting in a blend of medical and theological training, whereas at Bologna and Padua, theological education was handled by local religious communities. The most important institutional relationship was between the medical and arts faculties. Crucially, 'the needs and interests of the medical professoriate and students usually predominated in these organizations.[120] Hence the medical and arts faculties became institutionally linked within a single university and doctoral college. According to Siraisi, philosophical instruction, rather than theological training, was given priority, as it was seen as more relevant to medical education. By the fifteenth century, Padua had become a significant centre for philosophical teaching in its own right.[121]

Given the context of Latin humanism and the rise of new Galenism, the evident appeal and success of Bologna and Padua suggest that medical studies and the medical profession were becoming more highly valued in the culture, and that this reflected a societal need in the communities of northern Italy and regions north of the Alps. More broadly, it can be hypothesized that the increasing popularity of the medical faculty at Padua, evident in the number of foreign students and indeed the presence of Vesalius—a Fleming who was considered to be 'a northerner, a

[117] Berman (1982, p. 124).

[118] Berman (1982, p. 126).

[119] Siraisi (1990, p. 64).

[120] Siraisi (1990, pp. 65–66).

[121] Siraisi (1990, p. 69).

"German"'[122]—indicates a flow of cultural capital[123] away from theologically-oriented institutions and modes of cultural production, towards more practically-oriented institutions focused on the production and consumption of applicable knowledge.

Historical accounts depict the student universitas at Bologna as an organization that exerted considerable power over the curriculum and professorial body:

> The student universitas, or corporation, or guild, received from the city of Bologna a charter which permitted it to make contracts with the professors, to regulate the rents of student lodgings, to determine the kinds of courses to be taught and the material to be covered in each, to set the length of lectures and the number of holidays, to regulate prices for the rent and sale of books. The professors were paid directly by the students in their respective classes.[124]

In other words, the student body was an authority constituted by paying customers, often with very clear expectations regarding what and how they wanted to learn. This dynamic created a clear conflict of economic interests between students and professors, as well as competition and antagonism between the professors themselves. This situation entailed constant struggles over authority, as evidenced by students' accounts of Vesalius's demonstrations during Curtius's lectures at Bologna in 1540, students' accounts of his simultaneous lecture-dissections, and later by the complaints made against Fabricius at Padua.[125] It seems plausible to suggest that this unique teaching environment—characterized by empowered students, intergenerational conflict, and professorial rivalry—encouraged Vesalius to become increasingly bold and explicit in his criticisms of Galen's textual authority between 1538 and 1546.

Kenneth Bartlett enumerates several factors that made the University of Padua unique around the time of 1543. Firstly, Venice was to a large extent free from papal interference, and this autonomy extended to the University of Padua: 'The faculties were increasingly subject more to the Venetian Senate than to the Archbishop of Padua, and the cosmopolitan atmosphere drew students of various backgrounds, nationalities, and even religious beliefs'.[126] According to Bartlett, the University continued to admit Lutheran students even after Luther's excommunication in 1521, and Italians with reformed beliefs were not prevented from earning degrees. This policy was in line with Venice's policy of treating heresy as a political matter. The university's religious tolerance can be linked to a profit-oriented approach, where financial considerations outweighed religious affiliation. Cunningham notes that the university 'was run as a business': it aimed to attract foreign students, was sensitive to their complaints regarding the quality of teaching, and adopted the policy of

---

[122] Cunningham (1997).

[123] Bourdieu (1993).

[124] Berman (1982, p. 124).

[125] Cunningham (2017); Klestinec (2004).

[126] Bartlett (2018, p. 6).

'double professors', who lectured on the same subjects at the same time, to encourage competition.[127]

Considering the factors influencing the changes Vesalius introduced to the thought style of new Galenism, the University of Padua can be identified as contributing in three main ways. First, the University's well-attested policies on human dissection—established in the university statutes in 1465, with anatomy made a major subject in the 1530s-40s (rather than an annual event) as part of the embrace of medical humanism—allowed Vesalius to transform the ancient practice of human dissection into a participatory educational ritual in the anatomy theatre.

Second, during a period in which authority and fundamental assumptions were being challenged—e.g., by Copernicus (1509-14, 1543), who studied medicine at Padua in 1501-03; and by the Lutheran Reformation (1517)—the University of Padua acted as a communication hub in the two-way transmission of innovative ideas between northern Italy and German-speaking regions.

Third, the institutional arrangements, authority distributions, and intergenerational antagonisms within the University itself were conducive to questioning the authority of Galen's texts, especially when this authority was upheld by older professors who refused to get their hands dirty in the practice of dissection.

This exploration of the return to the practice of dissection, of the role of printing innovations, and of the communicative-pedagogical practices facilitated by the University of Padua, supports the thesis that Fleck's concept of intellectual unrest can illuminate changes in thought style if a variety of historically-oriented disciplines—in this case Renaissance studies, cultural history, and the history of science and philosophy—are carefully consulted to identify the factors that shaped ways of thinking and text production. This thesis asserts that such determinants do not merely provide additional contextual information about thought styles: rather, they actively shape and facilitate the emergence of new thought styles, becoming embedded and entangled in the thought collective's adoption of new practices and ways of thinking.

4.4.3 Proto-ideas

In *The Problem of Epistemology*, and *Genesis and Development of a Scientific Fact*, Fleck adds another component to his account of the emergence of scientific thinking, namely 'proto-ideas or pre-ideas'.[128]

Fleck describes the notion of foul blood in syphilitics' as a hazy proto-idea (*unklare Uridee*), a precursor to the modern conception of a disease entity detectable in the blood. He traces this proto-idea back to the theory of dyscrasia, which held that diseases resulted from the humours being combined in 'noxious, foul

[127] Cunningham (2018, p. 87).

[128] Fleck (1979, p. 23).

mixtures'. While Fleck asserts that the theory was largely abandoned as a general explanation for diseases, in the case of syphilis, it became more 'substantial and precise'.[129] The key characteristic of a proto-idea, as gleaned from these passages, is that it begins as a vague, general notion or is intertwined with other ideas in ways that prevent conceptual precision.

Fleck then lists further examples of proto-ideas in other fields of science: Democritus's concept of the atom is identified as the proto-idea of atomic theory, and the theories of the elements, the spherical Earth, and the heliocentric solar system are all described as developing from 'hazy proto-ideas' (*unklare Urideen*).[130]

Fleck warns that not all modern scientific ideas developed from proto-ideas (e.g., isomerism), and not all proto-ideas actually evolved into the modern ideas that seem similar, since the underlying concepts are actually dissimilar (e.g., ancient pregnancy tests based on urine). He also warns against assessing proto-ideas as right or wrong when judged in terms of current criteria of truth and validity. To do so would take the idea from its 'socio-cogitative foundation' and out of its 'chronological context':

> Any absolute criterion of judgment as to suitability is as invalid for fossilized theories as a chronologically independent criterion would be for adaptability of some paleontological species. The brontosaurus was as suitably organized for its environment as the modern lizard is for its own. If considered outside its proper environmental context, however, it could not be called either "adapted" or "unadapted".[131]

The truth and validity of ideas, Fleck argues, can only be assessed in terms of the criteria internal to a particular thought style. When there is significant temporal distance between thought styles, there is little common ground between a proto-idea and its descendent concept in terms of the underlying assumptions, content, rules of validity, or social function. (Here, Fleck comes close to Kuhn's conception of incommensurability defined as a lack of a common measure).[132]

In *The Problem of Epistemology* (1936), Fleck revisits his concept of proto-ideas through an analysis of the development of the notions of heat and cold. His first point is that if we read old medical books dating back to the sixteenth century, or books on alchemy, we cannot simply substitute the archaic concepts they contain with our modern equivalents. According to Fleck, the ideas expressed in such texts are inextricable from elements that we would now class as symbols, mystical correlations, and clumsy arguments. To us, the texts are often imbued with 'a strange mood of bombastic seriousness', and if we come across a description of a phenomenon that we think we can identify—such as an account of the plague that seems to describe syphilis—these will be embedded in other details that seem completely irrelevant to us, such as references to animals falling ill and meteorological phenomena. Thus, he concludes: 'the description cannot be transposed into today's

[129] Fleck (1979, p. 11, 23).

[130] Fleck (1979, p. 24).

[131] Fleck (1979, pp. 25-26).

[132] Kuhn (1982, p. 670).

thought language'.[133] (Again, this notion of incommunicability shares similarities with Kuhn's notion of semantic incommensurability).

Fleck's second point is that, despite this alien mood and these unfamiliar clusters of thought, it is possible to distinguish elements within these texts that would go on to develop genetically (rather than logically) into our 'present-day notions'. He analyses the varied conceptions of heat and cold contained in a sixteenth-century medical book to conclude that the examples of heat found in fire, temperament, spice, bodily warmth and hunger are considered 'identical'. Similarly, cold is treated as the same in weather, temperament, fear, and death. In this thought style, the link between 'life' and 'fire' is not merely symbolic:

> *Everything that excites, that increases vitality and all symptoms of vitality, is linked in some way with heat, or rather not separated from heat, from fire.* There is in it an implicitly contained view that 'fire' and 'life' are conjugated in a certain way, by no means a figurative or symbolic one; they are in its essence; to a certain extent identical.[134] [emphasis in the original].

As time went on, Fleck suggests, these proto-ideas of heat and cold became 'differentiated and divided'. For instance, the 'physical meaning' of heat became separated from the 'figurative meaning', and modern physics developed the physical meaning into 'the energy idea of heat'.

For Fleck, such developments are arbitrary, shaped by historical contingency rather than logical or objective necessity. Echoing Mach, he suggests that modern science could have taken alternative paths. For instance, had the conception of heat as a chemical element persisted, physics and chemistry would have developed differently (though it's difficult to see how, as Fleck speculates, the concept of 'caloric' would have simplified the problem of element transformation). More intriguingly, Fleck proposes that if life had been defined morphologically, as the ability to produce specific shapes rather than energy through combustion, crystals might now be classed as living.

The final element Fleck adds to his conception of proto-ideas is that in such early notions, words are 'spontaneous transpositions of experiences'.[135] Drawing inspiration from Erich von Hornbostel, Fleck suggests that with proto-ideas, words do not simply name things or function in logical deductions; instead, they operate as real equivalents. In the conviction that life and fire are identical, words transpose the direct experience of this analogy, invoking the 'magical equivalent' of the experience.

At this point, some inconsistencies in Fleck's thought begin to emerge. He continues:

> It is a vision of the thought-collective, which shocks its mental life so profoundly that it cannot be rejected any more. Being itself without any stable sense, since it provides the mutual relation of notions whose content has not yet been established, it becomes a guiding principle for assigning this content. Before the content of the notion 'life' had been fixed,

[133] Fleck (1986d, p. 91).

[134] Fleck (1986d, p. 91).

[135] Fleck (1986d, p. 94).

> there was an unclear proto-idea of the identity between the essence of life and fire. This unclear thought became the guiding principle of the development of the notions of life and fire.[136]

But for whom was this proto-idea and thought unclear? Given that Fleck's own theory of thought styles asserts that a later thought style can only interpret the concepts of an earlier thought style through the lens of its own socially determined assumptions, a proto-idea could only appear unclear to the thought-style that is interpreting from the outside. We cannot suppose that, from within the original thought style—i.e., for the thought collective of sixteenth-century physicians—the idea of life-fire identity seemed unclear or unstable. Like the brontosaurus, this idea must have been fully adapted to its social environment.

According to Fleck's theory, the only situation in which an idea—later identified as a proto-idea—could have appeared unclear to the thought collective that created it is during a period of intellectual unrest, when various contradictory ideas are competing and causing internal debate. An example of this would be Copernicus's heliocentric model, which took over 150 years to gain general acceptance among European scientific thought collectives, in part due to its unclear quantitative advantages and its competition with alternative models, such as those proposed by Tycho Brahe and Descartes. In this context, the Copernican system could be viewed as a proto-idea, one that appeared unclear to members of the target thought collective and served as a guiding principle as they sought clarity through proof. However, Fleck does not account for intellectual unrest in his discussion of proto-ideas, choosing instead to focus on the notion that vague ideas function as guiding principles.

Another possible example could be, following Lévi-Strauss' taxonomy of magical, mythical, and scientific thought,[137] periods when a thought collective was in the midst of a major shift in the type of thought style employed to process its experience, for example if a dominant mythical-poetic thought style began to give way to a more rational-scientific thought style. For instance, if a mythical-poetic thought style began to give way to a more rational-scientific one, the emerging thought style would inevitably retain and integrate elements of the old. During such transitional periods, it is conceivable that members of the thought collective would find these hybrid ideas vague or unsatisfactory. A perfect example of this might be the Socrates depicted in Plato's dialogues, who struggles with the haziness of new ideas emerging within his collective. However, Fleck does not address such major shifts in thought styles when discussing proto-ideas, focusing instead on their role as guiding principles within more stable thought collectives.

I would suggest that Fleck's concept of proto-ideas can be cautiously applied in two main ways. First, certain concepts may be inherited and preserved by thought styles until developments in the existing fund of knowledge render them obsolete or incompatible. As previously noted, ancient concepts like *pneuma* or animal spirits

---

136 Fleck (1986d, p. 94).

137 Lévi-Strauss (1963).

can be viewed as proto-ideas that were communicated across millennia, appearing in the writings of Vesalius, Harvey, and Descartes, until concepts such as oxygenated blood and nerve impulses were established. Secondly, some thinkers explicitly identify older concepts as the foundation for their own. One example, which will be explored in detail in Chap. 6, is Plato's *Charmides*, where Socrates, Charmides, and Critias analyse the concept of *sophrosyne*. This dialogue traces its transformation from the old aristocratic virtue of self-discipline and adherence to social norms that define one's social position, towards the more recent meaning of self-knowledge that was circulating in Socrates' circle. Another example is Hegel's depiction of *Bildung* as an updated version of the Greek concept of *paideia*, as defined by Plato's reconstruction of Protagoras (explored in Chap. 8). This justifies treating *paideia* as a proto-idea reactivated and developed by eighteenth-century German theorists.

Thus, in the subsequent investigations, the concept of proto-ideas is employed to track communication between thought collectives over time—especially during transitions to new thought styles—and to explore how older concepts are explicitly reformulated and reintroduced from the existing fund of knowledge.

4.5 The Circulation of Ideas

The fourth and final element Fleck posits to explain changes in ideas and thought styles is the transformation that occurs when ideas are communicated within and between thought collectives. As ideas circulate, they undergo significant changes and acquire new meanings.

Within a thought style, an idea is transformed as it moves from the esoteric elite (specialists) to the exoteric general population (non-experts and amateurs). In this process of popularization, ideas that require specialized knowledge are simplified or adapted for popular understanding: '[...] now circulating within the crowd the new thought interferes with the mental store and adjusts itself to the specific style of the thought-collective'.[138] Fleck refers to this as the 'legitimization transformation'. When a thought style remains stable over time, the popular circulation of ideas may involve only 'minimal transformation', but in times of unrest—marked by intellectual shock and creativity—the circulation process is disrupted, and a new process of transformative circulation begins.

While individuals may sometimes play key roles in transmitting ideas between collectives, Fleck argues that many transformations resulting from this communication must be considered 'authorless': '[...] *some elements of up-to-date thought content may be authorless.* Out of the understandings and misunderstandings, out of repeated transformations and recastings, a creation arises, during social circulation, for which no original, primary components can be found'.[139]

[138] Fleck (1986d, p. 87).

[139] Fleck (1986d, p. 88).

One crucial element of change is the fact that communication between thought collectives functions like a game of 'Chinese whispers': concepts inevitably undergo changes in content and acquire new meanings in the process of communication itself. Some changes cannot be traced to specific individuals, places, or times. The social nature of cognition and communication means that such transformations are the result of innumerable acts of anonymous cognition and thus appear 'authorless'. In *Genesis and Development of a Scientific Fact*, Fleck suggests that the Wassermann reaction emerged through just such authorless contributions.[140]

In a passage that seems to echo Plato's oligarchic, anti-democratic critique of writing in *Phaedrus*—which warns that written words can fall into the hands of those who have no business with them[141]—Fleck, an advocate for 'the democratic way of thinking',[142] as mentioned in Chap. 2, emphasizes that random and unpredictable transformations can occur when unintended recipients repurpose words and ideas:

> The intended circulation of ideas, motivated by a desire to communicate, is not the only possibility. Other social forces, *inter alia*, the force of curiosity, result in the thought reaching a recipient for whom it had not been intended. Such unintentional circulation of ideas is very important from the standpoint of the sociology of thinking, and it is linked to the most outstanding alterations, sometimes with a complete change of the meaning. Words and sentences pass from one thought-collective to another, transferred by an individual for whom they had not been intended, and their meaning during this migration changes sometimes to such an extent that only a loose, distant similarity remains.[143]

Fleck provides examples of this type of circulation: when an idea enters a different collective, it can take on a mystical aura, or become the subject of ridicule and caricature. More profound changes also occur, as Fleck illustrates: '[...] the content changes sometimes beyond recognition, even if the word has remained unchanged. May I give as an example the word and the notion of "race", which has been transferred from the natural science or anthropological style to the political one'.[144]

In contrast to problematic and negative borrowings, the transmission of ideas across thought collectives often results in creative mutations that lead to the emergence of distinctly new thought styles—ones that can have far-reaching repercussions in society and trigger significant cultural change. Examples discussed in later chapters include: Thucydides' borrowing from Hippocratic medicine to describe civil strife as a contagion that spreads through the body politic, contributing to the growing reflexive, diagnostic analysis of society during a period of devastating unrest (Chap. 6); the transmission of Greek philosophy from 5th/4th century BC

---

[140] Fleck (1979, pp. 68–69).

[141] Phaedrus (275d–e): 'And every word, when once it is written, is bandied about, alike among those who understand and those who have no interest in it, and it knows not to whom to speak or not to speak.' Fowler's 1925 translation is available at: http://data.perseus.org/citations/urn:cts:greekLit:tlg0059.tlg012.perseus-eng1:275e.

[142] Fleck (1986b, p. 50).

[143] Fleck (1986d, p. 87).

[144] Fleck (1986d, p. 88).

Athens to 1st century BC Rome, primarily through the labour of educated Greek slaves, which involved the translation of Greek philosophical concepts into the Roman imperial context, most notably through Cicero's modification of the Socratic turn toward practical moral philosophy that repositioned rhetoric as central to philosophy, recognizing its importance for exerting power in the Roman public sphere (Chap. 7); Hobbes' and Spinoza's application of Euclidean deduction and geometric proof to non-geometric phenomena, which, among other things, subjected Biblical texts to the same types of analysis as other phenomena, as well as enabling the dispassionate analysis of state power (Chap. 10); and the repurposing of Shaftesbury's concept of 'self-formation', originally developed within the individualist philosophy of politeness in England, but then adopted in the German universities, where the concepts of *bilden* and *Bildung*—translated as 'forming' and 'formation'—were redeployed within a more collectivist, state-oriented framework of self-formation fostered by educational institutions, as part of a questioning of values that facilitated the rise of the philosophy faculty at the expense of the theology faculty (Chap. 9).

These examples illustrate two important points: first, how ideas are not only transmitted but also transformed through translation into new linguistic and cultural contexts; and second, how these transformed-transmitted ideas can act as catalysts for cultural change when they are introduced into new cultural environments. By focusing on the dynamics of these cultural contexts, this study applies Fleck's framework to examine how changes in thought styles are deeply intertwined with broader social and cultural transformations.

4.6 Conclusion

In this chapter, I have reconstructed and expanded Fleck's framework to explore the dynamics of cultural change, emphasizing the interplay between thought collectives, intellectual unrest, proto-ideas, and the transformative circulation of ideas. These extensions address gaps in Fleck's original conception, particularly in explaining the mechanisms by which new thought styles emerge and the sociocultural determinants shaping their adoption and transmission.

Building on Fleck's evolving account of the Vesalian revolution—from his early emphasis on individual genius (1929) to his later recognition of the role of intellectual unrest (1935–1936)—I have demonstrated how changes in thought style rarely stem from isolated acts of genius. Instead, such transformations arise through the interaction of institutional, technological, and social forces. Vesalius's contributions to anatomy, for instance, were contingent on printing innovations, participatory pedagogical practices at the University of Padua, and intellectual shifts associated with Renaissance humanism. Rather than constituting a rupture with Galenic anatomy, his work demonstrates how new thought styles often reconfigure and integrate elements of their precursors.

The concept of proto-ideas provides a means to trace how enduring yet adaptable concepts—such as pneuma or the life-fire analogy—persist across thought collectives. These notions develop not through logical progression but through their entanglement with shifting intellectual and cultural contexts. At the same time, Fleck's insights into the circulation of ideas show how their meanings evolve as they traverse esoteric and exoteric circles, shaped by translation into new linguistic and cultural frameworks. Vesalius's innovations, for instance, became embedded within broader cultural configurations through the dissemination enabled by print technologies and mercantile networks.

Fleck's concept of intellectual unrest demonstrates the conditions under which new thought styles emerge. Periods of contradiction and instability—marked by challenges to authority and debates over fundamental assumptions—create opportunities for shifts in intellectual mood and the reconfiguration of epistemic boundaries. The Vesalian shift from textual authority to direct observation exemplifies how such periods foster both necessity and possibility for change.

This chapter has sought to extend Fleck's framework by emphasizing the role of socio-cultural determinants in shaping epistemic transformations. Factors such as institutional rivalries, economic infrastructures, and communication networks are integral to understanding how innovations emerge, stabilize, and disseminate. These determinants also shape the adoption and limits of new epistemic practices, as seen in the Vesalian reconfiguration of anatomical authority and pedagogy.

The next chapter will build on these insights to propose a methodological toolkit for applying Fleck's comparative epistemology to empirical studies of cultural change. By integrating Fleck's key concepts—thought collectives, thought styles, proto-ideas, and intellectual unrest—with supplementary approaches from Foucault, Laclau and Mouffe, and Bourdieu, the chapter will outline practical strategies for examining the migration of concepts, texts, and practices across institutional and social boundaries. Special attention will be given to the interplay of discourse, power, and collective cognition, providing a flexible methodology for identifying pivotal moments of 'heretical' innovation and analyzing their impact on cultural transformation.

References

Althusser L (2014) On the reproduction of capitalism (1995), (trans: Brewster B). Verso, London
Bartlett K (2018) The culture of Venice in the age of vesalius and the Aldine Press. In: Ciavolella ER (ed) Andreas vesalius and the fabrica in the age of printing. Turnhout, Brepols, pp 3–18
Bataille B, Wager M, Lapierre F, Goujon JM, Buffenoir K, Rigoard P (2007) The significance of the rete mirabile in Vesalius's work: an example of the dangers of inductive inference in medicine. Neurosurgery:761–768
Berman HJ (1982) Law and revolution. Harvard Univerity Press, Cambridge
Bourdieu P (1993) The field of cultural production. Columbia University Press, New York
Braudel F (2019). Out of Italy (1989) (trans: Reynolds S). Europa, London

Brown PF (2000) Behind the walls. The material culture of Venetian Elites. In: Romano J (ed) Venice reconsidered the history and civilization of an Italian City-State, 1297–1797. John Hopkins University Press, Baltimore, pp 295–338

Burke P (2000) Early modern Venice as a center of information and communication. In: Martin J, Romano D (eds) Venice reconsidered the history and civilization of an Italian City-State. John Hopkins University Press, Baltimore, pp 389–419

Caron L (2015) Thomas Willis, the restoration and the first works of neurology. Med Hist 59(4):525–553

Carpi [Berengario] JB (1959) A short introduction to anatomy (*Isagogae breves*) (1530) (trans: Lind LR). University of Chicago Press, Chicago

Carrier M (2004) Semantic incommensurability and empirical comparability: the case of Lorentz and Einstein. Philosophia Scientiæ:73–94

Chia L, De Weerdt H (eds) (2011) Knowledge and text production in an age of print: China, 900-1400. Brill, Leiden, https://doi.org/10.1163/ej.9789004192287.i-430

Choulant L (1920) History and bibliography of Anatomic Illustration (1852) (trans: Frank M). University of Chicago Press, Chicago

Condé ML, Jarnicki P (2023) Ludwik Fleck: thought style and thought collective in the historiography of science. In: Condé ML, Salomon M (eds) Handbook for the historiography of science. Historiographies of science. Springer, Cham. https://doi.org/10.1007/978-3-031-27510-4_5

Cornford FM (1912) From religion to philosophy: a study in the origins of western speculation. E. Arnold, London

Cunningham A (1997) The anatomical renaissance. The resurrection of the anatomical projects of the ancients. Routledge, London

Cunningham A (2018) 'Fair Padua' Asa centre of Rennaissance Aantomy. In: Ciavolella ER (ed) Andreas Vesalius and the Fabrica in the age of printing. Brepols, Turnhout, pp 85–99

Duffin J, Wolfe J (2014). The annotated Vesalius. CMAJ. 186 (11, 856–857)

Duhem P (1954) The aim and structure of physical theory (trans: Wiener PP). Princeton University Press, Princeton

Feingold M (2010) The war on newton. The History of Science Society, pp 175–186

Fleck L (1979) Genesis and development of a scientific fact [1935]. The University of Chicago Press, Chicago

Fleck L (1986b) On the crisis of 'Reality' [1929]. In: Cognition and fact. Boston studies in the philosophy of science, vol 87. Springer, Dordrecht. https://doi.org/10.1007/978-94-009-4498-5_3

Fleck L (1986c) Scientific observation and perception in general [1935]. In: Cognition and fact. Boston studies in the philosophy of science, vol 87. Springer, Dordrecht. https://doi.org/10.1007/978-94-009-4498-5_4

Fleck L (1986d) The problem of epistemology [1936]. In: Cognition and fact. Boston studies in the philosophy of science, vol 87. Springer, Dordrecht. https://doi.org/10.1007/978-94-009-4498-5_5

Galen (1999) On anatomical procedures (trans: Singer CJ). OUP, Oxford

Ghosh S (2015) Human cadaveric dissection: a historical account from ancient Greece to the modern era. Anatomy Cell Biol 48(3):153–169

Harvey W (2017) On the motion of the heart and blood in animals (1628), (trans: Willis RC, Jarrett A) (eds) Wipf and Stock, New York

Klestinec C (2004) A history of anatomy theaters in sixteenth-century Padua. J Hist Med Allied Sci 59(3):375–412

Kuhn TS (1957) The copernican revolution. Harvard University Press, Cambridge

Kuhn TS (1962) The structure of scientific revolutions. University of Chicago Press, Chicago

Kuhn TS (1982) Commensurability, comparability, communicability. Philosophy of Science Association, pp 669–688

Latour B (2008) A textbook case revisited. knowledge as mode of existence. In: Hackett EJ, Amsterdamska O, Lynch M, Wajcman J (eds) The handbook of science and technology studies. The MIT Press, Cambridge, pp 83–112

Lévi-Strauss C (1963) Structural Anthropology (1958) (trans: Jacobson C, Grundfest Schoepf B). Basic Books, New York
Lind LR (1975) Studies in pre-vesalian anatomy. The American Philosophical Society, Philadelphia
Longrigg J (2003) Greek rational medicine. Routledge, London
Marx K, Engels F (1987) Collected works, vol 25. International Publishers, New York
Nuovo A (2013) The Book Trade in the Italian Renaissance (trans: Cochrane LG). Brill, Leiden
Nuovo A (2018) Aldus Manutius and the World of Venetian Publishing. In: Ciavolella ER (ed) Andreas Vesalius and the Fabrica in the age of printing. Turnhout, Brepols, pp 19–45
Nutton V (2012) Vesalius revised. His annotations to the 1555 Fabrica. Med Hist 56(4):415–443
Nutton V (2013) Ancient medicine, 2nd edn. Routledge, London
Nutton V (2018) 1538, A year of Vesalian innovation. J Medieval Early Mod Stud 48:1, January 2018, 41–59
Nutton V (2020) Galen. A thinking doctor in imperial Rome. Routledge, London
Nutton V (2021) Medical humanism, a problematic formulation? Arts et Savoirs [Online], 15| 2021
Oh Y (2013) Engraving virtue: the printing history of a premodern Korean moral primer. Brill, Leiden
Persaud T, Loukas M, Shane Tubbs R (2014) A history of human anatomy, 2nd edn. Charles C Thomas, Springfield
Rheinberger HJ (2010) On historicizing epistemology. An essay (trans: Fernbacj D). Stanford University Press, Stanford
Rix R (2007) William Blake and the cultures of radical christianity. Routledge, London
Sady W (2000) Fleck. O społecznej naturze poznania. Prószyńki i S-ka, Warszawa
Sady W (2021) Ludwik Fleck. In: The Stanford Encyclopedia of Philosophy (Fall 2023 Edition), Zalta EN, Nodelman U (eds) Metaphysics Research Lab. Stanford University
Saunders J, O'Malley C (1950) The illustrations from the works of Andreas Versalisus of Brussels. Dover Publications, New York
Shanks J (2008) The newton wars and the beginning of the enlightenment. University of Chicago Press, Chicago & London
Siraisi NG (1990) Medieval and renaissance medicine. University of Chicago Press, Chicago
Thompson E (1963) The making of the English working class. Vintage, New York
Thompson W (2003) The Printed Image in the West: Woodcut. Retrieved October 18, 2024, from https://www.metmuseum.org/toah/hd/wdct/hd_wdct.htm
Trenn TJ (1979) Descriptive analysis. In: Fleck L (ed) Genesis and development of a scientific fact (pp. 154–165). The University of Chicago Press, Chicago
Vesalius A (1973) In: Saunders JB, O'Malley CD (eds) The illustrations from the works of Andreas Vesalius of Brussels. Dover Publications
Vesalius A (2015) The China Root Epistle (1546), edited and translated by Garrison, D.H. Cambridge University Press, Cambridge
Voltaire (2007) Philosophical letters, Or, letters regarding the English Nation (trans: Steiner PL). Hackett, Indianapolis

Chapter 5
Methodology and Supplementation

Abstract Building on the conceptual groundwork laid in the previous chapter, this chapter sets out a methodological approach for applying Fleck's comparative epistemology to the study of cultural change. It integrates Fleck's central concepts—thought collectives, thought styles, esoteric and exoteric circles, proto-ideas, and intellectual unrest—into a coherent research toolkit. Particular attention is given to how the functionalist concept of ideology helps illuminate the ways in which thought styles sustain or challenge structures of power within social formations.

The chapter then supplements Fleck's model with perspectives from Foucault, Laclau and Mouffe, and Bourdieu, developing an adaptable methodology for examining how concepts, texts, and practices migrate across institutional and social boundaries. These theoretical supplements extend Fleck's framework to a wider field of application, particularly by enabling analysis of discursive constructions of social identity and the positioning of thought styles within fields of cultural production. Special emphasis is placed on reflexive reading strategies and the identification of external determinants—technological, political, and institutional—that shape epistemic development.

By tracking how ideas embed themselves in new contexts and generate heretical breaks in otherwise stable intellectual environments, the methodology seeks to capture the interplay between discursive strategies, power structures, and the active/passive elements of cognition that underpin transformations in thought style. This flexible framework is intended for use in subsequent chapters, where it will be tested against a range of case studies in the history of ideas and cultural practices.

5.1 Comparative Epistemology

Fleck's approach to science is primarily descriptive: he explains how science is conducted, revealing its collective, contingent, and anonymous nature. Yet his approach to epistemology is also normative, as he argues that it should evolve into a comparative science:

S. Dersley, *Thought Collectives and Cultural Change*, Living Signs of Law 1,
https://doi.org/10.1007/978-3-031-97431-1_5

> If epistemology is meant to be a science capable of development, useful and rich in a substantial way, it ought to broaden the range of its interests. It must not be limited to the study of the domains and stages of science which are officially recognized at the given moment, but, taking into account the variety of thought-styles and the multiplicity of thought-collectives, it must become a *comparative science*. Likewise, it ought to take into account the developmental moment and, while including the embryonic stages of cognition, it should aim at the research methods of unclear, wavering and indistinct cognition. It must take into account fundamentally and in detail the *social nature of thinking and cognition*.
>
> Consequently it ought to include *psychological, sociological and historical methods*. [...] *Epistemology thus understood is a science of thought-styles*.[1] [emphasis in the original]

Although Fleck does not explicitly label them as such, his genealogy of syphilis conceptions in *Genesis and Development of a Scientific Fact*, his analysis of the life-fire proto-idea in *The Problem of Epistemology*, and his discussions of the Vesalian Revolution in *The Crisis of Reality* and *Scientific Observation and Perception in General* can all be seen as attempts at the comparative epistemology he envisions.

Fleck's method in these works is primarily based on the analysis of source texts, applying insights from Durkheimian sociology and Machian psychology within his own interactionist epistemology. Fleck seems to signal reflexive awareness when he acknowledges the absence of any 'absolute criterion of judgment' or 'chronologically independent criterion'. In other words, since the researcher belongs to specialized and general thought collectives, there is no privileged, neutral position from which the science of comparative epistemology can be conducted.

Zittel argues that Fleck's epistemology should not be considered relativistic but rather relationistic,[2] as it does not imply that all perspectives are equally valid but instead emphasises the interdependence and contextuality of knowledge claims. This relationist stance aligns with Fleck's view that the analysis and comparison of thought styles must acknowledge their situated, provisional, and limited nature. Any attempt to present an objective, neutral account of how changes in thought styles contribute to cultural change would be doomed to failure at the outset. The analysis, therefore, must be conducted with the reflexive awareness that it is itself embedded within the very dynamics it seeks to examine.

Fleck's theory of cognition fundamentally revolves around interaction and communication. The study of thought styles can thus be understood as an interactive and communicative practice, rather than an attempt to adopt a privileged position from which thought collectives and styles can be represented. Fleck's model of scientific cognition explains how scientists interact with 'natural phenomena,' such as human bodies and non-human agents (e.g., those cognized as bacteria), but it can also be applied to the cognition of cultural phenomena. In this case, the researcher of historical thought styles (the cognizer) interacts with the content communicated by temporally remote collectives (the cognized) through the conceptual lenses and training provided by their own culture (the existing fund of knowledge).

---

[1] Fleck (1986d, pp. 97–98).

[2] Zittel (2010, p. 192).

This interaction with source texts, as well as with the interpretations, traditions, and scholarship that have accumulated over time, can be approached with varying degrees of sensitivity. At one end of the spectrum are maximalist appropriations, where the passive elements communicated by the cognized are selectively used to support the cognizer's agenda (e.g., Hegel's requisitioning of history and the history of philosophy). On the other end is a more reflexive analysis that allows passive elements to 'speak for themselves' as much as possible (e.g., James Schmidt's return to the essays of eighteenth-century German *Aufklärer*).[3] Another approach problematizes passive elements, leading to recontextualizations, revisions, and reframings (e.g., Derrida's engagement with the *pharmakon* in *Plato's Pharmacy*, which teases out suppressed elements in Plato's text and uses them to unravel the network of hierarchized binaries that structure the post-Platonic fund of knowledge).[4]

This study attempts to engage in a reflexive critique, emphasizing the extratextual determinants of thought styles—factors that deliver shocks, provoke intellectual unrest, and contribute to cultural change. From this perspective, Derrida's deconstruction of Plato's *pharmakon* and the speech/writing binary can be fully accepted, but the focus shifts to the social and cultural factors that led to and motivated the production of Plato's texts, factors which, crucially, are seen as embedded within them.

Thus, *philosophia* is treated as an emergent thought style developed and (textually) transmitted by a specific Athenian thought collective—namely, an oligarchic collective opposed to the *demos*—one that defined and positioned itself in relation to other thought collectives, engaged in and advocated for particular social practices and forms of cultural production, while criticizing and ostracizing others. These practices and ideas were then transmitted across empires and centuries.

Information about historical relations and practices, as well as modes of production, distribution, and consumption, is reconstructed through texts, which are the primary elements cognized in the study of thought styles, whether as 'primary source texts', or 'secondary literature', or through 'scholarly literature'.[5] However, texts also refer to and are shaped by their contexts—the external factors that determine and produce them, which can thus be construed as indirectly cognized elements. The Platonic practice of distinguishing between and evaluating modes of cultural production (e.g., poetry and tragedy in *The Republic*) and social practices (e.g., rhetoric in *Gorgias*, sophistry in *The Sophist*) is a textual practice that had far-reaching repercussions. These included the suppression of sophist knowledge in the field of cultural production and the persistent bias towards theory in institutionalized education.

As the previous chapter sought to demonstrate, Fleck's concepts of collective mood, intellectual unrest, and the circulation of ideas are tools that enable

[3] Schmidt (1996).

[4] Derrida (1981).

[5] The distinction between primary source texts and secondary literature is obviously not clear cut or stable, for example the texts of doxographic traditions, or Roman commentaries on Greek philosophy, are both secondary and primary source texts.

provisional conclusions about the extratextual determinants of thought styles. The application of Fleck's epistemology demands sensitivity to the passive and active elements of cognition involved in the construction of historical accounts. Phenomena that register non-arbitrary, passive elements—such as examples of phonemic representation in ancient Greece, Roman translations of Greek medical and philosophical texts, or the combination of movable type and woodcut techniques in European anatomy books—are combined with active elements shaped by the existing fund of knowledge. These active elements include conventions of dating and naming, reconstructions of circumstances, events, networks, and relationships, as well as the interpretative layer of evaluations, references, refutations, and polemics.

My study of thought styles frequently overlaps with other approaches that seek to account for the external determinants of thought and texts, such as Marx's account of ideology, as well as Foucauldian and post-Foucauldian discourse analysis. The following sections explore the differences between thought styles and ideologies, and between thought styles and discourses. They also illustrate how Fleck's comparative epistemology can be supplemented by insights and tools from these approaches, contributing to a provisional methodology for studying cultural change.

5.2 Ideology

5.2.1 Incompatible Models

Previous sections have suggested that the classic Marxian identification of the economic foundation as the sole or primary driver of change in the superstructure underestimates the capacity of ideas to trigger cultural change. Moreover, when applied to certain historical periods, Marx and Engels' concept of class conflict as a dynamic of change has less explanatory power than other research tools, such as those focused on innovations introduced through commercial networks or intergenerational antagonism (see Chap. 4). This section argues that while the Marxist concept of ideology is problematic, it provides useful explanatory power when cautiously applied to the functions of certain thought styles.

The various conceptions of ideology presented in, hinted at, or extracted from the writings of Marx and Engels—along with Marx's solo works—have been extensively discussed across numerous traditions and schools of thought. These discussions have involved from a wide array of thinkers, including Weber, Lenin, Gramsci, Althusser, Laclau, G.A. Cohen, Rosen, and Žižek, to name but a few. The intricacies of these debates lie well beyond the scope of this work. Here, the goal is simply to isolate conceptual components that are incompatible with Fleck's theory, and to identify a concept of ideology indebted to Marx and Engels that can be useful in understanding specific thought collectives and styles in particular historical circumstances.

Fleck's theory is incompatible with any framework that insists on a stark opposition between false ideology and scientific truth, or that claims reality can be directly accessed through perception and experience once the chimeras of ideology have been dispelled. Although Žižek dismisses this distinction as a 'worn-out line of argumentation',[6] it remains strongly articulated in the writings of Marx and Engels and in the work of self-declared Marxists such as Lenin and Althusser.

The account of ideology as 'wrong ideas'—false, distorted, and misleading conceptions of real social relations, as presented in *The German Ideology*[7]—is grounded in the assumption that 'real, positive science' can access reality: real premises, real men, empirically perceptible processes, and real knowledge.[8] Even if Marx moved beyond this straightforward conception of ideology in his later writings, his analyses remain structured by the true/false dichotomy. His work is consistently driven by the attempt to expose secrets, false ideas, mystifications, apparitions, and spectres—for example, his criticism of 'the mystificatory side of the Hegelian dialectic'[9] and his analysis of 'the mystical character of the commodity'.[10] In Michael Rosen's reading of *Das Kapital*, the true/false dichotomy takes on an ontological status: capital is the deceptive, false phenomenal subject that conceals the underlying structure of the true ontological subject, i.e., collective labour.[11]

This framework is maintained by later exemplars of Marxist thought. For instance, Lenin's 1909 critique of Bogdanov's Machian revision of Marxism reflects this perspective. Lenin rejected Mach's 'sensationalist' epistemology, insisting, first, that objective truth is accessible through experience: 'Matter is a philosophical category denoting the objective reality which is given to man by his sensations, and which is copied, photographed, and reflected by our sensations, while existing independently of them.' Second, he maintained that science is distinguished from other ideologies because of its privileged access to truth: 'Every ideology is historically conditional, but it is unconditionally true that to every scientific ideology (as distinct, for instance, from religious ideology) there corresponds an objective truth, absolute nature'.[12]

Even in the wake of Kuhn's critique of science and the reflexive critiques of Western knowledge performed by the French post-structuralists, claims to privileged access resurfaced in Althusser's classification of non-Marxist social and human sciences as 'semi-sciences' or 'pseudo-sciences' due to the influence of bourgeois ideology. Althusser also asserted that Marx's scientific concepts provided the basis for 'a true scientific theory of history'.[13]

It could be argued that, despite all the Lacanian twists and turns, this same framework is ultimately detectable in Žižek's rejection of 'historicist relativism', which, in his view, 'suspends the inherent cognitive value of the term "ideology" and

[6] Žižek (2012).

[7] Marx and Engels (1975, pp. 23, 59–60).

[8] Marx and Engels (1975, pp. 36–37).

[9] Marx (1990, p. 102).

[10] Marx (1990, p. 164).

[11] Rosen and Wolff (1996, pp. 217–222).

[12] Lenin (2010, pp. 122–131, 136).

[13] Althusser (2014, p. 18).

reduces it to a mere expression of social circumstances'.[14] For Žižek, the cognitive value of ideology lies in its ability to testify to the '"repressed" real of antagonism': social reality is constituted through the primordial repression of social antagonism, specifically class struggle.[15] This brings us back to the catastrophe outlined in *The German Ideology*, where ideology is seen as emerging with the division of labour and thus inseparable from class conflict.[16]

Žižek, however, abandons the representationalist framework that seeks to dispel the myths of bourgeois ideology in order to access and represent reality (scientifically) as it truly is. Instead, he replaces this with a psychological framework that continues to posit class struggle as ontologically fundamental. For Žižek, social reality is constituted by the primordial and continuous repression of this antagonism—which is expressed in ideas, externalized in the Ideological State Apparatuses, and woven into the techno-economic fabric of everyday life.

Turning to Fleck's theory, the first point to make is that his framework does not allow ideas from fields such as medicine to be straightforwardly classified as false or inaccurate. Consequently, the same must apply to ideas and claims from political economy, dialectical materialism, history, economics, and other fields. Fleck firmly rejected the notion that past explanations of syphilis—such as the concept of the *carnal scourge*—'can be simply declared wrong'.[17] From the time of the first written accounts of 'the French disease' in the late fifteenth century, all concepts of syphilis were based on observation, and some on experimentation. As such, they cannot be dismissed as 'non-scientific' in any straightforward sense.

From Fleck's perspective, the medicine of his time had not reached an ultimate, objective truth with its concept of a bacterial disease entity. By 1935, European medical thought collectives had constructed active elements, such as the Wassermann test, to cognize the entity *Treponema pallidum* through interaction with the non-arbitrary relations detected using certain concepts, techniques, and apparatuses (e.g., distinguishing symptoms, disease progression, microscopic measurements, and observed reactions with the cardiolipin antigen).[18] Fleck's theory implies that the disease entity described in 1905 was not the same as that described in 1935, as the interaction between the cognizer and the cognized had evolved with developments in the existing fund of knowledge.

Much like Mach, who treated 'things' as abstractions imposed on the flux of sensations (elements) and rejected the concept of the 'thing-in-itself' as a metaphysical projection, Fleck's epistemology treats disease entities as results of the interaction between a thought collective and passive elements. There is no 'disease entity in-itself' isolated from this interaction; rather, passive elements are 'waiting to be discovered' through active constructions that facilitate further interaction (e.g.,

[14] Žižek (2012, p. 6).

[15] Žižek (2012, po. 16–18).

[16] Marx and Engels (1975).

[17] Fleck (1979, p. 8).

[18] Fleck (1979, pp. 53–81).

the genome sequencing of *Treponema pallidum*, the discovery of subspecies). This ongoing process of refinement and discovery cannot be seen as progressing towards absolute or objective truth, as each new conceptualization and technique takes the thought collective down a specific path, while countless alternative paths could have led to different interactions with other passive elements, generating alternative, cutting-edge conceptions of the disease entity[19]—and perhaps even more effective treatments. As Mach highlighted, each solution generated by a set of conventions merely defines the next set of problems to be solved.[20]

If Fleck's theory is applied to the Marxist theoretical tradition, the cognizers drew on the existing fund of knowledge to actively develop and construct concepts (productive forces, modes of production, feudalism, capitalism, the bourgeoisie, the proletariat, class struggle, ideology, etc.) in their interaction with the cognized (various social organizations and knowledge concerning them). Here, the concept of 'social class' functions as an abstract category applied to the flux of passive elements; it cannot be separated from the interaction between the cognizer and the cognized. Any claims to possess objective knowledge of 'the capitalist class', 'the proletariat', or 'the class struggle' overlook the fact that these are conceptual tools applied in interactions, and not entities that exist ontologically independent of cognition.

Lenin's critique of Mach explicitly denies this interactionist component, portraying cognition as akin to photography, where human sensation and the mind passively reflect an external reality—a world of objects great and small, including macro-objects like social classes. The continued Marxist focus on class struggle—as originally constructed to explain certain nineteenth-century European societies—into the twenty-first century, as seen in Žižek's work, exemplifies what Mach called a 'pernicious error': a projected metaphysical concept that obstructs the exploration of other phenomena (e.g., other forms of antagonism, such as intergenerational conflict), alternative concepts for investigating social formations, and other conceptions of productive forces that emphasize collaboration and competition (e.g., commercial networks).

From the perspective of Fleck's theory, both classical 'bourgeois' political economy and Marxist dialectical materialism must be understood as thought styles that developed conceptual tools through their interaction with the cognized. Each style 'discovered' certain aspects of social organization, shaped by its starting assumptions, conventions, and modes of investigation. Marx's reflexive insight—that the researcher's interaction with phenomena is determined by their social position—opened up a new field of inquiry: the examination of how cognition is influenced by social and economic factors. The active elements of cognition—those which determine what is studied in political economy—are themselves shaped by the social context of interaction. Specifically, the political economist's interaction with the cognized is determined by the social position (class) from which the analysis is conducted.

19 Fleck (1986d, pp. 93–94).

20 Mach (1900).

However, while the conclusions of bourgeois political economy are necessarily the result of a limited interaction—conducted with specific tools, from a particular perspective, and at a given time and place—Fleck's theory would resist the claims of dialectical materialism. Marxist investigations cannot, in Fleck's framework, claim a privileged position or special access to the cognized.

From the 'Fleckian' perspective advocated in this thesis, the Marxist project can be depicted as a thought style that produced profound theoretical insights through its intense interaction with the cognized (i.e., industrializing European societies, along with other thought styles such as Hegelian idealism, French political theory, British political economy, and English socialism) between 1844 and 1873. However, it can also be described as a style that, over time, ceased to engage in creative interaction with the cognized. This stagnation arose due to the psychological and methodological certainty provided by the metaphysical concept of the dialectic. As the processes described by concepts such as productive forces, modes of production, and social relations continued to evolve, Marxist concepts—once shaped by interactive engagement—became static once abstracted from that interaction. These concepts were subsequently applied dogmatically by later adherents of the thought style, who treated them as ontological claims about the nature of objective reality, based on supposed privileged access to scientific truth.

5.2.2 The Functionalist Model

However, while Fleck's epistemology has to reject any conception of ideology that classifies one thought collective's ideas as 'false' or 'wrong' purely due to the social position and economic interests of that collective—and conversely, which classifies another collective's ideas as 'true' or 'correct' for the same reason—his theory is compatible with other conceptions of ideology, such as the 'functionalist model' outlined by Rosen.[21] Based on Gerald A. Cohen's analytical Marxist reading of the base/superstructure model presented in Marx's *Preface to A Contribution to the Critique of Political Economy* (1859), the functional interpretation of ideology posits that 'certain beliefs (or other forms of consciousness) exist *just because* they maintain the social structure'. [22]

It is necessary to unpack Rosen's adaptation of Cohen's reading of this key passage from Marx's 1859 preface:

> The changes in the economic foundation lead sooner or later to the transformation of the whole immense superstructure. In studying such transformations it is always necessary to distinguish between the material transformation of the economic conditions of production, which can be determined with the precision of natural science, and the legal, political,

[21] Rosen and Wolff (1996, pp. 213–216).

[22] Rosen and Wolff (1996, p. 214).

> religious, artistic or philosophic—in short, ideological forms in which men become conscious of this conflict and fight it out.[23]

Cohen distinguishes between the superstructure and ideology: the former consists of institutions, while the latter is a set of ideas. He also maintains the classic distinction between science and ideology: science, according to Cohen, is a mental productive force, whereas ideology is unscientific mentation that can only influence the development of productive forces.[24] Rosen, however, rejects this distinction and argues that ideology is part of the superstructure: the superstructure 'corresponds' to the economic base, which means both the superstructure (in Cohen's terms) and ideology (in Rosen's terms) can be understood as being 'appropriate' to the development of productive forces. In other words, ideology exists because it performs a function tied to the economic base.[25]

Thus, extrapolating from this functionalist model, the set of ideas held by the ruling class functions—at least in part—to maintain its dominant position in society. If Marx's passage is read in a certain way, ideological forms can be seen as expressions of underlying conflict in the economic base, with the superstructure viewed as a zone of conflict and contestation ('*ideologischen Formen, worin sich die Menschen dieses Konflikts bewußt werden und ihn ausfechten*'[26]). In this view, while the ideas of the ruling class function to maintain its domination over the institutions of the superstructure—and thus over the productive forces—the ideas of the dominated classes function to resist and contest this domination.

This functional model also appears in reflections grounded in an entirely different (Lacanian-Althusserian) theoretical perspective—namely in Žižek's account of the legitimizing function of ideology which, crucially, also emphasizes the non-transparent, concealed nature of this function:

> We are within ideological space proper the moment this content – 'true' or 'false' (if true, so much the better for the ideological effect) -- is functional with regard to some relation of social domination ('power', 'exploitation') in an inherently non-transparent way: the very logic of legitimizing the relation of domination must remain concealed if it is to be effective.[27]

Thus, if the conception of ideology as false ideas (as opposed to true science) is dispensed with, a functional account becomes highly useful when applying Fleck's theory to cultural phenomena: the superstructure is a zone in which social groups articulate the relations, conflicts, and transformations occurring in the economic base, driven by productive forces. This articulation is characterized by varying degrees of consciousness and concealment, ranging from religious devotion and patriotic outpourings to political beliefs, manifestos, and cynical propaganda. However, to the extent that ideas and forms of cultural production 'fight it out [*und*

[23] Marx (1987, p. 263).

[24] Cohen (1978, pp. 45–46).

[25] Rosen and Wolff (1996, pp. 213–214).

[26] Marx and Engels (1971).

[27] Žižek (2012, p. 6).

ihn ausfechten]', i.e., engage in a relation of social domination, they can be classified as ideologies, or at least as fulfilling an ideological function.

Therefore, with regard to the application of Fleck's theory, a thought style can be identified as having an ideological component if the ideas, texts, or institutions through which it is transmitted are involved in a relation of social domination—whether this relation is one of resistance or hegemony. The closest Fleck comes to this functional conception of ideology is when he describes Vesalius's innovations in anatomy as a 'struggle' or 'battle' (*Kampf*) against tradition in 1929.[28] In 1935, Fleck also noted that the acceptance of Vesalius's approach was facilitated by the 'collective mood' of the period, which was characterized by 'intellectual unrest' and a 'dissimilarity of views'.[29]

In Vesalius's context, this 'struggle' and 'dissimilarity of views' can be described as ideological, or as having an ideological function, insofar as they can be linked to conflicts between thought collectives over the control of university institutions and knowledge production—conflicts ultimately shaped by the development of productive forces and emerging modes of production.

An important consequence of adopting this functional model of ideology is that the application of Fleck's theory to the investigation of cultural phenomena can draw on classical Marxist accounts of specific historical periods, such as Brunt's *Social Conflicts in the Roman Republic* (1971) and Perry Anderson's *Passages from Antiquity to Feudalism* (1974).[30] These provocative works shed light on the external determinants of ancient Athenian and Roman thought styles—specifically, on how the slave mode of production enabled the development, transmission, appropriation, and translation of *philosophia*;[31] how the concept of Greek liberty was inseparable from the systematic extraction of surplus value from slaves; and how the superstructural development of Roman property law was founded on the extensive use of slavery.[32]

While these Marxist accounts are valuable, they must be treated as partial perspectives rather than definitive accounts of 'objective history', bearing in mind the influence of the researcher's thought style on which external determinants are given attention, and which facts are reconstructed and posited as significant. The advantage of Fleck's 'open epistemology'[33] is that it allows—indeed, requires—different accounts of phenomena to be considered. Marxist accounts are particularly valuable because they seek to illuminate the external determinants of thought, whereas the traditions of academic philosophy often remain ensconced *within the thought style of institutionalized philosophy*, engaging in interpretative practices within layers of cross-referenced intertextuality.

[28] Fleck (1986b, p. 54).

[29] Fleck (1986c, p. 75).

[30] For more recent scholarship supporting these classical analyses, see (Ando 2011).

[31] Brunt (1971, pp. 20–41).

[32] Anderson (1974, p. 23, 66).

[33] Borck (2004).

5.3 Discourse, Hegemony and Cultural Production

Chapter 1 suggested that Foucault's distinction between discourse and non-discursive practices and events[34] leads to problems when it is applied to cultural change. However, aspects of Foucault's conception of discourse and discursive practices remain relevant to the application of Fleck's theory, especially in light of critiques of Foucauldian discourse offered by Laclau and Mouffe (1985), and by Bourdieu (1993).

5.3.1 Foucault's Archaeology

Fleck's comparative epistemology justifies a comparison between Foucault's conception of discourse and Fleck's conception of thought styles. Although significant overlaps exist, important differences remain. In this comparison, the focus is restricted to Foucault's *The Archaeology of Knowledge* (1969), since this work provides an extended and explicit account of discourse.

Foucault's fundamental aim in *The Archaeology of Knowledge* (1969) was 'to describe the relations between statements'. Since there are regularities between statements—such as *what* they refer to and *how* they do so—this project involved describing the relations between groups of statements. A key point in Foucault's analysis is that these groups of statements do not refer to a constant, unchanging object. For example, the 'madness' referred to by medical statements in the seventeenth and eighteenth centuries is not the same as the 'mental illness' referred to by later 'psychopathological discourses'. As Foucault notes, 'we are not dealing with the same madmen'. These objects—such as madness or mental illness—only emerge within discourses, which Foucault defines as 'practices that systematically form the objects of which they speak'.[35]

Thus, the first similarity between thought styles and discourses is that both construct the objects of their knowledge and can later reconstruct entirely different objects. For example, just as 'madness' was reconstructed as 'mental illness' through changes in discourse, so too was 'the carnal scourge' reconstructed as *treponema pallidum* through developments in thought style. Similarly, the disease entities (such as diphtheria and syphilis) described in 1905-1906 had, by the 1930s, been completely reconstructed due to further developments in the thought style.

At one point, Foucault even hypothesizes that 'style' is the characteristic feature that unites statements, forms a discourse, and determines perception:

> It seemed to me, for example, that from the nineteenth century, medical science was characterized not so much by its objects or concepts as by a certain style, a certain constant manner of statement. For the first time, medicine no longer consisted of a group of traditions,

[34] Foucault (1989).

[35] Foucault (1989, p. 54).

> observations, and heterogeneous practices, but of a corpus of knowledge that presupposed the same way of looking at things, the same division of the perceptual field, the same analysis of the pathological fact in accordance with the visible space of the body, the same system of transcribing what one perceived in what one said (same vocabulary, same play of metaphor); in short, it seemed to me that medicine was organized as a series of descriptive statements.[36]

However, Foucault ultimately abandoned this hypothesis, concluding that clinical discourse cannot be reduced solely to descriptive statements. It is also shaped by 'institutional regulations' and 'teaching models', along with a broader set of factors that influence the relationship between doctor and patient. These include 'masses of documentation, instruments of correlation, and techniques of analysis'.[37]

Foucault ultimately concludes that the heterogeneous statements forming a discourse—whether perceptual descriptions, instrument-mediated observations, laboratory procedures, statistical calculations, epidemiological or demographic observations, etc.—are articulated through a group of rules and dispersed through a system of secondary relations. It is this system of rules, rather than the *style* or *form* of statements, that produces the regularities which define discursive formation.[38]

This conception of discourse also allows Foucault to contextualize the knowing subject and open up a broader field of determination than that suggested by Fleck's concept of the cognizer as a representative of a thought style. The system and rules of discursive practice create the positions from which subjects produce their discourse about objects. In other words, an educational, institutional, and bureaucratic infrastructure underpins the systematic articulation of discursive statements. The position from which the questioning, listening, or observing subject (e.g., an epidemiologist, a doctor, or a judge) enunciates statements about the object (e.g., bacteria, a patient, or a criminal) is legitimized by 'institutional sites' (e.g., the laboratory, the hospital, or the court system), which are established by the system of relations internal to a discursive practice.[39]

Foucault suggests that while subject positions, objects, and institutional sites are constantly redefined and reorganized, a discursive practice maintains its stability and unity over time because 'it makes constant use of this group of relations'.[40] References to the authorities (e.g., the law, the government) that recognize and use the bodies of knowledge produced by discursive practices, such as medical knowledge, position this stable group of relations within a broader context, prefiguring the regimes of power that would become central in Foucault's later work. In this way, Foucauldian discourse allows the components encompassed by Fleck's active, socially-conditioned elements of cognition (the existing fund of knowledge, conventions, trained perception, instruments, and laboratory practices) to be repositioned within a far wider field of institutional, social, and power relations.

---

[36] Foucault (1989, p. 36).

[37] Foucault (1989, p. 37).

[38] Foucault (1989, pp. 37–50).

[39] Foucault (1989, pp. 56–61).

[40] Foucault (1989, p. 59).

However, when it comes to what is formed as an object of knowledge, Foucauldian discourse is significantly more restricted than Fleck's conception of the cognized. The project of *The Archaelogy of Knowledge* is explicitly restricted to a focus on discourse: 'we shall remain, or try to remain, at the level of discourse itself'.[41] As was mentioned in Chap. 1, Foucault's binary distinction between discursive practices and non-discursive practices leads to problems if his 1969 conception of discourse is applied to account for social and cultural change. While it has to be acknowledged that accounting for change was not the aim of Foucault's project, the issue nevertheless arises repeatedly, for example in the accounts of changes in the discourse of Natural History, and of the appearance and disappearance of positivities, like the French Revolution.[42]

The primary aim of Foucault's archaeology—to describe relations between statements, and thereby describe discourses and discursive practices—is rendered deeply problematic by the distinction between discourse and 'prediscursive' entities, the separation of discursive from non-discursive practices, the refusal to conceptualize the 'exterior', and the insistence on remaining strictly within the dimension of discourse.[43]

On the one hand, Foucault acknowledges the existence of an exterior to discourse, and even the interaction between discourse and this exterior. For example, a discourse (e.g., the *Analysis of Wealth*) is said to perform a function 'in a field of non-discursive practices' (e.g., the practices of emergent capitalism).[44] On the other hand, this exterior of discourse is consistently characterized as an inaccessible primordiality: as pre-discursive experience, as the primal ground free from the tyranny of the text, or as a foundational reality that lies beyond discursive articulation. For some reason, Foucault insists that in order to study a discursive practice, it is necessary 'to suppress the stage of "things themselves"'.[45] The exterior is thus temporalized as anterior and pre-textual, with the implicit suggestion that attempts to access it are motivated by pre-Kantian metaphysical prejudices.

In other words, Foucault allows for the interaction between discursive practices and their non-discursive exterior, but simultaneously suppresses investigation of this interaction—particularly the relationship between a discourse and its referent, i.e., what is formed as the object of discourse. Foucault does not deny the existence of the referent; subjects whose positions and perceptions are defined by a discourse still *see* something, even if this apprehension is inseparable from the textual codings and entanglements of the discourse itself. Foucauldian archaeology opts to focus on the interactions between the statements and concepts within a discourse, or between different discourses, rather than the interaction between a discourse and its non-discursive exterior. Thus, the concepts and methods of the Physiocrats are compared

[41] Foucault (1989, p. 53).

[42] Foucault (1989, pp. 61–70, 193–195).

[43] Foucault (1989, p. 85).

[44] Foucault (1989, p. 75).

[45] Foucault (1989, pp. 52–53).

with those of the Utilitarians, but not in relation to the economic base, modes of production, or other non-discursive practices.[46]

The consequence of Foucault's strategy is that his analysis often remains descriptive rather than explanatory. For example, he describes how the discourse of Natural History 'altered' in the seventeenth and eighteenth centuries: existing concepts (e.g., genus, species, signs) came to be used in new ways, and new concepts (e.g., structure) were invented. However, what Foucault emphasizes most is the reorganisation of the discursive field:

> … what was altered in the seventeenth century, and was to govern the appearance and recurrence of concepts, for the whole of Natural History, was the general arrangement of the statements, their successive arrangement in particular wholes; it was the way in which one wrote down what one observed and, by means of a series of statements, recreated a perceptual process; it was the relation and interplay of subordinations between describing, articulating into distinctive features, characterizing, and classifying; it was the reciprocal position of particular observations and general principles; it was the system of dependence between what one learnt, what one saw, what one deduced, what one accepted as probable, and what one postulated. In the seventeenth and eighteenth centuries, Natural History was not simply a form of knowledge that gave a new definition to concepts like 'genus' or 'character', and which introduced new concepts like that of 'natural classification' or 'mammal'; above all, it was a set of rules for arranging statements in series, an obligatory set of schemata of dependence, of order, and of successions, in which the recurrent elements that may have value as concepts were distributed.[47]

However, no explanation is offered for why such a fundamental transformation of this discourse and its practices occurred. Foucault's description stops at the level of the enunciative field in which the discourse is articulated. For instance, he identifies 'a field of concomitance' in which Natural History, during the period of Linnaeus, was defined by its relations with other contemporary discourses, such as 'cosmology, the history of the earth, philosophy, theology, scripture and biblical exegesis, mathematics'.[48]

In contrast, Fleck's theory posits that such concomitance—understood as the circulation of ideas between thought styles[49]—is a major driver of change. Applying Fleck's concepts to the transformation of Natural History identified by Foucault would involve tracking the transmission, reception, and transformation of concepts as they circulated between thought collectives during this period. More fundamentally, Fleck's epistemology requires us to consider how the new system and set of rules described by Foucault altered the interaction between the cognizer and the cognized. What new objects were formed as a result of this altered discourse? What new value was extracted when subjects enunciated statements within this new system? How did the roles and functions of botanists and naturalists change as a result of treating the natural world as an object of systematic classification?

[46] Foucault (1989, p. 82).
[47] Foucault (1989, p. 63).
[48] Foucault (1989, p. 64).
[49] Fleck (1986d, p. 87).

Or, to put it in explicitly Fleckian terms: why did various thought collectives in Sweden, Britain, and Holland—such as Linnaeus and his 'apostles' at Uppsala University, the 'scientific explorers' on Captain Cook's colonizing voyages, military-commercial enterprises like the Dutch East India Company, or the English landed aristocrats who established herbariums, nurseries, and botanical gardens—all become involved in the costly practices of seeking out, collecting, describing, classifying, transplanting, and cultivating botanical specimens in the mid-eighteenth century? What were the determinants that led Linnaeus to abandon polynomial nomenclature in favour of binomial nomenclature in *Species Plantarum* (1753)? Why did this thought style emerge in Northern Europe at this particular time, and why was it so readily embraced by institutions like the British Royal Society in the 1760s?

A general answer to these questions might begin by pointing to a fundamental shift in the practices and thought styles of certain European collectives, predominantly Protestant in origin and orientation. This shift is reflected in Bacon's exhortations for natural philosophers to *penetrate*, *investigate*, and *disclose* 'nature' for the sake of man's utility and dominion,[50] and in the utilitarian approach to nature expressed in the English, Dutch, German, and Swedish physico-theology that flourished between 1650 and 1750.[51] Even cursory research yields more specific answers, which can be briefly indicated.

For instance, Lisbet Koerner argues that Linnaeus's taxonomic innovations in natural history—a field that would later divide into geography, anthropology, geology, zoology, and botany—were inseparable from his views and projects in political economy. Linnaeus sent his students around the world in search of specimens he believed could be cultivated in Sweden (e.g., tea) or attempted to find Swedish replacements for imported commodities (e.g., coffee). His thought style combined physico-theological assumptions, which viewed nature as a benign, prelapsarian superorganism created for humankind's use,[52] with cameralist economic theory, aimed at ensuring Sweden's self-sufficiency. The Linnaean apostles were thus sent on national missions to appropriate specimens and technologies for use at home, rather than as agents of colonial conquest.

Linnaeus's obsession with acquiring tea trees from Guangzhou and establishing Swedish tea plantations stemmed from his critical view of the European practice of trading Latin American silver for Chinese tea. He saw this as a waste of silver—a substance he regarded as intrinsically valuable—squandered on imports from 'the barbaric countries of the distant East Indies'.[53] This cameralist perspective led him to denounce the importation of luxury goods like coffee and sugar as wasteful, advocating instead for local agricultural development. Linnaeus's scientific texts and sermons reveal that his detailed study of regional flora and fauna was also motivated by a desire to save peasants from the recurring famines that devastated

---

[50] Bacon (2000).

[51] Blair and von Greyerz (2020).

[52] Koerner (1999, p. 118).

[53] Koerner (1999, p. 136).

the Scandinavian countryside.[54] Knowledge—of edible wild flora, of crops and their failures, and of plants that could be acclimatized to Swedish conditions—was thus produced through interaction with 'nature' and intertwined with attitudes to imports and concerns about national self-sufficiency.

As Fleck's theory predicts, when Linnaeus's system was communicated to another thought collective, it triggered far-reaching changes in practices. Correspondence and Royal Society papers allow certain facts to be reconstructed. Linnaeus's new taxonomic system was transmitted to England via Daniel Solander, 'a qualified young scholar from Uppsala' who was sent 'to England to promote the study of natural history'.[55] This Linnaean apostle soon mastered the English language, obtained a position at the British Museum, and became a member of the Royal Society in 1764. Through his friendship with Sir Joseph Banks—an aristocratic landowner, naturalist, botanist, and later President of the Royal Society—Solander was taken as Banks's assistant on Captain Cook's first circumnavigation (1768–1771).

In this way, the Linnaean thought style, stripped of its Swedish nationalist-cameralism, was repurposed as a tool of colonialist military-scientific expansion. Cook's voyage, ostensibly to observe the transit of Venus from Tahiti, was a joint Royal Navy and Royal Society expedition funded by the British state, with the secret objective of acquiring new territories.[56]

Throughout the voyage, Banks and Solander were relentless in their application of the Linnaean system of knowledge gathering:

> At every opportunity, the naturalists trawled for fish, retrieved birds and insects caught in the ship's rigging, and hunted for plants and animals when they went on shore. The naturalists settled into a routine which they maintained throughout the voyage – Banks and Solander inspected the new specimen, Parkinson or one of the assistants drew it, and then its new name and details were added to their Linnaean textbooks. Banks brought back around 3,000 dried plants and almost 1,000 original drawings, many of them made at sea from specimens piled up beneath damp cloths to keep them fresh.[57]

Focusing on personalities, biographical details and first-hand accounts—elements which Foucault's abstract depictions of discourse in *The Archaeology of Knowledge* studiously avoid—allows the interaction between the discourse of Natural History and its objects to be reconstructed. The sub-discourse of Linnaean botany, when applied as a system of knowledge production by the British colonizing machine, interacted with both 'Nature' and indigenous knowledge in very specific ways. As Cook's journal entry of Thursday 30 November 1769 testifies, in New Zealand the botanists gained access to their objects of study literally at gunpoint:

> I went with the Pinnace and yawl Man'd and Arm'd and landed upon the Island accompan'd by Mr Banks and Dr Solander. We had scarce landed before all the Canoes left the Ship and landed at different parts of the Island and before we could well look about us we were surrounded by 2 or 3 hundred people, and notwithstanding that they were all arm'd they came

---

54 Koerner (1999, p. 131).

55 Banks and Rauschenberg (1964).

56 Fara (2003, p. 77).

57 Fara (2003, pp. 79–80).

> upon us in such a confused Stragleing manner that we hardly suspected that the[y] meant us any harm, but in this we were very soon undeceaved for upon our indeavouring to draw a line on the sand between us and them they set up the war dance and immidiatly some of them attempted to seize the two Boats; being disapointed in this they next attempted to break in upon us upon which I fired a Musquet load[ed] with small shott at one of the forwardest of them and Mr Banks and 2 of the men fired immidiatly after; this made them retire back a little; but in less than a minute one of the Chiefs rallied them again, Dr Solander seeing this gave him a peppering with small shott which sent him off and made them retire a second time; they attempted to rally several times after and only seem'd to want some one of resolution to head them; but they were at last intirely dispersed by the Ship fire[ing] a few shott over their heads and a Musquet now and than from us.[58]

Linnaean binomial nomenclature was explicitly used to appropriate and overwrite indigenous knowledge:

> Although the Maori called their plant *Harakeke*, Banks gave it a Linnaean label – *Phormium tenax* (he even christened one variety *Phormium cookii*). He gloated that 'so usefull a plant would doubtless be a great acquisition to England', and Parkinson carefully drew flax for the book they planned to publish together on their return.[59]

Thus, the discourse of Natural History was not simply 'a form of knowledge' or 'a set of rules for arranging statements in series':[60] it was a way of interacting with 'the exterior' constituted by the natural world and other cultures, and was manifested in practices as diverse as firing muskets at indigenous peoples, disseminating knowledge through books and scientific societies, or tending exotic cultivars in a botanical garden in London.

To sum up, there is considerable overlap between Foucault's 1969 conception of discourse and Fleck's thought styles. On one hand, Foucault's positioning of the subject within systems and groups of relations, and his identification of institutional sites as positions from which statements are enunciated, significantly broadens the range of determinants involved in Fleck's active elements of cognition. On the other hand, Fleck's epistemology and theory of thought styles requires a focus on the interactional functions of discourse—specifically, how human groups use discourse (systems of knowledge production) to engage with the exterior, including Nature, the Other, and other thought collectives within their material and social relations.[61]

---

[58] Cook (2003, pp. 94–95).

[59] Fara (2003, p. 89).

[60] Foucault (1989, p. 63).

[61] At this point, it is necessary to signal Edward W. Said's complex critique of Foucault's conception of discourse, the detailed consideration of which lies beyond the scope of this work. One key point to highlight is that Said's *Orientalism* considers Orientalist discourse not only in terms of how it constructed the Other, but also in terms of how this Other was treated: "[Orientalism] is, rather than expresses, a certain will or intention to understand, in some cases to control, manipulate, even to incorporate, what is a manifestly different (or alternative and novel) world; it is, above all, a discourse that is by no means in direct, corresponding relationship with political power in the raw, but rather is produced and exists in an uneven exchange with various kinds of power [...]" (2003, p. 12, italics in original). This uneven exchange with various kinds of power can be read as taking place between the various powers internal to the discourse (political, intellectual, moral), but also in the relationship (or perceissved relationship) between the discourse and the culture that is investigated, classified, and appropriated —e.g. Napoleon's Egyptian expedition: "the very

While Foucault's theory in *The Archaeology of Knowledge* explicitly suppresses investigation of such interactions in favour of examining the rules of anonymous discourse and inter-discursive relations, Fleck's theory provides an epistemological framework that allows us to explore how individuals interact with their natural and social environments through the lenses and tools of their thought styles.

5.3.2 Laclau & Mouffe's Articulatory Practices

Two key components of Laclau and Mouffe's discourse theory are particularly relevant for applying Fleck's concepts to cultural change: (a) their rejection of Foucault's distinction between discursive and non-discursive practices, which leads to their focus on articulatory practices; and (b) their conception of the relational and differential nature of social identity, which asserts that groups are constituted through antagonistic articulations. Both of these contributions stem from Laclau and Mouffe's rejection of the traditional Marxist base/superstructure distinction.

5.3.2.1 The Rejection of Non-discursive Practices

Laclau and Mouffe argue that Foucault's distinction between discursive and non-discursive practices is rooted in the classical dichotomy between thought and matter, which also underpins the Marxist distinction between the economic base and the cultural superstructure. While orthodox Marxism posits an objective material world outside the superstructural world of thought, Foucault's discourse similarly posits a world of non-discursive material complexes and practices that exist prior to and outside discursive practices. Laclau and Mouffe reject these distinctions, affirming that all discursive structures have a material character.[62]

For Laclau and Mouffe, Foucault's non-discursive field, comprising 'institutions, political events, economic practices, and processes',[63] is reconceived as a material field of discursivity that is continually produced by antagonistic articulatory practices. In this framework, all social practices, whether linguistic or behavioural, contribute to 'the social production of meaning, which is structured under the form of discursive totalities'.[64]

Thus, to extrapolate, practices as varied as ploughing a field, exploiting slave labour, exchanging commodities, establishing a university, dissecting a corpse in an

---

model of a truly scientific appropriation of one culture by another" (2003, p. 42). Thus, it could be argued that—with the concept of the Other and the uneven exchange between powers—Said brings the missing element of interaction into Foucauldian discourse.

[62] Laclau and Mouffe (1985, pp. 106–108).

[63] Foucault (1989, pp. 179–180).

[64] Laclau and Mouffe (1985, p. 107).

anatomy theatre, or firing a musket at indigenous people are all practices that have meaning by virtue of discourse, and can thus be defined as discursive practices.

Crucially, this model of discourse rejects 'the thesis that the productive forces are neutral'.[65] The blind productive forces that drove Marxist history are reconceived as social practices that organized the exploitation of natural and labour resources through structured systems of social relations that were always already immanently saturated with meaning. Once the model of one-directional determination in which 'the economy' always determines 'society' in the last instance, is abandoned, and when meaning is freed from the confines of explicit linguistic articulation, it becomes possible to posit multi-directional determination and feedback loops, whereby 'the social' produces meaning and meaning produces 'the social'.

To extrapolate, the economies of ancient Greece and Rome can be identified as discursive totalities that assigned relational functions, statuses, and identities to human beings through hegemonic articulatory practices. In ancient Athens, the dominant discourse—manifested through systems of commodity exchange, law, religion, and the institutions of the polis—positioned individuals as slaves, metics, foreigners, male citizens, or women.

Instead of conceiving the economic base as a one-directional determinant of the superstructure—where meaning is always assigned later as a result of reflection in thought and expression in language—Laclau and Mouffe's concept of 'the social' asserts that meaning is distributed throughout social processes and relations, including economic practices. As they put it, 'The practice of articulation, as fixation/dislocation of a system of differences, cannot consist of purely linguistic phenomena but must instead pierce the entire material density of the multifarious institutions, rituals, and practices through which a discursive formation is structured'.[66]

5.3.2.2 Discourse & Group Formation

Laclau and Mouffe's rejection of the distinction between the economic base and the superstructure also has significant consequences for their conception of social groups. This aspect of their theory of discourse is particularly relevant to my attempt to apply an updated version of Fleck's theory. Since, for Laclau and Mouffe, 'every object is constituted as an object of discourse', it follows that social classes themselves are constituted discursively.

A soft constructionist interpretation of Laclau and Mouffe's position suggests that 'both social and physical objects exist, but our access to them is always mediated by systems of meaning in the form of discourses'.[67] There is some unfortunate ambiguity in Laclau and Mouffe's clarification of the ontological status of objects.[68]

---

[65] Laclau and Mouffe (1985, p. 80).

[66] Laclau and Mouffe (1985, p. 109).

[67] Jorgensen and Phillips (2002, p. 35).

[68] Laclau and Mouffe (1985, p. 108).

They do not explicitly acknowledge the existence of physical or social 'objects' independent of discourse or thought; they merely assert that 'events' like an earthquake or falling brick 'exist'. These *events* can be constructed as different *objects*, such as 'natural phenomena' or 'expressions of the wrath of God', depending on how the discursive field is constructed. The conclusion comes in the form of a complex denial: 'What is denied is not that such objects exist externally to thought, but the rather different assertion that they could constitute themselves as objects outside any discursive condition of emergence'.[69]

To maintain consistency, I suggest a hard-constructionist interpretation is necessary here: there are no objects—physical or social—external to discourse. Objects constituted by discourse, such as social classes and categories, can be construed as having an empirical basis, or a basis in empirical reality,[70] since they are constructed on the basis of events and regularities. However, given Laclau and Mouffe's conception of the social as a field of antagonism and surplus meaning, the concept of social class cannot exhaust, close, or fix the groups and identities that emerge in this field.

For Marx, Engels, Kautsky and Lenin, the proletariat appeared to be a fact of experience: it was a class unity formed by the laws operating in the economic base. Hence, in the orthodox Marxist tradition, the working class assumed the status of an ontologically privileged agent, or even a transcendent subject. Laclau and Mouffe trace the unorthodox contributions of Luxemburg, Adler, and Gramsci, through which the proletariat came to be successively viewed as a symbolic unity, a discursively constituted subjectivity, and a set of collective wills that traversed social classes in their opposition to the hegemonic class. Laclau and Mouffe break from what they identify as Gramsci's lingering economic determinism, objectivism and essentialism[71] to assert that defining political subjects in terms of class is no longer necessary or useful in light of the 'constant emergence of new forms of political subjectivity cutting across the categories of the social and economic structure'.[72]

Since, for Laclau and Mouffe, classes and groups are not objectively existing entities formed by the laws of economics, they have to put forward an alternative mechanism that accounts for the existence of groups as discursive objects. The two key concepts brought into play are hegemony and antagonism: the field of discursivity is said to be an antagonistic terrain in which competing forces struggle for dominance or hegemony.[73] Following Derrida, they define meaning and identity differentially and relationally; thus, a group is constituted by an articulatory practice that confronts other articulatory practices and defines itself antagonistically in relation to this exterior. The interior of a hegemonic discourse is thus constructed through an articulatory practice that attempts the impossible: to seal itself off from other practices, to construct stable subject positions and identities, to fill signifiers

[69] Laclau and Mouffe (1985, p. 108).
[70] Laclau and Mouffe (1985, p. 132).
[71] Laclau and Mouffe (1985, p. 69).
[72] Laclau and Mouffe (1985, p. 13).
[73] Laclau and Mouffe (1985, p. 136).

with fixed meaning, to arrest the flow of difference, to close the political space, to attain conclusive hegemony over other discourses.[74]

A discourse achieves hegemony when its articulatory practices suppress alternative discourses and its meanings become naturalized: its subject positions are not questioned, since they have become part of 'basic common sense' (e.g., national identities). However, Laclau and Mouffe's Derridean position asserts that meaning is always overdetermined: there is no central, transcendental signified that stands outside the system of differences and fixes meaning once and for all; meaning is always deferred and defined by difference, and all identities are fundamentally unstable. Therefore, hegemony has to be continually maintained through articulatory practices (e.g., flags, monuments, rituals, history lessons, patriotic cultural production) that suppress competing discourses and alternative meanings. Laclau and Mouffe argue that sometimes the 'precarious' and 'contingent' nature of the identities constructed by the hegemonic discourse becomes apparent, and alternative subject positions become articulated in the field of discursivity.

As Marianne Jørgensen and Louise J. Phillips indicate, Eric Hobsbawm's traditional Marxist analysis of nationalist and class identification in Europe in the years before and during the First World War can be used to illustrate a historical moment when conflicting subject positions were articulated. Unfortunately, though, Jørgensen and Phillips focus exclusively on Hobsbawm's account of the run-up to the war, to suggest that 'the national articulation prevailed' over workers' class-based identifications.[75] In fact, Hobsbawm only concludes that 'Nationalism was victorious in the formerly independent nationalities of belligerent Europe', that is, in states like Britain and France. His account indicates that the issue of collective identification was far more complex in the regions of Central and Eastern Europe that were dominated by various forms of imperial rule.[76]

Hobsbawm suggests that prior to 1914, identification with the nation-state was a key part of the identities of the petty bourgeoisie and lower middle classes—in both independent countries (Britain, France) and those under the yoke of imperialism (e.g., Ireland, Poland, Hungary). In contrast, European workers who identified with the new proletarian movements were 'consciously and militantly *internationalist*, or at the very least non-nationalist'.[77] Thus, it caused consternation among the leaders of the socialist movement when working-class men (Welsh miners, for example) eagerly signed up to fight for the British nation-state against the working-class men from the German nation-state. Hobsbawm argues that this is because the collective identifications were not mutually exclusive: people had several different attachments and loyalties, and could entertain the appeals of various movements and claims on their identity simultaneously:

> For long periods of time these different attachments would not make incompatible demands on a person, so that a man might have no problem about feeling himself to be the son of an

[74] Laclau and Mouffe (1985, pp. 112–132).

[75] Jorgensen and Phillips (2002, p. 46).

[76] Hobsbawm (1991, pp. 122–130).

[77] Hobsbawm (1991, p. 123).

> Irishman, the husband of a German woman, a member of the mining community, a worker, a supporter of Barnsley Football Club, a Liberal, a Primitive Methodist, a Patriotic Englishman, possibly a Republican, and a supporter of the British empire.
>
> It was only when one of these loyalties conflicted directly with another or others that a problem of choosing between them arose.[78]

Hobsbawm suggests that the choices people made depended on complex and specific contexts: nationalism was victorious in independent states; thus, British, French, and German workers supported their national governments. Meanwhile, the workers and peasants in regions under the Habsburg, Tsarist, and German empires—who, insofar as they adopted any identity beyond that of their town or village, might identify as Poles, Hungarians, Czechs, Slovaks, Slavs, Jews, etc.—tended to support movements which articulated overlapping national, social, ethnic, and religious identities (e.g., Colonel Piłsudski's Polish Socialist Party).

When viewed from the perspective of Laclau and Mouffe's discourse theory, the years 1914–1918 can be described as a period in which the hegemonic discourses of Empire and Nation were challenged by a multiplicity of discourses that articulated new subject positions through the reconstruction of suppressed national, social, religious, ethnic, and political identifications. Thus, due to these resurgent discursive representations, by 1918 the 'citizens' of the collapsing Habsburg, Tsarist, and German empires became able to identify themselves in completely new contexts as Polish Socialists, Ukrainian nationalists, Czechoslovaks, Zionists, Bundists, Bolsheviks, Orthodox Slavs, etc. The subject positions offered by these new or resurgent discourses appealed to composite attachments and loyalties by constructing collective identities in opposition to both the hegemonic discourses of the collapsing empires and through demarcating other discursive enemies (Bundism vs. Zionism, Bolsheviks vs. Mensheviks, anti-Semitism). As Hobsbawm observes, while nationalism was victorious in the Allied nation-states, in the defeated or semi-defeated states 'collapse led to social revolution'. [79] The collapse of hegemonic discourse and the emergence of new collective identities in 1917–1918 provide a very clear example of how articulatory practices extend beyond linguistic representations and are embodied in the dynamic restructuring of social relations.

Laclau and Mouffe's own example focuses on the precarious nature of class identification in the second half of the twentieth century, particularly in light of 'struggles in the Third World':[80] when the identities of social agents were no longer exclusively constituted by relations of production, the agent's identification with a class was challenged by the possible adoption of other subject positions.[81] Thus, a person could also identify with a nation, a gender, a generation, an ethnicity, a culture, a region, etc., and often these criss-crossing identifications come into conflict due to the primary antagonisms that are constitutive of discourse.

---

[78] Hobsbawm (1991, pp. 123–124).

[79] Hobsbawm (1991, p. 130).

[80] Laclau and Mouffe (1985, p. 13).

[81] Laclau and Mouffe (1985, p. 58).

In Mouffe's more explicitly Schmitt-inspired conception of 'the political', which draws on the latter's friend-enemy distinction, antagonism is assumed to be an 'ineradicable' dimension of social life: it 'belongs to our ontological condition'.[82] Thus, discourses are necessarily grounded in this primary, ever-present antagonism and draw on the affective forces of the 'passions'. Collective identities are conceived as discursive constructs formed relationally through the creation of a 'we' defined in opposition to a 'they'; the positive construction of a 'we' is bound up with the negative identification and representation of enemies.[83]

5.3.2.3 The Relevance to Fleck's Theory

In terms of Fleck's theory, the first obvious consequence of Laclau and Mouffe's conception of discourse is that Fleck's thought collectives have to be conceived as objects constituted by discourse. Therefore, when Fleck asserts 'As a research worker he is part of that community with which he works. [...] As a member of a political party, a social class, a nation, or even a race, he belongs to other collectives',[84] the general thought collectives of class, nation or race cannot be treated as entities that exist exterior to or independent of the productions of discourse. They have to be viewed as generalisations produced by discourses which, while initially created as discontinuous categories to impose order on the flux and complexity of interaction with the social, have become remote from any referent based in sensation through circulation processes, to the point that they have become the taken-for-granted stereotypes of common sense.

If it is accepted that Fleck's thought collectives can be treated as objects constituted by articulatory practices, then the thought styles they carry have to be conceived as subject to the processes of discourse formation. Thus conceived, thought styles are constituted as structured discursive totalities by articulating a differential position in relation to other thought styles with which they interact antagonistically while striving for hegemony. Thus, a thought style is identifiable precisely as a *style* because it distinguishes itself from *other styles*. This is particularly relevant when a new thought style emerges by modifying the prevailing thought style (e.g., the emergence of the Vesalian thought style from new Galenism—see Chap. 4).

Such modifications are proclaimed and treated as revolutions through the articulations that assert discontinuity in the discursive field. However, bearing in mind that a new thought style is bound to strive for hegemony in its field, research has to be conducted with caution—that is, with the awareness that the rhetorical layer of differential articulation masks fundamental continuities (e.g., Vesalius's loyalty to Galenic assumptions, as reflected in the maintenance of divisions, procedures, etc.). As Laclau and Mouffe repeatedly point out, a final 'suture' is an impossibility: a

[82] Mouffe (2005, p. 16).

[83] Mouffe (2005, pp. 1–15) (Dersley 2020).

[84] Fleck (1979, p. 45).

discourse cannot completely cut itself out as a totality and closed space; its identity always contains elements of the other that it defines itself against. No matter how vehemently a thought style may insist on its originality and independence from its predecessors, such an articulation cannot escape the fundamental instability and interaction involved in the differential assertion of identity.

Fleck's concept of thought styles can be adapted to investigate this discursive instability and fluidity. In their Fleck-inspired investigation of 'research styles', Afeltowicz and Sojak steer the concept of style away from uses that give the researcher 'a sense of ontological security' towards a mode of investigation that 'does not require strict divisions and unambiguous criteria: a style is something fluid, something that merges with others, goes from one into another, splits into new streams, and constantly fluctuates' (my translation).[85]

The second consequence of Laclau and Mouffe's theory of discourse is that more elements become methodologically accessible as external determinants of a thought style. While orthodox Marxism posits developments in productive forces and modes of production as primary, and intellectual labour as delayed and secondary, and while Foucauldian discourse theory posits non-discursive practices as the material-economic exterior of discourse, Laclau and Mouffe's conception of articulatory practices allows techno-economic developments to be conceived as partially determined by discourse, since these developments arise from processes that involve meaning systems and articulatory practices. Once we dispense with the model of one-directional determination imposed by the classic base/superstructure dichotomy and Foucauldian discursive/non-discursive distinction, a thought collective can be identified as triggering economic transformation and cultural change with the innovations of its thought style.

We can recall that one of the key characteristics of a thought style, as defined by Fleck, is the 'technical and literary style characteristic of the given system of knowledge'.[86] Style can thus be presumed to extend far beyond the styles of writing used to communicate conclusions among the esoteric circle and to share knowledge with the exoteric community. The concept of 'technical style' can be stretched to encompass genres, textual formats, means of production, transmission, and dissemination, and even the commercial and institutional infrastructure which supports and enables the communication of a thought style.

Thus, referring back to the intellectual unrest explored in Chap. 4, the commercial networks responsible for book production in Venice and Basel in the first half of the sixteenth century—with which Vesalius interacted intensively in the years 1538–1546—can be conceived as thought collectives whose articulatory practices (e.g., the messy business of producing books from paper and ink, experimentation with new printing technologies and formats, complex cross-border trade and communication between disparate social circles, marketing at book fairs and the creation of consumer demand, the adoption of deliberate strategies for dissemination of

[85] Afeltowicz and Sojak (2015, p. 30).

[86] Fleck (1979, p. 99).

knowledge) both triggered and were triggered by a revolution in social relations. In other words, the thought style of this collective was involved in a kind of feedback loop whereby new cultural practices stimulated the development of new modes of cultural production, which in turn stimulated new cultural practices, and so on.

The centrality of hegemony and antagonism to Laclau and Mouffe's theory also leads to the conclusion that, while these commercial networks relied on complex cooperation and the reciprocities of trade, their articulatory practices were ultimately driven by antagonism, which could be framed as a conflict over knowledge production and dissemination waged between the hegemonic thought collectives and emergent thought collectives. Laclau and Mouffe's abandonment of the centrality of class struggle also allows the conflict between thought collectives (or discursive formations) to be characterised as multi-layered and multi-dimensional: economic, intergenerational, institutional, regional, etc.

5.3.3 *Bourdieu's Field of Cultural Production*

Afeltowicz and Sojak have demonstrated that Fleck's conception of thought styles and Pierre Bourdieu's concept of habitus are compatible and complementary when applied in the reconstruction of historical phenomena.[87] A detailed comparison of Fleck's social epistemology and Bourdieu's sociology of practices obviously lies beyond the scope of the present work. For the purposes of these investigations, I will merely draw on Bourdieu's concept of the field of cultural production (1993) as a possible environment in which Fleck's thought collectives can be positioned.

With this restricted aim in mind, it is still necessary to consider the ontological status of Bourdieu's social classes and fields, since these entities can be viewed as overlapping Fleck's thought collectives and socially determined thought styles. In order to address these issues, brief consideration has to be given to both contemporaneous critiques of Bourdieu's theory—the charges of ambiguity, ambivalence, and muddle,[88] and of ontological and epistemological confusion[89]—and the recent embrace of Bourdieu's concepts by proponents of cognitive externalism[90] and cognitive sociology.[91]

Bourdieu's concept of field denotes and probes the external environment in which the habitus of agents is situated. In opposition to intertextual approaches, which treat culture as a system of interrelated, mutually referential texts and limit their analyses to the interior domain of symbolic representation, Bourdieu focuses on the practices that produce culture, and on the environment in which this production takes place. His concept of the field of cultural production is differentially

[87] Afeltowicz and Sojak (2015, pp. 41–53).

[88] Elster (1983, p. 70).

[89] Jenkins (1992, pp. 52–62).

[90] Fogle and Theiner (2018).

[91] Lizardo (2019).

defined in contrast to Foucault's conception of discourse, which Bourdieu characterizes as refusing 'to relate works in any way to their social positions of production, i.e., to positions occupied within the field of cultural production'.[92]

Thus, in opposition to Foucault's insistence that 'one remains within the dimension of discourse',[93] Bourdieu creates a model that describes and analyses the social environments in which discourses are produced, diffused, and embedded. The field of cultural production is one such environment: works of art and literature, as well as the auxiliary infrastructure constituted by media reviews and scholarly discourse, are the products of social and cultural practices that agents engage in as they compete for cultural capital.

Culture is thus conceived as a space of struggle and contestation, a space structured by previous struggles and conflicts, which entails that the possible positions and the relations between them have been established in advance of any agent's actions in the field. So, when agents engage in practices in the field of cultural production, they take positions in the already established 'spaces of possible', the space of position-takings (*prises de position*). Historical reconstructions of the circumstances surrounding the production of cultural works tend to omit consideration of the network of relations that structure these positions; these relations are not mentioned in contemporary accounts—they are just 'part of the self-evident givens of the situation'.[94] Bourdieu's model treats the elements that tend to be suppressed in traditional intertextual accounts as crucial for understanding how texts and authors acquired their status and came to occupy their current positions.

One example of the effects of such suppression is the 'consecration' of certain writers and texts: at the time when works that later became elevated to the status of masterpieces were produced, their authors defined their positions through competition on an equal footing with their peers who are now considered 'minor' or have been 'relegated to oblivion'.[95] Studying the field of cultural production at a specific time and place in history therefore entails reconstructing the competition that took place between the agents that produced cultural products, and attempting to recover the suppressed relations hidden underneath what became the self-evident givens.

Chapter 6 considers the cultural field disrupted by the practices of an oligarchic thought collective between 432 and 403 BC, and Plato's strategic representations of this collective. When considered in terms of Bourdieu's model, *The Republic* can be read as an Athenian cultural product that defines its position through explicit reference to the practices associated with Homeric poetry and Athenian tragedy, and through implicit reference to the statements of Ionian and Eleatic reflective thought; while dialogues like *Protagoras*, *Gorgias*, and *The Sophist* can be read as cultural products that articulate a distinctly Athenian thought style (*philosophia*) through the characterization, castigation and suppression of the foreign practices associated with the agents of sophistry.

---

[92] Bourdieu (1993, p. 33).

[93] Foucault (1989, p. 85).

[94] Bourdieu (1993, p. 31).

[95] Johnson (1993, p. 12).

The consecration of Plato's dialogues as the fundamental texts of Western thought obscured both the context in which they were articulated and their antagonistic functions. *The Republic* can be read as the heretical challenge of philosophy (i.e., the written representation of dialogical argumentation) to the orthodox educational practices conveyed through the oral recitation of epic poetry.[96] Meanwhile the Platonic dialogues that depict the sophists can be viewed as homogenizing and violent distortions of the heterogenous anti-dogmatic, and practical thought styles that had been circulating in Athens in the fifth and fourth centuries BC.[97] It can be argued that Plato's representations of the sophists had a specific function—to suppress the practices and texts of itinerant foreign thinkers, and the success of this strategy is indicated by the fact that the positions articulated by the sophists in the cultural field have to be reconstructed from Plato's negative depictions.

According to Bourdieu's model, the publication of a text involves the distribution of various forms of capital—economic, social, cultural, symbolic, educational. The publication and sale of a book does not merely produce economic capital as a surplus value after material and labour costs have been met: it can also increase the legitimacy of a form of knowledge production, increase an agent's power in an institution through generating social prestige, or make an institution itself more prestigious. Cultural and symbolic capital are largely dependent on the participants of the field believing in the legitimacy and value of the capital at stake.[98] Without recognition or belief, a book is merely ink and paper; a university—just bricks and mortar.

Jenkins argued that Bourdieu's model of the field 'is essentially one of equilibrium and stability', and that it struggles to account for social change, since the dispositions of habitus and the 'objective structures' of the field tend to reproduce relationships of domination.[99] I would argue that this interpretation is only possible if certain potentials of the field of cultural production—as indicated by Bourdieu in essays published between 1983–1989—are ignored. Bourdieu's concept of 'heretical break' signals that some participants in the cultural field are able, as newcomers, to '"get beyond" ["*dépassent*"] the dominant mode of thought and expression'—for instance, through parody—and that this can even be considered as '*emancipation*'.[100] The model of cultural production clearly suggests that heretical innovation can impact social relations. Culture and society are not merely reproduced as the same: there are breaks from orthodoxy, rejections of the dominant ideas, and successful introductions of rival modes of production.

Thus, to extrapolate, the appearance of a new book—or other textual innovations, such as a new style of public speaking (e.g., Socrates, Cicero), or a new way of delivering lectures (e.g., Vesalius)—can bring about a change in 'the space of

96 Havelock (1963).

97 Wallace (2007).

98 Jenkins (1992, pp. 57–58).

99 Jenkins (1992, pp. 57–58).

100 Bourdieu (1993, p. 31).

possibles' and upset the power relations in the field. A text—or even a new textual format made possible by new technology—can disrupt the field and displace the 'previously dominant productions'.[101] Similarly to Laclau and Mouffe's concepts of hegemony, discursive struggle, and the social, Bourdieu's model of cultural production depicts the social world as an arena of perpetual struggle—between power, forces, institutions, and agents. The notion of 'heretical break' and evidence of changes in cultural production and consumption suggest that this struggle is not always 'typically doomed to merely reproducing the constraints against which it is pitted', as Jenkins argues.[102]

Crucially, since Bourdieu abandoned any form of reductive economism which would reduce struggle in the field of cultural production to a struggle between social classes,[103] this allows such struggle to be conceived as occurring between different social groups and over different forms of capital (i.e., not just economic capital and the material means of production). When focusing on the twentieth-century art world and elitist literature in the nineteenth and twentieth centuries, Bourdieu defines the struggle in the cultural field as an intra-class conflict: heretical forms of cultural production are introduced by the dominated fraction of the dominant class, while orthodox forms are upheld by the dominant fraction of the dominant class. The conflict is framed predominantly as a contest for symbolic and cultural capital, rather than economic capital.

Bourdieu's model has considerable explanatory power when applied to actions that economism would struggle to account for. For instance, it explains why Vesalius sank his own money into the publication of his prohibitively expensive *Fabrica*, or why aristocrats like Francis Bacon and Robert Boyle devoted time and energy to scientific pursuits and projects that generated no financial gain: sacrificing or wasting economic capital can lead to a dramatic increase in an agent's cultural and symbolic capital.

Bourdieu's analysis refers to the classical descriptions of French class structure (working class, petite bourgeoisie, bourgeoisie, upper bourgeoisie, aristocracy) and frames the struggle in late nineteenth-century literature in terms of a conflict within the dominant class: the young generation of the bourgeoisie positions itself as 'avant-garde' or 'bohemian' in opposition to the commercial art of the consecrated generation of older artists.

This model of heretical position-taking within the dominant or ruling class can be applied to phenomena from other periods: in addition to Plato's attack on Homer and poetry mentioned above, which can be construed as the younger generation's rejection of the dominant modes of thought and expression, Vesalius's vitriolic criticism of Galenism—supported by a circle of loyal university students and allied with international commercial networks involved in the book trade—can be framed as the younger, cosmopolitan generation's rejection of the dominant modes of knowledge production and dissemination operating in the universities.

---

[101] Bourdieu (1993, pp. 31–32).

[102] Jenkins (1992, p. 61).

[103] Bourdieu (1993, p. 35).

The model can also be applied to the ideas and practices advocated by the proponents of *Bildung* in the German universities roughly between 1730 and 1820 which, while less 'heretical' than the scathing criticisms of Plato and Vesalius, can still be viewed as oppositional articulations—typically those of the lower middle-class *burghers* who populated the philosophy faculties, and who, as the dominated fraction, attempted to wrest control of the university—as an institution—away from the dominant social group of state administrators, lawyers, and theologians.

When applying categories such as 'dominant class' and 'burghers', it has to be borne in mind that the ontological status of Bourdieu's classes is a complex and thorny issue.[104] On the one hand, there are 'classes on paper',[105] i.e., theoretical representations used to carve up the social space. In this aspect, classes are to some extent arbitrary, in the sense that agents can be 'organized in accordance with other principles of division – ethnic, national etc.'.[106] On the other hand, Bourdieu posits 'a space of relations' and 'a field of forces' that exist and operate prior to and outside of subjective representation, which shape perception and even structure the 'objects of the social world'. Thus, in a complex sense, certain objects—e.g. institutions, social classes—can be said to exist independently of agents' perception of them, and also exterior to the constructions of the current discourses.

If Bourdieu's model is applied to Foucauldian discursive and non-discursive practices, and to Laclau and Mouffe's articulatory practices and material discourse, these phenomena become situated in a 'pre-structured space' that contains both current discourses and an exterior social world that has been structured by forces, relations and past discourse. In other words, the world 'outside' the constructions of the current discourse is a world that has been shaped and embedded with past discourse. The previous couplings and 'reciprocal structuring of habitus and field' entail that 'the present state of the field is the result of its own prior construction'.[107] While Laclau and Mouffe insist that 'every object is constituted as an object of discourse', meaning we cannot access objects except through the mediation of discourse, Bourdieu's model posits that such mediation encounters a world that has always already been structured by discourse and populated with socially constituted objects.

Bourdieu's contextualization of discourse posits that before agents perceive the social world through 'the labour of representation' and articulate their symbolic collective identities, a great deal of historical structuring has always already taken place:

> The perception of the social world is the product of a double social structuring: on the 'objective' side, this perception is socially structured because the properties attached to agents or institutions do not make themselves available to perception independently, but in combinations whose probability varies widely […]; on the 'subjective' side, it is structured because the schemes of perception and evaluation susceptible of being brought into

[104] For an example of a highly critical assessment of Bourdieu's conception of class, as presented in Distinction, see (Elster 1983).

[105] Bourdieu (1984, pp. 4–5), Bourdieu (1991, pp. 231–234).

[106] Bourdieu (1991, p. 233).

[107] Fogle and Theiner (2018, p. 230).

> operation at a given moment, including all those which are laid down in language, are the product of previous symbolic struggles and express, in a more or less transformed form, the state of symbolic relations of power.[108]

If this framework of double social structuring is applied to classes, when agents perceive themselves as belonging to a social class, or perceive other agents as belonging to the same or other social classes, they draw on pre-existing concepts and categories that were produced in previous symbolic/discursive struggles (the 'subjective' side of the social structuring), but at the same time this perception is shaped by the environment of forces and relations that pre-structure the social world (the 'objective' side of the social structuring).

Thus, while an agent's perception of the social world is necessarily subjective and mediated by discourse, the position from which the agent perceives this world can be described 'objectively', because it is possible to situate the agent within an environment that is independent of their subjective perception, and to identify the factors (e.g., relations, social position, discourses) that determine how the agent perceives the social world.

To begin bringing Bourdieu's model into alignment with Fleck's theory, it can be said that the position an agent occupies in a field is determined by non-arbitrary elements. An agent's economic capital can be subjected to statistical analysis, and thus be measured and compared with other agents who have similar properties attached to them (type of profession, income, educational background, the place of residence etc.). Although the choice of measure is arbitrary, since other categories (e.g. gender, ethnicity) and other forms of capital (e.g. social, cultural) could be the main focus of the analysis, and because the category of social class divides the continuous field of the social into discontinuous aggregates, the *relationships* identified between agents on the basis of arbitrary measures are not themselves arbitrary.

As was mentioned in Chap. 3, Fleck argued that the fact that oxygen has the atomic weight of 16 is conventional and arbitrary, but that if this measure is related to the atomic weight of hydrogen, i.e. 1.008, the ratio of the two weights 'is a passive element of knowledge'.[109] In other words, *the active constructs of a thought style do not determine the ratio discovered through the use of these constructs*. In a similar way, Bourdieu's model suggests that *the relationships between the positions agents occupy in a field are not arbitrary*: no amount of discursive manipulation will equate the social standing of a homeless person with that of a superyacht-owning oligarch, even though the terms 'homeless' and 'oligarch' are arbitrary and conventional.

Thus Bourdieu's frequent uses of the word objective—e.g., 'objective power relations', 'the objective structure of the social world', 'the objective world',[110] 'objective positions', 'objective competition between positions', 'objective

[108] Bourdieu (1991, p. 234).

[109] Fleck (1979, p. 83).

[110] Bourdieu (1991, pp. 229–240).

chances', 'objective probabilities'[111]—can be viewed as designating epistemic content that contains elements exterior to the active constructions of the perceiving or cognizing subject. In this sense, Bourdieu's objective relations refer to similar external determinants to those indicated by Fleck's passive elements.

Bourdieu's objective world can be defined as objective in two key senses: first, the positions, power relations and structures of this world always already exist prior to a given agent's perception of the field. Second, this world in which the agent finds itself is populated with socially constituted objects that are both the result of previous discursive struggles and the embodiment of current power relations. Socially constituted objects—art galleries, universities, libraries, law courts, parliament, etc.—are recognized as such by agents, who accept and perpetuate the correct practices associated with each object and its field. At the same time, as the remnants of previous conflicts, such objects also perpetuate the relationships manifested in the field, and are often the instruments through which the ruling class maintains its position of dominance.

Following Jon Elster's criticism of Bourdieu's allegedly ambivalent, ambiguous and muddled theoretical framework,[112] Jenkins argued in the early 1990s that Bourdieu's writings are plagued by contradictions between ontology and epistemology—i.e., issues associated with how the social world is constituted are conflated with issues associated with how we know or explain this world. Thus, for Jenkins it is not clear whether Bourdieu's field is a 'real' entity, a common-sensical category, or a purely analytical concept.[113]

I would suggest that Bourdieu's concept of double structuring allows a field to be conceived of as both a real entity (a component of the pre-structured objective world of forces, relations and positions) *and* a partially arbitrary analytical concept (a category used to describe aspects of the agent's environment). Bourdieu's model is necessarily ambiguous because—like Marx's productive forces, Fleck's conception of passive elements, Foucault's indication of non-discursive practices, and Laclau and Mouffe's articulatory practices—it attempts the seemingly impossible: to get outside thought to think the external determinants of thought; to represent from within discourse the external social environment in which discourse is produced.

In stark contrast to Elster and Jenkins' near-contemporaneous criticism of Bourdieu's work, Nikolaus Fogle and Georg Theiner's recent juxtaposition of Bourdieu's sociology of practice with the theses of cognitive externalism shows how Bourdieu's theoretical apparatus can be shorn of ontological and epistemological muddle and applied to enhance 'externalist accounts of culture and society'.[114] Stemming from the analytic tradition, philosophy of mind, and cognitive science, the various strands of cognitive externalism are united in the conviction that human organisms and brains can be straightforwardly described as being situated in a world replete with externalized cognition.

---

[111] Bourdieu (1993, pp. 29–64).

[112] Elster (1983, p. 70).

[113] Jenkins (1992).

[114] Fogle and Theiner (2018, p. 221).

Thus phenomena like language, pen and paper, calculators, computers and smartphones can be conceived as tools that extend cognition beyond 'the boundaries of skin and skull', as Andy Clark and David Chalmers put it in their key contribution to the externalist debate,[115] while libraries, museums and universities can be viewed as repositories of social knowledge that constitute socio-cultural extensions of the human brain, which enable agents to accumulate and bank cultural capital.[116]

A pertinent externalist debate arose between Clark's extended epistemology and Edwin Hutchins' distributed cognition. Hutchins' critique of Clark's *Supersizing the Mind* (2008) argues that Clark, despite indicating the role of cognitive ecosystems, ultimately remains bound to 'the Hypothesis of Organism Centred Cognition'.[117] Put simply, Clark's model of cognitive externalism tends to be based on individual mental representations, such as the classic example of Otto, who suffers from Alzheimer's and uses a notebook to replace his biological memory.[118] Otto strategically extends *his* individual cognition beyond *his* skull and skin into a tool in *his* environment.

Hutchins argues that this individualistic framework neglects the role of culture in organizing and distributing cognition: in Clark's model, culture is conceived as static, and Hutchins suggests that 'cognitive science has adopted ways of speaking and thinking that render cultural practices invisible'.[119] Instead of organism centred cognition, Hutchins advocates a mental flip that would focus on *cultural practices* as the drivers and carriers of 'enculturated cognition'.

Hutchins defines cultural practices as

> the things people do and their ways of being in the world. A practice is cultural if it exists in a cognitive ecology such that it is constrained by or coordinated with the practices of other persons. Above all else, *cultural practices are the things people do in interaction with one another*" Virtually all external representations are produced by cultural practices. All forms of language are produced by and in cultural practices.[120] (emphasis in original).

Thus, speaking, reading, and writing are classed as cultural practices, as are ways of perceiving the world. In contrast to (his framing of) Clark's model of mental representation and static culture, Hutchins describes cultural practices as 'fully embodied skills', and culture as the result of 'dynamic historical processes' through which human cognition has constructed 'assemblies' or 'products' which have shaped the environment and created cognitive ecosystems. Human organisms act in environments that have been modified and organized by other brains. As a result of this 'mental flip', the contributions of an individual brain and its mental representations to externalized cognition become rather negligible: the real forces that assemble and organize cognitive ecosystems are cultural practices.

[115] Clark and Chalmers (1998).

[116] Fogle and Theiner (2018, p. 234).

[117] Hutchins (2011, p. 440).

[118] Clark and Chalmers (1998, pp. 12–13).

[119] Hutchins (2011, p. 445).

[120] Hutchins (2011, p. 440).

Hutchins' emphasis on cultural practices, embodied skills, assemblies and cognitive niches clearly resonates with Bourdieu's focus on practices and his concept of the field. Hutchins' characterization of assemblies as culturally constructed products[121] can be viewed as designating the same kind of entities as Bourdieu's concept of social objects (i.e., institutions). Fogle and Theiner also draw on other recent contributions that are compatible with Bourdieu's theoretical apparatus, such as cultural niche construction theory (NCT), and the concepts of scaffolding and entrenchment as used in educational theory, to argue that cognitive processes both modify the environment and are modified by it.

Cognition is externalized, distributed, and stored throughout the environment in which agents find themselves (e.g., in the cultural practice of language, in repositories and centres of knowledge production, in the techno-mediation of the Internet), but agents are also able to exploit these cognitive resources in order to shape their environment. Thus understood, cognitive externalism can posit that the cognition and cultural practices of habitus are coupled with the cognition-rich environments of the field in positive feedback loops of co-constitution, co-dependence and mutual modification. It bears emphasizing that this model stands in stark contrast to the classical models of one-directional determination (economic base > cultural superstructure, non-discursive > discursive practices).

In Fogle and Theiner's reading, cognitive externalism can enrich Bourdieu's sociology through rigorous and explicit focus on cognition and epistemology, which were neglected in Bourdieu's writing due to his reaction against 'scholastic' intellectualism and his emphasis on practical knowledge and embodied skills. Thus, when viewed through the lens of cognitive externalism, habitus is coupled to a field which— in addition to being pre-structured by forces, positions, and relations—is pre-organized by the cognition embodied and distributed in bio-external cultural practices. At the same time, cognitive externalism, which has tended to neglect explorations of culture and society, benefits from a Bourdieu-inspired focus on cognition as an aspect of habitus: i.e., as practical and embodied forms of knowledge acquired through socialization and acculturation.[122]

Bourdieu's theoretical model shows that the socially extended cognition that is distributed through the environment, which shapes and is shaped by habitus, is not politically neutral. From the perspective of the agent, cognition is a differential activity that identifies agents with other agents in similar positions and that distinguishes them from other groups; from the perspective of the field, it was externalized cognition that pre-structured the environment and that is instrumental in maintaining relations of dominance within the social space.

A particularly refreshing aspect of this cognitive externalist reading of Bourdieu, as well as Omar Lizardo's treatment of Bourdieu as a cognitive sociologist who can be interpreted as advocating a form of 'embodied cognition',[123] is that Bourdieu's

[121] Hutchins (2011, p. 442).

[122] Fogle and Theiner (2018, p. 222).

[123] Lizardo (2019).

theoretical apparatus can be used to escape from the binaries of the Western rationalist tradition (e.g., mind/body, nature/culture) and the reflexive paralysis that characterizes the post-Kantian critical tradition (e.g., the prohibitions and hesitation regarding reference to the world outside of representation).

The restriction epitomized in Foucault's dictum 'one remains within the dimension of discourse/*On demeure dans le dimension du discours*'[124] is circumvented by positioning discursive representation in socio-cultural contexts that are full of externalized and distributed cognition. Cognition is matter-of-factly treated as embodied in both the physical, material bodies of agents and in 'a variety of extra-personal sites'.[125] In such cognitivist approaches, the residual hesitation and reflexive entanglement that is found in Bourdieu's writing, due to the legacy of structuralist discourse analysis, is simply discarded, and the muted elements of embodiment and externalization are brought to the fore.[126]

To sum up, Fleck's thought collectives and thought styles can be situated within Bourdieuan fields of cultural production if such fields are conceived as the result of the interaction between, on the one hand, cognizing thought collectives that represent their environment and articulate positions with the concepts and categories of their thought styles, and, on the other hand, a cognized, already-cognition-rich environment consisting of socially constituted objects, as well as the structures, forces and relations which determine 'objective' positions—objective in the sense that cognition does not determine the relations between them.

Thus, Fleck's 'passive elements of knowledge', as the non-arbitrary relations encountered in the cognized, can be reconceived as partially produced by Bourdieu's fields. In addition to the 'natural' objects constructed by a thought style, such as disease entities, species, anatomical organs etc., whose 'passive elements' are in no way generated by a Bourdieuan symbolic field, thought collectives are also located in specific positions in the field of cultural production, and are thus in the midst of cultural objects and the social structures produced by earlier and other cognizing agents and groups.

In other words, Fleck's thought collectives perceive and cognize both 'natural phenomena' (which become constructed as entities like bacteria) and 'cultural products' (whose elements already contain earlier constructions, e.g., language, discourse, concepts, externalized cognition, other thought styles etc.). The 'passive elements' of cultural products are thus formed from both non-arbitrary relations (Bourdieu's 'objective' social positions) and the results of earlier externalized active construction.

Just as the objects constructed from natural phenomena are the result of mutual interaction between the enculturated cognition of a thought style and non-arbitrary perceptual content, there is mutual interaction when a thought style relates to the externalized cognition distributed through the pre-structured cultural field.

[124] Foucault (1980), Foucault (1989, p. 85).

[125] Lizardo (2019).

[126] Lizardo (2019).

Bourdieu's concept of double structuring entails that, on the subjective side, a thought collective discursively and differentially represents itself and other thought collectives, while being discursively and differentially represented by other self-representing thought collectives; and that, on the objective side, these representations are determined by the position the members of the thought collective occupy in a pre-structured field (thought of cultural production, for instance).

Bourdieu's theory also posits the underlying forces driving in this double structuring: the cognitive interaction and symbolic-discursive representational struggle occurring between networks/thought collectives in the field of cultural production ultimately concerns the distribution of cultural capital. When a thought collective articulates a new (heretical) thought style in the form of utterances and publications that are distinguished from the (orthodox) style and products of the dominant thought collective in the field, what is ultimately at stake is a redistribution of social and cultural capital from one thought collective to another. Such redistribution is manifested in book sales, the widespread acceptance of a scientific theory, the consecration of artists, scientists and philosophers, the funding and patronage of scientific societies, the control, transformation and creation of educational institutions, the establishment of canons, schools and traditions.

While Fleck's theory of thought collectives and styles sheds light on the social determinants of perception and cognition and indicates the factors that are involved in the emergence and transmission of new ways of thinking, Bourdieu's theory provides conceptual tools for exploring the external factors that position thought collectives and shape their styles.

5.4 Conclusion

This chapter developed a flexible methodological framework by combining Fleck's comparative epistemology with functionalist-ideological, discourse-theoretical, and sociological perspectives to investigate cultural change. It synthesized Fleck's key concepts—thought collectives and styles, proto-ideas, esoteric/exoteric circles, and intellectual unrest—with Marx-inspired functionalist notions of ideology and Foucauldian discourse analysis, enabling the investigation of how ideas both shape and are shaped by broader relations of dominance.

The discussion also incorporated Laclau and Mouffe's concept of articulatory practices to demonstrate how social identities and knowledge are discursively constructed, and adapted Bourdieu's notion of the field of cultural production to situate these processes within specific institutional and historical contexts. By tracking how ideas migrate, embed themselves, and generate heretical breaks in otherwise stable intellectual environments, the methodology aims to capture the interplay between discursive strategies, power structures, and the active/passive elements of cognition.

The chapter has assembled a versatile toolkit for analysing source texts, identifying extratextual determinants of knowledge production, and tracing the complex network of external forces—economic, political, and technological—that shape evolving thought styles. The subsequent chapters of this thesis attempt to apply Fleck's theory of thought collectives and thought styles to account for cultural change, using the following methodology:

1. Fleck's key concepts—thought collectives, thought styles, esoteric and exoteric circles, collective mood, intellectual unrest, proto-ideas, the circulation of ideas—can be applied in the direct interpretation of source texts (including translated texts).
2. However, it is necessary to support the interpretation of source texts with historical and cultural studies to consider the broader contexts in which these source texts emerged and in which thought collectives operated. References to scholarly accounts of these contexts must be made with caution, as contextual facts are constructed through the interpretations of the authors' thought styles, which, of course, are not neutral.
3. The functionalist conception of ideology (Rosen and Wolff 1996; Žižek 2012) can be applied to explain the relations of dominance involved in the articulation and transmission of a thought style.
4. The concept of discourse is necessary for the application of Fleck's concepts: firstly, to position Fleck's active, socially-conditioned elements of cognition within a system of relations and practices that defines possible subject positions (Foucault, 1969); and secondly, to reflexively treat thought collectives as discursive constructs, and thought styles as differential articulations (Laclau and Mouffe 1985).
5. The concepts of material discourse (Laclau and Mouffe 1985) and the field of cultural production (Bourdieu 1993) allow Fleckian thought collectives and thought styles to be conceived as situated within environments that are already structured with meaning and externalized cognition (Fogle and Theiner 2018). Thought collectives and thought styles are both shaped by and modify these pre-structured environments, and cultural change arises when—as a result of Fleckian factors such as intellectual unrest and the circulation of ideas—a heretical articulation challenges the orthodox, dominant thought style.

The following chapters should be viewed as an experimental and always provisional application of Fleck's concepts in an attempt to account for cultural change. The application is made with acute awareness of the fact that Fleck's model lacks a criterion for evaluating the accounts provided by alternative or conflicting thought styles. In this regard, Leszek Nowak's concept of explanatory power may prove useful. Nowak's idealizational theory of science suggests a model for evaluating competing theories (paradigms) in the social sciences: consideration should be given to 'the proportion of facts explained by the theory to the facts in a given domain'.[127] During the subsequent chapters, a factor that can always be borne in mind is whether the application of Fleck's concepts sheds light on new facts or new aspects of accepted facts in the domain of cultural change.

[127] Nowak (2012, p. 38).

References

Afeltowicz Ł, Sojak R (2015) Arystokraci i rzemieślnicy. Synergia stylów badawczych. Wydawnictwo Naukowe Uniwersytetu Mikołaja Kopernika, Torun

Althusser L (2014) On the Reproduction of Capitalism (1995) (trans: Brewster B). Verso, London

Anderson P (1974) Passages from antiquity to feudalism. NLB, London

Ando C (2011) From Republic to Empire. In: Peachin M (ed) The Oxford handbook of social relations in the roman world. OUP, Oxford, pp 37–68

Bacon F (2000) In: Jardine L, Silverthorne M (eds) The New Organon (1620). CUP, Cambridge

Banks J, Rauschenberg R (1964) A Letter of Sir Joseph banks describing the life of Daniel Solander. Isis 55(1):62–67

Blair A, von Greyerz K (2020) Introduction. In: Blair A, von Greyerz K (eds) Physico-theology religion and science in Europe, 1650–1750. John. Hopkins University Press, Baltimore, pp 1–20

Borck C (2004) Message in a bottle from 'the crisis of reality': on Ludwik Fleck's interventions for an open epistemology. Stud Hist Philosophy Sci Part C Stud Hist Philosophy Biol Biomed Sci 35(3):447–464

Bourdieu P (1984) Espace social et genèse des "classes". Actes de la recherche en sciences sociales. Vol. 52–53, Le travail politique, 3–14

Bourdieu P (1991) Language and symbolic power. Polity Press, Cambridge

Bourdieu P (1993) The field of cultural production. Columbia University Press, New York

Brunt P (1971) Social conflicts in the Roman Republic. W. W. Norton, New York

Clark A, Chalmers D (1998) The extended mind. Analysis 58(1):7–19

Cohen G (1978) Karl Marx's theory of history a defence. Princeton University Press, Princeton

Cook J (2003) The journals. Penguin, London

Derrida J (1981) Plato's pharmacy (trans: Johnson B). In: Dissemination (pp. 61–171). The Athlone Press, London

Dersley S (2020) A discourse analysis of news media articles on the polish 'Rule of Law Crisis'. comparative legilinguistics. Int J Legal Commun 44(1):4–49

Elster J (1983) Sour grapes. CUP, Cambridge

Fara P (2003) Sex, botany and empire. Icon Books, Cambridge

Fleck L (1979) Genesis and development of a scientific fact [1935]. The University of Chicago Press, Chicago

Fleck L (1986b) On the crisis of 'Reality' [1929]. In: Cognition and fact. Boston studies in the philosophy of science, vol 87. Springer, Dordrecht. https://doi.org/10.1007/978-94-009-4498-5_3

Fleck L (1986c) Scientific observation and perception in general [1935]. In: Cognition and fact. Boston studies in the philosophy of science, vol 87. Springer, Dordrecht. https://doi.org/10.1007/978-94-009-4498-5_4

Fleck L (1986d) The problem of epistemology [1936]. In: Cognition and fact. Boston studies in the philosophy of science, vol 87. Springer, Dordrecht. https://doi.org/10.1007/978-94-009-4498-5_5

Fogle N, Theiner G (2018) The "Ontological Complicity" of Habitus and field: bourdieu as an externalist. In: Pritchard D et al (eds) Socially extended epistemology. Oxford University Press, Oxford, pp 220–252

Foucault M (1980) Truth and power. In: Gordon C (ed) Power/knowledge. Selected interviews and other writings 1972–1977. Harvester Press, Hemel Hempstead, pp 109–133

Foucault M (1989) The archaeology of knowledge (1969) (trans: Sheridan Smith AM). Routledge, London and New York

Havelock EA (1963) Preface to plato. Harvard University Press, Cambridge

Hobsbawm E (1991) Nations and nationalism since 1780: programme, myth, reality. CUP, Cambridge

Hutchins E (2011) Enculturating the supersized mind. Philos Stud 152:437–446

Jenkins R (1992) Pierre Bourdieu. Routledge, London

Johnson R (1993) Editor's introduction. In: Bourdieu P (ed) The field of cultural production. Columbia University Press, New York, pp 1–25
Jorgensen M, Phillips L (2002) Discourse analysis as theory and method. Sage Publications, London
Koerner L (1999) Linnaeus: nature and nation. Harvard University Press, Cambridge Mass
Laclau E, Mouffe C (1985) Hegemony and socialist strategy. Verso, London and New York
Lenin V (2010) Materialism and Empirio-criticism. Collected Works Volume 14 1908–1909. Progress Publishers, Moscow
Lizardo O (2019) Pierre Bourdieu as cognitive sociologist. In: Brekus WE, Ignatow G (eds) The Oxford handbook of cognitive sociology. Oxford University Press, Oxford
Mach E (1900) Principles of the theory of heat (trans: Jourdain PEB, Heath AED). Reidel, Dordrecht
Marx K (1987) A contribution to the critique of political economy (1859). In: Marx K, Engels F (eds) Collected works, vol. 29. International Publishers, New York, pp 257–389
Marx K (1990) Capital Volume I (trans: Fowkes B). Penguin, London
Marx K, Engels F (1971) Werke, Band 13, 7. Auflage 1971, unveränderter Nachdruck der 1. Auflage 1961. Dietz Verlag, Berlin
Marx K, Engels F (1975) Collected Works, vol 5. International Publishers, New York
Mouffe C (2005) On the political. Routledge, Abingdon
Nowak L (2012) On the hidden unity of social and natural sciences. In: Brzechczyn K, Paprzycka K (eds) Thinking about provincialism in thinking (Poznań Studies in the Philosophy of the Sciences and the Humanities, vol. 100) pp 15–50
Rosen M, Wolff J (1996) The problem of ideology. Proc Aristotelian Soc Suppl Vol 70:209–241
Said EW (2003) Orientalism. Penguin, London
Schmidt J (ed) (1996) What is enlightenment. University of California Press, Berkeley
Wallace RW (2007) Plato's sophists, intellectual history after 450, and sokrates. In: The Cambridge companion to the age of pericles. CUP, Cambridge, pp 215–237
Zittel C (2010) The politics of cognition: genesis and development of Ludwik Fleck's 'Comparative Epistemology'. In: Epple M, Zittel C (eds) Science as cultural practice: Vol. I: cultures and politics of research from the early modern period to the age of extremes. De Gruyter (A), Berlin, pp. 183–200. https://doi.org/10.1524/9783050087092.183
Žižek S (2012) The spectre of ideology. In: Žižek S (ed) Mapping ideology. Verso, London, pp 1–33

Chapter 6
The Emergence of Philosophy as a Cultural Practice in Ancient Greece

Abstract This chapter examines the emergence of philosophy as a cultural practice in ancient Greece by analysing the socio-political forces that shaped new modes of inquiry and discursive engagement. Building on existing critiques of the 'myth to logos' paradigm, it challenges triumphalist narratives that obscure the argumentative structures and problem-solving strategies evident in earlier texts, such as Hesiod's poetry. Drawing on Fleck's theory of thought collectives and thought styles, the chapter reconstructs how distinct collectives—including oligarchic networks in Athens, thinkers who came to be labelled as sophists, and early philosophical schools—debated the roles of gods, poetry, and power within the polis.

A central argument is that Plato's *Republic* responds to Athens' cultural trauma following its defeat in the Peloponnesian War, the oligarchic coups, and decades of civil strife. By analysing key Platonic dialogues (*Charmides*, *Phaedrus*, *Republic*) alongside the texts of the 'Old Oligarch' and Thucydides, the chapter identifies shared preoccupations with control over manual labour, cultural production, and social hierarchy. Plato's assertion of philosophy's supremacy over other modes of discourse—such as poetry and rhetoric—is framed as a strategic adaptation to this unsettled context, attempting a broader realignment of elite interests and discursive practices.

The chapter uses Fleck's framework to show how philosophy was articulated in response to a prolonged period of intellectual unrest and socio-political conflict. It argues that Plato's dialogues articulate a desire to establish philosophy as a controlling discourse—one that could suppress and pathologize rival thought styles and assert itself as the dominant epistemic force within Athens' contested cultural landscape.

6.1 Scope and Aims

Ancient Greece is the classic, prototypical example of cultural change. Diverse scholarly traditions—including academic philosophy, classical philology, historiography, cultural studies, and the philosophy of science—have identified and framed

S. Dersley, *Thought Collectives and Cultural Change*, Living Signs of Law 1,
https://doi.org/10.1007/978-3-031-97431-1_6

two key epistemic shifts that occurred between 700 and 350 BC in Greek-speaking cities and colonies. Through complex layers of sedimented discursive practice, these epistemic shifts have been variously identified, constructed, and positioned as foundational to Western thought and as catalysts for the subsequent development of European culture. The two key changes can be broadly identified as the emergence of 'naturalist' thinking in Ionia during the sixth century BC and the self-differentiation of Athenian philosophy in the fifth and fourth centuries BC.

There is broad scholarly consensus that 'naturalist', 'scientific', or 'non-mythological' thinking emerged in Miletus and the Ionian colonies in the course of the seventh and sixth centuries. Scholars have variously reconstructed this shift as 'the discovery of the mind/intellect',[1] 'the birth of philosophy',[2] the emergence of 'rational thought',[3] 'the Ionian Enlightenment',[4] and 'the Presocratic Enlightenment'.[5] The scant surviving textual fragments have been interpreted as evidence that a qualitative shift occurred in the style of thinking of a specific epistemic community—namely, the elite 'knowledge specialists'[6] in Miletus and the Ionian colonies. However, this shift within a specific epistemic community was soon reframed as a broader transformation in 'Greek thought'.

The self-differentiation of Athenian philosophy in the fifth and fourth centuries BC is identified as a response to Ionian, Eleatic, and sophist thought. This articulation is framed either as a discontinuity, dubbed the 'Socratic caesura', or as a continuation, particularly through Aristotle's appropriation, which suggests teleological development rather than a rupture.[7]

The initial emergence of 'naturalist' thinking in Ionia was famously framed as a transition from *mythos* to *logos*—from a religious, mythopoeic mentality to philosophical-scientific rational thought. In authoritative accounts and analyses of the history of philosophy and science, this shift was treated as an absolute discontinuity by scholars such as Wilhelm Nestle (1940), W.K.C. Guthrie (1962), G.S. Kirk and J.E. Raven (1957), and Jonathan Barnes (1979). Guthrie dramatically framed it as 'pre-philosophical man' suddenly becoming 'philosophical man'.[8]

However, significant works of scholarship have complicated and challenged this simplistic binary transition 'from myth to logos'. For instance, F.M. Cornford's *From Religion to Philosophy* (1912) emphasized the persistent presence of mythological and religious elements in Ionian-Milesian thought. Drawing on Durkheim-inspired approaches, Cornford argued that religious beliefs continued to influence early philosophical thinking. Similarly, F.J. Teggart (1947) highlighted that rational

---

[1] Snell (1953).

[2] Guthrie (1962, p. 29).

[3] Barnes (1979, p. 3).

[4] Schrodinger (1954, pp. 53–68).

[5] Popper (1998, pp. 8–10).

[6] Sandywell (1996, p. 104).

[7] Laks (2018, pp. 1–18).

[8] Guthrie (1962, p. 26).

arguments and justifications can be identified in 'pre-philosophical' texts, such as Hesiod's poetry, and other scholars like E.R. Dodds (1951) and Eric A. Havelock (1978) explored rational elements in pre-Platonic works. G.E. Lloyd (1979) traced the emergence of critical attitudes and rational argumentation in Greek culture, noting the empirical research initiated in nascent medicine and astronomy, which suggests that rational thought was developing in various fields simultaneously. Additionally, J. P. Vernant (1982) argued that Greek rationality appeared primarily due to new social relations and practices that emerged in the *polis* (city-state). These practices were subsequently codified in laws and externalized in political institutions. According to Vernant, the rationality articulated in Greek philosophy reflects a deeper rationalism already distributed throughout the social realm.[9]

From the perspective of Fleck's theory, at first glance, the emergence of an ostensibly 'naturalist philosophy' in Miletus in the seventh and sixth centuries BC might suggest a straightforward change in the thought style of a specific thought collective, which was subsequently transmitted from the colonies back to the mainland, resulting in a more general change in the 'Greek thought style'. However, cursory analysis reveals that this change is complex and entangled. All the utterances and statements authored by representatives of the Milesian thought collective were preserved, filtered, represented, and interpreted by later 'schools', particularly Athenian ones. These schools had their own agendas, and their reconstructions are deeply intertwined with discursive struggles focused on the control of cultural production and the distribution of cultural capital.

Reconstructing Ancient Greek thought collectives requires attention to the strategies and struggles embodied in these representations. It is especially important to examine the role of specific Athenian thought collectives in the filtering and transmission of Ionian cultural production. Scholarly accounts accept that the Homeric epics, originally Ionian poems, were standardized in Athens during the sixth century, a process known as the Pisistratean Recension. In the process, a thin layer of Attic diction was added to the dominant Ionic dialect.[10] By the fifth and fourth centuries, Athenian discursive practices and strategies aimed at representing and transmitting non-Attic thought had become more aggressive. The self-differentiation of Athenian philosophy, as articulated by thought collectives associated with Socrates, Plato, and Aristotle, necessitated a critique of the practices linked to Homeric poetry, the suppression of itinerant and 'foreign' sophist thought through homogenizing and negative representations, and the reinterpretation of Ionian naturalism through an Attic interpretative lens.

Evidence of this conflict is found in surviving texts. In Plato's works, such as *Republic*, Socrates is dramatically represented attacking Homer's epics, Hesiod's poetry, and Attic tragedy throughout the dialogue. In *Phaedo* (96a8, 97c–99d), Socrates criticizes 'natural science' and Anaxagoras's explanations of reasons/causes. *Timaeus* presents a mathematical-teleological cosmology, which can be

---

[9] Cornford (1912), Teggart (1947), Dodds (1951), Havelock (1978), Lloyd (1979), Vernant (1982).
[10] Finkelberg (2020, pp. 182–196).

viewed as a response to the Milesian 'physical' cosmology and Democritus's atomic theory. Plato's texts consistently attack, denigrate, and exclude the practices and knowledge production associated with alien *metoikoi* (resident foreigners)—often rendered in English as 'metics'—and sophists, particularly those involved in maintaining and manipulating the power of the *dēmos*.[11] Additionally, Aristotle's *Metaphysics* (983b) includes textual reconstructions of 'the first philosophers', further shaping the understanding of earlier thought, often through an Athenian lens.

Thus, rather than identifying a straightforward shift in thought styles, the application of Fleck's theory necessitates constant uncovering of layers, revealing a complex and entangled field of cultural production. Fleck's open epistemology resists reductive explanations, encouraging us to approach thought collectives as evolving through dynamic interaction. While certain thought collectives—such as the 'Oligarchic thought style' articulated in the texts of Thucydides, the Old Oligarch, Aristophanes, and Plato—can be reconstructed with some clarity and confidence, other thought styles remain obscured, accessible only through strategic representations shaped by Athenian collectives that achieved cultural hegemony through their own discursive strategies and the transmission of later collectives and styles (e.g., Cicero's Roman philosophy, German philology, and German academic philosophy in the eighteenth and nineteenth centuries).

The aim here is not to find evidence that validates Fleck's theory, but to use it as a lens through which new aspects of intellectual interactions and conflicts can be uncovered. Fleck's framework exposes how the transmission of ideas was not a neutral process but one of reconfiguration, suppression, and contestation. As a result, many thought styles are partially hidden or distorted, discernible only in the traces left by their opponents. Any attempt to reconstruct the evolution of thought in Ancient Greece must engage with this complexity, and Fleck's theory is particularly useful in this regard, as it highlights the contingent, contested, and multi-layered nature of epistemic change, providing a richer understanding of the cultural forces and power struggles at play.

6.2 The 'from Myth to Logos Paradigm'

As Richard Buxton noted, for an extended period, German and Anglophone scholars found it unproblematic to interpret the reconstructed, fragmentary statements of Thales and Anaximander as evidence that ancient Greek civilization had 'undergone a development from myth to reason'.[12] Following the central thesis of Nestle's *Vom Mythos zum Logos* (1940), scholars such as Guthrie (1953) and Kirk, Raven and

[11] Transliterations follow standard conventions using macrons to indicate long vowels (ē, ō), and are italicized when used analytically. Greek terms are occasionally accompanied by the original script where relevant for clarity or precision.

[12] Buxton (1999).

Schofield (1983) propagated the triumphalist 'from… to' account of Greek thought which posits the occurrence of a 'fundamental shift towards rationality'.[13]

According to Buxton, this scholarly paradigm identified a broad trend across various forms of Greek thought during the sixth and fifth centuries BC—now categorized under disciplines such as 'philosophy, historiography, medicine, and technology'—where mythical or mythopoeic explanations were gradually replaced by rational ones. While there may have been debates over the pace or permanence of this shift, there was little doubt within the scholarship that such a transformation occurred, with Thales positioned as its 'standard-bearer'.[14]

Thus, according to the 'from … to' perspective, the following translated excerpts can be treated as evidence that a clear shift occurred in the way that certain Greek-speaking people perceived and thought about the world:

i) Homer, *The Iliad*, Book XV (190-199) – c. 800 BC.

The world was split three ways. Each received his realm.
When we shook the lots I drew the sea, my foaming eternal home,
and Hades drew the land of the dead engulfed in haze and night
and Zeus drew the heavens, the clouds and the high clear sky,
but the earth and Olympus heights are common to us all.[15]

ii) Hesiod, *Theogony* – c. 800-700 BC

And Earth first bore starry Heaven, equal to herself, to cover her on every side, and to be an ever-sure abiding-place for the blessed gods. (126)[16]

iii) Thales c. 624 – c. 545 BC

Thales, the founder of this school of philosophy, says the permanent entity is water (which is why he also propounded that the earth floats on water). (Aristot. *Met.* 1.983b)[17]

iv) Anaximander c. 610–c. 546 BC

Anaximander said that the first principle and element of existing things was the boundless; it was he who originally introduced this name for the first principle. He says that it is not water or any of the other so-called elements, but something different from them, something boundless by nature, which is the source of all the heavens and the worlds in them. And he says that the original sources of existing things are also what existing things die back into 'according to necessity; for they give justice and reparation to one another for their injustice in accordance with the ordinance of Time', as he puts it, in these somewhat poetic terms.

From Simplicius, *Commentary on Aristotle's 'Physics'*, CAG IX, 24.14–25 Diels[18]

v) Plato c. 428- c.347 BC

When I was young, Cebes, I was tremendously eager for the kind of wisdom which they call investigation of nature. I thought it was a glorious thing to know the causes of everything,

---

[13] Buxton (1999, p. 2).

[14] Buxton (1999, p. 2).

[15] Homer (1990).

[16] Hesiod (1914a).

[17] Aristotle (1933).

[18] Waterfield (2000).

why each thing comes into being and why it perishes and why it exists; and I was always unsettling myself with such questions as these: Do heat and cold, by a sort of fermentation, bring about the organization of animals, as some people say? Is it the blood, or air, or fire by which we think? (*Phaedo* 96a-b)[19]

vi) Aristotle 384–322 BC

How much knowledge, then, does a natural scientist have to have about form and what a thing is? Just as much as a doctor has about sinews or a metal-worker has about metal, which is to say as much as it takes to know what the purpose of a given thing is? And only about those forms which are found in matter, although they may be separable in form? After all, a man is created by a man, and by the sun as well. Questions remain—in what sense is anything separable? What is it that is separable?—but it is the job of first philosophy to answer them. (Aristot. *Phys*. II.3. 194)[20]

The classic 'from … to' model identifies a clear shift in how natural phenomena were conceived and explained, as reflected in the above textual fragments: from the earth, sea, and sky being governed by supernatural forces, to a domain governed by rational principles, 'united under a common law'.[21] In this new framework, external deities are replaced by immanent elements, principles, and causes. The questioning in the passages from Plato and Aristotle can be seen either as a reflexive deepening and continuation of this shift toward rationality, or as the emergence of a rupture, often referred to as 'the Socratic caesura'.[22]

At first sight, this model of a clear-cut paradigm shift in Ancient Greek thought seems to suggest that there is substantial scholarly evidence that could be used to support Fleck's theory, i.e., to claim that a straightforward change in thought style occurred: from a 'mythopoeic' thought style to a 'rational-scientific' or 'philosophical' thought style. However, there are two main problems with identifying such a straightforward shift. The first is that classifying all pre-Milesian thought and textual products as 'mythological' or 'mythopoeic' is a simplification that reduces heterogeneous forms of cultural production to a single homogeneous category.

This tendency was epitomized by the academic philosopher Jonathan Barnes, who credited the Presocratics with being 'the fathers of rational thought', while simultaneously classifying all pre-Milesian narratives as 'dogma':

Scholars often, and rightly, contrast the naturalistic cosmogonies of the Milesian philosophers with such mythological stories as we find in Hesiod's *Theogony*. Yet the essence of the contrast is sometimes misrepresented: what is significant is not that theology yielded to science or gods to natural forces, but rather that unargued fables were replaced by argued theory, that dogma gave way to reason.[23]

Here, the diverse, complex, and multifunctional narrative forms that came to be classed as epic poetry, lyric poetry, and wisdom texts are reduced to two

[19] Plato (1966).

[20] Aristotle (2008).

[21] Vlastos (1947).

[22] Laks (2018, p. 17).

[23] Barnes (1979, p. 3).

distinguishing features: the genre of 'mythological stories', and the negative definition of 'unargued fables', i.e., narratives lacking rational argument. When reduced and categorized in this manner, Hesiod's *Theogony* is lumped together with an indefinite and undifferentiated mass of 'theology' that is strategically evaluated as pre- and non-rational.

If it seems unfair to seize on passages from a work of academic philosophy written in 1979, a more recent example of how *Theogony* is exploited for strategic contrastive purposes is provided by Cohen, Curd, and Reeve in *Readings in Ancient Greek Philosophy* (2011), this time with some rather astounding suppositions concerning the poet's thought processes and attitudes towards his audience: 'Since Hesiod feels no compunction about asserting his claims without reasons to support them, he seems to think that the proper response to the story is acceptance. The hearer or reader should not subject it to critical scrutiny followed by rational agreement or disagreement'. This characterization is leveraged to assert that, in contrast to Hesiod, the Milesians 'took a bold leap in adopting a critical attitude'.[24]

These representatives of relatively recent academic philosophy managed to set up and pillory Hesiod for his supposed lack of argumentation, despite the fact that prominent scholars of the 1930s and 1940s had already highlighted the explanatory qualities and purposes of Hesiod's didactic poetry. For instance, in response to the positivist depictions put forward by John Burnet and Theodor Gomperz in the late nineteenth century, which cast the pre-Socratics as empirical and scientific thinkers, Werner Jaeger argued in 1936 that the image of Greek philosophy as purely rational and scientific is based on minimizing or neglecting the continuous development of theological content in Greek poetry and philosophy.

TIn other words, *theologia* (θεολογία), a term coined by Plato in *The Republic* to denote accounts of the divine, can be identified as the fundamental preoccupation of Hesiod's *Theogony*. In this framing, Hesiod's 'original explanations and constructions', which account for the origin of the gods and address 'the problem of toil and hardship' in *Works and Days*, constitute a preparatory stage in the development of Greek thought focused on the divine, exemplified by Empedocles, Parmenides, Plato's *Republic* and Aristotle's *Metaphysics*; a tradition which was then continued by the Roman philosophy of Cicero and the Christian theology of St. Augustine. Thus, rather than the emergence of Milesian 'naturalism' and Athenian philosophy constituting a shift from myth to logos, these later thought styles developed the *logoi* presented in the poetry of Homer and Hesiod, but restated them with greater reflective consistency 'in a new and generalized philosophical form'.[25]

Similarly, in *The Argument of Hesiod's Works and Days* (1947), Teggart argued that Hesiod's use of myth to address both conceptual and social problems signalled the arrival of 'a new mode of thought'. Like the Hebrew prophets who were his contemporaries, Hesiod recognized that his audiences required explanations for certain problems: 'Homer tells a tale. Hesiod faces a problem, that of accounting for

[24] Cohen et al. (2011, pp. 3–4).

[25] Jaeger (1947, p. 17).

the existence of toil. But the recognition of this problem was not peculiar to the Greek poet. It is the very problem that is dealt with in the early chapters of *Genesis*'.[26]

Crucially, Teggart highlighted how Hesiod's arguments were shaped by the form of cultural production through which they were conveyed: because *Works and Days* was 'written for the ear' and recited with musical accompaniment, the audience needed pauses to absorb the chain of thought. This format entailed that—to our modern eyes—the topics and arguments seem to shift abruptly.[27] For example, there is a sudden transition from the story of Pandora to the account of the five races of humanity (Hes. *WD* 90–110), as well as a shift from the general problems of human nature, toil, and scarcity in the first 383 lines to very specific advice in the later sections of the poem (e.g., the direction in which a man should urinate, Hes. *WD* 727–8)[28]

The intriguing possibility that emerges when the context of oral performance is considered is that such breaks and pauses may have allowed for audience response and interaction. In contrast to the later arguments of Athenian philosophy, which were conveyed through continuous written prose and perhaps aimed at readers who could revisit the text in silence, Hesiod's arguments might have functioned more like Heraclitus' *logoi*. As M.M. McCabe suggests, these *logoi* were deliberately dense and abrupt, intended to stimulate audience reaction.[29]

Teggart's comparative analysis claims that Hesiod and the Hebrew prophets offered 'identical' explanations for the widespread social demoralization that characterized the era, which Hesiod captures with the concept of Wicked Strife (*WD* 11–26), but also suggests that they propose divergent solutions. While the prophets emphasized the ideal condition that would be received as the gifts of Yahweh, Hesiod repurposed the Homeric conception of the practice of justice: in Homer, justice is 'attributed to the good guidance of a noble king; in Hesiod, it is to be attained through the efforts of the people themselves'.[30] This framing positions Hesiod's poetry as an essential element of the Greek tradition: in addition to presenting a new form of argumentation to account for social problems, it also begins the investigation into the acquisition of culture—with the myth of Prometheus (*WD* 48–52), later repeated in Plato's *Protagoras*—and introduces the idea that human progress can be attained through 'common regard for justice'.[31]

The 'from myth to logos' paradigm, which excludes Hesiod's *Theogony* and *Works and Days* from the sphere of *logos*—an exclusion that also extends to the Homeric epics—can only be maintained by suppressing certain functions and

[26] Teggart (1947, p. 50).

[27] Teggart (1947, p. 57). Barry Gordon (1975, p. 4) made a similar point in *Economic Analysis Before Adam Smith*: 'Its 828 verses are broken up into small groups suited to the requirements of solo vocal presentation. Rather than a continuous logical development appropriate to an academic treatise on the nature of work, different groups of verses take up individual aspects of the central theme in a pattern appropriate to song'.

[28] Hesiod (1914b).

[29] McCabe and Adamsom (2010).

[30] Teggart (1947, p. 68).

[31] Teggart (1947, p. 77).

features of these texts within the context of broader cultural-intellectual developments. This includes overlooking the continuous tradition of attempts to account for the divine, failing to appreciate that arguments can take various forms beyond Socratic dialogue and syllogistic reasoning, disregarding the 'self-evident givens of the situation'[32]—such as the impact of oral performance on the transmission and reception of thought—and ignoring the contributions of scholars from the 1930s and 1940s who embraced a more interdisciplinary approach.

Moreover, the application of the 'from myth to logos' paradigm is vulnerable to more fundamental criticisms. First, it involves the uncritical projection of certain oppositional categories—established in the fifth-century writings of Pindar, Herodotus, and Thucydides, and later consolidated in Platonic philosophy—back into an earlier field of cultural production. Second, it perpetuates the Platonic strategy of reducing heterogeneous genres and cultural practices into homogenized caricatures. These issues will be explored in more detail in the following sections, but for now, it is sufficient to note that categorizing Hesiod's *Theogony* as 'unargued fables'[33] or as dogmatic assertions of 'claims without reasons to support them'[34] essentially reiterates an ancient discursive antagonism and uncritically applies the conceptual weaponry of the victorious party.

Jean-Pierre Vernant's observation on the treatment of myth is pertinent here: 'Here again modern scholars have simply followed in the footsteps of the ancient authors, remaining in a sense a part of the classical tradition that they had set out to study'.[35] The signifiers 'myth', 'logos', 'philosophy', and 'theology' are by no means neutral; they were coined and imbued with meaning through discursive struggles that ultimately resulted in the dominance of Athenian thought styles, genres, and cultural practices.

As Lowell Edmunds notes in his overview,[36] in the poetry of Homer and Hesiod, the words μῦθος (*muthos*) and λόγος (*logos*), along with their associated forms, were originally synonymous and neutrally used to denote speech, story, or account, with *muthos* being the more frequently used term. However, by the time of Pindar and Herodotus, *muthos* had begun to take on negative connotations. This shift suggests that—following the focus on *logoi* in the texts of Heraclitus and Parmenides—a standardised opposition was emerging, with *muthos* denoting 'misleading tales' (Pindar, *Nemean* 7) and *logos* becoming associated with true accounts and understanding. By the time of Thucydides, *muthos* had solidified its pejorative meaning in opposition to *logos* and *historia* (ἱστορία), signifying misleading or exaggerated tales versus true, evidence-based histories.

Edmunds frames the development of Herodotean and Thucydidean history as part of a discursive conflict: 'both historians seek to oppose a new kind of discourse,

[32] Bourdieu (1993, p. 31).

[33] Barnes (1979, p. 3).

[34] Cohen et al. (2011, p. 3).

[35] Vernant (1988, p. 220).

[36] Edmunds (2021).

even if it is different in each case, to another kind, represented by Homer and the poets'.[37] Thus, Plato's attack on the poets and *muthos* in *The Republic*—culminating in strict control over the form and content of poetic texts and the banishment of certain kinds of poetry from the ideal state—can be seen as a decisive blow in an ongoing intellectual struggle. The continued exclusion of Homer and Hesiod's poetry from the canon of ancient philosophy, or philosophy's frequent claims to supremacy over other disciplines in the modern era, indicates that this conflict remains very much alive.

Although the *Iliad*, the *Odyssey*, *Theogony*, and *Works and Days* share common features, such as the prominent role of divine beings in influencing human affairs, there are also significant distinctions between the Homeric epics and between the poetry attributed to Homer and Hesiod, particularly in terms of their social functions and the cultural practices they exemplify and support.

For example, in his monumental three-volume *Paideia* (1933–1947), Werner Jaeger contrasted the *Iliad*, which looks back to a bygone era and glorifies war and military prowess, with the *Odyssey*, which he viewed as more contemporaneous and representative of Ionian civilization during peacetime:

> In the *Odyssey* as in the *Iliad*, the highest standard of manly character is the traditional ideal of warlike valor. But the *Odyssey* also exalts the intellectual and social virtues. It is the man who is never at a loss for an apt word or a clever plan. His chief merit is his cunning—the fertile practical insight which saves his life and wins his return to his home through lurking dangers and powerful enemies.[38]

For Jaeger, the fundamental function of the Homeric epics was to educate by providing *paradeigmata*—examples or pattern-lives—for imitation. Thus, the shift from the conduct exemplified by Achilles in the *Iliad* to the schooling of Telemachus in social skills and responsibilities in the *Odyssey* marks a key transition in aristocratic ethics: from war and prowess on the battlefield to the discipline and courtesy necessary for life in the Greek states during peacetime.[39]

In turn, Eric B. Havelock also emphasized the educational role of Homer's epics, arguing that they functioned as 'a sort of tribal encyclopedia', containing detailed descriptions and re-enactments of customs and attitudes—from how public debate should be conducted and how oaths should be sworn, to how ships should be unloaded. Moreover, these texts served as living encyclopaedias, with public performances, rhythmic participation, and emotional involvement being essential to the maintenance of the community.[40]

According to Jaeger, and later Barry B. Powell, Hesiod's *Theogony* served a more doctrinal purpose: in response to an influx of Eastern creation stories and motifs—Mesopotamian, Hittite-Hurrian—Hesiod situated the emergence of the traditional Greek gods within a broader narrative framework that both explained and

[37] Edmunds (2021).

[38] Jaeger (1946, p. 22).

[39] Jaeger (1946, pp. 29–34).

[40] Havelock (1963, pp. 61–84).

justified their ascendancy.[41] Then, while *Theogony* clearly inscribes itself within the tradition of creation stories, modern scholarship has assigned Hesiod's *Works and Days* to the genre of 'Wisdom Poetry' or 'Wisdom Literature', 'a genre well represented in Sumerian, Akkadian, Egyptian, Aramaic, and Hebrew documents', the purpose of which is to provide explicit guidelines on correct behaviour through direct advice.[42]

The evolution from Homeric *paradeigmata* to Hesiod's general rules of conduct can be treated as evidence of a tendency to abstract from the current situation and form generalised conclusions. Thus *Works and Days* can be considered 'the first essay into economic analysis' in the European tradition, while Hesiod can be treated as a forerunner both of the sophists, who provided instruction on economics, and the philosophers, who continued his reflection on the organization of law.[43]

The categorization of the *Iliad*, the *Odyssey*, *Theogony* and *Works and* Days as 'mythological stories' and 'unargued fables' is a strategy that suppresses generic and functional heterogeneity and ignores developmental continuity. As the next sections will attempt to demonstrate, this strategy is straight out of Plato's playbook.

6.3 The Scholarly Quarrel About 'the Ancient Quarrel'

A clear example of an attempt to suppress generic heterogeneity is found in Plato's *Republic*. In Book 2, poetic narratives are reduced to a single trait—fabrication—and assigned a single permissible function—educating children. In Book 10, poetry—now encompassing Athenian tragedy in addition to the Homeric epics—is considered in terms of its effects on the adult population and is reduced to harmful *mimēsis* that appeals to the worst elements of the human psyche, which justifies its banishment from the ideal *polis*.

This section examines how Plato's attacks on poetry in the *Republic* have been variously framed by different academic thought collectives. In the twentieth century, these attacks—presented by Plato as the latest salvo in the ancient 'quarrel between poetry and philosophy' (607b)[44]—became the focus of intense scholarly debate. The opposing positions centred on how the arguments in lines 595a–608b (now known as 'Book 10') relate to the *Republic*'s overarching conceptual structure and to Plato's other dialogues.

---

[41] Powell (2017).

[42] Powell (2017, p. 102); Stallings (2018).

[43] Gordon (1975, pp. 2–3).

[44] Plato (1969, p. 465). Henceforth all references to Plato's Republic are to Paul Shorey's Loeb translation, unless indicated otherwise.

6.3.1 The Attack on Poetry Treated as a Gratuitous Appendix

On one side of the quarrel, Book 10's renewed attack on poetry and its scathing rejection of Homer's epistemic authority were depicted as poor-quality, inconsistent, and unnecessary additions to the main argument of the *Republic*. The tone was set in 1897, when Richard Lewis Nettleship asserted that the attack on poetry in Book 10 is 'disconnected from the rest of the *Republic*'.[45] For Nettleship, Plato's 'digression on poetry' in Book 10 was an overgeneralization written in response to the behaviour of the Athenian *dēmos* during the performances of tragedies, and thus only applies to lower forms of literature, which had 'degenerated into indiscriminate catering for common excitement'.[46]

Cornford consolidated the scholarly consensus in his 1941 translation of the *Republic*, explicitly indicating that he had truncated Plato's attacks on Homer, Hesiod, and Aeschylus in Book 2,[47] before dismissing the renewed attack on poetry in Book 10 as having 'the air of an appendix, only superficially linked with the preceding and following context'.[48] An identical position was adopted by Julia Annas in 1981, who described Book 10 as 'gratuitous and clumsy' and 'an excrescence'.[49]

In these accounts, it is the concept of *mimēsis* (μῑμησις) elaborated in Book 10 that receives the brunt of the scholarly ire. Nettleship notes that the concept of 'imitation' presented in Book 10 has a broader sense than that outlined in Book 3 (395–396), where it was decided that the guardians would only be exposed to imitations of virtuous conduct, while all other forms of the mimetic art would be prohibited. Nettleship acknowledges that Book 10's designation of poetry as three removes from the truth—as imitation of imitation—draws on the epistemological and ontological framework established after Book 3, notably the analogy of the divided line (509d–511e) and the definition of 'conjecture' (*eikasia*) as inferior to *doxa* (511e).

Thus, Nettleship recognizes the consistency between the epistemological and ontological distinctions outlined in Book 6, on the one hand, and, on the other, the consequences of these distinctions presented in Book 10, where the ontological status of *mimēsis* is defined and it is implied that 'the knowledge of the artist' is limited to the epistemologically inferior *eikasia*.[50] However, Nettleship simply rejects Plato's conceptual framework and asserts his own views. While recognizing that Plato is focused on 'a certain kind of production or making', Nettleship bluntly insists, 'this is not a true account of artistic production'.[51] In his view, the idea that the poet 'represents, and only represents' is simply wrong: artists do more than

45 Nettleship (1951, p. 340).
46 Nettleship (1951, p. 353).
47 Cornford (1941, p. 66).
48 Cornford (1941, p. 314).
49 Annas (1981, p. 335).
50 Nettleship (1951, p. 347).
51 Nettleship (1951, p. 345).

merely hold up a mirror to nature and create superficial resemblances that cater to the worst instincts of the populace.[52]

Annas also focused on the apparent inconsistencies between the concept and role of *mimēsis* presented in Book 3 and in the 'gratuitous' excrescence of Book 10, adopting a similarly evaluative stance. For Annas, Plato's attack on poetry in Book 10 is unsuccessful, since it is based on 'hopelessly bad arguments'.[53] Her first charge is that the second attack on poetry 'changes the meaning and scope of "imitation"'. In terms of meaning, *mimēsis* shifts from the notion of expressing and representing conveyed in Book 3 to copying or holding up a mirror to things in Book 10, through what she considers the weak analogy between painting and poetry. Annas argues that the optical illusions created by a *trompe-l'œil* painter do not bear comparison with poetic images, so 'all the reasons for claiming the painter "lacks knowledge" do not carry over to the poet'.[54]

Then, in terms of scope, while Book 3 casts only some poetry as mimetic—there is also 'narrative' poetry,[55] or 'simple narration'[56] (396e)—in Book 10 all poetry is reduced to imitation. Her second criticism is that, while Book 3 recognised that poetry can shape human character and hence acknowledged that the poets wield an 'important and dangerous' power justifying stringent controls on the content and form of poetry in the ideal *polis*, the arguments of Book 10 contradict this by trivialising poetry and suggesting that poets are not respected for their knowledge. Annas thus concludes that the *Republic* presents 'two inconsistent views about poetry'.[57] In her evaluation, the weak arguments focused on the ontological degradation of poetry and the rejection of the poet's epistemic authority cannot be taken seriously, while the stronger arguments, which acknowledge the power and potential danger of poetry in civic life, are more consistent with the position assigned to poetry and poets in other dialogues (e.g., *Ion*, *Phaedrus*).

These scholars explicitly register their sense of encountering something alien in Plato's concepts and strategies. For example, Nettleship states: 'it is very difficult to make sense of';[58] Cornford remarks: 'the point of view seems as perverse, and even stupid, as Tolstoy's in *What is Art?*';[59] Annas notes: 'it is full of oddities'.[60] From the perspective of Fleck's theory,[61] these reactions can be treated as clear examples of a later thought style encountering 'alien' and 'foreign' elements in its interaction with an earlier thought style. More precisely, a specific scholarly community of twentieth-

[52] Nettleship (1951, pp. 344–353).

[53] Annas (1981, p. 344).

[54] Annas (1981, pp. 337–338).

[55] Plato (1991)—Jowett's translation.

[56] Plato (1969)—Shorey's translation.

[57] Annas (1981, p. 342).

[58] Nettleship (1951, p. 345).

[59] Cornford (1941, p. 314).

[60] Annas (1981, p. 335).

[61] For instance, Fleck (1979, pp. 125–126).

century academic philosophers—which Havelock described as representing 'the magisterial scholarship on Plato'[62]—had a uniform and sustained reaction to certain unpalatable strategic positions articulated in a text produced by a representative of a particular Athenian thought style that emerged in the fourth century BC.

Fleck's theory predicts that communication between distant thought styles inevitably involves a transformation or distortion of concepts, especially when the communication occurs over a distance—spatial, temporal, or in terms of subject matter.[63] In the transmission of Plato's *Republic* and its reception by twentieth-century academic philosophy—via various interpretative filters such as Byzantine and Renaissance Neoplatonism, German classical studies (*Altertumswissenschaft*), and Anglophone positivist Plato scholarship—the inevitable distortion took the form of what can be described as a suppressive accommodation. The incompatible elements of Plato's text are suppressed through criticism and rejection to ensure it aligns with the humanistic thought style of modern academic philosophy, which tolerates the presence of poets, playwrights, and novelists within the canon of European thought.

In contrast to this accommodating position, Plato's *Republic* has also been reconstructed as articulating a far more extreme and unorthodox position in the field of cultural production—one that cannot be comfortably reconciled with the humanist orthodoxy institutionalized in post-Renaissance universities. From this perspective, the educational program proposed in the *Republic* was entirely incompatible with the *studia humanitatis* of the Renaissance, which introduced the study of poetry to the curricula of Italian schools and universities, and with the subsequent institutionalization of the study of classical languages and literature in English and German universities in the eighteenth and nineteenth centuries.[64] Plato's multipronged attack on the authority and educational role of Homer and Hesiod, along with his evaluation of the impact of tragedy and drama on the psyche of Athenian citizens, cannot be reconciled with the status assigned to poetic texts, narrative literature, theatre, and other forms of artistic representation in later European fields of cultural production. As Thomas Gould astutely observed, 'the removal of all that Plato found objectionable in Greek literature would take the heart out of Shakespeare, the Bible, Dostoevsky, and much of the best of the whole western tradition'.[65]

The dismissal of Book 10 of the *Republic* as an inconsistent appendix requires a suppression or neglect of the cultural context in which Plato's text articulates its position. Nettleship acknowledged that Plato 'was writing in a different atmosphere from our own',[66] in which tragedy and comedy had greater influence on human conduct. Yet this atmosphere is only apprehended through its representations in Plato's dialogues: no effort is made to consider the connections between Plato's texts and other works, or to situate his arguments in a broader cultural context.

[62] Havelock (1963, p. 15, footnote 12).

[63] Fleck (1986, p. 87).

[64] On Renaissance education: Grendler (1989); on German and English Universities: Hofstetter (2001).

[65] Gould (1990, p. 12).

[66] Nettleship (1906, p. 58).

In contrast, Cornford's denigration of Plato's attack on poetry is somewhat perplexing. Citing T. B. L. Webster's 1939 essay 'Greek Theories of Art and Literature down to 400 BC',[67] Cornford indicates that Plato's account of *mimēsis* adopts (and pillories) a theory that rose to prominence at the end of the fifth century, which viewed art as a likeness (*eikon*) of an original. In other words, Cornford actually acknowledges that Plato's second attack on poetry—the *mimēsis* argument—was culturally determined; it was embedded within and responded to ongoing debate and theorization that had been taking place in the cultural field prior to the emergence of Plato's texts.

Webster's study is particularly interesting, as it situates the arguments of Book 10 of the *Republic* within a broader context of cultural production, theory, and criticism initially centred on the concept of *mimēsis*. From the imitation of voices in Homer's *Odyssey*, through the Hippocratic treatise *On Diet*, which describes 'sculptors making an "imitation" of the body', to Pindar's account of Athena inventing the flute to imitate the Gorgon's shrieks, Webster traces the development of the *mimēsis* theory over a period of at least one hundred years, leading to its dominance in the time of Socrates and Plato.[68]

At the same time, Webster also situates the *Republic* at the end of a period of substantial and more wide-ranging theoretical reflection on the nature and effects of poetry and tragedy. While Plato's accounts of the sophists' rhetorical theory provide evidence that by the fourth century '[g]rammar, vocabulary, argument, composition, and all the various ways of playing on the emotions of the audience have been worked out and reduced to a system', evidence of complex theorizing can also be located outside of Plato's texts. Aristophanes' *Frogs* shows that he 'was well versed in literary criticism and that the craft of poetry had been well examined before he wrote', and the plays of Sophocles and Euripides bear witness to the consciousness that the task of artists was 'the education of their fellow citizens'.[69]

In effect, Cornford referred to a study that provided a detailed investigation of the context that Plato's arguments addressed and engaged with, yet avoided any discussion of how deeply the interaction between the *Republic* and this context might have shaped Plato's attacks on poetry. Webster argued that the *mimēsis* theory had attained dominance by 400 BC, and that the ancient quarrel between poetry and philosophy to which Plato refers can be traced back to Xenophanes and Heraclitus and their rejection of the authority of Homer and Hesiod.[70] These intertextual arguments clearly undermined Nettleship's depiction of Book 10 as an appendix or afterthought, yet Cornford—strangely—failed to address them, instead opting to consolidate Nettleship's framing.

While Nettleship's and Cornford's accounts at least signalled awareness of contextual determination and cultural difference, Annas remained firmly focused on the internal consistency of the conceptual framework constructed in the *Republic* and

[67] Cornford (1941, p. 316).
[68] Webster (1939, p. 168).
[69] Webster (1939, pp. 170–171).
[70] Webster (1939, p. 169).

across Plato's dialogues. In this perspective, poetry and philosophy are juxtaposed as purely abstract opponents, or at most, as genres that somehow influence people's behaviour.[71] In other words, the quarrel between poetry and philosophy is investigated as a phenomenon occurring within the boundaries of Plato's texts, which, in turn, are treated as if they exist in a cultural vacuum.

6.3.2 The Attack on Poetry Treated as the Core Argument

The other side of the scholarly quarrel responds to a provocative thesis that was put forward as a challenge to traditional academic philosophy, namely in Havelock's *Preface to Plato* (1963). Havelock rejected the scholarly consensus to argue that the attack on poetry in Book 10 of the *Republic* actually constituted the core argument and purpose of Plato's text.[72]

In a nutshell, Havelock argued that Plato's attack on poetry was first and foremost an attack on the practices and states of mind associated with the oral performance of poetry. In Havelock's framing, as mentioned previously, Homer's poems functioned as 'a sort of tribal encyclopedia' that provided models of correct conduct and procedures, and their oral performance in educational and public settings served to maintain the customs, habits and attitudes of the community.[73] For Havelock, Plato's text epitomizes the shift from a predominantly oral culture to a literate one: with its musical accompaniment and gestures, oral poetry was geared to memorization, and while the introduction of the Greek alphabet in the seventh century and the coding of poetic texts in writing initially facilitated memorisation, by the fifth century the unique capacity of the Greek alphabet to capture speech triggered a switch to prose. Havelock explicitly framed this development in communication technology in terms of discursive conflict:

> The contrary conception of poetic inspiration was born in Greece precisely at that time, toward the end of the fifth century, when the requirements of oral memorisation were no longer dominant and when the functional purposes of poetry as a tribal education were being transferred to prose. At this point those who thought in prose and preferred prose—that is the philosophers, who were intent upon constructing a new type of discourse which we can roughly characterise as conceptual rather than poetic—were driven to relegate the poetic experience to a category which was non-conceptual and therefore non-rational and non-reflective.[74]

Here, Plato's attack on poetry is depicted as an attack on the practices and state of mind associated with a specific communication technology—oral poetry, on behalf of the practices and a state of mind associated with a new communication technology—philosophical prose.

---

[71] Annas (1981, p. 340).

[72] Havelock (1963, pp. 15–16, footnote 13).

[73] Havelock (1963, pp. 66–84).

[74] Havelock (1963, p. 156).

In Havelock's reconstruction of the conflict, those who had adopted the new communication technology began to differentiate between the discourses by means of antagonistic binaries: the prose of the philosophers was defined as conceptual, rational, and reflective, while poetry was pilloried as non-conceptual, non-rational, and non-reflective. Thus, on Havelock's reading, the main purpose of the *Republic* was to show how philosophy could usurp the hegemony of oral poetry: by controlling the role of poetry in education (*paideia*) and banning any performances of narrative poetry or tragedy in the adult community that did not conform to the strict ethical requirements of philosophy.

The new discourse of philosophy could not simply disseminate its texts and leave oral poetry alone, because this older communication technology was thoroughly embedded in the practices and institutions of Athenian society: the '"oral" state of mind' stands in the way of philosophy and constitutes 'the chief obstacle to scientific rationalism'.[75] Only when oral poetry had been dislodged and supplanted could the practices associated with philosophy—i.e., critical reading, analysis, classification, generalization, dialectical argumentation—come to dominate in the culture and society. Oral poetry was thus identified as the 'arch-enemy' that had to be defeated and mastered before philosophy could rule the *polis*.

In *Literacy and Orality and Ancient Greece* (1992), a study of key importance for the Plato scholarship of Penelope Murray (1996), Rosalind Thomas problematised what she saw as Havelock's reductive technological determinism. First, she characterized Havelock as an overly enthusiastic follower of Goody's absolute image of the consequences of literacy, which, despite modifications and increasing sensitivity over the course of decades, essentially argued that writing and literacy are 'a force for logical and scientific thought, bureaucracy and the modern state, and law'.[76] Thus in this research current, societies tended to be divided into literate and non-literate, with the introduction of literacy being treated like the addition of a catalyst in a chemical reaction: it causes certain predictable changes in any society. Second, Thomas suggests Havelock was an exponent of McLuhan's strain of technological determinism, which reduced all methods of communication to matters of technology, and attributed social and cultural change primarily to developments in communication technology. This single-factor deterministic approach is succinctly summed up by Walter Ong's assertion: 'Writing restructures consciousness'.[77]

In contrast to these reductive positions, Thomas refers to comparative evidence showing that the arrival of writing was not always followed by a cultural shift towards rationality and analytical thinking (e.g. in Sparta, Tibet); she then highlights the long period following the invention of the Greek alphabet during which orality predominated and co-existed with literacy, when writing was used in the service of orality, as a storage technology that aided the oral performance of poetry,

[75] Havelock (1963, p. 47).

[76] Thomas (1992, p. 18).

[77] Ong (1982, pp. 77–113).

until growing professionalism enhanced the status of writing in the fourth century;[78] and lastly draws on G.E.R. Lloyd's *Magic, Reason and Experience* (1979), which argues that factors other than literacy also contributed to the Greek intellectual revolution, such as the practice of public debate, the ethos of competition, and the structure of the *polis* itself.[79]

So, in contrast to the absolute image of literacy and single-factor technological determinism, Thomas adopts a more complex and fluid conception of literacy: rather than a catalyst with predictable consequences, the impact of writing depends on the structures and practices already present in the society in which it appears; and, in turn, these features of the society have an impact how the technology of writing itself develops.[80]

In *Plato on Poetry* (1997), Murray took Thomas's critique of Havelock's account on board but essentially adopted the latter's interpretation of the *Republic*'s attack on poetry as forming the core arguments and discursive purpose of Plato's text. Firstly, Murray identifies a consistent position on poetry running through *Ion*, *Republic* and *Laws* which degrades the epistemic status of poets and rhapsodes, characterizes poetry as a dangerous and corrupting influence on society, and insists on philosophy's control over poetry and the poets, to be implemented through censorship and/or banishment. Thus, in contrast to the traditional treatment of the *Republic*'s Book 10 as an inconsistent appendix, Murray reads Books 2 and 3 as preparation for 'the final assault on poetry in book 10'.[81]

Secondly, Murray reaffirms Havelock's core thesis on what is fundamentally at stake in the *Republic*: '[Socrates'] emphasis on the triviality of poetry and his insistence on Homer's ignorance about all matters human and divine strike at the heart of Greek *paideia*. Homer, the educator of Greece, must be banished in order to make way for a new system of *paideia* in which poetry will be replaced by philosophy'.[82] At the end of the section 'Plato and Homer', Murray acknowledges Thomas's critique of Havelock's thesis, but aligns her reading with the latter's basic thrust:

> No doubt Havelock exaggerated his case in claiming that P. was at the centre of a revolution in communications, and that he was himself instrumental in bringing about a transition from an oral to a literate mentality in Greek society. Clearly the concepts of orality and literacy are more flexible, and the interplay between them more complex, than Havelock's analysis suggested.[54] Nevertheless it cannot be denied that P.'s attack on poetry represents a radical break with the past. Greece in many ways continued to be an oral society: historians, for example, regularly recited their works in public, and Greek social and political life was dominated by oratory, a performance art if ever there was one. But after the fifth century, despite the enormous popularity of drama, the performance of poetry was no longer at the centre of Greek culture as it had been in earlier times.[83]

---

[78] Thomas (1992, pp. 13–14).

[79] Thomas (1992, p. 20).

[80] Thomas (1992, pp. 24–25).

[81] Murray (1997, p. 22).

[82] Murray (1997, p. 22).

[83] Murray (1997, p. 24). In footnote 54, Murray refers to: Thomas (1992), passim, but especially 3–5, 17–28, and 102–117.

Murray's position was consolidated and expanded by Susan B. Levin's meticulously argued *The Ancient Quarrel between Philosophy and Poetry Revisited* (2001). Levin focused on the concept of *technē,* and the epistemological status assigned to various practices in the *Gorgias*, *Cratylus*, *Ion* and *Republic*, to argue that Plato's conceptual threads are woven together to form a sustained and systematic critique of poetry. Following Gould and Murray's Havelock-inspired position, Levin frames Plato's attacks on Homer and the poets as part of a broader assault on tradition, which is ultimately aimed at supplanting poetry and installing philosophy as 'the educator of Greece'.[84] On this reading, the Theory of Forms and related doctrines, such as the Divided Line and the Allegory of the Cave, which appear in between the attacks on poetry in Books 2 and 10, were specifically constructed to counter the authority of poetry and the poets in Greek society.

For Levin, the *technē* framework plays a pivotal role in Plato's critique: the criteria for *technai* established in the *Gorgias*, namely goodness, knowledge and subject-matter, are identified as shaping the distinctions that Socrates makes between poetry, sophistry, and true philosophy throughout *The Republic*. Thus, according to Levin, while poetry and the false wisdom of the sophists cannot be classed as *technai*, *philosophia* is placed 'at the top of the hierarchy of *technai*', as the *technē* par excellence.[85] The fundamental point of the *Republic* Book 6 (493) is thus interpreted as being to link the sophists and the poets in terms of their destructive impact of society (lack of goodness), their low level of cognition (opinion—*eikasia*), and their low-level subject matter: *semblances* of virtue and wisdom.[86] In contrast, true *philosophia* fulfils all the criteria of *technai*: a positive impact on society (if philosophers ruled), knowledge of the Good and the intelligible world of being, and the subject matter of the Forms.[87]

The *technē* framework rigorously excludes poets from the possibility of attaining true knowledge and subordinates their production to the control of the philosophers: if poets did have real knowledge of virtue and vice, they would actually be philosophers. However, the necessity of the division of labour established in Book 2 ('the Principle of Specialization'[88]) entails that philosophers will not be tasked with writing the kind of poetry that will be acceptable in the ideal *polis*: carpenters or bedmakers will make beds, poets will write poetry.

In contrast to Annas' charge that Plato's attacks of poetry in Books 2 and 10 are inconsistent and weak, particularly when the concept of *mimēsis* comes into play, Levin highlights the threads of Plato's text that specify the role of poetry and *mimēsis* in the ideal *polis*: poets will have true, stable beliefs (*orthē doxa*) inculcated by the new *paideia*, and will assist the philosophers by providing desirable role models for young children before they are able to form their own judgments

[84] Levin (2001b, p. 129).

[85] Levin (2001b, p. 135).

[86] Levin (2001b, pp. 133–135).

[87] Levin (2001b, p. 140).

[88] Levin (2001b, p. 148).

concerning the Good, and by writing poems for important social occasions that contain *mimēsis* of reasonable and moderate conduct, which will unify the community.[89]

In her complex critique of previous scholarship, Levin returns to Nettleship's acknowledgement of the consistency between the epistemological distinctions presented in Book 6 and status assigned to the poets' knowledge in Book 10,[90] i.e., *eikasia*, but extends the scope of this consistency to Book 7's Allegory of the Cave to align this representation of epistemological deception with Plato's thoroughly pessimistic view of typical human cognition.[91] Thus, at the point where Nettleship and Annas introduce their own judgments to suppress the unpalatable aspects of Plato's critique of poetry, Levin does not flinch in her description: the fundamental purpose of Plato's epistemological, ontological, and ethical frameworks is to reduce poetry to the supervised production of stories for early childhood and special state-organized civic occasions. Such a power grab would give philosophy absolute control over the field of cultural production and enculturation: 'by functioning as the community's ultimate authority regarding the content and form of admissible constructions, philosophy clearly supersedes poetry as the educator of Greece'.[92]

6.4 Strategic Consistency in Plato's Treatment of Cultural Practices

6.4.1 Ion *and* Phaedrus*: Exclusion, Homogenization, and Assimilation*

Interpretations that focus on Plato's texts in isolation from their cultural context tend to neglect their communicative purpose and suppress consideration of how they interacted with and were shaped by this context. Focusing exclusively on the logical-conceptual consistency of Plato's arguments—taken from within the interior of his texts—obscures the strategic consistency of his engagement with rival thought styles and discourses. It also overlooks his attacks on the cultural practices these discourses maintain and promote.

For example, Annas[93] argues that Plato's true views on poetry can be found in the *Ion* and *Phaedrus*. Yet the strategies deployed in these texts are entirely consistent with the most extreme attacks on Homer and the poets in the *Republic*. In the *Ion*[94] Socrates challenges the epistemic authority of rhapsodes by denying their practice

[89] Levin (2001b, pp. 153, 158).
[90] Nettleship (1951, p. 347).
[91] Levin (2001b, p. 156).
[92] Levin (2001b, p. 166).
[93] Annas (1981, p. 342).
[94] Plato (1925a).

the status of a craft or skill (*technē*) and demonstrating their lack of knowledge (*epistēmē*) (537c–538a). Socrates also indirectly challenges Homer's epistemic authority by questioning whether Ion has the necessary knowledge to judge Homer's knowledge—for example, of chariot driving (536e–537e). Since Socrates defines *technē* as the ability to know a particular occupation (537c), the implication is that if Homer does not have knowledge of chariot driving, his poetry is not a *technē*.

Furthermore, Socrates' interrogation of Ion is not restricted to challenging the status of rhapsodes and poetry; it also questions the practice of public poetry recital, by focusing on how rhapsodes affect their spectators. The practice of recital is described as a chain of collective derangement or possession: the poet is possessed by gods and divine things, the rhapsode is possessed by Homer, the spectators by the rhapsode (535a–536d). Thus, if the *Ion* does indeed reveal Plato's true views on poetry, the core arguments suggest that poems are textual products lacking genuine knowledge, and that recitals exert a questionable or malign influence on the spectating public.

The notion that Plato assigns poets a positive status or role through acknowledging their divine inspiration ignores that this concession comes bundled with two strategic attachments: the exclusion of poetry from the status of *technē* and *epistēmē*, and the taint of possession or madness ('are you then in your right mind, or outside yourself?' (535c).[95] As Murray notes, the *Ion*'s characterization of the poet, the rhapsode and the audience as divinely possessed also serves to position these participants of poetic recitals as 'devoid of reason' and emphasizes the 'irrational nature of the poetic process'.[96] It is precisely the charge that poetry 'impairs reason' and 'indulges the irrational nature' that leads to the poet's banishment from the ideal *polis* in Book 10 of the *Republic* (605–608).

In the *Phaedrus*,[97] the strategies that Plato deploys to tackle poetry are more complex and ambiguous, particularly when the issue of madness and divine inspiration is raised (244a–245c). Nevertheless, Plato deploys recognizable strategies consistent with those in the *Ion*, *Gorgias* and the *Republic*.

The *Phaedrus* covers such a wide range of issues that its thematic unity has been called into question and subjected to rigorous debate (e.g., Heath (1989), Rowe (1989)). However, it can be safely argued that the *Phaedrus* is, like the closely related *Gorgias*, fundamentally concerned with *the best way of life* and thus with the choices that have to be made between the different practices that one can engage in. Since the *Phaedrus* ultimately argues that the philosophical way of life is superior to a life focused on other pursuits—for example, speaking and acting in the world of men (*Phaedrus* 273 e)—Heath's conclusion is convincing: 'The dialogue,

[95] Allen (1996, p. 15). Lamb's 1925 translation: 'Well now, are we to say, Ion, that such a person is in his senses at that moment'.

[96] Murray (1997, pp. 8–9).

[97] Plato (1925b).

therefore, is not about love, or about rhetoric, or about both love and rhetoric, as such, but about philosophy—which, for Plato, happens to be a matter of love and discourse'.[98]

The fundamental issue addressed in both the *Gorgias* and *Phaedrus* is *what one does*, and *what one does with one's life* (with the 'one' in question obviously restricted to male citizens/aristocrats). While the *Gorgias* takes aim at the practices of public speaking and political involvement, the *Phaedrus* can be boiled down to the question of *education*: whether the soul should be *persuaded* by the public speech of oratory or *educated* by the private conversation of philosophy (277c). In both dialogues, the elevation of philosophy as the best way of life and best educator is achieved by downgrading the status of other practices and attacking other uses of spoken and written words (oratory, sophistry, poetry).

In the *Phaedrus*, poetry is—as in *Ion*—associated with madness and divine possession. The theme of madness—*maníē* (μανία)—appears in Socrates' first speech in response to Phaedrus' recitation of Lysias' written speech. After invoking the Muses and defining love as what happens when irrational desire—and thus the pursuit of pleasure and physical beauty—gain the upper hand over thought and self-control, Socrates breaks off to ask 'Anyway, my dear Phaedrus, do you think I've been inspired by a god? I do' (238c).[99] Before continuing, he attributes his inspiration to the bucolic setting and warns Phaedrus 'so don't be surprised if, as may happen, I become possessed by the Nymphs as my speech progresses. As it is I'm already more or less chanting dithyrambs' (238d).[100] Thus Socrates playfully (and flirtatiously) signals that his speech is mimicking divine inspiration and poetic affectation.

He goes on to outline the course of a homoerotic love affair, in which the older lover starts off driven by obsession and compulsion, but then falls out of love, recovers his sanity, and flees from the beloved (240c–241b). Socrates' first speech ostensibly repeats the main conclusion of Lysias' speech, i.e., that it is better to gratify a non-lover than a lover, but really serves to introduce the theme of madness and loss of control, which is framed as a conflict between desire and reason, and thus to lay the ground for distinguishing philosophy from other thought styles and discursive practices.

Socrates' second speech, the famous palinode delivered in response to a reprimand from his 'divine sign', begins with a reconception of madness as a divine gift and source of blessings, and then proceeds to distinguish four kinds of madness: the possession of prophecy (244a–b), the purificatory madness that provides relief from guilt (244d–e), the Muses' madness that possesses poets (245a), and the apparent madness of philosophers who recollect the beauty of the true reality (249c–e). The strategy from *Ion* is redeployed: the acknowledgement that competent poetry is

[98] Heath (1989, p. 170).

[99] Plato (2002, p. 18)—Waterfield's translation. Fowler's 1925 translation: 'Well, my dear Phaedrus, does it seem to you, as it does to me, that I am inspired?'

[100] Plato (2002, p. 18).

divinely inspired and 'educates future generations by glorifying the countless deeds of the past' is accompanied by the more loaded suggestion that truly inspired poets compose in a frenzy—a sane poet cannot compete with 'poetry composed by men who are mad' (245a).[101]

The charioteer allegory running through the palinode establishes an epistemic hierarchy that assigns a privileged status to philosophy. The region beyond heaven, full of true being, true knowledge and divine intelligence, is described as inaccessible to earthly poets (247c), since it is only visible to immortal souls without bodies. Needless to say, Socrates courageously attempts to describe it himself: it is a region full of fierce competition, where souls vie to see the plain of truth, with much pushing and trampling; hence some souls gain more access than others. Not surprisingly, it is the souls who see the most truth that 'enter the seeds of men who will become philosophers, lovers of beauty, men of culture, men who are dedicated to love' (248d).[102] Socrates enumerates eight groups of souls below the philosophers, hierarchically organized in accordance with how much truth they glimpsed:

> [...] the second group those of law-abiding kings or military commanders or civic leaders; the third group those of politicians, estate- managers or businessmen; the fourth group those of men who love exercising in a gymnasium or future experts in bodily health; the fifth group will live as prophets or as initiators into one of the mystery cults; the sixth group will most suitably live as poets or some other kind of representative artist, the seventh as artisans or farmers, the eighth as sophists or demagogues, and the ninth as tyrants (248c–d).[103]

Two points can be emphasized here. First, grouping poets together with representative/imitative artists is fully consistent with the *mimēsis* argument in Book 10 of the *Republic*. Second, it is no accident that poets are placed one rank above artisans and farmers, and two ranks above sophists.

As Ellen Meiksins Wood has argued, 'the outright contempt for labour and labourers displayed by Plato and Xenophon' was a unique class prejudice, rather than a universal cultural norm: while disdain for *dependent* labour and slaves was the norm, Plato and Xenophon's contempt for manual workers set them against democracy and the "'banausic' multitude".[104] The sophists are ranked even lower than craftsmen and other manual labourers, along with demagogues and just above tyrants, because they are identified and targeted as the chief rival and opponent of the new discourse of philosophy that is consistently and antagonistically articulated across Plato's texts.

The text of the *Phaedrus* refers to and incorporates external texts, genres, and discourses: the alien discourses of poetry and rhetoric are cited (sometimes verbatim), parodied and subjected to critique, but oblique reference is also made to Plato's

---

[101] Plato (2002, p. 27).

[102] Plato (2002, p. 31). Fowler's translation of ἀνδρὸς γενησομένου φιλοσόφου ἢ φιλοκάλου ἢ μουσικοῦ τινος καὶ ἐρωτικοῦ: 'the birth of a man who is to be a philosopher or a lover of beauty, or one of a musical or loving nature', Plato (1925b).

[103] Plato (2002, pp. 31–32).

[104] Wood (1989, p. 139). Also Nightingale (1995, p. 56).

own *Gorgias* and its account of *technē*.[105] The genres of speech represented and addressed in the *Phaedrus* contrast with those depicted in the *Gorgias*: while the *Gorgias* ends in failure—dialogical breakdown with ominous overtones—*Phaedrus* hints at what true philosophical discourse might look like.

Thus, although in *Gorgias* Socrates successfully demolishes the claims of sophist oratory in a public debate involving many participants, downgrading *rhētorikós* from *technē* to mere flattery (*kolakía—κολακεία*), the dialogue ultimately ends as a monologue, with Socrates debating with himself and delivering a long, uninterrupted account (*logos*), despite his repeated insistence that Gorgias and Polus engage with him through questioning and short answers rather than extended refutations (449, 467, 474). Socrates' extended *logos* effectively silences Callicles, who has been steadfastly unpersuaded by dialogical browbeating, and who has insisted that Socrates' philosophical discourse will not protect him from those who will seek to put him to death (521–22). Socrates can thus be read as resorting to a 'true' account of the afterlife—a *logos* which is pointedly defined as *not* being *muthos* (523a), even though it features Cronus, Zeus, Prometheus, the Isles of the Blessed and Tartarus—in response to his failure to convince Callicles, who had brutally called into question the purpose and utility of philosophy in Athenian society. In fact, Socrates' focus on the judgment and punishments that await in the afterlife can be read as acknowledging that philosophy has no utility in the present society, that it is in fact an *anti-social* practice. At the end of the *Gorgias*, Callicles' charge from earlier in the dialogue, when he paraphrased Euripides' *Antiope*, are still all too relevant: 'You couldn't put a speech together correctly before councils of justice or utter any plausible or persuasive sound' (485e–486a).[106] Thus the question that lingers at the end of the *Gorgias* is what exactly is the 'true political craft' and 'true politics' that Socrates claims to practice? (521)—because it clearly cannot consist in the public articulation of a suppressive, silencing *monologos*.

By contrast, the *Phaedrus* provides a closer representation of what true philosophical discourse might look like: a *dialogos*—a dialectical exchange in which the speech techniques of poetry and rhetoric are appropriated to lead and educate a young man's soul. After Socrates' palinode has established the epistemic superiority of philosophers over poets, and that the philosophical life ensures both a better afterlife (the soul will regain its wings more quickly (249a)) and a harmonious life on earth (256a), the topic of the dialogue takes a reflexive turn to consider what makes speech and writing good or bad (259e).

This analytical shift is the basis for arguing that the *Phaedrus* lacks fundamental unity and is 'intolerably misshapen'.[107] However, as mentioned previously, if, following Heath (1989), we take the fundamental focus of the text to be the education of the soul, then the analysis of speech and writing in terms of their impact on the soul becomes strategically consistent with the palinode's assertion of philosophy's

[105] Heath (1989, pp. 154–155).

[106] Plato (1986).

[107] Rowe (1986).

epistemic supremacy and its claim to the best 'way of life'. This approach is also fully aligned with the discursive strategies employed across Plato's texts—such as *Charmides*, *Ion*, *Gorgias*, *Republic*, and *Sophist*—and can be viewed as a defining characteristic of Plato's thought style. Three examples will serve to illustrate this strategic and discursive consistency.

6.4.1.1 The Incorporation of Court Procedure and Technique

Socrates' analysis of speech and writing in the *Phaedrus* is not focused on abstract forms of text production, but on specific social practices associated with particular Athenian institutions, such as the Council (258a) and the lawcourts (261a), and with the oratory of notable public figures, such as Pericles (269). The first question addressed in the protagonists' analysis of what makes speech good is whether knowledge of the truth is required for the speaker to speak well. This reactivates the issue tackled in the *Gorgias*—whether there is such a thing as an art or science (*technē*) of speaking.

In the *Phaedrus*, while the *technē* of speaking is allowed to defend herself and claim that knowledge of the truth is necessary for persuasion, Socrates refers to certain pre-existing arguments (*logoi*): those that testify she is an art, and those that accuse her of lying, of being 'an unsystematic knack (ἄτεχνος τριβή/*atechnos tribē*)' (260e).[108] It thus becomes clear that the *technē* of speaking is actually on trial, with the procedure resembling that of the Athenian courts: the defendant speaks for herself, arguments testify as witnesses for the defendant and are presented by the prosecutor. Phaedrus makes this explicit by suggesting they incorporate or imitate the procedure and techniques of the lawcourt: 'We need these arguments, Socrates. Bring them here to take the stand, and cross-examine them to see what they are saying and how they put it' (261a).[109]

The first point to make here is that this strategy of incorporating or parodying the legal procedure of public examination in a private conversation—where philosophers analyse a specific social practice—is also deployed in *Republic* Book 10 (605–07) with the trial and banishment of poetry. The second point is that the incorporation of Athenian court procedure into the text of the *Phaedrus* exemplifies what Andrea Wilson Nightingale describes as Plato's engagement with 'alien' *logoi*: a strategy that appropriates, parodies and exploits other discourses and genres to assert the claims of philosophy as a distinct, rival discourse.[110]

[108] Plato (2002, p. 48).

[109] Plato (2002, p. 48). For comparison, Fowler's Loeb translation opts for 'examination' rather than 'cross-examination', perhaps because the cross-examination of witnesses was not a part of Athenian court procedure: 'Socrates: Yes, if the arguments that are coming against her testify that she is an art. For I seem, as it were, to hear some arguments approaching and protesting that she is lying and is not an art, but a craft devoid of art [...]. Phaedrus: We have need of these arguments, Socrates. Bring them here and examine their words and their meaning.' Plato (1925b).

[110] Nightingale (1995, p. 132).

6.4.1.2 Homogenizing Heterogeneous Cultural Practices

When he begins the analysis of what makes good speech, Socrates' first move is to reduce heterogeneous phenomena to one common denominator:

> Wouldn't rhetoric, in general, be a kind of skilful leading of the soul by means of words, not only in public gatherings such as the lawcourts, but also in private meetings? Isn't it the same skill whether it is dealing with slight or great issues, and something which, seen aright, is no more valuable when it is concerned with important matters than it is when it is dealing with trivia? (261a)[111]

Thus, various forms of public discourse—such as a speech given before the Athenian Assembly or a litigant's speech before a court—are reduced to a single characteristic: the attempt to persuade the audience. Any differences between public and private discourse, or between weighty deliberation and casual conversation, are also eliminated when Socrates gathers disparate forms and contexts of spoken discourse together under the single class of rhetoric (i.e., speech aimed at persuasion).

Socrates subsequently describes this homogenizing technique as the principle of 'collection'—bringing scattered particulars under a single class (265d). Along with the complementary principle of 'division'—cutting things up according to their natural joints—this practice distinguishes those whom Socrates describes as 'dialecticians' (διαλεκτικοί/*dialektikoi*) (266b).[112] As Heath stresses,[113] these principles of dialectic do not exhaust the practice of philosophy: Socrates reveals that he had used the principle of division in his 'poetic' speeches when analysing the different forms of madness (266a), and he later asserts that good rhetoricians will make use of the techniques of collection and division when tailoring their speeches to the souls of their audience (272a, 273e). Thus both rhetoric and philosophy are discursive practices that have to use dialectical collection and division in the fulfilment of their distinct purposes.

Heath suggests that the final cut that divides rhetoric from philosophy is Socrates' distinction between persuasion and teaching: the conventional (i.e., non-*technē*) practice of rhetoric persuades without systematic knowledge, while the true practice of rhetoric that persuades with systematic knowledge ultimately dissolves into philosophy, which seeks to educate rather than merely persuade.[114]

The first point to make here is that the discursive strategy of homogenizing (collecting) diverse cultural practices and forms of cultural production and reducing them to one defining characteristic is replicated in *Republic* Books 2 and 10. There, diverse text types are reduced to the production of *pseudos*—fables/fiction/falsehood, and to *mimēsis*—imitation/representation, respectively. Similarly, in *Gorgias*,

---

[111] Plato (2002, p. 48).

[112] Fowler's Loeb translation: 'That of perceiving and bringing together in one idea the scattered particulars. […] That of dividing things again by classes, where the natural joints are, and not trying to break any part, after the manner of a bad carver. […] I have called them hitherto dialecticians' Plato (1925b).

[113] Heath (1989, p. 156).

[114] Heath (1989, p. 158).

the practices of cooking and rhetoric are reduced to *kolakeia*—pandering or flattery. Secondly, Plato's texts employ the strategy of dividing to distinguish between practices that are uncomfortably similar from the perspective of Plato's project of articulating *philosophia* as a hegemonic, master discourse. Thus Plato's philosophy—which reaches for *muthos* and *poiēsis* in moments of need, when rational analysis and *logos* are insufficient, and which represents men speaking in a range of private and public situations—had to be distinguished in its form and content from the ostensibly similar practices of poetry recital and public oratory. Lastly, in Plato's texts the strategies of homogenizing (collecting) and distinguishing (dividing) are frequently deployed alongside the strategy of evaluating cultural practices and forms of production with epistemic criteria in order to delegitimize, assimilate, and control them—the strategy covered in the next section.

6.4.1.3 The Delegitimization, Assimilation and Control of Traditional and Rival Practices

The narrower definition of rhetoric provided in the *Gorgias* (454–459)—persuasion concerning matters that are just and unjust—excludes rhetoric from the status of *technē* by deploying the knowledge criterion: the orator only provides conviction/belief (*pistis*) without knowledge (*epistēmē*) of this subject matter (454c–e).[115] This criterion assigns the practice of rhetoric the status of producing conviction-persuasion in the law courts and public gatherings, rather than teaching-persuasion or true instruction.

The knowledge criterion also comes into play in the *Phaedrus*, but the broader definition of rhetoric as a kind of leading the soul by means of words (261a) entails that considerations as to whether speaking can be classed as a *technē* need to cover *all* kinds of persuasive speaking (261d–e)—not just serious public speaking in the lawcourts and political arena, but also private conversations focused on persuasion, even trivial ones. The knowledge criterion is introduced when Socrates considers the practice of making opposing speeches in the lawcourts and the political arena: speakers can only lead listeners deceptively across similar views and get them to change positions if they are acquainted with the truth of the matter (262b).

But the critical moment comes with the shift of focus from knowledge of the subject matter to knowledge of the listener's soul: an expert practitioner of the art of speaking would proceed in a scientific manner and focus all his efforts on the soul (271a). In other words, an expert/true rhetorician would apply the dialectical principles of collection and division to different kinds of speech and souls, a practice which clearly requires the use of systematic knowledge:

> [...] once he has classified the types of speech and of soul, and the ways in which the various types of soul are acted upon, he will go through all the causes, fitting each type of

[115] For a more detailed discussion of the criteria that distinguish between *technai* and pseudo-*technai*, see Levin (2001b, pp. 82–84).

> speech to each type of soul and explaining what it is about the nature of particular kinds of soul which makes them inevitably either persuaded or unpersuaded by speeches of a particular kind. (271b)[116]

Such experts are rare, however. When Socrates surveys contemporary practitioners and the current state of rhetoric in Athens, he finds no evidence of systematic knowledge: the writers of rhetorical manuals are scoundrels who hide their knowledge of the soul (271c), and in the lawcourts orators aim for persuasive probability (*eikōs*) rather than truth (272d–e). Yet the current state of affairs does not rule out the possibility of a rhetorician using systematic knowledge to persuade his listeners. Nor does it exclude the possibility of a master using such knowledge to teach pupils how to persuade. However, at the point where rhetoric becomes a *technē* it also becomes philosophical, but a wise man/man of sound mind (*sōphrōn*) would not invest all his energy in public speaking (273e) and mere persuasion.

The subsequent famous analysis of writing leads to the conclusion that the written representation of philosophical speech can at best provide a reminder of genuine, serious philosophy—a practice that uses the spoken words of private conversation 'for explanation and teaching' (278a). Heath highlights the paradoxical position that Plato's text wrestles rhetoric into: 'So if conventional rhetoric does not become philosophical it is not a *technē* and cannot achieve its ends systematically; but if it does become philosophical it no longer wishes to achieve those ends. Either it dissolves itself, or it remains unfulfilled'.[117] Thus, ultimately, rhetoric is pinned down as a cultural practice that is either excluded from the status of *technē*—insofar as it focused on persuading the public and inculcating beliefs, or is assimilated to the supreme *technē*—the practice of philosophy, focused on educating souls in private conversation.

Once again, like the strategy of homogenization, the strategies of epistemic exclusion and genre assimilation applied to rhetoric are fully consistent with the *Republic*'s treatment of poetry. As was mentioned in the previous section, Levin highlighted how the epistemological and ontological architecture erected in Books 6 and 7 of the *Republic* serves to exclude poetry from knowledge (thus denying this cultural practice the status of *technē*): 'If poets actually did have knowledge of virtue and vice, hence qualifying as *technē* practitioners, they would be none other than philosophers'.[118] In the *Republic*, the strategies of epistemic exclusion and genre assimilation are taken a step further, with the banishment of poetry from the *polis*, unless the productions of this genre meets the strict approval of the philosopher-rulers. The pincer move of exclusion or assimilation ultimately serves to bring other modes of cultural production—practices, discourses, genres and text types—under the control of the master *technē*: philosophy.

[116] Plato (2002, p. 63).

[117] Heath (1989, p. 158).

[118] Levin (2001b, p. 148).

6.4.2 Charmides*: A Preliminary Attempt at Controlling Cultural Practices*

The *Republic*'s multi-layered justification for philosophy's control over all forms of cultural production is prefigured in the more hesitant probing of Plato's *Charmides*. This section outlines the strategic continuities between the two texts, engages with recent interpretations of academic philosophy, and proposes a broader contextual framework—drawing on Fleck's theoretical insights—for understanding the *Charmides*. The details of this contextualization will be developed in the subsequent sections.

In the *Charmides*, Socrates, just returned from the Battle of Potidaea (432 BC), discusses the virtue *sōphrosyne* (σωφροσύνη)—translated as 'temperance',[119] but also as 'moderation' and 'sound-mindedness'[120]—with two scions of ancient Athenian families: the mature Critias and the youth Charmides. At the time when Plato was writing (c. 399–390 BC), these two individuals were infamous for their roles in the oligarchic coup of 404–403 BC. Both had died in the battles associated with Thrasybulus' restoration of the democracy, and Critias in particular was in the process of being discursively villainized—for example in Xenophon's *Hellenica* (2.3), written c. 393–380[121]—as the leader of 'the Thirty Tyrants' who had ruled Athens with a reign of murder and rapacious appropriation. The fact that Critias and Charmides were also Plato's maternal great-uncle and uncle, respectively, is significant for the position that Plato's text occupied in the broader field of cultural production.

The *Charmides* is an incredibly complex text that looks back to 432 BC—the eve of the Peloponnesian War—but also forward through the events that led up to 399 BC. Plato's textual markers emphatically position the *Charmides* within a contested field of symbolic representation and intense, ongoing antagonism involving the following historical and political developments:

- The Peloponnesian War (431–404 BC): A disastrous conflict, which led some Athenian elites to accuse the radical democracy of being responsible for the defeat.
- Oligarchic Opposition to the *dēmokratia*: This opposition can be traced through texts from the 420s to Thucydides' account of the oligarchic coup of the Four Hundred in 411 BC.
- Post-War Decline of Athens: Following its loss in the Peloponnesian War, Athens was transformed from the dominant Aegean power—a superpower with unmatched wealth and resources—to a weakened subject under Spartan

[119] Plato (1955, 1992).

[120] Tuozzo (2011).

[121] Brownson (1961, p. ix).

hegemony. The city had been ravaged by plague and war and only narrowly escaped complete destruction by the Peloponnesian alliance.[122]
- The Oligarchic Coup of 404–403 BC: Pro-Spartan oligarchs seized power, murdered leading democrats and moderates, attacked democratic institutions, and attempted to 'efface the democratic culture deeply embedded within the various religious, social, and political institutions of Athens'.[123]
- The Civil War of 404 BC and the Restoration of Democracy: After the tumultuous civil strife, the restoration led to discursive countermeasures—such as legal reforms and the codification of ancestral laws—creating a charged atmosphere that ultimately contributed to the execution of Socrates in 399 BC.[124]

In other words, Plato's *Charmides* was just one salvo in an ongoing culture war. It articulated a complex and deliberately ambiguous position in a multi-layered discursive struggle that can be traced back through the previous decades. This context is, therefore, an ideal testing ground for applying Fleck's concepts of 'intellectual unrest', 'collective mood', 'the circulation of ideas', and 'proto-ideas', to identify the emergence of a specific thought style.

To begin with, Plato's choice of the virtue *sōphrosynē* is far from a neutral subject for discussion: it was an ancient aristocratic virtue that had become associated with Spartan self-discipline (Thuc. 1.68.2) while its opposite, *akolasia* (indiscipline), was associated with the excesses of the radical democracy—exemplified in Alcibiades' address to the Spartans (Thuc. 6.89.5)).[125] Thucydides has Peisander, one of the instigators of the 411 oligarchic coup of the Four Hundred, declare that the Athenians would not be able to save the city without 'adopting a more σώφρων [prudent] government and putting the offices to a greater extent into the hands of a few' (Thuc. 8.53.3).[126] Thus, as Thomas M. Tuozzo highlights, during the Peloponnesian War, Athenian oligarchic circles came to use *sōphrosynē* as a term 'to describe their own political program'.[127] Bearing in mind that Athenian citizens were highly sensitive to the negative connotations of the term '*oligarchia*', since it was associated with schemes for the potential return of the treacherous Alcibiades, the use of *sophrosyne* and its cognates (e.g., *sōphrōn*) functioned as a more palatable slogan or codeword.[128]

---

[122] 'When they arrived, the ephors called an assembly, at which the Corinthians and Thebans in particular, though many other Greeks agreed with them, opposed making a treaty with the Athenians and favoured destroying their city.' (Xen. *Hellenica*. II. 2.17-22) Xenophon (1918/1921).

[123] Wolpert (2002, p. 23).

[124] Wolpert (2002, pp. 37–38, 63–65).

[125] Powell (1988, p. 87).

[126] Tuozzo (2011, p. 94). Mynott's translation: 'This is not going to happen unless we govern ourselves more prudently and restrict office to fewer people than now, […]' Thucydides (2013, p. 542).

[127] Tuozzo (2011, p. 94).

[128] Raphael Sealey (1973, pp. 277–280) notes that in Thucydides, *oligarchia* is a narrator's term rather than one used by advocates of the political shift. Even Peisander, when proposing an oligar-

Therefore, *sōphrosynē* can be identified as a Fleckian proto-idea:[129] a concept which by the 420s still retained its core meaning (discipline, restraint) but which was undergoing a process of differentiation and acquiring new meanings due to its circulation among an Athenian thought collective which actively adapted the idea to its present circumstances.

When Socrates presses Charmides to define *sōphrosynē* at the start of the investigation, the initial definitions he supplies (doing things in an orderly and quiet way (159b); modesty (160e)) derive from the long-established aristocratic value system. However, his third definition, which he apparently heard from Critias, i.e., 'minding one's own business' (161b) (*to ta heautou prattein*—literally 'to do the things of oneself',[130] or 'doing one's own things'[131]) was associated with more recent modifications and connotations. This shift of meaning entails a shift in interlocutor: from now on in the dialogue, Socrates will examine the meaning and functions of *sōphrosynē* with Critias.

Tuozzo reconstructs the range of meaning associated with *sōphrosynē* defined as doing one's own things: 'σωφροσύνη in this sense involves refraining from transgressing social norms constitutive of one's social position and, in particular, from transgressions that would infringe on the prerogatives of another'.[132] Since different people and social groups occupied different social positions, the appropriate temperance or prudence expected from them varied. Tuozzo writes: 'For elites, σωφροσύνη consists in refraining from abusing their power for their own profit; for common citizens, it consists in submitting to the rule of their betters'.[133] Crucially, the concept of *sōphrosynē* as 'minding one's own business' applied from the level of the individual to the level of the polis: 'the term also had a use in discussions of foreign policy, to describe the nonimperialistic, noninterfering foreign policy associated with Sparta'.[134] In other words, the Athenian Empire, characterized as violating established Hellenic social norms by subjugating and enslaving rebellious subject-allies (Thuc. 1.97.4), and encroaching on the territories and alliances of the Peloponnesian city-states, did the exact opposite of minding its own business. Athens was unrestrained and undisciplined, upsetting the peace and calmness (*hēsychiotēs* – ἡσυχιότης) associated with Spartan discipline.

Socrates' response to the notion of *sōphrosynē* as minding one's own business prefigures three elements that reappear in the *Republic*: need as the founding principle of the *polis* (*Rep.* 369b), the resulting division of labour (*Rep.* 369d–374e), and the concern with the control and supervision of cultural production that runs

chic program, avoids the word, and Thucydides summarises it euphemistically as a rejection of *demokratia*.

[129] Fleck (1979, p. 23).

[130] Plato (1992, p. 70, Sprague's footnote 33).

[131] Tuozzo (2011, p. 66).

[132] Tuozzo (2011, p. 91).

[133] Tuozzo (2011, p. 94).

[134] Tuozzo (2011, p. 94).

throughout Plato's masterpiece. In the *Charmides*, Socrates makes an abrupt transition from the notion of *not* doing other people's business (161e) to the concept of the division of labour and the issue of a well-governed city in order to highlight the problematic implications of Critias' conception of *sōphrosynē*:

> "Well then," I said, "do you think a city would be well governed by a law commanding each man to weave and wash his own cloak, make his own shoes [sandals] and oil flask and scraper, and perform everything else by this same principle of keeping his hands off of other people's things and making and doing his own?"
>
> "No, I don't think it would," he said.
>
> "But," said I, "if a city is going to be temperately governed, it must be governed well."
>
> "Of course," he said.
>
> "Then if temperance is 'minding your own business', it can't be minding things of this sort and in this fashion." (161e–162a)[135]

In other words, a well-governed polis requires people to do other people's business, at least in the sense of producing material goods. Therefore, the virtue of *sōphrosynē* cannot be a norm applicable to each man. By implication, Socrates has drawn attention to the tension between the aristocratic notion that people should not transgress the norms constitutive of their social position and the concept of a democratic *polis* wherein the law applies equally to all men.

This provocation prompts Critias to take over from Charmides. The first tussle between Socrates and Critias concerns the latter's distinctions between doing (*πράττειν—prattein*), working (*ἐργάζεσθαι—ergazesthai*), and making (*ποιεῖν—poiein*). According to Rosamund Kent Sprague's reading,[136] Critias is prepared to allow that people who do other people's business are temperate (*σώφρων—sōphrōn*), but cannot accept that people who make other people's things are temperate (163a). By means of this distinction, and drawing on the authority of Hesiod, Critias hopes to exclude specific modes of production and forms of labour from the sphere of *σωφροσύνη* (*sōphrosynē*):

> "No, I don't," he said; "neither do I call working (*ἐργάζεσθαι/ergazesthai*) and making (*ποιεῖν/poiein*) the same thing. I have learned this from Hesiod, who said that work (*ἔργον/ergon*) is no disgrace. Now do you think that, if he called things such as those you just now mentioned works (*ἔργα/erga*) and working (*ἐργάζεσθαι/ergazesthai*) and doing (*πράττειν/prattein*), he would say that it is not a disgrace for anyone to make sandals or sell salt-fish or work in a brothel? You mustn't think so, Socrates, but he in fact, I think, considered a making (*ποίησιν/poiesin*) to be something other than a doing (*πράξεως/praxeōs*) and working (*ἐργασίας/ergasias*), and that what is made (*ποίημα/poiēma*) is sometimes a disgrace, when it is not accompanied by the noble (*μετὰ τοῦ καλοῦ/meta tou kalou*), but that no work (*ἔργον/ergon*) is ever a disgrace. For he called things that are made nobly (*καλῶς/kalōs*) and beneficially (*ὠφελίμως/ōphelimōs*) works (*ἔργα/erga*), and such makings he called workings (*ἐργασίας/ergasias*) and doings (*πράξεις/praxeis*). And one must say that he considered only such things to be proper to one (*οἰκεῖα/oikeika*), and all harmful (*βλαβερά/blabera*) things alien (*ἀλλότρια/allotria*); so one must think that both Hesiod

[135] Plato (1992, p. 71).

[136] Plato (1992, p. 73).

> and anyone else who is wise (*φρόνιμος/phronimos*) calls this person who does his own things temperate." (163b4–c8) (163b4–c8)[137]

Although forms of craft production and labour are mentioned explicitly, Critias refrains from giving examples of things 'made nobly and beneficially'. Tuozzo suggests: 'We may hazard a guess that Critias has in mind the activities proper to a well-born, wealthy gentleman, and in particular, political engagement. These are the things that are nobly done, and are far removed from the craft activity of those who must work for a living'.[138]

It can thus be observed that Critias is represented as deploying the Socratic-Platonic strategy of exclusion identified in the previous section. However, while in the *Ion*, *Gorgias* and *Phaedrus* Socrates is shown using the strategy of making conceptual distinctions to exclude certain cultural practices (rhetoric, poetry recital, poetry) from the class of *technē*, Critias uses semantic distinctions to exclude certain social practices (the manual labour of sandal making, the selling of a fishmonger, providing sexual services) from the value associated with the virtue of *sōphrosynē*. Unlike the sophists depicted in other dialogues, whose practices bear the brunt of Socrates' exclusionary strategy, it becomes apparent that Plato is portraying Critias as more aligned with Socrates' practice of *philosophia*. His distinctions may be somewhat forced and clumsy, requiring prompting and guidance from Socrates—Critias is almost immediately made to abandon his distinctions and concur that he is really asserting temperance is doing good things (163e10–11)—but his method and concerns are far more 'Socratic' than those of the long-winded or blustering sophists whom Socrates ultimately humiliates and silences in other dialogues (e.g., Gorgias, Thrasymachus).

When considered in the light of Fleck's theory, these two elements—the focus on and concern with a range of practices (political engagement, productive crafts, prostitution) and the use of distinctions to assign a hierarchy of values (from noble to disgraceful) and enforce exclusion—suggest that Socrates and Critias share the same thought style. That is, they share 'the problems of interest to the thought collective' and the 'methods which it applies as a means of cognition'.[139] The subsequent conceptual steps of Plato's rigorously constructed dialogue provide further support for this reading.

First, Socrates introduces the issue of whether 'temperate men can be ignorant of their temperance' (164a). Since Critias allows that certain craftsmen who *do* other people's business can be temperate (e.g., politically engaged noblemen, and probably doctors), Socrates suggests he must believe that it is also possible for them to not know they are temperate while doing this business. Socrates then takes a second step: *doing* other people's business can be beneficial or harmful, but craftsmen do

[137] Tuozzo (2011, p. 176), transliterations added.

[138] Tuozzo (2011, p. 177).

[139] Fleck (1979, p. 99).

not always know whether they have acted beneficially or not.[140] Therefore, Critias must allow that a craftsman can act beneficially when doing other people's business without knowing it (164b–c).

Critias' response to these steps is to insist that *sōphrosynē* necessarily entails knowledge, even at the cost of withdrawing his previous statements: 'As a matter of fact, this is pretty much what I say temperance is, to know oneself, and I agree with the inscription to this effect set up at Delphi' (165d).[141] Thus, at this point the dialogue moves from the proto-idea of *sōphrosynē* (sound-minded restraint, modesty), through Critias' reformulated conception of minding one's own business, to the epistemological terrain traditionally associated with Socrates and the Delphic inscription "Know thyself (*gnōthi sauton*)" (Phaedrus 229e).

The fact that it is Critias who introduces the definition of *sōphrosynē* as self-knowledge has been construed differently by scholars. On the one hand, Laurence Lampert[142] reads it as marking a break between Critias and Socrates, since Critias assumes that he is a knower and that he can use this definition as a basis for knowing and ruling other knowledges, while Socrates—of course—only knows that he does not know, and thus will ultimately refrain from claiming knowledge of all knowledges. Furthermore, for Lampert, Critias' willingness to abandon his previous definitions reveals that he is no philosopher; he is an opportunist who uses truths to further his own agenda.

On the other hand, Tuozzo suggests that Plato was sympathetic towards the aristocratic tradition of pro-oligarchic thinking that Critias represented. He argues that Plato depicts Critias as a serious thinker who makes fruitful contributions to the dialogue and demonstrates 'relative philosophical and dialectical sophistication'.[143] On Tuozzo's reading, by allowing Critias to make an extended speech on the Delphic inscriptions, which asserts that '"know thyself" and "be temperate" are the same' (164c165c),[144] Plato makes a clear reference to Critias' poetry, which associated the Delphic recommendation of moderation with Spartan values.[145] Moreover, for Tuozzo, Critias' speech revives the divine aspects of the concept of *sōphrosynē* hinted at previously—for example, in Socrates' account of Zalmoxis, the necessity of curing the soul, and the soul's acquisition of *sōphrosynē* (156d–157a)—and emphasizes how unique this value is: 'one that both is central to human social life and links human beings with the gods'.[146]

The reference to the Delphic inscriptions and the identification of *sōphrosynē* with self-knowledge marks a thematic shift in the dialogue. Socrates' response to

---

[140] On the issue of whether Socrates can be interpreted as meaning that crafts are other- or self-benefiting, see Tuozzo (2011, pp. 181–183), who concludes that "only a self-benefiting interpretation does justice to the letter of the text" (183).

[141] Plato (1992, p. 76).

[142] Lampert (2010, pp. 185–192).

[143] Tuozzo (2011, pp. 66, 70, 177).

[144] Plato (1992, p. 76).

[145] Tuozzo (2011, p. 75).

[146] Tuozzo (2011, p. 188).

Critias' third definition is to infer that 'if *sōphrosynē* is knowing [*gignōskein*] something, it is clear that it would be a kind of knowledge [*epistēmē*] and of something, wouldn't it?' (165c4–5).[147] Henceforth the conversation is focused on the status of *sōphrosynē* as a knowledge/science, which entails considering this knowledge reflexively—how a knowledge can know itself as knowledge, its relation to the knowledges involved in various *technai*, and ultimately its relation to the knowledge/science of the good and bad. Since the *Charmides* is one of Plato's aporetic dialogues, in this case ending with an explicit acknowledgement of failure (175a–e), the dialogue can be read as raising issues that are eventually solved more satisfactorily in the *Republic.*[148]

Thus, just as the setting of the *Charmides* steps back to the outbreak of the Peloponnesian War in 432–1 BC, while the characters of Critias and Charmides point forward to the oligarchic coup of 404–3 BC, and even to Socrates' execution in 399 BC, the dialogue similarly steps back through the conceptual field to trace the development of the idea of *sōphrosynē*—from ancient notions, through Critias' modification, to Socrates' epistemological and moral additions, but it also points forward to developments in the field of *philosophia* that are yet to come (e.g., Socrates' reference to 'the great man' who is needed (169a)).[149]

Once *sōphrosynē* is redefined as a knowledge/science (*epistēmē*)(165c), the first issue to be addressed is what this knowledge produces (165e). Critias insists that *sōphrosynē* is unlike other knowledges/sciences—such as the science of housebuilding, which produces houses; or the *technai* of geometry and calculation, which have an object distinct from themselves (they are 'of something' in Critias' formulation)—since *sōphrosynē* 'is the only science which is both of other sciences and of itself' (166c).[150] Thus, rather than maintaining the definition of *sōphrosynē* as the science of the self (Know thyself), it becomes a knowledge of itself as knowledge.[151] This reflexive twist enables Critias to bring all other *technai* and knowledge practices under the control of *sōphrosynē*: if this knowledge knows itself as an *epistēmē*, it is in effect the knowledge of knowledge, the science of science.

Socrates adds yet another conceptual twist: if *sōphrosynē* is the science of science, it could also be 'a science of the absence of science' (166e). This would place the temperate man in a unique position in society:

> Then only the temperate man will know himself? and will be able to examine what he knows and does not know, and in the same way he will be able to inspect other people to see when a man does in fact know what he knows and thinks he knows, and when again he does not know what he thinks he knows, and no one else will be able to do. (167a)[152]

---

[147] Lampert (2010, p. 77).

[148] For instance, Lampert (2010, p. 169) and Tuozzo (2011, pp. 313–314).

[149] Lampert (2010, p. 169) even argues that the dramatic date of the *Republic* is just a few weeks after the *Charmides*.

[150] Plato (1992, p. 79).

[151] Sprague describes this as Critias' 'shift from knowledge of self (*heautou*) to knowledge of itself (*heautes*)'—Plato (1992, p. 79).

[152] Plato (1992, p. 80).

Despite being condemned to a strange reflexivity and producing nothing that has any obvious benefit, due to the unique nature of his knowledge, might not the temperate man be able to inspect other people's knowledge and 'divide things and say that one is science and the other not?' (170a).

However, Socrates is acutely aware that the temperate man cannot lay claim to omniscient knowledge: when inspecting other people, the man possessing *sōphrosynē* is not able to know *what* the other person knows; he can only claim to know *that* the other person knows or does not know something: 'Nor, when another person claims to know something, will our friend be able to find out whether he knows what he says he knows or does not know it. But he will only know this much, it seems, that the man has some science; yes, but of what, temperance will fail to inform him' (170d).[153] Tuozzo frames this as the difference between 'a full-fledged knowledge of knowledge (knowing *what*)' and 'a reduced knowledge of knowledge (knowing *that*)'.[154] In other words, without being a doctor himself, a temperate man cannot know *what* a doctor knows, only *that* a doctor knows something/has some science.

In crucial passages, Socrates reveals what is really at stake in the definition of *sōphrosynē* as the science of science: the true benefit of *sōphrosynē*—as the ability to inspect and supervise other people's knowledge—is that it would also allow them to rule over these people and govern the *polis*:

> "[…] Because if, as we assumed in the beginning, the temperate man knew what he knew and what he did not know (and that he knows the former but not the latter) and were able to investigate another man who was in the same situation, then it would be of the greatest benefit to us to be temperate. **Because those of us who had temperance would live lives free from error and so would all those who were under our rule**. Neither would we ourselves be attempting to do things we did not understand—rather we would find those who did understand and turn the matter over to them—**nor would we trust those over whom we ruled to do anything except what they would do correctly, and this would be that of which they possessed the science**. And thus, by means of temperance, **every household would be well run, and every city well-governed, and so in every case where temperance reigned**. And **with error rooted out and rightness in control**, men so circumstanced would necessarily fare admirably and well in all their doings and, faring well, they would be happy. Isn't this what we mean about temperance, Critias," I said, "when we say what a good thing it would be to know what one knows and what one does not know?" (171d–172a) (emphasis added)[155]

If such a supervisory science were possible, it would legitimize the division of labour—the necessity of which was signalled earlier (161e–162a), since the rulers would be able to recognize their own cognitive limitations and delegate tasks to those who have passed inspections to determine *that* they possess knowledge, and who could be trusted not to stray beyond their expertise. It is noteworthy that it is precisely during this fantasy of domination that Socrates introduces the very element that will ultimately threaten the whole argument and conception of *sōphrosynē*

[153] Plato (1992, pp. 86–87).

[154] Tuozzo (2011, pp. 257–263).

[155] Plato (1992, pp. 88–89).

as the ruling science of science: the claim that in a *polis* thus governed the people 'would be happy'.

This element is also emphasized when Socrates provides further details on the benefits that would result from their epistemic supervision of specific crafts:

> "Listen then," I said, "to my dream, to see whether it comes through horn or through ivory. If temperance really ruled over us and were as we now define it, surely everything would be done according to science: **neither would anyone who says he is a pilot (but is not) deceive us, nor would any doctor or general or anyone else pretending to know what he does not know escape our notice**. This being the situation, wouldn't we have greater bodily health than we do now, and safety when we are in danger at sea or in battle, and **wouldn't we have dishes and all our clothes and shoes and things skill fully made for us, and many other things as well, because we would be employing true craftsmen**? [...] I grant that the human race, if thus equipped, would act and live in a scientific way—because temperance, watching over it, would not allow the absence of science to creep in and become our accomplice. But whether acting scientifically would make us fare well and be happy, this we have yet to learn, my dear" (173a–d) (emphasis added).[156]

These passages provide us with an uninhibited expression of a will to power. The articulation of the claim to have knowledge of knowledge is tightly bound up with the articulation of the desire to rule over other knowledges and their uses. Plato's interlocutors—acutely aware that they produce no goods of tangible value in a city entirely dependent on the crafts and professions involved in the import of commodities and production of goods—dream up ways of claiming the authority to supervise all professions and modes of production.

My argument is that in these passages Plato offers a clear representation of the concerns and longings that were articulated by a specific thought collective on the outbreak on the Peloponnesian War and in the following decades. Plato's focus on the concept of *sōphrosynē* can be treated as a window onto the thought style of Athenian *aristoi* (or *oligoi*) who were dissatisfied with the governance and policies of the *demokratia*. In the 420s, their opposition to the radical democracy was initially restricted to purely articulatory practices, such the intrigues and sympotic texts read and discussed at the meetings of political clubs (*hetaireiai*) and sworn associations (*synōmosiai*),[157] but with the opportunities afforded by Athenian military disaster (411 BC) and ultimate defeat at the hands of Sparta (404 BC), this thought collective engaged in practices aimed at abolishing the democratic political culture, reorganizing the constitution, and returning Athens to its ancestral laws (*patrioi nomoi*).[158]

Thus, Plato's contemporary readers would have been all too aware that, about three decades after the fictional conversation presented in the *Charmides*, the real Critias tried to make the dream of ruling a reality, by seizing power with a group of oligarchs that sought 'to remake Athens on the model of Sparta, or on the model of

[156] Plato (1992, pp. 88–89).

[157] Hornblower (2008, pp. 916–920).

[158] Wolpert (2002).

an idealized Sparta'.[159] In the last decades of the fifth century, the Spartan model of social organization, i.e., a narrow oligarchy based on agrarian production with a tightly-controlled slave population (*heilōtes*), was discursively framed as the antithesis of the Athenian model, i.e., a direct democracy based on an aggressively expansionist empire (*archē*) with subjugated and exploited subject-allies. The Athenian shift from the traditional agrarian economy to a thalassocracy entailed a structural transformation in the modes of production that ultimately undermined Solon's hierarchy of property classes.

Athens' successful maritime strategy in the Persian Wars, the founding of the Delian League (477 BC) and the rise of the radical democracy (462 BC) are associated with the Athenian economy being increasingly oriented away from an agrarian economy based on small farms and dependent on the labour of the *zeugitae* (the hoplite rank) and slaves, to a maritime empire dependent on seaborne commerce for the import of corn and wheat, and on the tribute (*phoros*) collected from subject-allies. The sources of Athens' power—the control of trade routes, the ability to brutally suppress resistance, colonial settlements (*klērouchiai*), the imposition of Athenian coinage, a monetized economy based on the import of foodstuffs and the export of commodities and manufactured goods, the cultural capital accrued from public expenditure on architecture and theatre—were all ultimately based on the labour of the *thētes* (the lowest and poorest class), who manned the ships and were sent out as colonizers, and on the prized craftsmanship of the *metoikoi*, who were particularly associated with the port of Piraeus.[160]

The development of Piraeus as a military harbour and commercial port under the guidance of Themistocles (completed c. 471 BC) had, in effect, created an alternative power centre outside of Athens proper. This centre was associated with the *metoikoi* and a proliferation of trades, as signalled by the disgruntled 'Old Oligarch'[161] in 431–424 BC: 'the city needs metics because of the great number of their skills and the requirements of the fleet' ([Xen] *Ath. Pol.* 1.12).[162] The skilled labour involved in shipbuilding required a plethora of other specialized crafts, such as timber wholesaler, woodcutter, saw maker, ropemaker, rope dealer sail stitcher, glue seller etc.; then a flourishing port required yet more specializations, such as stevedore, cartwright, basket maker, net maker; and all these labourers had to be fed, clothed and provided with tools.[163]

According to Diodorus, who probably based his account on lost fourth-century sources, the growth of professions and professionalism was a direct result of Themistocles' encouragement: 'He also persuaded the *demos* every year to

[159] Krentz (1982, p. 64).

[160] On the historical context: de Ste. Croix (1954, 1981), Kagan (1969, 1987), Meiggs (1972), Powell (1988), Kallet (2013).

[161] For the dating of the *Constitution of the Athenians* and the use of the name 'the Old Oligarch' as opposed to Pseudo-Xenophon etc., see Marr and Rhodes (2015, pp. 1–6).

[162] Marr and Rhodes (2015).

[163] David M. Lewis' (2021, pp. 158–167) *Labour Specialization in the Athenian Economy: Occupational Hazards* contains an extensive list of Athenian occupations with testimonia.

construct twenty triremes as additions to the existing fleet and to make resident aliens and craftsmen tax free, the object being to bring crowds of immigrants into the city from every quarter, and thus provide manpower for a greater number of skilled occupations' (Diod. xi.43.3).[164]

When viewed in this light, Critias' disdain for manual labour and his attempt to exclude certain professions from the virtue of *sōphrosynē,* and Socrates' obsession with identifying true craftsmen and rooting out charlatans by means of the supervisory category of *epistēmē*, can be interpreted as Plato's representations of the reactionary responses of a specific group of elite citizens who lamented their loss of power and control over the productive forces in Athenian society. In the face of structural economic transformation and the accompanying social upheaval—with the Solonic hierarchy and traditional value system under immense pressure—a section of the elite came to articulate a set of highly critical positions with regard to various forms of production and the specialised practices associated with them.

Crucially, this criticism was also targeted at the leaders and statesmen who initiated and facilitated the economic transformation with specific policy decisions, and at the representatives of the democratic consensus that supported and ostensibly benefited from these policies, or at least acquiesced to them. Thus, Plato's dialogues can be read as historical-fictional representations of what Josiah Ober described as 'intra-elite competition'.[165] In a somewhat similar vein, Wood argued that the 'outright contempt for labour and labourers' displayed by Plato and Xenophon was also aimed at 'the prevailing cultural ideal': 'In other words, those who were most vociferous in their expressions of contempt for labour were clearly not *reflecting* but *attacking* the dominant world-view'.[166]

However, Plato's complex representational strategies make it impossible to straightforwardly identify his texts with one specific discursive position. At most, the dialogues can be treated as reconstructing and representing a range of conflicting and differentially defined positions.

Nevertheless, I contend that representational consistencies within and across Plato's dialogues, as well as consistent positions articulated in the textual field outside of Plato's texts—and with which his texts interact—allow the identification of a specific aristocratic-oligarchic thought style that developed between 432 and 403 BC. This thought style self-identified in opposition to the prevailing democratic consensus and other rival thought styles, such as those which came to be strategically conflated with the homogenizing designation 'sophistry'.

In *Plato's Charmides Positive Elenchus in a "Socratic" Dialogue*, Tuozzo analyses and rejects the ancient and modern depiction of Critias as a sophist and atheist. He suggests that this image of Critias, which persists in relatively recent Plato scholarship (e.g. Schmid 1998; Lampert 2010), is filtered through the hostile

[164] Diodorus Siculus (2010, p. 50).

[165] Ober (1989, p. 85).

[166] Wood (1989, p. 139).

historiographic tradition of the fourth century BC, and is rooted in the criticism of Epicurus and the second-century AD account of Philostratus.[167]

Since the phenomenon of recycling ancient representations without reflexive analysis and questioning can be construed as a clear-cut example of a modern or near-contemporary thought collective (Anglophone academic philosophers) uncritically applying the biased characterisations of earlier thought collectives, tracing the interactive transmission of these representations across centuries and millennia will both shed light on the perceptions of Plato's *Charmides* and further justify the application of Fleck's theory.

6.4.3 *The Transmission of Critias*

6.4.3.1 Critias the Tyrant

The earliest surviving evidence for the vilification of Critias appears in Xenophon's Hellenica, written c. 393–380. There, Critias is portrayed as the most tyrannical of the Thirty—vicious, cynically self-interested oligarchs who seized power in 404–3. Xenophon's Critias is singled out as being uniquely eager to execute informers and enemies of the aristocracy. While these vengeful actions are described as initially having the support of the Senate and the citizens (*Hell.* 2.3.12), Critias is then depicted as leading a killing spree that targeted personal enemies and—crucially, in the light of the hostility to craftsmen that Plato's Critias expresses in the *Charmides*—the Athenian *metoikoi*:

> And now, when this had been accomplished, thinking that they were at length free to do whatever they pleased, they put many people to death out of personal enmity, and many also for the sake of securing their property. One measure that they resolved upon, in order to get money to pay their guardsmen, was that each of their number should seize one of the aliens residing in the city, and that they should put these men to death and confiscate their property. (*Hell.* 2.3.21)[168]

The centrepiece of Xenophon's account is the dramatic clash between Critias and Theramenes, who are positioned as symbolic representatives of extreme and moderate oligarchy, respectively. In contrast to Theramenes' position of pragmatic restraint—he describes the Thirty's executions as unjust, but also stresses their negative impact on public opinion and the danger of turning the *metoikoi* against the government (2.3.40)—Critias is depicted as a pro-Spartan traitor and tyrant who has abandoned all restraint, using violence to subvert legal procedure (he 'went out and ordered the men with the daggers to take their stand at the railing in plain sight of the Senate' (2.3.50)).[169]

---

[167] Tuozzo (2011, pp. 59–79).

[168] Xenophon (1961, p. 123).

[169] Xenophon (1961, pp. 139–141).

Thus, in Xenophon's symbolic representation, Critias is pointedly cast as the exact opposite of the temperate man: it is Theramenes who embodies aristocratic *sōphrosynē* as he argues the case for moderation and faces his execution with calm dignity (2.3.55).

In *The Athenian Constitution,* long attributed to Aristotle but probably written by one of his pupils c. 332–322 BC,[170] Critias is not listed as one of the Thirty.[171] Although the text refers to Theramenes' opposition to the violent excesses of the Thirty, no mention is made of any public confrontation with Critias or of the latter's role in his execution (*Ath. Pol.* 34–38).[172] The contrast with Critias' central role in Xenophon's dramatic re-enactment is stark, suggesting that this absence could have been due to cultural pressure to erase Critias as a historical figure, or that by the time of writing Critias had been thoroughly expunged from the collective memory of Athenian citizens.[173]

6.4.3.2 Critias the Atheist

In the Hellenistic period, Epicurus (341–270 BC) is credited with including Critias among the Greek atheists that he criticized in Book 12 of his lost work, *On Nature* (*Peri physeōs*). This criticism was probably based on Critias' *Sisyphus*, the surviving fragment of which has been traditionally interpreted as asserting that the gods were a human invention:

> […] it seems to me,
> that first a certain man, shrewd and wise in mind (σοφὸς γνώμην),
> invented fear of the gods for mortals, so that
> base men have some fear, even if
> they do or say or think a thing in secret.[174]

According to *On Piety* by Philodemus, an Epicurean philosopher and poet of the first century BC, Epicurus described Prodicus, Diagoras, Critias, and others as "raving lunatics" and "Bacchant revellers" for eliminating the divine from existing things (Col. XVIII 518–33).[175] Interestingly, then, Epicurus—whose philosophy became associated with atheism in the seventeenth century, when the term 'Epicurean' was used to exclude the certain philosophies from the public sphere and

[170] Rhodes (2002).

[171] For a detailed comparison of ancient accounts of the Thirty, see Wolpert (2002).

[172] Aristotle (2002).

[173] Tuozzo (2011, p. 60) also adduces a passage from Aristotle's *Rhetoric* which indicates that Critias' deeds were not very well known: 'But if you wish to praise Critias, narrative is necessary, for not many people know [what he did]' (Rhet. 1416b26–29). Tuozzo also cites Umberto Bultrighini's *Maledetta democrazia* as a key text for Critias' 'virtual *damnatio memoriae*', but this text was not accessible at the time of writing.

[174] Tuozzo (2011, p. 82).

[175] Spinelli and Verde (2020).

the universities (see Chap. 10)—seems to have been responsible for stigmatizing Critias with the charge of atheism.[176]

In the mid-second century AD Sextus Empiricus, a Pyrrhonian Skeptic, consolidated the tradition of categorizing Critias as an atheist with his interpretation of Critias' *Sisyphus* fragment:

> And Critias, one of the Tyrants at Athens, seems to belong to the company of the atheists when he says that the ancient lawgivers invented God as a kind of overseer of the right and wrong actions of men, in order to make sure that nobody injured his neighbours privily through fear of vengeance at the hands of the Gods. (Ad. Math. 1.54)[177]

The main basis for Epicurus' and Sextus Empiricus' classification of Critias as an atheist is a fragment of a dramatic speech delivered by the mythological trickster Sisyphus. This raises the question of whether the speech reflects the views of Critias himself. Tuozzo's subtle and convincing interpretation of this and other fragments suggests that Critias recognized most people need something more than law to deter them from wrongdoing, but this does not necessarily entail atheism: 'The fact that the many need the fear of the gods to act in ways that are socially beneficial does not require that the gods be a mere fiction concocted for that purpose'.[178]

A fragment from a dramatic work is clearly an insufficient basis for inferring the author's religious beliefs. What is evident is that, in the light of other surviving fragments, Critias considered the gods from the perspective of social utility, and in terms of different needs: the majority of people need the fear of the gods to supplement the coercive power of the law, whereas some aristocrats are capable of cultivating their characters (through internalizing values such as *sōphrosynē*) to the point where they avoid injustice independently, without the fear of divine vengeance.[179]

6.4.3.3 Critias the Sophist

In the Roman imperial period, Philostratus (c. 170–247 AD), a Greek sophist and writer, was able to comfortably add a third element to the discursive representation of Critias, namely his supposed sophistry. In the *Lives of the Sophists* (written c. 230–38 AD), Philostratus describes Critias as a pupil of Gorgias (along with Alcibiades, Thucydides and Pericles) (1.9.1), which initially justifies the subsequent use of the epithet 'sophist' at the beginning of a list of Critias' crimes:

> Critias the sophist, even though he did overthrow democratic government at Athens, was not thereby proved to be a bad man; for the democracy might well have been overthrown from within, since it had become so overbearing and insolent that it would not heed even

---

[176] Emidio Spinelli and Francesco Verde (2020) analyse the *Epistles* and ancient sources to conclude that Epicurus was far from an atheist: his theory was 'also a theological theory' in which the gods and the divine play key roles.

[177] Sextus Empiricus (1936, pp. 29–31).

[178] Tuozzo (2011, p. 85).

[179] Tuozzo (2011, pp. 85–86).

> those who governed according to the established laws. But seeing that he conspicuously sided with Sparta, and betrayed the holy places to the enemy; that he pulled down the walls by the agency of Lysander; that he deprived the Athenians whom he drove into exile of any place of refuge in Greece by proclaiming that Sparta would wage war on any that should harbour an Athenian exile; that in brutality and bloodthirstiness he surpassed even the Thirty; that he shared in the monstrous design of Sparta to make Attica look like a mere pasture for sheep by emptying her of her human herd; for all this I hold him to be the greatest criminal of all who are notorious for crime. (1.16.1)[180]

This passage clearly indicates that, as the image of Critias was transmitted across six centuries, thought collectives interacted with the representations they received, actively emphasizing certain elements and articulating positions with regard to them. Thus Critias' attack on Athenian democracy is excusable for Philostratus' thought style, while his pro-Spartan treachery and his treatment of the Athenian people are singled out for the strongest condemnation.[181]

Philostratus' position as a Greek sophist living in Imperial Rome, and in close proximity to the imperial family, determines what he focuses on in his account of the Greek 'sophists'. At a time when the Roman Republic had been discursively positioned as a distant memory of civil strife followed by two centuries of stability under the *Pax Romana*, but also at a time when Imperial Rome was on the verge of a new period of civil strife in the 'Crisis of the Third Century', Philostratus' *Lives of the Sophists* contains frustratingly little detail on the contribution of the fifth-century sophists to the deliberative practices of the Athenian democracy. Adam M. Kemezis points out that Philostratus' 'very unusual sort of narrative history of the Greek people' attempts to present sophistic activity as a cultural movement and set of cultural practices that were entirely dependent on the creativity of unique individuals. Thus Philostratus suggests—provocatively, according to Kemezis—that the appearance of the sophistic art at certain times and locations 'does not need to be related to any outside causal factors':

> Philostratus wants his readers to contemplate the idea of a narrative history of Greek culture independent of political circumstances, and at the same time to ask themselves whether such a history can be made to function, or whether political and dynastic changes really are the critical factors.[182]

Philostratus provides details that acknowledge fifth-century sophists were deeply involved in public life, and in political and religious controversies—he indicates there was a connection between Gorgias and Pericles (1.9.1), that Pericles' had a great reputation as an orator due to his extempore eloquence (1. praef), that Gorgias played a role in religious festivals and delivered orations on Greek reconciliation

[180] Philostratus (1922, pp. 45–47).

[181] A similar emphasis is found in Philostratus' assessment of Antiphon, the orator who Thucydides describes as the brains behind the oligarchic coup of 411 BC (Thuc. 8.68). According to Philostratus, he was a bad man because: 'He broke up the democracy; he enslaved the Athenian people; he sided with Sparta, secretly at first, but openly later on; and he let loose on the public life of Athens the mob of the Four Hundred Tyrants' (1.15) Philostratus (1922, p. 41).

[182] Kemezis (2014, p. 203).

and unity (including at Athens) (1.6.2), that the Athenians mistrusted the sophists and banned them from the lawcourts (1. praef), that Protagoras was banished from Athens for heresy (1.10.0), and that Antiphon and Critias betrayed the people of Athens in the coups of 411 and 404–3 BC (1.15, 1.16).

Yet these circumstances are incidental to Philostratus' main concern, which is to offer an *internal* account of how 'the sophistic art' developed and was transmitted through Greek communities across the centuries. In other words, according to Kendra Eshelmnan, Philostratus presents

> the circle of sophists as an almost incestuously self-contained, self-generating, self-regulating community. As he presents it, this community is constituted entirely from within, by the consensus of insiders whose insider status is confirmed in part by their assent to this same consensus, which is thus imagined as having an objective, self-evident reality independent of the negotiations by which it is created.[183]

For Philostratus, the sophistic art is defined as an overriding focus on eloquence, and particularly the ability to demonstrate 'extempore eloquence' (1. praef). This definition is the key conceptual tool that Philostratus uses to distinguish between those who can be counted among the sophistic community, and those who cannot. Thus Critias, despite his treachery and heinous crimes, is included in the canon of the Old Sophistic by virtue of his style:

> As regards the style of his oratory, Critias abounded in brief and sententious sayings, and he was most skilful in the use of elevated language, but not of the dithyrambic sort, nor did he have recourse to words borrowed from poetry ; but his was the kind of elevated language that is composed of the most appropriate words and is not artificial. I observe, moreover, that he was a master of concise eloquence [...] (1.16)[184]

In Philostratus' project, Critias' language sets him apart from ancient philosophers who were definitely not sophists, as well as from ancient philosophers who had a reputation for being sophists, due to the ease and fluency with which they expounded their theories, but who were not in fact genuine sophists (1. praef, 1.8).

Bearing in mind the claims to self-knowledge and knowledge of knowledges that Plato's Critias articulates in the *Charmides*, one component of Philostratus' distinction between philosophy and the sophistic art is particularly relevant: philosophers are said to 'set snares for knowledge' and assert that they have 'no sure knowledge', whereas 'the sophist of the old school assumes a knowledge whereof he speaks' (1. praef).[185] This distinction, articulated as part of a revalorization and recategorization, rejects Plato's suppressive representation of the sophists, and his concomitant elevation of Socratic philosophy, to present an alternative, revisionist counter narrative. Philostratus downplays Socrates, and dismisses the Socratic practice of laying traps for interlocutors while professing to lack certain knowledge, to reappraise the practice of speaking persuasively in public on a wide range of themes, in response

---

[183] Eshelman (2008, p. 396).

[184] Philostratus (1922, pp. 49–50).

[185] Philostratus (1922, p. 5).

to audience demand. This reappraisal also allows Philostratus to recover Antiphon and Critias from their fourth-century vilification and suppression.

Despite Philostratus' attempt to present sophistic art as a cultural practice that was generated and sustained independently of cultural circumstances, his own project was deeply determined by his context. The fact that he was able to recover and reconfigure the history of the fifth-century sophists and re-evaluate their contributions with such evident comfort and ease is indicative of broader cultural shifts and changing social needs. As Kemezis points out, Philostratus' narrative fits into—but barely mentions—losses and transfers of hegemony: from Athens to Sparta, from Sparta to Macedonia, from Macedonia to Rome; and as an account of the cultural practices characteristic of a new periphery, i.e., the eastern Greek territories of the Roman Empire, it revolves around 'an inescapable center of imperial gravity'.[186]

The Roman appropriation of Athenian philosophy—which was made possible by the physical transfer of Greek libraries and intellectual slave labour (scribes, grammarians, philosophers) to Rome in the first century BC, and Cicero's subsequent Roman version of Plato's philosophy, which emphasized the positive value of oratory (see **Chap. 7**)—entailed that Philostratus' rehabilitation of the fifth-century sophists could rely on widespread knowledge and acceptance of sophistic cultural practices.

However, a key component of Philostratus' project was the emphasis on sophistic art as a fundamentally Greek cultural practice. According Barbara Levick's study of the empress Julia Domna, Philostratus chronicled the resurgence of Greek sophistry that had begun in the Greek territories of the Roman Empire in the first century AD. Due to the extended period of the Augustan peace and renewed prosperity, the wealthy elite could afford to pay Greek sophists for training and lectures, and were able to devote the necessary time to learning the art of oratory, which was seen as having practical benefits for the governing of cities. Such was the cultural capital associated with these professional speakers and lecturers that distinguished families would have a resident sophist in the household. Talented sophists like Philostratus had access to regional and imperial courts, and thus exerted considerable influence on political life.[187]

The criteria used to identify and rehabilitate the fifth-century sophists (the Old Sophistic) is thus determined by Philostratus' project of defining the canon of the Second Sophistic. Eshelman argues that Philostratus in effect created the Second Sophistic by simultaneously defining and chronicling the canon, and established himself as the canonizing authority in the process. Since this canon is defined in highly partisan terms, Philostratus' narrative excluded other canons and networks, which have largely been effaced from the historical record.[188]

Thus Philostratus' phrase 'Critias the sophist [Κριτίας δὲ ὁ σοφιστὴς / *Kritias de ho sophistēs*]' is determined by a complex interplay of cultural processes and

[186] Kemezis (2014, p. 198).

[187] Levick (2007, p. 108).

[188] Eshelman (2008, p. 408).

transformations. Fleck's theory asserts that the members of a thought collective are only able to perceive something new and different if the thinking style is changed (e.g., due to intellectual unrest and changing moods).[189] Thus, due to the Ciceronian revaluation of oratory and the resurgence of Greek sophistry in the eastern territories of the Roman Empire—cultural developments shaped by numerous factors, such as political crises, transfers of hegemony, imperial conquest and appropriation, the reassertion Greek identity at the periphery—Philostratus was able to recover the figure of Critias from the discursive suppression of the fourth-century historiographical tradition and bring to light aspects of his writing that had long passed out of view, namely his eloquent style.

Philostratus' revisionist reconstruction of the canon of the Old Sophistic can therefore be construed as the articulation of a thought style that defined itself in explicit opposition to the thought style of the Athenian philosophy of the fifth and fourth centuries, by identifying itself with a suppressed lineage. I would even suggest that Philostratus positions the Old Sophistic as a counter to the imperial tendencies of the Athenian democracy and its associated discourses and practices. This can be detected in his account of Gorgias, which emphasizes his opposition to war and implies that his Olympian Oration contained a coded message: 'it was addressed to Athenians who had a passion for empire' (1.9.2).[190]

At the same time, Philostratus' construction of the Second Sophistic attempts to define a contemporary Greek community as the rightful heirs to this ancient line of sophists by, on the one hand, tracing networks, alliances and master-student chains of transmission on the basis of gossip and anecdotes, and on the other, explicitly dismissing certain second- and third-century *sophistai* and *rhētores* from the canon, and excluding others (who were thereby effectively effaced).[191] Philostratus' thought style was articulated in a fierce competition over cultural capital: with the revaluation and appreciation of public speaking, a premium was put on genuine sophists—those who could demonstrate their pedigree and credentials. Hence this thought style from the eastern periphery was able to gain access to prestige and influence at the centres of imperial power through a process of revisionist reconstruction, self-definition, and exclusion.

It bears emphasizing that the scholarly analyses specifically identify cultural practices—Kemezis (2014), and discourse—Eshelman (2008) as central concerns in Philostratus' project. In contrast to philosophy, the sophistic art is depicted as a practice that can educate, edify and entertain a receptive public. Though Philostratus based his canon on some examples of written style (e.g., Critias), eloquent improvised speech was defined as the primary medium for attracting the public and conveying content. However, unlike Plato's written texts, which represent, re-enact and contrast the practices of delivering sophistic monologues and engaging in the dialectical exchange of philosophical conversation, Philostratus' text predominantly

189 Fleck (1979, pp. 74–75).

190 Philostratus (1922, p. 33).

191 Eshelman (2008, pp. 408–409).

contains descriptions of sophists and anecdotal accounts of their lives rather than representations of their art. Thus the sophistic art is consistently positioned as a cultural practice that occurs outside the textual field of written texts, in direct engagement with the public, while Philostratus' written text functions as canon-defining discourse. In Fleckian terms, it defines *who* belongs to the thought collective and describes *what* the thought style does, but it does not represent the thought style in action, as Plato's texts do. However, on another level of functionality, Philostratus' text ultimately employs the antagonistic and exclusionary discursive strategies that characterize Plato's texts.

6.4.3.4 Critias in the Twentieth and Twenty-First Centuries

In the twentieth century, Philostratus' categorization of Critias as a sophist is adopted and exemplified by the collection *The Older Sophists* edited by Sprague (1972). This handbook eschews the earlier inclusion of Critias under the broader category of the Pre-Socratic Philosophers by Harmann Diels in 1903 and Kathy Freeman in 1948, and instead presents 'a complete translation of the sophist material in Diels-Kranz'.[192] The criteria for extracting this sophist material from the Diels-Kranz fragments is not made explicit, but the introductory notes to the translated fragments emphasize reputations for eloquence and teaching rhetoric (Protagoras), familiarity with rhetoric (Gorgias), being an accomplished speaker (Prodicus), oratory (Thrasymachus), lecture tours and oratorical displays (Hippias), and oratorical style and speeches (Antiphon). However, when it comes to stereotypical sophistic practices, Donal Norman Levin's introductory note on Critias only mentions that 'Critias produced both prose and verse'.[193] Then, tellingly, the fragments on Critias' Life and Writings begins with Philostratus' account from *Lives of the Sophists*: 'Even if Critias the sophist brought down the democracy …'.[194]

W. Thomas Schmid's 1998 study, *Plato's Charmides and the Socratic Ideal of Rationality*, recycled all the key components of the characterisation of Critias passed down through Xenophon, Epicurus, and Philostratus. So Critias is described as 'a sophist', 'an atheist', 'a sensualist' and 'a bloodthirsty reactionary'.[195] In Schmid's reading, Plato's *Charmides* is aligned with the other early dialogues that expose the dangers of sophistry: 'The drama of the *Charmides* will take us a long way toward understanding Plato's view of the relation between Sophistry and Critias' future tyranny, and of why Socrates did not have a more benign effect on him and his ward'.[196] Lastly, rather than seeing any value in Critias' definitions of *sōphrosynē*,

[192] Sprague (2001, p. vii).

[193] Levin (2001a, p. 241).

[194] Levin (2001a, p. 242).

[195] Schmid (1998, p. 12).

[196] Schmid (1998, p. 14).

Schmid treats them as examples of a traditional virtue corrupted by atheist sophistry and a nihilistic, self-interested desire for power.[197]

More recently, Lampert reproduced the image of Critias as an atheist-sophist in his Nietzschean *How Philosophy Became Socratic* (2010). Despite advocating a contextual approach to Plato's dialogues that pays close attention to their dramatic dates and personae, as well as to the broader background of the history of Athens, Lampert's reconstruction remains firmly anchored within Plato scholarship, and thus his recontextualization is actually rather limited. Critias is described as a second-generation sophist, 'a future sophist and future tyrant',[198] and is presented as a subtle, sophistic atheist who has misunderstood Socrates' philosophy.

Hence for Lampert, the *Charmides* is essentially the story of Socrates returning to Athens after the battle of Potidaea to find that his philosophy has been misinterpreted and distorted by Critias, whose claim to a knowledge of other knowledges will ultimately be used to justify his claim to a right to rule.[199] On Lampert's reading, Socrates' reduced definition of knowledge of knowledges (i.e., knowing whether a knowledge's claims to knowledge are possible, thus knowing the absence of knowledge) allows him to counter Critias' claim to knowledge of *what* other knowledges know. In Lampert's Nietzschean reading, this strategy allows Socrates to subordinate knowledge of good and evil to *sōphrosynē*—which can therefore rule absolutely, 'by ruling in or ruling out what can count as knowledge'.[200] Critias' claim to the right to rule is thus revealed to be unjustified, while Socrates' has laid the foundations for asserting the rule of the philosopher in the *Republic*. So the *Charmides* fits within Lampert's overarching framework which casts Socratic philosophy as responding to and overcoming 'the Greek enlightenment', or 'the sophistic enlightenment'—a cultural phenomenon which Lampert does not define explicitly, but which he suggests was intimately bound up with the rise of the Periclean democracy.[201] In a nutshell, as with Schmid, Lampert treats the Charmides as a key moment in the emergence of Socratic philosophy through its confrontation with sophistry—represented here by Critias' uniquely dangerous distortion of Socratic thought, which appropriates philosophical language in the service of authoritarian ambition.

[197] Schmid (1998, p. 38).

[198] Lampert (2010, pp. 148, 157).

[199] Lampert (2010, pp. 198, 219).

[200] Lampert (2010, pp. 213, 222).

[201] Lampert (2010, pp. 27, 62, 132).

6.4.4 The Attempt at 'Nonachronistic Interpretation'

As was mentioned, Tuozzo (2011) rejects both the ancient-traditional representations of Critias and recent scholarly works that reproduce their key components. He draws extensively on historical studies and recent Italian scholarship to set aside the standard view of elenctic argument—one underpinned by what he calls 'the broad philosophical framework of twentieth-century Anglo-American philosophy'. In its place, he attempts to develop a 'nonanachronistic interpretation' of the philosophical reasoning presented in Plato's dialogues.[202] While Fleck's theory will be applied to the issue of nonanachronistic interpretation in the next section, the present discussion will focus exclusively on Tuozzo's interpretation and conclusions.

In Tuozzo's interpretation, Plato's characterization of Critias is broadly sympathetic. In the *Seventh Letter* Plato admits to hoping that when the oligarchs took power in the coup of 404–403 BC, they would lead Athens from an 'unjust way of life to a just way and then administer it' (324d4–5);[203] Critias is assigned a positive role in Plato's *Timaeus*, as a member of the educated class who has knowledge beyond that of the layman.[204]

Then, as mentioned previously, Tuozzo reads Critias' definition of *sōphrosynē* as a serious contribution to the dialogue and a basis on which Socrates (and Plato) can develop this concept—through dialectical conversation—from aristocratic awareness of the restraints imposed by social position, and thus self-knowledge, towards reflexive epistemology and knowledge of the Good.

The idea that Plato depicted Critias as a philosopher rather than a sophist can actually be brought into alignment with Xenophon's report that during the rule of the Thirty Critias was responsible for a law that 'made it illegal "to teach the art of words"' (*Mem.* 1.2.31).[205] Xenophon adduces this fact as evidence of a split and conflict between Socrates and Critias, suggesting that the decree specifically targeted Socrates' practices. Yet Xenophon is forced to acknowledge that, if such was the purpose, the law made no sense: 'For I myself never heard Socrates indulge in the practice, nor knew of anyone who professed to have heard him do so' (*Mem.* 1.2.31).[206]

Lampert, who trusts Xenophon's account without question, treats this law as evidence of Critias' cynicism, borne of his atheism and unbridled pursuit of self-interest.[207] In contrast, Tuozzo argues that the decree would have been entirely consistent with Critias' social theorizing: according to his Spartan ideal, a man belongs

---

[202] Tuozzo (2011, pp. 6, 14).

[203] Tuozzo (2011, p. 62). Tuozzo (2011, p. 21) assumes the Seventh Letter is genuine: 'The letter was either written by Plato or by someone whose understanding of Plato is deep and whose views will prove useful in developing a fruitful methodology for interpreting Plato's dialogues'.

[204] Tuozzo (2011, p. 65).

[205] Xenophon (1923, p. 27).

[206] Xenophon (1961, p. 27).

[207] Lampert (2010, p. 189).

to the aristocratic elite not by virtue of good birth and wealth, nor by 'training in skillful speech', but by 'a lifelong practice of aristocratic self-cultivation' and self-mastery.[208]

Thus, textual evidence—Critias' fragments, Xenophon's accounts, Plato's dialogues—justifies constructing the following facts: the historical Socrates and Critias were opposed to those who taught the art of speech; the historical Critias went beyond the desire to rule over and supervise all cultural practices expressed by the fictional Socrates and Critias in the *Charmides* and actually crafted laws to this effect, with a specific focus on the practices associated with the *sophoi/sophistai*.

If the *Charmides* is not another instance of Socrates articulating his thought style at the expense of a sophistic opponent and the sophistic art in general, what exactly is the strategic purpose of this text? Tuozzo emphasizes the dialogue's aporetic function: Plato is read as *representing* philosophy as a cultural practice.[209] The actual practice of philosophy is not contained in the text; the written dialogues merely represent what philosophers do, namely engage in the dialectical activity of private philosophical-educational conversation (rather than in the public practice of oratory, delivering legal speeches etc.). Thus, if the practice of philosophy is defined as existing outside the written text, as indicated in the *Phaedrus* (275–77), the most that a written text can do is provide reminders of philosophy or, as Tuozzo suggests, recommend the practice to readers. Suitable readers who encounter one of Plato's aporetic dialogues should be intellectually provoked: prompted to make their own connections, to believe they can go further, to seek a philosophical community, and ultimately to take up the philosophical life as a living practice.[210]

The crucial point here is that, on this interpretation, Socrates, Critias, and Charmides are represented as engaging in the same cultural practice: they are all *doing* philosophy. Thus the purpose of the dialogue is not to show how Critias distorted Socrates' philosophy with sophistry, and hence to lay the blame for the oligarchic coup of the Thirty Tyrants in 404–403 BC on Critias' sophistic corruption. The aim is rather to present philosophers grappling with a set of problems connected with knowledge, and ultimately failing, due to the gaps in their reasoning, and thereby to force the reader to interact with the concepts presented in the text. Thus construed, Plato's aporetic dialogues functioned as a kind of marketing strategy that was intended to attract readers outside the school.[211]

At the end of the *Charmides*, Socrates highlights that the reduced knowledge of knowledges—i.e., knowing *that* a person who claims to be a doctor or craftsman knows or does not know something—is not in itself a productive knowledge that produces any tangible benefit: 'Then how will temperance [*sōphrosynē*] be useful when it is the craftsman of no useful thing?' (175a). Since Socrates and Critias had just reached the conclusion that the knowledge that makes men happy and that ensures the other sciences are well and beneficially done is the knowledge of good

[208] Tuozzo (2011, p. 86).

[209] Tuozzo (2011, p. 14).

[210] Tuozzo (2011, p. 18).

[211] Tuozzo (2011, pp. 16, 280).

and bad (174b–d), it is evident that a connection could be made between *sōphrosynē* and the knowledge of good and bad.

Knowledge of good and bad clearly produces benefit, which is what is lacking in the definitions of *sōphrosynē* as knowledge of knowledges, but neither Critias nor Socrates make the connection and redefine *sōphrosynē* with an additional knowledge-of-good-and-bad component—this is left to the reader:

> [...] the elaborate discussion of the various formulations of self-knowledge is to be brought into relation with, and so help illuminate, what is in itself the rather opaque notion of a knowledge of good and bad. This is the non-trivial philosophical task that the reader is invited to take up.[212]

The ominous, ambiguous, and much-discussed ending of the *Charmides*, where Critias and Charmides are said to be plotting out of Socrates' earshot, leading Socrates to ask 'Are you going to use force, [...] and don't I get a preliminary hearing?' (176c),[213] reminds us of the setting of the conversation, i.e., Socrates' return from the Battle of Potidaea and the outbreak of the Peloponnesian War, which would have prompted Plato's contemporary readers to consider the dialogue in the light of Critias and Charmides' later roles in the oligarchic rule of 404–403 BC. Nevertheless, there is no explicit condemnation in Plato's text. Tuozzo concludes that the ending points to 'the fact that any attempt to reform society so that it is directed toward the good requires more than reflection on the relations of the various kinds of knowledge that must be in play in the city'.[214]

The aporetic gap between *sōphrosynē* as knowledge of knowledges and knowledge of good and bad is finally closed in the *Republic*, where Socrates identifies the Form of the Good as the source of all usefulness and benefit (505a2–b3), and argues that knowledge of this Form has 'epistemic priority',[215] over all modes of knowledge and forms of production. Thus, when read in the light of the *Seventh Letter* and the *Republic*, the message that can be construed from the *Charmides* is that Critias' error was not his attempt to rule and change the constitution of Athens; it was rather that he failed to base his rule on the knowledge of the Good, and based it purely on his aristocratic claim to self-knowledge and his claim to superior knowledge over other arts and practices.

6.4.5 Summary Reflections: Anachronism, Bias, and Comparative Epistemology

When formulated through the lens of Fleck's theory, Tuozzo's interpretation gives grounds for concluding that Plato represented Socrates and Critias as belonging to the same specific thought collective, and hence that their communication can be

[212] Tuozzo (2011, p. 280).

[213] Plato (1992, p. 96).

[214] Tuozzo (2011, p. 303).

[215] Tuozzo (2011, p. 314).

treated as the expression of a distinct thought style. This thought collective can provisionally be identified with a section of the Athenian elite (*aristoi*) who were conscious of the position of their social group within the broader collectives constituted by the classifications of the Athenian imperial democracy: hierarchically ranked male citizens, resident non-citizens (*metoikoi*), imperial subject-allies, women, slaves.

This elite thought collective consciously attempted to maintain its intellectual lineage by redefining and adapting inherited aristocratic concepts (the proto-idea of *sōphrosynē*), by engaging in elite cultural practices (sympotic poetry, the private speeches and recitations associated with symposia, the secretive discourse of political clubs (*hetaireiai*) and sworn associations (*synōmosiai*))—which in Fleck's terms can be described as esoteric circles.[216] Between 431 and 403 BC, they articulated increasingly vocal opposition to other, more public- and *dēmos*-oriented thought collectives whose thought styles were communicated through political oratory, legal speeches, rhapsodic recitations, and theatre performances.

On the basis of this perspective, it can be posited that Plato's thought style emerged from the historical thought collective represented in the fictional *Charmides*, and therefore that he inherited many of its preoccupations and prejudices, such as the hostility towards other thought styles associated with the Athenian *dēmokratia* and *dēmos*, which was consistently communicated through reflections on how to classify, evaluate and supervise their communicative practices.

Plato's complex text can thus be identified as having several key functions:

1) Representing the historical thought style of philosophia as it emerged from the aristocratic tradition and the oligarchic thought style that was communicated in the 420s and went on to seize power in 411 and 404 BC;
2) Highlighting the internal divisions and failures of this historical thought style, in response to which Plato's thought style offers solutions;
3) Self-defining and establishing the thought style of philosophy at the time of writing, through discursive representations that antagonistically and intertextually elevate philosophy at the expense of other styles and practices—consistently homogenized, devalued, and subordinated across Plato's texts—with the ultimate aim of assimilating, supervising, or excluding them.

The success of Plato's discursive strategies is evident, *inter alia*, in the overwhelmingly negative image of the sophists and the sophistic art transmitted from fourth-century Athens through to the present day; in the pejorative connotations of the word 'sophistry'; in the transmission of fragments of 'sophist' authors rather than entire works; and in the persistently uncritical use of Platonic categories and frameworks—such as the opposition between philosophy and sophistry, or the continued maintenance of the Socratic caesura in modern academic philosophy.

Plato's texts present themselves as representing the thought style of philosophy—conceived as an elite oral practice. Yet these written representations ultimately

[216] Fleck (1979, pp. 105–107).

achieved many of the aims of the Athenian oligarchic thought collective c. 431–403 BC—such as excluding *dēmos* -oriented oral practices from cultural transmission, by ensuring the study of philosophy remained an elite thought style (propagated behind the walls of educational institutions, beginning with the Academy).

As was mentioned, Tuozzo highlighted and attempted to avoid the anachronistic bias implicit in the interpretative layers of accreted traditions, in order to develop 'a nonanachronistic interpretation' of the reasoning represented in Plato's dialogues.[217] Thus, in Fleckian terms, Tuozzo attempted to discard the lenses of previous thought styles through which Plato's texts have been viewed, specifically those of twentieth century Anglo-American scholarly philosophy, Philostratus' second century AD sophistic reconstruction, and the historiographical tradition of the fourth century BC. By using historical studies, recent Italian scholarship and his own careful reading of the Greek originals, Tuozzo successfully sheds light on aspects of the historical Critias and Plato's texts that had been obscured by the previous lenses. However, the notion of achieving a nonanachronistic interpretation is deeply problematic, particularly in the light of Fleck's theory.

Fleck's interactionist model of comparative epistemology suggests that anachronism, which for historians is 'the worst of all sins, the sin that cannot be forgiven',[218] is in fact inevitable. We can recall that Fleck describes communication between thought collectives as 'feasible' but subject to complexity, as it is 'always connected with a more or less marked modification of the ideas'.[219] The closer thought collectives are to each other—in terms of subject matter, adopted terminology, communicative function and purpose, spatial and temporal proximity—the less the ideas will be modified in the communication; and vice versa, the greater the distance, the more the ideas will be modified in the communication, to the point that communication actually becomes minimal or non-existent. Therefore, even if we were able to discard the lenses of previous thought styles that stand between us and a source text like Plato's *Charmides*—a possibility which is very questionable, given that the transmission of the text has been determined by the evaluations, formatting, and editing of other thought collectives—we would still inevitably bring the biases of our own thought styles to bear in our interaction with the text.

Using historical studies to counter the biases implicit in the tradition of academic philosophy may uncover aspects and determinants of the textual phenomena that eluded or were suppressed by the latter thought style, but they in no way guarantee that our fresh interpretation is based on an unbiased account of historical facts. The history of fifth and fourth-century Greece has been highly-contested and filtered through the lenses of competing thought styles, ranging from Thomas Hobbes' 1629 pro-monarchical reading of Thucydides,[220] George Grote's 1957 reading of

---

[217] Tuozzo (2011, pp. 6–14).

[218] Febvre (1982, p. 5).

[219] Fleck (1986, p. 85).

[220] Hobbes (1843, p. xvii): 'He praiseth the government of Athens, when it was mixed of *the few* and *the many;* but more he commendeth it, both when Peisistratus reigned, (saving that it was an usurped power), and when in the beginning of this war it was democratical in name, but in effect

Thucydides through the lens of the English legal system and the British Empire,[221] through G. E. M. de Ste. Croix's 1954 pro-Soviet reading of the Athenian Empire[222] and Donald Kagan's NATO-inspired 1969 justification of the Delian League,[223] to Lisa Kallet's more recent critique of the transformationist model and 'Athenocentric' discourse.[224]

The *Oxford Dictionary* defines 'anachronism' as 'The misplacing of any person, thing, custom, or event outside its proper historical time'.[225] Some of the most esteemed historians of the twentieth century were clearly guilty of projecting attitudes and convictions characteristic of the Cold War back into the historical Greece of the fifth century BC. I would argue that the reassessment of Critias—beginning with Peter Krentz's *The Thirty at Athens* (1982), continuing in Andrew Wolpert's *Remembering Defeat* (2002), and culminating in a kind of rehabilitation in Tuozzo's *Plato's Charmides* (2011)—is not free from such anachronism, since it is determined by a broader shift in attitudes to empire, coloniality, and democracy that has led to changing perceptions of the Athenian Empire in scholarly reconstructions.

The classic twentieth-century accounts of the Athenian Empire provided by de Ste. Croix and Kagan are characterized by idealism and ultimately side with the Athenian democracy against the Spartan oligarchy, despite acknowledging the aggressive and often brutal expansionism of the Athenian *arche*.[226] Russell Meiggs offered a more critical account in *The Athenian Empire* (1972), which attempted to reconstruct contemporary perceptions of the Empire and argued that even those who were critical of the democracy (Thucydides, Aristophanes) still assumed that Athens was justified in subjugating its neighbours in the pursuit of self-interest. Meiggs highlights the difference in mentality between, on the one hand, the Athenians' sophist-inspired celebration of their power and dominance, and on the other, mod-

monarchical under Pericles. So that it seemeth, that as he was of regal descent, so he best approved of the regal government'.

[221] Grote (1879, p. 48 footnote 91): 'It is to be recollected that the Athenian empire was essentially *a government of dependencies*; Athens, as an imperial state, exercising authority over subordinate governments. To maintain beneficial relations between two governments, one supreme, the other subordinate, and to make the system work to the satisfaction of the people in the one as well as of the people in the other, has always been found a problem of great difficulty. Whoever reads the instructive volume of Mr. G. C. Lewis (Essay on the Government of Dependencies), and the number of instances of practical misgovernment in this matter which are set forth therein, will be inclined to think that the empire of Athens over her allies makes comparatively a creditable figure. It will, most certainly, stand full comparison with the government of England, over dependencies, in the last century; as illustrated by the history of Ireland, with the penal laws against the Catholics; by the Declaration of Independence, published in 1776, by the American colonies, setting forth the grounds of their separation; and by the pleadings of Mr. Burke against Warren Hastings'.

[222] de Ste. Croix (1954, p. 23).

[223] Kagan (1969, pp. 41–42).

[224] Kallet (2013, 2017).

[225] Oxford Reference: https://www.oxfordreference.com/display/10.1093/oi/authority.20110803095410147.

[226] de Ste. Croix (1954), Kagan (1969).

ern rights-based sensitivities and constitutional niceties,[227] and concludes: 'The evidence that has so far been examined suggests that the Athenians, both rich and poor, thought primarily of the benefits that empire brought to them and were not ashamed to say so'.[228] Anton Powell added a reflexive component to this critical perspective in his handbook *Athens and Sparta. Constructing Greek Political and Social History from 478 BC* (1988), which reviews the biases of modern historians' accounts in the chapter on the Athenian Empire.[229]

Krentz's reassessment of Critias, which for example argues that the Thirty did not take power through a coup but were instead elected as a government,[230] and which Tuozzo describes as being part of an attempt 'to arrive at a more balanced account of the motives, aims, and program of the Thirty',[231] can thus be situated within a broader shift towards more critical analysis of the Athenian Empire and its historiography.

In the twenty-first century, with the rise of discourse analysis, decoloniality, and subaltern studies, the study of the Athenian Empire became more critical and aware of the limitations of the twentieth century framework. For example, Kallet criticized the transformationist model, which assumes 'the Athenians changed from leaders of an alliance to hardened imperialists; the *hegemonia* became an *arche*',[232] arguing that the Delian League was expansionist from the outset. Her critique of Meiggs and other scholars leads her to signal the need to access the exterior of 'Athenocentric' discourse, entailing a valorization of studies that focus 'as much on the *poleis* and communities in the *arche* as on Athens'.[233] As an example of such studies, Kallet cites Christy Constantakopoulou's *The Dance of the Islands: Insularity, Networks, the Athenian Empire, and the Aegean World*, which explores how the Delian League, under Athenian hegemony, exploited archaic religious networks as the basis of its thassalocracy.[234] Kallet also recommends dismantling 'the standard periodizations', such as 'sixth and fifth centuries, Archaic and Classical, pre-Persian Wars and post-Persian Wars', and focusing on continuities instead.[235]

The point here is that, according to Fleck' s epistemology, even if a philosopher manages to discard the interpretative layers that stand between them and Plato's text, or if a researcher manages to abandon the inherited periodizations of Athenocentric discourse and adopts a methodology that allows them to valorize phenomena excluded by the traditional framework, such projects could not claim to produce nonanachronistic or unbiased accounts, since these very acts of discarding,

---

[227] Meiggs (1972, pp. 377–396).

[228] Meiggs (1972, p. 404).

[229] Powell (1988).

[230] Krentz (1982, p. 50).

[231] Tuozzo (2011, p. 61).

[232] Kallet (2013, p. 43).

[233] Kallet (2013, p. 44).

[234] Constantakopoulou (2007).

[235] Kallet (2013, p. 52).

abandoning and revalorizing are determined by the thought styles of contemporary thought collectives. Tuozzo's rehabilitation of Critias as a serious oligarchic philosopher who seized power at a moment when the democratic constitution was in mortal danger had clear contemporary resonance in 2011, in the aftermath of the 2007–8 Financial Crisis, the subsequent challenges to elite authority and the liberal-democratic consensus.[236] Similarly, Kallet's repositioning the Athenian *hēgemonia* of the 470s and 460s BC as an already aggressively expansionist form of ancient coloniality—that is, before the supposed hardening of the arche—an assumption built into the standard transformationist models around 454 BC assumed in the standard transformationist models—seems to be determined by the broader critique of Western hegemony exemplified by discourse analysis and deconstruction (e.g. Foucault, Said, Derrida, Spivak) and challenged by Mignolo's concept of decoloniality.[237]

Thus, as far as Fleck's comparative epistemology is concerned, research that challenges, reframes, or abandons standard accounts, narratives, categorizations, and periodizations can perhaps claim to have brought to light other phenomena, aspects of phenomena, histories, ways of constructing histories, networks, knowledge practices, and even epistemologies that have been excluded by the standard models and accounts, but this research cannot claim to have accessed unbiased or nonanachronistic facts, knowledge or accounts.

In *The Problem of Unbelief in the Sixteenth Century*, Lucien Febvre made the following recommendation: 'As always, anachronism comes into play. For in the end—to get back to Rabelais—we have to reread the words after taking off our modern eyeglasses, the ones of today; we have to read them with the eyes of another time'.[238] This may be a paradoxical ideal, but according to Fleck, it is simply impossible: we cannot take off our modern eyeglasses, all we can do is use them to look at how people saw things in the past. We are unable to see or understand anything without our contemporary thought style, so, to reiterate, bias and anachronism are inevitable. The ancient Athenians organized and marked time with Archon years, so using the symbols '431 BC' instead of 'the year of Pythodorus' to designate the start of the Peloponnesian War is a purely anachronistic projection in and of itself.

So, if we are condemned to anachronism and bias, what are our options as researchers? The maximalist option would be the Hegelian strategy of unashamedly appropriating concepts from the past and designating them as under-developed versions of modern concepts, whereby Protagoras' *paideia* can be treated as an early form of *Bildung*, and the sophists were cast as near-German Burghers—lacking only Platonic philosophy and the Christian God (see **Chap. 8**). A more minimalist option would involve a conscious and critical application of contemporary concepts, theoretical tools and explanatory frameworks aimed at bringing new phenomena to

---

[236] See e.g. Martin Gurri's *Revolt of the Public* (2018) on the epistemic crisis and distrust of democracy exacerbated by the financial crisis, and my essay on Gurri: *The Networked Public Sphere and the Sectarian Public*, Dersley (2024).

[237] Mignolo and Walsh (2018, pp. 105–242).

[238] Febvre (1982, p. 289).

light, always trying to bear in mind that research phenomena are produced in interactive act of cognition. Fleck's project of *comparative* epistemology[239] can be treated as a way of pursuing the minimalist option: the act of identifying and characterizing historical thought styles is inherently comparative: not just in terms of comparing two historical thought styles to explain the emergence of one from the other (e.g., the emergence of the Platonic thought style from the oligarchic thought style communicated between 432 and 403 BC), but also attempting to be aware of one's own thought style in the process of cognition.

6.5 Reconstructing the Oligarchic Thought Style (432–403 BC)

Section 6.3.2 suggested that in the *Charmides*, Plato portrayed the concerns and practices of certain members of the Athenian elite who, in Fleckian terms, can be understood as a specific thought collective. This collective developed an 'oligarchic' thought style that explicitly opposed the democratic orthodoxy. Its members also distinguished their cultural practices from those associated with public communication aimed at or representing the *dēmos*, such as political oratory, legal speeches, and theatre performances.[240]

Certain characteristics of this thought collective and its style can be reconstructed both from Plato's texts and from the wider field of cultural production with which they interacted. This includes accounts, representations, and indications in Athenian texts produced between c. 430 and c. 322 BC and, more problematically, from Greek authors writing during the period of Roman rule (60 BC–AD 119):

1) 431–400 BC: texts such as those of the 'Old Oligarch', Thucydides, Aristophanes, and Euripides, written, circulated or performed in the decades prior to the composition of the *Charmides* and *Republic*.
2) 399–380 BC: This period includes Xenophon's *Hellenica*—the relevant sections of which were probably composed around the same time as Plato's *Charmides* (i.e. 393–380)[241]—and Callicles' nomos/physis argument in *Gorgias* (482–492), which may date to 387–385.[242]
3) 375–353 BC: Thrasymachus' argument on self-interest in *Republic* I.338–9; and the *Seventh Letter* attributed to Plato.
4) 332–322 BC: *The Athenian Constitution* written by Aristotle and/or a student/students

[239] Fleck (1986, pp. 97–98).

[240] On the role of public discourse in the Athenian democracy, see Ober's *Mass and Elite in Democratic Athens* (1989).

[241] Brownson (1961, p. ix).

[242] Dodds (1959).

5) Diodorus' *Bibliotheca historica* (60–30 B.C), Plutarch's Parallel Lives (100–119 A.D.)

A considerable degree of caution must be exercised when attempting a cultural-historical reconstruction of this oligarchic thought collective, due to the biases and scant details of the historical accounts—'so little of the iceberg is visible above the water'[243]—and because of the use of analogy, symbols, and comic exaggeration in the dramatic works. However, some key characteristics can be tentatively and provisionally identified.

6.5.1 478–461 BC: A Projected Mirage

Aristocratic opposition to the Athenian democracy is traced back, via the Aristotelian *Athenian Constitution* (c. 332–322 BC) and Plutarch's anecdotal accounts (c. 100 AD), to the 470s and 460s.[244] In the traditional accounts, these decades are conventionally marked by the supremacy of Cimon—the wealthy, pro-Spartan noble (479–461 BC), Athens' taking over the hegemony from Sparta with the creation of the Delian League (478 BC), the ostracism of the democrat Themistocles (472 or 471 BC), Cimon's ostracism as a result of his humiliating treatment by Sparta (461 BC), and the onset of the radical democracy and Periclean era (461 BC).[245]

However, reconstructing thought collectives from the years 478–461 BC is particularly difficult, as this period lies within the nearly fifty-year gap between Herodotus and Thucydides, i.e., between the end of the Persian Wars (479 BC) to the beginning of the Peloponnesian War (431 BC). The events of these years are only sketched in Thucydides' notoriously selective digression known as the '*Pentecontaetia*' (1.89–117).[246] Crucially, the *Pentecontaetia* contains no references to the aristocratic/noble opposition to the *dēmos* which appears in the later accounts.

Both *The Athenian Constitution* and Plutarch's *Pericles* characterize this period as one of intense polarization or cleavage: Ephialtes and Pericles are cast on the side of the *dēmos*, or the people, with their attack on the Council of the Areopagus—the constitutional bastion of aristocratic conservatism—while Cimon and Thucydides (son of Melesias) are cast on the side of the few (*oligoi*) and the wealthy (*euporoi*):

---

243 Rhodes (2000, p. 135).

244 Rhodes (2000).

245 Hornblower and Spawforth (1999).

246 For the debate on the *Pentecontaetia*, see Gomme (1971, pp. 361–389), who describes this section of Thucydides' text as 'scrappy', lacking chronological precision and full of omissions, and Meiggs (1972, p. 445), who views it as a hurried and unintended digression. For a critique of these traditional assessments, see Kallet (2017, p. 77), who argues that these historians exhibit a 'tendency to judge Thucydides' *Pentecontaetia* by their own standards of what those interested in demonstrating Athens' rise to power should include'.

> [...] Ephialtes was champion of the people and Cimon son of Miltiades champion of the wealthy; then Pericles was champion of the people and Thucydides, a relative of Cimon, champion of the others. (*Ath. Pol.* 28.2)[247]

> Now there had been from the beginning a sort of seam hidden beneath the surface of affairs, as in a piece of iron, which faintly indicated a divergence between the popular and the aristocratic programme but the emulous ambition of these two men cut a deep gash in the state, and caused one section of it to be called the 'Demos,' or the People, and the other the 'Oligoi,' or the Few. (Plut. *Per.* 11)[248]

In Plutarch's account, this gash or 'cleavage'[249]—τομήν (*tomēn*)—is described as having been fully healed during the Periclean era, when Athens became 'altogether united' (Plut. *Per.* 15).

P.J. Rhodes suggests that aspects of the account of the 470s and 460s presented in *The Athenian Constitution*, such as the dominance of the Council of the Areopagus, are 'clearly anachronistic' and 'a product of fourth-century rationalizing'.[250] If this Aristotelian account can be described as anachronistic, then the same has to be said of Plutarch's account, which drew on *The Athenian Constitution* and other fourth-century historical accounts that are completely or mostly lost to us (e.g., those of Ephorus and Theopompus).[251]

In *The Lame Hegemony* (2017), Matteo Zaccarini highlights the problematic nature of Plutarch's *Cimon*, the main source of Cimon's image as a pro-Spartan aristocrat (Plut. *Cim.* 16).[252] Firstly, Plutarch was not focused on a factual reconstruction—his aim was rather to provide instructive examples; secondly, Plutarch tended 'to interpret Greek history through typically Roman categories – and vice versa';[253] and thirdly, the way that Plutarch used his sources makes reconstruction immensely problematic:

> The fact that Plutarch's *Cimon* combines, juxtaposes, and (rarely) compares so many different ancient sources – each, in turn, originally arguing for its personal agenda – represents both a boon and a problem for modern scholarship. The original context of most of these fragments is indeterminable, just like the extent and scope of Plutarch's own intervention on his sources: as a consequence, the *Cimon* is as rich as troublesome a resource for the construction of the period under study.[254]

It bears mentioning that the problematic nature of Plutarch's *Lives*, written over five centuries after the events they describe, is not registered in twentieth-century accounts. For example, Kagan cites Plutarch as the main source for his

---

247 Aristotle (2002).

248 Plutarch (1932, p. 33).

249 Scott-Kilvert's translation in Plutarch (1960).

250 Rhodes (2000, pp. 121, 124).

251 Stadter (1989).

252 Plutarch (1968, pp. 451–457).

253 Zaccarini (2017, p. 19).

254 Zaccarini (2017, p. 19).

reconstruction of the 470s and 460s ('Plutarch is certainly right when he reports …').[255] Then, de Ste. Croix states in the footnote to support his assertion that Cimon was 'a staunch believer in the 'dual hegemony' of Sparta and Athens': 'It will be sufficient to cite Plut., *Cim.* 16'.[256] In contrast to this approach, which simply took the only available reported facts for granted and used them for the basis of reconstruction and interpretation, Zaccarini's methodology shifts the focus away from the reconstruction of facts and circumstances to interpreting information in terms of its nature, aims and its 'intellectual reception through the tradition'.[257]

In short, the image of Cimon as the philolaconian champion of the *oligoi* is not an authentic reflection of contemporary political conflict. It is a retrospective projection—a 'mirage'—cast back onto the 470s and 460s through the entangled categories of the 420s, fourth-century nostalgia, and Plutarch's didactic project. Textual-discursive evidence for the perception of a polarized, conflict only appears in the 440s–420s, in the texts of Herodotus, the Old Oligarch (Pseudo-Xenophon), and Thucydides.

6.5.2 Herodotus: Reflection on Constitutions

According to Rhodes,[258] apart from a few oblique indications in Solon (sixth century BC), Pindar (468 BC)[259] and Aeschylus (462 BC),[260] the earliest surviving explicit uses of the terms *dēmos*, *dēmokratia* and *oligarchia* appear in Herodotus (3.80–82), specifically in the famous Debate of the Persian Nobles on the merits of tyranny, oligarchy and democracy.

In this debate, while Otanes associates the rule of the *dēmos* with *isonomia*, the principle of equality,[261] Megabyzus dismisses this form of government as the rule of the violent and ignorant mass, and characterizes *oligarchia* as the rule of the best, also indicating that this form of government would conveniently include the present debate participants:

> Let those stand for democracy who wish ill to Persia; but let us choose a company of the best men and invest these with the power. For we ourselves shall be of that company; and where we have the best men, there 'tis like that we shall have the best counsels (3.81.1)[262]

---

[255] Kagan (1969, p. 60).

[256] de Ste. Croix (1972, p. 172).

[257] Zaccarini (2017, p. 24).

[258] Rhodes (2000, p. 124).

[259] Pindar, *Pythian 2* (86–88): 'In every polity the straight-speaking man is best—whether under a tyranny/or when the violent mob or wise watch over it' Pindar (2007, p. 49).

[260] Aeschylus (1926), *The Suppliants* (604): 'and to what course does the majority of the people's (*dḗmou*) votes incline?'

[261] Ostwald (1969, pp. 107–108).

[262] Herodotus (1928, p. 107).

Darius' argument for monarchy is based on the recognition that oligarchy leads to rivalry and strife, which is said to always be resolved by the return of monarchy:

> But in an oligarchy, the desire of many to do the state good service ofttimes engenders bitter enmity among them; for each one wishing to be chief of all and to make his counsels prevail, violent enmity is the outcome, enmity brings faction and faction bloodshed ; and the end of bloodshed is monarchy; whereby it is shown that this fashion of government is the best. (3.82.3)[263]

Thus Darius concludes that the optimal constitution is 'the rule of the one best man', who will 'govern the multitude with perfect wisdom' (3.82.2)[264]

The neat triple classification articulated in this debate, which has a dramatic setting of 522 BC but was probably composed c. 435, suggests that Herodotus was drawing on stock contrasts and characterizations[265] that were commonplace in contemporary intellectual discourse. In the light of Herodotus' praise of the Athenian democracy (5.78) and Agariste's dream of giving birth to a lion of before giving birth to Pericles (6.131)—which can be viewed as an unambiguously positive symbol and 'triumphant climax' of the Alcmeonid genealogy[266]—it is recognized that Herodotus' reconstruction of a sixth-century debate about tyranny, oligarchy and democracy tells us more about the preoccupations of his contemporaries.[267] An implicit evocation of Pericles can be read into Darius' assertion that 'one best man' is needed—one who resolves factional division and rules wisely.

Thus, in Fleckian terms, it is evident that the concept of oligarchy was circulating among Herodotus' thought collective (e.g., the audiences at wisdom-performance recitals[268]) and that the terminology was in the process of becoming established in 'the existing fund of knowledge'.[269] While it would be a bit far-fetched to construe Megabyzus as a full-fledged fictional representative of the oligarchic thought style, Herodotus' text does suggest that a key conceptual framework was in place or was emerging.

The three constitutions are conceived on a scale that slides from two extremes with key attributes: the ignorant multitude at one extreme, the perfectly wise monarch at the other. Rule is conceived is ranging from broad to narrow: the broadest constitution of democracy spreads power through the principle of *isonomia*, oligarchy narrows the distribution of power to the best men, and monarchy is the narrowest possible constitution, with power in the hands of one man. This conceptual framework establishes the basis for the distinctions between moderate, narrow and extreme oligarchy that were articulated between 411 and 403 BC, reflected in the oligarchic coups which narrowed from the Four Hundred (411 BC), to the Thirty

---

263 Herodotus (1928, p. 109).

264 Herodotus (1928, p. 109).

265 Sealey (1973, p. 273).

266 Harvey (1966, p. 255).

267 Roberts (1994).

268 Thomas (1992), Oliver (2010).

269 Fleck (1979, p. 38).

(404–3 BC), and in Xenophon's depiction of Critias wielding power almost single-handedly.

Herodotus' text does not so much represent an oligarchic thought style as indicate that the possibility of oligarchy had become a subject of conversation. The comparative nature of the Debate of the Persian nobles, featuring explicit criticisms of both democracy and oligarchy, suggests that a critical-reflexive awareness of possible constitutional forms was emerging, including a clear perception of how different forms of rule distributed power in the polis.

I would suggest that the Athenian experience of transformative top-down social engineering (Solon's legislative reforms c. 594 BC, Cleisthenes's state reforms c. 508 BC), and of Peisistratus' attempt at tyranny (561–560 BC), combined with Athens' existential struggle with the Persian empire (480–479 BC) and its subsequent conflict with Sparta during the First Peloponnesian War (461–445 BC), entailed that Athenians were acutely aware both that their constitution—i.e., social, legal, and political organization—could be completely reorganized, and that the constitutions of their rivals were organized along completely different lines.

Thus, the possibility of a narrower constitution c. 435 BC, at the time Herodotus was probably writing and reciting in Athens, was not just idle speculation: the Periclean era was one of Athenian imperial domination, entailing great wealth and vast public expenditure, so the radical democracy held the consensus, but discontent, crisis and revolt were never far away,[270] and war with Sparta and its allies was brewing. The conceptual distinctions and framework that Herodotus projects back to the safe distance of 522 BC were ideas that could be and were put into practice; they concerned things that could be done in the here and now of the 430s. Therefore, many of the elements that Fleck identified as being necessary for a change of thought style, or the emergence of a new thought style, were in place: social and intellectual unrest, the circulation of ideas, strong individuals.

Herodotus' text also provides evidence that the concept of oligarchy had entered into written discourse: a field of cultural production becomes visible to us, as do a range of cultural practices: the representation of debate, the textual basis of wisdom-performance, the valorization and dissemination of written texts among the Athenian elite.

6.5.3 The Old Oligarch: Explicit Opposition to the **Demokratia**

The first surviving articulation of the oligarchic thought style is found in the Old Oligarch's *Athenaion Politeia* (The Constitution of the Athenians). The text's authorship and circumstances of composition have long been the subject of debate, but in the introduction to their edition and commentary, J.L. Marr and P.J. Rhodes

[270] Meiggs (1972, pp. 152–158).

date the text to between 431 and 425 BC and suggest that the treatise has the textual features of 'an academic composition, a lecture or paper, a classroom orator's exercise'.[271] So, rather than being Xenophon or an actual old oligarch, the author was probably a young man who was being schooled in the art of constructing and presenting arguments. As such, it sheds light on the thought style of 'certain upper-class Athenians' who formed 'a hard core of anti-democratic irreconcilables'.[272] The work directly articulates many discursive positions that are only represented or dramatized in the texts of Aristophanes, Thucydides, and Plato. These features are extracted and analysed below.

6.5.3.1 Discursive Antagonism

The author consistently uses a 'restricted and partisan sense of *demos*' which is identified with the poor majority[273] in order to define an enemy that is inherently opposed to and in conflict with his own group, the *oligoi*. For example:

> Next, a thing which some people are surprised at, namely the fact that in every area they assign more to the worthless and the poor and the common people than they do to the valuable; but it will become clear that it is precisely through this practice that they preserve their democracy. For the poor and the common people and the inferior classes will increase the strength of the democracy by doing well and by increasing the numbers of themselves and their like. If, however, the rich and the valuable do well, the common people make the opposition to themselves strong. (1.4)[274]

Marr and Rhodes do not hesitate to describe such passages as expressions of 'class hatred'.[275] Similarly, Roberts described the text as 'the first extant account of democracy as the calculated suppression of one class by another'.[276] The Old Oligarch's consistent use of a network of oppositions, which are organized around the core structural opposition of the *ponēroi* (worthless, base, bad), vs. *chrēstoi* (the valuable, good, noble), create an image of a binary conflict and ineradicable antagonism[277] between political and social classes, in which the Athenian state, legal system, and empire are depicted as captured by the *dēmos* and are being wielded against the *oligoi*.

The references to trade and commerce (1.2), self-interest (1.6), the importance of slaves and *metoikoi* (1.10–12), the appropriation of property (1.14), the connection between lawsuits, jury pay and the *dēmos* (1.16), and trade interdependencies (2.11) justify describing the author's perceptions in terms of class and drawing on the

---

271 Marr and Rhodes (2015, pp. 5, 15).

272 Marr and Rhodes (2015, pp. 16, 20).

273 Marr and Rhodes (2015, p. 19).

274 The 'Old Oligarch' (2015, p. 37).

275 Marr and Rhodes (2015, pp. 16, 24–26).

276 Roberts (1994).

277 Mouffe (2005).

functional conception of ideology outlined in **Chap. 5** of the present work. The Old Oligarch's thought style articulates a position of resistance with regard to the radical democracy, which is depicted as representing the economic interests of the *ponēroi*—the lowest class in terms of value, but the dominant class in terms of power.

Meiggs described the Old Oligarch's depiction of Athenian democracy as 'a cynical analysis'.[278] Marr and Rhodes describe his basic assumptions as flawed, arguing that the analysis which can be attributed to his circle 'just did not correspond to contemporary reality'.[279] This contemporary reality is supposedly accessible outside of the Old Oligarch's text through reconstructing the universal and inclusive sense of the word *dēmos* more commonly used by his contemporaries (e.g. Pericles in Thucydides' reproduction of his Funeral Oration of 430 BC (Thuc. 2.34–46)), and through a reconstruction of the social organization of Athens: the Attic farmers of the hoplite rank did not belong to the *oligoi*, but the Old Oligarch cannot include them in his pejorative designation of the *dēmos* as the worthless urban poor, so his binary *dēmos vs. oligoi* conflict does not match up with reality.[280]

Thus, setting questions of reality aside, the question from the perspective of Fleck's theory is whether the Old Oligarch's perception of the Athenian *dēmokratia* being geared towards the benefit of the urban poor (and *metoikoi*, as we shall see) was a commonly-shared perception among the general thought collective constituted by the Athenian elite, or whether his treatise marks the emergence of a new thought style—a heretical position articulated in the field of cultural production, in Bourdieuan terminology.

6.5.3.2 The Evocation of Broader Antagonism and Intra-Class Conflict

Though ostensibly focused on the specific constitution of the Athenians, after a few dozen lines the author generalizes the structural division and binary antagonisms (the best—*beltistoi*, the valuable vs. the worthless, the ignorant) to a more universal level:

> Throughout the world the best element is opposed to democracy. For within the best men there is the least amount of licentiousness and injustice, and the most scrupulousness over what is valuable; whereas within the *demos* there is the greatest ignorance, indiscipline and worthlessness. (1.5)[281]

Later on, when the Old Oligarch's account turns the focus to the democracy's empire, he explicitly indicates that the antagonism between the *dēmos* and the *oligoi* is not peculiar to Athens:

> But with regard to their allies, and the claim that they sail out there and bring malicious charges against, and hate, the valuable among them – it is because they know that the ruler

[278] Meiggs (1972, p. 115).

[279] Marr and Rhodes (2015, p. 20).

[280] Marr and Rhodes (2015, pp. 21–22).

[281] The 'Old Oligarch' (2015, p. 37).

> is necessarily hated by the ruled, and that, if the rich and strong come into power in the allied states, the empire of the Athenian *demos* will only last for a very short time. That is the reason why they take away the political rights of the valuable, and confiscate their property, and exile and kill them, and, correspondingly, promote the interests of the worthless. But the valuable men at Athens try to protect the valuable men within the allied states, since they realise that it is good for themselves always to protect the best men in the allied states. (1.14)[282]

From this section and others (e.g., 2.17, 2.20) it is evident that the author believes the allied states and other Greek *poleis* are either oligarchically-governed or oriented towards the interests of the *dēmos*. Thus, as de Ste. Croix noted, the Old Oligarch simply 'takes it for granted that the Greek states were deeply divided on social and economic lines into broad groups between which there existed a permanent and deep-seated antagonism'.[283] On this account, when it sailed overseas, the Athenian *dēmos* encountered the universal structural division wherever it went and exploited existing class hatred. Writing from a Marxist perspective, de Ste. Croix both stressed the value of the Old Oligarch's viewpoint and claimed he painted an accurate picture of the social and economic reality:

> [...] his pamphlet is particularly valuable for the light it sheds on the viewpoint of the upper classes in states other than Athens. The picture he draws, with its extremes of black and white, is of course somewhat exaggerated and over-simplified, but its basic division of the citizens of the Greek states into two broad economic and social categories between which there existed a deep-seated political tension, is amply confirmed by other contemporary evidence.[284]

The other contemporary evidence that ostensibly confirms this social and economic binary antagonism is, according to de Ste. Croix, provided by Thucydides and Xenophon; that is, by the representations of other elite Athenians whose writing is, while more complex than the stark simplifications of the Old Oligarch, nevertheless driven by their own specific agendas.[285]

In contrast to this Marxist model which treats the *oligoi* as a broadly homogenous social and economic entity, a unified class with shared interests, other scholars have argued that the last decades of the fifth century saw the emergence of divisions within the ruling class, that is, between members of the elite who supported and benefited from the radical democracy and those who opposed it. The latter group could include members of the old aristocracy (e.g., Critias and Charmides) who probably drew on an established tradition of opposition to the *dēmokratia*, but it could also encompass newly-rich Athenians whose families had risen to prominence during the fifth century, who might have benefited from the influx of wealth from empire and/or Pericles' largesse, but whose loyalty was contingent and opportunistic.[286] This intra-class conflict is clearly signalled by the closing section of the

---

[282] The 'Old Oligarch' (2015, p. 41).

[283] de Ste. Croix (1954, p. 24).

[284] de Ste. Croix (1954, p. 25).

[285] Powell suggests a five-part model, also inspired by Thucydides' comments.

[286] Rhodes (2000, pp. 131–133).

Old Oligarch's treatise, which accuses the *oligoi* who are politically active in democracies of injustice and wickedness:

> Now I forgive the demos themselves for their democracy. For one has to forgive anyone for looking after himself. But whoever is not a member of the *demos*, and yet has chosen to have a political life in a democratic city rather than an oligarchic one, has deliberately set himself to act unjustly, and has realised that it is easier for a man who is wicked to escape notice in a democratically governed city than it is in an oligarchic one. (2.19)[287]

So, in addition to the permanent structural division between the *dēmos* and the *oligoi* in Athens and across the empire, the author also signals a division within his own class that is framed in terms of an unforgivable betrayal of class interests.

The Old Oligarch's text can therefore be construed as marking the emergence of a self-identifying, oppositional thought style, or an ideology, which disassociates itself from the elite thought style identified with the social, economic and imperial policies associated with the radical-Periclean democracy. As such, the pamphlet articulates a discursive position that is defined by its two-fold opposition to both the *dēmos* and those members of the *oligoi* who can be accused of disloyalty to their class. That this position was more widely articulated (i.e., that it was an established position in 'the space of possibles'[288]) is supported by Marr and Rhodes' argument that the text was produced in an educational setting, and by similar articulations and framings in other contemporary or near-contemporary works. For instance, the notion that the Athenian *oligoi* perceived themselves as having more in common with the *oligoi* from other *poleis* than with the Athenian *dēmos*, in terms of economic interests and maintaining the privileges associated with rank, is theme that recurs throughout Thucydides' History (especially in his account of the oligarchic coup of 411 (Thuc. 8.64–99)). Furthermore, over three decades later, the framework of intra-class conflict establishes the discursive coordinates for Xenophon's depiction of the clash between Critias and Theramenes (extreme oligarch vs. moderate oligarch) (*Hell.* 2.3).

6.5.3.3 The Theory of Self-interest

The author of the treatise does not criticise the Athenian *dēmos* or *dēmokratia* through reference any absolute moral criteria. The declared purpose of the text is to explain how effectively the Athenian constitution works to further the interests of the worthless *dēmos* (1.1). The implication is that if the *oligoi* govern the *polis*, they do so in their own interests (not for the interests of the *polis* itself). It is suggested that the *oligoi* would govern better, because there would be less ignorance, licentiousness and injustice among such rulers (1.5), and would stand by their oaths due to the public prominence associated with the rule of the few (2.17), but their primary motivation would be self-interest.

---

[287] The 'Old Oligarch' (2015, p. 51).

[288] Bourdieu (1993, p. 30).

Rhodes identifies this worldview as being the result of the sophists' theoretical innovations:

> The idea that the lower classes prefer democracy because it serves their own interests is a product of the sophists' distinction between *physis* ('nature') and *nomos* (human 'convention'): the form of government belongs to the realm of *nomos*; there is no absolutely right form; but each man will prefer the form from which he stands to benefit, and this is in accordance with *physis*.[289]

Rhodes supports this interpretation with a footnote citing Lysias' *Defense Against a Charge of Subverting the Democracy* (c. 401–399 BC),[290] Xenophon's representation of Alcibiades' questioning of Pericles on the issue of law and violence in *Memorabilia* 1.2.40–46[291] (written after 371 BC), and Aristotle's *Politics*[292] (c. 330s). In other words, the attribution of the theory of self-interest to the sophists is based on works written after the rule of the Thirty 404–403 BC, at a time when oligarchy was being vilified, following the restoration of the democracy and the subsequent discursive measures (e.g. the legal-constitutional reforms begun in 403).[293] It would also seem that Rhodes implicitly classed Lysias and Alcibiades as sophists, yet the former has been described more precisely as a metic-businessman who made a living as a speechwriter.[294] At the same time, in the light of the previous sections of these investigations, Alcibiades can be identified as a member of the Athenian elite who, like Critias and Charmides, drew on the aristocratic tradition of opposition to the *dēmokratia*, and who, from the 430s onwards, can be identified as communicating a new thought style.[295]

The theory of self-interest is represented across the Athenian field of cultural production, most prominently in Thucydides' *History* (1. 75–76), in Plato's *Gorgias* (481b–527e) and *Republic* (I. 336b–343); hence, bearing in mind Tuozzo's rejection of the traditional classification of Critias as a sophist analysed in the previous

---

[289] Rhodes (2000, p. 129).

[290] Lysias (1930) 25.8: 'Now, first of all, you should reflect that no human being is naturally either an oligarch or a democrat: whatever constitution a man finds advantageous to himself, he is eager to see that one established; so it largely depends on you whether the present system finds an abundance of supporters.

[291] Xenophon (1923) *Mem.* 1. 2.44-45: 'But force, the negation of law, what is that, Pericles? Is it not the action of the stronger when he constrains the weaker to do whatever he chooses, not by persuasion, but by force? [...] "And when the minority passes enactments, not by persuading the majority, but through using its power, are we to call that force or not?'

[292] Aristotle (1998, p. 77) *Pol.* 1279, 25–31: 'Since "constitution" and "governing class" signify the same thing, and the governing class is the authoritative element in any city-state, and the authoritative element must be either one person, or few, or many, then whenever the one, the few, or the many rule for the common bene- fit, these constitutions must be correct. But if they aim at the private benefit, whether of the one or the few or the MULTITUDE, they are deviations (for either the participants should not be called citizens, or they should share in the benefits)'.

[293] Wolpert (2002, pp. 41–42), Carawan (2013).

[294] Carawan (2013).

[295] This framing of the sophistic origins of the theory of self-interest is repeated in Marr and Rhodes' Introduction to *The Athenian Constitution* (2015, pp. 16–17).

section, I suggest that self-interest theory articulated by the Old Oligarch is not reducible to sophistic relativism. While the theory may have been shaped by the deliberative-argumentative practices associated with sophistry, the Athenian democracy, and the Periclean supremacy, its consistent distribution and representation across the field of cultural production suggests that it came to function as a discursive tool. Specifically, it enabled a section of the Athenian elite to reject the orthodox, inclusive sense of the word *dēmos* and to construe their own interests as incompatible—indeed, irreconcilable—with those of the *dēmokratia* and its imperial policies. My hypothesis is that this theory was actively reworked and developed by the Athenian anti-democratic oligarchic thought collective after 431 BC, in response to the outbreak of war. It served to articulate and justify political opposition to the democratic order—justifying disloyalty, siding with Sparta, and attacks on the institutions of the *dēmokratia*. These became defining practices of the oligarchic thought style between 411 and 403 BC.

6.5.3.4 The Economic Analysis of Empire and Its Ramifications

While the Old Oligarch's account of political division in Athens in 431–424 is widely described as simplistic and exaggerated,[296] the same cannot be said of the awareness of economic interdependencies and the analysis of the machinery of empire. In the light of fourth-century writings on economics, such as Xenophon's *Oeconomicus* and Aristotle's *Oeconomica*, which are focused on household management or raising money, the Old Oligarch's text is exceptional for its diagnoses of how the political and legal system serve the interests of the ruling social group, of how maritime power can be used for coercion, domination and imperial exploitation, and of how the necessities associated with creating and maintaining a fleet were fundamentally transforming the social structure and norms of Athens. If the author was merely repeating analyses that had become commonplace in his social network, as Marr and Rhodes suggest, this indicates that a certain section of the Athenian elite was conscious of—and acutely concerned by—these economic entanglements. As I argued in the previous section, these concerns are evident in Socrates and Critias' obsessive focus on craftsmen throughout the *Charmides*. These economic grievances can also be construed as the trigger for the reflections on the division of labour and the optimal organisation of the polis in the *Republic*.

The Empire sidelines the hoplites. The Old Oligarch recognises that the imperial democracy has fundamentally transformed the traditional power relations in Athens:

> [...] it is the *demos* who operate the ships and who confer its strength on the city; the steersmen, the boatswains, the lieutenants, the look-outs and the naval engineers – these are the people who confer its strength on the city, much more so than the hoplites and the well-born and the valuable. (1.2)[297]

[296] de Ste. Croix (1954), Roberts (1994), Marr and Rhodes (2015).

[297] The 'Old Oligarch' (2015, p. 37).

Athenian naval supremacy is inseparable from the labour of *thētes* and the empowerment of this class is explicitly identified with a devaluation of the hoplite class and the nobles. Furthermore, the needs of the fleet entails a demand for specialised labour, and thus another social group acquires status and preferential treatment: '[...] the city needs metics because of the great number of their skills and the requirements of the fleet. So that is why we have, naturally, established equality of free speech for the metics too' (1.12).[298] According to the Old Oligarch, this transformation led to a kind of levelling and the collapse of social norms: the *dēmos*, *metoikoi*, and slaves all dress alike and are indistinguishable; they do not step aside for nobles; the *metoikoi* can speak freely, like citizens.

The Empire rules through economic coercion. The Old Oligarch takes it for granted that, by 431–424 BC, Athens' subject-allies have little remaining autonomy:

> As for those states subject to Athens' rule which are situated on the mainland, the big ones are kept in subjection through fear, the small ones very much so through need. For there is no state which does not need to import or export something, and these activities will not be open to it, unless it is compliant with the rulers of the sea. (2.3)[299]

This state of affairs is attributed to Athens' naval presence and policies, such as the requirement that the subject-allies' lawsuits have to be heard in Athens (which, the author concludes, makes them the slaves of the Athenian *dēmos,* who are paid for their jury service (1.16)).

> They alone of Greeks and non-Greeks are able to possess naval wealth. For if some city is rich in timber for shipbuilding, where will it dispose of it, if it does not have the consent of the ruler of the sea? What if a city is rich in iron or copper or flax? Where will it dispose of it, if it does not have the consent of the ruler of the sea? And yet it is from these very materials that I get my ships, taking timber from one place, iron from another, copper from another, flax from another, and wax from another. Furthermore, they will prevent any of our rivals from transporting these materials as a cargo to any other place, with the threat that, otherwise, they will be stopped from using the sea at all. Thus, despite producing nothing from my land, I possess all these materials because of the sea. (2.11–12)[300]

One interesting aspect of this characterisation is the suggestion that Athens has ceased to be a productive agrarian economy ('despite producing nothing from my land'), which links back to the assertion that the hoplite class had been side-lined (1.2). The Athenian pursuit of naval wealth is thus portrayed as not just involving a shift from an agrarian economy to an economy based on import and export, but also on controlling trade between other *poleis*.

The Old Oligarch's analysis thus stands in stark contrast de Ste. Croix's (1954) framing of the Athenian Empire as a popular Panhellenic assertion of the power of the *dēmos* against the propertied class, which—given de Ste Croix's comparison of Athenian sense of 'democratic' with the Soviet sense[301]—conjures up images of the

---

[298] The 'Old Oligarch' (2015, p. 41).

[299] The 'Old Oligarch' (2015, p. 44).

[300] The 'Old Oligarch' (2015, p. 47).

[301] de Ste. Croix's (1954, p. 23).

democratic revolution being exported across the seas during the fifth century. From the Old Oligarch's perspective, the Athenian *dēmos* simply used the empire as an instrument of subjugation and exploitation:

> [...] the common people think that it is more of a good thing that each and every Athenian should individually own the resources of their allies, and that they, the allies, should have only what is enough to survive on, and should continue to cultivate the land, but without being able to plot revolt. (1.15)[302]

In other words, there was little solidarity with the *dēmos* across the Aegean and beyond.

The Old Oligarch's supposedly 'cynical' view of the Athenian Empire as ruthlessly expansionist and exploitative was rejected by Meiggs, who concluded:

> From such evidence as we have it would be dangerous to conclude that the Athenians drained the wealth of the Aegean world and exploited the allies to improve their own standard of living. Athens' secure control of the seas increased the total volume of trade, but though Athens was the main beneficiary others shared the benefits.[303]

As was mentioned, this rose-tinted view of the Athenian *archē* has been subjected to criticism (relatively) recently, by Kallet, who argued that the imperial democracy not only continued existing exploitative practices but took them to a whole new level in terms of 'success and scale'.[304]

To sum up, the Old Oligarch's treatise discursively constructs an enemy that is both local and universal: on the local level, the target of antagonism is the Athenian *dēmos* and the *oligoi* who engage with and profit from the Athenian *dēmokratia*; but the antagonism is extended to all Greek *poleis*, so that Athenian *oligoi* who are (justly) opposed to the empowerment of the *dēmos* can align with the *oligoi* from other *poleis*. The theory of self-interest has been modified by a specific Athenian oligarchic thought collective to identify all the institutions, machinery and practices of the *dēmokratia* (the law courts, jury service, the empowerment of the *thētes* and preferential treatment of *metoikoi*, the expansionist and coercive empire) as geared towards the interests of the *dēmos*, which justifies opposition, disloyalty, and ultimately siding with Sparta, as such practices will ultimately further the interests of the *oligoi*.

6.5.4 Thucydides: Stuck in the Middle

Building on the reflections above, I would suggest that Thucydides' *History of the Peloponnesian War* can be viewed as an offshoot of the oligarchic thought style identified earlier. In his extensive work, Thucydides offers only a few explicit authorial comments, such as those in the excursus on *stasis* (3.82–84). However, the

302 The 'Old Oligarch' (2015, p. 43).

303 Meiggs (1972, p. 272).

304 Kallet (2013, p. 54).

general heft of his representations and arguments indicates a position that is both sharply critical of Athenian democracy—particularly its imperial policies and the actions of post-Periclean demagogues—and of extreme oligarchs, whose secretive, treacherous, and violent practices he also condemns. Thucydides positions himself 'in the middle' (3.82.0), distancing his stance from the factional extremes he criticizes. Yet, bearing in mind Herodotus' scale that ranges from the broad extreme of democracy and *isonomia*, through oligarchy, to the narrowest extreme of monarchy, this position of moderation is, in fact, a position of moderate oligarchy. This alignment is made explicit in his positive account of the 'good government' of the Five Thousand in 411–410 BC (8.97), a form of moderate oligarchy defined by a broader—but still restricted—citizen body comprising those who could supply their own hoplite armour. Hence, this is the provisional basis for describing Thucydides' text as a communication of the Athenian oligarchic thought style—albeit one situated at the moderate end of a spectrum that also included extremist variants like the conspiratorial violence of the Thirty. Only an outline of this manifestation of the thought style can be offered here.

6.5.4.1 The Athenian Empire as a Tyranny

Thucydides has both the enemies of Athens and its own representatives describe the Athenian Empire as a form of tyranny. For instance, the Corinthian envoy accuses the Athenians of enslaving states and steadily encroaching on their neighbours (1.68–69). Later, the Corinthians describe Athens as 'a tyrant city' that threatens the whole of Greece (1.122, 124).

In his 'last speech' (2.60–64), Pericles himself is portrayed as acknowledging that the Athenian Empire resembles a tyranny:

> You all take pride in the prestige the city enjoys from empire, and you should be prepared to fight in defence of it. You cannot shirk the burden without abandoning also your pursuit of the glory. Do not think that the only issue at stake is slavery or freedom: there is also loss of empire, and the danger from the hatred incurred under your rule. You no longer have the option to abdicate from your empire, should anyone out of present fear affect this idea as a noble-sounding means of disengagement. The empire you possess is by now like a tyranny [ὡς τυραννίδα γὰρ ἤδη ἔχετε αὐτήν /*hōs turannída gar ēdē echete autḗn*]—perhaps wrong to acquire it, but certainly dangerous to let it go. If people of that sort managed to persuade the others they would quickly ruin a city, and even if they set up their own independent state somewhere they would ruin that too. The disengaged can survive only when men of action are ranked beside them. Their policy has no place in an imperial state, but it belongs in a subject city, and what it means is safe servitude. (2.63)[305]

The key points here are, firstly, that Thucydides' Pericles asserts that *all* Athenians take pride in the empire;[306] secondly, his acknowledgement that the Athenian hegemony is *like* a tyranny (τῦραννίς /*turannís*), one that is hated by those subject to its

[305] Thucydides (2009, p. 104).

[306] Hornblower (1991, p. 337).

rule; and, thirdly, his indication that that some Athenians, faced with the hardships of the Peloponnesian invasions, devastation, and plague (2.59), seem to have been advocating disengaging from the empire and hegemony, possibly even suggesting setting up their own new state.

Thucydides has Cleon echo this theme of tyranny when, following the revolt of Mytilene, he argues for brutal measures (killing all the adult males and enslaving the women and children), and addresses the Athenians: 'You do not reflect that your empire is a tyranny, exercised over unwilling subjects who will conspire against you. Their obedience is not won by concessions, made to your own detriment, but by a domination based on force rather than popularity' (3.37).[307] It is telling that that Thucydides attributes this characterization of the empire as a tyranny to both Pericles—the personification of the radical democracy and a statesman whom Thucydides clearly admired—and Cleon, a demagogic hardliner whom he clearly despised.

Thucydides' account of how the Athenians came to take the *hēgemonia* from Sparta in his *Pentecontaetia* focuses on the shift in Athens' treatment of the islands in the Aegean, the city-states in Ionia, Thrace and the Hellespontine region—from the 'autonomous allies' (1.97) of the defensive Delian League to the subject-allies under the increasingly coercive and often brutal control of the *archē*. This shift has been much discussed in the scholarly literature (e.g., de Ste. Croix 1954; Meiggs 1972; Kallet 2013, 2018); here it will suffice to highlight that Thucydides explicitly frames Athenian practices as coercive, oppressive and contrary to established Greek norms (e.g., enslaving populations after revolts were crushed) (1.98–99).

Furthermore, the Athenian approach is explicitly contrasted with that of the Spartans:

> The Spartan hegemony did not involve the imposition of tribute on their allies, but they took care to ensure oligarchic rule exclusively in their own interest: whereas the Athenians in time came to deprive all subject cities of their ships and require payment of tribute, with the exceptions of Chios and Lesbos (1.19)[308]

Thus, while Thucydides ultimately attributes the outbreak of the Peloponnesian War to Spartan fear of Athens' expanding power (1. 88), his narrative carefully builds the case that this fear was justified. At the very least, Thucydides' account indicates the perception that the Athenian *hēgemonia* was maintained through exploitation and coercion was shared across contemporary thought collectives—from the bitterest enemies to the democratic statesmen responsible for Athens' imperial policies and military strategies.

---

[307] Thucydides (2009, p. 146).

[308] Thucydides (2009, p. 11).

6.5.4.2 The Theory of Self-interest as a Defence of Imperialism

Thucydides has the Athenian envoy at Sparta explicitly defend the Athenian *hēgemonia* with reference to the theory of self-interest, which is now grounded in appeals to typical behaviour, established practice, and the rule of the stronger:

> In the same way, there is nothing remarkable or contrary to normal human behaviour in what we have done, just because we accepted an empire when one was offered and then declined to let it go, overcome by these strongest of all motives – honour, fear and self-interest. Nor were we the first to take this course but it has always been established practice for the weaker to be ruled by the stronger. Besides, we believed ourselves worthy of this role and you agreed, until now when in a calculation of your own interests you started appealing to "justice" – though no one ever let that consideration stop them getting an advantage when presented with an opportunity to gain something by force. (1. 76)[309]

Here, Thucydides is arguably invoking the notion of 'the natural right of the stronger to act as he would (τὸ δίκαιον τοῦ κρείττονος – *to dikaion tou kreittonos*)', a conceptual motif often associated with sophistic thought.[310] Whether or not this articulation directly echoes the supposed sophistic doctrine that 'might is right',[311] it is evident that the Athenian speaker gives expression to a theoretical framework that justifies the use of violent, coercive, and exploitative practices in the pursuit of self-interest.

Thus, in addition to the Old Oligarch's use of the theory of self-interest to justify oligarchic opposition to the *dēmos*, Thucydides' representation suggests the theory of self-interest had become part of the 'the existing fund of knowledge'[312] and could be drawn on by all elite thought collectives in their articulatory practices—e.g., to justify hegemony and the encroachment upon neighbouring city-states. Of course, Thucydides may have added or projected these theoretical elements to the speech of the Athenian representative—there are no alternative accounts, so we have no way of peering behind Thucydides' representation. All we can reasonably conclude is that Thucydides presented the theory of self-interest as a commonly available conceptual framework, capable of being adapted to various rhetorical and political ends.

[309] Thucydides (2013, pp. 46–47). I have quoted Mynott's translation because of the emphasis on typical human behaviour and established practice rather than 'human nature', the phrase chosen by Hammond (2009, p. 38). Hornblower argues that since Thucydides does not use the term φύσις in this passage, it is implausible to suggest Thucydides is referring to the *phusis/nomos* debate or theory—Hornblower (1991, pp. 121–122).

[310] Gomme (1971, p. 236).

[311] Hornblower (1991, p. 121) argues that it does not. A more explicit Athenian articulation of the 'might is right' doctrine can be construed from the Melian Dialogue (5.89).

[312] Fleck (1979, p. 38).

6.5.4.3 Polarisation and Socio-cultural Trauma

While the Old Oligarch focuses on an Athens bitterly divided by class and intra-class antagonism, Thucydides shifts the focus outward. He depicts a Greek world polarized on two distinct levels: the devastating and interminable war between the Peloponnesian League and the Athenian alliance, and the numerous civil wars ignited between factions aligned with either Athens or Sparta. Thucydides' account registers a shift from the antagonistic and coercive practices described in the Old Oligarch's text to the violent practices unleashed by outright war:

> That is how savagely the civil war progressed, and it was the more shocking for being the first of the revolutions. Because later virtually the whole of the Greek world suffered this convulsion: everywhere there were internal divisions such that the democratic leaders called in the Athenians and the oligarchs called in the Spartans [...] So then civil war spread among the cities, and those who came to it later took lessons, it seems, from the precedents and progressed to new and far greater extremes in the ingenuity of their machinations and the atrocity of their reprisals. (3.83)[313]

At the same time, Thucydides stresses the importance of discursive practices as instruments of justification and persuasion once the descent into depravity had begun:

> They reversed the usual evaluative force of words to suit their own assessment of actions. Thus reckless daring was considered bravery for the cause; far-sighted caution was simply a plausible face of cowardice; restraint was a cover for lack of courage [...] The dominant men on each side in the various cities employed fine-sounding terms, claiming espousal either of democratic rights for all or of a conservative aristocracy, but the public whose interests they professed to serve were in fact their ultimate prize. (3.83)[314]

In wartime, articulatory practices become entwined with acts of violence—in what Timothy Snyder describes as the 'escalation from rhetoric to action'.[315]

Back in 1929, Charles Cochrane argued that Thucydides' approach to history and his method for the analysis of society was profoundly influenced by the Hippocratic school: like the authors of the Hippocratic texts, Thucydides assumes that 'all human actions and sufferings are subject to natural causes' and attempts to explain them on this basis.[316] Just as Thucydides' famous account of the plague at Athens in 430 BC (2.47–55) provides a detailed description of the symptoms and consequences of the plague as it spread through Athens, his analysis of war and civil strife is couched in medical terms, as an 'infliction'.[317] Human nature is viewed as 'a relatively uniform and stable entity' influenced by varying circumstances, and

[313] Thucydides (2009, pp. 169–170).

[314] Thucydides (2009, pp. 170–171).

[315] Snyder (2003, p. 155).

[316] Cochrane (1929, p. 17).

[317] Hornblower (1991, p. 480).

stasis, or civil strife, is described as a contagion that spreads through the body politic and the Hellenic world.[318]

While Thucydides' method and style were influenced by the dispassionate analysis of Hippocratic medicine, his historical account was evidently deeply affected by the events he described (e.g., the evocation of unparalleled suffering, desolation, and widespread death in 1.23). As Roberts observed: '[…] he approached his work with a curious blend of clinical detachment and missionary zeal. Tremendous anguish and ambivalence underlie Thucydides' writing. The principal process under scrutiny in his *History* is the progressive decay of his native polis'.[319]

The 27-year-long disaster of war is primarily blamed on human nature and emotions, and secondarily on collectives succumbing to these emotions—the Spartan oligarchy succumbs to fear, the Athenians are driven by greed, and the civil strife is perpetuated by resentment and cycles of vengeance. However, the use of words and persuasion to trigger decision and action is constantly emphasized as a key factor.

6.5.4.4 The Organisational and Ruling Practices of the Oligarchic Thought Collective

Thucydides' account of the oligarchic coup of 411–410 BC sheds some light on how the oligarchic thought collective communicated and put their ideas into practice, as well as on some key characteristics of their ruling practices.

Thucydides identifies several causal factors and triggers leading up to the oligarchic coup: he focuses on the Athenian defeat in Sicily, with the loss of men and ships; the lack of funds in the treasury (8.1); the machinations of Alcibiades, who promised the Persian satrap Tissaphernes and the Athenian *beltistoi* (the 'best' men) that he would return if an oligarchy were established to replace 'the villainous democracy that had driven him out' (8.47.2);[320] and the oligarchic revolt at Samos. Kagan draws on various mid-twentieth century studies on manpower and population to stress the economic roots of the coup: by 411 BC, Athens had a catastrophically reduced population due to the plague, years of war, and the Sicilian disaster. This factor, combined with the inability to squeeze more funds from the subject-allies, many of whom were in open revolt, resulted in an intolerable fiscal burden being placed on the propertied classes of Athens, whose farms had been ravaged and abandoned.[321]

In Thucydides' account, the attempt to destroy the Athenian democracy and establish an oligarchy (8.47–8), was made possible by the existence of a network of political clubs (*hetaireiai*) and sworn associations (*synōmosiai*) across the allied

[318] Cochrane (1929, pp. 19, 133).
[319] Roberts (1994).
[320] Hornblower (2008, p. 893).
[321] Kagan (1987, pp. 2–4).

city-states[322] and in Athens. The instigators of the coup, Phrynichus and Peisander, are depicted as sending letters to and communicating with these associations. This enabled Peisander to sail 'along the coast, unseating the popular parties from power', so that when they arrived at Athens 'they found that most of their work had already been done by their associates'. It transpires that this 'work' entailed the killing of popular leaders and other 'inconvenient people' (8.65).[323]

Thucydides describes the practices used by the oligarchs in their attempt to dismantle the *dēmokratia*: assassinating opponents, intimidating critics, suspending legal enforcement—'Anyone who did speak out against them met with a sudden death in some convenient way; and there was neither any search for the perpetrators of the deed nor any legal action taken against suspects' (8.66.2);[324] disseminating distrust (8.66.5); suspending the procedures of the *dēmokratia* to enact a resolution to disenfranchise citizens (narrowing the constitution to the Four Hundred) (8.67); seizing the council building with the threat of violence (8.69); imprisoning and banishing opponents; opening negotiations with the Spartans, and, ultimately, planning to hand the city over to the Spartans (8.91.3).

Thucydides' account of how the Four Hundred were defeated and replaced by the broader, 'moderate' oligarchy of the Five Thousand echoes key elements of the Old Oligarch's picture of the Athenian social structure and allegiances: the popular party and the 'inveterate opponents of oligarchy' (8.73.5)[325] are identified with the fleet and the *thētes*—the lowest property class, who man the ships—so that in effect the *dēmos* was literally at sea while the extreme oligarchs ruled Athens. Key factors leading to the fall of the Four Hundred were an intra-class split between extreme and moderate oligarchs (8.89), the treason of the extreme oligarchs as the Peloponnesian fleet approached the Piraeus, and the hoplites fortifying Piraeus siding with the moderate oligarchs due to the promise of broader enfranchisement under the Five Thousand, which would 'consist of all those who could provide their own hoplite armour' (8.97.1).[326]

The eventual restoration of the democracy was achieved by an alignment between 'dissidents',[327] i.e., pro-democratic oligarchs, and the hoplite class (*zeugitae*) whose economic side-lining the Old Oligarch had bemoaned (Ath. Pol. 1.2). Thucydides' account also positions the role of the Piraeus, the bastion of the *metoikoi* and the 'urban proletariat',[328] as crucial to these events. Consistencies can thus be identified in the representations of collectives, networks, antagonisms and practices.

Consistencies can also be found in later accounts. Most importantly for the purposes of the present study, Xenophon's account of the rule of the Thirty in 404–403 BC (*Hellenica* Book 2), represents Critias and the other oligarchs as employing

[322] Hornblower (2008, pp. 916–917).

[323] Thucydides (2013, p. 549).

[324] Thucydides (2013, p. 550).

[325] Thucydides (2013, p. 555).

[326] Thucydides (2013, p. 572).

[327] Kagan (1987, p. 189).

[328] Gomme (1938, p. 98).

exactly the same practices as those employed by the Four Hundred, but with greater violence and the addition of property seizure. Xenophon describes them as appointing a Senate without any public consultation; arresting, prosecuting and executing democrats, as well as moderate oligarchs who opposed them; installing a Spartan garrison; killing *metoikoi* and appropriating their property; confiscating arms and convening the Senate with young men with concealed daggers in attendance; disenfranchising citizens; and evicting them from their estates etc. (*Hell.*2.3–4).

The Aristotelian *The Athenian Constitution*, which—as previously noted—completely suppresses any mention of Critias, provides a more condensed and depersonalised account of the Thirty, focusing on their attack on the constitution and concluding with the following description of their practices:

> They eliminated malicious prosecutors, and those who curried favour with the people contrary to what was best and were harmful and wicked; and the city was pleased with these achievements, thinking that the Thirty were acting from good motives. But when they had a firmer hold on the city they left none of the citizens alone, but put to death those who were outstanding for their wealth, birth or reputation, cunningly removing those whom they had cause to fear and whose property they wanted to plunder. Within a short space of time they had killed no fewer than fifteen hundred. (35.3–4)[329]

This version of events adds two more elements of the extreme oligarchs' practices: deceptively hiding their true agenda and appealing to the worst instincts of the populace.

According to the sources, the defining characteristic of the oligarchic thought style in its extreme manifestations between 411 and 403 BC was the transition from the practices associated with purely spoken and written antagonism, e.g., discussions and speeches at secret political associations, the circulation of letters and treatises, to the use of violence and intimidation. Wolpert concluded:

> […] we can find significant agreement in our sources which is worth emphasizing. They are in complete accord about the brutality of the oligarchy: violence created, sustained, and destroyed the regime. But unlike Xenophon, who represents the reign of terror as senseless, and Aristotle, who shows it to be a reaction to internal and external threats, I argue that it was systemic. The Thirty depended upon violence to seize power, to rid the community of the previous political culture, and to block opposition.[330]

The rejection of the *dēmokratia* ultimately came to entail the rejection of the norms and cultural practices that were associated with this broad constitution.

6.5.5 Concluding Observations on the Oligarchic Thought Style

The Athenian texts covered above—as well as others that have not, such as Aristophanes' *The Archanians*, *The Knights*, *Lysistrata*, and Euripides' ironic tragedies, such as *The Suppliant Women* and *Orestes*—indicate that the period between

[329] Aristotle (2002).

[330] Wolpert (2002, p. 16).

432 and 403, the historical setting inferred from the dramatic context of Plato's *Charmides*, was marked by extreme social unrest.

The source texts explicitly describe antagonisms on multiple levels. At the local level, they depict tensions between social groups occupying different positions in the hierarchy—for instance, between the *dēmos*, the *metoikoi,* and the *aristoi*—as well as internal conflicts within the same rank, particularly among rival factions of the elite. These local antagonisms are then situated within a broader contest for hegemony over the Greek world, in which *poleis* positioned themselves in relation to competing constitutional models. This larger conflict is predominantly framed as a political struggle over whether power should be shared among a broad section of the populace (the *dēmos*, composed of adult male citizens), or restricted to a narrow elite (the *oligoi*).

The economic dimension underlying the political struggles is registered with varying degrees of explicitness, ranging from the Old Oligarch's focus on the gains of the *dēmos* and the *metoikoi*, and the empire's control of trade, to Thucydides' references to self-interest and revenue collection, to Aristophanes' depictions of struggling farmers (*The Archanians*) but thriving sausage-, hemp- leather-, sheep-sellers etc. (*Knights* 128–148).

Scholarly studies of the period have brought to light further dimensions of this already multidimensional conflict: the intergenerational transition from oral to literate culture (Havelock); the consolidation of an urban ruling class based on the exploitation of enslaved rural labour (Anderson 1974); a broader cultural-linguistic tension between Dorian and Ionian identity (Powell 1988); and a shift in discursive practices from elite-elite communication (e.g. Thucydides and Plato) to elite-mass address in public oratory (Ober 1989).

Thus, on the basis of contemporary and modern accounts, the period of 432–403 BC clearly qualifies as a period characterised by the kind of social and intellectual unrest that Fleck's theory requires for the emergence of a new thought style.[331] I suggest that a new thought style began to emerge within a segment of the Athenian elite in response to its loss of status, control over the means of production, and political power—losses precipitated by the empowerment of the *thētes* (manual labourers, rowers, and farmhands) and *metoikoi* (skilled noncitizen labourers, especially in shipbuilding and trade-related crafts), following the reorientation of the Athenian economy towards commerce, monetization, and imperial expansion.

Fleck's theory also posits that the circulation of ideas between distinct thought collectives is a factor which contributes to the emergence of a new thought style. My analysis of the Old Oligarch's treatise and Thucydides' *History* suggest that the theory of self-interest was communicated across thought collectives, perhaps from sophistic wisdom-performances, and was clearly developed by the Athenian elite for their own discursive purposes, and by the thought collective of the anti-democratic *oligoi* to allow them to define their interests in opposition to those of the *dēmokratia*. Thucydides' 'scientific' analysis of polarised Greek *poleis* was also

[331] Fleck (1986, pp. 76–77).

clearly influenced by another distinct thought style—the Hippocratic school and its theory of causality.

In the *Charmides*, Plato portrays Socrates, Critias, and Charmides analysing the inherited proto-idea of *sōphrosynē*, and Critias is shown adapting the concept to the contemporary context, to argue that one should not transgress the social norms constitutive of one's social position. As the above analysis has shown, this was precisely the problem for the anti-democratic oligarchic thought collective as the Peloponnesian War was breaking out: the *dēmos* and the *metoikoi* had been allowed to rise out of the position assigned to them in traditional society, and the *oligoi* and *zeugitai* had fallen in importance as a consequence. On a broader level, Athens, by pursuing its expansionist *archē*, was transgressing the norms applicable to a Greek *polis*.

Thus, to reiterate, on the basis of the above analysis of the Athenian oligarchic thought collective, in the *Charmides* Plato can be construed as depicting the representatives of a specific, historical thought collective and as dramatizing their thought style in action. Socrates and Critias are both shown to be preoccupied with controlling and supervising the knowledge practices and craft production that are clearly now beyond the control of their class. Plato's audience—traumatized by decades of war, disaster and coups, and the loss of Athenian hegemony and status—would have been all too aware that Critias had resorted to violence and seized control of Athens. Socrates stands in explicit contrast to Critias' treachery: crucially, the opening of the *Charmides* emphasises Socrates' loyalty to the ruling *dēmokratia*: he has just returned from fighting for the empire, having participated in crushing the revolt of the subject-ally Potidaea. In other words, he is a loyal opponent of the regime: 'an obedient dissident; a critic of democratic culture who takes up public office and is a stickler for the legal rules'.[332] Plato thus positions Socrates as the alternative to resorting to violence and seizing power in the name of self-interest and on the basis of claims to self-evident elite knowledge.

In the next section, I argue that Plato continues and develops the Athenian oligarchic thought style in the *Republic* by adopting a new strategy: focusing on the control of cultural production, through the control of education (*paideia*).

6.6 The *Republic* and the Control of Cultural Production

6.6.1 *Injustice and Collective Trauma*

In light of the preceding analysis of the *Charmides* and the broader corpus articulating the oligarchic thought style, it is surely no coincidence that the *Republic* opens with Socrates returning from the Piraeus—the harbour zone symbolically linked to naval power, the *dēmos*, and the skilled labour of the *metoikoi*. In fact, the

[332] Ober (2017, p. 84).

conversation takes place in the house of Cephalus, a rich and successful *metoikos* from Syracuse,[333] who participates in the conversation when it concerns money and sex, withdraws, leaving his son Polemarchus to continue, once the discussion shifts to justice and more abstract matters (331d).

The overall structure of conversation in the *Republic* can be read as an ascent from lower concerns—such as the Piraeus, manual labour, skilled labour, sex, and money—to higher-level dialectical exchanges with Plato's aristocratic brothers. This upward progression is mirrored by a process of exclusion, as figures such as Cephalus and Polemarchus (both *metoikoi*), along with the foreign sophist Thrasymachus, are successively sidelined.

Without examining the details of Thrasymachus' articulation of the theory of self-interest or Socrates' refutations, the main functions of this passage can be outlined. First, Thrasymachus articulates—or rearticulates for Plato's contemporaries—the discursive issues that preoccupied the Athenian elite in the 430s and 420s: the idea that the strong rule for their own advantage (338c, more precisely 341a); that the three possible constitutions are tyranny, democracy, and aristocracy (338d); and that each type of constitution serves those in power (338d–e). The preference for *aristokratia* over *oligarchia* suggests that, after 403 BC, the latter term came to be avoided—most likely due to its negative political associations.

Socrates' responses to Thrasymachus' arguments begin to differentiate his philosophy from the oligarchic thought style associated with Critias and the Thirty: a ruler is like a good craftsman and does not rule for his own advantage, but for the advantage of his subjects (342d–e). Thrasymachus' counter argument—that injustice brings more advantages than justice—seems to allude directly to Critias and the Thirty Tyrants: 'And this is tyranny, which both by stealth and by force takes away what belongs to others, both sacred and profane, both private and public, not little by little but at one swoop' (344a).[334]

Socrates' eventual response to this argument makes similarly direct references to the Athenian Empire: 'A city, you would say, may be unjust and try to enslave other cities unjustly, have them enslaved and hold many of them in subjection' (351a-b). He then seems to allude to the civil strife that spread across Greek city-states during the Peloponnesian War:

> For factions, Thrasymachus, are the outcome of injustice, and hatreds and internecine conflicts, but justice brings oneness of mind and love. Is it not so?
>
> "So be it," he replied, "not to differ from you."
>
> That is good of you, my friend; but tell me this: if it is the business of injustice to engender hatred wherever it is found, will it not, when it springs up either among freemen or slaves, cause them to hate and be at strife with one another, and make them incapable of effective action in common? (351d–e)

---

[333] Carawan (2013, p. 9).

[334] Unless otherwise indicated, all English translations are taken from the Loeb edition of *Republic* in Plato (1969) translated by Paul Shorey. Available online at https://www.perseus.tufts.edu/hopper/text?doc=Perseus:text:1999.01.0168.

Without having defined justice as yet, Socrates' asserts that the theory of self-interest and the strong ruling to their own advantage lead to injustice and warring factions within the *polis* and the individual (352a). Cooperation and 'self-agreement' become impossible; nothing can be accomplished. In effect, Socrates silences Thrasymachus by invoking the threat and associations of civil strife rather than by dialectical argument. For Plato's contemporaries, Socrates' references to civil strife may well have evoked the collective trauma of recent factional violence and political collapse. In any case, immediately after Thrasymachus makes his final utterance, Socrates admits they have not answered the question of what justice is (354b–c).

6.6.2 Crafts, Goods and Production

The interactions with Polemarchus and Thrasymachus also serve to reintroduce the concerns articulated in the *Charmides*: the classification of certain practices (medicine, cooking, captaincy, music, soldiering, shepherding) as crafts (*technai*); the problem that knowledge fails and craftsmen seem to make errors (340e); and the argument that crafts compensate for deficiencies and produce benefits (341e–342c, 346c). Socrates explicitly asserts that ruling is a craft and that rulers practice the craft of ruling for the benefit of their subjects (342e),[335] and implies that the craft of justice is what makes it possible for the city and the individual to have a unified purpose and achieve anything (351c–352a).

With Polemarchus and Thrasymachus now silent, Socrates, Glaucon and Adeimantus begin defining justice. Glaucon shifts the emphasis from crafts to goods (*agatha*), and Socrates classes justice among the finest kind of good—one that is valued in and of itself (357d–358a). Glaucon puts forward the argument that people do not practice justice for its own sake, but for the sake of reputation and consequences: just as a clever craftsman's errors go undetected, an unjust man can have a reputation for justice (360e–361b).

Adeimantus' contribution, which contains a slew of references to Homer, Hesiod, Musaeus, and Pindar, introduces the question of whether poetic portrayals of injustice are beneficial—a point that raises the crucial issue of their impact on young men.

> What, Socrates, do we suppose is the effect of all such sayings about the esteem in which men and gods hold virtue and vice upon the souls that hear them, the souls of young men who are quick-witted and capable of flitting, as it were, from one expression of opinion to another and inferring from them all the character and the path whereby a man would lead the best life? […] (365a-b)

Socrates' response to the task set by Glaucon and Adeimantus—to explain why justice is good in and of itself, and why injustice is bad; without appealing to

[335] In this passage, Plato uses the term **δημιουργῇ** (*dēmiourgēi*)—often translated as 'exercises his craft'—instead of **τέχνη** (*technē*), which more directly denotes 'art' or 'skill'.

reputation or consequences—and to Adeimantus' question about the effect of poetry on the young, is to embark on an extended analysis of material and cultural production in the *polis* (369a).

The hypothetical *polis* constructed by Socrates is far from Spartan: it relies on imports and exports, so, in addition to farmers and craftsmen, it also needs merchants, retailers, money, and labourers (370e–371e). Following Glaucon's prompting, Socrates goes further and allows that it will be 'a luxurious city', with tables, couches, delicacies, perfumed oils etc. In fact, it will be filled with many things that go beyond what is necessary, entailing a plethora of professions, including those connected with the arts: 'the poets and their assistants, rhapsodists, actors, chorus-dancers [...]' (373b). In other words, the hypothetical *polis* comes to resemble Athens, especially as expansion is viewed as inevitable, once the unlimited acquisition of wealth becomes the overriding aim: 'Then we shall have to cut out a cantle of our neighbor's land if we are to have enough for pasture and ploughing [...]' (373d).

This inevitability of expansion and the conflicts it brings means that guardians will be needed, and they must undergo training and education (376e). As Adeimantus has pointed out, however, existing poetry contains many representations of injustice, leading to the conclusion that control over educational texts must be established to ensure proper guidance for the guardians and the young citizens.

6.6.3 *Republic II: The Regulation of* Muthos *and the Emergence of* Theologia

In the *Republic*, Plato tends to lump Homer and Hesiod together (e.g. 363a, 612b), while those who engage in diverse forms of cultural production are broadly described as creating ψεῦδος (*pseudos*)—a term encompassing not only fables or fiction but also falsehood and lies (376e). These creators are collectively referred to with terms like μυθοποίος (*mythopoios*), meaning 'a maker of myth,' or μυθολόγος (*mythologos*), 'a teller of myth'.[336] Translators vary in their interpretations, from 'fabulists or poets' (Shorey) to creators of 'mythology and poetry' (Jowett) and 'writers of poetry or prose' (Griffith).[337]

Socrates employs the homogenizing technique established in the *Phaedrus*—the principle of 'collection', which gathers dispersed particulars under a single class (265d). By reducing diverse forms of cultural production to a single category, this method initiates a process that ultimately subjects them to regulation and, by Book 10 of the *Republic*, to the full force of the law.

The position assigned to the creators of *pseudos* and *muthos* becomes increasingly bleak as Plato's narrative progresses. The attack on Homer and Hesiod begins

[336] Moors (1982, p. 36).

[337] Plato (1969, p.225), (1991, p. 85), (2000, p. 80).

with the analysis of how justice and injustice are portrayed by poets—or, more literally the 'fabricators'. First, the poets are taken to task for aligning with popular opinion in describing the path of injustice as easy, and the wicked and unjust as happy, then they are associated with itinerant prophets who claim to be able to influence the will of the gods.

Adeimantus (364d) brings attention to how the poets are cited as authorities on the nature of vice and virtue:

> And for all these sayings they cite the poets as witnesses, with regard to the ease and plentifulness of vice, quoting:
>
> "Evil-doing in plenty a man shall find for the seeking;
> Smooth is the way and it lies near at hand and is easy to enter;
> But on the pathway of virtue the gods put sweat from the first step," (Hes. *WD* 287–289)
>
> and a certain long and uphill road. And others cite Homer as a witness to the beguiling of gods by men, since he too said:
>
> "The gods themselves are moved by prayers,
> And men by sacrifice and soothing vows, "And incense and libation turn their wills
> Praying, whenever they have sinned and made transgression." (Hom. *Il*. 9.497)

These passages from *Works and Days* and *The Iliad* are deemed reprehensible in terms of their educational function: intelligent or quick-witted young men could draw the conclusion that it pays to behave unjustly and bribe the gods. This concern recurs throughout the *Republic*, a point that Havelock emphasises in *Preface to Plato* (1963): Socrates and his interlocutors approach the fabrications of the poets as powerful forms of cultural production with clear social and educational functions, rather than as mere entertainment or intellectual titillation. Poetic tales are understood as transmitting and reinforcing societal norms of conduct. Thus, the first prong of Socrates' critique focuses on challenging the social norms embedded in the works of Homer and Hesiod.

The second prong of the attack comes later in Book II, when the interlocutors revisit the issue of education, now cast in terms of the preparing the philosopher-guardians of a healthy, ideal *polis*. Firstly, it is decided that children's education should introduce them to music before gymnastics. Music is defined broadly to encompass 'tales'—that is, epic or lyric verse—and these tales are further divided into two categories: the true and the false (*pseudos*).

Socrates then elaborates on the role of *pseudos* in early education, stating: '"Don't you understand," I said, "that we begin by telling children fables (*muthos*), and the fable is, taken as a whole, false (*pseudos*), but there is truth (*alēthē*) in it also? And we make use of fable with children before gymnastics"' (377a). This introduces a distinction between general tales, which may contain elements of truth or falsehood (*alēthē* or *pseudos*), and pedagogical *muthoi* designed for children, whose fictional surface may nonetheless convey formative moral instruction.

Socrates and his interlocutors decide that strict supervision must be exercised over the makers and tellers of *muthos* (377b–c). Mothers will only be permitted to tell their children stories from the accepted list of good fables—those containing truth—while the tales that consist of bad *pseudos* will simply be discarded. As the discussion unfolds, it becomes apparent that Socrates has the works of Homer and Hesiod in mind, since their tales contain bad images of the gods (377d–e). Examples of those who 'image badly' (Shorey) / 'make erroneous representations' (Jowett) are specified in detail, including Cronus' castration of his father Uranus in Hesiod's *Theogony*, as well as the conflicts and squabbles between the gods found in Homer (377e–378d).

Since the makers of *pseudos* and *muthos* have been found guilty of (a) transmitting norms of conduct that might encourage injustice in the *polis*, and then of (b) producing false images of the gods, any role they might hold in the ideal *polis* must be rigorously supervised. This leads Socrates and Adeimantus to seek and define a new means of control:

> And I replied, "Adeimantus, we are not poets, you and I at present, but founders of a state. And to founders it pertains to know the patterns on which poets must compose their fables and from which their poems must not be allowed to deviate; but the founders are not required themselves to compose fables."
>
> "Right," he said; "but this very thing—the patterns or norms of right speech about the gods, what would they be?"[338]
>
> "Something like this," I said. "The true quality of God we must always surely attribute to him whether we compose in epic, melic, or tragic verse."
>
> "We must."
>
> "And is not God of course good in reality and always to be spoken of as such?" (379a).

According to Jaeger, a new branch of thought is distinguished in this passage for the first time, namely θεολογία (*theologia*), which he defines as 'the approach to God or the gods (*theoi*) by means of the *logos*'.[339] It is clear that this approach is introduced at the expense of the makers of *pseudos* and *muthos*: the emergence of theology is immediately followed by a rule or law to which poets must adhere.

In Book II of the *Republic*, the proposed legislative supervision over the makers of *muthos* imposes strict requirements on their productions: to meet state approval, their fables must contain good *pseudos*, and their tales in epic or lyric verse must represent the deity, *theos*, as he truly is—that is, as good.[340] Nevertheless, at this point, despite being subject to such draconian restrictions, the makers of *muthos* are still assigned a role and place in the ideal *polis* emerging in the Socratic dialogue.

---

[338] ***οἱ τύποι περὶ θεολογίας τίνες ἂν εἶεν*** *(hoi typoi peri theologias tines an eien)*. Other translations 'forms of theology' (Jowett), 'patterns for stories about the gods' (Griffith), and 'the lines on which our poets must work when they deal with the gods' (Lee).

[339] Jaeger (1947, p. 4).

[340] Notably, as the dialogue progresses and the interlocutors' intentions become increasingly stringent, a notable shift occurs from the plural form 'gods' (*θεῶν*, 377e) to the singular 'God' (*θεὸς*, 379a).

6.6.4 *Republic X:* Mimēsis *and Deception*

In Book X, when Plato deploys the theory of *mimēsis* to assign an ontological status to the products of various makers or craftsmen, the position of the makers of epic and lyric verse, along with the makers of tragedies and comedies, becomes particularly dire. It is noteworthy that at this point of the *Republic*, where the ideal *polis* has been constructed upon the pillars of the 'metaphor of the sun', the 'analogy of the divided line', and the 'allegory of the cave', the theory of *mimēsis* draws on this theoretical framework to explicitly put 'poetry' on trial.[341]

The judicial metaphor here is far from arbitrary; it underscores a deliberate structural consistency across Plato's dialogues. As mentioned in Sect. 6.3.1, court procedure in the *Phaedrus* (260–261) is employed to examine the *technē* of speech (and, by extension, rhetoricians), while in the *Republic*, it serves as a powerful tool for asserting cultural hegemony. Just as the subject-allies of Athens in the Delian League were obliged to submit their appeals before an Athenian law-court,[342] Plato's *Republic* brings the Ionian *muthos* of Homer to Athens to face judgment before a jury of philosophers. The prosecution brings the combined resources of the conceptual apparatus erected by Socrates throughout the dialogue and the institutions and procedures of the Athenian legal system to bear on the 'makers of tragedies', with Homer at their head. Throughout the trial, Socrates behaves as the presiding magistrate (*archon basileus*), steering the procedure, while his interlocutors function as a panel of *dikastes*—judges/jurors who collectively determine guilt.[343]

Socrates begins the prosecution with an ontological framing: while (the singular) God made the one, original true bed or couch, 'which really and in itself is' (597c), a carpenter creates a bed in imitation of this form. A painter, in turn, imitates this imitation, becoming 'the producer of the product three removes from nature' (597e). Similarly, the maker of tragedies (*tragōidopoios*) is deemed an imitator 'in his nature three removes from the king and the truth'. With this status assigned to tragedy, Socrates and his interlocutors are now able to present their case against poetry. Two main charges can be identified.

The first is that of deception, echoing the association of *muthos* with *pseudos* from Book II. Just as painters can use their imitations to trick people into thinking they have created the real thing (598c), Homer and other makers of tragedy deceive their audiences with imitations of virtue and vice (598e), when in fact they make 'phantoms, not realities' (599a). This leads to the extraordinary assertion—given the status of Homer's poetry in Athenian culture and its role in education—that Homer did not have genuine knowledge of the things he imitates, such as war, generalship, administration, and education. This culminates in a direct challenge to Homer himself:

[341] Levin (2001).

[342] Meiggs (1972, pp. 179–180).

[343] Carey (1997, pp. 5–7).

> Friend Homer, if you are not at the third remove from truth and reality in human excellence, being merely that creator of phantoms whom we defined as the imitator, but if you are even in the second place and were capable of knowing what pursuits make men better or worse in private or public life, tell us what city was better governed owing to you, even as Lacedaemon was because of Lycurgus, and many other cities great and small because of other legislators. But what city credits you with having been a good legislator and having benefited them? Italy and Sicily say this of Charondas and we of Solon. But who says it of you? (599d–e)

This critique is followed by further scathing attacks on Homer's person (e.g., that he was not a renowned sage like Thales, was not credited with public service, had no followers etc. (600a–e)).

6.6.5 *Republic X:* Mimēsis *and the Inferior Part of the Soul*

The second charge brings one more doctrine into play, namely the theory of the soul gradually introduced throughout *Republic* (e.g., Books 4, 8 and 9). This theory posits that the soul is divided—a battleground over which the competing aspects of reason, spirit, and appetite vie for dominance. In Book X, this theory of the soul is coupled with the theory of *mimēsis* to put forward the accusation that the poets' imitations target the feelings and passions and, for this reason, should be banned from the ideal *polis*.

Socrates' argument proceeds by drawing on the epistemological framework established over the course of the dialogue. The sense of sight, for instance, is identified as liable to deception and contradiction (a straight object looks crooked in water); yet such contractions can be resolved by 'the part of the soul that reasons and calculates' (602e), which deemed 'the best part of the soul', while the part of the soul with holds opinions that contradict the calculations of measurement is identified as one of 'the inferior elements of the soul'. Since the mimetic arts produce 'a product far removed from the truth', they are associated with this inferior part of the soul: 'Mimetic art, then, is an inferior thing cohabiting with an inferior and engendering inferior offspring' (10.603a–b).

Since this analogy is initially based on vision and painting, Socrates senses the need to extend it more convincingly to 'hearing and to what we call poetry' (*poiēsis*) (603b). Here, Plato draws on an arsenal of concepts and legal tools that enable Socrates to build his case: the theory of the divided psyche, the identification of law with reason, crowd psychology, the *polis*-soul analogy, and the institution of ostracism.

The key element justifying the ostracism of poetry is the *polis*-soul analogy. This is based on comparing the individual's behaviour when alone with their behaviour in public, and then, again, with the behaviour of crowds at performances of tragic poetry or a comedies. The argument begins by analysing behaviour associated with sorrow and grieving. A person afflicted with sorrow or in grief will resist or struggle against this emotion when observed by their peers, but when alone will say or do things that they would be ashamed of in public: 'Now is it not reason and law (*logos* and *nomos*) that exhorts him to resist, while that which urges him to give way to his grief is the bare feeling itself?' (604a–b). Thus, the rational element of the soul, *logos*, gains mastery over the soul when supported by and allied with law or custom—*nomos,* which exerts its power over the individual through the gaze of others.

However, Socrates then argues that whereas the irrational, cowardly part of us that succumbs to useless lamentation provides rich material for imitation, the higher principle of reason which resists sorrow—somewhat oddly, given that it is supported by *nomos*—'is neither easy to imitate nor to be understood when imitated, especially by a nondescript mob assembled in the theater' (604e). This entitles Socrates to conclude that the art of the mimetic poet, like that of the painter, is aimed at the irrational, passionate part of the soul.

Once the connection between mimetic poetry and the inferior part of the soul is established, Socrates deploys the *polis*-soul analogy to ban poets from entering the ideal *polis*:

> And so we may at last say that we should be justified in not admitting him into a well-ordered state, because he stimulates and fosters this element in the soul, and by strengthening it tends to destroy the rational part, just as when in a state one puts bad men in power and turns the city over to them and ruins the better sort. Precisely in the same manner we shall say that the mimetic poet sets up in each individual soul a vicious constitution by fashioning phantoms far removed from reality, and by currying favor with the senseless element that cannot distinguish the greater from the less, but calls the same thing now one, now the other. (605b–c)

Just as corrupt rulers tend to corrupt citizens in a *polis*, the mimetic poet corrupts the individual's soul. Good individuals who can manage their own private grief give way to sympathy when *listening* to Homer or other tragedians who rouse their feelings, such as pity. The more one indulges such emotions in the theatre, the more difficult it becomes to control them in private. This effect is further illustrated by comedy: laughing at unseemly jokes at the theatre means that one will become a buffoon at home (606c–d).

The case against poetry culminates in an explicit attack on the status and role of Homer as the educator of Greece (606e). Socrates acknowledges Homer is the greatest poet, but repeats that in the ideal *polis* his poetry would be banned (only hymns to the gods and encomia of famous men will be permitted): 'For if you grant admission to the honeyed muse in lyric or epic, pleasure and pain will be lords of your city instead of law (*nomos*) and that which shall from time to time have approved itself to the general reason (*logos*) as the best' (607a). Although Socrates initially frames the poets' exclusion in terms of non-admission—'we should be justified in not admitting him into a well-ordered state' (605b)—it gradually becomes clear that the poets are not merely refused entry but effectively expelled. The judgment, more precisely, is one of removal from the *polis*, stripping poetry of its traditional cultural authority. This expulsion sets the stage for the final turn in Book X, where poetry is imagined as returning only under tightly controlled conditions—if, and only if, she can prove her political and ethical worth through rational discourse.

Socrates then famously refers to an ancient quarrel between philosophy and poetry (607c), citing some unknown fragments of poetry which appear to be critical of philosophers.[344] The judgment concludes by allowing poetry to return from exile if she can plead her defence in lyric metre, and if her defenders can show, in prose, that she is beneficial to 'orderly government and the life of man' (607c).[345]

It is noticeable that poetry is not afforded the opportunity to defend itself before being dismissed from the *polis*: it is judged in absentia, already implicitly banished even before a formal judgment is issued (as it is said to be prohibited from entering the *polis* before a verdict of banishment has been officially pronounced). In this metaphorical trial, Plato does not allow any of the dialogue's participants to mount a defence on behalf of poetry—not even a weak, token defence for Socrates to dismantle. This exclusion may reflect the reality that the interlocutors, raised in a culture steeped in poetry—as Havelock pointed out in 1963—have already heard all she has to offer. Alternatively, poetry's exclusion could signal the worry that the 'honeyed Muse' (607a) might prove too alluring if granted the chance to speak.

As early as 1939, T. B. L. Webster argued that Plato's elaboration of *mimēsis* in the *Republic* reflects a culmination of sustained reflection on poetic representation dating back to the late fifth century. Plato's invocation of the 'ancient quarrel' between philosophy and poetry, moreover, aligns Socrates with pre-Socratic figures such as Xenophanes and Heraclitus, who had already rejected Homer and Hesiod as authoritative sources. Thus, Plato situates himself within a longstanding cultural conflict. In the aftermath of the Peloponnesian War, the disastrous oligarchic coups, and the execution of Socrates, the *Republic* can be read as recognizing that cultural conflict over values is the new battleground, and that the path to power lies in the control of cultural production.

6.7 Conclusion: *philosophia* as a Thought Style

In light of the previous sections, we can conclude that *philosophia*, the thought style communicated in the *Charmides*, *Phaedrus* and *Republic*, developed from a thought style communicated by a section of the Athenian elite, the *oligoi* opposed to the democracy, in the period between 431 and 403.

To recap, the oligarchic thought style of the late fifth century was characterized by discursive antagonism, articulated through a narrowed definition of the *dēmos* as the enemy; by resentment and hostility towards the *metoikoi* and the skilled urban labour that had been empowered by the Athenian Empire; by the identification of a broader conflict between the *dēmos* and the *oligoi* across the Greek world; by deploying the theory of self-interest to justify opposition to the Athenian *dēmokratia* and siding with Sparta; by organizing opposition through secret political associations and symposia; and by attempts to replace the institutions and cultural practices

[344] Perhaps Aristophanes' Clouds could be considered just such an example of a poet's criticism of philosophy.

[345] Webster (1939, pp. 168–171).

of the *dēmokratia* with a narrow, oligarchic constitution that would return the traditional social hierarchy.

Plato's *philosophia* can be characterized as a thought style that emerged from the oligarchic tradition and perpetuated many of its preoccupations, prejudices, and practices, even as it reframed them within a philosophical and educational project. However, while the oligarchic thought collective emerged during wartime, and while its practices transitioned from purely discursive opposition to the active adoption of violent and intimidatory practices, and actually seized control and wielded power, Plato's *philosophia* emerged during a period of trauma, when Athens had lost its hegemony and control, and was recovering from the devastation of war, coups and civil strife. Thus, rather than advocating the overthrow of the restored democracy or seizing power through political means, Plato's project redirects the claim to rule into a pedagogical strategy: the long-term transformation of the polis through control of cultural production and elite education.

The following conclusions encapsulate the unique traits and strategic goals of this thought style:

1) The thought style's core concepts—*technē*, *epistēmē*, and *mimēsis*—serve to differentiate, evaluate, and suppress various forms of cultural production and practices. Thus, the attack on poetry and tragedy in *Republic* Book X is not an appendix (as argued by Nettleship 1987; Cornford 1941; Annas 1981) but a core purpose of the text (Havelock 1963; Murray 1997; Levin 2001b).
2) The thought style is strategically reductive: concepts like *muthos* and *mimēsis* identify general features shared across heterogeneous practices—such as fabrication, representation, and persuasion—allowing them to be treated as homogeneous cultural products or practices. Consequently, diverse modes of public communication (e.g., political oratory, legal speeches, sophistic lectures) are all reduced to a single essence—persuasive speech—and thus classed inferior to philosophical conversation, defined as private and educational in nature (Heath 1989; Tuozzo 2011).
3) This thought style shapes its identity through the negative identification and characterisation of other styles (analogous to the discursive antagonism described by Laclau and Mouffe (1985) and Mouffe (2005)).
4) The thought style was focused on the subjugation and control of rival thought styles: once forms of communication are homogenised, they can be assimilated (e.g., through genre hybridisation (Wilson Nightingale 1995)), supervised, and subordinated to *philosophia*—pilloried, silenced, or excluded.
5) The thought style of *philosophia* inherited the hostile, suspicious attitude to craftsmen and the production of goods expressed by the oligarchic thought style; the desire to rule over and supervise different forms of knowledge is at the core of Plato's project.
6) More broadly, the thought style was deeply imbued with the arrogance and sense of superiority associated with the Athenian mentality (as described in Thucydides' *History*). Despite its anti-imperial origins—the core code of the initial oligarchic thought style—Plato's thought style perpetuates the Athenian

assertion of cultural superiority, shifting the locus of dominance from political control over Ionia to intellectual hegemony over its cultural legacy—particularly in poetry and natural philosophy.

7) *Philosophia*'s method of argumentation was determined by, and explicitly invoked, the Athenian legal system: in the *Phaedrus* and *Republic*, Socrates and his interlocutors assume the role of magistrate and jurors; charges are brought, the case is argued, the judgment is made, the sentence is pronounced.
8) Plato's use of writing is a key addition to the Socratic practice of dialectical conversation, but Plato's adoption of the concept of *mimēsis* actually condemns his written text to the representation of philosophy; his texts do not *do* philosophy, they can only *represent* it—the cultural practice of philosophy is defined as something that occurs outside the text, in active real-life engagement in philosophical conversation (Heath 1986; Tuozzo 2011). In Plato's own terms, his texts function more like advertisements than carriers of truth.
9) Fleck's theory can lead to a greater appreciation of Plato's texts than perhaps Plato would have allowed. Plato's texts are the communication of a thought style shaped by, and responding to, multiple determinants from a traumatic period marked by economic upheaval, war, civil strife, plague, and cultural conflict. While his works can stand alone, reading them through the lens of the Peloponnesian War and the oligarchic coups illuminates the immense subtleties and complexities embedded within these texts.
10) Fleck's theory suggests that uncovering the subtleties within Plato's texts emerges from an engaged, inquisitive interaction: their richness reveals itself in response to the reader's depth of inquiry. Moreover, a coherent description of Plato's thought style should resonate with readers who share a similar cognitive approach.

In the next chapter, this analysis extends to the transmission of the Socratic caesura—a conceptual boundary framing Socrates as a decisive rupture in the history of Western thought and the founder of civic—or *polis*-oriented—philosophy. By tracing its reinterpretation from Plato to German scholarship the chapter explores how this pivotal construct shaped philosophy's evolving role as both an intellectual and ideological force.

References

Aeschylus (1926) Suppliant Maidens, Persians, Prometheus, Seven Against Thebes (trans: Smyth). Harvard University Press, Cambridge

Allen R (1996) The dialogues of Plato, vol 3. Yale University Press, New Haven

Annas J (1981) An introduction to Plato's Republic. Clarendon Press, Oxford

Aristotle (1933) Metaphysics. In: Aristotle in 23 Volumes, vols 17, 18 (trans: Tredennick H). Harvard University Press, Cambridge

Aristotle (1998) Politics (trans: Reeve C). Hackett, Indianapolis

Aristotle (2002) The Athenian Constitution (trans: Rhodes P). Penguin, London

Aristotle (2008) Physics (trans: Waterfield R). OUP, Oxford

Barnes J (1979) The Presocratic Philosophers. Routledge, London
Bourdieu P (1993) The field of cultural production. Columbia University Press, New York
Brownson CL (1961) Introduction. In: Xenophon's Hellennica Books I-V. Harvard University Press, Cambridge
Buxton R (1999) Preface. In: Buxton R (ed) From myth to reason?: Studies in the development of Greek thought. OUP, Oxford, pp 1–21
Carawan E (2013) The Athenian amnesty and reconstructing the law. OUP, Oxford
Carey C (1997) Trials from classical Athens. Routledge, London
Cochrane C (1929) Thucydides and the science of history. Oxford University Press, London
Cohen SM, Curd P, Reeve C (2011) Readings in Ancient Greek philosophy. Hackett Publishing, Indianapolis
Constantakopoulou C (2007) The dance of the islands. Insularity, networks, the Athenian Empire, and the Aegean world. OUP, Oxford
Cornford FM (1912) From religion to philosophy: a study in the origins of western speculation. E. Arnold, London
Cornford FM (1941) The Republic of Plato. Clarendon Press, Oxford
de Ste. Croix GEM (1954) The character of the Athenian Empire. Historia: Zeitschrift für Alte Geschichte 3(1):1–41
de Ste. Croix GEM (1972) The origins ofthe Peloponnesian War. Duckworth, London
de Ste. Croix GEM (1981) The class struggle in the Ancient Greek world: from the Archaic age to the Arab conquests. Cornell University Press, New York
Dersley S (2024) Chapter 5 The Networked Public Sphere and the Sectarian Public. In: Postcollectivity. Brill, Leiden, The Netherlands. https://doi.org/10.1163/9789004694880_007
Diodorus Siculus (2010) The Persian Wars to the Fall of Athens (trans: Green P). University of Texas Press, Austin
Dodds ER (1951) The Greeks and the Irrational. University of California Press. Berkeley and London
Dodds ER (1959) Plato. Gorgias. A revised text with introduction and commentary. Clarendon Press, Oxford
Edmunds L (2021) Greek myth. De Gruyter, Berlin
Eshelman K (2008) Defining the circle of sophists: Philostratus and the construction of the second sophistic. Class Philol 103(4):395–413
Febvre L (1982) The problem of unbelief in the sixteenth century (trans: Beatrice Gottlieb). Harvard Univesity Press, Cambridge
Finkelberg M (2020) Homer and early Greek epic. De Gruyter, Berlin
Fleck L (1979) Genesis and development of a scientific fact [1935]. The University of Chicago Press, Chicago
Fleck L (1986) The problem of epistemology [1936]. In: Cognition and fact. Boston Studies in the Philosophy of Science, vol 87. Springer, Dordrecht. https://doi.org/10.1007/978-94-009-4498-5_5
Gomme AW (1938) Aristophanes and politics. Class Rev 52(3):97–109
Gomme AW (1971) A historical commentary on Thucydides, vol 1. Clarendon Press, Oxford
Gordon B (1975) Economic analysis before Adam Smith. Macmillan Press, London
Gould T (1990) The ancient quarrel between poetry and philosophy. Princeton University Press, Princeton
Grendler PF (1989) Schooling in Renaissance Italy. John Hopkins University Press, Baltimore
Grote G (1879) History of Greece, vol VI. Harper and Brothers, New York
Gurri M (2018) The revolt of the public. Stripe Press, San Francisco
Guthrie WKC (1962) A history of Greek Philosophy, vol 1. CUP, Cambridge
Harvey F (1966) The political sympathies of Herodotus. Historia: Zeitschrift für Alte Geschichte 15(2):254–255
Havelock EA (1963) Preface to Plato. Harvard University Press, Cambridge

Havelock EA (1978) The Greek concept of justice: from its shadow in Homer to its substance in Plato. Harvard University Press, Cambridge
Heath M (1989) The unity of Plato's Phaedrus. Oxford Stud Ancient Philos 7:151–173
Herodotus (1928) Books III and IV (trans: Godley A). William Heinemann, London
Hesiod (1914a) Theogony. In: The Homeric Hymns and Homerica with an English Translation by Hugh G. Evelyn-White. Harvard University Press, Cambridge
Hesiod (1914b) Works and Days. In: The Homeric Hymns and Homerica with an English Translation by Hugh G. Evelyn-White. Harvard University Press, Cambridge
Hobbes T (1843) The history of the Grecian War written by Thucydides, vol 1 (1629). John Bohn, London
Hofstetter MJ (2001) The Romantic Idea of a University England and Germany, 1770–1850. Palgrave, New York
Homer (1990) The Iliad (trans: Fagles R). Penguin, New York
Hornblower S (1991) A commentary on Thucydides, vol I, Books I-III. Clarendon Press, Oxford
Hornblower S (2008) A commentary on Thucydides, vol III, Books 5.25-8.109. OUP, Oxford
Hornblower S, Spawforth A (1999) The Oxford classical dictionary. Third edition. OUP, Oxford
Jaeger W (1946) Paideia. The Ideals of Greek Culture, vol I. Blackwell, Oxford
Jaeger W (1947) The theology of the early Greek philosophers. Oxford University Press, London
Kagan D (1969) The outbreak of the Peloponnesian War. Cornell University Press, Ithaca and London
Kagan D (1987) The fall of the Athenian Empire. Cornell University Press, New York
Kallet L (2013) The origins of the Athenian Economic Arche. J Hell Stud 133:43–60
Kallet L (2017) The Pentecontaetia. In: Balot RK, Forsdyke S, Foster E (eds) The Oxford handbook of Thucydides. Oxford Univerity Press, New York, pp 63–80
Kemezis AM (2014) Greek Narratives of the Roman Empire under the Severans: Cassius Dio, Philostratus and Herodian. CUP, Cambridge
Kirk G, Raven J (1957) The Presocratic Philosophers. CUP, Cambridge
Krentz P (1982) The thirty at Athens. Cornell University Press, New York
Laks A (2018) The concept of Presocratic philosophy: its origin, development, and significance. Princeton University Press
Lampert L (2010) How philosophy became Socratic. University of Chicago Press, Chicago
Levick B (2007) Julia Domna. Syrian Empress. Routledge, Abingdon
Levin DN (2001a) Critias. In: Sprague RK (ed) The Older Sophists (1972). Hackett. Cambridge, pp 241–278
Levin SB (2001b) The Ancient Quarrel between philosophy and poetry. OUP, Oxford
Lewis DM (2021) Labour specialization in the Athenian economy. In: Stewart E, Harris E, Lewis D (eds) Skilled labour and professionalism in Ancient Greece and Rome. CUP, Cambridge, pp 129–174
Lloyd GE (1979) Magic, reason and experience: studies in the origin and development of Greek science. CUP, Cambridge
Lysias (1930) Lysias with an English translation by W.R.M. Lamb, M.A. Harvard University Press, Cambridge
Marr J, Rhodes P (2015) Introduction, Translation and Commentary. In: The 'Old Oligarch', The Constitution of the Athenians. Oxbow Books, Oxford
McCabe M, Adamsom P (2010) MM McCabe on Heraclitus. Retrieved July 30, 2022, from History of Philosophy Without any Gaps: https://historyofphilosophy.net/mccabe-on-heraclitus
Meiggs R (1972) The Athenian Empire. OUP, Oxford
Mignolo WD, Walsh CE (2018) On decoloniality: concepts, analytics, praxis. Duke University Press
Moors KF (1982) Platonic myth: an introductory study. University Press of America, Washington DC
Mouffe C (2005) On the political. Routledge, Abingdon
Murray P (1997) Plato on poetry. Cambridge University Press, Cambridge
Nestle W (1940) Vom Mythos zum Logos. Die des griechischen Denkens Selbstentfaltung von Homer bis auf die Sophistik und Sokrates. A. Kröner, Stuttgart

Nettleship RL (1906) The theory of education in the Republic of Plato. University of Chicago Press, Chicago
Nettleship RL (1951) Lectures on the Republic of Plato (1897). Macmillan, London
Nightingale AW (1995) Genres in Dialogue. CUP, Cambridge
Ober J (1989) Mass and elite in democratic Athens. Princeton University Press, Princeton
Ober J (2017) The trial of Socrates as a political trial. In: Meierhenrich J, Pendas D (eds) Political trials in theory and history. Cambridge University Press, Cambridge, pp 65–87
Oliver IC (2010) The Audiences of Herodotus: the influence of performance on the histories (Doctoral Thesis). University of Colorado
Ong W (1982) Orality and literacy. Routledge, Abingdon
Ostwald M (1969) Nomos and the beginnings of Athenian democracy. Clarendon Press, Oxford
Philostratus (1922). The Lives of the Sophists. In: Philostratus and Eunapius (trans: Wright WC). William Heinemann, London
Pindar (2007) The Complete Odes (trans: Verity A). OUP, Oxford
Plato (1925a) Ion. In: Plato in Twelve Volumes, vol 9 translated by W.R.M. Lamb. Harvard University Press, Cambridge
Plato (1925b) Phaedrus/ In: Plato in Twelve Volumes, vol 9 translated by Harold N. Fowler. Harvard University Press, Cambridge
Plato (1955) Plato in Twelve Volumes, vol 8 translated by W.R.M. Lamb., Harvard University Press, Cambridge
Plato (1966) Phaedo. In: Plato in Twelve Volumes, vol 1 (trans: Fowler HN). Harvard University Press, Cambridge
Plato (1969) Plato in Twelve Volumes, vols 5 & 6 translated by Paul Shorey. Harvard University Press, Cambridge
Plato (1986) Gorgias (trans: Zeyl DJ). Hackett, Indianapolis
Plato (1991) The Republic (trans: Jowett B). Vintage Classics, Toronto
Plato (1992) Laches and Charmides (trans: Sprague RK). Hackett, Indianapolis/Cambridge
Plato (2000) The Republic (trans: Griffith P). CUP, Cambridge
Plato (2002) Phaedrus (trans: Waterfield R). OUP, Oxford
Plutarch (1932) Lives, vol III (trans: Perrin B). Heinemann, London
Plutarch (1960) The Rise and Fall of Athens. Nine Lives by Plutarch (trans: Scott-Kilvert I). Penguin, London
Plutarch (1968) Lives, vol II (trans: Perrin B). Heinemann, London
Popper K (1998) The World of Parmenides: Essays on the Presocratic Enlightenment. Routledge, London
Powell A (1988) Athens and Sparta constructing Greek political and social history from 478 BC. Routledge, London
Powell BB (2017) The Poems of Hesiod. University of California Press
Rhodes P (2000) Oligarchs in Athens. In: Brock R, Hodkinson S (eds) Alternatives to Athens. Varieties of political organization and community in Ancient Greece. OUP, Oxford, pp 119–136
Rhodes PJ (2002) Introduction. In: Aristotle (2002) The Athenian Constitution (trans: Rhodes P). Penguin, London
Roberts JT (1994) Athens on Trial. Princeton University Press, Princeton
Rowe C (1986) The argument and structure of Plato's Phaedrus. Camb Class J 32:106–125
Rowe C (1989) The Unity of the Phaedrus: A Reply to Heath. Oxford Stud Ancient Philos 7:175–188
Sandywell B (1996) Presocratic reflexivity: the construction of philosophical discourse c. 600-450 B.C.: logological investigations: Volume Three. Routledge, London
Schmid WT (1998) Plato's Charmides and the Socratic Ideal of Rationality. State University of New York Press, New York
Schrodinger E (1954) Nature and the Greeks. CUP, Cambridge
Sealey R (1973) The Origins of "Demokratia". Calif Stud Class Antiq 6:253–295

Sextus Empiricus (1936) Sextus Empiricus Volume III (trans: Bury RG). Harvard University Press, Cambridge

Snell B (1953) The discovery of the mind. Blackwell, Oxford

Snyder T (2003) The reconstruction of nations. Poland, Ukraine, Lithuania, Belarus, 1569–1999. Yale University Press, New Haven & London

Spinelli E, Verde F (2020). Theology. In: Mitsis P (ed) The Oxford handbook of Epicurus and Epicureanism. OUP, Oxford

Sprague RK (ed) (2001) The Older Sophists: A Complete Translation by Several Hands of the Fragments in Die Fragmente der Vorsokratiker, Edited by Diels-Kranz. With a New Edition of Antiphon and of Euthydemus (1972). Hackett, Indianapolis

Stadter PA (1989) A Commentary on Plutarch's Pericles. The University of North Carolina Press, London

Stallings AE (2018) Introduction to Hesiod's Works and Days. Penguin, London

Teggart FJ (1947) The Argument of Hesiod's Works and Days. J Hist Ideas 8(1):45–77

The 'Old Oligarch' (2015) The Constitution of the Athenians (trans: Marr J, Rhodes P). Oxbow Books, Oxford

Thomas R (1992) Literacy and orality in Ancient Greece. CUP, Cambridge

Thucydides (2009) The Peloponnesian War (trans: Hammond M). OUP, Oxford

Thucydides (2013) The War of the Peloponnesians and the Athenians (trans: Mynott J). CUP, Cambridge

Tuozzo TM (2011) Plato's Charmides. Positive Elenchus in a "Socratic" Dialogue. CUP, Cambridge

Vernant JP (1982) The origins of Greek thought. Cornell University Press, New York

Vernant JP (1988) Myth and society in Ancient Greece. Zone Books, New York

Vlastos G (1947) Equality and justice in Early Greek cosmologies. Class Philol 42(3):156–178

Waterfield R (2000) The first philosophers. OUP, Oxford

Webster TB (1939) Greek theories of art and literature down to 400 B. C. Class Q 33(3/4):166–179

Wolpert A (2002) Remembering defeat. Civil war and civic memory in Ancient Athens. John Hopkins University Press, Baltimore

Wood EM (1989) Peasant-citizen and slave: the foundations of Athenian democracy. Verso, London

Xenophon (1923) Memorabilia (trans: Marchant E). In: Xenophon, Memorabilia, Oeconomicus, Symposium, Apology. Harvard University Press, Cambridge

Xenophon (1961) Xenophon's Hellennica Books I-V (trans: Brownson CL). Harvard University Press, Cambridge

Zaccarini M (2017) The Lame Hegemony. Cimon of Athens and the Failure of Panhellenism, ca. 478–450 BC. Bononia University Press, Bologna

Chapter 7
The Transmission of Philosophy: The Socratic Caesura

Abstract This chapter explores the transmission of the Socratic caesura—a conceptual break framing Socrates as the founder of civic, or polis-oriented, philosophy—through successive reinterpretations, from Plato's original articulation to its reimagination in German scholarship of the late eighteenth century. Applying Fleck's theory of thought styles and thought collectives, the chapter traces how this framing evolved across historical and cultural contexts, shaped by ideological struggles and institutional transformations.

Beginning with Aristophanes' *Clouds* and the charges brought at Socrates' trial, the chapter examines early hostile representations that conflated naturalist, sophistic, and Socratic thought styles. It then turns to Plato's *Apology* and *Phaedo*, where Socrates is redefined through a decisive rupture with naturalism and rhetoric. This caesura was reinforced and transformed by Xenophon, Aristotle, and Cicero, each adapting Socrates' legacy to their own cultural frameworks. Cicero's version integrated Greek philosophy with Roman ideals, casting Socrates as a model of practical wisdom and oratory in service of the Republic.

The chapter concludes by tracing how the caesura became a vehicle for philosophical legitimation in early modern and modern Europe. From Cicero's assimilation into Christian thought to Eberhard's coinage of 'Presocratic' and Hegel's institutionalization of philosophy in the Humboldtian university, the caesura was reactivated to consolidate disciplinary authority. Viewed through Fleck's framework, the caesura emerges not as a neutral historical marker but as a long-range discursive strategy for elevating philosophy and marginalizing rival modes of knowledge.

7.1 Scope and Aims

André Laks, in *The Concept of Presocratic Philosophy: Its Origin, Development, and Significance* (2018), coined the term 'Socratic caesura' to describe the model that positions Socrates as a radical discontinuity in the history of Western

S. Dersley, *Thought Collectives and Cultural Change*, Living Signs of Law 1,
https://doi.org/10.1007/978-3-031-97431-1_7

rationality.[1] Laks traces the caesura back to Plato's *Apology* and *Phaedo*, emphasizing Cicero's focus on Socrates as the initiator of practical philosophy.[2] He then outlines how this model was developed and transmitted in German eighteenth and nineteenth-century thought, from Johann Augustus Eberhard's coinage of the term *Vorsokratiker* (Presocratic) in 1788, through Friedrich Schleiermacher and Hegel's problematizing and relativizing Socrates' contribution, to Eduard Zeller's return to Socrates' pivotal position (1844), which became consolidated in Nietzsche's *Birth of Tragedy* (1872) and Hermann Diels's authoritative *Fragmente der Vorsokratiker* (1903).[3]

This model of Socratic thought as a rupture or decisive pivot was articulated through projects involving extensive comparison and intense self-reflection. Cicero, for instance, drew an explicit comparison between Greek and Roman culture to assert the supremacy of the latter, thereby justifying his appropriation and Romanization of Greek philosophy. In the German context, the University's scholarly reconstruction of Greek culture did more than shape philosophy and philology; it also constituted the University itself as the authoritative site of discursive practice, with the distinctions it imposed on Greek cultural production both reflecting and reinforcing the disciplines that emerged within the university walls. These distinctions, in turn, conferred cultural capital on fields like Philosophy, which was shaped by the institutional roles of its professors. Hegel's definition of Philosophy, shaped by his interaction with Plato's texts, was inextricably bound up with the subject positions he articulated from within the German university system.

The aim of this chapter is to consider the transmission of the Socratic caesura, as a model of emergence and discontinuity, from a Fleckian perspective. The model is grounded in the notion that Socrates marked an entirely new way of thinking—a new thought style in Fleck's terms. Subsequent traditions that transmitted this model (e.g., Ciceronian, Shaftesbury, various German university disciplines, contemporary academic philosophy that retains the term 'Presocratic') repurposed the idea of Socrates to suit their cultural, political, and institutional contexts. Each version enacted a distinct Socratic caesura, a term introduced by Laks but here developed into a wider analytic framework. In accordance with Fleck's theory, this transmission and repurposing involved complex interactive cognition: various thought collectives over the centuries interacted with the texts of Plato and Xenophon as these texts were filtered, interpreted, and transmitted by other thought collectives. Crucially, key moments when new interpretations emerged—such as Cicero's combination of Socratic practical philosophy with Roman oratory, and Hegel's revalorization of the sophists and his purification of Platonism—occurred during periods of social upheaval and wide-ranging cultural change. This context provides fertile ground for examining Fleck's concepts of thought styles and the interplay between thought collectives.

---

[1] Laks (2018, pp. 1–18).

[2] Laks (2018, pp. 8–10).

[3] Laks (2018, Chapter 2).

7.2 Plato's Socratic Caesura

In the ancient sources, the Socratic rupture was most powerfully articulated in Plato's texts. When Plato's Socrates publicly defends himself against the charges of impiety and corrupting the youth of Athens in the *Apology*, he cites his accusers' statement: 'Socrates is a criminal and a busybody, investigating the things beneath the earth and in the heavens and making the weaker argument stronger and teaching others these same things' (19b).[4]

This charge can thus be construed as alleging that Socrates was an exponent of what we would now identify as *two distinct thought styles*: one focused on naturalist investigations, the other on rhetorical persuasion. Socrates suggests that the source of this public image is Aristophanes' comedy (i.e., *Clouds*), which had 'a Socrates being carried about there', providing naturalistic accounts of phenomena, such as thunder, and also agreeing to train a young man in rhetorical techniques. However, Plato's Socrates explicitly distinguishes his thinking from both naturalist philosophy and sophistry: 'I, men of Athens, have nothing to do with these things' (19c).

Socrates explains that his investigations are rather focused on wisdom (*sophiā*) and examining those who claim to be, or who are reputed to be, wise (*sophos*) (20d-e). Later in the text (26b-e), Socrates addresses the specific charges of impiety (*asébeia*) ('teaching them [the youth] not to believe in the gods the state believes in') by countering Meletus' attempt to associate his teaching with ideas attributed to Anaxagoras. When Meletus claims that Socrates 'says that the sun is a stone and the moon earth', Socrates responds: 'Do you think you are accusing Anaxagoras, my dear Meletus, and do you so despise these gentlemen and think they are so unversed in letters as not to know, that the books of Anaxagoras the Clazomenian are full of such utterances?' (26d).

Socrates employs reasoning by analogy to demonstrate that, in contrast to Anaxagoras, he believes in supernatural matters and beings, and thus, in gods (27b-c). Hence, in the *Apology* the Socratic caesura is articulated in a denial of impiety, as a disassociation and distancing from Anaxagorean naturalism, and as an assertion that the Socratic examination of wisdom is entirely distinct from naturalist investigations.

However, in *Phaedo* 96a-99a, when speaking to an informal circle of friends, Socrates acknowledges that in his youth, he had indeed been enthusiastic about 'the investigation of nature'. He then explains how he came to reject Anaxagoras' naturalist account of causes in favour of accounts of causes that could be construed as political, i.e., pertaining to the practical motivations of the men of Athens. This is exemplified by a comparison: rather than accounting for his sitting and talking in prison with an explanation based on natural causes ('bones and sinews', 'air currents and auditory sensations'), Socrates would now focus on '[...] the real causes, which are, that the Athenians decided it was best to condemn me'.[5]

---

[4] Plato (1914, p. 75). All quotations from Plato's *Apology* were taken from Fowler's 1914 Loeb translation.

[5] Plato (1914, pp. 331–341) Again, all quotations from Plato's *Phaedo* are taken from Fowler's 1914 Loeb translation.

Thus, Plato's texts present two sides of the Socratic caesura: public and private. In Fleckian terms, the public face is a defensive denial delivered to the exoteric thought collective constituted by the 'men of Athens', while the private face is an admission and explanation shared within an esoteric thought collective, an inner circle of like-minded friends or acolytes.[6]

In the *Phaedo*, Plato allows his Socrates—after his trial, when facing imminent death—to reveal that he once held an interest in naturalistic investigations, thereby contradicting his public disavowal. Moreover, rather focusing on something *entirely different* to the investigations of the naturalists, i.e., practical wisdom instead of natural phenomena, it can be argued that by shifting the focus from natural or physiological causes to political (*polis*-based) explanations, Socrates in some sense continued the naturalists' investigations of causes/ reasons/ explanations (*aitiai*).[7]

Thus, to reiterate, Plato's texts present a Socrates who publicly dissociates himself from Anaxagorean naturalism in a denial that asserts his investigations into wisdom as fundamentally distinct and discontinuous with naturalist inquiries. Yet privately, Socrates appears to acknowledge some continuity with Anaxagorean naturalism—at least in terms of investigative purpose, method, and practice.

Plato's Socrates' public disavowal of naturalism seems to have been a dissimulation necessitated by cultural and political factors. The reports on Anaxagoras' life from Plato's *Phaedrus*, Clement of Alexandria, and Diogenes Laertius have allowed a handful of salient facts to be constructed: he introduced Milesian/Ionian naturalism to Athens; he lived in Athens for thirty years and was the teacher of Archelaus and Pericles; he was indicted for impiety, sentenced to death, and subsequently released, before leaving—or being banished from—Athens for Lampsacus.[8]

Plutarch's account of Anaxagoras in the *Pericles* registers the tensions and positioning that had become fossilized in centuries of discursive layering. On the one hand, Anaxagoras is portrayed a source of cultural capital (he 'did most to clothe [Pericles] with a majestic demeanour' (*Per.* 4.4)[9] and as a model of composure and public speaking (*Per.* 5.1). Yet, on the other, Plutarch's defence of Pericles from the charges of Ion of Chios (a contemporary of Anaxagoras and Pericles) suggests that Anaxagoras was partly held responsible for Pericles' haughty demeanour and arrogance (*Per.* 5.3-5.4).

Furthermore, Plutarch's account of Anaxagoras' natural philosophy—which comfortably contrasts rational knowledge of natural causes with superstition and

[6] Fleck (1979, pp. 105–107).

[7] In *How Philosophy Became Socratic* (2010), Laurence Lampert distinguishes between Plato's 'politic' and 'impolitic' philosophy. The former is concerned with the 'public appearance of philosophy' and is conveyed in dialogues such as *Protagoras*, *Charmides* and the *Republic*, while the deeper, impolitic philosophy is articulated to the initiated in the more private dialogues—*Phaedo*, *Parmenides* and *Symposium*—Lampert (2010, p. 8). This distinction converges with Fleck's model of the exoteric and esoteric circles of a thought collective—Fleck (1979, pp. 111–125).

[8] On Anaxagoras biography: Diogenes Laertius (1925), Sider (2005, pp. 1–11), Curd (2007, pp. 129–137).

[9] Plutarch (1916).

ignorance (Per. 6.2)—depicts a thought style that dismissed traditional practices in a manner that would have shocked the sensibilities of fifth-century Athenians:

> A story is told that once on a time the head of a one-horned ram was brought to Pericles from his country-place, and that Lampon the seer, when he saw how the horn grew strong and solid from the middle of the forehead, declared that, whereas there were two powerful parties in the city, that of Thucydides and that of Pericles, the mastery would finally devolve upon one man,—the man to whom this sign had been given. Anaxagoras, however, had the skull cut in two, and showed that the brain had not filled out its position, but had drawn together to a point, like an egg, at that particular spot in the entire cavity where the root of the horn began. (*Per.* 6.2)[10]

Writing over five centuries later, in the era of imperial Rome—by which time Athenian philosophy had long been appropriated and Romanized—Plutarch still felt the need to stress that the accounts of 'the naturalist and the seer' were not incompatible, by distinguishing between the cause and meaning of the one-horned ram (*Per.* 6.3). Whether or not there is truth to the story of Anaxagoras and Lampon, the key point is that over the course of centuries Anaxagoras had become a consolidated symbol of a naturalist philosophy that, firstly, posed a threat to traditional knowledge practices and, secondly, was embraced by the main representative of the radical democracy.

In the setting of Plato's *Apology*, thirty years after Pericles' death, the 'men of Athens' of 399 BC are represented as still viewing the mechanical explanations offered by naturalists as a threat to the authority of the state and civic religion based on traditional stories and rituals.[11] One explanation for this apparently renewed emphasis on traditional explanations and practices is the context of collective trauma:

> With the democratic restoration, Athens was freed from the Thirty, but remained in dire straits: Perhaps half the citizen population of Athens had been killed in the later years of the war and the civil war; the economy was a shambles; the fleet and walls that had protected the city were destroyed. Surviving Athenians had lost much: In many cases their ancestral property was lost forever. Once-wealthy families struggled to make ends meet. The Athenians held civic festivals stressing national unity. [...] Meanwhile, the Amnesty meant that the people's anger and pain at the losses suffered during the reign of the Thirty could not be satisfied by seeking justice through the legal system. It was an agonizing era; everyone's life was in disarray.[12]

At the time of Socrates' trial in 399 BC, the restored democracy seems to have been distancing itself from the policies and mindset of the Periclean-radical democracy, which was perceived as having embroiled Athens in decades of war. Efforts were made to bolster the restored democracy's claims to traditional legitimacy: for example, after the first oligarchic coup, in 410 BC, transcribers had been tasked with recovering and writing up the laws of Solon, a project resumed after 403 BC.[13]

---

[10] Plutarch (1916).

[11] Irwin (1992, pp. 51–52), Miller and Platter (2010, p. 30).

[12] Ober (2017, pp. 69–70).

[13] Wolpert (2002, p. 37).

There was some debate in the scholarly literature as to whether the trial of Socrates was primarily political or religious in nature. Ober, for example, argues that Meletus grounded his accusation in the charge of impiety in order to circumvent the Amnesty prohibiting prosecutions of those associated with the coup of the Thirty.[14] According to this account, Socrates was prosecuted because he refused to change his behaviour after the oligarchic coup of 404–403 BC: he continued to criticize the democratic culture publicly, at a time when the mood had evidently changed: 'The Athenian willingness to tolerate potentially dangerous behavior and apparently irresponsible public attitudes reached a low point'.[15]

However, Carawan had previously made a crucial point: 'At Athens there was no wall of separation. Every aspect of political activity was sanctified by ritual, and much of religious life was regulated by laws and decrees'.[16] Thus the distinction between political and religious reasons for the prosecution can be viewed as an anachronistic projection by a modern thought style that obscures aspects of the mentality in question due to contemporary biases. Carawan suggests that Socrates' frequent references to his *daimonion*, his private divine voice mentioned by both Plato and Xenophon in their accounts of the trial—were seen as 'undermining the sacred practice of the polis'.[17] The criminal charge of corrupting the youth of Athens probably contained a key religious component: 'Thus Meletos and Anytos seem to have argued that Socrates alienated young men from the proper authorities who should have guided them in cult ritual and family obligations'.[18]

The historical analyses ultimately resort to speculation, because the accounts of Plato and Xenophon, the only available sources for this trial, are driven by agendas and attempts to shape the image of Socrates and transmit alternatives. From the perspective of Fleck's theory, we have representations of a conflict between thought styles, but viewed through the lenses of thought styles aligned with (their interpretations of) Socrates' thought style. In the light of the previous sections of this thesis that attempted to highlight the oligarchic, anti-democratic determinants of Socrates' thought and practices, and given the historical evidence for a less tolerant restoration of the *dēmokratia* after 403 BC, it has to be borne in mind that both Plato and Xenophon inevitably suppressed or downplayed certain aspects of Socrates' discursive activity, while emphasizing others.

The two-sided articulation of the Socratic caesura in Plato's texts—a public-exoteric disavowal and assertion of discontinuity in the *Apology*; a private-esoteric admission of shared concerns and common practices in the *Phaedo*—can be interpreted as representations which register the power struggles and interactions taking place between specific thought collectives in 399 BC. In turn, Plato's apologetic representations, written in the aftermath of Socrates' execution, were determined by these struggles and, in a sense, continued them.

[14] Ober (2017, p. 71).

[15] Ober (2017, p. 72).

[16] Carawan (2013, p. 210).

[17] Carawan (2013, p. 207).

[18] Carawan (2013, p. 211).

Hence, Plato's Socratic caesura can be viewed as a component of a strategy that retrospectively represented a complex conflict between networks and discourses by reconstructing at least three competing thought collectives: (1) the 'men of Athens'—the jurors who can be identified with the restored democracy, endowed with legal authority and power upheld by the traditions of civic religion and education; (2) the diverse itinerant wise men (homogenized as 'sophists'[19] or 'natural philosophers') who brought new ideas and practices from other Greek cities (including former subject-allies and colonies), and who famously exerted influence over public figures (statesmen-orators) and the rich young men of Athens; and (3) Socrates and his circle of followers, who, as can be inferred, were inveterate critics of the restored democratic regime.

It is suggested that the itinerant wise men who roamed across the Greek-speaking world in the fifth century BC evolved from the touring poets of previous centuries. The transition from poets to wise men (*sophoi*)—reflected in the shift from poetry to prose, and from recitals to lectures—responded to the practical needs emerging in the increasingly interconnected and complex Greek city-states,[20] where the use of speech became essential for exerting power in the public sphere of the *polis*.[21] In the fourth century, the previously overlapping roles of these knowledge specialists were subjected to a process of definition and professionalization: 'philosophers, rhetors, playwrights, politicians, generals, and sometimes even sophists became distinct cultural categories'.[22]

Plato's texts consistently portray these wandering wise men as a malign foreign influence by reducing their heterogeneity to a set of shared characteristics. This facilitated the discursive construction of thought collectives and styles, in particular: (1) the Sophists, who charged money for instruction focused on rhetoric and political *areté*, and who tended to question and relativize traditional beliefs and practices; and (2) naturalists, such as Anaxagoras and his predecessors, who were apparently satisfied with materialist or mechanistic explanations of phenomena—accounts which are both incompatible with traditional religious explanations and insufficient from the perspective of Platonic philosophy, since they either render intellect (νοῦς / *nous*) unnecessary or incoherent (i.e., Anaxagoras's account, as presented in *Phaedo*).[23]

Plato's texts also clearly signal the influence of these foreign thought styles on Pericles. Thus while 'Anaxagoras the Clazomenian' is identified with naturalism in the *Apology* and *Phaedo*, in the *Phaedrus* he is also said to have influenced Pericles' 'art of speaking' (270a). In *Protagoras*, the oldest representative of the Sophists acknowledges he is perceived as exerting a foreign and pernicious influence: 'A foreigner who comes to great cities and persuades the best of the young men to abandon the society of others, kinsmen or acquaintances, old or young, and

---

[19] Wallace (2007, p. 218).

[20] Jaeger (1946, pp. 291–298).

[21] Vernant (1982, pp. 50–52; 1988, p. 99).

[22] Wallace (2007, p. 217).

[23] Gerson (2020, pp. 48–65).

associate with himself for their own improvement – someone who does that has to be careful …' (316c).[24]

In his contextual analysis of the emergence of Socratic philosophy, Lampert highlights that the fact Protagoras had been Pericles' teacher haunts the debate between Protagoras and Socrates. Notably, two of Pericles' sons are present at the confrontation, sons whom—Socrates suggests (319e-320a)—Pericles evidently failed to educate in political *areté*. Set in 433, just prior to the Peloponnesian War, Plato's *Protagoras* can be read as implicitly raising the question of whether this sophist might have been partially responsible for the outbreak of war with Sparta. According to Lampert, Pericles encouraged and imported 'the Protagorean enlightenment', and this ultimately endangered 'the whole Achaian enterprise'.[25] In this reading, which follows the hints in Thucydides (1.23) and Plutarch (Pericles 31) that the disastrous imperial war was caused by Athens' growing strength and Pericles' arrogance, the enlightenment fostered by Protagoras and enshrined by Pericles' building projects was based on a confused and limited conception of virtue: one in which hedonism is restrained by the threat of punishment, rather than through the power of knowledge.[26]

These interpretations justify treating Plato's depiction of the Socratic *philosophia* as an intervention which sought to counteract the influence that foreign thought styles had on the ruling class of Athens and its future representatives. The favourable reception of Ionian-Anaxagorean naturalism and Protagorean sophistry indicates the eroding authority of traditional stories and values, and thus an epistemic crisis. The Socratic thought style, as represented in Plato's texts, mounted a response to this crisis, first by exposing the shortcomings and pernicious aspects of naturalism and sophistry, then subjecting traditional *muthos* and *paideia* to sustained critique in the *Republic*. Thus, the Platonic-Socratic caesura was articulated from within a complex nexus of representation strategies that constructed, homogenized and prosecuted rival thought styles. At its core, this conflict concerned the cultural-educational practices and norms of the restored *dēmokratia*.

7.3 Anti-Socratic Representations of Socrates: The Charge and Aristophanes' *Clouds*

The suppressive and exclusionary strategies of the Platonic thought style succeeded: no sophist representations of Socrates' thought style have survived. As one of the 'philosophies of the losers',[27] the sophist thought style was unilaterally represented by the denigrating, homogenizing, and suppressive strategies of Socrates' allies and heirs (Plato, Xenophon, Aristotle).[28] Likewise, there are no substantial representa-

[24] Plato (1976, p. 9).

[25] Lampert (2010, pp. 62, 121).

[26] Lampert (2010, pp. 62, 116).

[27] Laks (2018, p. 34).

[28] Jaeger (1946, pp. 291–298), Wallace (2007, p. 218).

tions of the Socratic philosophy in extant naturalist accounts, such as those that can be reconstructed from fragments of Democritus, whose writings were subjected to more oblique suppression in Plato's texts.[29] Thus the one-sided representations of the Sophists and naturalists, and in all likelihood their fragmentary nature, can be viewed as the result of the discursive suppression and devaluation inseparable from the articulation of the Socratic caesura.

The main depictions of Socrates that were not aligned with his thought style are found in the charges of Socrates' accusers and Aristophanes' *Clouds*. Both these representations can be linked to the position of the traditional thought style, even if such an identification is far from straightforward in the case of Aristophanes' satire.

The statement of Socrates' accusers, as cited by Plato (*Apol.* 19b)—'investigating the things beneath the earth and in the heavens and making the weaker argument stronger'—indicates, somewhat conveniently, that the ruling thought collective viewed the diverse new thought styles as a homogenous threat. It can be surmised that the ostensibly non-mythological *logoi* of naturalism were viewed as challenging the authority of traditional *muthoi*, and that the rhetorical techniques demonstrated by the foreign Sophists and the native Socrates in the public spaces of Athens were recognized as a threat to the traditional practices maintained by the older generation. Hence, naturalist prose accounts and the new spoken language games played by the Sophists and Socrates' circle could be strategically lumped together and subjected to public disapproval.

The new thought styles and the intergenerational nature of the conflict were pitilessly satirized in Aristophanes' *Clouds*, first performed in 423 BC, over twenty years before Socrates' trial. Aristophanes' famous caricature of Socrates as an amalgamated intellectual type, who is both an absurd natural philosopher and a depraved teacher of sophist rhetoric, has been the focus of conflicting interpretations.

Most notably, in his classic edition of *Clouds* from 1968, Sir Kenneth Dover asserted that Aristophanes saw no meaningful distinction between Socrates and the Sophists nor would he have considered such a distinction significant, since 'He drew one basic distinction, between the normal man and the abnormal man'.[30] In Dover's view, Aristophanes simply considered Socrates and his ilk to be abnormal parasites, and philosophy to be antithetical to civilized society. Thus, Dover suggests, *Clouds* can be viewed as an attempt to arouse public hostility toward philosophers, inviting 'violence, or repressive legislation, against such teachers'.[31]

---

[29] Diogenes Laertius famously cited a source that claimed Plato wanted to suppress Democritus' writing by burning surviving copies: 'Aristoxenus in his *Historical Notes* affirms that Plato wished to burn all the writings of Democritus that he could collect, but that Amyclas and Clinias the Pythagoreans prevented him, saying that there was no advantage in doing so, for already the books were widely circulated' Diogenes Laertius (1925) (D. L. 9.7). Ferwerda considers this story to be grounded in fact, even thought its source, Aristoxenus, was an Aristotelian who was 'prejudiced against Plato' Ferwerda (1972).

[30] Dover (1968, p. liii).

[31] Dover (1968, p. lvi).

In contrast, Stephen Halliwell, in his 2015 edition of *Clouds*, situates Aristophanes' comedy within the community tradition of the *kômos* and the Dionysia festivals in which civic seriousness and the 'norms of shame and inhibition' were abandoned for a few days. At such times, authors of comedies enjoyed great satirical freedom: public figures could be subjected to ridicule and abuse without fear of political or legal reprisals. Thus, when considering the mockery of Socrates in *Clouds*, it should be borne in mind that this occurred in a very specific social context—one in which the legal and social norms that normally regulated the public sphere were briefly set aside, in order to provide the community with temporary release from social pressures.[32]

In Halliwell's reading, rather than being ignorant or indifferent to the differences between the naturalists, Sophists and Socrates, Aristophanes was actually poking fun at the general public's ignorance. In other words, the homogenizing treatment of the diverse new intellectual currents, placing them all under one roof and under the tutelage of a grossly caricatured Socrates, was in itself a joke—perhaps at the audience's expense. Aristophanes taunts his '*clever* audience', hoping they would be able to appreciate the ludicrousness of housing all these heterogeneous thought styles under the roof of the Thinking Institute (*phrontistērion*).[33]

In the play, the intergenerational conflict brewing in Athens is primarily represented in the *agon* between the hapless bumpkin Strepsiades and his profligate son Pheidippides; but it is also mirrored and reflected in the *agones* between Strepsiades and Socrates and his acolytes at the Thinking Institute, and between the personified arguments Moral/Right and Immoral/Wrong.

All of the conflicts dramatized in *Clouds* ultimately boil down to the issue of *paideia*: the ways that young men's behaviour can be guided and trained. On the side of tradition stand Strepsiades, with his unquestioned belief in Zeus and the divinities, and the Moral/Right argument, who defends the way boys were taught in 'the old days', i.e., traditional forms of *paideia*, involving discipline at the gymnasium, singing traditional songs, and unquestioning respect for elders (who, in Aristophanes' depiction, are of course lecherous old men). On the side of '*new* ideas' stand Socrates, who explicitly denies the existence of Zeus and offers naturalistic explanations for phenomena as diverse as the humming sound that gnats make (159–165) and thunder (375–8), and the Immoral/Wrong argument, who draws on the populist crowd, denies the existence of Justice, disrespects elders, celebrates loitering in the agora, advocates abandoning self-control, and offers a range of rhetorical strategies for evading lawsuits and legal consequences (889–1110).

---

[32] Halliwell (2015, pp. xix–xx).

[33] Halliwell (2015, pp. 12–13). Robin Waterfield (1990, p. 10) provided partial support of this interpretation, arguing that Aristophanes' Socrates is used as 'a figurehead for intellectuals of all types', 'a catch-all character'. Aristophanes' comedy exploits the popular fear of intellectuals and chose Socrates as the butt of his joke because he was a native Athenian who would have been immediately recognizable to the audience.

The inter-generational conflict comes to a head when Pheidippides turns the arguments and the moral education he received from Socrates against his own father, since he can now prove that it is 'right to beat your own father' (1330–1340). The new thought styles emanating from the Thinking Institute are thus comically depicted as training young men to undermine both traditional social relations (paternal-filial) and the legal and commercial order (breaking promises, denying creditors, evading lawsuits).

The homogenizing treatment of heterogeneous thought styles is satirized in Strepsiades' naive view of those who live in the Thinking Institute, which conflates naturalist cosmology with sophistry:

> Inside this building are men who say the sky
> Is not what it seems—no, it's really a baking-lid
> Which curves all round us here, so we're the charcoal.
> These people will teach anyone who pays them a fee
> How to argue and win, regardless of right and wrong (96–99).[34]

As Halliwell points out, it would have been quite common knowledge among Athenian audiences that most natural philosophers did not teach rhetoric and that the Sophists did not engage in cosmological speculation: the fact that Strepsiades is unable to distinguish between these intellectual pursuits and uses a clichéd image of philosophers is part of the joke, emphasizing his rustic backwardness.[35]

However, at the same time, Aristophanes' depiction of the Thinking Institute and Socrates draws on and perpetuates—for comedic purposes—the cliché of the new fields and methods of enquiry being housed under one roof. As soon as Strepsiades enters the Thinking Institute and begins examining various pieces of equipment and artefacts, a student identifies the objects with different sciences 'Well this is astronomy here... That's geometry ... And this is a map of the whole wide world, you see?' (200–205).

Aristophanes' Socrates then espouses ideas and methods that are far broader than the sphere of practical wisdom suggested by the Platonic-Socratic caesura: aside from denying the existence of the traditional gods, praying to the new divinities of Air, Aither and Clouds, and offering naturalist explanations for biological and meteorological phenomena, he also attempts to instruct Strepsiades in the use of words, grammar and rhythm, and introduces him to the Thinking Institute's linguistic innovations (470–670). In a passage that is worth quoting at length, Halliwell identifies all the types of enquiry practiced at the Thinking Institute:

> As the play develops, we are given a picture of the Thinking Institute as housing at least five types of intellectual/philosophical enquiry: first, cosmology, astronomy, 'meteorology', and physics of the kind particularly ascribed to the Ionian tradition of early Greek philosophy; second, a further group of scientific subjects, including geometry, zoology, and geography; third (though overlapping with the first category), a kind of philosophical theology which critiques traditional religion and sets up a new, more abstract conception of the divine (even if it also shows signs of being able to dispense with the divine altogether); fourth, language-related matters ('proto-linguistics', one might say), including systems of grammatical and

[34] All subsequent quotations are taken from Halliwell's translation: Aristophanes (2015, p. 24).

[35] Halliwell (2015, p. 11).

> metrical classification; fifth, rhetorical debating skills, as enacted in the play's showpiece contest between the two personified arguments, Moral and Immoral. We can see that Aristophanes has taken (and distorted) material related to a large range of thinkers, among them the early Milesians (Thales, Anaximander, Anaximenes), Empedokles, Anaxagoras, Diogenes of Apollonia, Hippon of Samos, Protagoras, the music-theorist Damon, the Pythagoreans(?), as well as the historical Sokrates himself (especially in hints of his one-to-one dialectical methods and his concern for intense self-scrutiny or 'the examined life').[36]

The comedy of *Clouds* depends on the audience being able to appreciate the humour in, firstly, Strepsiades' ignorance of the heterogenous thought styles present in Athens, and secondly, Aristophanes' deliberately mixing up these diverse thought styles and ridiculing their pretensions. Aristophanes' *parabasis* explicitly taunts the audience, insisting that the play requires 'clever' and '*sophisticated* spectators' (521) and suggesting that the failure of the play's first performance was due to the first audience's lack of sophistication. Since *Clouds* mocks both rustic ignorance and intellectual ridiculousness, any spectators who failed to see that Aristophanes' Socrates was a pastiche and caricature of philosopher types, and the Thinking Institute as housing an implausible mix of schools, would be viewing the play at the intellectual level of the play's hapless Strepsiades, and thus would themselves have been the butt of Aristophanes' jokes.

Aristophanes' satire of inter-generational conflict and emergent thought styles sheds light on the fact that these phenomena were associated with various social practices, many of which had the potential to undermine the traditional social order. The primary reason for Strepsiades' resorting to the Thinking Institute is that his son Pheidippides has let 'his hair grow long' and incurred debts due to his obsession with horses and chariot-racing. Rather than continuing the family tradition of agricultural production, Pheidippides—encouraged by his 'city girl' mother—is an unproductive drain on his father's resources. Thus, the shift from rustic life to city life is a form of corruption: young men are becoming idle and are living beyond the family's means. Then the horse-obsessed Pheidippides describes the students at the Thinking Institute as a 'pale-faced, shoeless crowd', suggesting that the ascetic, intellectual lifestyle pursued by Socrates and his acolytes entails certain bizarre behaviour—e.g., staring at the ground—that is at odds with traditional sporting and military prowess. Finally, Socrates himself enumerates a range of collectives and social practices that are sustained by the heavenly Clouds:

> You don't know then that they keep alive great hordes of *clever* people:
> Purveyors of prophecy, medical experts, long-haired signet-ring-wearers,
> Composers of intricate dithyramb lyrics, and cheats with their heads in the clouds.
> Layabouts like these they keep alive for treating the Clouds as their Muses. (330–334)[37]

Aristophanes' Socrates thereby offers a glimpse of the heterogeneous epistemic communities at large in the broader society outside the Thinking Institute: numerous new types of intellectuals engaged in social practices that—from the traditional perspective—are perceived as bizarre, dishonest, unproductive and parasitic. By

[36] Halliwell (2015, p. 11).

[37] Aristophanes (2015, p. 34).

having this caricatured Socrates express approval of all these '*clever* people', and shortly thereafter having the Chorus of Clouds describe him as a 'priest of subtle drivel', Aristophanes' satire represents Socrates as a leading figure in the widespread counter-cultural movement corrupting Athens.

Although *Clouds* resists any facile ascription of a 'conservative' position to Aristophanes, since all forms of *logos* are equally subjected to ridicule[38] and are ultimately consumed by Strepsiades' arson, the text clearly signals that the heterogenous thought styles emerging in Athens at that time were, firstly, perceived as posing a homogenous threat to the existing social order, and were, secondly, all guilty of ludicrousness. Hence *Clouds* pre-empts and rejects the articulation of the Socratic caesura: regardless of their nit-picking distinctions and internecine conflicts, the naturalists, Sophists, and Socrates' circle are all represented as engaged in the same ridiculous and socially corrosive practices.

It is worth reiterating that *Clouds* was produced in 425 BC, thus six years into the Peloponnesian War, and just two years after the outbreak of civil strife ('the great stasis') described by Thucydides (3.82-85). It is also contemporaneous with the discursive antagonism described and articulated in the Old Oligarch's *Athenaíōn Politeía*. The intergenerational and cultural conflict and collapse of social norms depicted by Aristophanes can thus be situated within a broader context of bitter division and tumultuous upheaval.

7.4 The Consolidated Caesura: Xenophon and Aristotle

As we have seen, Plato's Socrates simply disavows and distances himself from Aristophanes' Socrates, dismissing him as 'uttering a vast deal of other nonsense, about which I know nothing, either much or little' (*Apol.* 18b-c). In direct contrast to Aristophanes' caricature of the philosopher type, Plato's Apology constructs the image of a relentless and deeply principled questioner who values truth and intellectual integrity above personal safety or social conformity. The Platonic-Socratic caesura thus distinguishes Socrates from the image conveyed first by Aristophanes, and later by his accusers, emphasizing his unique focus on the examination of virtue, justice, and the nature of good conduct.

This caesura was discursively reinforced by Xenophon's portraits of Socrates, supported by Aristotle's comments on Socrates, and ultimately consolidated by Cicero's emphasis on Socrates' philosophical shift. A detailed examination of Xenophon and Aristotle's didactic or critical intentions lies beyond the scope of this work, as the next section will focus on Cicero's crucial role in reformulating and transmitting the Socratic caesura. For now, a few paragraphs on Xenophon and Aristotle will have to suffice.

Like Plato, Xenophon primarily dissociates Socrates from naturalist philosophy by portraying him as a participant in the public sphere, focused on 'human affairs'

[38] Freydberg (2008, p. 54).

in the agora, who emphatically dismissed the then-popular discussions about the 'Nature of Universe' and 'the laws that govern the phenomena of the heavens' as 'sheer folly' (Xen. *Mem.* 1.1.10-11).[39] Xenophon also performs a more subtle, secondary dissociation: he explicitly contrasts Socrates with the Sophists by emphasizing that he does not accept payment (Xen. *Apol.* 12–20), while Protagoras, Gorgias and Prodicus are described as receiving 'a great deal of money' for 'expert instruction' (Xen. *Symp.* 1.5).[40] This distinction is further reinforced implicitly through Xenophon's repeated emphasis on Socrates' moral earnestness and clear opinions on how to live a good life—qualities contrasted with sophistic relativism.

Though Aristotle's reconstruction of the history of philosophy in the *Metaphysics* avoids the Platonic-Socratic caesura, embedding Socrates instead within a continuist narrative that culminates in Aristotle's own philosophy, his comments on Socrates' project provide additional support for the Socratic caesura: 'And when Socrates, disregarding the physical universe and confining his study to moral questions, sought in this sphere for the universal and was the first to concentrate upon definition, Plato followed him [...]'. (Aristot. *Met.* 1.987b).[41] This depiction of Socrates pursuing universal moral principles—rather than political *areté*—also allows Aristotle to exclude the Sophists from his account of philosophy. As Jaeger notes, 'The history of philosophy given by Aristotle in the *Metaphysics* excludes the sophists'.[42]

Thus, even though Plato's texts clearly depict the sophist Prodicus addressing both ethical issues and the accurate use of words (e.g. *Laches* 197d, *Meno* 75e, 96d), Aristotle's narrative positions Socrates' shift from the physical universe to moral universals and logical definitions as a unique discontinuity—even if this discontinuity is then subsumed within his incremental, continuist narrative.

7.5 The Ciceronian-Socratic Caesura

7.5.1 Socrates the Model Citizen: Practical Philosophy and Oratory—Not Sophistry

Laks argues that Cicero decisively consolidated the Socratic caesura, largely due to the 'large diffusion' and 'apparent simplicity' of his *Tusculanae Disputationes* (45 BC).[43] In a key passage from this work, which both affirms the break from natural philosophy and subtly erases the contributions of the Sophists, Cicero asserts:

---

39 Xenophon (1923a, p. 9).

40 Xenophon (1923b).

41 Aristotle (1933).

42 Jaeger (1946, p. 294).

43 Laks (2018, pp. 9–12).

> But numbers and motions, and the beginning and end of all things, were the subjects of the ancient philosophy down to Socrates, who was a pupil of Archelaus, who had been the disciple of Anaxagoras. These made diligent enquiry into the magnitude of the stars, their distances, courses, and all that relates to the heavens. But Socrates was the first who brought down philosophy from the heavens, placed it in cities, introduced it into families, and obliged it to examine into life and morals, and good and evil.[44]

While the break from naturalism is explicitly signalled, the designation of Socrates as the first urban moral philosopher implicitly and effectively eliminates the Sophists from the history of Greek philosophy reconstructed in Cicero's dialogues.

The Sophists are more overtly excluded in Book II of Cicero's *De Finibus Bonorum et Malorum* (45 BC), where Cicero describes Socrates as 'the father of philosophy' and contrasts his method of questioning with the Sophists' lecturing style, particularly that of Gorgias.[45] By casting Socrates as the progenitor of philosophical inquiry, Cicero implies that whatever the Sophists practiced, it was not philosophy.

In essence, Cicero's project of repurposing Greek philosophy for the Late Republic reiterates the Platonic-Socratic caesura as a movement away from abstract natural philosophy toward practical moral philosophy. At the same time, the Ciceronian-Socratic caesura sustains the exclusion of the Sophists and leverages Aristotle's *Topics* and *Rhetoric* to counter Plato's Socrates' denigration of oratory.[46] In this synthesis, Cicero combined elements of diverse thought styles to present philosophy as an activity that integrates leisurely theorizing in rural villas with practical involvement in the Senate, ultimately aiming for the moral improvement of the Republic.

In broad outline, this fusion of intellectual cultivation with civic duty made the Ciceronian tradition appealing to Italian humanists in fifteenth- and sixteenth-century Italy, who sought an alternative to scholasticism,[47]and to English and Scottish empiricists in the seventeenth and eighteenth centuries, who aimed to counter dogmatism.[48]

On closer analysis, however, matters are not quite so straightforward, since the identification of Socrates as a rupture or starting point becomes complicated in Cicero's multi-layered *Academica*. Circulated in 45 BC—the same period as his *Tusculanae Disputationes* and *De Finibus*—the *Academica* essentially dramatizes an 'inheritance dispute' among Roman adherents of the sceptical and dogmatic (Stoic) schools, both of whom claimed Socratic ancestry.[49] From a Fleckian perspective, *Academica* is perhaps Cicero's most complex text. Fragmentary in form, it navigates disputes between thought collectives separated by vast spatial and temporal distances: the divergence of the Platonic Academy and Aristotle's Peripatetic

---

44 Cicero (1877, pp. 166–167).

45 Cicero (2004, p. 26).

46 Long (1995, pp. 52–58).

47 Marsh (2013).

48 Stuart-Buttle (2018).

49 Glucker (1997, pp. 59–74).

school; the conflict between Greek Stoic and Academic schools from the second and third centuries BC; the intra-Academic disputes of the first century BC; and Cicero's direct knowledge of recent or contemporary conflicts among Greek and Roman Stoics, Epicureans, and Academic Sceptics (62–45 BC).[50]

Cicero's interlocutors represent an idealized Roman thought collective—including generals like Catulus and Lucullus, who demonstrate detailed knowledge of Greek philosophical traditions—capable of navigating exegetical layers constructed by past thought collectives over generations and across regions. Since Cicero's text serves as the main evidentiary source for some of the philosophers and ideas discussed, such as the sceptical Academic philosophy of Philo of Larissa, scholarly interpretations remain somewhat inconclusive and ongoing.[51] John Glucker points out—very much in line with Fleck—that reconstructing ideas and modes of thought conveyed in ancient texts is constantly at risk of distortion by 'contemporary attitudes and modes of thought'.[52] Thus, the fragmentary and multi-layered nature of *Academica* makes it a uniquely problematic text, especially given Cicero's strategically elusive scepticism.

One of the central issues addressed in the *Academica* is whether Socrates articulated a genuinely sceptical position and, if so, whether this scepticism was dogmatic-negative or mitigated. Concerning the first issue, Lucullus, who represents one version of Antiochus' Stoic position, argues that Socrates' scepticism is not genuine: 'As for Socrates, he used to ascribe the larger part in arguments to the people he was trying to refute by deprecating his own contribution. So, since he said one thing and thought another, it was his practice to use the kind of dissimulation the Greeks call eirôneia ['irony']' (*Ac.* 2.15).[53] By contrast, Varro, presented as another follower of Antiochus, reiterates the Platonic-Socratic caesura articulated in *Apology* 23b:

> As I see it, Socrates was the first (this is a point accepted by all) to summon philosophy away from the obscure subjects nature itself has veiled—the questions all his philosophical predecessors had been concerned with—and to direct it towards ordinary life. He set it onto investigating virtue and vice and good and bad in general, considering celestial subjects to be far beyond our knowledge or, even if they were perfectly knowable, still completely irrelevant to the good life. (*Ac.* 1.15)[54]

However, Varro then follows his initial commentary with a description of Socrates' scepticism, suggesting it was consistent and genuine but possibly dogmatic and hypocritical:

> His manner of argument is the same in practically all the conversations his students wrote up so eloquently and variously: he makes no affirmation of his own, but refutes other people and says that he knows nothing except just that. This, he says, is his advantage over every-

[50] Cicero (2006).

[51] Powell (1995, pp. 19, 32).

[52] Glucker (1997, p. 64), Brittain (2006, p. xxxvii).

[53] Cicero (2006, p. 10).

[54] Cicero (2006, p. 92).

> one else: while they think they know what they don't know, he knows just the fact that he doesn't know anything—and that, he thinks, is why he was declared the wisest of all men by Apollo, because not thinking you know what you don't know is the sum of human wisdom. And yet, though he kept making these claims and stuck with this view, every speech of his was taken up with praising virtue and exhorting people to pursue it, as one can see from the books of the Socratics, and especially Plato's (*Ac.* 1.16)[55]

Here, Varro's Socrates can be construed as asserting a form of dogmatic scepticism based on the idea that he knows what does not constitute knowledge, yet he simultaneously engages in practices that suggest an understanding of virtue and how it should be pursued. Varro, in any case, contrasts Socrates' scepticism with the systematic art of philosophy institutionalized by the Academics and Peripatetics, something he implies that Socrates 'was far from approving' (*Ac.* 1.17).[56]

While the two Antiochian interlocutors present conflicting views of Socrates' scepticism—one ironic and the other dogmatic—both Lucullus and Varro trace their Stoic lineage back to Plato's dogmatic certainty. The alternative to this dogmatism, as reconstructed from the 'Cicero' of the dialogue's fragmentary contributions, is mitigated scepticism or Academic probabilism. This stance stands in opposition to the rational certainties of the Stoics and the materialist certainties of the Epicureans.[57] Accordingly, the 'Cicero' of *Academica* includes Socrates among a non-dogmatic group of thinkers who preceded him—'Democritus, Anaxagoras, Empedocles, and virtually all the early philosophers'—and who agreed 'that nothing could be cognized, apprehended, or known' (*Ac.* 1.44).[58]

While 'Cicero' identifies the Academic sceptic Arcesilaus as rejecting Socratic dogmatic scepticism and withholding assent on the basis of universal inapprehensibility, he also implies it is possible to recover a non-dogmatic Plato from his works, where 'nothing is affirmed, there are many arguments on either side, everything is under investigation, and nothing is claimed to be certain' (*Ac.* 1.46).[59]

Based on this complex, multi-layered exegesis, it is suggested that Cicero primarily employed Academic scepticism for epistemological purposes, a strategy that broadened the scope of his philosophical inquiry.[60] In positioning himself with respect to Socrates, *Academica* aligns with the Platonic-Socratic caesura articulated in the *Apology*, reaffirming the shift from natural to moral philosophy and the suppression of sophist oratory. However, Cicero also repurposes Socrates' confession of ignorance (Plat. *Apol.* 20c-22e) to place him among a group of 'early philosophers' who had arrived at sceptical positions out of epistemological despair. Through Academic scepticism, Cicero could distinguish a mitigated, probabilistic form of scepticism from the dogmatic scepticism associated with early philosophers. The strategic withholding of consent allowed Cicero to treat ideas from Plato's texts—

55 Cicero (2006, p. 93).
56 Cicero (2006, p. 93).
57 Powell (1995, p. 23).
58 Cicero (2006, p. 106).
59 Cicero (2006, p. 107).
60 Long (1995, pp. 41–42).

such as the immortality of the soul in *Tusculanae Disputationes*—as plausible or probable theses (*probabilia*) rather than absolute doctrines.[61] More broadly, Academic probabilism enabled Cicero to resist the dogmatic certainties of post-Socratic schools, including the Platonic, Aristotelian, Stoic, and Epicurean.[62]

The Academic sceptical practice of withholding assent also enabled Cicero to incorporate another key element into his philosophical position: the use of Aristotle's *Topics* and *Rhetoric*, or at least Peripatetic handbooks,[63] to counter Plato's Socratic dismissal of oratory as mere *kolakeia* (pandering) and deny its status as a *technē* (Plat. *Gorg.* 463–466a). In addition to critiquing Socrates' dogmatism, Cicero criticizes him for separating philosophy and rhetoric[64]—in other words, for dividing 'the knowledge of forming wise opinions and of speaking with distinction' (*de Orat.* 3.59 et seq.). By resisting the closure of dogmatic certainty, Cicero revives Plato's dialogical form to enable the rhetorical presentation of 'many arguments on either side'. In contrast to the Sophists' mercenary relativism, as Plato depicts it, and Aristotle's critique of making 'the weaker seem the better cause' (Aristot. *Rh.* II.24.1402a), Cicero's presentation of arguments for and against each position aims to reveal the strengths of various perspectives, including ethical theories.[65]

The Ciceronian-Socratic caesura, therefore, entails a sophisticated conceptual-discursive approach: it critiques the Platonic-Socratic caesura, synthesizes Peripatetic rhetoric and Academic scepticism, and establishes a uniquely Roman conception of philosophy as a theoretical-rhetorical practice grounded in civic duty.

7.5.2 Scholars and Spoils: How Plunder Shaped Roman Philosophy

Cicero's texts dramatize and embody the process by which one thought collective reinterprets and adapts the thought styles of another, shaping them to meet the demands of a new context. On one level, creating a distinctly Roman philosophy required the importation of Greek concepts, methods, and practices—transmitted interactively through layers of exegesis and translation. At the same time, developing a Roman thought style capable of challenging Greek cultural hegemony involved critical self-reflection and contrastive self-identification. Thus, Ciceronian philosophy was not an isolated intellectual pursuit; it responded directly to the social

[61] Long (1995, pp. 41–42).

[62] On Cicero's adherence to Philo's fallibilism, i.e., 'a mitigated skepticism', see Zarecki (2014, pp. 17–24).

[63] On the issue of whether Cicero read Aristotle's texts or only had indirect access through the Peripatetic tradition and the filtering of Hellenistic intermediaries, see Long (1995, p. 55), Barnes (1997, p. 24).

[64] Long (1995, pp. 50–55).

[65] Annas (2001, p. xii).

upheaval of Roman society and sought to engineer a far-reaching cultural transformation.

Cicero's project of Romanizing Greek philosophy identified and synthesized aspects of the Hellenic legacy that could be restructured into a practical philosophy to serve educated Romans in the Late Republic—a period when Rome was rapidly expanding its territories, particularly in Greece.[66] This intellectual appropriation of Plato's Socratic caesura, establishing a practical philosophy for Roman life, was both preceded and supported by the material acquisition of Greek libraries and the exploitation of Greek slaves and immigrants. Cicero's self-positioning as the Roman Plato, as indicated by titles like *De Re Publica* and *De Legibus*, depended heavily on the material resources, recording technologies, and intellectual capital acquired through military conquest and political dominance.

Cicero's emphasis on the practical value of philosophy can be better understood within this social and cultural framework. In Book I of *Tusculanae Disputationes*, Cicero asserts Roman supremacy over Greece, claiming that Roman discoveries have surpassed or refined those of the Greeks and that Roman private and public life is superior in its manners, customs, and laws. Roman excellence in military valour and discipline reinforces this claim. While Cicero acknowledges Greek dominance in learning, literature, and philosophy, he attributes this to the high regard these pursuits have in Roman culture. When arts and skills are esteemed in Rome, they flourish, and Roman practitioners excel, which explains why Roman orators have equalled or even surpassed their Greek counterparts in reputation. Having raised Roman oratory to prominence, Cicero now aims to elevate philosophy from its low standing, as a service to his countrymen (*Tusc.* 1.1-3).

To raise the status of philosophy, Cicero needed to counter the negative perception of philosophy that prevailed in his broader thought collective. Sean McConnell highlights the Roman distinction between intellectual pursuits seen as escapism and those compatible with 'active political or public life'.[67] Therefore, when Cicero praises philosophy:

> The force of these passages relies largely on established negative attitudes on the part of the Roman audience towards philosophical pursuits, which they associated with Greeks, the apolitical Epicurean life of pleasure, idle *otium*, debauchery, useless theorising, and so forth. Cicero took care to justify his own intellectual pursuits in such a way as to avoid adverse criticism of this kind.[68]

Cicero's alignment with Plato and the practically-oriented Socrates was part of a strategy to distance philosophy from idle speculation and establish it as integral to political life. His goal was to bring ancient philosophy 'down to the forum, the

---

[66] Corbeill (2013, p. 11), Hind (1992, pp. 153–154).

[67] McConnell (2014, p. 57). See also Zarecki (2014, pp. 31–38) on Cicero's dismantling of the barriers between philosophy and statesmanship, and his countering of 'philosophical objections to civic engagement' in *De Re Publica*.

[68] McConnell (2014, p. 56).

council chamber, and the very camp itself', as he expressed in a letter to Cato (*Fam.* 15.4).[69]

In this revaluation, Cicero sought to make philosophy honourable by redistributing cultural capital in a way that aligned it with Roman values. His analysis of poets' status in Greek and Roman society offers insights into how he intended to achieve this. In *Tusculanae Disputationes*, Cicero argues that 'Honour sustains the arts. The possibility of glory makes everyone an enthusiast, whereas activities regarded as shameful are always neglected' (*Tusc.* 1.4).[70] He observes that music, highly esteemed in Greek culture, flourished because 'everybody learned it, and anyone who didn't was thought to be uncultured'. This proto-Bourdieuan view on cultural capital reflects Cicero's mission to elevate philosophy: by aligning it with honourable pursuits and distancing it from pursuits deemed idle or shameful, he aimed to integrate it into Roman social ideals.

In essence, Cicero's *otium* project appropriated a thought style from the subjugated Greek city-state—once known for its colonizing, imperial, and hegemonic inclinations—and adapted it for the Late Republic's imperialist aims. Sulla's siege of Athens in 88–86 BC and the wholesale plunder that followed brought Greek philosophical works to Rome, including Aristotle's library.[71] This conquest, along with Pompey's later Greek campaigns, led to an intellectual exchange: educated Greeks arrived in Rome as slaves or refugees (with figures like Philo of Larissa among the latter), where their literacy and knowledge made them prized as teachers, scribes, and librarians. Conversely, young Romans like Cicero, Caesar, and Cato the Younger travelled to Greece to study philosophy, often for extended periods in places like Athens and Rhodes, engaging directly with Stoic, Epicurean, and Sceptic thought[72] in what was essentially a 'classical grand tour'.[73]

As predicted by Fleck's conception of communication between thought collectives,[74] Cicero's transmission of Greek thought styles across geographic and temporal divides involved deliberate transformations—through selective appropriation, suppression, and emphasis. Thus, in addition to adopting the Socratic thought style (as defined by Plato) and the rehabilitation of oratory, Cicero countered Aristotle's view of knowledge for its own sake as the highest wisdom (*Met.* 982a). In *De Re Publica*, Cicero insists that 'virtue is not some kind of knowledge to be possessed without using it: even if the intellectual possession of knowledge can be maintained without use, virtue consists entirely in its employment' (*Rep.* I.2).[75]

---

[69] Cicero (1908–1909).

[70] Cicero (2012). Latin text: '*Honos alit artes, omnesque incenduntur ad studia gloriae; iacentque ea semper, quae apud quosque improbantur*' from Perseus: http://data.perseus.org/citations/urn:cts:latinLit:phi0474.phi049.perseus-lat1:1.4.

[71] Griffin (1994, p. 693), Marsh (2013).

[72] Rawson (1985), Zetzel (1999), Corbeill (2013).

[73] Everitt (2001, p. 118).

[74] Fleck (1986b, p. 88).

[75] Cicero (2014).

Cicero emphasizes Plato's real-world application of philosophy (as best exemplified in the *Seventh Letter* and his work in Sicily) and rejects the Aristotelian valorization of disinterested theorizing, which was largely disdained in Roman culture. In positioning himself as the Roman Plato, Cicero's ideal state was not a theoretical construct or hypothetical thought experiment but rather the Roman state 'restored to its idealized past condition'.[76] A key modification to Athenian philosophy, the Ciceronian thought style emphasized practical experience over theoretical study, advocating 'for *phronêsis* over *sophia*, for *prudentia* over *sapienta*'.[77] The Roman philosopher was thus portrayed as the ideal guide for the Republic, committed to using his broad education, oratory skills, and sceptical openness to address ethical-political issues within the Senate.

The emergence of Ciceronian-Roman philosophy as a unique thought style—distinct from Athenian Greek philosophies and their Hellenistic offshoots[78]—resulted from centuries of interaction between specific Greek and Roman philosophical thought collectives, as well as between Cicero, his contemporaries, and a more general Roman thought collective composed of ruling-class representatives and educated citizens who often viewed philosophy as a foreign practice. These philosophical thought collectives, or 'schools' (e.g., the Platonic Academy, the Peripatetic school, the Stoa, and the Epicureans), were reconstructed from the ideas and positions attributed to specific figures and their followers (e.g., Zeno of Citium, Epicurus, Arcesilaus, Philo of Larissa, Antiochus). Interaction between these collectives was either remote and textual—a one-way transmission of ideas from earlier periods responded to by later thought collectives—or more immediate, involving direct exchanges, as seen in Hellenistic Athens with the Stoics, the Academy, and the Epicurean community coexisting in the third century BC,[79] or in Cicero's letters and dialogues with his contemporaries, such as Varro, Brutus, and Atticus.

The interaction between philosophical thought collectives and the broader Roman collective can largely be reconstructed through the texts of the pro-Hellenic Roman thought collective, which report on the public mockery of and hostility towards philhellenism (e.g., *Fin.* 1.8-9). The extent of this general odium toward Greek culture and philosophy is illustrated in *De Oratore*, where Cicero describes the strategies used by L. Crassus and M. Antonius to conceal their knowledge of and fluency in Greek:

> There was nevertheless this point of difference between the two men, that Crassus did not so much wish to be thought to have learned nothing, as to have the reputation of looking down upon learning, and of placing the wisdom of our own fellow-countrymen above that of the Greeks in all departments while Antonius held that his speeches would be the more

[76] Griffin (1994, p. 717).

[77] Zetzel (2003, p. 131).

[78] The term 'Hellenistic,' used in modern scholarship (Long and Sedley 1987) to denote the period from Alexander's death to the emergence of the Roman Empire, is a later organizational category that Cicero himself did not employ. Cicero generally referred to this period's philosophers simply as 'the Greeks' (*Graeci*).

[79] Long and Sedley (1987, pp. 1–6).

> acceptable to a nation like ours, if it were thought that he had never engaged in study at all. Thus the one expected to grow in influence by being thought to hold a poor opinion of the Greeks, and the other by seeming never even to have heard of them. (*de Orat.* 2.4)[80]

In this passage, Cicero, writing in 55 BC, reveals that in 91 BC—the time when his fictional dialogue was set—philosophy had yet to become a dominant or securely established discourse in Roman society. Although philosophical ideas and practices may have gained acceptance by Cicero's time, his explicit advocacy for a Romanized philosophy in 55 BC, and again during the prolific years of 45–44 BC before his assassination by the Second Triumvirate in 43 BC, suggests that the thought style of Cicero and his circle was far from destined to achieve dominance or secure transmission to future generations.

Fleck's account of how a new thought style develops from a traditional one argues that periods of intellectual unrest allow dissimilar views to emerge, creating a different intellectual mood in which new phenomena can be seen, and alternate perspectives, interests, and forms take shape. Content and motives from other fields are incorporated, but the new thought style must overcome inhibiting resistance.[81] The Late Republic—particularly the years 91–44 BC covered by Cicero's writing—was a period of unprecedented social turmoil, involving two civil wars and the eventual defeat of the Republic as a political form. Cicero's works, by combining elements of Greek and Hellenistic thought styles with Roman political oratory and by explicitly stating their educational function, can be seen as attempts to overcome the resistance of the traditional, nativist, and xenophobic thought collective. Thus, to a certain extent, Cicero fulfils the function of a strong individual who, like Vesalius, in the midst of intellectual unrest, imposes his vision on the traditional thought collective: 'One has to create another mental readiness and to educate people to live in it'.[82] However, as with Vesalius (as covered in **Chap. 4**), the emergence and transmission of Cicero's thought style was facilitated by a range of social and cultural factors.

Firstly, the construction of a self-identified Roman philosophy on the basis of collected rival Athenian and Hellenistic philosophies required the widespread availability of technologies and resources that could be allocated to recording, storing, organizing and evaluating this extracted repository. Hence, before a public figure like Cicero could even begin to single out and reformulate the elements of Greek thought that might be beneficial to Roman statecraft, an apparatus of cultural appropriation and reproduction had to be firmly in place.

On the material level, manuscripts, entire libraries, and educated Greeks had to be captured and brought to Rome. The influx enabled members of the patrician class to amass private libraries in their villas. Before the emergence of public libraries and a book trade in the imperial era, these private libraries were built through aristocratic social networks and the use of slaves: Greek texts were exchanged and circulated between the villas dotted around the countryside outside of Rome, in which

[80] Cicero (1942, pp. 199–201).

[81] Fleck (1986a, pp. 72–77).

[82] Fleck (1986a, p. 77).

educated Greek slaves were prized 'possessions'—from copyists to expert grammarians like Tyrannion of Amisus, who organized Cicero's library.[83]

Secondly, on the intellectual level, the construction of a distinct Roman thought style required both adopting analytical tools from Athenian and Hellenistic philosophical schools and developing new attitudes toward education. Roman writers like Varro, Nepos, and Cicero used Greek methods of analysis and self-reflection to examine Roman institutions, traditions, and values, explicitly comparing Greek and Roman culture.[84] This comparative approach fostered awareness of Roman society's unique identity and virtues by juxtaposing them with Greek norms. James Zetzel argues that this reflection on the roles Greek cultural artifacts played in Roman society constituted an 'anthropology of culture', and in Cicero's case, even a 'sociology of culture', since his approach was both comparative and normative.[85]

Like Plato, Cicero viewed philosophy as entailing the introduction of transformative educational and communicative practices. For Roman philosophy to surpass and supplant Greek hegemony, its ideas needed to be accessible to the general thought collective of the ruling class—and thus communicated in Latin. Since Greek remained the lingua franca in the Mediterranean well into the imperial period, asserting the dominance of Roman philosophy required complex, long-term strategies for balancing Greek and Latin.

Firstly, because Greek culture provided the primary source of philosophical models, importing these ideas into Roman culture required large-scale translation. Translation became a central area of Roman cultural innovation: 'As the Greeks rarely translated works from other languages for their own use, there were no treatises on the subject to guide Roman writers. [...] Latin translators had to grasp the difference in character of two languages and preserve the genius of their own while developing its full potential'.[86]

Secondly, the valorization of Greek culture posed challenges, as Greek was also the language of a subjugated people, and some Romans viewed Hellenic culture as a source of moral decline, linking it to Greece's debauchery and defeat: 'Greek learning, which had been deracinated by excessive cleverness from its own society, could only be rescued, or even understood, by anchoring it once more in a social and moral context – in the service of Roman tradition and Roman values'.[87] Thus, while it was crucial for pro-Hellenic Romans that Roman boys learn Greek and be exposed to Greek rhetorical models—whether at private schools or in domestic settings—over the course of decades, increasing importance was placed on studying language and literature (*grammatica*) in both Greek and Latin. Cicero's broad conception of education ultimately held that training in Latin rhetoric was essential for preparation for public life in the Republic.[88]

---

[83] Griffin (1994, pp. 693–694).

[84] Griffin (1994, pp. 706–707).

[85] Zetzel (2003, p. 134).

[86] Griffin (1994, p. 700).

[87] Zetzel (2003, p. 137).

[88] Griffin (1994, pp. 690–692).

7.5.3 Cultural Hegemony in the Midst of Turmoil

Studies of social and class conflict in Roman society during Cicero's lifetime support Fleck's contention that transformations in thought style occur during periods of 'intellectual unrest' and 'general social confusion'.[89] According to Peter Brunt's classic revisionist account (1971), the internal strife that beset the Republic from 133 to 27 BC—epitomized by two major civil wars—was caused, or at least exacerbated, by wars of conquest and the mass importation of slaves into the Italian peninsula. Though conflicts among patricians, wealthy plebeians, and the poor were temporarily relieved by distributing annexed land to the poor, imperial expansion ultimately deepened the economic divide.

The Republic's economy shifted from agriculture and trade to one dominated by war and government. This influx of slave labour from conquest had two main consequences: first, the Roman army drew on this surplus labour through conscription, and second, free men, no longer needed to work the lands feeding the armies, struggled to make a living and sustain families.[90] Meanwhile, 'the profits of empire enabled the upper classes to import hundreds of thousands of slaves, entire shipments of Greek art, luxury goods of all kinds, and to buy up lands, stock them with cattle, or turn them into the orchards Varro admired'.[91]

A more recent study by Clifford Ando estimates that between two and four million slaves were imported into Italy in the last two centuries of the Republic. Ando reiterates Brunt's thesis that this influx destabilized the Republic, as it led to growing demands for imperial revenues to 'restore some measure of economic and demographic stability,' demands that ultimately placed unsustainable pressures on the Roman aristocracy and 'proved fatal to the republic.'[92]

Cicero himself benefited from the imperial project and explicitly defended the interests of the propertied class in his speeches. In 51 BC, the year in which *De Re Publica* was probably written, Cicero reluctantly went to southern Anatolia to serve as proconsul of Cilicia, managing to amass 550,000 denarii in a single year without resorting to corruption.[93] While the patricians accumulated wealth and indulged their Hellenic tastes in luxurious villas and estates, the urban populace faced deteriorating conditions. Unemployment, soaring grain prices, and cramped, unsanitary living quarters fuelled discontent. Food and rent riots became common, armed gangs roamed both cities and countryside, and violence escalated amid the two civil wars that defined Cicero's lifetime—first in 83–81 BC and later in 49–45 BC—making violence an endemic feature of Roman life.[94]

---

[89] Fleck (1986a, pp. 76–77), Fleck (1979, p. 177).

[90] Brunt (1971, p. 19).

[91] Brunt (1971, p. 40).

[92] Ando (2011).

[93] Brunt (1971, p. 40).

[94] Brunt (1971, pp. 111–127).

In his Marxist account of class struggle in the Late Republic, de Ste Croix demonstrates that, throughout these tumultuous times, Cicero consistently sided with the senatorial class, using his oratory to scorn the *populares*—figures like Gracchus, Saturninus, Catiline, and Caesar—and their lower-class supporters.[95] Cicero was staunchly opposed to 'the wretched half-starved populace' (*Att* 1.16) and to democratic institutions like popular assemblies. In his 59 BC defence of L. Valerius Flaccus, Cicero reveals the limits of his Hellenism: while Greek republics allowed popular assemblies, Rome, he notes, did not give them 'any authority to make laws'. Greece, which 'once flourished with riches, power, and glory, fell owing to that one evil, the immoderate liberty and licentiousness of the popular assemblies' (*Flac.* 16). Cicero's class contempt is explicit in his description of shopkeepers, artisans, and the common people as the worthless and ignorant 'dregs of the city' (*Flac.* 18–19).[96]

From this perspective, the Ciceronian thought style functioned as an ideology—a tool of control and repression serving the propertied class (see Chap. 5). By combining selective elements of Greek thought—such as Socratic *polis*-based moral philosophy, Plato's anti-democratic political philosophy, and Peripatetic rhetoric—with uniquely Roman ideals of oratory, civic values, and education, Cicero and his social network constructed a thought style that upheld traditional hierarchies and resisted the demands of the *populares*, who claimed to represent the common people's interests. The emergence of the Ciceronian thought style, a distinctly Roman philosophy formed amid the Late Republic's internal strife, can be seen as an innovation that applied reformulated Greek concepts and strategies in order to maintain the traditions of the past. In other words, a change in thought style came about through an effort to prevent social change.

In sum, based on source texts and scholarly literature, the Ciceronian-Socratic caesura—which reiterated the Platonic-Socratic caesura's rejection of naturalism and suppression of sophistic philosophy, while further emphasizing the practical, civic focus of the Socratic thought style by reuniting philosophy and oratory—can be framed as a discursive strategy developed by Cicero's patrician social network. Cicero's *De Oratore* and *De Re Publica* dramatize the emergence of this thought style, as this erudite network deliberately defined their philosophy as distinct from, and superior to, that of the Greeks. The techno-economic context of appropriating educated slaves, texts, libraries, and analytical tools allowed this thought collective to challenge the cultural dominance of Greek thought styles.

At the same time, the influx of slave labour—a consequence of mass enslavement—destabilized social relations across the Italian peninsula, fuelling the social conflict that ultimately fractured the Republic. On one level, the emergence of this new thought style during the Late Republic—a period marked by internal political upheaval and territorial expansion—enabled Rome to see itself as a cultural hegemon as well as the dominant military and political power. Yet, this thought style also operated as a political ideology: a conceptual framework and set of discursive practices intrinsically linked to the underlying class conflicts of the era.

[95] de Ste Croix (1981, p. 354).

[96] Cicero (2014).

7.6 Conclusion: The Transmission of the Socratic Caesura

The image of Socrates as the first to turn philosophical inquiry from the cosmos to civic life is not a neutral portrayal; it was crafted and perpetuated by thought collectives with clear ideological objectives. Plato's Socratic caesura was entangled in the suppression and devaluation of rhetors and their public oratory; of elite communication with the *dēmos* concerning the *polis*; of tragedy and comedy as media that allowed complex religious, social, and political issues to be presented to the public; and of various forms of social theorizing and wisdom-sharing in fifth and fourth-century Athens. This caesura was later repurposed by Cicero and his patrician network as they appropriated Greek thought, deploying it against the *populares* who claimed to represent the common people. Ultimately, the image of Socrates was shaped by elite thought collectives who defined philosophy as intellectual engagement about, rather than with, the *polis* and the *dēmos*. As Ober notes in *Mass and Elite in Democratic Athens*, the elevation of elite forms of discourse entailed the marginalization of more *dēmos*-oriented communicative practices.[97]

The term 'Presocratic' is fundamentally rooted in the Socratic caesura and has had lasting consequences for the study of ancient thought. This label reinforces Plato's homogenizing strategy, effectively suppressing the diverse philosophical inquiries of the sixth and fifth centuries BC. As A. A. Long observes, the 'Presocratic' label obscures the range of early thinkers' interests—ethics, psychology, theology, and epistemology—by grouping them under a term that emphasizes their non-Socratic features.[98] Consequently, the term conceals the fluidity and diversity of early Greek thought—qualities that Fleck's theory of thought styles helps us appreciate more fully.

Cicero's adaptation of the Socratic caesura had a profound impact on intellectual traditions from 1350 to 1789. Rediscovered and disseminated through translations and printings before Plato's key dialogues were widely accessible, Cicero's works offered Renaissance thinkers a philosophical model that countered Aristotelian orthodoxy. Italian humanists initially deployed Cicero's writings to challenge scholasticism, while British philosophers, such as Toland, Shaftesbury, Locke, and Hume,[99] later drew on Cicero's moral philosophy to explore the possibility of a moral framework distinct from theological control. Unlike Plato's rather extreme philosophy, which contained numerous elements incompatible with Christian doctrine and led to public denunciations,[100] Cicero's urbane republicanism and his

---

[97] Ober (1989).

[98] Long (1995, pp. 6–7).

[99] Fox (2013), Stuart-Buttle (2018).

[100] A public denunciation of Plato was delivered in 1458 by George of Trebizond, whose *Comparitio philosophorum Aristotelis et Platonis (Comparisons of Aristotle and Plato)* defended Aristotle as inspired by the Holy Spirit and attacked the Plato and the (Florentine) Platonists as sexual deviants, hedonists, heretics and corrupters of public morality. In George's apocalyptic vision, Plato was the inspiration for the Great Apostasy and Platonism would trigger the end of Latin Christianity (Monfasani 1976, pp. 157–159).

reworking of Greek thought provided a mediating thought style that could be aligned with Christian doctrine while fostering new intellectual traditions.[101] It was precisely because Cicero's writings were aligned with the Socratic caesura, i.e., focused on moral philosophy and rhetoric rather than natural science or metaphysics, that they could be readily assimilated into the textual and educational environment of Christian Europe, becoming a component of an apparently benign alternative to the prevailing scholastic Aristotelian thought style.[102]

While Plato's philosophy influenced the scientific revolution in its Neoplatonist derivation, as is evident to varying degrees from the writings of Copernicus, Kepler, and Galileo, Renaissance Neoplatonism largely bypassed Socrates' practical philosophy to focus on metaphysical and cosmological themes. For example, Marsilio Ficino, the Renaissance philosopher and leading figure of the Florentine Platonic Academy, translated and interpreted Plato through a Neoplatonic lens that emphasized metaphysics, the soul, and the ascent to divine knowledge. Ficino, deeply influenced by the Neoplatonists—especially Plotinus and Proclus—viewed Plato not primarily as a practical philosopher but as a mystical teacher whose dialogues conveyed a path to spiritual enlightenment and divine understanding.[103]

The Socratic caesura re-emerged with new intensity in German scholarship of the late eighteenth and early nineteenth centuries, amid revolutionary wars and institutional transformation. In these decades, scholars in German philosophy faculties, including specialists in *Altertumswissenschaft* (classical studies), asserted and finally achieved institutional independence from the theology faculty. In contrast to the British and French focus on Ancient Rome, German scholars like Friedrich August Wolf, Wilhelm von Humboldt, and Georg Wilhelm Friedrich Hegel identified the culture of Ancient Greece as primary and of unique spiritual importance.[104] The liberation of the philosophy and classical studies faculties from theological control, and the elevation of philosophy to the status of master discipline in Hegel's writing and in the Humboldtian university, was inseparable from a critical reflection

[101] Cicero's letters, orations and principal works, including *De Oratore,* were rediscovered by Petrarch and others between 1345 and 1421. They were first printed in 1465 and translated into European languages between 1481 and 1561; and by 1700 there were 300 editions and commentaries on Cicero's rhetorical works (Marsh 2013, pp. 306–310). Though it was his oratory that received the most attention, by the eighteenth century complete editions of Cicero's corpus were available, and in translation in the nineteenth century (Fox 2013, p. 320). For most Italian humanists, the evident value of Cicero's elegant Latin style far outweighed the dangers posed by the fact he was a pagan; for example, it sufficed for Petrarch to condemn the polytheism endorsed in *De natura deorum.* Leonardo Bruni, who had grave reservations about certain ideas expressed in Plato's *Republic*, deemed Cicero's writing suitable for women (Wilson 1992, p. 21) (Marsh 2013, pp. 307–308).

[102] Wilson (1992), Marsh (2013).

[103] On Neoplatonism and modern science, see Carré (1955), Martens (2000). For Ficino's Neoplatonic reading of Plato, see Ficino (2001) and Celenza (2002). For a more historically grounded interpretation that highlights Ficino's treatment of Socrates and the philosophical function of Platonic dialogue, see Robichaud (2022).

[104] Hegel (1995, pp. 150–155), Marchand (1996, pp. 3–35).

that considered German culture in light of Ancient Greek culture. This identified the beleaguered German states with the embattled Greek states of antiquity and constructed both Ancient Greeks and modern Germans as unique spiritual *Völker*, distinguished by their philosophical consciousness.

Johann Augustus Eberhard's coining of the term '*vorsokratische Philosophie*' (Presocratic Philosophy) in 1788,[105] while employed as a philosophy professor at the University of Halle, reintroduced the Platonic-Socratic caesura as a significant demarcation in philosophical history, setting in motion its eventual institutionalization. Eberhard's definition was but one step in a larger process whereby, in the eighteenth century, the German philosophy faculty asserted its autonomy from theology and aligned more closely with the natural sciences. This shift had already been set in motion by confrontations such as those of Christian Wolff, who, also at Halle, faced theological opposition as he sought to establish a rationalist framework for philosophy distinct from theological oversight.[106] Likewise, Kant's critique of theological assumptions in the *Critique of Pure Reason* exemplifies the broader process of German philosophy asserting its institutional autonomy and societal influence. The positioning of Socrates as the true beginning of philosophy thus reflects a deeper shift—one that would ultimately reframe philosophy as a distinct intellectual authority and, following Kant, as a mediator between government, the university, and the public. It is to this evolving role that we now turn.

References

Ando C (2011) From republic to empire. In: Peachin M (ed) The Oxford handbook of social relations in the Roman world. OUP, Oxford, pp 37–68

Annas J (2001) Introduction. In: Cicero (ed) On moral ends. CUP, Cambridge, pp ix–xxvii

Aristophanes (2015) Clouds, women at the thesmophoria, frogs, a verse translation, with introductions and notes (trans: Halliwell S). OUP, Oxford

Aristotle (1933) Aristotle in 23 volumes, vols 17, 18 (trans: Tredennick H). Harvard University Press, Cambridge

Barnes J (1997) Roman Aristotle. In: Barnes J, Griffin M (eds) Philosophia Togata II: Plato and Aristotle at Rome. OUP, Oxford

Brittain C (2006) Introduction. In: Cicero (ed) On academic scepticism. Hackett, Indianapolis, pp viii–xlv

Brunt P (1971) Social conflicts in the Roman Republic. W. W. Norton, New York

Carawan E (2013) The Athenian amnesty and reconstructing the law. Oxford University Press, Oxford

Carré MH (1955) Platonism and the rise of science. Philosophy 30(115):333–342

Celenza CS (2002) Late antiquity and Florentine Platonism: The 'Post-Plotinian' Ficino. In: Allen MJB, Rees V (eds) Marsilio Ficino: His Theology, His Philosophy, His Legacy. Brill, Leiden–Boston–Köln, pp 71–97

Cicero (1877) Tusculan disputations (trans: Yonge C). Harper and Brothers, New York

[105] Laks (2018, p. 1).

[106] Saine (1997).

Cicero (1908–1909) The Letters of Cicero; the whole extant correspondence in chronological order, in four volumes (trans: Shuckburgh ES). George Bell and Sons, London
Cicero (1942) De Oratore I, II (trans: Sutton E). Harvard University Press. Cambridge
Cicero (2004) On moral ends (trans: Woolf R). Annas J (ed). CUP, Cambridge
Cicero (2006) On academic scepticism (trans: Brittain C). Hackett, Indianapolis
Cicero (2012) On living and dying well (trans: Habinek T). Penguin, London
Cicero (2014) Complete works (trans: Yonge C). Delphi Publishing Ltd, Hastings
Corbeill A (2013) Cicero and the intellectual milieu of the late Republic. In: Steel C (ed) The Cambridge companion to Cicero. CUP, Cambridge, pp 9–24
Curd P (2007) Anaxagoras's life and work. In: Anaxagoras of Clazomenae: Fragments and Testimonia: a text and translation with notes and essays by Patricia Curd. University of Toronto Press Incorporated, Toronto, pp 129–152
de Ste Croix GEM (1981) The class struggle in the ancient Greek world. from the Archaic Age to the Arab conquests. Cornell University Press, New York
Diogenes Laertius (1925) Lives of eminent philosophers (trans: Hicks RD). Harvard University Press, Cambridge
Dover KJ (1968) Introduction. In: Aristophanes, Clouds. Clarendon Press, Oxford, pp xvii–xcviii
Everitt A (2001) Cicero: the life and times of Rome's greatest politician. Random House, New York
Ferwerda R (1972) Democritus and Plato. Mnemosyne, Fourth Series, vol 25, Fasc. 4, 337–378
Ficino M (2001) Platonic theology: Books I–IV. Allen MJB (trans), Warden J (with), Hankins J (ed), Bowen W (with). Harvard University Press, Cambridge, MA/London
Fleck L (1979) Genesis and development of a scientific fact [1935]. The University of Chicago Press, Chicago
Fleck L (1986a) Scientific observation and perception in general [1935]. In: Cognition and Fact. Boston Studies in the Philosophy of Science, vol 87. Springer, Dordrecht. https://doi.org/10.1007/978-94-009-4498-5_4
Fleck L (1986b) The problem of epistemology [1936]. In: Cognition and fact. Boston Studies in the Philosophy of Science, vol 87. Springer, Dordrecht. https://doi.org/10.1007/978-94-009-4498-5_5
Fox M (2013) Cicero during the enlightenment. In: Steel C (ed) The Cambridge companion to Cicero. CUP, Cambridge, pp 318–336
Freydberg B (2008) Philosophy and comedy: aristophanes, logos, and eros. Indiana University Press, Bloomington
Gerson LP (2020) Platonism and naturalism. Cornell University Press, New York
Glucker J (1997) Socrates in the Academic books and other Ciceronian Works. In: Inwood B, Mansfield J (eds) Assent and argument. Studies in Cicero's Academic Books. Brill, Leiden, pp 58–88
Griffin M (1994) The intellectual developments of the Ciceronian age. In: Crook J, Lintott A, Rawson E (eds) The Cambridge ancient history, vol IX. CUP, Cambridge, pp 689–728
Halliwell S (2015). Introduction. In: Aristophanes. Clouds, women at the thesmophoria, frogs. A verse translation with introduction and notes. OUP, Oxford, pp 3–19
Hegel GW (1995) Lectures on the history of philosophy (trans: Haldane ES). Bison, Nebraska
Hind JG (1992) Mithridates. In: Crook JA, Lintott A (eds) The Cambridge ancient history second edition. The last age of the Roman Republic, 146-43 B.C. CUP, Cambridge, pp 129–164
Irwin TH (1992) Plato: the intellectual background. In: Kraut R (ed) The Cambridge companion to Plato. Cambridge University Press, Cambridge, pp 51–89
Jaeger W (1946) Paideia. The Ideals of Greek Culture Volume I. Blackwell, Oxford
Laks A (2018) The concept of presocratic philosophy: its origin, development, and significance. Princeton University Press
Lampert L (2010) How philosophy became socratic. University of Chicago Press, Chicago
Long AA (1995) Cicero's Plato and Aristotle. In: Powell J (ed) Cicero the Philosopher. Clarendon Press, Oxford, pp 37–62
Long AA, Sedley D (1987) The Hellenistic Philosophers Volume 1. CUP, Cambridge

Marchand S L (1996) Down from Olympus: Archaeology and philhellenism in Germany, 1750–1970. Princeton University Press, Princeton
Marsh D (2013) Cicero in the Renaissance. In: Steel C (ed) The Cambridge companion to Cicero. CUP, Cambridge, pp 306–317
Martens R (2000) Kepler's philosophy and the new astronomy. Princeton University Press, Princeton
McConnell S (2014) Philosophical life in Cicero's letters. CUP, Cambridge
Miller PA, Platter C (2010) Plato's apology of socrates: a commentary. University of Oklahoma Press, Norman
Monfasani J (1976) George of Trebizond. Brill, Leiden
Ober J (1989) Mass and elite in democratic Athens. Princeton University Press, Princeton
Ober J (2017) The trial of socrates as a political trial. In: Meierhenrich J, Pendas D (eds) Political trials in theory and history. Cambridge University Press, Cambridge, pp 65–87
Plato (1914) Euthyphro. Apology. Crito. Phaedo. Phaedrus (trans: Fowler HN). Harvard University Press, Cambridge
Plato (1976) Plato's Protagoras (trans: Taylor C). Clarendon Press, Oxford
Plutarch (1916) Plutarch's Lives (trans: Perrin B). Harvard University Press. Cambridge
Powell J (1995) Introduction. In: Powell J (ed) Cicero the Philosopher. Twelve papers. Clarendon Press, Oxford, pp 1–36
Rawson E (1985) Intellectual life in the late Roman Republic. Duckworth, London
Robichaud DJ-J (2022) Plato's persona: Marsilio Ficino, Renaissance humanism, and Platonic traditions. University of Pennsylvania Press, Philadelphia
Saine TP (1997) The problem of being modern or the German pursuit of enlightenment from Leibniz to the French Revolution. Wayne State University Press, Detroit
Sider S (2005) The fragments of Anaxagoras. Academia Verlag, Ankt Augustin
Stuart-Buttle T (2018) From moral theology to moral philosophy Cicero and visions of humanity from Locke to Hume. OUP, Oxford
Vernant JP (1982) The origins of Greek thought. Cornell University Press, New York
Vernant JP (1988) Myth and society in Ancient Greece. Zone Books, New York
Wallace RW (2007) Plato's Sophists, intellectual history after 450, and Sokrates. In: Samons II LJ (ed) The Cambridge companion to the age of Pericles. CUP, Cambridge, pp 215–237
Waterfield R (1990) Introduction. In: Xenophon, Conversations of Socrates (trans: Tredennick H, Waterfield R). Penguin Books, London, pp 5–26
Wilson N (1992) From Byzantium to Italy. Greek studies in the Italian Renaissance. Duckworth, London
Wolpert A (2002) Remembering defeat. Civil war and civic memory in ancient Athens. John Hopkins University Press, Baltimore
Xenophon (1923a) Memorabilia (trans: Marchant E). In: Xenophon, Memorabilia, Oeconomicus, Symposium, Apology. Harvard University Press, Cambridge
Xenophon (1923b) Symposium (trans: Todd OJ). In: Xenophon, Memorabilia, Oeconomicus, Symposium, Apology. Harvard University Press, Cambridge
Zarecki J (2014) Cicero's ideal statesman in thoery and practice. Bloomsbury, London and New York
Zetzel J (1999) Introduction. In: Cicero, On the commonwealth and on the laws. CUP, Cambridge, pp vii–xxiv
Zetzel J (2003) Plato with pillows: Cicero on the uses of Greek culture. In: Braund D, Gill, C (eds) Myth, History and Culture in Republican Rome: Studies on Honour of T. P. Wiseman. University of Exeter Press, Exeter, pp 119–137

Chapter 8
Hegelian *Bildung* as a Development of *Paideia*

Abstract This chapter examines Hegel's concept of *Bildung*, contextualizing it as a synthesis of Greek *paideia* and German educational ideals shaped by the evolving institutional forces of the German University. Ludwik Fleck's theory of thought styles and thought collectives is used to explore how Hegel's vision of *Bildung*—as a process of cultural and intellectual self-formation—served to position philosophy as the master discipline, distinct from mythology, religion, and poetry. Hegel's engagement with these forms of cultural production is analysed as part of his broader project of philosophical demarcation, most notably reflected in his critique of Georg Friedrich Creuzer's interdisciplinary methodology in the *Symbolik*.

The chapter situates Hegel's conceptualization of *Bildung* within the Humboldtian educational reforms and broader nationalist currents of the early nineteenth century. It examines how Hegel's interpretation of Greek culture and philosophy was mediated by the institutional dynamics of the German University, which shaped his distinction between explicit philosophical thought and representational forms like mythology. Drawing on Fleck's framework, the chapter demonstrates that Hegel's reconstruction of Greek thought reflects both the constraints and opportunities afforded by competing academic disciplines and thought collectives, including German Idealism and neo-humanist philology.

By integrating Fleckian, Foucauldian, and Bourdieusian approaches, the chapter reveals the interplay between Hegel's thought and the institutional forces shaping it. Ultimately, Hegel's strategic positioning of philosophy as an autonomous *Wissenschaft*, capable of subsuming and redefining other disciplines, emerges as a product of his engagement with the cultural, political, and academic transformations of his time.

8.1 Scope and Aims

This chapter examines Hegel's conceptualization of *Bildung*—as a distinctive form of cultural and intellectual self-development emerging within the German philosophical tradition—as both an academic and institutional phenomenon. Hegel's

S. Dersley, *Thought Collectives and Cultural Change*, Living Signs of Law 1,
https://doi.org/10.1007/978-3-031-97431-1_8

notion builds on Greek *paideia* yet is explicitly redefined in terms of the German *Bildung* ideal, and was thus shaped by institutional, philological, and nationalist currents at the turn of the nineteenth century. Within this framework, Hegel reactivated and repurposed a Platonic thought style that strategically elevated philosophy as a master discipline, distinct from other forms of cultural production, including mythology, religion, and poetry.

The analysis applies Fleck's theory of thought collectives to examine how Hegel's understanding of Greek and German philosophy operates as a framing of parallel national-spiritual unities in the *Lectures on the History of Philosophy*. It demonstrates that Hegel's reinterpretation of Greek *paideia* is inseparable from the specific cultural and institutional pressures shaping the German university system, where figures such as Fichte and Humboldt promoted an integrated model of *Bildung* and *Wissenschaft* for national renewal.

By tracing Hegel's critical engagement with Georg Friedrich Creuzer and the intellectual controversy surrounding Creuzer's *Symbolik*, the chapter highlights Hegel's rigorous exclusion of mythology from the domain of philosophy. While Hegel acknowledges philosophical elements within mythology, he ultimately rejects Creuzer's interdisciplinary methodology, establishing strict boundaries around philosophy as a methodologically autonomous science (*Wissenschaft*) of explicit thought. In his response to Creuzer's perceived disciplinary encroachment, Hegel's approach reflects a broader strategy of establishing philosophy's primacy over other disciplines within the university hierarchy. The chapter situates Hegel's differentiation strategies within the currents and conflicts occurring in the German University, highlighting how his thought style both drew on and contributed to the state-aligned discursive practices and educational reforms of his era.

8.2 Hegel's Conception of *Bildung* in the *Lectures on the History of Philosophy*

The following sections will first analyse Hegel's internal differentiation of philosophy as a cultural practice and then apply Fleck's theoretical tools to illuminate the cultural-historical and institutional factors that significantly influenced Hegel's textual strategies.

In the study of Greek thought, Hegel operates as a professional, university-based philosopher who made a decisive contribution to the 'from myth to logos' paradigm discussed in Chap. 6. His reconstruction of the history of philosophy can be read as a prototypical example of philosophy's habitual self-positioning as a master discipline. Hegel's philosophy asserts this claim by tracing its lineage back to an absolute discontinuity in the history of human thought—in Fleck's terms, the appearance of an entirely new thought style.

Although Johann August Eberhard had coined the term *Vorsokratiker* (Presocratic) in 1788, signalling that the arrival of Socrates was a crucial caesura in the development of Greek philosophy,[1] Hegel notably avoids using this term in his *Lectures on the History of Philosophy*. Instead, Hegel structures Greek philosophy into three periods: *From Thales to Aristotle*, *Dogmatic and Skeptical Philosophy*, and *Neoplatonic Philosophy*. Within the first overarching period, *From Thales to Aristotle*, Hegel delineates three specific progressions: *From Thales to Anaxagoras* and *From the Sophists to the Socratics*, culminating with *Plato and Aristotle*. Here, rather than positioning Socrates as an absolute rupture, Socratic thought is subsumed within a series of progressions that constitute the universal dialectical process through which the universal world spirit gradually unfolds its self-awareness.

Hegel's *Lectures on the History of Philosophy (1825–6)*, which both engaged with and contributed to the burgeoning field of German scholarship on ancient Greek philosophy, explicitly highlight two primary formations: Greek philosophy and German philosophy. Hegel presents philosophy as developing organically within these formations, with progress being gradual yet at times interrupted, or punctuated by periods of 'fermentation'. In Hegel's view, such pauses occur because the world spirit requires time and 'has the wherewithal to make its way through a multitude of nations, peoples, and the like'.[2]

A pivotal aspect of Hegel's analysis is his characterization of the Greeks as a unified people (*Volk*), conceptualized as a homogenous spiritual entity in direct contrast with 'the Orientals'. In cultural terms, he positions 'the Greek World' as a distinct and superior counterpart to 'the Orient'.[3] Despite the geographical spread of Greek thinkers—from the 'Oriental' figures of Asia Minor, such as Thales, Anaximander, Heraclitus, and Democritus, to the 'Greek Italians' in the West, including Pythagoras, Parmenides, Zeno, and Empedocles[4]—Hegel maintains that 'Greek philosophy' can be regarded as a singular, cohesive tradition.

Because Hegel famously excluded the Oriental world from the realm of philosophy, citing the dominance of the objective domain over individual subjectivity in the Orient and the single individual lacking political freedom and rights,[5] he frames the emergence of Greek philosophy as the birth of an entirely new epoch in the world spirit's history. In Hegel's conceptualization, the philosophical activity in Greece represents a critical, unprecedented shift, distinct from anything that had appeared in the Oriental world.

In *The Problem of Epistemology*, Fleck observes our tendency to 'involuntarily substitute today's content' for the language and ideas found in 'scientific literary monuments'.[6] Hegel's identification of 'die Griechen' as a distinct *Volk* exemplifies this tendency, though we can surmise that, in Hegel's case, it is more a deliberate choice. Following Prussia's defeat by Napoleonic forces at the Battle of Jena–

[1] Perilli (2018, p.105).

[2] Hegel (2009, p. 96).

[3] Hegel (2006, pp. 11–12).

[4] Hegel (2006, p. 16).

[5] Hegel (2009, pp. 89–90).

[6] Fleck (1986, pp. 89, 91).

Auerstedt (1806), the focus on Germans as a unique people was exemplified by Johann Gottlieb Fichte's shift from internationalist ideals toward a more nationalistic conception of German unity and culture. This shift, which was central to the founding of the 'Humboldtian' University of Berlin in 1810, formed part of the intellectual unrest that framed Hegel's *Lectures on the History of Philosophy*. Delivered during the turbulent years between 1806 and 1831, at the Universities of Jena, Heidelberg, and Berlin, these lectures trace the evolution of philosophical consciousness against the backdrop of an emergent German identity. Thus, when Hegel describes the spiritual unity of the Greek people and their culture—despite their geographical dispersal, with the polarized East-West branches of Greek philosophy converging in Athens 'for the first time at a central point'[7]—he could just as well be describing the German *Volk*, German philosophy, and Berlin.

A key point here is that, while Fleck cautions against such substitutions—implying a need for sensitivity to the 'passive' elements present in ancient texts—Hegel, in contrast, consciously adopts these appropriations and substitutions. As this section will demonstrate, Hegel's thought style positions Modern Philosophy as distinct from Ancient Philosophy through precisely these conscious substitutions.

In Hegel's framework, philosophy arrives through a 'spiritual rebirth' (*geistige Wiedergeburt*). The first birth provides natural life, consciousness, and knowledge, but it is only the rebirth that brings true spiritual life. For Hegel, the Greeks experienced this rebirth *as a people*, thus ushering in a critical stage in the world spirit's development of self-awareness.

Hegel acknowledges the influence of external stimuli on Greek art and science but emphasizes Greek agency and creativity:

> In dealing with Greek art and life we are led to Asia and Egypt. But [...] we can locate the germination, growth, and blossoming of Greek science and art within Greek life itself; even the source of its decay is already embedded in it. What came from elsewhere was but the raw material or impetus for them; and they transformed or recast it. The spiritual ethos is precisely characteristic of the Greeks themselves, the form of art and science that is the pure form of thinking.[8]

For Hegel, the Greeks were thus fundamentally a distinct spiritual people, whose thought emerged internally, from their unique 'primordial elements' (*uranfänglichen Elementen*). In the following passage, Hegel seems to indicate, obliquely, that poetry played a key role in the first phase of this emergence:

> They have preserved all of their beginnings—a history of the world (a cosmogony) and of the gods (a theogony), and also a history of how the human race came to possess fire, agriculture and the olive tree. The memories of these earliest beginnings of all culture, which constitute the initial transition out of primeval savagery, the Greeks have gratefully preserved. Thus they are at home with themselves even in their outward, historical aspect. So too the development of their thought emerged or unfolded from their own primordial ele-

[7] Hegel (2006, p. 16).

[8] Hegel (2006, p. 10).

ments, and we need not seek for some further external stimulus, some historical tie [with other peoples].[9]

The reference to cosmogony and theogony, history and the beginnings of culture would seem to suggest, at the very least, that Hesiod contributed to the Greeks' 'initial transition' from primeval savagery.

Hegel's explicit references to Homer and Hesiod in Lectures on the History of Philosophy, though sparse, are deeply telling, particularly in his reconstruction of the Sophists, which draws heavily on Plato's Protagoras. Hegel's highly original interpretation is crucial, as it demonstrates how his conception of *Bildung* hinges on his treatment of mythology, religion, and poetry.

In his recap of Plato's text, Hegel tends to treat Plato's depiction of Protagoras as providing a reliable account of sophist thought, as he reproduces key points without significant commentary or interpretation. The following passage from Plato's text, where Protagoras suggests that Homer and Hesiod engaged in sophistry cloaked as poetry, exemplifies this:

> Now I tell you that sophistry is an ancient art, and those men of ancient times who practised it, fearing the odium it involved, disguised it in a decent dress, sometimes of poetry [ποίησις/*poiēsis*], as in the case of Homer, Hesiod, and Simonides sometimes of mystic rites and soothsayings, as did Orpheus, Musaeus and their sects; and sometimes too, I have observed, of athletics,. [...] Hence the road I have taken is one entirely opposite to theirs: I admit that I am a sophist and that I educate men [παιδεύειν ἀνθρώπους /paideuein anthrōpous]; and I consider this precaution, of admitting rather than denying, the better of the two. (Prot. 316d, 317d)[10]

Hegel paraphrases and expands on this as follows:

> He [Protagoras] maintains that the art of the Sophists is ancient, although just in order to avoid giving offense those who have practised it have given it a cloak under which they concealed it. Some of the ones from whom culture derived, such persons as Homer and Hesiod, employed poetry [as a cloak], others such as Musaeus and Orpheus employed the mysteries and oracular sayings, other again gymnastics, and others music. All of these arts are modes whereby human beings impart culture. [...] Protagoras himself professes to have gone the other way and says openly that he is a Sophist, a teacher of culture, that his business is to give people spiritual culture (παιδεύειν ἀνθρώπους), just as the other have done—Homer, Hesiod and the like.[11]

---

[9] Hegel (2006, pp. 10–11). The original German for the last sentence: 'Die Entwicklung des Gedankens ist bei ihnen von ihren uranfänglichen Elementen hervorgetreten, hat sich entfaltet, und wir können sie betrachten, ohne weitere äußere Veranlassungen aufsuchen zu müssen' (Hegel 1986, pp. 175–176).

[10] Plato (1967).

[11] Hegel (2006, pp. 112–113). The German text: 'Hierüber spricht er weitläufig und sagt dabei: »Ich aber behaupte, daß die sophistische Kunst alt ist, daß aber die von den Alten, welche sie übten metacheirizomenous, in Besorgnis, damit anzustoßen« phoboumenoi to epachthes, denn das Ungebildete ist dem Gebildeten feind), »ihr ein Gewand machten und sie verdeckten.« Diese Kunst ist Bildung überhaupt, dasselbe was »ein Teil, wie Homer und Hesiod, in Poesie vorgetragen, andere, wie Orpheus und Musaios, in Mysterien und Orakelsprüche eingehüllt. [...] Wenn man sich aber so verhält, so macht man sich verhaßter, setzt sich selbst dem Scheine (Verdachte) aus, Täuscher (Betrüger, panourgon) zu sein. Ich bin darum den entgegengesetzten Weg gegangen

Crucially, Hegel's gloss—*Diese Kunst ist Bildung überhaupt*[12]—casts the art of the Sophists as *general culture*, thereby highlighting a conception of culture distinctly rooted in the German university-based philosophy of the late eighteenth and early nineteenth centuries. In treating the Greek *paideia* that Plato's *Protagoras* attributes to the Sophists as embodying physical mastery (as in athletic training), the rituals and models of behaviour represented in poetry, and the shaping of human minds practised by the Sophists, Hegel presents it as an early, more rudimentary form of *Bildung*. This conception of *Bildung* synthesizes cultural formation, enlightenment, and self-cultivation, reflecting Hegel's broader philosophical project of aligning these diverse practices under a coherent developmental arc.[13]

Terry Pinkard emphasizes that the concept of *Bildung* had preoccupied Hegel since his youth, when he encountered Moses Mendelssohn's *What is Enlightenment?*, an essay that seemed to equate Enlightenment with Bildung.[14] For Hegel, *Bildung* was inseparable from his passionate support for the French Revolution, which he saw as a stimulus for the moral and spiritual renewal of Germany—a renewal that would unfold, he believed, when 'men of Bildung' governed the nation:

> The idea itself of *Bildung* was one of those things that was in the air at the time and came with considerable controversy attached to it. By Hegel's time, the idea had been distinguished from that of *Erziehung*, education. *Bildung* incorporated within itself the notion of true education and cultivation as in turn demanding self-formation. As it were, one could become educated (in the passive tense, represented by the term *Erziehung*), but one had to make oneself into a cultivated-educated person (in the active tense, represented by the term *Bildung*). *Bildung* required self-activity, self-development, and self-direction.[15]

Thus, Hegel's treatment of Bildung as a later, more developed form of *paideia*—a direct conceptual descendant—is by no means neutral. While the Hegelian system justifies this strategy as a reflection of the world spirit's gradual awakening, Hegel's choice of words can also be seen as reflecting the changing institutional status of philosophy in the German and Prussian states.

Marek Kwiek has observed that *Bildung* was a 'strongly politicized' notion, inseparable from a national dimension and a specific vision of the university's role within the state, as conceived and promoted by figures like Fichte and Humboldt.[16] Nigel Tubbs further emphasizes that, in the Hegelian system, the state is essential to this conception of education: *Bildung*, for Hegel, becomes the process by which

und bekenne offen und leugne es nicht homologô, ein Sophist zu sein« (Protagoras führte zuerst den Namen Sophist), und daß mein Geschäft sei, »den Menschen Geistesbildung zu geben *(παιδεύειν ἀνθρώπους)*«, wie die anderen, Homer, Hesiod usf., es auch getan'. (Hegel 1986, p. 415).

[12] Hegel (1986, p. 415).

[13] Pinkard (2000, pp. 26, 49).

[14] Pinkard (2000, p. 49).

[15] Pinkard (2000, p. 49).

[16] Kwiek (2006).

ethical life replaces natural need, and it is the maturation of the person from particular to universal, and of family to civil society and state'.[17]

The twenty-five-year period during which Hegel worked on and delivered his *Lectures on the History of Philosophy*, from 1806 to 1831, was marked by considerable upheaval, spanning from Napoleon's defeat of Prussia at the Battle of Jena–Auerstedt to the wide-ranging reforms of the Prussian Reform Movement and the territorial consolidations following the Congress of Vienna. The intellectual unrest of this era aligns with Fleck's conception of a period in which the intellectual mood of a thought collective shifts, becoming conducive to a change in thought style and facilitating new perceptions and interpretations—of texts, for instance.

In terms of Fleck's theory, Hegel's reconstruction of sophistry presents a clear example of a modern thought style interpreting an earlier one through its own conceptual lens, with the passive elements of the original style obscured in the process. For instance, Hegel equates the German concept of *Bildung* directly with the Greek *paideia*. When Plato attributes to Protagoras the words *παιδεύειν ἀνθρώπους* (train/teach/educate man), Hegel translates this as *den Menschen Geistesbildung zu geben* (to impart spiritual education to man), explicitly referencing the Greek in his lectures; thus, *Geistesbildung* functions as a direct substitution for *paideia*. From the perspective of Fleck's theory of thought styles, Hegel's interpretive move might be seen as a somewhat forceful projection of contemporary concepts back into an older, 'appropriated' proto-idea.

However, the Hegelian framework possesses the 'conceptual antibodies' to counter Fleck's critique: Hegel's system conceives of the world spirit as a unified process of self-realization, whereby *paideia* and *Bildung* represent stages of the same underlying development. Within this framework, *Bildung* can be viewed—if one accepts the Hegelian tenets—as a mature outgrowth of *paideia*. This aspect of Hegel's method illustrates what might be termed 'Hegelian autoimmunity', or, put differently, a 'rigorous acknowledgment of complicity in the imperialisms of the age' that manifests as a conscious and unapologetic engagement with the transmission and transformation of ideas over time.[18]

In his lectures on the Sophists, Hegel repeatedly contrasts the *Bildung* of ancient Greece with that of *der modernen Zeit* (modern times) or the *europäischen Welt* (European world).[19] He defines *Bildung* as an indeterminate concept (*unbestimmt*), suggesting its essence lies in one's 'acquaintance with the general viewpoints that pertain to any object or issue' and the capacity 'to grasp these perspectives in a general way'. In Hegel's view, an educated person (*gebildeter Mensch*) is someone able to engage with diverse issues and approaches, and is familiar with the various perspectives that inform them.[20]

[17] Tubbs (2008, p. 44).

[18] Tubbs (2008, p. 42).

[19] Hegel (1986, pp. 420–421).

[20] Hegel (2006, p. 111; 1986, pp. 410–411).

Hegel credits the Sophists with introducing such intellectual cultivation, or *Bildung*, to Greek society. Importantly, he frames this as a break from inherited customs and norms: the Sophists, he argues, fostered a new consciousness in individuals, awakening in them the need to reflect critically and to adjust their thinking in response to particular circumstances. Hegel's reading of Plato's *Protagoras* suggests that the Sophists provided instruction not only in theoretical knowledge but also in practical political virtue. Young men, he argues, were guided to understand both their personal best interests and those of the state, learning how to articulate these interests within the civic sphere.[21]

By cultivating a reflective stance in Greek citizens, the Sophists contributed to a shift in political *Bildung*—a form of cultural and civic education that engaged citizens in active participation and ethical reasoning within the *polis*. For Hegel, then, the Sophists' role transcended mere rhetorical instruction; they fostered a critical awareness essential to the *Bildung* of the modern European world, where knowledge is not just passive but actively woven into the moral and political fabric of society.

Ultimately, Hegel's description of the Sophists' practices has a distinctly modern ring: for the Sophists, political virtue pertains to all citizens (*Bürger*); education is directed toward training children in custom and right, so that they become accustomed to 'self-regulation in accordance with a law or a rule'.[22] Upon completing their instruction in political virtue, they then enter the state's constitution, which exerts its influence on the individual and keeps them 'within the bounds of law and order'.[23] Hegel's most interpretive moment comes in his admiration for Protagoras' analogy between instruction in flute-playing and political virtue. In Plato's *Protagoras* (327a–e), Protagoras asks Socrates to consider the consequences of flute-playing being mandated by the state and all citizens receiving instruction in it. Hegel summarizes this as follows:

> All citizens would master flute-playing to a certain degree, and they would at all events be more proficient than those who had received no instruction. In the same way, the worst citizens of a rational state (*auch die schlechtesten Bürger eines vernünftigen Staats*) are at all events better than those who belong to a people that has no culture, no education, no law (*keine Bildung ist, keine Gerichte, keine Gesetze, keine Nötigung, sie zum Recht zu bilden*). The citizens owe this superiority to the laws, instruction, and culture in their state (*den Gesetzen, dem Unterricht, der Bildung in ihrem Staate*).[24]

If Hegel's reading is compared with Plato's original, his paraphrase, due to additions and selective word choices, casts the Sophists' attempts to educate Greek citizens in distinctly German or Prussian terms:

> Likewise, in the present case, you must regard any man who appears to you the most unjust (*ἄδικος – ádikos*) person ever reared among human laws (*νόμος – nomos*) and society as a

[21] Hegel (2006, pp. 111–113).

[22] Hegel (2006, p. 115).

[23] Hegel (2006, p. 115).

[24] Hegel (2006, p. 116).

just (*δίκαιος* – *díkaios*) man and a craftsman of justice, if he had to stand comparison with people who lacked education (*παιδεία* – *paideia*), law courts and laws (*νόμος* – *nomos*), and any constant compulsion to the pursuit of virtue (*ἄρετή* - *aretē*), but were a kind of wild folk [...] (327c–d)[25]

Thus, the most unjust men reared within the customs and laws of Plato's hypothetical *polis* become, in Hegel's gloss, the worst citizens of a rational state. Once again, *paideia* is treated as a straightforward equivalent of German *Bildung*, and the coerced pursuit of *aretē* is equated with the German civic virtue (*politische Tugend*). In Fleckian terms, this substitution illustrates the conceptual transformations and distortions that inevitably accompany the communication of ideas between distinct thought collectives. Yet, based on the student notes that form the basis of the *Lectures*, it appears that Hegel did not highlight the gaps in equivalence nor the conceptual differences between the Greek and German terms. Instead, he seems to have substituted, without reservation, the Greek *polis* with the rational German *Staat* and Greek *paideia* with German *Bildung*.

One of Hegel's purposes in his lecture on the Sophists was to contrast the culture of ancient Greece with that of modern Europe. Crucially, this contrast is key to the distinction Hegel makes between poetry and religion on the one hand, and philosophy on the other. And since Hegel's original interpretation of the Sophists—which, radically, also classifies Socrates as a sophist—presents them as the teachers who brought *Bildung überhaupt* (general culture) into existence in Greece, the educator-citizens who trained individuals to reflect on multiple viewpoints and consider both their own interests and those of the (rational) state, the question that arises here is: What stopped the Sophists from becoming fully-developed Prussian philosopher-burghers and purveyors of fully-fledged *Bildung*?

Hegel's answer centres on the limitations of the religion underlying the Sophists' *Bildung*. He describes their approach as 'defective' (*Mangelhaftes*), embracing 'one-sided principles' (*einseitige Prinzipien*) and overly favouring subjective determination due to inherent deficiencies in Greek religion:

That the Sophists embraced one-sided principles correlates above all with the fact that in Greece and in Greek Culture there was no such firm foundation as we have in the modern world. Culture (*Bildung*) has entered into the modern world too, but under the aegis and presupposition of the spiritual religion—not under that of a religion of a fanciful imagination (*Religion der Phantasie*). [...] In modern Europe the foundation has been a principle that is secure and indeed spiritual, one that in that way satisfies the needs of subjective spirit. All subsequent relationships, [including] the categories of duty and morality, determine themselves on the basis of this absolute, universal principle and are made dependent on it. The inevitable result was that culture did not adopt the multiplicity of orientations that it had among the Greeks and those who disseminated culture in Greece, namely, the Sophists. Confronted there with the religion of fanciful imagination and with undeveloped principles of political relationships, culture could splinter into a great variety of points of view; as a result private or subjective points of view could be established as supreme principles.[26]

---

[25] Plato (1967).

[26] Hegel (2006, pp. 116–117; 1986, p. 421).

This passage indirectly reinforces the point Hegel makes in the *Introduction* to the *Lectures on the History of Philosophy*: it is only within the Christian-Germanic world that philosophy fully advances to the 'thought of spirit'. Hegel notes that while Greek religion was the fertile ground for philosophical growth, Greek philosophy ultimately 'developed thought to the point of the idea'.[27] On one side, Greek philosophy advances the principle of the free, self-determining subject; on the other, it reaches the concept of an objective 'intellectual or ideal world'.[28] Yet, for Hegel, one final synthesis—attainable only through Christian doctrine—remains necessary: uniting the subject and objective ideal in the 'self-knowing idea, the principle of Christian philosophy'.[29] Christianity, Hegel contends, illuminates 'the unity of the divine nature with human nature [...] This is the Germanic principle, in which the objective idea and humanity are thus united'.[30]

In Hegel's system, the *Bildung* of the Sophists is rooted in the soil of the fanciful Greek religion, which lacks both the unifying principle of the Christian religion and the structural support of modern European political institutions. Consequently, the discovery of the subjective principle in this context leads to a splintering into multiple viewpoints and the limitless expansion of subjective determinations. Protagoras' assertion that 'man is the measure of all things,' which grants absolute determinative power to the subject, thus arises after abandoning the abstract focus on nature as the singular, sensuous universal object characteristic of Ionian natural philosophy and prior to Socrates and Plato's establishment of an objective, non-sensible ideal world—an independent realm of 'being-in-and-for-self,' or the self-generated content of thought.[31]

The *Bildung* of the Sophists is, therefore, inherently ambiguous, as it leaves open the question of which subject is to be educated or cultured. Hegel asks: 'Is it each human being according to private individuality, so as to make one's particular self the purpose, or is it the human being according to its rational nature and universal essence?'[32] In other words, within sophistic thought, the movement from the particular to the universal is incomplete: sophistic thought equips the individual citizen of the *polis* to pursue personal interests through subjective measures, or 'one-sided principles.' While Protagoras appears to acknowledge the state's interests, sophistic thought stops short of establishing an objective measure to subordinate private, subjective principles to external 'supreme principles [*höchste Prinzipien*].' It thus fails to elevate the individual citizen to the status of a universal subject fully aware of themselves through the *Bildung* imparted and regulated by the rational state.

To conclude, the Greek *paideia* offered by the Sophists remains an underdeveloped form of *Bildung*, limited to subjective determinations, bound by the limitations

---

[27] Hegel (2009, pp. 91–92).

[28] Hegel (2009, p. 93).

[29] Hegel (2009, p. 94).

[30] Hegel (2009, p. 95).

[31] Hegel (2009, p. 121).

[32] Hegel (2009, p. 121).

of a fanciful Greek religion. It stands in contrast to the matured *Bildung* of modern European (Prussian) statehood, developed within the universal principles of Platonic philosophy and the spiritual, unifying foundation of the Christian religion.

8.3 The Status of Religion, Myth and Poetry in Hegel's *Lectures on the History of Philosophy*

Given the significant limitations that Hegel suggests religion imposed on the development of Greek philosophy, it is necessary to give broader consideration to the status assigned to religion, mythology, and poetry in his *Lectures on the History of Philosophy*, particularly in terms of how philosophy is distinguished from these forms of cultural production.

In the *Introduction* to the *Lectures*, Hegel presents religion, mythology, and poetry as sharing certain characteristics that distinguish them from philosophy. First and foremost, they are all classed as forms of representation, with the thinking expressed in them described as sensuous and 'representational' (*sinnliche Vorstellung*).[33] In the Hegelian system, this is because the content of spirit takes an objective form in religion and mythology: it is apprehended by the sensual imagination as an external object, represented in sensuous forms (e.g., the burning bush that confronted Moses, the Greeks' marble statues of the gods) drawn from living nature. Similarly, poetry also 'clothes' its content in sensuous representations.[34] Crucially, philosophy is distinct from these representational forms of portraying spirit: while philosophy deals with the same content—spirit—it is 'grasped and posited in the form of thought'.[35]

While situating the thought of Socrates and Plato within a deterministic historical process, Hegel redeploys the negative concept of *mimesis*—thus reactivating key Platonic distinctions—to differentiate Greek philosophical thought from the thought that can be found in Greek religion and mythology. The thought specific to philosophy is explicit, non-representational thought, through which spirit becomes conscious of itself as such; here, thought itself becomes the content of thought, in the unity of self-knowing oneness.[36] In excluding mythology from philosophy, Hegel follows Aristotle's condemnation of myth in *Metaphysics* (III. 4), taking a more uncompromising position than Plato's critique of *mythos* in the *Republic*. Despite his criticisms of myths and poetry, Plato still resorts to myth to add clarity to pure

[33] Hegel (2009, p. 78).

[34] Hegel (2009, pp. 78–79). Hegel's German text: 'Allerdings muß die Wahrheit—es sei auf welcher Stufe sie selbst stehe—zuerst in äußerlicher Weise an die Menschen kommen, als sinnlich vorgestellter, gegenwärtiger Gegenstand; wie Moses Gott im feurigen Busch erblickte und sich die Griechen den Gott in Marmorbildern oder sonstigen Vorstellungen zum Bewußtsein gebracht haben' (Hegel, 1986, p. 92).

[35] Hegel (2009, p. 79).

[36] Hegel (2009, pp. 78–79; 1995, p. 83).

thought, but according to Hegel no matter how helpful Plato's use of myth might be, 'this form is not suitable to Philosophy'.[37]

Thus, Hegel views Plato's *Parmenides*, which avoids mythic elements entirely, as a superior work to those that use poetic myth. From this perspective, Hegel's ambition to position Philosophy as the master discipline of pure thought, grounded in the Absolute, draws on a rigorously purified form of Platonism, one that completely excludes mythology and poetry from philosophy's domain.

A key issue can be highlighted at this point. While there are internal factors within Hegel's conceptual system that lead him to re-enact the Platonic exclusion in a more purist form—such as his assumptions about the ontological status of thought and spirit—external factors also shape and guide Hegel's strategies of differentiation and exclusion.

The reading of Hegel's *Lectures on the History of Philosophy* proposed here is that, just as Plato's *Republic* can be read as fundamentally concerned with supervising, assimilating, and excluding practices associated with particular forms of education and cultural production, Hegel's conception of Philosophy is closely connected with a specific, historically, socially, and culturally determined notion of education: *Bildung*. I argue that this conception was externally determined by the shifting status and role of philosophical faculties within the German university institution, reflecting class struggles within both society and the scholarly community. Furthermore, the status of the philosophical faculty and Philosophy was asserted, defended, and maintained in a struggle with other faculties, disciplines, and conceptions of philosophy.

According to Fleck's theory, the thought collectives to which Hegel might be said to have belonged ranged from the immediate networks of philosophers, poets, and educators with whom he interacted, to broader, discursively constructed thought styles such as 'German Idealism', 'German Romanticism', and 'Lutheran Protestantism', which collectively influenced and shaped his ideas. Individuals with whom Hegel directly studied, worked, or corresponded—such as Friedrich Wilhelm Joseph Schelling and Friedrich Immanuel Niethammer—are readily identifiable, with some also aligning with the broader category of 'German Idealism' (e.g., Schelling). However, categorizing certain individuals as 'German Idealists' and thus as members of a general thought collective narrows rather than opens up the phenomena; despite instances of self-identification or explicit influence (as with Samuel Taylor Coleridge), such broad attributions, in my view, obscure the specific dynamics of these intellectual interactions rather than elucidate them.

Aside from these specific and general thought collectives, one of the most powerful determinants of Hegel's thought style was the institution of the German University itself. I propose that the emergence of Hegel's unique philosophy was inseparable from the emergence of a new model of this institution as he wrote and worked. The university, as an educational institution, can be understood as a dynamically evolving social entity that shaped thought styles and, in turn, was shaped by them. From their founding in the fourteenth century through to Hegel's time,

[37] Hegel (1995, p. 87).

German universities formed, hierarchized, and directed various competing thought collectives, while simultaneously being influenced, occupied, and reshaped by these collectives. In the European context, German philosophy was uniquely institutionalized; as a cultural practice, German Philosophy was far more influenced by the interplay between the university institution and specific thought collectives than were the types of philosophy that developed, for example, in England and France during the seventeenth and eighteenth centuries.

Immanuel Kant famously addressed the conflict between the philosophy faculty and the theology faculty in his polemic *The Conflict of the Faculties* (*Der Streit der Fakultäten*) (1798), asserting the right of the philosophy faculty—then the 'lower faculty' to exercise 'the free play of reason' and even to 'control' the higher faculties. He went so far as to insist that the philosophy faculty 'must be conceived as free and subject only to laws given by reason, not by the government'.[38] This polemic, along with his *Religion within the Limits of Bare Reason* (1793), which brought Kant into conflict with the King's censor, Johann Christoph von Wöllner, retroactively casts light on an institutional subtext of Kant's *Critique of Pure Reason*. Viewed through this lens, the *Critique* can be read as an act of philosophical demarcation, in the Platonic sense, but one that was performed within an institutional context. Thus, when Kant laid out principles and rules of cognition and morals with his Critical Method, he was simultaneously staking out a newly claimed terrain for the philosophy faculty within the German University.

By the time Hegel entered this conflict, and particularly when he delivered his lectures in Berlin in the 1820s, Philosophy was no longer the 'lower faculty' but had played a central role in redefining the university's conception in Germany, rising to a position of prominence.[39] Thus, whereas Kant and Fichte had come into conflict with the theological faculty and faced reprimands and penalties, Hegel, in his *Introduction to the Lectures on the History of Philosophy*, operated with greater freedom to 'separate' Philosophy from 'other Departments of Knowledge'. While his *Introduction* is less explicit than *The Conflict of the Faculties* in terms of addressing university power relations—this was Kant's last published book, when he had little to lose[40]—Hegel's work nonetheless engages in a departmental and disciplinary struggle, consolidating the gains made by Philosophy and reasserting its status as 'the discipline of disciplines', 'the sovereign and imperialist metadiscipline'.[41]

Crucially, the study of ancient Greek thought, the role Hegel assigns Greek philosophy in the history of philosophy, and the status he assigns to Greek religion and mythology in relation to Greek philosophy, were thoroughly entangled in and shaped by the struggles that took place between various disciplines in German universities during Hegel's lifetime. I propose that these struggles were determining factors that led Hegel to choose the word *Bildung* to describe the practice of the Athenian Sophists, rather than the available alternative, *Erziehung*.

[38] Kant (1979, pp. 35, 43).

[39] Kwiek (2006, pp. 4–5).

[40] Gregor (1979, p. vii).

[41] Kelley (1997, p. 22).

8.4 The Creuzer Affair

One clue to this institutional conflict can be extrapolated from Hegel's reference to 'my friend Creuzer'.[42] Georg Friedrich Creuzer (1771–1858) was a professor of philology and ancient history at the University of Heidelberg for over 50 years and belonged to the network forming Hegel's immediate thought collective. Apart from working at the same university for a couple of years, Hegel socialized with Creuzer and later maintained correspondence with him during his Berlin years.[43] In 1810–1812, Creuzer published his most famous book, *Symbolism and Mythology of the Ancients, particularly the Greeks* (*Symbolik und Mythologie der alten Völker, besonders der Griechen*)—henceforth *Symbolik*. This work was extremely controversial, drawing fierce criticism from all quarters and sparking what came to be known as 'the Creuzer Affair'.

The Creuzer Affair was a pivotal controversy in the history of German Philhellenism, a cultural movement of great complexity that has been the focus of much scholarly analysis following Martin Bernal's *Black Athena: The Afroasiatic Roots of Classical Civilization* (1987) and Susan L. Marchand's *Down from Olympus. Archaeology and Philhellenism in Germany, 1750–1970* (1996). The key issues will only be briefly highlighted here, insofar as they pertain to Hegel's comments on Creuzer's project.

Creuzer's *Symbolik* is treated as a key contribution to the 'Oriental Renaissance' or 'new Orientalism', a movement that emerged in German cultural circles towards the end of the eighteenth century.[44] New Orientalism opposed and radically undermined the German Philhellenism established by Johann Joachim Winckelmann (1717–1768) and popularized by figures like Friedrich Schiller (1759–1805) and the early works of Schelling (1775–1854). German Philhellenism held up Greek art, religion and republicanism as models for a renewal of public and aesthetic life in Germany, while simultaneously downgrading or at least challenging the role of Christianity—a strategy that went hand-in-hand with a strident anti-Orientalism. However, from the 1780s onwards, the dominance of Philhellenism in German universities and intellectual circles was increasingly countered by a growing interest in Indian, Egyptian, and Persian culture, spurred by William Jones' Sanskrit discoveries. Unlike earlier, dilettantish forms of Orientalism that can be traced back to the sixteenth century, the German New Orientalism carried considerable scholarly weight, as it was championed by figures such as Johann Gottfried Herder (1744–1803) and Friedrich Schlegel (1772–1829), who asserted 'the primacy or at least the deep antiquity of Indian culture'.[45]

The publication of Creuzer's four-volume *Symbolik* in 1810–1812 (and an expanded version in 1819–1821) added further weight to the new Orientalist case, since his huge scholarly erudition and rigor—typical for works claiming the status

[42] Hegel (2009, p. 83).

[43] Pinkard (2000, p. 373).

[44] Williamson (2006, pp. 147–154).

[45] Williamson (2006, p. 150).

of *Wissenschaft*—simply could not be ignored. Creuzer's central argument was that Greek religion and mythology were derivative, having borrowed key aspects from Egypt, India and Persia.[46] Drawing on Herodotus' claim that the Greek Gods had Egyptian origins, Creuzer suggested that representatives of the Indian and Egyptian priestly castes had actually migrated to Greece via Thrace and transmitted their revealed religion to the indigenous population[47]; hence, in Creuzer's account, the Greek religion was adopted as a result of migration, rather than through seafaring Greeks importing foreign ideas. This claim enraged philhellenists, classical philologists and Romantics alike. If this was not enough, Creuzer also claimed that Judaism and Christianity had their origins in an ancient Indian monotheism. At the start of the nineteenth century, the suggestion that German culture, as a Christian culture, was ultimately founded on religious symbols revealed to ancient Hindus was simply unacceptable. For Johann Heinrich Voss (1751–1826), a classicist and supporter of the Enlightenment, Creuzer's focus on ancient India was tantamount to treason, and his emphasis on eroticism and sexual imagery were scandalous.[48]

At the same time, another aspect of Creuzer's book infuriated German Romantics, who saw mythology as a counterbalance to the Enlightenment's emphasis on Reason and Universalism. In Creuzer's reconstruction, Greek religion and mythology were depicted as impoverished derivatives of a monotheistic Indian religion. The original revelations had been communicated to Indian priests in pure symbolic forms, but when these priests migrated to Greece, 'the symbols had to be adjusted to the crude native polytheism and demand for stories or myths'.[49] Creuzer thus undermined one of the central tenets of German Romanticism, propounded by Herder and Fichte, namely that distinct nations or peoples (*Volk*) exist and are expressed primarily through language, with the German nation holding a unique place among them.

Firstly, Creuzer's account does not merely propose that Greek mythology borrowed from Oriental sources, a view that was broadly compatible with German Romanticism; it actually suggests that the transmission of religion resulted from migration and the mingling of races and peoples. Secondly, Creuzer's model downgrades the status of language, which was primary in the Romantic conception of *Volk*. According to Creuzer, the divine originally revealed itself in 'dark, portentous symbols':

> Such symbols or pictographs preserve the wondrous primal union of spirit and matter. Image, precedes speech, then, as symbols precede myth or narration. Or put most drastically, the symbolic or direct contemplation of spirit precedes or is higher than indirect *told* or narrated stories about the gods. Symbols directly show mystic oneness, myths portray this through human action and history; symbols teach monotheism, myths polytheism.[50]

On this model, if the fundamental truth of monotheism is indeed symbolic and premythological, then mythology must be understood as reflecting the disintegration of

[46] Stewart (2018, p. 34).

[47] Williamson (2006, p. 151).

[48] Stewart (2018, pp. 35–36) and Williamson (2006, p. 152).

[49] Creuzer (2000, p. 387).

[50] Creuzer (2000, p. 388).

monotheism—an issue that Schelling grappled with for decades.[51] Thus, rather than offering classicist scholars and Romantic poets a source of primordial religious truth, Creuzer's depiction of mythology instead provides proof of the loss of unity and the emergence of multiplicity.

Creuzer employs binary imagery of darkness and light to argue that 'all Greek poetry draws a most decisive line between the shadowy indefiniteness of Near Eastern worship and the bright and variously formed warrior of the mythical gods'. The bright mirror of Homeric poetry reveals the actions of mankind and the gods, but on the other side of this mirror lies the darkness of the forgotten; clarity emerges from forgetfulness: 'What the Near East had taught and practiced, partly openly, partly esoterically, was forgotten by the Greeks amid the full clarity of their Olympus'. In its Homeric form, Greek religion embodies a shift from the 'old peace and Asiatic contemplativeness' to legends focused on action and a multiplicity of actors, the deeds of heroes and gods.[52]

A key component of Creuzer's historical analysis was the emphasis he placed on the relationship between religion and society. He credits Homeric poetry with unifying Greek religion for a century. However, when the 'old royal houses disappeared' and were succeeded by citizen lawgivers who established free constitutions, the role of religion in society was reshaped:

> This transformation of the nature of the community had great effects on the spirit of religion. The performance of devotions became one with the claims of the state, and the organization both of the holy choral dances and of the drama was at the same time a fulfillment of the duties of citizens. So tragedy and comedy, deriving anciently from the old worship of nature, now betray such a public and external spirit.[53]

With the emergence of the state, or *polis*, religion was subjected to further fragmentation, as each state employed legends 'to promote the renown of the city'. Based on this model of disintegration, Creuzer casts the emergence of Ionian philosophy as an attempt to regain the lost unity of the original monotheism:

> Cultivated men, wearied by the confusion into which the One and the Divine had been splintered, expressed healthy doubts, complained about the innumerable and absurd myths and—distinguished by an honest spirt of enquiry—departed from the vulgarities of the mob. These were the masters of old Ionian philosophy who had grasped the harm being done to religion and philosophy by the tyranny of Homeric poetry through the entrenched power of myth.[54]

Creuzer's book—with its radical conception of Greek myths as polytheistic narratives in a derivative relationship to a monotheistic symbolic core, as the hollow linguistic disintegration of a lost unity; with its challenge to the Philhellenic neohumanism that had prevailed in German classical scholarship since the times of Winckelmann; and with its challenges to the notions of European racial purity and supremacy and its undermining of the Romantic notion of *Volk*—provoked

[51] Schelling (2007).

[52] Creuzer (2000, pp. 390–391).

[53] Creuzer (2000, p. 391).

[54] Creuzer (2000, p. 391).

widespread intellectual outrage. The controversy surrounding Creuzer broke disciplinary boundaries: aside from classical philologists like Voss, Christian August Lobeck (1781–1860), and Karl Otfried Müller (1797–1840), philosophers such as Humboldt, Schelling, and Hegel all felt compelled to express a position on the Creuzer affair.

As Jon Stewart points out, Hegel's reference to Creuzer as 'my friend' and his acknowledgment of Creuzer's contributions in other works, such as the *Lectures on the Philosophy of History*[55] and *Aesthetics: Lectures on Fine Arts*,[56] constitute a public declaration of Hegel's allegiance regarding 'the Creuzer Affair'.[57] Hegel was clearly influenced by Creuzer's account of religion and mythology being transmitted between societies, and by Creuzer's conception of a primordial, unified monotheism that fragmented into multiplicity. However, in the *Lectures on the History of Philosophy*, Hegel also explicitly rejects a key aspect of Creuzer's thought, namely its interdisciplinary character.

In the Introduction to the *Lectures*, Hegel refers to Creuzer when, after discussing the differences between religion and philosophy, he broaches the question of whether mythology can be included in the history of philosophy. He writes:

> The first point concerns mythology as such, which is said to contain implicit philosophical themes [*Philosopheme*]; to that extent mythology may be considered in the history of philosophy. My friend Creuzer is renowned for his special project of treating the mythology or, in general, the religious representations, of all peoples, so as to recognize the philosophical themes or the rational element in them.[58]

Since Hegel is engaged in disciplinary demarcation at this point—justifying his exclusion of various forms of cultural production from the history of philosophy—Creuzer's 'special project' can be read as one that blurs disciplinary boundaries.

When Creuzer's *Symbolik* was first published, and even at the time of its second edition, philology was still an amorphous field—one which would eventually branch into more narrowly defined disciplines, such as literary criticism, textual criticism, historical studies, classical studies, and Oriental studies. In purely methodological terms, Creuzer's project clashed with the historicist, text-critical approach then prevailing in north-German philology, since it incorporated ideas from secular history and aesthetics and proposed novel conceptions of language that would later fall under linguistics and semiotics.[59] So, another controversial aspect of Creuzer's *Symbolik* was precisely its interdisciplinary character.

Had Hegel accepted Creuzer's methodology and conception of human thought, it would have required adopting a continuous approach to mythology and philosophy, rather than a discontinuous one. This would mean that the history of philosophy would have had to begin with the rational elements contained in myths—or

[55] Hegel (2011, pp. 217–218).

[56] Hegel (1975, pp. 310–311).

[57] Stewart (2018, p. 37).

[58] Hegel (2009, p. 83).

[59] Marchand (1996, p. 45), Stewart (2018, p. 36) and Williamson (2006, pp. 153–154).

'theomyths (*Theomythien*)' as Creuzer termed them. Thus, Hesiod's *Theogony* could have been treated as a text that contained discrete but implicit philosophical elements, such as logical development and rational arguments (see Chap. 6).

However, despite Hegel's evident sympathy for Creuzer's project, he establishes a firm disciplinary boundary, insisting that mythology be excluded from the history of philosophy. In a typically complex strategy, Hegel reinforces this boundary indirectly, by critiquing Creuzer's critics. While Creuzer's opponents argued that his methodology was 'unhistorical'—here Hegel probably had Voss in mind—suggesting that he had 'read into' his material, or projected rationality into ancient mythology, Hegel acknowledges Creuzer's claim that rationality is present in mythology, and at the same time praises his methodology:

> The religions of the various peoples, and their mythologies too, are products of rational human beings who have set down in mythology their highest consciousness, a consciousness of what is true. It follows in any event that mythology does contain reason, thoughts, general insights and determinations, in short, what one calls 'philosophical themes'. [...] All religions, no matter how natural, simple, or childish they may seem, are products of the reason that is becoming self-conscious, however meager their religious configurations may still be. So Creuzer should be acknowledged for employing the methodology that is, in and for itself, authentic and essential.[60]

Since Hegel concedes that mythology and religion contain philosophical themes, he must rely on another strategy to exclude them from philosophy. He adopts a distinction between implicit thought (entangled with sensuous imagery) and explicit thought:

> It is not our task to deal with philosophical themes as such, that is, with general ways of representing what is true or with thoughts presented in just any fashion. Instead we deal with thoughts that are out in the open [*heraus sind*] and only to the extent that they are out in the open—only insofar as religion has attained consciousness in the form of thought [... *die Religion hat, in der Form des Gedankens zum Bewußtsein gekommen ist*]. This is a momentous distinction. Reason is present in the child too, but in the child it is merely the capacity for reason; in the history of philosophy, however, we are dealing with its form, with the fact that this content is set forth in the form of thought. Philosophical themes contained implicitly in religion are not our concern.[61]

This 'momentous distinction' (*ungeheurer Unterschied*) thus significantly narrows the scope of philosophy: it encompasses only thought that is explicitly articulated in the form of thought, thereby excluding content that is implicitly conveyed through sensuous images or representations, as in religion, mythology, art, and poetry.

This exclusionary principle is further refined in Hegel's delineation of the relationship between Philosophy and scientific knowledge, which excludes natural philosophy from the history of Philosophy and self-differentiates German Philosophy from English Philosophy.[62] Hegel's comments on the broad content covered by other examples of 'Philosophy' in other contexts, and his contribution to the methodological controversy surrounding 'the Creuzer Affair', demonstrate that Hegel

---

[60] Hegel (2009, pp. 83–84).

[61] Hegel (2009, pp. 84–85).

[62] Hegel (2009, pp. 73–74).

was well aware of other disciplinary possibilities and forms that 'Philosophy' could assume.

Ultimately, Hegel's demarcation of Philosophy's exclusive domain is primarily a disciplinary assertion, a thought style positioning itself institutionally. Hegel's *Lectures on the History of Philosophy* are thus concerned with Philosophy as a *university discipline*, specifically as a German university discipline that seeks to differentiate itself from other fields, particularly philology and, more broadly, classical scholarship. By the 1820s, within the context of the German University, both philosophy and philology/classical studies had finally managed to break free from the long-standing oversight of the theological faculty.

8.5 The Evolving University Institution as a Determinant of Hegelian Thought

To understand Hegel's distinctions and demarcations within Philosophy, it is essential to situate his thought within the broader cultural and institutional context of the German University. These were not issues he addressed in isolation but within a landscape of competing academic disciplines and thought collectives. Indeed, Hegel's system, with its historical-determinist model of consciousness, acknowledges that the dominant preoccupations of an era pervade and unify its culture. In Hegelian terms, the singular, overarching spirit was 'thinking' and 'recognizing' content through the intersubjective consciousness of a wide network of individuals.[63]

However, certain theoretical approaches resolutely resist Hegel's systematic ambitions. For instance, his thought can be analysed through Fleck's theory of thought styles, Foucauldian discourse analysis, and Bourdieu's praxeological sociology of power (see Chap. 5)—each shedding light on different facets of Hegel's thought and texts. Fleck's theory[64] would suggest, firstly, that Hegel's perception of ancient Greek texts, mythology, religion, and philosophy was both guided and constrained by various thought collectives, particularly those operating within the Universities of Jena, Heidelberg, and Berlin; and, secondly, that the revolutionary mood and intellectual unrest allowed him, as a strong individual, to see new elements and aspects of ancient texts.

From a Foucauldian perspective,[65] Hegel's texts emerged as discursive productions that did not merely describe their objects but actively created them. Thus, professorial subjects within the institutional site of the German University produced discourses that shaped and delimited 'Philosophy', 'Greece', 'myth', 'the German Volk', and so forth. Applying Foucauldian discourse analysis—at least following its 1969 formulation—would track Hegelian references to *Bildung*, *Volk*, *Philosophie*,

[63] Hegel (2009, pp. 66–67).

[64] Fleck (1979).

[65] Foucault (1989, 1980).

etc., across the discursive field, examining relations between Hegel's statements and those of others to identify the rules and regularities constituting a discursive formation. One regularity, clearly articulated in references to 'philosophy' in the statements of Plato, Kant, and Hegel, is the use of distinctions and demarcations to supervise and control the field of knowledge production. Laclau and Mouffe's revision of Foucauldian discourse analysis[66] enables us to analyse such statements as products of articulatory practices that position a discourse antagonistically and relationally to other discourses in a constant striving for hegemony.

Finally, Bourdieu's sociology[67] would situate Hegel's philosophy within a pre-structured cultural field shaped by previous struggles over cultural capital. The German University—a source of significant prestige, authority, and power in Hegel's society—determined which positions could be articulated. Amidst the philosophy faculty's revolutionary rise, Hegel insisted on orthodox boundaries between disciplines. Creuzer's *Symbolik* attempted to occupy a heretical position within this field, posing an interdisciplinary challenge to established academic boundaries between religion, myth, and philosophy and provoking intense controversy. Hegel's response to Creuzer brought the might of purified Platonism to bear on this heretical position, giving full rein to the urge to control and reasserting Philosophy's role as the master discipline.

Historical events of the late eighteenth and early nineteenth centuries underscore the dramatic shifts in the role of the university and the philosophical faculties. In 1788, Wilhelm von Humboldt, alongside his brother Alexander, transferred from the Prussian University at Frankfurt-on-Oder to the University of Göttingen to study jurisprudence, also enrolling in the theological seminar 'not because he wished to become a pastor, but because that seminar taught the newly fashionable classical sciences in an unparalleled way'.[68] Thus, classical philology—one of the fields shaping Hegel's *Bildung* concept—was at that time under the aegis of the theological faculty. Christian Gottlieb Heyne's philological seminar at Göttingen embodied a neo-humanist approach to education and introduced students to the concept of *Bildung* (understood as cultural and self-formation) that Hegel would come to consider fundamental in his reading of Greek culture and the Sophists.[69] Humboldt's fascination with *Bildung*, shaped by his time in Jena, Paris, and Rome, would drive him to spearhead educational reforms and establish the University of Berlin in 1809. Under the influence of Schiller and Fichte, Humboldt aimed to 'join "objective *Wissenschaft*" with "subjective *Bildung*"'[70] in a vision of the university as an instrument of national renewal and identity.[71] Although philosophy was to be the 'queen

[66] Laclau and Mouffe (1985).

[67] Bourdieu (1991, 1993).

[68] McClelland (1980, p. 112).

[69] McClelland (1980, p. 62).

[70] Hofstetter (2001, p. 106).

[71] Kwiek (2006).

of the sciences' in this institution, classical studies also played a crucial role in Humboldt's vision, exemplified by his efforts to employ Friedrich August Wolf.[72]

The development of classical philology into a scientifically rigorous discipline was another milestone in the institutional consolidation of German academic culture. While Heyne is credited with treating the study of Greek mythology as *wissenschaftlich* (scientific),[73] it was Wolf who introduced the term *Altertumswissenschaft* (the scientific study of antiquity) and established Germany's first department for classical philology at the University of Halle (1783–1807).[74] Wolf's attempt to demonstrate that philology could be conducted scientifically provides a clear example of Fleck's notion that ideas can revolutionize thought when applied in new disciplinary settings. Inspired by the empirical rigor and mathematical deduction of English natural philosophy, particularly as exemplified by Newtonian physics, Wolf applied these principles to antiquity, using literary texts, inscriptions, and coins to establish factual knowledge about ancient Greece and Rome.[75]

Moreover, Wolf's contribution extended to the Romantic concept of *Volk*. For Wolf, while natural science produced knowledge of nature, philology provided insights into ancient human cultures:

> The philologist's goal is the knowledge of ancient man himself. Examining the remains of antiquity, he achieves an "organically developed" picture of the national character of the Greeks and the Romans and so learns about human nature itself: "its original powers and tendencies, and all the restrictions and limitations [which act upon them]."[76]

This shift toward defining distinct peoples and national spirit, found in Wolf's *Darstellung der Altertumswissenschaft* (1807), reflects the growing nationalism of German scholars during the Napoleonic Wars.[77] By this time, universal humanism, which had characterized the French-led Enlightenment, had shifted to a preoccupation with peoples and national identity.

In this historical context, three core concepts—*Bildung*, *Wissenschaft*, and *Volk*—emerged as key forces shaping Hegel's thought style and his approach to Greek culture and philosophy. While some of these concepts were championed by neo-humanist figures in philology, such as Creuzer, and in educational reform, such as Immanuel Niethammer, these thought collectives left an indelible mark on Hegel's philosophical work. Despite his reliance on these ideas, Hegel also carefully positioned Philosophy to maintain its unique status and role within the German University. Hegel's attempts to distinguish Philosophy as a distinct field—superior and separate from philology and broader classical studies—exemplify his strategic

[72] Hofstetter (2001, p. 105).

[73] Hofstetter (2001, p. 23).

[74] Stewart (2018, pp. 227–228).

[75] Bolter (1980, pp. 86–87).

[76] Bolter (1980, p. 87).

[77] Hofstetter (2001, p. 89).

stance: he sought to appropriate elements of other disciplines to serve Philosophy's systematic ends while rejecting their interdisciplinary methodologies.

In summary, while the Hegelian thought style was deeply indebted to other thought collectives for key concepts such as *Bildung*, Hegel drew disciplinary boundaries to maintain Philosophy's role as an autonomous master discipline within the German University. The following chapter will reconstruct the changing status of the philosophical faculty in relation to these broader institutional dynamics and its role in articulating the German Enlightenment, or *Aufklärung*.

8.6 Conclusion

Hegel's concept of *Bildung*, framed as an evolution of Greek *paideia*, represents a deliberate effort to position philosophy as a distinct and preeminent discipline. This project was deeply shaped by the institutional structures and ideological currents of the early nineteenth-century German University, including the aftermath of the Napoleonic Wars, the Prussian Reform Movement, and the Humboldtian educational reforms.

This chapter, drawing on Ludwik Fleck's theory of thought collectives, has examined how Hegel's reconstruction of Greek philosophy operated within the intellectual constraints and opportunities of his era. His critique of Creuzer's *Symbolik*, alongside his strict differentiation between mythology, religion, poetry, and philosophy, was not merely theoretical but part of a broader strategy to assert philosophy's institutional autonomy and reinforce its claim to intellectual supremacy.

At the heart of Hegel's notion of *Bildung* lies an effort to define a modern German identity through a synthesis of Christian theological principles, civic ideals, and the cultural prestige of Greek antecedents. Greek *paideia*, in Hegel's system, appears as a preliminary stage in the development of the world spirit, hindered by what he described as a 'religion of fancy' and lacking the structural coherence of the Christian-Germanic synthesis. By reframing *paideia* as a kind of proto-*Bildung*, Hegel sought to articulate a vision of modern subjectivity grounded in rational statehood and philosophical self-awareness.

Hegel's demarcation of philosophy from other forms of cultural production—particularly his exclusion of myth and poetry—was as much an act of institutional self-assertion as it was a methodological clarification. His insistence on philosophy as a domain of explicit thought reflects both his intellectual commitments and his engagement with the institutional dynamics of the German University.

Hegel's efforts to position philosophy as the master discipline were shaped by the evolving status of the philosophical faculty within this institutional framework. These developments, and the philosophical faculty's rise to intellectual authority, form the focus of the next chapter. By tracing its medieval origins, its transformations during the Reformation, and its role in shaping *Bildung* as a contested concept, the next chapter situates Hegel's project within the broader history of the German University as a determinant of cultural and intellectual production.

References

Bolter J (1980) Friedrich August Wolf and the scientific study of antiquity. Greek, Roman and Byzantine Studies, pp 83–99

Bourdieu P (1991) Language and symbolic power. Polity Press, Cambridge

Bourdieu P (1993) The field of cultural production. Columbia University Press, New York

Creuzer GF (2000) Excerpt from symbolism and mythology of ancient peoples. In: Feldman B, Richardson R (eds) The rise of modern mythology, 1680–1860. Indiana University Press, Bloomington, pp 390–396

Fleck L (1979) Genesis and development of a scientific fact [1935]. The University of Chicago Press, Chicago

Fleck L (1986) The problem of epistemology [1936]. In: Cognition and fact. Boston studies in the philosophy of science, vol 87. Springer, Dordrecht. https://doi.org/10.1007/978-94-009-4498-5_5

Foucault M (1980) Truth and power. In: Gordon C (ed) Power/knowledge. Selected interviews and other writings 1972–1977. Harvester Press, Hemel Hempstead, pp 109–133

Foucault M (1989) The archaeology of knowledge (1969), trans. Sheridan Smith, A. M. Routledge, London

Gregor MJ (1979) Translator's introduction. In: Kant I (ed) The conflict of the faculties. Anaris Books, New York, pp vii–xxxiv

Hegel GW (1975) Aesthetics, lectures on fine art, trans. Knox, T. M. Oxford University Press, Oxford

Hegel GW (1986) Vorlesungen über die Geschichte der Philosophie I. Suhrkamp, Frankfurt am Main

Hegel GW (1995) Lectures on the history of philosophy (trans: Haldane ES). Bison, Nebraska

Hegel GW (2006) Lectures on the history of philosophy volume II, trans. Brown, R. F. and Stewart, J. M. Clarendon Press, Oxford

Hegel GW (2009) Lectures on the history of philosophy volume I, trans. Brown, R. F. and Stewart, J. M. Clarendon Press, Oxford

Hegel GW (2011) Lectures on the philosophy of history, trans. Alvarado, R. Wordbridge, Aalten

Hofstetter MJ (2001) The romantic idea of a university England and Germany, 1770–1850. Palgrave, New York

Kant I (1979) The conflict of the faculties, trans. Gregor, M. J. Abaris, New York

Kelley DR (1997) The problem of knowledge and the concept of discipline. In: Kelley D (ed) History and the discipline. University of Rochester Press, New York, pp 13–28

Kwiek M (2006) The Classical German Idea of the University Revisited, or on the Nationalization of the Modern Institution. CPP RPS Volume 1

Laclau E, Mouffe C (1985) Hegemony and socialist strategy. Verso, London

Marchand SL (1996) Down from Olympus: archaeology and philhellenism in Germany, 1750–1970. Princeton University Press, Princeton

McClelland CE (1980) State, society and university in Germany 1700–1914. Cambridge University Press, Cambridge

Perilli L (2018) The Presocractics. In: Taormina L (ed) Ancient philosophy: textual paths and historical explorations. Routledge, New York, pp 103–215

Pinkard T (2000) Hegel. A biography. Cambridge University Press, Cambridge

Plato (1967) Protagoras. In: Plato in twelve volumes, Vol. 3, transl, Lamb, W.R.M. Harvard University Press, Cambridge, MA

Schelling FW (2007) Historical-critical introduction to the philosophy of mythology (1842). State University of New York Press, Albany

Stewart J (2018) Hegel's interpretation of the religions of the world. Oxford University Press, Oxford

Tubbs N (2008) Education in Hegel. Continuum, London

Williamson GS (2006) Gods, titans, and monsters: philhellenism, race, and religion in early-nineteenth-century mythography. In: Eigen S, Larrimore M (eds) The German invention of race. State University of New York Press, Albany, pp 147–166

Chapter 9
The Rise of the Philosophical Faculty in the German University

Abstract This chapter examines the philosophical faculty's rise in the German university, tracing its development from a subordinate preparatory faculty to a distinct intellectual force. Beginning with the medieval foundations of German universities, it explores the arts faculty's marginalized yet indispensable role within the traditional four-faculty model and the influence of the Reformation. Particular attention is given to Melanchthon's synthesis of Renaissance humanism and Lutheran theology, which laid early conceptual groundwork for *Bildung* as an educational ideal linked to civic and state service.

The chapter then investigates the transformative reforms at Halle and Göttingen in the seventeenth and eighteenth centuries. At Halle, the confluence of Pietist educational reforms, the waning authority of the theological faculty, and the ascendancy of Christian Wolff's rationalist philosophy fostered conditions for the philosophical faculty to begin asserting a more autonomous role. At Göttingen, by contrast, curricular innovations in classical studies advanced *Bildung* as a neo-humanist programme of self-cultivation. These reforms redefined the faculty's purpose, while debates over education's utility and cultural value exposed tensions between practicality and humanistic ideals.

The evolution of *Bildung* is traced from its religious origins in Meister Eckhart's mysticism, through its transformation by Pietist introspection, to its rearticulation within Enlightenment and neo-humanist frameworks. Shaftesbury's philosophy of politeness—appropriated and reshaped in the German context—played a formative role in Herder's vision of *Bildung*. Drawing on Fleck's theory, the chapter analyses how *Bildung* was adapted by competing thought collectives, reflecting the transformation of religious and classical traditions into new forms of philosophical self-understanding.

S. Dersley, *Thought Collectives and Cultural Change*, Living Signs of Law 1,
https://doi.org/10.1007/978-3-031-97431-1_9

9.1 The Founding of German Universities: Secular Endowment

According to Friedrich Paulsen's classic *The German Universities and University Study* (1885), secularization is what distinguishes the first German universities, founded in the fourteenth century, from their French and Italian counterparts, which had been founded in the twelfth and fourteenth centuries. While the latter evolved spontaneously and later acquired the status of public legal corporations, German universities were intentionally established by territorial governments, with autonomy, rights, and exemptions granted by the local ruler.[1] Paulsen asserts that the secular endowment of German universities marked the beginning of the secularization of instruction and knowledge in late-medieval Germany.[2]

However, In *Protestant Theology and the Making of the Modern University* (2006), Thomas Howard, drawing on Overfield's (1984) work,[3] explicitly questions Paulsen's secularization thesis, arguing that the German universities did indeed have religious missions:

> [...] all faculty members were also members of religious orders or had received some form of clerical training in monasteries or cathedral schools. University routines and rituals were, in large measure, modelled after life in the cloister. Papal bulls recognizing universities assumed that knowledge was the business of the church. It is thus most accurate to regard the earliest German universities, although no longer ecclesial in the strictest sense, as religious institutions in the broadest sense and therefore as key agents of cultural unity in the world of medieval Christendom.[4]

In Overfield and Howard's reconstructions, the fact that German universities were founded by princes and local governments would come to have significant repercussions during the Reformation. With the rise of territorial-confessional states, the autonomy of universities became increasingly restricted.

The issue of the secularization of knowledge is thus complex. If the German universities can be described as broadly religious institutions prior to the Reformation, it can be argued that they became *fundamentally* religious in the sixteenth and seventeenth centuries. Territorial-confessional states established their own universities and exerted direct control over theological faculties, making appointments contingent on oaths of confessional fidelity. The theological faculties, in turn, exerted authority over the other faculties, for instance through the practice of censorship (*Censurrecht*).[5]

If the secularization of instruction and knowledge is understood as the process by which the education system—its institutions, professoriate, teaching staff, curricula, and texts—is freed from the control of religious authority (whether in the form

---

[1] Paulsen (1906, p. 16).

[2] Paulsen (1906, p. 27).

[3] Overfield (1984).

[4] Howard (2006, p. 50).

[5] Howard (2006, pp. 46, 109).

of Catholic or Protestant churches, theological faculties, or rulers enforcing ecclesiastical orthodoxy), evidence suggests that this process was not achieved in Germany until the late seventeenth and early eighteenth centuries, driven by the policies of progressive rulers. Direct evidence of this secularization can be found in the statutes of the Universities of Halle (1692) and Göttingen (1734), which explicitly promoted tolerance and allowed for greater academic and teaching freedom.[6]

Nevertheless, when Hegel began his studies at Tübingen in 1788, on the eve of the French Revolution, universities like Tübingen remained very much under ecclesiastical control. As Terry Pinkard observes:

> Universities remained semifeudal "corporations," institutions governed by the professoriate, who were far more interested in exercising their inherited medieval privileges than in anything else, and who thus tended to resist strenuously all efforts to reform the universities. Moreover, like many other German universities, Tübingen maintained an idea of its educational mission as that of passing on orthodox, correct belief to its students, a pedagogical idea reinforced by the predominance of the theological faculty of the university.[7]

Although Pinkard's observation generalizes somewhat, neglecting developments at Halle, Göttingen, and Jena, historical scholarship agrees that these institutions stood out as progressive exceptions. By contrast, German universities in general had, by the seventeenth century, become the butt of jokes in Europe and the target of criticism from intellectuals such as Leibniz, Lessing, Goethe, and Schiller.[8]

Howard's description of fourteenth-century university life being 'modelled after life in the cloister' still held true four centuries later, when Hegel embarked on his studies in the theological faculty at Tübingen's seminary, on route to becoming a pastor:

> [...] The Protestant Seminary was built on the foundations of an older Augustinian seminary, and, for the duration of their studies, the students became in effect Protestant monks. They were required to wear long black coats (which vaguely resembled cassocks) with white cuffs and collars. The seminarians' hours were strictly regulated, and they were regularly scrutinized and watched. Failure to abide by the rules meant punishment, usually in the form of being deprived of one's ration of table wine for the day or being incarcerated in the student jail (the Karzer).[9]

9.2 Academic Structure and Hierarchy

In terms of structure, German universities adopted the Parisian four-faculty model: the lower arts faculty (*facultas artium*), later referred to as the 'philosophical faculty', and the three higher faculties of theology, law, and medicine. The function of the arts/philosophical faculty was to prepare students for the higher faculties, and

[6] Howard (2006, pp. 91–92, 106–109).

[7] Pinkard (2000, p. 19).

[8] Paulsen (1906, p. 42), McClelland (1980, p. 79) and Howard (2006, p. 81)

[9] Pinkard (2000, p. 21).

there was a particularly close connection between the philosophical and theological faculties—with the former subservient to the latter.[10]

The fact that the arts/philosophical faculty occupied the lowest rung of the university hierarchy was also evident in economic terms. Government funding and church subsidies for salaries were channelled to the higher faculties, and thus to a handful of professional theologians, jurists and physicians who tended to have other sources of income anyway. The teaching staff of the arts faculty was far more numerous, consisting of a few full-time lecturers on modest salaries, and students with teaching duties, all of whom had to rely on the fees they charged for extra, private tuition to make a living.[11]

This situation of economic deprivation persisted after the Reformation and into the early nineteenth century: the financial prospects for aspiring professional philosophers like Kant and Hegel were somewhat parlous in the early stages of their careers, when they worked as tutors and *Privatdozenten*—private, unpaid lecturers.[12]

To enter the theological faculty at a pre-Reformation German university, students were required to obtain a Master of Arts degree (*magister artium*). The Parisian scholastic curriculum was uniformly adopted at all German universities,[13] hence the bachelor's course was primarily focused on the mastery of scholastic logic, entailing the study of Aristotle's *Organon* (chiefly *Prior Analytics*, *Sophistical Refutations*, *Posterior Analytics*), while the study of grammar and Latin were of secondary importance: 'To be a "scholastic" was first and foremost to be a logician'.[14] On the master's course, students were introduced to Aristotle's other works (*Politics*, *Metaphysics*, *Economics* etc.) and Euclid's Geometry.[15] Only after many years of study under the philosophy faculty could candidates finally enter the higher faculties. According to Howard, the entire curriculum entailed 16 years of study, and a doctorate in theology was typically not awarded until the age of 35.[16]

Hence, on the one hand, teachers of the arts/philosophy faculty were explicitly assigned the lowest position in the university hierarchy (e.g., in public processions they had to walk behind the doctors from the theology, law, and medicine faculties).[17] On the other hand, their teaching of logic and philosophical works was essential for the higher faculties, particularly the theological faculty. In real terms, this meant that 'teachers of the arts were the cornerstone of the university',[18] and at the same time constituted an exploited economic class, in terms of remuneration for their intellectual labour.

---

[10] Howard (2006, pp. 53–56).

[11] Paulsen (1906, pp. 19–20) and Overfield (1984, p. 18).

[12] Paulsen (1902, p. 35) and Pinkard (2000, pp. 45–52, 106).

[13] Overfield (1984, pp. 27–28).

[14] Overfield (1984, p. 44).

[15] Overfield (1984, pp. 29–43).

[16] Howard (2006, pp. 56–57).

[17] Overfield (1984, p. 26).

[18] Overfield (1984, p. 26).

9.3 The First Wave of Reform: The Reformation

In Paulsen's outline, a second wave of German universities appeared in response to the Renaissance-humanistic movement (e.g. Freiburg—1460, Tübingen—1477, Wittenberg—1502). These foundations were soon followed by far-reaching curricular changes, such as the abandonment of scholastic Latin in favour of classical or humanistic Latin and—most importantly for these considerations—the inclusion of the study of the ancient Greek language and literature. The first German scholars of Greek were given positions at German universities during this period, including Johann Reuchlin at Tübingen and Philip Melanchthon at Wittenberg.[19]

Howard points out that the Reformation began as a university event, instigated by a professor in the theological faculty at the University of Wittenberg, and Lewis W. Spitz argues that Martin Luther's Reformation would not have triumphed without the support of the universities.[20] While Luther insisted that nothing could be more wicked than 'unreformed universities', it was his friend, Melanchthon, who was to be tasked with designing and implementing educational reforms. Rejecting the anti-rationalist and anti-cultural elements of the Protestant Reformation, such as Luther's abhorrence for Aristotle, Melanchthon managed to synthesize the ideas of Renaissance humanism and Lutheran evangelical theology into a coherent philosophy of education for the German states.[21]

Melanchthon's allegiance to the humanist movement was made public in the inaugural address he gave at Wittenberg University in 1518, entitled *On Improving the Studies of Youth* (*De corrigendis adolescentiae studiis*). In this speech, the 21 year old Melanchthon recommended that 'Greek letters should be added to Latin, so that reading the philosophers, theologians, historians, orators, poets, wherever you turn, you may gain the very substance, not the shadow of things [...]', and advocated reading Homer and Plato in addition to Aristotle.[22] Two key elements of Renaissance Humanism were expressed here: firstly, the conviction that Greek authors had to be read in the original Greek, rather than in Latin translation, if the essence of their thought is to be grasped; and, secondly, that the study of Greek thought and writing must go beyond the narrow confines of Aristotelian scholasticism and embrace a range of 'pagan' authors and genres.

Moreover, in this oration Melanchthon also begins to give expression to an idea which in Fleck's terms could be seen as a proto-idea for the eighteenth-century concept of *Bildung*. After stressing the importance of history for public concerns and civil activities, Melanchthon offers a broader definition of philosophy:

> With the name "philosophy" I therefore include the science of nature, the principles and examples of behavior. Whoever has been properly imbued with these has secured for himself the way to the summit. The attorney at law will have the source for preparing an oration

---

[19] Paulsen (1906, pp. 29–30).

[20] Spitz (1984, p. 42) and Howard (2006, p. 62).

[21] Paulsen (1906, pp. 32–33).

[22] Melanchthon (1974).

> rich in content and forceful; the statesman the source from which he may acquire formulas for the peaceful, the good, the just …[23]

Here philosophy is defined broadly, as reflection on history, nature and behaviour which— crucially—has civic utility, since it can and should be applied and in the practice of law and statecraft. For Melanchthon, 'renascent studies' are aimed at 'cultivating good minds', but in the context of the German university—and this is where the emergent concept of *Bildung* can be detected—these good minds are prepared for service of the state.

The synthesis of Renaissance humanism and Reformation theology becomes even clearer in a later oration, entitled *On the Study of Languages*, given at Nuremberg in 1533, in which Melanchthon justifies the study of the Hebrew and Greek languages on University arts courses. First, he refers to both Erasmus and Luther in short succession to emphasize that knowledge of Holy Scripture is essential for the good young men that make up the state and country, and that knowledge of languages—the cornerstone of Erasmus's humanism—is indispensable for understanding the Scriptures and the will of God, and for the study of theology.[24] Second, Melanchthon insists that knowledge of Greek is crucial for understanding philosophy and Aristotle, thereby jettisoning scholastic Latin translations of 'the philosopher'. Third, he sets the path for German classical philology over the next three centuries, by asserting the supremacy of the Greek poets and historians over the Latin ones, due to their universal truths and practicality. Lastly, Melanchthon stresses the importance of Greek for the knowledge of medicine and law:

> Medicine is to a large extent Greek, and cannot be grasped without philosophy. And those who dedicate themselves to the law do not only strive to acquire the rhetoric of the law-court in order to apply it to their occupation, but they also seek a teaching that will be of use to the state and, as they themselves say, a philosophy that is not feigned. In order to protect themselves with dignity they will surely also need some other kind of teaching, that is, the knowledge of religion and of antiquity, eloquence and those writings which, because they contain the sources of laws, are no less often employed for deliberations on public duties than the laws themselves.[25]

A few points can be highlighted here: for Melanchthon the arts course served a purpose within 'the state', and he argued that ancient Greek and Greek philosophy should be essential components of this course. While the utility of ancient Greek and Greek philosophy for prospective theologians more apparent—since they are key to understanding Scripture and Aristotle—he also argues that these studies will benefit doctors and jurists, as they are the 'source' of medicine and law. The underlying suggestion in the oration is that incorporating Hellenic studies into the arts course would prepare students for the higher faculties and, ultimately, their professions, by fostering the essential general knowledge and intellectual awareness required for public service in the state, and in the service of the Church and God.

---

[23] Melanchthon (1974, p. 170).

[24] Melanchthon (2012, pp. 30–32).

[25] Melanchthon (2012, p. 34).

Once again, the explicit connection between the broad cultivation of young minds and their subsequent civic duty reinforces the argument that Melanchthon's nascent conception of education serving the state—when combined with a synthesis of Renaissance Humanism and Reformation theology—can be regarded as a proto-idea for the concept of *Bildung* that would emerge in the eighteenth century.

Paulsen goes as far as to assert that Melanchthon single-handedly laid the foundations for the later successes of German philosophy and science:

> It was primarily due to him that the Protestant half of Germany won the ascendency over Catholicism in the realm of education and culture. There can be no doubt whatever about the final outcome: German philosophy and science, German literature and culture grew up in the soil of Protestantism, and they may be described as the result, although perhaps remote, of that spirit of freedom and independence of thought which the Reformation called into being.[26]

However, this 'final outcome' would not be realized until the late eighteenth and early nineteenth century. According to Howard, Renaissance humanism and the Reformation led to significant changes in the curricula of German universities, but not their structure; thus it amounted to 'an alteration in university *content* but not *form*'.[27]

In the decades following Melanchthon's educational reforms, German universities and schools turned their back on the universality championed by the Renaissance, became more restrictive and inward-looking, and ultimately entered a period of decline that would last for centuries—until late in the eighteenth century. Among the complex cultural and political factors driving this process, the emergence of states defined by creed and the strengthening of territorial boundaries played a crucial role. In a nutshell, the Reformation and Counter-Reformation entailed that the German-speaking regions became a patchwork of variegated, competing states. Numerous universities were founded in both Protestant and Catholic states, Königsberg (1544) and Jena (1556) being famous examples of the former, and Dillingen (1549) being the prime example of the latter. Paulsen describes the emergence of these 'territorial-confessional universities' as follows:

> The chief impetus leading to these numerous foundations was the accentuation of the principle of territorial sovereignty from the ecclesiastical as well as the political point of view. The consequence was that the universities began to be *instrumenta dominationis* of the government as professional schools for its ecclesiastical and secular officials. Each individual government endeavored to secure its own university in order, in the first place to make sure of wholesome instruction, which meant, of course, instruction in harmony with the confessional standards of its established church; in the second place, to retain the training of its secular officials in its own hands; and, finally, render attendance at the foreign universities unnecessary on the part of its subjects, and to keep the money in the country.[28]

[26] Paulsen (1906, p. 33).

[27] Howard (2006, p. 60).

[28] Paulsen (1906, p. 36).

The rise of princely territorial states was concomitant with the growth of bureaucracies and a demand for public servants.[29] Hence, education and the universities primarily became tools for producing both the servants (*Beamte*) essential for the administration of the state—bureaucrats, jurists, and judges, as well as the pastors and churchmen necessary for maintaining the presence and authority of the church throughout the state. While the medical faculty remained the weakest of the higher faculties, the law faculty began its steady rise in importance and prestige during this period: from this time on, the state bureaucracy would come to operate as 'an independent entity, like the Church', the law faculty would open the door to the esoteric science of law and judges and jurists would become an increasingly privileged class.[30]

However, during this period of heightened religious passion and conflict following the Reformation, and then during the Counter-Reformation and the Thirty Years War, when denomination became a defining element of state identity—there was an increased need for theological expertise and justification. Consequently, the theological faculties tightened their grip on the universities, in both Protestant and Catholic states (with the latter supported by Jesuit colleges). Hence the previously noted argument that German universities can be characterized as fundamentally religious institutions during this period. Due to the pressing need for 'doctrinal purity', the theological faculties at reformed universities came to be dominated by 'protestant scholasticism', a method of philological and logical analysis that would prevail in German universities well into the eighteenth century.[31]

Howard suggests that following the Reformation the 'subservient role of the arts faculty' actually became more pronounced:

> In fact, under medieval scholasticism, all-important logic, though nominally the servant, regularly dictated the terms of theological study. Because of the Reformation, however, the imperatives of doctrinal purity (defined for Lutherans by the Augsburg Confession of 1530) and the practical exigencies of making the Reformation a social success (through the training of committed clergymen) reinforced the notion that time spent in the philosophical faculty was a mere prelude to serious theological study.[32]

In the philosophical faculty, the study of Aristotle—even when it included reading passages in Greek—remained fundamentally scholastic in its approach and was treated as purely preparatory for theological study.[33] The post-Reformation focus on doctrine ultimately meant that the supposedly humanistic study of philosophical texts was subordinated to theological concerns. Steven Ozment concludes: 'The humanities became for Protestant theologians what Aristotelian philosophy had been to late medieval theologians – the favoured handmaiden of theology; the rhetorical arts served the more basic task of communicating true doctrine'.[34]

---

[29] Spitz (1984, p. 48).

[30] Paulsen (1906, pp. 38–39), also Bruford (1935, p. 236).

[31] Howard (2006, p. 68).

[32] Howard (2006, p. 71).

[33] Paulsen (1906, p. 45).

[34] Ozment (1980, p. 315).

Despite Melanchthon's calls for the study of Greek and Hebrew, Bruford notes that Latin retained its dominance: as the tool for studying the Catechism, as the *lingua franca*, and as the model of eloquence. Thus, in the state grammar schools, such as the one in Württemberg where Hegel was educated,[35] over three centuries after Melanchthon's reforms, Latin remained the medium of instruction:

> Greek if taught at all was given far less attention. The only other important subject was religious instruction. The elements of rhetoric and dialectics, arithmetic and geometry, physics and cosmogony were thrown in, all taught in the medieval way. It will be seen that there was a very great deal in the school curriculum that had remained unchanged since the Middle Ages.[36]

Latin remained the language of instruction at all German universities until the foundation of the University of Halle in 1694. This institution was strongly influenced by developments in France, such as the growing fashion for the use of vernacular French in court circles and the salons, which at this time were the centres of intellectual activity in France rather than the universities.

In English and French Philosophy a decisive break had been made from scholasticism in the first half of the seventeenth century, which was associated with the use of the vernacular in philosophical writings. While Francis Bacon's relentless critique of scholasticism was delivered in Latin, for instance in *Novum Organum* (1620), subsequent ground-breaking works—such as Thomas Hobbes's *Leviathan* (1651), Robert Boyle's *The Sceptical Chymist* (1661) and John Locke's *An Essay Concerning Human Understanding* (1689)—were all written in English. Similarly, René Descartes used vernacular French to deliver his personal and accessible attack on 'the schools' in *Discours de la Méthode* (1637). Crucially, these philosophical innovations largely took place outside the universities, often in opposition to them (see Chap. 11).

In Germany, however, no equivalent break occurred in the seventeenth century. This was due to the disastrous impact of the Thirty Years' War (1618–1648) on the German states and the continued dominance of Protestant scholasticism in its universities. Gottfried Wilhelm Leibniz cuts a rather odd figure in this regard. After earning his doctorate in law from the University of Altdorf in 1666, Leibniz declined a professorship,[37] began his autodidactic scientific studies in Paris and London, gravitated towards scientific societies and court circles, and treated German universities and scholarship with disdain.[38] In 1700, he founded the *Kurfürstlich Brandenburgische Sozietät der Wissenschaften* (Society of Sciences of the Elector

---

[35] When Leibniz began his formal education at the Leipzig Latin school in 1653, the study of Latin dominated the first three classes, amounting to 24 h per week, and Greek was not introduced until the fourth class: 'Whereas teacher and pupils were required to speak Latin within the confines of the school, instruction in such disciplines as ethics, physics, and astronomy was restricted to four hours per week during the final year' (Antognazza 2009, p. 31).

[36] Bruford (1935, p. 241).

[37] Antognazza (2009, p. 66).

[38] Howard (2006, p. 81).

of Brandenburg) as an alternative to the universities.[39] He also wrote his philosophical works in French and Latin rather than in German.

Nevertheless, it could be argued that Leibniz never fully abandoned the Protestant scholasticism of his youth: unlike Descartes, Leibniz did not abandon the rigour of Aristotelian scholasticism. Indeed, his philosophy could be described as a synthesis of scholasticism with the new science that was emerging in England and France.[40] It was not until the works of Christian Wolff appeared in the eighteenth century—works written in German and later translated into Latin—that a definitive break from the scholastic philosophy was effected in German Philosophy.[41] Significantly, Wolff's decision to write and publish in German was part of a desire to 'educate and enlighten a broader public' beyond the university walls.[42]

9.4 The Second Wave of Reform: Halle and Göttingen

9.4.1 The University of Halle

The University of Halle was founded in 1694 with the explicit aim of addressing the failings and widespread decline in German Universities. It grew out of a practically oriented *Ritterakademie*, an alternative educational institution to universities which prepared young men for careers in the military and state administration. When Halle was established as a university, several factors played a decisive role in shaping the distinct characteristics of its philosophical faculty.

Firstly, the theological faculty was strongly influenced by Pietism rather than Protestant scholasticism and was therefore more focused on 'worldly engagement' than 'scholastic subtlety'. This granted the other faculties greater freedom to provide instruction with more practical relevance, ostensibly enabling them to better meet the needs of the state and society. Consequently, the university 'attracted law students from the wealthier classes from all over Germany'.[43] This marked a decisive shift from the dominance of Protestant scholasticism, which emphasized the training of clergy and theologians, to a more utilitarian model of education that addressed the growing demand for educated bureaucrats and state officials.

Secondly, the Brandenburg state revoked the privileges of the medieval university in order to implement a policy of religious tolerance and prevent the kind of doctrinal controversies that had driven students away from the universities of neighbouring principalities. This policy of tolerance was expressly stipulated in the university's statutes:

---

39 Paulsen (1906, p. 42).

40 Antognazza (2009, pp. 37, 46–47) and Hösle (2017, pp. 44–45).

41 Paulsen (1906, p. 45).

42 Saine (1997, p. 125).

43 McClelland (1980, pp. 34–35).

> Indeed, the very first statute of the university explicitly called for the four faculties to live in harmony with one another and stipulated that no faculty attempt to suppress another. Each faculty was supposed to concern itself only with matters appropriate to it; therefore, a law professor should not venture into theology or vice versa. Yet within the individual faculties, the statutes granted more teaching freedom.[44]

Thus, the power of the theological faculty was explicitly curtailed. Although the faculty retained its power of censorship, and professors were still required to take an oath of confessional loyalty, the theological faculty was the 'first faculty' in name only.[45]

Thirdly, due to its progressive stance, the university attracted leading reformers or 'progressives'. These included Christian Thomasius (1655–1728), who had been reprimanded in Leipzig for lecturing in German rather than Latin; the Pietist August Hermann Francke (1663–1727); and, above all, the towering figure of the German Enlightenment—the philosopher Christian Wolff (1679–1754), who, according to Bruford, succeeded and 'displaced' Melanchthon in his impact on German education.[46]

In Paulsen's account, Wolff's work at Halle marks the definitive break from scholasticism in German philosophy and constitutes the beginning of 'modern philosophy' in the German University:

> The aim of philosophical instruction up to this time had been to inculcate the scholastic Aristotelianism, primarily as a preparation for the study of theology. The new philosophy now defiantly appealed to its own reason. Wolff's *Verniinftige Gedanlien*, the general title of his German works, positively denies the dependence of philosophy upon theology. Basing himself upon the modern sciences of mathematics and physics, he declares that philosophy should seek the truth free from all assumptions, regardless of what may happen to the theologians. Similarly as in the case of theoretical philosophy, the theological basis of practical philosophy was also positively repudiated: law and morals, he declared, must be based upon a rational knowledge of human life and society.[47]

Wolff's deterministic philosophy tested the limits of the tolerance stipulated in the university statutes, culminating in the famous events of 1723, when Francke and the theological faculty petitioned the King of Prussia to expel Wolff from Halle on the grounds that his teachings 'contradicted revealed religion'. Friedrich Wilhelm I complied: Wolff was forced to leave the city, and his writings were banned in Prussia and other German states.[48] Wolff thus became the first of a series of German philosophers—including Kant and Fichte—who would come into direct conflict with the theological faculty and face penalties or reprimands as a result. As Howard notes, Wolff explicitly championed the philosophical faculty and rejected its subordinate, propaedeutic role:

---

[44] Howard (2006, p. 92).

[45] Howard (2006, p. 92).

[46] Bruford (1935, pp. 242–243).

[47] Paulsen (1906, p. 45).

[48] Howard (2006, p. 96).

> 'The philosophical faculty,' he wrote, 'has hitherto been regarded merely as that which prepares young people for the other faculties of theology, law, and medicine.... [I]t is called the lower faculty and the others the higher faculties. But this prejudice must be done away with, and one must regard the philosophical faculty not merely as a lower one, but also as a higher one' (*sondern auch als eine Obere Facultät*).[49]

Wolff's eventual reinstatement at Halle by Frederick the Great in 1740 marked a significant victory in the philosophical faculty's ongoing struggles with the theological faculty. It also represented a triumph for the German Enlightenment and the broader process of secularization, ultimately paving the way for Kant to assert further claims for the remit and authority of philosophy in his *Critiques*.

One notable consequence of the curricular reforms at Halle was the neglect of humanistic studies—driven by an emphasis on practical education and Prussian organizational efficiency on the one hand, and Wolff's focus on natural philosophy, mathematics, and Reason on the other. While the practical utility of subjects such as law, statecraft, economics, modern languages, and the natural sciences was undeniable, this modernizing trend severely undermined the study of the classics, which had been a cornerstone of German education since Melanchthon's time.[50] Interest in ancient Greece and the Greek language, which would become essential to Hegel's conception of philosophy, only began to revive in the latter half of the eighteenth century, particularly at the University of Göttingen.

9.4.2 The University of Göttingen

Following Halle's example, the University of Göttingen was also established with reform in mind, opening in 1734. According to McClellan, the curricular innovations were specifically aimed at attracting upper-class students who would pass though the law faculty, the 'backbone of the university', and take up careers in the state bureaucracy and courts. A university education became increasingly associated with enhanced social prestige, and Göttingen sought to combine the practical aspects of a *Ritterakademie* (courtly arts, equestrian skills, and modern languages) with a career-oriented university education, aiming to equip students with the specialist knowledge required to fulfil the functions of a civil servant. However, as discussed by Andre Wakefield, the extent to which this aim was fully realised remains debatable.[51] Nevertheless, some subjects taught within the philosophical faculty, such as history and modern languages, evidently gained clear practical utility for careers in fields like diplomacy, a fact reflected in the salaries of the professors who taught these subjects.[52]

---

[49] Howard (2006, p. 122).

[50] Bruford (1935, p. 243).

[51] Wakefield (2009).

[52] McClelland (1980, pp. 38–59).

Gerlach Adolph von Münchausen (1688–1770), the founder and curator of the university, insisted that the theological faculty should 'play a quiet role' at Göttingen and appointed 'doctrinally neutral professors of theology'.[53] As in the case of Halle, tolerance and a progressive approach were explicitly provided for in the university statutes. And, as at Halle, this curtailment of the theological faculty's historic privileges was counterbalanced by a rise in the status of the philosophical faculty. This allowed for the introduction of new subjects into the faculty's sphere, such as 'empirical psychology, natural law, politics, modern physics, mathematics, modern history, geography, diplomacy and modern languages'.[54]

Crucially, three areas that 'belonged' to the philosophical faculty were subject to curricular innovation: history, classical philology, and classical studies (or the study of antiquity, which would later become *Altertumwissenschaft*): 'At Göttingen, these subjects began a metamorphosis, whereby they ceased to be minor, subordinate (and often neglected) fields of study and began to take shape as autonomous "disciplines" in their own right'.[55] The development of these disciplines at Göttingen influenced the unique shape that German philosophy would take in the first decades of the nineteenth century, determining its focus: the preoccupation with history of philosophy, the textual analysis of philosophical concepts, and the focus on ancient Greece (rather than Rome, which was more typical of French and English scholarship).

Furthermore, as mentioned in the previous chapter, the discipline of classical philology at Göttingen was a key source of the neo-humanist approach to education and contributed to the development of the concept of *Bildung*. The principal classical philologists—who, it is worth noting, were members of the philosophical faculty—were Johann Matthias Gesner (1691–1761) and Christian Gottlob Heyne (1729–1812). Gesner downgraded the role of grammar in classical education and recommended that students should immerse themselves in reading the classics, in order to absorb 'broad intellectual nourishment from the aesthetic, moral, and cultural sensibilities present in Greek and Roman literature'.[56] Heyne placed an emphasis on culture: classical texts should be treated as sources of information and insight into aspects of ancient culture, such as religion and civic life, which provide models for reflection and personal development.[57]

Hence, within the philosophy faculty, the study of the classics came to be viewed as an essential component of a man's education: to be 'cultivated' meant to have absorbed classical culture internally, into one's character and subjective worldview.[58] This marked a decisive shift from Melanchthon's conception of the role of classical learning in education. While Melanchthon viewed knowledge of ancient

[53] McClelland (1980, p. 39).
[54] Howard (2006, pp. 115–116).
[55] Howard (2006, p. 116).
[56] Howard (2006, p. 118).
[57] Howard (2006, pp. 118–119).
[58] Bruford (1935, p. 245).

Greek and the classics as useful for the state—enabling jurists and physicians to perform their duties objectively—classical studies at Göttingen emphasized the subjective benefits of students internalizing the knowledge gained from the classics through an 'inwardly oriented Bildung'.[59]

The sources and scholarship suggest that Göttingen was an institution whose purpose was the subject of intense debate. While the philosophy faculty pioneered innovative curricula, emphasizing character formation through classical learning, the cameralist officials overseeing the university and its town—ensuring, for instance, a plentiful supply of taverns[60] —primarily regarded students as a means to fill the coffers of the *Kammer*[61]:

> Göttingen had been designed and run as a financial and personnel resource for the state. One Göttingen graduate compared his alma mater to a royal factory: "You, Mr. Curator, are the factory director; the teachers at the university are workers; the young people studying and their parents... are the customers; the sciences taught are the wares. Your King is the master and owner of his [scholarly] factory." The university and its resources—faculty, students, scholarship—were goods to be managed and exploited by the state.[62]

Between 1768 and 1776, Johann David Michaelis, a biblical scholar and professor at Göttingen, published a four-volume critique of Protestant universities in Germany. He expressed disdain for the cameralist approach, which treated the university as a mechanism for advancing the fiscal interests of the state, and for the reduction of the university to 'a factory or glassworks designed to use up any excess wood'.[63] Evidently, both support for and opposition to this administrative and financial vision circulated within the university and shaped contemporary debates about its role.

When the University of Jena emerged as a centre of German Idealism and Romanticism in the late eighteenth century, critiques of this administrative and economic orientation grew sharper. Friedrich Schiller intensified and weaponized this opposition through his polemical articulation of a discursive 'us versus them' antagonism, which pitted philosophers—tasked with 'forming and educating themselves as human beings' (*sich als Menschen auszubilden*)—against the careerist 'bread scholars' (*Brodgelehrte*) of the legal, medical, and theological faculties, who, as Schiller put it, were primarily focused on securing material benefits and social status.[64]

---

[59] Horlacher (2017, pp. 5, 12–15). See also McClelland (1980, p. 60) The emphasis on *Bildung* as character development was not without its practical utility, however: the student community at German Universities in the seventeenth and eighteenth centuries was notorious for its drunkenness and brawling hence the cultivation of character leading to the improvement of students' behaviour could have immediate consequences.

[60] Menand et al. (2017, p. 23).

[61] Wakefield (2009).

[62] Menand et al. (2017, p. 14).

[63] Menand et al. (2017, p. 26).

[64] Schiller (2017, p. 32). The German text is available at: https://www.projekt-gutenberg.org/schiller/universl/universl.html.

I would argue that our understanding of Hegel's characterization of the Sophists as pre-Christian men of *Bildung* is deepened when we recognize that this radical reconception was inseparable from the fact that Hegel articulated his thought style—or, to adopt a more Foucauldian perspective, his subject positions and the discourse he produced—within the philosophy faculties of specific universities—Jena, Heidelberg, and Berlin—which occupied distinct and powerful positions in the field of cultural production. In other words, Hegel's characterization of the Sophists was made possible by the thought collectives that, over the preceding decades, had developed and articulated the concept of *Bildung* both within the university and in the public sphere. In the next section, I turn to these intellectual and institutional developments to trace how they shaped the environment in which Hegel's ideas emerged.

9.5 The Evolution and Transmission of *Bildung:* Communication and Conflict Between Thought Collectives

9.5.1 Religious Roots

Bildung was a signifier that, in its temporal and spatial meanderings, acquired a succession of varied and at times bewilderingly diverse meanings and associations, as disparate thought collectives redefined and repurposed it to suit their specific contexts and agendas. In *The Educated Subject and the German Concept of Bildung* (2017), Rebekka Horlacher traces the development of this multifaceted concept across centuries: from its initial coinage by Meister Eckhardt in the thirteenth century, through its literary elaboration in the *Bildungsroman* inspired by Weimar Classicism, its aesthetic theorization, and its educational reformulation and institutionalization within the German university in the latter half of the eighteenth century, to its eventual migration into North American schooling systems in the nineteenth and twentieth centuries. Certain elements and transformations particularly pertinent to this study warrant further exploration.

Meister Eckhardt originally used the term *Bildung* to describe 'the mystical experience of sinking into Christ while thinking about oneself as made in the image of Christ',[65] and this subjective and introspective dimension remained central to *Bildung*, even as it evolved into an educational concept in the mid-eighteenth century. For instance, Friedrich Gottlieb Klopstock's poetry (1748) and Johann Gottfried Herder's theoretical writings (e.g. 1769) emphasized *inwardness*—the sentiment and self-examination accessible through encounters with poetry, culture, or a conducive educational setting.[66]

[65] Horlacher (2017, p. 8).

[66] Horlacher (2017, pp. 10–12).

The religious roots and connotations of *Bildung* meant it was compatible with Pietism, which had hegemonic control over the Prussian universities and enjoyed the support of the Prussian monarchy. Unlike Protestant scholasticism, which emphasized adherence to dogma, Pietism centred on individual belief and constant introspection as the path to correcting and forming a perfectible humanity. This Pietist inwardness remained at the core of the *Bildung* concept as it was transmitted through the German *Aufklärung*, which was a uniquely religious strand of the European Enlightenment.[67]

However, *Bildung* took on meanings and discursive power that went far beyond its religious origins. When German philosophy faculties and literary movements encountered the writings of the third Earl of Shaftesbury, the concept took on more radical connotations. The reception and adaptation of Shaftesbury's *Characteristics of Men, Manners, Opinions* (1711), translated into German in 1738–1740 and again in 1776–1779,[68] exemplifies Fleck's suggestion that the communication of one concept from one thought collective to another can trigger a change in thought style.[69]

9.5.2 Shaftesbury: Character Formation and the Public Sphere

Lawrence E. Klein's seminal 1994 study of Shaftesbury's philosophy essentially framed it as a paradigm shift that was bound up with the appearance of the public sphere in eighteenth-century Britain. Drawing on Habermas's 1962 study of bourgeois society,[70] Klein situated Shaftesbury's project within a broader process of economic, political, social, and cultural transformation.

In this model, the turmoil and trauma of the mid-seventeenth century—epitomized by the Civil War (1642–1651), the execution of Charles I (1649), and Cromwell's Protectorate (1653–1659)—was followed by a repressive attempt to restore traditional control under the Stuart Restoration (1660), exemplified by measures such as the Licensing of the Press Act (1662). The Glorious Revolution of 1688 is thus positioned both as a response to this period of breakdown and repression and as a catalyst for far-reaching structural and discursive transformations.

These transformations included the political ascendancy of Parliament, with royal prerogatives curtailed by the Bill of Rights (1689), the extension of freedom of worship through the Toleration Act (1689), and the establishment of the Bank of England (1694) under parliamentary authority, which ensured financial stability and laid the groundwork for growing prosperity. Economic liberalization during this period is often portrayed as marking a decisive departure from the centralized, mercantilist policies of James II toward a more liberal model that encouraged free trade,

67 Horlacher (2017, pp. 12–14). Also: Epstein (1966) and Whaley (1981).

68 Grean (1967, p. 265).

69 Fleck (1986, p. 87).

70 Klein (1994, pp. 13—14) and Habermas (1992).

manufacturing, and the rise of the commercial class, contributing to a reshaping of social structures and fostering a more dynamic society.[71]

Another crucial transformation was the lapse of the Licensing Act in 1695, which ended pre-publication censorship.[72] While the end of censorship was not necessarily driven by a commitment to press liberty, it created conditions conducive to a freer press, enabling public criticism of individuals, institutions, and ideas to thrive.[73] This relaxation of censorship coincided with significant developments in media: pamphlets, broadsides, news-books, news-sheets, and periodical journals became increasingly common, alongside smaller, cheaper formats such as chapbooks, octavos, and duodecimos.[74] These new media forms were distributed through an expanding urban commercial infrastructure, which included coffeehouses, commercial lending libraries, book clubs, and reading societies. These venues are often regarded as having provided spaces for readers to access, discuss, and critique texts, thereby contributing to what is frequently characterized as the emergence of a more engaged and critical public.[75]

Additionally, rising literacy rates[76] and an increasingly secular orientation in reading habits are treated as key factors in shaping this environment. Readers turned to texts addressing political, social, and cultural issues, aligning with the Whiggish emphasis on self-improvement and rational public debate. These intersecting factors—the economic, cultural, and discursive transformations catalysed by the Glorious Revolution—help to explain the emergence of what has been described as 'the public sphere' in eighteenth-century England.[77]

In Klein's framing, these rapid structural and cultural transformations meant that 'traditional authoritative institutions were unable to order and control this new discursive and cultural environment. As a result, a new way of comprehending discourse in society arose, the paradigm of politeness'.[78] Shaftesbury's philosophy is thus positioned as both a product of and a reflection on this new public sphere, which developed in tension with institutions such as the Court and Church.

---

[71] For example, Pincus (2009, pp. 366–399).

[72] Downie (2005) and Barber (2022, p. 14).

[73] Downie (2005, pp. 58–62) challenges the assumption that the expiration of the Licensing Act in 1695 reflected a principled shift toward press liberty. He argues that it was largely the result of practical concerns about the ineffectiveness of pre-publication censorship, with subsequent efforts to reinstate stricter press controls continuing well into the eighteenth century. Downie also highlights that state intervention in the press persisted through libel prosecutions, arrests, and regulations, suggesting that a truly free press did not emerge in this period. Moreover, he questions Habermas's emphasis on 1695 as a pivotal moment for the public sphere, noting earlier breakdowns in press control (1642 and 1679) and the development of effective distribution networks as equally significant factors.

[74] Steinberg (1996, pp. 121–126) and Burke (2008, p. 169).

[75] Klein (2012, p. xvi).

[76] Our World in Data (n.d.) Historical Literacy in England, by Sex. https://ourworldindata.org/grapher/historical-literacy-in-england-by-sex (accessed 4 May 2025).

[77] Cressy (1980) and Spufford (1981).

[78] Klein (1994, pp. 11–12).

For Klein, the paradigm shift exemplified by and advocated for in Shaftesbury's writing is closely tied to a broader Whiggish cultural ideology, which articulated a polarized opposition to the established power centres of the Tory Party, the Anglican Church, the princely Court, and the Universities, while simultaneously championing civil society and advocating for the civil oversight of cultural production:

> Notwithstanding the project of restoration, both the Court and the Church were declining as centers of discursive and cultural production. [...] As for the Church, the overwhelming lesson of seventeenth-century history for the English mind was the need for religious sentiment and ideology to be under psychological and intellectual discipline and for religious institutions to be firmly under civil control. The later seventeenth century and the early eighteenth did not see a decay of the religious spirit but rather its rigorous submission to social and civil discipline. This process weakened the Church's presumption of authority over discourse and culture. The best evidence for this is the decline in prestige of the English universities in this period and their abandonment by the English elite.[79]

The Whiggish cultural ideology had a broad range of addressees. On the one hand, Shaftesbury's philosophy of politeness, as 'an elite ideology of sociability', can be seen as representing the high level of an intra-elite conflict (Whig vs. Tory).[80] As Klein emphasized in a more recent essay from 2018, Shaftesbury was an aristocrat who primarily addressed persons like himself: 'men of property and leisure, men with an education and a stake in politics, and men who might acknowledge some interest in the arts'.[81] Thus, his advice on new norms of sociability, which emphasized the importance of self-improvement and character formation over the claims of birth and inherited status that traditionally distinguished the landed aristocracy, was primarily—but not solely—focused on helping the elite navigate and distinguish themselves in the new public sphere.

By contrast, Joseph Addison and Richard Steele adopted a more inclusive approach, targeting a broader 'bourgeois' audience with their *Spectator* project. This 'moral weekly', founded in 1711–1712, focused on 'manners, morals, and letters' and aimed at a wide readership spanning the gentry, merchants, and professionals.[82] As Klein notes, 'they aimed more explicitly to widen the audience for what they called "philosophy" and to include women and also various ranks of the middling sorts who sometimes appear to have been beneath Shaftesbury's notice'.[83]

In his 1994 study, Klein argued that the Whig cultural ideology of politeness 'should not be dismissed simply as an irrelevant ideological gloss on a reality of an entirely different nature'.[84] This comment, I would suggest, arises from the problematic connotations inherent in the concept of ideology, as highlighted in Chap. 5 of the present study—ideology as 'wrong ideas'; false, distorted, and misleading conceptions of real social relations. Pre-empting the charge that the philosophy of

[79] Klein (1994, p. 10).

[80] Jost (2018, pp. 137–139).

[81] Klein (2018, p. 201).

[82] Melton (2004, p. 96).

[83] Klein (2018, pp. 203–204).

[84] Klein (1994, p. 12).

culture was merely an obfuscatory smokescreen, Klein contends that it 'helped shape a wide range of cultural institutions and practices in the eighteenth century',[85] suggesting that the philosophy of politeness played an active role in shaping reality.

If the Whiggish cultural transformation and the philosophy of politeness are to be understood as forming an ideology, the functionalist model of ideology is more appropriate: a framework of concepts, practices, and technologies employed by a specific group in a relation of social domination, whether in the pursuit of or resistance to cultural hegemony. Importantly, the philosophy of politeness cannot be reduced to the ideology of a single socio-economic class, as the collective that articulated it and the audience it addressed spanned the social hierarchy—from aristocrats, through the aspiring gentry and the new commercial elite, to self-taught artisans.

Furthermore, the notion that the Whigs or bourgeois society strategically shaped a singular and unified public sphere as 'an intersubjective domain' in opposition to the apparatuses and bastions of traditional control (the Court, Church, the Tories, the Universities) is deeply problematic, not least because High Church Tories participated in complex public discussion in tracts and pamphlets, for instance on the issue of the free expression of orthodox opinions.[86]

Historians have argued, against Habermas's idealized model of publicity and accessibility, that between 1688 and 1720, the so-called public sphere in England was constituted and riven with class and gender exclusions; that there was no single public sphere, but 'a plurality of competing publics', and 'a host of competing counterpublics, including nationalist publics, popular peasant publics, elite women's publics, and working class publics';[87] and that it was the propertied gentry, not the rising middle 'bourgeois' class that truly benefited from the 1688 settlement.[88]

Klein's contextualization of Shaftesbury's philosophy within the emerging English public sphere draws directly on Habermas's 1962 framework of structural transformation, itself grounded in the Marxian base-superstructure model. While this model sheds light on aspects of the relationship between economic structures and cultural forms, it also tends to impose analytical categories and identify homogenized, unified entities—a tendency exemplified in Habermas's characterization of the public sphere as 'a Category of Bourgeois Society'.[89]

J.A. Downie argues convincingly that Habermas's projections are a direct result of his Marxist assumptions, under which the assertion 'it is essential that England became a bourgeois state by the end of the seventeenth century' functions as a historical fact.[90] Fleck's theory allows us to view this fact as a product of interactive

[85] Klein (1994, p. 12).

[86] Barber (2022, p. 14).

[87] Fraser (1990, p. 61).

[88] Downie (2005, p. 62).

[89] The full title of Habermas's 1962 study: *Strukturwandel der Öffentlichkeit. Untersuchungen zu einer Kategorie der bürgerlichen Gesellschaft.*

[90] Downie (2005, pp. 64–65).

cognition—Habermas engaging with historical data and texts through the lens of a particular thought style. The problem is that Habermas's treatment of new ideas and discursive practices as mere superstructural reflections—or delayed echoes—of economic transformations in the base necessarily entails a systematic oversimplification of the complex interplay of processes at work, reducing multifaceted conflicts to simplistic binary oppositions.

A less rigid, Fleck-inspired approach to examining the public sphere suggests that ostensibly superstructural elements—such as philosophy, law, new textual genres, parliamentary debates, and coffeehouse discussions—were not merely reflections of an underlying economic base, but were produced by collectives and networks that both responded to and actively shaped economic transformations. These interactions can be understood in terms of positive feedback loops, whereby the innovative thinking of specific groups—conceivable in various ways, including socio-economic class, thought collective, discursive formation, epistemic community, or social network—initiates structural reforms and generates economic value, which in turn reinforces the appeal and influence of the group's cognitive orientation. Such dynamics expose the limitations of a rigid, one-directional model and underscore the analytical value of a more open, relational, and epistemologically sensitive framework.

These broader theoretical issues will be explored in greater detail in the next chapter through an analysis of Koselleck's conception of critique and Habermas's model of structural transformation. For the purposes of this chapter, however, the focus will shift to Shaftesbury's thought, with particular attention paid to the characteristics that facilitated its transmission and reception in the German universities.

In his *A Letter Concerning Enthusiasm* (1707), Shaftesbury defends the nation's newly-gained freedom of criticism and explicitly upholds the liberty to subject the court, the nobility, and the church to public judgement—and even ridicule:

> Never was there in our nation a time known when folly and extravagance of every kind were more sharply inspected or more wittily ridiculed. [...] It is only in a free nation, such as ours, that imposture has no privilege and that neither the credit of a court, the power of a nobility, nor the awfulness of a church can give her protection or hinder her from being arraigned in every shape and appearance. It is true, this liberty may seem to run too far. We may perhaps be said to make ill use of it. So everyone will say when he himself is touched and his opinion freely examined. But who shall be judge of what may be freely examined and what may not, where liberty may be used and where it may not?[91]

Shaftesbury's implied answer to these rhetorical questions is that no authority can be the arbiter of what can be examined and judged, and that it is within the realm of polite and candid conversation that liberty finds its proper balance.

In the *Letter*, Shaftesbury mentions the public (but not the public sphere), the effects of company, and the 'rage of the people'. Groups are depicted as sources of inspiration—an actor will perform better for an audience of 'the better sort', we can

[91] Shaftesbury (2012, p. 7).

discover a new power of eloquence when we speak in public[92]—but also sources of enthusiasm (i.e., fanaticism), popular fury, and infectious rage.[93] He depicts people as particularly vulnerable to 'the testimony of others':

> The combustible matters lie prepared within and ready to take fire at a spark, but chiefly in a multitude seized with the same spirit. No wonder if the blaze rises so of a sudden when innumerable eyes glow with the passion and heaving breasts are labouring with inspiration, when not the aspect only but the very breath and exhalations of men are infectious, and the inspiring disease imparts itself by insensible transpiration.[94]

To counter such susceptibility, Shaftesbury offers two remedies. The first is raillery, or good-humoured criticism, which exposes superstition and deflates religious inspiration. The second is 'the homespun philosophy of looking into ourselves':[95] a disciplined understanding of human passions and their origins, with a particular focus on the self. Self-scrutiny, he argues, enables individuals to recognize and resist the internal seeds of fanaticism, preventing them from igniting under external influences.

These remedies reflect Shaftesbury's belief in the power of polite conversation and introspection to safeguard against collective irrationality. His *Letter*, framed as an anonymous appeal to a Lord, exemplifies an individual seeking company that will 'raise his thoughts', emphasizing his view of the mutual exchange of ideas—intersubjective communication in more modern parlance—as a means to refine judgment and temper enthusiasm.

At the heart of Shaftesbury's work lay a vision of philosophy as a cultural activity free from the constraints of theological authority. This aspect of his thought resonated deeply with German philosophers in the latter half of the eighteenth century, who, operating under the *Censurrecht* and shaped by very different institutional frameworks, were similarly preoccupied with emancipating philosophy from the oversight of theology faculties. While Shaftesbury's philosophy of politeness was formulated in direct opposition to Hobbes and Spinoza—both of whom he regarded as modern exponents of Epicurean thought—he nonetheless shared with these thinkers a commitment to championing philosophy as a distinct mode of reasoning and argumentation, independent of theological control.[96]

Crucially, Hobbes and Spinoza were regarded as anathema within German universities and the broader cultural milieu of the disparate German states from the 1670s through much of the eighteenth century. Jakob Thomasius, a professor at Leipzig University, attacked Spinoza's *Theologico-Political Treatise* in a lecture given in 1670, the very year this controversial work was first published, scandalizing many contemporary readers.[97] Samuel Pufendorf, writing in 1672, took pains to

[92] Shaftesbury (2012, pp. 5–6).

[93] Shaftesbury (2012, pp. 9–10).

[94] Shaftesbury (2012, p. 23).

[95] Shaftesbury (2012, p. 22).

[96] Israel (2018).

[97] Begley (2018).

distance himself from Hobbesian philosophy, despite having previously acknowledged drawing on Hobbes's ideas.[98] Leibniz, following his correspondence with Thomasius in the early 1670s concerning the mysterious author of the *Theologico-Political Treatise*, developed his own metaphysics in opposition to key tenets of Spinozism. In the 1720s, the spectre of Spinoza loomed over Christian Wolff's determinism, which conceptualized the soul as an automaton—a 'sensation machine'—provoking accusations of Spinozism from the theological faculty at Halle (see Chap. 10)[99] Even as late as the 1780s, Spinoza's name sparked controversy, with the posthumous accusation that Lessing had become a Spinozist in his final years, igniting a scandal that reverberated throughout German intellectual circles.[100]

However, Shaftesbury's advocacy on behalf of philosophy and his polite insistence on the liberty to criticize theologians and Churchmen originated from a completely different position compared to Hobbes's mechanistic materialism and naturalistic analysis of Biblical texts, as well as Spinoza's Biblical hermeneutics. Shaftesbury's intellectual alignment with the Cambridge Platonists,[101] his belief in universal morality (articulated in opposition to Locke's empiricist relativism), and his reverence for the moral and philosophical authority of Antiquity—signalled through careful references to Plato, Xenophon, and Cicero—rendered his thought significantly more palatable within the German context.

His conception of philosophy as a cultural endeavour was framed within a moral and aesthetic tradition that resonated strongly with the values of German classicism and idealism—values not only compatible with, but actively celebrated by, many German thinkers and institutions, particularly those involved in neo-humanist educational reform. Moreover, the shared Protestant background between England and many German territories provided an additional layer of affinity: Shaftesbury's natural religion—rational, anti-clerical, and independent of revelation—could be received not as a threat to Christian belief, but as a means of refining it: a philosophical deepening of religion through reason, aesthetic appreciation, and inner virtue.[102] In this respect, his focus on ethical inwardness could even resonate with aspects of Pietist sensibility. This made Shaftesbury's ideas far safer for adoption

[98] Parkin (2007, pp. 451–452) and Palladini (2020, pp. 149–155).

[99] Saine (1997, pp. 146–152).

[100] Saine (1997, pp. 224–225).

[101] Cassirer (1953, pp. 157–165).

[102] While John Andrew Bernstein carefully situated Shaftesbury within the transition toward deism, he emphasizes that Shaftesbury's form of deism does not involve explicit attacks on Christian doctrine, but rather a reorientation of religion away from Pauline themes of sin, redemption, and divine forgiveness, and toward a moral-theistic framework rooted in harmony, inner virtue, and natural law. Shaftesbury is, in Bernstein's words, 'a deist in the simplest sense of the term, a moral theist without belief in revelation', yet this stance is not reducible to Enlightenment Deism. As Michael B. Gill observes, Shaftesbury's natural religion emphasized *reasonable enthusiasm* and a love of the cosmic order, aligning him only partially with English Deists. His theology blends Stoic, aesthetic, and theistic elements in a way that resists strict categorization. See Bernstein (1978) and Gill (2024).

and adaptation within German universities and society, as they offered a vision of philosophical liberty without the overtly subversive implications associated with Hobbes or Spinoza.

As Klein has emphasized, Shaftesbury's project can be understood as a 'reclamation' of philosophy—an effort to 'extricate philosophy from "Colleges" and "Cells" (as he put it) and return it to "the World" and worldly conversation'.[103] Central to this reclamation was his strategic activation of the Socratic caesura (analysed in Chap. 7)—the deployment of Socrates as a discursive rupture through which philosophy could be reimagined as a form of public engagement rather than a scholastic or esoteric discipline. Shaftesbury recovered Socrates by bypassing the Renaissance Neoplatonist readings of Plato, instead turning to the more accessible and civic portrayals in Xenophon and Cicero. From these sources, Shaftesbury derived an image of Socrates as 'the greatest of philosophers, the very founder of philosophy itself'.[104] For Shaftesbury, Socratic philosophy was inseparable from the life of the polis—his self-examination was a civic practice 'carried out in public through a process of public conversation in the midst of the city-state'.[105]

By foregrounding this image of Socrates as the exemplar of self-scrutiny and character formation through public engagement with a diverse range of citizens, Shaftesbury established a conceptual bridge linking the civic philosophies of Ancient Greece and Rome with the intellectual traditions of the German universities. His reinterpretation of the Socratic caesura—as a redefinition of philosophy's role in fostering moral and civic responsibility—laid the groundwork for its adaptation within a new intellectual and cultural milieu. Viewed through the lens of Fleck's theory, Shaftesbury's engagement with Xenophon and Cicero facilitated a significant interaction between temporally distant and culturally distinct thought styles, transmitting and transforming this philosophical legacy for German contexts.

When Shaftesbury's notions of self-examination and character formation were translated into High German and merged into the terms *bilden* and *Bildung*, significant conceptual shifts reshaped the German understanding of *Bildung*. As Horlacher has observed, Shaftesbury emphasized education as an inner process of moral and aesthetic transformation—rooted in character formation—rather than a superficial familiarity with culture or dependence on external instruction. Crucially, this understanding transcended the acquisition of useful knowledge or technical skills, instead representing a holistic transformation of the individual subject that integrated ethical refinement, aesthetic sensibilities, and inner truth claims.[106] This reinterpretation stood in stark contrast to early *Aufklärung* ideals of rational instruction and cameralist models of utilitarian reform.

Shaftesbury's ideas, however, emerged from a cultural and discursive context vastly different from that of the German philosophers who later adapted them.

[103] Klein (2018, pp. 202–203).

[104] Shaftesbury (2012, p. 441).

[105] Klein (2012, p. xxv).

[106] Horlacher (2017, p. 43).

Disseminated through entrepreneurial publishing networks in an environment of relaxed censorship, his reflections benefited from a level of intellectual autonomy that was unthinkable for many German philosophers, who operated under much tighter supervision. While Shaftesbury worked largely outside institutional constraints, German philosophers engaging with his ideas were still striving to assert philosophy's independence from the control and censorship imposed by theological faculties and state authorities. Their intellectual environment was more tightly regulated, with restrictions not only on their engagement within the university—shaping communication with students and colleagues—but also in the broader public domain, where theological authorities and state officials could block the publication of their works.

Despite these contextual differences, Shaftesbury's vision of self-examination and character formation resonated with German critiques of the instrumentalization of education. For those grappling with the cameralist view of universities as institutions focused on producing wealth, status, and state functionaries, Shaftesbury's rejection of inherited privilege and emphasis on inner character offered a compelling alternative. His focus on moral and aesthetic self-cultivation, rather than practical or economic aims, served as a conceptual bridge between Enlightenment England and the emerging thought style of German philosophy faculties during the late *Aufklärung*—a period marked by Herder's writings in the 1760s and 1770s, the public debates conducted in the *Berlinische Monatsschrift* journal during the 1780s and 1790s,[107] the contributions of Lessing and Mendelssohn in the late eighteenth century, and culminating in Kant's more political writings from the 1790s, particularly *The Conflict of the Faculties*, which is analysed in detail in the next chapter.

Herder's reception of Shaftesbury underscores the profound significance of these ideas for the evolving German concept of *Bildung*. Calling Shaftesbury the 'amiable Plato of Europe',[108] Herder recognized his critical role in elevating philosophy beyond scholasticism and institutional control. For Herder, Shaftesbury rescued philosophy from the 'school-prisons' of lifeless abstractions and hollow conceptual systems, which disconnected reason, sensation, and language from direct human experience.[109] Shaftesbury's insistence on grounding philosophy in public conversation and worldly engagement resonated deeply with Herder's critique of the German intellectual tradition. This vision not only revived the Socratic ideal of philosophy as a civic practice but also inspired a more dynamic, culturally engaged understanding of *Bildung*, rooted in moral and aesthetic self-formation rather than the mechanistic accumulation of knowledge for state utility.

Beyond Herder's philosophical engagement, Shaftesbury's reception in Germany was shaped by broader cultural and nationalist aspirations. Early German translations of his works—such as Georg Venzky's rendering of *Soliloquy*—were part of a wider effort to refine and elevate the German language to the cultural level of French

[107] Hellmuth (1998).

[108] Herder (2004, p. 283).

[109] Herder (2004, p. 227).

and English.[110] But Shaftesbury's appeal extended beyond linguistic concerns. For thinkers seeking to define a distinctively German philosophical tradition, he offered a constructive alternative to the perceived atheism and political radicalism of figures like Hobbes and Spinoza. His emphasis on moral and aesthetic self-cultivation aligned with emerging ideals of rational autonomy and cultural formation, providing a framework that supported the rejection of empiricism and mechanistic materialism. In this sense, Shaftesbury became a resource for German thinkers striving to assert their intellectual independence while linking philosophy to national renewal and cultural identity.

From the perspective of Fleck's theory, the communication of Shaftesbury's ideas to German audiences involved both interaction and resistance. German philosophers critically adopted Shaftesbury's ideas, incorporating them into their emerging thought style while simultaneously defining their philosophy in opposition to French *philosophes*, whose atheism and disregard for tradition made them less assimilable, and to the empiricists of England and Scotland, who were seen as mired in the contingent and coarse realities of sensory experience. Herder's response to Shaftesbury exemplifies this process of discursive antagonism. By linking Shaftesbury's emphasis on moral philosophy and public engagement to an explicitly patriotic agenda, Herder reinforced the notion of German philosophy as an integral part of the national character, uniquely suited to bridging the cultural and intellectual demands of the age.[111]

Shaftesbury's affirmation of the Socratic caesura—his insistence that philosophy engage with public life rather than remain confined behind the walls of the University—provided German philosophers with a powerful conceptual tool as they sought to claim a vital role for philosophy in the public sphere and within the state—particularly the Prussian state. By appropriating and adapting Shaftesbury's ideas, they critiqued their subordination to theological and state oversight while asserting philosophy's capacity to shape individual character and contribute to the moral fabric of society. From the perspective of Fleck's theory, this process of appropriation exemplifies a dynamic interaction between temporally and culturally distinct thought styles, with Shaftesbury serving as a bridge that transmitted the Socratic caesura into a new intellectual context.

[110] Horlacher (2017, p. 41).

[111] See for example Herder's *How Philosophy Can Become More Universal and Useful for the Benefit of the People* (1765): 'England is full of deep observers of nature, full of natural philosophers, politicians, mathematicians. France is full of literary types (*Schöngeister*), full of men, experts in statecraft, full of geometers. Germany—hardworking Germany—has only the national virtue of being philosophical (*weltweise zu sein*). The former cannot reach up to us, and so they belittle us. Oh, is it not therefore a task for everyone who has German blood in his veins and a German philosophical spirit to develop this patriotic theme, to show how philosophy stands in relation to political science, mathematics, and the literary arts (*den schönen Wissenschaften*), so that he cedes nothing belonging to philosophy and to its standing? Herder (2004, p. 6).

9.5.3 Class Struggle

Class dynamics played a significant role in shaping both the development of the concept of *Bildung* and the growing status of the philosophical faculties within German universities. According to McClelland, while the law faculty attracted upper-class students and the nobility, the neo-humanistic seminars of classical philology 'appealed to young men from the poorer sectors of society'. McClelland elaborates:

> In the midst of social betters trained principally in courtly arts and law, these students gained a new respect for their own fields of study and a heightened prestige as contributors to a reinterpretation of the classical and biblical worlds. They could begin to look askance at the richer and more aristocratic law students for the mundanity and shallowness of their man-of-the-world training.[112]

This dynamic fostered a growing sense of intellectual self-confidence among students in the philosophical faculty, even as they operated within an institutional hierarchy that privileged the law faculty's careerist and elitist values.

This class contrast is echoed in the characterizations of German philosophers by both Paulsen and Bruford. Paulsen notes that German philosophers often came from lower-middle-class or middle-class backgrounds: Kant's father was a harness maker, Fichte's a ribbon weaver, and Schlegel's a pastor. These modest origins sharply contrasted with the French and English philosophers, such as Voltaire, Locke, Shaftesbury, and Hume, who moved in aristocratic or gentlemanly circles. Unlike their sociable counterparts, German philosophers were predominantly university professors—reclusive scholars rather than conversationalists or social figures. Raised in deeply pious families, they carried the values of hard work and seriousness over into their professional lives.

Bruford similarly highlights this social disparity within German universities, observing that the philosophical faculty differed markedly from the law faculty, which was dominated by the nobility:

> As study in the philosophical faculty had a preparatory character, the arts professors did not enjoy the same standing as the rest. They were glorified schoolmasters, who taught the elements of a fairly wide range of subjects for about as many hours a week as a schoolmaster teaches today. Being overworked and poor, and having had few opportunities of mixing in society, scholars usually lived the life of recluses.[113]

From the perspective of Fleck's theory, these philosophical faculties can be understood as constituting a broad thought collective, internally divided into smaller thought collectives based on disciplinary demarcations. Within this context, the concept of *Bildung*, as developed by the classicists, acquired class-determined elements. It was constructed in opposition to the careerist values espoused by the upper-class thought collective dominating the law faculty, which the state assigned

[112] McClelland (1980, pp. 60–61).

[113] Bruford (1935, p. 250).

the highest value in terms of social prestige and cultural capital. By contrast, the philosophical faculty articulated *Bildung* as a defining concept of their distinct thought style, rejecting inherited privilege and emphasizing moral and cultural self-formation over material success.

This dynamic reveals how *Bildung* came to embody a class struggle within the German university system in the late eighteenth century, with the concept itself being shaped by the conflict between competing visions of the university, education, and the state. Pinkard highlights the class tension underlying Hegel's use of *Bildung*, particularly in his disdain for the ruling class's sense of entitlement. Reflecting on Hegel's time as a tutor to the aristocratic von Steiger family, Pinkard writes:

> To be a person of *Bildung* had nothing to do with one's birth but with how one directed and formed oneself; men (and women) of *Bildung* thus had a claim to status that directly contradicted the traditional claims of birth and estate. [...] For Hegel, [...] an educated-cultivated man, who had *Bildung*, to be treated as a lowly servant by a family that in his eyes represented a dying and corrupt social order with no right to be at the center of things - all this was destined not to sit particularly well with him.[114]

On this reading, the rise of the philosophical faculty within the German university system coincided with the societal transformations of the Napoleonic era, particularly the expansion of state bureaucracy and civil service roles that demanded a new class of educated professionals. This thought collective, shaped by institutional reforms, societal pressures, revolutionary intellectual upheavals, and cross-disciplinary influences, exemplified the transformation of *Bildung* from its neo-humanist philological roots into a broader moral and cultural critique.

9.6 Conclusion

Klein frequently framed Shaftesbury's contributions as part of a broader cultural transformation, which he characterized using the term 'paradigm'. He described politeness as both 'a new cultural paradigm' and 'a dominant paradigm', presenting Shaftesbury's writings as epitomizing the 'paradigm of polite writing' and portraying Shaftesbury as viewing conversation itself as the 'paradigm of discourse'.[115] These formulations evoke an image of a comprehensive shift from a conservative mode of cultural production—rooted in state authority and theological control of texts and social practices—to a liberal, individualistic model embedded in the new media technologies, practices, and distributed authority of a self-regulating public.

This framing acknowledges that the cultural transformation involved both base and superstructural factors—a legal and economic environment that enabled an unprecedented expansion in the production, consumption, and discussion of texts—while also positing that at its core lay an intellectual innovation: a reimagining of

[114] Pinkard (2000, pp. 50–51).

[115] Klein (1994, pp. 9–11, 6, 96, 100).

education, shifting from top-down clerical instruction rooted in Biblical texts to self-directed, critical learning inspired by classical ideals and models.

Yet, describing this transformation as a neat binary switch that amounts to a Kuhnian paradigm shift introduces conceptual challenges. Kuhn's original conception of a paradigm shift in science involves the replacement of one explanatory model with another due to the accumulation of anomalies that the existing paradigm cannot resolve. A new paradigm is accepted or rejected based on a complex interplay of factors, such as its explanatory power, aesthetic appeal, generational dynamics, and the broader social and historical context. Crucially, a paradigm accounts for observed phenomena systematically and empirically, serving as a comprehensive framework for understanding and conducting research.[116]

Cultural transformations, such as the 'cultural ideology' of politeness and Shaftesbury's emphasis on self-scrutiny, character formation, and civic engagement, resist such a framework. First, what anomalies did politeness, as a new paradigm, resolve? How did Shaftesbury's model provide a superior account of cultural phenomena? Dissatisfaction with existing educational models or their inadequacy in meeting societal or group needs does not align neatly with Kuhn's concept of anomaly, which presupposes empirical failure within a systematic framework.

For instance, considering Melanchthon's Humanistic-Reformed educational model, the cameralist approach to universities, and the Classicist-*Bildung* model as distinct paradigms reveals that their emergence, acceptance, and rejection were driven by more than just the resolution of anomalies. These models were normative frameworks that articulated values, assigned meaning, and reflected the agendas of specific groups engaged in antagonistic relationships.

Melanchthon's model valued classical texts for their moral significance and their role in establishing standards for education and conduct, shaping how they were studied and perceived. The Classicist-*Bildung* model, by contrast, enriched this tradition by emphasizing the individual's subjective experience of classical texts, asserting that these individual perceptions held social and cultural value. At the same time, the concept of *Bildung* was articulated in opposition to the cameralist view of universities as state-driven institutions focused on producing wealth and functionaries.

These transformations arose from a confluence of factors: secularization and the weakening of Christian values, the growth of state power, economic upheavals and class shifts, discursive antagonism, and institutional power struggles within universities. Kuhn's concept of paradigm shift cannot adequately account for these dynamics without either the concept being diluted into a vague gesture toward cultural change or its definition being radically reformulated to fit cultural contexts. Unlike Kuhn's paradigms, Fleck's theory emphasizes the continuous evolution of thought styles, where intellectual unrest—dissatisfaction, contradiction, or insufficiency within a prevailing thought style—creates the conditions for change.

---

[116] Kuhn (1962).

Another pitfall of applying the paradigm-shift model to cultural transformations, such as the emergence of the philosophy of politeness or the development of *Bildung* in the German university, is that it imposes an assumption of discontinuity and rupture: politeness is framed as suddenly emerging from the events of 1688 and the Whig supremacy. However, as Steven Shapin and Simon Schaffer demonstrated in *Leviathan and the Air-Pump* (1985), civility and politeness were central to Robert Boyle's experimental method and his dispute resolution in public debates with Hobbes in the 1660s and 1670s.[117] Viewed in this light, Shaftesbury's philosophy—rooted in polite conversation, reasoned engagement, and self-scrutiny—can be traced back genetically to the cultural practices established by Boyle and, before him, Francis Bacon. Bacon's vision of scientific inquiry as collaborative and methodical, rejecting individual bias, rhetorical excess, and dogmatic authority, informed Boyle's experimental norms and ultimately shaped the intellectual milieu that Shaftesbury inherited.

At the same time, the thought style associated with Shaftesbury marks a significant transformation. While clearly indebted to Boyle and Bacon, whose cultural practices he inherited, Shaftesbury positioned himself as resolutely non-empirical and even anti-empiricist, as seen in his critique of Locke.[118] His philosophy of politeness emerged as an elite articulation within a broader Whiggish thought style, shaped both by his return to classical sources like Xenophon and Cicero, and by the broader intellectual unrest circulating within the Whig thought collective. His contribution to this new thought style synthesized classical ideals with contemporary concerns, reframing politeness not merely as a mode of scientific inquiry but as a broader framework for civic and moral life.

My use of Fleck's theory challenges Klein's framing of politeness as a sudden innovation tied to political events like 1688. Instead, it highlights the continuous evolution of thought styles—and the emergence of new ones—through dynamic interactions within thought collectives, where cultural practices, classical revivals, ideology, and political circumstances converged to produce new discourses and modes of cognition. Fleck's theory also emphasizes the role of intellectual unrest in creating the conditions necessary for such transformations. Shaftesbury's philosophy, rather than representing a rupture, reflects the adaptation and transformation of Baconian and Boylean ideals into the broader cultural and moral discourse of his time.

This transformation extended beyond intellectual inheritance, involving the circulation and reinterpretation of ideas across contexts. Shaftesbury's contribution to the new thought style exemplifies how cross-temporal and cross-cultural transmission reshapes thought styles as they respond to new intellectual and social challenges. The interaction between existing cultural practices and broader political

[117] Shapin and Schaffer (1985, pp. 74–75). Klein covers Shaftesbury's critique of Hobbes's supposed Epicureanism and egoism in Klein (1994, pp. 28–30, 63–65) but does not address Hobbes's confrontations with Boyle.

[118] Klein (1994, pp. 65–67).

circumstances within the Whig thought collective was key to the synthesis of these classical ideals with contemporary civic and moral concerns.

Similarly, the concept of *Bildung* developed gradually, shaped over decades of circulation through German universities and public debate, with disparate thought collectives adding new content and purposes to suit their contexts. The writings of Herder, Kant, Fichte, and Hegel exhibit shared features indicative of a common thought style—marked by intellectual seriousness, a concern with status (whether of the discipline, the nation, or the individual), and a deep commitment to inward moral and philosophical reflection, shaped by the broader traditions of German Protestant thought.

Nietzsche's cutting observation in *The Anti-Christ* (§10) that German philosophy 'really is an underhand theology'[119] captures something essential about the thought style's entanglement with German Protestantism. Despite their conflicts with theological orthodoxy, Herder's cultural individualism, Kant's moral law, Fichte's call to duty, and Hegel's concept of Spirit all reflect the intellectual and moral framework of German Protestantism, particularly its Lutheran and Pietist forms. These thinkers transposed religious structures into philosophical systems, preserving key elements of inwardness, moral rigor, and redemptive teleology. Like the philosophy of politeness, which evolved through the gradual adaptation and interaction of thought styles rather than through a sudden, discontinuous paradigm shift, the emergence of *Bildung* reflects a continuous development shaped by the interplay of intellectual traditions, institutional contexts, and broader political and economic transformations.

References

Antognazza MR (2009) Leibniz an intellectual biography. Cambridge University Press, Cambridge

Barber AW (2022) The restraint of the Press in England, 1660–1715: the communication of sin. The Boydell Press, Woodbridge

Begley B (2018) Naturalism and its political dangers: Jakob Thomasius against Spinoza's theological-political treatise. A study and the translation of Thomasius' text. Seventeenth Century 34(2018):649–670

Bernstein JA (1978) Shaftesbury's reformation of the reformation: reflections on the relation between deism and Pauline Christianity. J Religious Ethics 6(2):257–278. http://www.jstor.org/stable/40014915

Bruford W (1935) Germany in the eighteenth century: the social background of the literary revival. Cambridge University Press, Cambridge

Burke P (2008) A social history of knowledge. Polity Press, Cambridge

Cassirer E (1953) The platonic renaissance in England, trans. Pettegrove. J.P. Thomas Nelson and Sons, Edinburgh

[119] Nietzsche (2005, p. 9). See also Schopenhauer's critique in *On Philosophy at the Universities* (1851) (*Parerga and Paralipomena*), and Nietzsche's *Schopenhauer as Educator* (1874) in *Untimely Meditations*, both of which articulate early expressions of what can be described as an anti-university philosophical thought style.

Cressy D (1980) Literacy and the social order. Cambridge University Press, Cambridge
Downie JA (2005) Public and private: the myth of the bourgeois public sphere. In: Wall C (ed) A concise companion to the restoration and the eighteenth century. Blackwell, Oxford, pp 58–79
Epstein K (1966) The genesis of German conservatism. Princeton University Press, Princeton
Fleck L (1986) The problem of epistemology [1936]. In: Cognition and fact. Boston studies in the philosophy of science, vol 87. Springer, Dordrecht. https://doi.org/10.1007/978-94-009-4498-5_5
Fraser N (1990) Rethinking the public sphere: a contribution to the critique of actually existing democracy. Social Text (25/26):56–80
Gill MB (2024) Lord Shaftesbury [Anthony Ashley Cooper, 3rd earl of Shaftesbury]. In: Zalta EN, Nodelman U (eds) The Stanford Encyclopedia of philosophy (fall 2024 edition). Stanford University, Stanford. https://plato.stanford.edu/archives/fall2024/entries/shaftesbury/
Grean S (1967) Shaftesbury's philosophy of religion and ethics. Ohio University Press, Athens
Habermas J (1992) The structural transformation of the public sphere: an inquiry into a category of bourgeois society [1962], trans. Burger,T and Kert, L. Polity Press, Oxford
Hellmuth E (1998) Enlightenment and freedom of the press: the debate in the Berlin Mittwochsgesellschaft, 1783-1784. History 83(271):420–444
Herder JG (2004) Philosophical writings, trans. Forster M. N. Cambridge University Press, Cambridge
Horlacher R (2017) The educated subject and the German concept of Bildung. Routledge, New York
Hösle V (2017) A short history of German philosophy, trans. Rendall, S. Princeton University Press, Princeton
Howard TA (2006) Protestant theology and the making of the modern German university. Oxford University Press, Oxford
Israel J (2018) Shaftesbury, an early voice of the radical enlightenment. In: Müller P (ed) Shaping enlightenment politics. Peter Lang, Berlin, pp 89–97
Jost JS (2018) Party politics in characteristics. In: Müller P (ed) Shaping enlightenment politics. Peter Lang, Berlin, pp 135–147
Klein LE (1994) Shaftesbury and the culture of politeness. Cambridge University Press, Cambridge
Klein LE (2012) Introduction. In: Shaftesbury, A. Characteristics of men, manners, opinions, Time*s*. Cambridge University Press, Cambridge
Klein LE (2018) Taste, the people and the public according to the third earl of Shaftesbury. In: Müller P (ed) Shaping enlightenment politics. Peter Lang, Berlin, pp 197–213
Kuhn TS (1962) The structure of scientific revolutions. Chicago University Press, Chicago
McClelland CE (1980) State, society and university in Germany 1700–1914. Cambridge University Press, Cambridge
Melanchthon, P (1974) De corrigendis adolescentiae studiis, trans. Spitz, L.W. In: Kingdon, R (ed) Transition and revolution: problems and issues of European renaissance and reformation history (pp. 168–171). Burgess Pub. Co, Minneapolis
Melanchthon P (2012) In: Kusukawa S (ed) Orations on philosophy and education, trans. Salazar, C. F. S. Cambridge University Press, Cambridge
Melton JV (2004) The rise of the public in enlightenment Europe. Cambridge University Press, Cambridge
Menand L, Reitter P, Wellmon C (2017) The rise of the research university: a sourcebook. The University of Chicago Press, Chicago
Nietzsche F (1997) Schopenhauer as educator. In: Breazeale D (ed) Untimely meditations. Cambridge University Press, Cambridge, pp 125–194
Nietzsche F (2005) The anti-Christ, ecce homo, twilight of the idols, trans. Norman, J. Cambridge University Press, Cambridge
Overfield JH (1984) Humanism and scholasticism in late medieval Germany. Princeton University Press, Princeton
Ozment S (1980) The age of reform 1250–1550. Yale University Press, New Haven
Palladini F (2020) Samuel Pufendorf disciple of Hobbes, trans. Saunders, D. Brill, Leiden

Parkin J (2007) The reception of Hobbes's leviathan. In: Springborg P (ed) The Cambridge companion to Hobbes's leviathan. Cambridge University Press, Cambridge, pp 441–459

Paulsen F (1902) Immanuel Kant: His life and doctrine, trans. Creighton JE, Lefevre A. C. Scribner, London

Paulsen F (1906) The German universities and university study. Charles Scribner's Sons, New York

Pincus S (2009) 1688: The first modern revolution. Yale University Press, New Haven and London

Pinkard T (2000) Hegel. A biography. Cambridge University Press, Cambridge

Saine TP (1997) The problem of being modern or the German pursuit of enlightenment from Leibniz to the French revolution. Wayne State University Press, Detroit

Schiller F (2017) What is universal history and why study it? An inaugural academic lecture [1789]. In: Menand L, Reitter P, Wellmon C (eds) The rise of the research university: a sourcebook. The University of Chicago Press, Chicago, pp 31–44

Schopenhauer A (1974) On philosophy at the universities In: Payne EFJ (trans) Parerga and Paralipomena, vol 1. Clarendon Press, Oxford, pp 137–197

Shaftesbury A (2012) In: Klein LE (ed) Characteristics of men, manners, opinions, times. Cambridge University Press, Cambridge

Shapin S, Schaffer S (1985) Leviathan and the air-pump: Hobbes, Boyle, and the experimental life. Princeton University Press, Princeton

Spitz LW (1984) The importance of the reformation for universities: culture and confession in the critical years. In: Kittelson JM, Transue PJ (eds) Rebirth, reform, and resilience: universities in transition, 1300–1700. Ohio State University Press, Columbus, pp 42–67

Spufford M (1981) Small books and pleasant histories: popular fiction and its readership in seventeenth-century England. Methuen, London

Steinberg SH (1996) Five hundred years of printing. Oak Knoll Press and The British Library, London

Wakefield A (2009) The disordered police state. German Cameralism as science and practice. University of Chicago Press, Chicago

Whaley J (1981) The Protestant enlightenment in Germany. In: Porter R, Teich M (eds) The enlightenment in National Context. Cambridge University Press, Cambridge, pp 106–117

Chapter 10
Philosophy, Censorship, and the Public Sphere

Abstract This chapter examines the complex relationship between philosophy, censorship, and the public sphere in early modern and Enlightenment Europe, focusing on Kant's *The Conflict of the Faculties* (1798). It engages competing reconstructions of the German *Aufklärung*—from binary reductions to open-ended analyses of multidimensional antagonisms and positional struggles. Given that Kant's later polemical texts articulated positions within a prestructured field of cultural production, the chapter adopts an archaeological approach to uncover the earlier conflicts that shaped this field.

Taking up Koselleck's identification of Hobbes's *Leviathan* (1651) as marking the onset of the Enlightenment, the chapter critically assesses both his pathogenetic model—structured by Schmittian dualism—and Habermas's base–superstructure account, which reduces philosophy to ideological function. While drawing on Israel's triangular model of the Early Enlightenment, it departs from his Spinoza-centric emphasis by foregrounding the earlier, institutionally embedded conflicts surrounding Hobbes—his rejection by Boyle, the Cambridge Platonists, Nonconformists, the legal profession, and the universities. It repositions Hobbes and Spinoza as discursively paired *Epicurean* outcasts, excluded by multiple European thought collectives, especially in the German university context.

Fleck's theory is used to trace the emergence of epistemic positions formed through antagonistic differentiation. The chapter concludes with a Fleckian reading of Kant's institutional thought style: the philosophy faculty emerges not as a neutral site of reason, but as a mediating organ between state and public—regulating cultural production and constraining the public articulation of thought under censorship.

10.1 Approaching Kant's *The Conflict of the Faculties*

Kant's *Der Streit der Fakultäten*, published in 1798, is a pivotal polemical text in the historical development of German universities; it also retroactively sheds light on many facets of Kant's broader thought and writings.

S. Dersley, *Thought Collectives and Cultural Change*, Living Signs of Law 1,
https://doi.org/10.1007/978-3-031-97431-1_10

First, in this collection of essays, Kant explicitly examines distinct social groups, defining their roles and functions within the university, the state, and society at large. It is here that Kant most clearly and extensively turns his attention to what, from Fleck's perspective, may be understood as specific thought collectives. More broadly, his portrayal of the university as an institution that both served the state and retained the capacity for autonomous rational inquiry, coupled with his effort to redefine the role and function of the philosophy faculty, was foundational for the emergence of the Humboldtian Berlin University.[1] Furthermore, the self-reflexivity involved in a state-employed philosopher critically considering the role of university faculties within the state—and the university's broader place in society—prefigures Hegel's more expansive exploration of institutions and intersubjective thought.

Second, in his effort to demarcate the proper sphere of philosophical inquiry and adjudicate the legitimacy of claims and conflicts among the faculties, Kant's essays in *The Conflict of the Faculties* retrospectively illuminate the political-institutional embeddedness of the *Critiques* themselves. These writings show how deeply Kant's critical project was shaped by the social, cultural, and institutional tensions of the German *Aufklärung* prior to the French Revolution (and, in the case of the *Critique of Judgment*, during the Revolution as well).

Third, as Hannah Arendt observed, Kant's later writings, with their new focus on 'constitutional and institutional questions', register the profound impact of the French Revolution.[2] The first essay in *The Conflict of the Faculties* (written in 1794, during the Revolution's descent into the Terror) addresses the structure of the university, advocating for the philosophy faculty's independence from theological oversight. The second essay, ostensibly addressing the conflict between the law and philosophy faculties, implicitly engages with the Revolution ('an event of Our Time', 'this event') and asserts a nation's right to establish 'a republican constitution'. Kant's *Toward Perpetual Peace* (1795) continues this trajectory by turning explicitly to questions of constitutional law. John Christian Laursen's *The Subversive Kant* (1986) compellingly argues that *The Conflict of the Faculties* links back to Kant's earlier polemics—especially *An Answer to the Question: What is Enlightenment?* (1784)—and reflects his evolving views on 'the public' and the scholarly community in response to revolutionary developments in France and the shifting political climate in Prussia.[3]

In Fleckian terms, Kant's real-time commentary on the conflicts among the thought collectives of his era reflects the social upheaval and intellectual unrest that both shaped emerging thought styles and were, in turn, intensified by them. These conflicts range from power struggles between particular groups to broader confrontations involving increasingly general formations: the philosophy faculty,

[1] Mittelstraß (2005).

[2] Arendt (1992, p. 15).

[3] Laursen (1996).

the scholarly community, the German reading public, the nation, the European reading public, and even the network of European states.

Kant's *Conflict of the Faculties* was itself entangled in a confrontation with the Prussian government. The first essay, *The Conflict of the Philosophy Faculty with the Theology Faculty*, was originally written in response to Kant's reprimand by the king's censor, Johann Christoph von Wöllner, in 1794, following the publication of *Religion within the Bounds of Mere Reason* in 1793. To better understand the stakes of this conflict, it is necessary to briefly examine the controversial nature of this earlier work.

10.2 *Religion Within the Bounds of Mere Reason* (1793)

In this book, Kant essentially subordinated revealed religion to rational religion. His hierarchical schema sets up a contrast between, on the one hand, 'purely rational religion/faith' and 'purely moral laws', and, on the other, 'historical/ecclesiastical faith' and 'statutory laws'.[4] In Kant's conception, purely rational religion is universal: there is only one true religion, and all human beings have access to its purely moral laws—and, through them, to the will of God—by means of their individual consciousness and use of reason. Consequently, Kant asserts that revealed religion is not strictly necessary—or at least would not be, were it not for the 'weakness of human nature'.[5]

Since human cognition is impotent when it comes to *knowing* the supersensible realm, human beings must rely on faith; however, purely rational faith often lacks the persuasive power necessary to assuage human nature: people are not convinced that merely fulfilling their duties toward other human beings is sufficient for God, and they come to believe that they must instead perform *service* for God. This shift devalues the intrinsic worth of actions in favour of their extrinsic demonstration as acts of service, so that actions are now 'performed for God to please him through passive obedience'. The political overtones and ramifications of Kant's schema are unmistakable:

> Since every great lord of this world has a special need of being *honored* by his subjects, and of being *praised* by signs of submissiveness; nor can he expect, without this, as much compliance with his orders from his subjects as he needs to rule over them effectively and, in addition, however reasonable a human being may be, he always finds an immediate pleasure in attestations of honor: so we treat duty, to the extent that it is equally God's command, as the transaction of an *affair* of God, not of humans; and thus arises the concept of a religion of divine service instead of the concept of a purely moral religion.[6]

[4] Kant (1998a, pp. 112–4).

[5] Kant (1998a, p. 113).

[6] Kant (1998a, p. 113).

Hence, rather than using reason to access purely moral laws and thereby fulfil their duties to one another, human beings extend their need to serve and obey—from human rulers to God. In a purely rational faith, reason would recognize that the divine will requires obedience to purely moral laws. By contrast, revealed faith requires human beings to honour God through the obedience to divine statutory laws, 'laws which let us recognize them as obligatory, not of themselves, but only inasmuch as they are the revealed will of God'.[7]

The key and most contentious consequence of this distinction between rational and revealed religion is that the latter is, by definition, contingent: a revealed religion cannot reach all human beings, and 'hence does not bind all human beings universally'.[8] Its status as contingent and historical—that is, empirical—entails that revealed or *ecclesiastical* religion is, in principle, subject to change and possible improvement. Moreover, its observances and professions of faith are, for Kant, 'morally indifferent'. While a revealed religion can preserve its faith and statutory laws in a community through tradition and the institution of a church, it commands the greatest respect when rooted in scripture. The fact that Christianity happens to contain 'the purest moral doctrine of religion' in its holy book is described by Kant as 'fortunate'—a matter of luck rather than necessity.[9]

The contingent—historical, empirical—nature of revealed religion entails that ecclesiastical faith can 'transition' to pure religious faith. Kant's conceptual schema accordingly positions ecclesiastical faith as a mere 'vehicle' that should ultimately be abandoned: 'as the faith of a church, it carries a principle for continually coming closer to a pure religious faith until finally we can dispense of that vehicle'.[10] His teleological leanings lead him to suggest that, despite current diversity, any ecclesiastical faith 'tending to its goal of pure religious faith' can flower into the 'all-unifying church triumphant'.[11]

Kant's position acquires significant political implications in the second part of the book, where he addresses 'the counterfeit service of God', and particularly when he turns his attention to 'priestcraft (*Pfaffenthum*) as a regime' in §3. Here, Kant recasts the opposition between the revealed faith and rational faith through the deployment of sets of binary pairs: coerced observance vs. free homage; the yoke of statutory law vs. the moral law; statutory commands vs. the principles of morality; and counterfeit service/*fetish-service* (*ein Fetischdienst*) vs. true *enlightenment* (*die wahre Aufklärung*).[12] Kant's text reaches a particularly sensitive moment when he turns to the practical effects of the clergy on the state and minds of its subjects. In Kant's view, a church dominated by fetish-service—which demands outward

[7] Kant (1998a, p. 114).
[8] Kant (1998a, p. 114).
[9] Kant (1998a, p. 116).
[10] Kant (1998a, p. 122).
[11] Kant (1998a, p. 122).
[12] Kant (1998b, pp. 173–4).

professions of faith and obedience—leads to a situation where 'the masses are ruled and robbed of their moral freedom':

> Where articles of faith are included in the constitutional law, a *clergy* rules which believes that it can actually dispense with reason, and ultimately with scriptural scholarship itself, because, since it is the single authoritative guardian and interpreter of the will of the invisible lawgiver, it has the exclusive authority to administer the prescriptions of faith; hence, thus equipped with this absolute power, it need not convince but *only give orders*. - Now, since apart from this clergy all that is left is the *laity* (the head of the political commonwealth not excepted), the church finally rules the state, not indeed through force, but through influence over minds, and also, in addition, through pretense of the benefit which the state could allegedly derive from the unconditional obedience to which a spiritual discipline has habituated the very *thinking* of the people.[13]

In this passage, Kant moves beyond the critique of reason (and the various cognitive faculties) and beyond a critique of religion (in its revealed and rational forms) to a critique of the church as a social institution within the state.

Kant depicts a scenario in which the church suppresses both philosophy (*Vernunft*) and theology (*Schriftgelehrsamkeit*), seizing absolute power and exerting control over the state. This domination is achieved not through force or physical coercion but through influence over minds. In Fleckian terms, a specific thought collective—the clergy (*Clerus*)—dominates society through its thought style, priestcraft (*Pfaffenthum*). From a discursive perspective, the clergy's discourse, rooted in articles and prescriptions of faith, attains hegemony over competing discourses, such as scholarly philosophy and scriptural studies, enabling a discursive formation to exert control over society.

In *Religion*, Kant was careful not to refer explicitly to Prussian or German churches or to the Prussian state: apart from scant references to the Lutheran faith,[14] the Connecticut Puritans,[15] and the Protestants—who are said to have attained a modest beginning in freedom of thought[16]—his depictions of 'the church' remain general and abstract. Nevertheless, given the overtly political nature of his analysis of the church's function in society, even in this abstract form, it is unsurprising that the book drew the censure of Prussian state authorities, particularly under the influence of figures like Johann Christoph von Wöllner, whose counter-revolutionary policies had come to dominate by 1788.

---

[13] Kant (1998b, p. 174).

[14] Kant (1998a, p. 116).

[15] Kant (1998b, p. 171).

[16] Kant (1998b, p. 181).

10.3 The *Edict Concerning Religion* of 1788 and the Censoring of Kant: Conflicting Perspectives

To convey the tone and stakes of the conflicts surrounding Kant's *Religion within the Limits of Mere Reason* (1793), and the interplay between Enlightenment ideas and the Prussian state's regulation of intellectual and religious discourse, we turn to two significant texts: an excerpt from the 1788 *Edict Concerning Religion* issued by Wöllner, the Minister of Justice, and the full text of the 1794 royal proclamation reprimanding Kant. Together, they illuminate the rhetoric, priorities, and underlying tensions shaping the Prussian authorities' response to perceived threats to orthodoxy.

Excerpt from the *Edict Concerning Religion*, issued by Wöllner, Minister of Justice, July 9, 1788:

> We have noted with regret ... that many Protestant pastors allow themselves unbridled liberty in the treatment of the dogma of their confession; they repudiate several essential parts and basic truths of the Protestant Church and indeed of the Christian religion; and they preach in a frivolous manner completely incompatible with the spirit of true Christian piety, and calculated to shake the foundations of the faith of their Christian flock. They are not ashamed to warm up the miserable, long refuted errors of the Socinians, deists, naturalists and other sectarians, and to spread them among the people with impertinent impudence under the much abused banner of *Aufklärung*! They denigrate the respect in which the Bible has been hitherto held as the revealed word of God, and do not hesitate to falsify, twist or even repudiate this divine guarantee of the welfare of the human race.[17]

The Royal Proclamation of 1794, Addressed to Kant:

> First, our gracious greetings, worthy, most learned, dear and loyal subject! Our most high person has long observed with great displeasure how you misuse your philosophy to distort and disparage many of the cardinal and basic teachings of the Holy Scriptures and of Christianity; how you have done this particularly in your book *Religion within the Limits of Mere Reason*, as well as in other shorter treatises. We expected better things of you, as you yourself must realize how irresponsibly you have acted against your duty as a teacher of youth and against our paternal purpose, which you know very well. We demand that you give at once a most conscientious account of yourself, and expect that in the future, to avoid our highest disfavor, you will be guilty of no such fault, but rather, in keeping with your duty, apply your authority and your talents to the progressive realization of our paternal purpose. Failing this, you must expect unpleasant measures for your continuing obstinacy.
>
> With our favorable regards.
>
> Berlin, 1 October 1794
>
> By special, most gracious order of His Majesty *Wöllner*[18]

The context surrounding these texts has been interpreted in two principal ways. The first, long the dominant scholarly consensus, presents a straightforward narrative rooted in what Paulsen's 1902 intellectual biography, *Immanuel Kant, his Life and Doctrine*, termed 'the classic Enlightenment/Counter-Enlightenment dichotomy'.[19] In this view, figures such as Frederick the Great, Baron von Zedlitz, and Kant rep-

[17] Epstein (1966, p. 143).

[18] Kant (1979, p. 11).

[19] Sauter (2009, p. 7).

resent the Enlightenment ideals of freedom of thought, progress, and liberalism. In contrast, Frederick William II and Wöllner embody the Counter-Enlightenment values of orthodoxy, obscurantism, and conservatism.

Paulsen's biography vividly illustrates this classic dichotomy:

> The successor of Frederick the Great had appointed in Zedlitz's place a priestly-minded enthusiast, the former preacher Wöllner, with whom he was connected by a Rosicrucian mysticism and a common hatred of the illumination. With the religious edict of July 9, 1788, there began the systematic uprooting of the illumination in Prussia. By means of the censorship and inquisition, by removals and punishments, Frederick William II and Wöllner undertook to destroy the spirit of their predecessor, a regular regime of priestly resentment.[20]

This narrative was further consolidated by Paul Schwartz's 1925 *Der erste Kulturkampf in Preußen um Kirche und Schule: (1788–1798)* (*The First Culture Struggle in Prussia Regarding Church and Education*), which explicitly projected contemporary concerns—such as Bismarck's persecution of the Catholic Church—back onto the eighteenth century by associating Wöllner's *Edict* with that later conflict.[21] The same framing was perpetuated in Mary J. Gregor's introduction to her translation of Kant's *Conflict*, where Frederick William II (described as 'orthodox and mystically inclined') and Wöllner are said to have 'launched a campaign to "stamp out the Enlightenment"'.[22]

The second, alternative perspective—found in works such as Klaus Epstein's *The Genesis of German Conservatism* (1966), the essays by Joachim Whaley and T.C.W. Blanning in *The Enlightenment in National Context* (1981), the essays by James Schmidt and John Christian Laursen in the collection *What is Enlightenment?* (1996), and Michael J. Sauter's *Visions of the Enlightenment* (2009)—offers a more nuanced analysis that avoids simplistic dichotomies and moves beyond inherited categories. Epstein, for instance, highlighted features that distinguished the German *Aufklärung* from the Western (Anglo-French) Enlightenment, particularly its preoccupation with religion and the unique dynamics of the competing social groups that staked out conflicting positions regarding progressive ideas.[23] Sauter, reconstructing the intellectual background of late eighteenth-century Prussia, argued that the German *Aufklärung* was fundamentally a contest over freedom and social control between 'two complicated and dynamic entities—the state and the educated elite—both of which feared uprisings by the common folk'.[24] In his account, Wöllner emerges not as a figure of pure Counter-Enlightenment reaction but as a product of the German/Prussian *Aufklärung*, representing a current within it that sought to safeguard the state and public sphere from practices deemed socially destabilizing, such as unchecked criticism and inflammatory preaching.

[20] Paulsen (1902, p. 48).

[21] Sauter (2009, pp. 5–6).

[22] Gregor (1979, p. ix).

[23] Epstein (1966, pp. 29–84).

[24] Sauter (2009, p. 9).

The binary reconstruction of the Edict and royal proclamation points to the existence of two distinct yet general thought collectives or discourses: Enlightenment vs. Counter-Enlightenment. This dualism can be elaborated through further oppositions, such as liberal vs. conservative, secular philosophy vs. orthodox religion, the bourgeoisie vs. the first and second estates, or the state vs. the public sphere. Yet such an approach either neglects the complex cultural context in which Kant and Wöllner's texts appeared, or reduces it to fit a set of inherited binaries, squeezing it into an entrenched narrative about 'the Enlightenment'.

In contrast, the alternative framing situates Wöllner and Kant within the same intellectual milieu: the state-employed educated elite of Prussia. From this perspective, their conflict can be seen as a struggle between two distinct thought styles that arose within the same specific thought collective. Alternatively, viewed through the lens of discourse analysis, Wöllner and Kant articulated competing positions within a shared (state-institutional) discursive formation. Their clash represents a struggle for discursive hegemony, as each sought to define the dominant discourse within this shared framework.

10.4 Perspectives on the German *Aufklärung*

Klaus Epstein, in *The Genesis of German Conservatism* (1966), highlighted four key features that distinguish the German *Aufklärung* from the Anglo-French Enlightenment: (1) a weak bourgeoisie, due to economic backwardness; (2) monarchical-authoritarian patterns of government, coupled with a low level of civic consciousness; (3) the high prestige of the universities, which meant intellectual movements tended to be scholarly; and (4) a national preoccupation with religious controversy.[25] These factors shaped the German public sphere, such that, unlike their English and French counterparts who addressed an established or emerging bourgeois reading public, German authors primarily addressed 'university professors, progressive bureaucrats, marginal intellectuals, and a *bourgeoisie* which was half-embryonic and half-decadent'.[26]

As a result, while the Anglo-French Enlightenment was disseminated outside the universities, which had declined in influence in England and France, the German *Aufklärung* was primarily a university phenomenon—an academic, 'professorial *Aufklärung*'. As a result, writers of the Aufklärung were generally invested in maintaining the status quo: moderate rather than radical, and conducting their debates out of earshot of the lower classes—the despised 'mob'.[27]

[25] Epstein (1966, p. 33).

[26] Epstein (1966, p. 33).

[27] Epstein (1966, p. 34). The primarily scholarly nature of the *Aufklärung* was also emphasized by Notker Hammerstein (1977), and by Tim Blanning (1981).

Then, while England had long since grappled with the tensions between Christianity and natural religion by the late seventeenth century, and France had absorbed Voltaire's anti-clerical attacks and Deism in the 1720s, the writers associated with the German Aufklärung—Lessing, Nicolai, and Mendelssohn—remained deeply engaged with religious debates into the 1770s and 1780s. The fact that Whaley could write an essay on "The Protestant Enlightenment in Germany" and Blanning on "The Enlightenment in Catholic Germany"—while other contributions in *The Enlightenment in National Context* simply addressed "The Enlightenment in England," "France," "the Netherlands," or "Sweden"—underscores how uniquely entangled the German Aufklärung was with religious questions and confessional identities. Of course, the distinction between Protestant and Catholic Enlightenments within the German principalities also reflects broader cultural, political, and geographical divides, often summarized as the 'Catholic south' and the 'Protestant north'.[28]

Epstein also highlighted the unique features of German society in the late eighteenth century. Since his approach fundamentally distinguishes between progressive ideas and conservatism (defined as resistance to progressive ideas and a desire to maintain the status quo), he identifies three main groups: 'progressive groups', 'ambivalent groups', and 'conservative groups', while acknowledging that this 'general categorization is subject to many individual exceptions'.[29]

The **progressive groups** included the entrepreneurial class, the emerging proletariat, and the intelligentsia. These groups were weak due to factors such as the fundamentally agrarian nature of German society, widespread illiteracy, exclusion, and precarity. Epstein's account describes the intelligentsia as consisting of embittered university-educated men ('literary vagabonds') who had failed to gain secure employment in the bureaucracy, clergy, or universities, alongside impoverished students (the 'academic proletariat') who aspired to such positions. These sub-groups, Epstein argues, were among the primary sources of the 'flood of books, pamphlets, magazines, and fly sheets which propagated the cause of *Aufklärung*'.[30]

The **ambivalent groups** comprised university professors, bureaucrats, professionals, and clergymen—men who had passed through the German universities and secured employment. Epstein categorized them as ambivalent because, while their worldview was shaped by the university-driven *Aufklärung*, their attitudes were tempered by the authoritarian and paternalist tendencies of the bureaucracy and state institutions.

On the one hand, many members of this group had been exposed to progressive ideas in the Wolffian philosophy faculties, to the *neo-humanism* spreading from Göttingen, to the concepts of natural law taught in many law faculties, and perhaps to professors who espoused forms of liberal theology. They were thus familiar with contemporary currents in French and English thought, including developments in

[28] Whaley (1981), Blanning (1981).

[29] Epstein (1966, pp. 47–48).

[30] Epstein (1966, pp. 48–52).

political economy, such as *laissez-faire* doctrines. They were often socially and geographically mobile, and many bureaucrats entered public service motivated by the university-taught ideals of progress, service, and legal equality.

On the other hand, the emphasis for this group was on 'good government' rather than 'self-government'. Moreover, the fierce competition for positions often led to a conservative outlook once employment was secured: state functionaries had a vested interest in preserving the status quo. Epstein emphasizes the difficulty of generalizing about this 'ambivalent group': for instance, doctors and lawyers, while largely autonomous and enjoying leisure time that allowed them to espouse progressive ideas, were also embedded within communities and often served conservative clients.

Similarly, there was significant diversity within the clergy. Protestant clergy tended to be more pro-Enlightenment than their Catholic counterparts, at least until the late 1780s, but internal stratification within the clergy complicates generalization. Higher clergy might have embraced advanced theological ideas while rejecting social radicalism, whereas lower clergy and village pastors often lacked intellectual sophistication, faced frustration and bitterness due to their status, and resisted radical ideas in order to maintain their social position above the peasantry.[31]

This ambivalent attitude towards the *Aufklärung* was exemplified by the Berliner Mittwochsgesellschaft, a semi-secret debating society active from 1783 to 1798, whose mouthpiece journal, *Berlinische Monatsschrift* (1783–1796), famously published Kant's essay *Beantwortung der Frage: Was ist Aufklärung?* (*Answer to the Question: What is Enlightenment?*) in 1784. Eckhart Hellmuth's account of the society highlights that the majority of its members were state-employed bureaucrats who espoused an elitist-paternalistic view of 'the masses' and enlightenment. For them, the intellectual freedom integral to the *Aufklärung* was generally seen as a privilege reserved for the educated elite, something to be withheld and jealously guarded from the uneducated masses, who were deemed incapable of enlightenment. At the same time, the society counted independent thinkers among its members—most notably Moses Mendelssohn and Friedrich Nicolai—who espoused a more optimistic stance on the people's capacity for self-determination and enlightenment. These fundamental differences in attitude led to splits in the society over pressing social issues of the day, such as whether there should be censorship of the press. The debates conducted within the society and in the pages of the *Berlinische Monatsschrift* support Epstein's claim that some groups were characterized by a deep-seated ambivalence toward aspects of the *Aufklärung*.[32]

The **conservative groups** included the princes and their courts, the aristocracy and officer corps, the guild masters, and the peasantry.[33] Epstein's crucial insight at this point is that a conservative outlook—one oriented towards preserving the status quo—did not necessarily preclude support for certain elements of the *Aufklärung*.

[31] Epstein (1966, pp. 52–58).

[32] Hellmuth (1998).

[33] Epstein (1966, pp. 58–59).

For instance, princes could legitimize their rule by aligning themselves with the principles of 'enlightened absolutism'. Thus, they could embrace reason, science, and the notion of progress, as long as these served to reinforce their autocratic authority. However, they stood on shakier ground with those elements of the *Aufklärung*, such as the doctrine of natural law, that posed fundamental challenges to their inherited positions.[34]

Karin Friedrich's (2012) account argues that the Wolffian Enlightenment dovetailed with Frederick II's claim to enlightened absolutism: in a rational universe designed by perfect intellect, the most legitimate ruler would be a rational law-giver, a philosopher king who had himself submitted to reason, as 'first servant of the state'. As Friedrich points out, the formula of enlightened absolutism encapsulated the contradictions inherent to the German *Aufklärung*, since it combined 'the Enlightenment precept of individual emancipation from the bondage of tradition and ignorance with the demand for subjection to a ruler whose priority was above all to consolidate the power and efficiency of his state'.[35] Thus, on the one hand Frederick II's autocratic reign saw both the publication of Kant's *Critique of Pure Reason* and the introduction of the Prussian General Law Code, and on the other, it was responsible for unprecedented warmongering, the Partition of Poland, and the exclusion of Prussian Jews and Polish Catholics from Frederician toleration.[36]

While some enlightenment ideas were variously promoted, adopted or tolerated by a broad range of groups with different orientations to the status quo, some core principles of the *Aufklärung* were resolutely opposed by certain groups with conservative outlooks: Junker officers, whose worldviews were grounded in discipline, hierarchy and particularism; the urban patriciate, whose families monopolized government functions; and guild masters, who were opposed to the new entrepreneurial class. The peasantry, meanwhile, was, according to Epstein, not so much opposed to the Enlightenment as unaware of it, steeped—in his view—in traditionalism, acquiescence, and illiteracy.[37]

At least until the 1760s, the German *Aufklärung* is not identified in the literature as a distinct ideology that was articulated by a specific social class. The Enlightenment was transmitted predominantly from English and French intellectual circles, as a set of ideas, attitudes and discursive practices that were received, reshaped and retransmitted through the German states via the universities. Whaley emphasizes that Enlightenment ideas were partially absorbed into the utilitarian educational reforms that had already begun at Halle (1694) and Göttingen (1734).[38] The cameralist philosophy, which prioritized vocational training and preparing young men for service in the bureaucracies and armies of the German states, could be characterized as a 'progressive' movement when compared with the university curricula dominated by

[34] Epstein (1966, p. 61).

[35] Friedrich (2012, p. 95).

[36] Friedrich (2012, pp. 101–113).

[37] Epstein (1966, pp. 60–64).

[38] Whaley (1981, pp. 109–117).

Protestant confessionalism and Jesuit scholasticism. Thus, enlightenment notions of reason and progress were incorporated into a pre-existing but developing state-oriented philosophy. The utilitarian rationalization of education came to be viewed as 'enlightened' because it aimed to improve the rational functioning of the state and implement a form of organizational progress.[39]

In contrast to the English class of professionals, entrepreneurs, and industrialists—who, in the absence of government interference, had accumulated economic and social capital and increasingly came to treat the state as an instrument for pursuing their self-interest, licensed by a national ethos of economic liberalism and individualism—and contrary to the emerging French bourgeoisie, who were beginning to exert external pressure on the French state, the chief opportunities for middle-class social mobility in the German states lay in gaining access to positions within the state bureaucracy. The *Estates* remained firmly intact, and an 'inherently conservative nobility in Germany could be enlightened since the "true enlightenment" posed no threat to its position'.[40]

Blanning highlights how the Protestant *Aufklärung* spread to Catholic Germany via the universities: 'a significant and growing number of Catholics went north to study at Leipzig, Jena, Halle or Gottingen and then returned to their *alma mater* with quite a new conception of what and how they should teach'.[41] He further emphasizes that Catholic universities selected compatible elements of Enlightenment thought to deploy against the Jesuit monopoly on Catholic educational institutions. Representatives of the Italian Enlightenment, the *Illuministi*, such as Cesare Beccaria, tended to be preferred over the French *philosophes*: 'When French thinkers did find an audience, their ideas were refracted out of all recognition by native intellectual traditions'.[42]

The key point here is that German universities—whether Protestant or Catholic—were far from passive recipients of Enlightenment thought. In the process of reception and transmission, ideas were selectively adopted, refracted, blended, and reinterpreted to fit within domestic meaning systems. In terms of Fleck's theory, this is an example of the transformations that inevitably arise as a result of the 'circulation of ideas'.[43] Let us recall: Fleck's theory asserts that the communication of ideas between thought collectives is determined by the distance between them. The greater the temporal and spatial distance, the more significant the communicative obstacles, and the more transformative—or distorting—the effects of translation and transmission.[44]

[39] For a skeptical perspective on the rationalization of state and society during this period, see Wakefield (2009), which questions the coherence and efficacy of cameralist reforms and their alignment with Enlightenment ideals.

[40] Whaley (1981, p. 111).

[41] Blanning (1981, p. 121).

[42] Blanning (1981, p. 121).

[43] Fleck (1986, p. 87).

[44] Fleck (1986, p. 85).

In eighteenth-century Europe, multiple factors constituted and determined the distances between thought collectives: language barriers, national boundaries, religious denominations and allegiances, the role of institutions in censoring, filtering, and disseminating ideas, the size and quality of the reading public, and the existence of deeply entrenched domestic thought styles.

Jonathan I. Israel draws on the evidence of foreign language publications that were contained in libraries across Europe in the eighteenth century to highlight the paradoxical nature of the intellectual and social elites that drove the Early Enlightenment: their peculiar combination of cultural cosmopolitanism and 'universal intellectual concerns' with 'remarkably parochial' and narrow outlooks.[45] British libraries tended to contain works in English, Latin, and French, but hardly any in Dutch, German, Spanish, or Italian. Similarly, other national libraries exhibited limited linguistic diversity, with their collections dominated by works in the local language, Latin, and occasionally French. If English authors like Hobbes and Locke appeared in Northern European collections, they tended to be in Latin translations.

Nevertheless, in the same section of his monumental study, Israel concludes that, despite such cultural and linguistic parochialism, 'the great cultural transformation' of the eighteenth century should still be seen as 'a single European Enlightenment', rather than as 'many different national Enlightenments'. In Israel's preferred framing, the Enlightenment was a continent-wide cultural transformation, shaped by intellectual innovations emerging at different times and progressing with varying pace and intensity in five national contexts: France, Britain, Germany, Italy, and the Netherlands.[46] Given that neither Germany nor Italy can be straightforwardly identified as nations in the eighteenth century, Israel's later reformulation is more compelling: he argues that the great cultural transformation had its centre of gravity in north-western Europe and was driven by the 'ebb and flow of ideas' among an inner circuit of key cities—Amsterdam (and other Dutch cities), Paris, London, Hamburg, and Berlin.[47]

Considering Fleck's framework, two points can be made at this stage. First, Israel draws on quantitative data to construct historical facts and derive conclusions regarding their historical significance. Library contents can be treated as examples of Fleck's passive elements of cognition: once the arbitrary measure of 'a volume' is applied to collections of printed material, statements such as the following can be made: 'Locke's personal library of over 3000 volumes was entirely typical'. This measure, in turn, enables non-arbitrary relations between the volumes to be established and significance to be attached to their ratios:

> Over a third of his books were in English and another third in Latin, with a further 18 per cent in French. The rest amounting to under 5 per cent, mostly comprised works in Greek

[45] Israel (2001, p. 137).

[46] Israel (2001, p. 140).

[47] Israel (2001, p. 141).

> and Italian, leaving Dutch, German, and Spanish almost totally excluded, despite his having lived and worked for six years in the Netherlands and knowing some Dutch.[48]

Following Fleck's theory, the statement that Locke's library was 'entirely typical' can be viewed as a historical fact constructed through indirect cognitive interaction with two passive elements: collections of printed materials associated with specific historical individuals and institutions, and the linguistic systems of signs identifiable as characteristic of European languages of the period. If definitions of 'volume' and specific languages are accepted (keeping in mind that distinctions between 'Low Dutch', 'Low German', and 'High German' were by no means straightforward), the data incorporates non-arbitrary elements. For instance, a researcher cannot arbitrarily claim that Locke's library contained 18 per cent Dutch-language volumes when the data indicates otherwise.

Since Israel refers to Harrison and Laslett's *The Library of John Locke* (1971), his cognitive interaction with Locke's library is indirect, as is his engagement with other collections used for comparison in the assertion that Locke's library was 'entirely typical'. Historical facts regarding European libraries of the late seventeenth and early eighteenth centuries are thus constructed through indirect scholarly interaction with passive elements (printed materials and linguistic systems), the application of arbitrary measures and criteria (volumes and languages), and comparisons of non-arbitrary ratios within and between collections (percentages, fractions, and typologies).

As a historian of intellectual history, Israel's thought style is exemplified in his methodological approach: historical facts are constructed through layers of scholarly interaction—both direct and indirect—with passive elements such as source texts and scholarship on physical artefacts. He then argues positions by assigning significance to these facts. For example, Locke's neglect of Dutch is presented as emblematic of English thinkers' and readers' prioritization of works in English, Latin, and French. Israel's positions are also established through discursive struggles with other members of his thought collective, whose divergent approaches and interpretations reveal variations within the collective's thought style.

Israel's assertion that the cultural transformation of the eighteenth century should be viewed as 'a single European Enlightenment' implicitly challenges Roy Porter's thesis of multiple, localized Enlightenments.[49] In Fleckian terms, the late twentieth-century and early twenty-first-century thought collective of intellectual historians was itself divided over how to frame the cultural change generated by eighteenth-century thought collectives. This division influenced both the research objects and the methodologies employed to investigate these collectives, ultimately shaping the facts constructed to support their respective positions.

The second—and perhaps more significant—point is that both framings, whether of a single Enlightenment or multiple, local Enlightenments, emphasize the importance of distance and barriers in shaping the emergence of cultural change. In

[48] Israel (2001, p. 137).

[49] Porter (1981).

Israel's account, factors such as lack of synchronicity and entrenched linguistic parochialism are identified as catalysts for change within the broader context of a drive toward universality. While certain developments facilitated the rise of an increasingly pan-European or 'universal' public sphere—epistolary networks, numerous journals summarizing key contributions in the emerging genre of the review, reading and debating societies, transnational debates in print, the burgeoning translation industry, newspapers, and periodicals—change is depicted as unfolding across the continent precisely because transmission between regions involved delays, adaptations, and distortions. This view envisions change as occurring in waves of communication that wash back and forth across local European cultures. These waves encounter obstacles, such as censorship and translation delays, swirl into urban whirlpools, are processed through institutions like universities and scientific societies, and intermix with local currents before recirculating toward their points of origin.

By contrast, the model proposed by Porter, Whaley, Blanning, and others (1981) resembles a family tree. A plausible extrapolation from their framework suggests that when a local tradition absorbs ideas from another cultural context, this 'marriage' generates a new branch and line of descent, with national contexts forming distinct limbs of the Enlightenment. If the main trunk of the Enlightenment originated in the Late Renaissance challenge to church authority, exemplified by the Lutheran Reformation and the Copernican hypothesis, it subsequently divided into English, Italian, and French branches with the advent of Baconian, Galilean, and Cartesian philosophies. These branches occasionally intermarried, as with Voltaire's *Letters on the English* or the eventual French embrace of Newtonianism, yet they retained their distinctiveness as national 'Enlightenments'. Within this framework, the German *Aufklärung* would trace its lineage through local developments in Protestantism, Confessionalism, Pietism, and Cameralism. This trajectory formed a distinctly German branch of the Enlightenment as the rationalist contributions of Leibniz and Wolff absorbed and responded to ideas transmitted through the English, French, and Dutch Enlightenments. According to Blanning (1981), this predominantly Protestant German Enlightenment further diversified into a German Catholic Enlightenment through its assimilation of Italian intellectual currents.

Both these models of cultural change—emphasizing intellectual innovations as key determinants—are fully consistent with Fleck's concepts of the circulation of ideas between thought collectives and the role of distance between them in shaping changes in thought styles. In this framework, cultural change arises from two distinct but interrelated factors: (1) developments in communication technologies and practices that tend toward universality and homogenization, and (2) barriers that disrupt seamless communication, persistently generating heterogeneity. Such barriers include distance (temporal and spatial), linguistic differences, translation delays and distortions, resistance from local traditions, censorship, and institutional filtering by universities and scientific societies.

To put this in counterfactual terms: in the seventeenth and eighteenth centuries, amid dramatic advancements in communication technologies, if European cultures had adhered to a relatively homogenous set of norms and practices; if Latin had remained the lingua franca; and if European thought collectives had not begun to express and disseminate ideas in the vernacular, then the transmission of ideas across European regions would likely not have contributed to such profound cultural transformations. According to Fleck's theory, smooth and rapid communication between thought collectives—when minimally distorted—is not conducive to substantive transformations in thought styles. Rather, such change requires friction: obstacles, distance, and distortion.

To summarize, the analysis of scholarship on the German *Aufklärung* supports two key conclusions. First, the transmission, absorption, and articulation of non-traditional ideas; the adoption of new social practices (e.g., debating, and reading and writing non-religious texts); and the emergence of new forms of cultural production (e.g., journals, novels, political pamphlets, and philosophical essays and tomes increasingly written in the vernacular) were shaped by interactions between a wide array of thought collectives. These collectives were both internally divided and defined by antagonisms with others. Second, cultural change in Prussia and the broader German principalities was driven by how these diverse social groups received, adapted, and responded to the ideas transmitted through non-German waves or branches of the Enlightenment.

In the light of such complexity, it is evident that the Enlightenment/Counter-Enlightenment dichotomy, while a convenient heuristic, oversimplifies the textual phenomena by suppressing evidence of the complex interactions within and between thought collectives. Yet, the source texts—most notably Wöllner's *Edict* and reprimand, and Kant's *The Conflict of the Faculties*—do provide clear evidence of antagonism and resistance between representatives of divergent thought styles. The challenge, then, is to frame this resistance in a way that acknowledges its complexity without collapsing it into reductive binary oppositions. This is the issue explored in the following sections.

10.5 The Challenge to Theology: Hobbes, Spinoza and the Claims of Philosophy

If a broader, European-level perspective is adopted, Kant's clash with Wöllner in 1794 and the blows Kant delivered on behalf of the philosophy faculty in *The Conflict of the Faculties* (1794–98) can be viewed as just one skirmish in a longer conflict stretching back to the mid-seventeenth century. For example, Reinhart Koselleck and Jonathan I. Israel—scholars with very different approaches to the Enlightenment—both identify the mid-seventeenth century as a watershed moment when antagonism in Europe underwent a crucial shift: intra-religious, confessional conflicts began to recede in significance, while theologians and state authorities increasingly recognized 'philosophy' as the new enemy.

The measures employed to suppress works by authors like Hobbes and Spinoza in the ostensibly tolerant environments of late seventeenth-century England and

Holland—personal vilification, branding as 'atheist', censorship, court trials, imprisonment, seizing books, and punishing printers—became standard strategies in the German states throughout the eighteenth century, persisting even into the 1790s. Nearly 50 years after Spinoza's death, Wolff's expulsion from the University of Halle in 1726 was justified by charges—brought by the theologians Lange and Buddeus—that Wolff's system opened the gates to Spinozism.[50] Even as late as the 1780s, Fritz Jacobi caused a scandal with his (posthumous and contentious) claim that Lessing had become a Spinozist in his final years, and that §73 of Lessing's *The Education of the Human Race* could only be understood as an expression of Spinozist pantheism. It can be argued that the punitive measures taken against Kant in the 1790s—censorship of his *Religion within the Limits of Mere Reason* (1791), the royal reprimand of 1794, and the 1795 ban on lectures about his philosophy of religion—were reactions to a work that, in many respects, echoed the claims Spinoza had made—anonymously but with devastating clarity—in the *Tractatus Theologico-Politicus* (1670).

The following sections trace three interconnected phenomena: first, the challenges posed by a new 'naturalist-critical' form of philosophy that emerged in the second half of the seventeenth century; second, the theological and conservative reactions to this philosophy's claims of autonomy and its right to analyse religion and Scripture; and third, the strategic efforts of other emergent strains of philosophy to distance themselves from the image of atheism projected onto naturalist criticism.

The ultimate aim of this reconstructive analysis is to illuminate the determinants of Wöllner's and Kant's textual actions: the former's *Edict* and official reprimand, and the latter's advocacy for the philosophy faculty in *The Conflict of the Faculties*. These texts occupied positions in a cultural field where the available positions had already been shaped and encoded by over a century of discursive and institutional conflict. To fully appreciate Kant's unique contributions to the conception and development of the German university, it is crucial to discern which elements of his text were determined by these established discursive layers and antagonisms, and which introduced concepts from other thought styles, thereby laying the groundwork for cultural change.

In terms of Fleck's theory, the tendency of seventeenth-century naturalist-critical philosophy to increasingly identify itself as *philosophy* and define itself in explicit opposition to theology and ecclesiastical authorities—a trend evident in the works of Hobbes, Lodewijk Meyer, Spinoza, and the Koerbagh brothers—indicates the emergence of a new thought style. Following Hobbes's foundational contributions, this thought style was predominantly articulated by an anti-authoritarian and confrontational Dutch thought collective, drawing inspiration from natural philosophy, Bible hermeneutics, and democratic republicanism. The radical claims of this thought style provoked a backlash from theological thought collectives across Europe, which relied on vilification and suppression to maintain control over universities and state institutions (e.g., Jakob Thomasius at the University of Leipzig).

[50] Saine (1997, p. 121).

This emergent philosophy was also criticized by other thought styles seeking to distance themselves from its more radical aspects, as seen in the responses of German natural law philosophers (e.g., Samuel Pufendorf, Christian Thomasius), English empiricists (e.g., Boyle), and proponents of theodicy (e.g., Leibniz).

The circumstances and processes underpinning the emergence of this new thought style align closely with Fleck's concepts. Most obviously, the intellectual unrest driving these developments is exemplified by well-documented historical crises. The turmoil of the English Civil War, for instance, shaped the problem that Hobbes sought to address in *Leviathan*. Similarly, Spinoza's *Tractatus Theologico-Politicus* reflects the conflict between the Remonstrants and Counter-Remonstrants and aligns with the Republican Dutch States Party in its long-standing struggle against the Royalist Orangists. Few philosophical texts are as deeply embedded in the socio-political crises of their time as *Leviathan* and the *Tractatus Theologico-Politicus*. Composed amid political turmoil and socio-economic upheaval, these works sought to offer solutions to the normative and epistemic crises that engulfed English and Dutch societies.

In terms of the Fleckian circulation of ideas, both Hobbes and Spinoza borrowed concepts and methods from other fields of inquiry, with revolutionary results. First, both philosophers famously suffered from 'geometrophilia'[51] and sought to emulate the deductive certainty of Euclidean geometry in their analyses of non-geometric phenomena, with Spinoza even adopting Euclidean procedure as the expository form in his *Ethics*. Though their Euclidean preoccupations ultimately led to unfortunate consequences—Hobbes's damaged reputation as a scientist and Spinoza's questionable deductive leaps—the necessity inherent in geometric proof nevertheless served as a normative benchmark, raising the clarity and confidence of their reasoning to unprecedented heights.

Fleck's claim that a thought style determines perception suggests that Hobbes and Spinoza's infatuation with Euclidean demonstrations conditioned their perception of natural phenomena. The irresistible necessity of geometric deductions did not merely reflect the mechanical causality perceived in nature—it acted as a perceptual framework that shaped how nature itself was seen. Applying Fleck's interactionist social epistemology to Hobbes's materialist determinism and Spinoza's necessitarianism reveals how these views emerged from the interplay of non-arbitrary passive elements and theoretical projections. Sequences of events observed in the natural world cannot be arbitrarily reordered or reversed; this observation appeared to confirm the appropriateness of mechanical causality (developed in natural philosophy/physics) and necessity (developed in mathematics/geometry). These concepts came to structure how nature was perceived, and—through repeated confirmation—were eventually treated as essential features of natural reality. The radical concept of nature as the sole substance, where all things happen of necessity

[51] Gottlieb (2017, pp. 50–51; 100–01).

according to a 'fixed and unalterable order' (*TTP* Ch. 3, §3),[52] can thus be traced to communication between thought styles: the mathematical concept of demonstrative necessity was adopted by philosophy and projected into 'nature' as a metaphysical concept.

Second, as will be explored in more detail in the following sections, Hobbes, Meyer, and Spinoza adopted and adapted methods of scriptural exegesis developed in diverse traditions: Renaissance humanism, Protestant Scholasticism, the school of Saumur, and even Cartesian exegesis.[53] When the thought style of naturalist philosophy borrowed these interpretative tools, the consequences were *momentous*. Techniques originally intended for analysing sacred texts were repurposed to investigate the Bible as if it provided descriptions of natural events and phenomena, and religion itself was treated as a natural phenomenon.

Third, twentieth-century historians of culture and intellectual history framed the onset of the Enlightenment using assumptions, methods, and intellectual fashions characteristic of their own thought styles. Despite occupying opposing positions on the political spectrum, both Reinhart Koselleck and Jürgen Habermas reconstructed the Enlightenment as a fundamental dichotomy between the public sphere and state authority. In this big picture model, intellectual critique (Koselleck) and bourgeois production and communication (Habermas) are portrayed as relentlessly undermining the authority of the church and the absolutist state, culminating in crisis and revolution, thereby perpetuating the Enlightenment/Counter-Enlightenment dualism.

In contrast, more recent scholarship and popular history have framed the period as one of multi-dimensional antagonisms and complex interactions among diverse intellectual communities. For example, Jonathan I. Israel's in-depth analysis presents the Early Enlightenment as a threefold conflict between radical democrats, the moderate mainstream, and traditional power structures—all mutually opposed across Europe.[54] Similarly, in his detailed work of popular history, Ritchie Robertson describes the emergence and cross-fertilization of *multiple* Enlightenments—religious, scientific, practical, aesthetic, political.[55] This shift—from sweeping dualisms that reduce history to a struggle between abstract, homogeneous entities (e.g., 'Reason' vs. 'the State') to more nuanced accounts attentive to complexity, heterogeneity, and historical particularity—marks a transformation in the way cultural change is conceptualized—no longer as a dialectical, dualistic unfolding, but as the product of intersecting discourses, institutional pressures, and historically situated thought styles.

[52] All references to Spinoza's *Tractatus Theologico-Politicus* (TTP) are to the 2007 translation of Michael Silverthorne and Jonathan I. Israel: Spinoza (2007).

[53] Rice and Pastijn (2005, pp. 3–4).

[54] Israel (2001).

[55] Robertson (2020).

10.6 Hobbes's *Leviathan* (1651) and the Onset of the Enlightenment

Reinhart Koselleck (1957) identified the publication of *Leviathan* in 1651 with the inception of the Enlightenment, as it is here that Hobbes suggests for the first time that an alliance between Reason and the Absolutist State is essential to suppress religious conflict and end civil war. For Koselleck, this empowerment of Reason had both foreseeable and unforeseen consequences. The secularization of morality was a predictable and, in retrospect, perhaps even inevitable outcome of Hobbes's effort to recast moral philosophy as a science grounded in natural principles (*Leviathan*, Ch. XV §40). However, Hobbes failed to anticipate that Reason would one day emancipate itself from state control—a decoupling that would have far-reaching consequences when Reason turned its critique upon the state itself.[56]

In Koselleck's framing, the Enlightenment is presented as a single pathogenetic process. Reason, portrayed as an abstract cultural entity, gradually freed itself from theological constraints and discarded successive layers of theological and institutional constraint. This trajectory saw Reason apply its critique first to the church and religion, then to the State and monarchy, and finally, in Kant's *Critique of Pure Reason*, to itself.

Leviathan also constitutes an early example of a naturalistic account of the phenomenon of religion and of philosophical 'criticism' of Scripture. In Chapter XII, Hobbes observes that 'from all Living Creatures, the seed of Religion is found onely in Man',[57] and this phenomenon is attributed to a range of propensities: the desire to know causes, anxiety about the future, and assigning reality to 'creatures of the Fancy' such as ghosts. This leads Hobbes to the distinction between natural religion and revealed religion: the former ('human Politiques') grows from a natural seed, and the variety of its inventions is attributable to differences in culture, while the latter ('Divine Politiques') is directed by God's commandment. Crucially, for Hobbes, both kinds of religion serve the same purpose: 'Obedience, Lawes, Peace, Charity, and civill Society'. Thus, from a purely naturalistic perspective, the function of religion—whether natural or revealed—is the same: to teach the duty 'required from Subjects'.

In Part III of *Leviathan*, Hobbes shifts from a naturalistic description of human society organized in accordance with 'the Principles of Nature' and 'naturall Reason' to a consideration *Of A Christian Commonwealth*, one which depends on 'Supernaturall Revelations'. The focus thus shifts from a causal analysis of *Natural Man* to a rational examination of the *Word of God*. Employing a combination of Protestant Biblical exegesis and mechanistic-Cartesian reasoning, Hobbes cites chapters and verses to dissect phenomena such as revelation, prophecy, miracles, the authorship and interpretation of the Scriptures, angels, demons, hell, salvation, heaven, the Trinity, martyrdom, excommunication, and ecclesiastical law.

---

[56] Koselleck (1988, pp. 34–40).

[57] All quotations from Hobbes's *Leviathan* are taken from the Penguin 1986 edition: Hobbes (1986).

Hobbes's analysis of angels exemplifies his method: he contrasts Angels as Messengers of God with the imagery of the brain, which Gentiles and Jews mistakenly regarded as truly existing incorporeal substances. When constrained by the text of the Old Testament, *Angel* signifies nothing more than the presence of God performing supernatural work. Hobbes concludes with the following functional interpretation:

> There you see Motion, and Speech, which are commonly attributed to Angels, attributed to a Cloud, because the Cloud served as a sign of Gods presence; and was no lesse an Angel, than if it had had the form of a Man, or Child of never so great beauty; or with Wings, as usually they are painted, for the false instruction of common people. For it is not the shape; but their use, that makes them angels. But their use is to be significations of Gods presence in supernatural operations; as when Moses (Exod. 33· 14) had desired God to goe along with the Campe, (as he had done alwaies before the making of the Golden Calfe,) God did not answer, *I will goe, nor I will send an Angell in my stead;* but thus, *My presence shall go with thee*. (*Leviathan*, Ch. XXXIV)

He then asserts that 'no text in that part of the Old Testament, which the Church of England holdeth for Canonicall' permits the conclusion that permanent, incorporeal entities exist in space. Angels, Hobbes contends, are nothing but 'signs of God's special presence' (*Leviathan*, Ch. XXXIV). With his unique combination of uncompromising materialism and Scriptural exegesis, Hobbes effectively eliminates an entire class of supernatural beings.

Hobbes's philosophical analysis of Scripture exemplifies what Reinhart Koselleck describes as 'the new art of criticism', or *critique*, which emerged in the seventeenth century and came to characterise Enlightenment thought in the eighteenth. Koselleck traces the term 'criticism' (French *critique*, German *Kritik*) to Renaissance humanists, who drew on the Greek term χρίνω (*chrino*, to differentiate, select, judge, decide) to signify the evaluation and study of ancient texts. When Scripture itself became subject to similar philological analysis, this process was also termed 'criticism'.[58] The term acquired its polemical edge during confessional disputes, as critics increasingly employed rationality, rather than Revelation, as the ultimate criterion of truth. As Koselleck observes: 'Thus, in the context of the textual criticism of Holy Scripture, and from out of the religious conflicts, a new front was formed, remarkable for the novel fact that the spokesmen of the warring Churches were confronted by a common enemy'.[59]

In contrast to the early seventeenth-century natural philosophies of Bacon, Galileo, and Descartes—which employed various strategies to mask their challenge to theology and seek compromise with ecclesiastical authorities—Hobbes openly identified religion as a potential source of 'Faction and Civil war in the Commonwealth, between the Church and State', unless the Civil Sovereign was also the Chief Pastor, governing both State and Religion (*Leviathan*, Ch. XXXIX).

Hobbes's argument for subordinating religion to the absolute control of the civil sovereign is reinforced in Part 4, Chapter XLVI, with a lengthy critique of 'Vain

---

[58] Koselleck (1988, p. 105).

[59] Koselleck (1988, p. 107).

Philosophy'. This critique targets the scholastic philosophy dominant in universities, which Hobbes characterizes as the handmaid to theology. He contends that the combined errors of Vain Philosophy and theology constitute a false philosophy that suppresses true philosophy, as evidenced by those who 'supposed' the heliocentric doctrine and were punished for it by 'Authority Ecclesiasticall'. Crucially, Hobbes asserts that if philosophers are to be silenced—whether for inciting rebellion or sedition—it must be by 'the Authority Civill'. Ecclesiastical attempts to censor philosophy, he argues, amount to an unauthorized seizure of power: 'Usurpation' (*Leviathan*, Ch. XLVI).

Hobbes's oblique reference to the trial and sentencing of Galileo in 1633, and to the prohibition of his *Dialogue*, implicates *Leviathan* in the broader struggle between theological authorities and and the new philosophy taking shape in seventeenth-century Europe. Prohibition and censorship were the first weapons wielded by ecclesiastical and state authorities to suppress philosophical texts. These power struggles—between theologians, the state, universities, philosophers, and the reading public—ran through the entirety of the Enlightenment, from the banning of the works of Hobbes and Spinoza in the 1670s, to the debates of the Berliner Mittwochsgesellschaft in the 1780s, and Wöllner's attempt to silence Kant in the 1790s. Hobbes's position on censorship merits particular analysis, as it is bound up with key conceptual distinctions and dualities that subsequently structured the field in which various Enlightenment thought styles staked out their positions.

The issue of censorship—in Hobbes's terms, the governance of Opinions and Doctrines—is addressed in Part II, Chapter XVIII, where he enumerates the rights of an instituted Sovereign and the limitations of his subjects. Since the Sovereign is instituted for the purpose of peace and defence, Hobbes argues that the Sovereign must act as Judge of 'the meanes of Peace and Defence', with the authority to do whatever is necessary to prevent 'Discord at home'. Therefore:

> Sixtly, it is annexed to the Soveraignty, to be Judge of what Opinions and Doctrines are averse, and what conducing to Peace; and consequently, on what occasions, how farre, and what, men are to be trusted withall, in speaking to Multitudes of people; and who shall examine the Doctrines of all bookes before they be published. For the Actions of men proceed from their Opinions; and in the wel governing of Opinions, consisteth the well governing of mens Actions, in order to their Peace, and Concord. (*Leviathan* Ch. XVIII)

Alongside Hobbes's familiar insistence on the Sovereign's absolute right to control society for the sake of peace, here focused on public speaking and the publication of books, this passage also highlights his crucial distinction between Actions and Opinions. Hobbes recognizes that opinions and doctrines can directly incite actions that 'awake the Warre', since some men 'dare take up Armes, to defend, or introduce an Opinion'.[60] Therefore, the governance of opinions and doctrines becomes inseparable from the governance of actions and is essential to preventing 'Discord and Civill Warre' (*Leviathan* Ch. XVIII).

[60] Hobbes's debt to Thucydides is evident here. See Chap. 6.6.3 of the present study for an analysis of how Thucydides describes the use of words and persuasion to provoke decision and action—how articulatory practices became entangled with acts of violence, ultimately instigating civil war.

Hobbes's *Leviathan* thus exemplifies a philosopher diagnosing the causes of social and political turmoil and identifying opinions and doctrines as the chief culprits. In Hobbes's analysis, the tumult of the English Civil War is reducible to two key determinants: first, that society is 'only a Cessation of Armes', with men 'still in Warre' (*Leviathan* Ch. XVIII); and second, that men are willing to fight for opinions. Patricia Springborg argues that, for Hobbes, it was the opinions of the Presbyterians and Papists that plunged England into civil war. Both Protestant Puritans and Roman Catholics denied the Sovereign's authority, the former insisting on greater independence and the latter appealing to supranational authority.[61]

Hobbes's proposed remedy for such challenges to authority—and for mankind's propensity to return to the state of war for the sake of opinions and doctrines—was to ensure that the Sovereign exercised total control over public speaking and the publication of books.

The distinction between action and opinion maps onto another crucial duality that structures Hobbes's reasoning throughout *Leviathan*: the internal vs. external binary opposition. The key point is that the Sovereign has no jurisdiction over 'internall Faith' or 'inward thought', but only over 'externall Worship' or 'external acts' (*Leviathan* Ch. 31, 40, 42, 43, 45). This distinction is most explicitly connected to the control of speech as an action in Chapter 42, where Hobbes reduces the doctrine of the New Testament to advice rather than Law, which pertains only to the Commonwealth: 'For internall Faith is in its own nature invisible, and consequently exempted from all humane jurisdiction; whereas the words, and actions that proceed from it, as breaches of our Civill obedience, are injustice both before God and Man'. Thus, the Sovereign has no control over invisible thought, only over words and actions, and this jurisdiction is civil, or secular, not ecclesiastical or divine.

10.7 Koselleck vs. Habermas: Hobbes, the Privatization of Conscience, and the Emergence of the Public Sphere

In a tantalizing footnote,[62] Koselleck acknowledges that Hobbes's separation of inward thought and external acts draws on a long-established Western tradition. This lineage can be traced back to Augustine's two-world doctrine, through Thomas Aquinas's distinction between external acts and the inner world of God, to Luther's separation between the spiritual realm and the external office of the rulers. However, according to Koselleck, Hobbes's unique contribution lies in his 'functionalist interpretation of conscience', which analyses the inner realm in terms of political motivations and outcomes.

---

[61] Springbourg (1996, pp. 366–67).

[62] Koselleck (1988, p. 29).

In this framing, Hobbes adopts an extra-religious, supra-partisan position that identifies conscience as a cause of instability on two fronts. On the one hand, the 'prophets of Revelation', such as Luther, followed their conscience and thereby encroached upon the external realm, while Presbyterians even sought to subjugate the secular realm entirely to the spiritual realm. On the other hand, Puritans and Independents opposed their good conscience to the evil external world, leading to a self-righteous rejection of secular authority. Hobbes thus identified conscience—unmoored from unified religious authority—as one of the causes of civil war. Koselleck reads Hobbes's reduction of the inner realm to 'opinion' as an attempt to neutralize the potential of conscience as a motivation for action.[63]

Koselleck's complex account of Hobbes's intervention requires some unpacking. He suggests that Hobbes's strategy of simultaneously removing conscience (inward thought) from the jurisdiction of the Civil Sovereign and endowing the same Sovereign with complete control over the external realm of actions and words (including ecclesiastical doctrine and publicly expressed opinions) achieves several functional outcomes. First, on the individual level, the subject's internal opinions are protected from external interference by the state and/or ecclesiastical authority; the Sovereign only has the right to intervene if the subject's inward thought manifests in disobedient action or seditious speech. Second, on the level of civil society, the Civil Sovereign's control over religious doctrine protects the Commonwealth and its laws from usurpation by ecclesiastical authorities and the destabilizing influence of self-righteous religious sects.

The crucial outcome of Hobbes's diagnostic framing and proposed solution in *Leviathan* is that 'Hobbes's man is fractured, split into private and public halves: his actions are totally subject to the law of the land while his mind remains free, "in secret free"'.[64] For Koselleck, this fracturing marks the onset of the pathogenetic process of the Enlightenment, whereby man's private inner space steadily expanded and—through the emergence of forms of cultural production and social practices, such as the 'Republic of Letters', philosophical criticism, secret societies, and the stage—came to express the opposition of 'the bourgeois stratum' to the 'absolutist state and ruling church'.[65] Thus, for Koselleck, Hobbes's internal/external dichotomy underpins the cascade of dualistic concepts and counter-concepts that structure Enlightenment thought: 'reason and Revelation, freedom and despotism, nature and civilization, trade and war, morality and politics, decadence and progress, light and darkness'.[66]

In terms of Koselleck's main thesis, the most crucial dichotomy is that between morality and politics. Since Leviathan had absolute control over the sphere of external action—in other words, over politics—and since Hobbes freed inward thought

[63] Koselleck (1988, pp. 27–30).

[64] Koselleck (1988, p. 37).

[65] Koselleck (1988, p. 122).

[66] Koselleck (1988, p. 100).

from the jurisdiction of church and state, this became an autonomous sphere of moral judgement. Piet Strydom succinctly summarizes Koselleck's argument:

> Politics, the preserve of the state, was separated from morality, the domain in which the subjects found a refuge. The Enlightenment was an articulation of this latter domain, developing the universalistic morality excluded by the state and critically playing it out against the state as soon as the critique of its legitimation foundation, religion, had been completed.[67]

In this conception, the Enlightenment was an emancipatory process whereby the suppressed and controlled terms in a set of dualisms became liberated and turned on the dominant terms. The thought and opinion confined to the private domain escaped to construct a bourgeois public sphere which subjected the Sovereign to criticism and, ultimately, to the moral judgement of its dualistic concepts.

Koselleck's dualistic account aligns with the textual evidence: the fracturing of man that emerges in Hobbes's philosophy can be traced through subsequent Enlightenment discourses and identified in reformulations which retain the key Hobbesian distinction—the dichotomy of the (inwardly critical) private citizen and the (externally obedient) subject. Most pertinently for the purposes of the present work, over a 130 years after Hobbes's English intervention on behalf of the new philosophy, this structural fracture reappeared in Kant's 'two-hats' conception of the public sphere, the *Aufklärung*, and the German University. In 1784's *What is Enlightenment?*, Kant famously argued that one and the same person must use their reason freely when playing the role of a scholar (*Gelehrte*), but passively obey the government when reasoning as a civil servant (*Beamte*).[68] In *The Conflict of the Faculties* (1794), he reformulated this duality by dividing the university institution into two distinct domains: the theology, law, and medicine faculties, which must obey the commands of the external legislator, and the philosophy faculty, which is subject only to the laws of reason.[69]

More broadly, for Koselleck and Habermas (circa 1962)—despite their methodological differences and opposed evaluations—the demarcation of religion as a private matter in the late seventeenth century opened up a space of autonomy that ultimately, in the eighteenth century, set civil society and the public sphere in opposition to the state.[70] Thus, the dualistic conception of a pan-European cultural and political conflict between the public sphere and the state, which is also cast as the Enlightenment vs. Counter-Enlightenment polarity, is rooted in the conviction that the emancipation of the individual's private opinion from theological and state jurisdiction marked a critical moment and turning point in European culture.

In Koselleck's intellectualist account, this occurred through philosophy's relentless deployment of dualistic formulations. Hobbesian conceptual dichotomies underpinned and triggered the cultural and political conflict of the eighteenth century; then, once set in motion, the pathogenetic process of philosophical critique

---

[67] Styrdom (2000, p. 258).

[68] Kant (2008, p. 19).

[69] Kant (1979, pp. 31–47).

[70] Habermas (1992, pp. 11–12).

took on a cultural and political agency of its own—while hypocritically claiming political neutrality—and ultimately came to engulf the French King as well as philosophers themselves with its utopian morality.[71]

In contrast, the Habermas of *The Structural Transformation of the Public Sphere* (1962)—clearly written partly in response to Koselleck's thesis—treats the public sphere as a normative 'ideological template' shaped by underlying structural transformations. From this perspective, the polarization that positioned the bourgeois public sphere against the state was driven by economic changes and advances in communication technology, which fundamentally altered power structures in European societies.

While Habermas does not explicitly outline his methodology, it becomes evident through his focus on economic factors, communication technologies, and social relations, rather than on conceptual developments. This approach is particularly clear in Chapter IV, *The Bourgeois Public Sphere: Idea and Ideology*, where philosophers begin to receive sustained attention, and Habermas traces the term 'opinion' from Hobbes to Rousseau. The terms 'opinion', 'public opinion', *opinion publique*, and *öffentliche Meinung* are thus treated as ideological reflections of primary transformations in the economic base and as downstream effects of developments in communication technology.

In Habermas's account, these underlying structural transformations included the rise of capitalist commercial relations and modes of production, which coincided with the emergence of new communication genres and institutions. Merchants, financiers, and entrepreneurs required up-to-date information, giving rise to private *news letters* and postal services, which eventually became public commodities in the form of newspapers and a social institution in the form of the press. Habermas identifies two key functions that the press fulfilled in European societies from the end of the seventeenth century: first, providing commercial information essential to an emerging class whose economic interests and dependencies extended beyond the self-contained household (*oikos*), thereby acquiring public relevance; and second, disseminating the instructions and ordinances of state administrations, which sought to regulate the economy through mercantilist policies.

As the state evolved into an administrative entity distinct from the sovereign's personal property—in other words, as a public authority focused on taxation and regulation—it required regular communication with its subjects. The increasing availability of newspapers and rising literacy levels ensured this need was met: 'the addressees of the authorities' announcements genuinely became "the public" in the proper sense'.[72] However, antagonism between the public authority and the bourgeois public sphere was structurally inevitable.

While a segment of the emerging bourgeois class was assimilated into the state administration and civil service (e.g., jurists, pastors, professors, and schoolteachers), another segment—bankers, entrepreneurs, and manufacturers—remained

[71] Koselleck (1988, pp. 120–23).

[72] Habermas (1992, p. 21).

outside the state apparatus. This independent stratum constituted the core of the bourgeois public sphere: 'This stratum of "bourgeois" was the real carrier of the public, which from the outset was a reading public'.[73] Addressed by state authorities yet distinct from the administration, the public sphere became an 'abstract counterpart of public authority' and, in turn, subjected the state to 'the critical judgement of a public making use of its reason'.[74]

Newspapers provided the literate bourgeois stratum with essential information on trade and state policy. However, it was the emergence of periodicals and journals across Europe in the latter half of the seventeenth century that truly facilitated the articulation of *critical judgment* in the public sphere. Habermas highlights Christian Thomasius's *Monatsgespräche* of 1688 as a pioneering example of the scholarly periodical: a genre that significantly influenced the text types later adopted by the daily press. The reviews and criticism featured in such periodicals gradually permeated newspapers in the form of learned articles, enabling critical reasoning to expand beyond the narrow audience of scholars and educated laymen. As a result, the broader general public increasingly sought to 'compel public authority to legitimate itself before public opinion'.[75]

Thus, in Habermas's framing of the emergence of the public sphere (in Britain, France, and Germany, at least), the articulation of critical public opinion in opposition to the state is treated, firstly, as a *reflection* of the underlying structural transformations and antagonisms occurring at the primary level of production, commodity exchange, and social labour, and secondly, as facilitated by the emergence of communication technologies that distributed critical reasoning in accessible forms, such as articles and reviews, rather than being driven by the top-down dissemination of philosophical tomes. Hence, this position, ultimately grounded in the Marxist base-superstructure account of cultural change, implicitly critiques the agential power assigned to critical philosophy in Koselleck's account.[76]

For Habermas, the struggle between the bourgeois public sphere and the state/public authority was most clearly expressed in the controversy over law, encapsulated in the dualism of absolute sovereignty vs. constitutional law. This explicit conflict centred on how civil society was to be regulated: by the secret decisions and decrees of the monarch, or in accordance with the general and abstract norms and laws established publicly and legitimized by public opinion. Again, in Habermas's framing, this conception of law as the embodiment of external, universal, and abstract norms reflects underlying structural determinations and dualities:

> These rules, because they remained strictly external to the individuals as such, secured space for the development of these individuals' interiority by literary means. These rules, because universally valid, secured a space for the individuated person; because they were

---

[73] Habermas (1992, p. 23).

[74] Habermas (1992, pp. 23–24).

[75] Habermas (1992, pp. 25–26).

[76] Habermas's explicit critique of Koselleck's *Kritik un Krise* appeared in 1973, in *Kultur und Kritik*.

> objective, they secured a space for what was most subjective; because they were abstract, for what was most concrete.[77]

This passage draws on Habermas's division of the public sphere into the 'world of letters' and the 'political realm'. The literary public sphere emerged first, following the liberation of opinion from religious control and the explosion of literacy and communication technologies. It was also more inclusive, allowing women to participate in letter writing and the consumption of literature. The public sphere in the political realm rode on the back of the literary public sphere, converting the forums of discussion developed in the world of letters into a sphere of political debate, which was, however, restricted to male participants. In both cases, the autonomy of the individual was grounded in the ownership of property and the privacy of the bourgeois family:

> As a privatized individual, the bourgeois was two things in one: owner of goods and persons and one human being among others, i.e., *bourgeois* and *homme*. This ambivalence of the private sphere was also a feature of the public sphere, depending on whether privatized individuals in their capacity as human beings communicated through critical debate in the world of letters, about experiences of their subjectivity or whether private people in their capacity as owners of commodities communicated through rational-critical debate in the political realm, concerning the regulation of their private sphere.[78]

Thus, following the Glorious Revolution and the triumph of the Protestant middle class in the Whig supremacy, the Hobbesian fracturing of the individual into private and public halves was carried over into the emergent public sphere, which was divided into two complementary modes of communication:

1. Via intersubjective communication in the world of letters, the property-owning individual shares experiences from the private confines of their subjectivity with equivalent property-owning individuals.
2. Via rational-critical communication in the political realm, the property-owning individual makes claims upon the public authority, ultimately regarding the law.

When Habermas finally addresses the contributions of philosophers to this process in Chapter IV, tracing the history of the idea of public opinion and the ideology of the public sphere, Hobbes is credited with two key contributions. First—following the accounts of Schmitt and Koselleck, though Habermas only cites the former—Hobbes is credited with the 'momentous' reduction of conscience to opinion, a move that privatized religion. Second:

> [...] on the level of intellectual history he nevertheless provided the commentary on a development that, with the privatization of religion and of property and with the emancipation of civil society's private people from the semi-public bonds of the Church and the intermediate powers of the estates, increased the importance of these people's private opinions even more. Hobbes's devaluation of religious conviction actually led to an upward evaluation of all private convictions.[79]

---

[77] Habermas (1992, p. 54).

[78] Habermas (1992, pp. 55–56).

[79] Habermas (1992, p. 91).

The implicit conception of causality in this passage is complex and arguably unstable. On the one hand, Habermas reduces Hobbes's texts to providing 'a commentary on a development' that increased the importance of private opinion. In this view, the rational dissection of man and the critical analysis of the Christian Commonwealth in *Leviathan* are merely epiphenomenal, reflecting transformations already occurring in the economic base: private opinion gained cultural and political significance as the individual (and family unit) acquired economic significance in the transition from feudal to capitalist society, and Hobbes's texts simply reflect this after the fact.

On the other hand, Habermas claims that Hobbes's devaluation of religious conviction 'led to an upward evaluation of all private conviction' (*Aufwertung*). Here, it seems to be acknowledged that Hobbes's contributed to the increased value of pri vate opinion, implying causal agency. A possible reconciliation might be that, in terms of rational-critical analysis, Hobbes's texts function as commentary, but in the normative field (devaluation/upward evaluation—*Abwertung/Aufwertung*), they exert causal influence and reinforce socio-cultural change.

By way of conclusion, a few key points can be made. First, Habermas's inclusion of economic and communication technology factors sheds additional light on the Hobbesian fracturing of the seventeenth-century subject into private and public halves. Koselleck's epistemic model, which identifies Hobbes's philosophy as a key determinant of cultural change, is critiqued and repositioned within a broader framework of socio-economic, technological, and institutional determinants. However, the ambiguous role assigned to philosophy within the ideology of the public sphere—as both mere commentary and a determiner of value (and thus an agent of cultural change?)—remains entangled with the inherent tensions of the Marxist conception of ideology, particularly its tendency to treat thought as an epiphenomenal reflection of processes occurring in the economic base.

Second, despite their opposing evaluations of the Enlightenment and the bourgeois public sphere, Koselleck and Habermas's accounts share a dualistic framing of historical phenomena. Both identify abstract entities and pitch them against one another in a fundamental, totalizing binary conflict: on one side, the bourgeois stratum, criticism, reason, and the public sphere; on the other, the state, the public authority, and the church. While these dualistic frameworks stem from distinct intellectual allegiances—the existential, polar antagonisms of Carl Schmitt in Koselleck's case, and the dialectical antitheses of Hegelian and Marxist reasoning in Habermas's case—they can both be seen as falling into the trap identified by Jean-Pierre Vernant.[80] Just as modern scholars of ancient Greek thought often remained embedded within the classical tradition they aimed to study, projecting Attic philosophical concepts and distinctions back onto the 'Presocratic' cultural field, Koselleck and Habermas project categories and methodological strategies of later German post-Enlightenment philosophy onto the diverse cultural fields that began emerging in England and the Dutch Republic in the late seventeenth century, and in France and the German-speaking regions in the eighteenth century. While their interpretations

[80] Vernant (1988, p. 220).

retain valuable insights, over 60 years later it is clear that their approaches also bypassed or suppressed key aspects of the cultural phenomena they sought to investigate.

Thus, Koselleck identifies Enlightenment thought—which, in his view, homogenizes the diverse currents of English, French, and German philosophy—as profoundly dualistic, and critiques it for this tendency. Yet he reproduces this dualism in his own framing, casting the eighteenth century as a pan-European existential confrontation between bourgeois critique and the state. Enlightenment criticism is portrayed as fundamentally one-sided, with 'postulated concepts in turn positing their counter-concepts, which were generally disposed of and "criticized" in the course of being posited'.[81] However, as Habermas observed,[82] Koselleck's narrative is itself one-sided, attributing all agency to the process of critique. By assuming that the Enlightenment was a homogenous, unstoppable pathogenetic-philosophical process, Koselleck's analysis overlooks significant heterogeneity and conflict within the Republic of Letters itself, the adoption of Enlightenment ideas by some state authorities and theologians, and the concerted resistance from thinkers and institutions. These resistant forces deployed various strategies to demonize and suppress radical Enlightenment thought, while also redefining traditional conceptions of society and state power in response.

In turn, while Habermas's application of Marxist categories and methodology sheds light on the economic and communicative determinants of the public sphere, it also results in the reconstruction of an abstract dialectical conflict. Habermas's analysis ultimately assumes that the heterogeneous thought articulated in diverse local contexts across Europe, from 1650 to 1800 and beyond, can be generalized and captured as an abstract superstructural entity: the bourgeois public sphere. Crucially, Habermas describes the notion that the public sphere was homogenous as 'the fiction of the one public [*die Fiktion der einen Öffentlichkeit*]'; a useful fiction which was accepted because it 'had positive functions in the context of the political emancipation of civil society from mercantilist rule and from absolutistic regimentation in general'.[83] To unmask this fiction, Habermas identifies 'the two forms of the public sphere' discussed above: the literary public sphere and the political public sphere, and addresses variants of the latter: the British case and 'Continental Variants'.[84]

However, while Habermas acknowledges heterogeneity in the public sphere in terms of form and national context, the Marxist emphasis on the determinative power of the economic base entails that this heterogeneity could only be conceived as occurring on the level of ideological articulation:[85] the underlying economic transformations were essentially the same wherever they occurred, since in all cases

[81] Koselleck (1988, p. 122).

[82] Habermas (1973, pp. 357–58).

[83] Habermas (1992, p. 56).

[84] Habermas (1992, pp. 51–73).

[85] On Habermas's later critique of Marx's dialectical materialism, see Flood (1977) and Love (1995, pp. 50–51).

they involved the emergence of a bourgeois class within feudal-absolutist power structures, only varying in terms of when this class emerged and the resistance it met. Thus, even if the *one* public sphere was a useful ideological fiction masking heterogeneous forms and local variation, the multiple public spheres that emerged at different times and places were nevertheless homogenous in terms of their underlying determinants: they followed the same basic blueprint or floorplan [*Der Grundriß*].[86]

In Habermas's narrative, Marx's critique of the Hegelian conception of the public sphere exposed the fictions underpinning the bourgeois public sphere, revealing it as a mask for bourgeois class interests, a generator of new power dynamics, and a structure that, far from enabling universal access, excluded non-property owners—particularly those 'who possessed their own labour power as their sole commodity'.[87] Despite the resulting fracturing of society into competing social classes, Habermas retains Marx's view of the bourgeois public sphere as a fundamentally homogenous entity. Andrew Edgar succinctly summarizes:

> The working classes are excluded, and this entails that a number of fundamental issues are excluded from the debate. The contributors to the public sphere are homogeneous in terms of power and economic interests. Any individual differences between members of the bourgeoisie are typically economic interests, and are worked out in the market. The enormous conflict of economic interests that existed between the working classes and the bourgeoisie is not debated. In effect, it is not even politically recognised.[88]

The notion that all iterations of the public sphere were essentially homogenous and necessarily followed the same blueprint is what enables Habermas to construct a narrative populated by abstract entities engaged in a pan-European dialectical struggle, such as the following: 'A political consciousness developed in the public sphere of civil society which, in opposition to absolute sovereignty, articulated the concept of and demand for general and abstract laws and which ultimately came to assert itself (i.e., public opinion) as the only legitimate source of this law'.[89]

Even if the public sphere emerged according to a broadly shared structural blueprint—replicated across Europe through new textual genres (e.g., newspaper articles, journal reviews) and common social settings (e.g., salons, coffee houses, debating societies)—it is possible to extrapolate from Habermas's model that the distinct religious, political, legal, infrastructural, linguistic, and cultural contexts in which it arose necessarily would have given rise to diverse and dynamic content. While the transformations in production and consumption might suggest structural uniformity, the temporal and spatial variation in their application necessarily would have produced heterogeneous public spheres. Viewed through Fleck's lens, the public sphere can be seen as not only mediating interaction between the bourgeoisie and state authorities but also facilitating intellectual exchange between thought collectives in different urban centres. These interactions, shaped by local conditions and

86 Habermas (1992, p. 26).

87 Habermas (1992, p. 124).

88 Edgar (2006, p. 126).

89 Habermas (1992, p. 54).

antagonisms, would have circulated ideas, fostered dialogue, and provoked intellectual conflict, thereby reinforcing its dynamic heterogeneity.

Habermas's identification of the 'one public sphere' as a functional fiction of self-representation hints at these fractures but stops short of fully embracing the complexity of its internal dynamics.[90] Instead, the Habermas of 1962 frames the phenomena in terms of dialectical struggle, assigning agency to abstract entities in a manner that echoes Hegel and Marx. Like Koselleck, Habermas retrojects later dialectical categories onto earlier cultural fields, perpetuating the image of the Enlightenment as a dualistic conflict. Yet, while Koselleck's framing is informed by Schmittian antagonism, Habermas's account remains tied to Marxist dialectics, as evidenced in his analysis of the bourgeois public sphere in Chapter IV, §14.[91]

These dualistic conceptions of the Enlightenment and the bourgeois public sphere were imposed on cultural phenomena at the expense of currents and dimensions of Early Enlightenment thought that resisted tidy categorization within such dichotomies. For instance, both Koselleck and Habermas concentrated their analyses on England, France, and the German-speaking states, entirely overlooking the significant contributions of thinkers from the Dutch Republic to Enlightenment thought and the development of the public sphere. Neither Koselleck's *Critique and Crisis* nor Habermas's T*he Structural Transformation of the Public Sphere* engages with Spinoza, despite his pivotal role in shaping early modern conceptions of naturalism, toleration, and the critique of ecclesiastical authority. Nor do they offer a detailed exploration of the complex and ambivalent role universities played in simultaneously resisting and advancing the dissemination of Enlightenment ideas across Europe. Yet from the 1670s onwards, and particularly in the German universities in the first half of the eighteenth century, Spinoza was persistently coupled with Hobbes: they came to symbolize all that was bad—atheism, materialism, naturalism, determinism and libertinism—in the image constructed to designate the radical destination to which certain currents of the new philosophy would inevitably lead.

10.8 The Fractured Public Sphere and the 'Epicurean' Outcasts

To illustrate the suppressive tendencies resulting from the dualistic framings of Koselleck and Habermas, we turn briefly to Jakob Thomasius's lecture against Spinoza's *Theologico-Political Treatise* (TTP), delivered in 1670—the very year Spinoza's work was published anonymously, before its authorship became widely

[90] For an account emphasizing the plurality of public spheres and the existence of diverse and competing publics—including nationalist, peasant, elite women's, and working-class counterpublics—see Fraser (1990).

[91] On the influence of Marxist assumptions and projections in Habermas's account of the post-1688 public sphere in England, see Downie (2005).

known. Thomasius, Professor of Moral Philosophy at Leipzig University—a bastion of Protestant scholasticism—was a pivotal figure whose influence extended to his student Leibniz, with whom he corresponded, including on the authorship of the *TTP*. Jakob Thomasius was also the father of Christian Thomasius, whose lectures at the University of Halle, delivered in German, are often seen as marking the inception of the German Enlightenment.

Bartholomew Begley provides invaluable context for Jakob Thomasius's lecture, noting that it formed part of a series targeting innovators such as the English physician Edmund Dickinson. Thomasius, Begley recounts, 'defended the hegemony of one philosophy in the schools and universities, against what he calls "democratic philosophy" where everyone, even paid from the public treasury, can teach what they like'.[92] In this specific lecture, as translated by Begley, Thomasius directly associates the anonymous author of the *TTP* with atheism, naturalism, and libertinism, and explicitly links him to Hobbes:

> [...] a man of course of that religion which [...] opens an obvious door to atheism. We tend to call it Naturalism, rudiments or elements of which are in large part made up of the most pestilential principles of the two innovators of our age, sewn together and adulterated. In naming his book, maybe the author hits the nail on the head. For the author conceived the work in two parts, of which one part claims that this libertinism agrees with true faith or religion, the other that it agrees with peace in the republic; the former part smacks of the theology of Edward Herbert, the latter of the politics of Thomas Hobbes. Nor does it seem to owe nothing to the Pre-adamite Peyrère.[93]

Here we see a professor from the philosophy faculty at a prestigious German university associating the anonymous author of the TTP—a Jewish philosopher living in Amsterdam—with the proponents of 'new teachings' in England and France: Herbert's proto-deism,[94] Hobbes's political science, and La Peyrère's radical Bible criticism,[95] all of which were propagated beyond the confines of the universities. Thomasius clearly identified these new thought styles as a threat to the hegemony of university-based philosophy and to the foundations of Christian society. Furthermore, Thomasius devotes the greater part of his lecture to refuting Spinoza's arguments against censorship—a crucial component of the *TTP* which got lost in the slew of vituperative attacks on Spinoza's supposed atheism.

The issue of censorship, which Hobbes touched on and Spinoza tackled at length, was of paramount importance at the onset of the Enlightenment. During the reign of Charles II, Anglican bishops and royalists denounced *Leviathan* as 'an atheist's handbook for rebellion', and it was rumoured that Hobbes would be tried for heresy. In 1666, *Leviathan* was investigated by a Commons Committee for atheism, and thereafter the book was effectively prohibited, which led to the enduring image of Hobbes in popular culture—of a dangerous, 'immoral Epicurean atheist'.[96] In the

[92] Begley (2018, p. 3).

[93] Begley (2018, p. 14).

[94] Waligore (2012).

[95] Popkin (1987, pp. 42–59).

[96] Parkin (2007, pp. 447–449).

Dutch Republic, long considered a tolerant haven for freedom of thought and the country with the most liberal publishing climate, both Hobbes's *Leviathan* and Spinoza's *Tractatus Theologico-Politicus* were banned in 1674: bookshops were raided, and copies confiscated.[97]

The dons and lawyers at the English universities responded to Hobbes's attacks by publishing a slew of refutations of his theology and theory of law. At Oxford, *Leviathan* and *De Cive* were 'formally banned by university decree in 1683 and publicly burnt'.[98] In 1668, Cambridge expelled Daniel Scargill and deprived him of his fellowship for espousing 'Atheistical Tenets'; he was only reinstated after making a public recantation in the University Church, in which he admitted to having been 'an Hobbist and an Atheist' and renounced these 'execrable Positions'.[99]

The campaign against Hobbes and Spinoza extended beyond governments, religious authorities, and universities. The official vilification directed at these figures compelled more mainstream thinkers to declare their orthodoxy by distancing their philosophies from those of the alleged 'atheists'. For instance, in the preface to *Elementorum Jurisprudentiae Universalis* (1660), Samuel Pufendorf acknowledged his intellectual debt to Hobbes's *De Cive*.[100] However, fierce criticism from Protestant scholastics who associated Pufendorf with Hobbes—and by extension, atheism—prompted Pufendorf in 1672 to repudiate Hobbes's influence, accusing him of propounding 'the old hypothesis of the Epicureans', which amounted to an allegation of atheism.[101]

These efforts to marginalize Hobbes and Spinoza were not confined to formal institutions. They also crystallized in the positioning strategies of a number of English thought collectives, which sought to define their philosophical legitimacy by demarcating themselves from the perceived threat of materialism and atheism.

10.8.1 Anti-Hobbesian English Thought Collectives

Three groups in particular illustrate this dynamic: the thinkers retrospectively labelled the 'Cambridge Platonists' (Ralph Cudworth, Henry More, Anne Conway); the empiricists associated with the Royal Society (Henry Oldenburg, Robert Boyle); and Protestant nonconformist dissenters (notably Richard Baxter).

---

[97] Deijl (2020).

[98] Mintz (1996, p. 50), Springborg (1996, p. 348).

[99] Mintz (1996, pp. 50–51).

[100] Pufendorf (2009, pp. 10–11). Pufendorf draws on and obliquely alludes to Hobbes's *De Cive* throughout the text, as in the following typical passage (2009, p. 127): 'Nay, if that fear should prevail over good faith, no civil society could be formed or preserved, but life would have to be spent in perpetual warfare, and therefore in the status of brute beasts'.

[101] Parkin (2007, pp. 451–452), Palladini (2020, pp. 149–155).

10.8.1.1 The Cambridge Platonists

The designation 'Cambridge Platonists' is an eighteenth-century coinage, not one the group used to describe themselves.[102] The position of this thought collective is perhaps best encapsulated by Lady Anne Conway's rejection of 'Hobbesianism' in her *Principles of the Most Ancient and Modern Philosophy* (1690). While Conway describes her philosophy as 'anti-Cartesian', since she opposes her vitalist ontology to Descartes' mechanistic conception of nature, she acknowledges that at least Descartes was not a materialist, unlike Hobbes and Spinoza:

> BUT, Secondly, as to what pertains to Hobbs's Opinion, this is yet more contrary to this our Philosophy, than that of Cartes; for Cartes acknowledged God to be plainly Immaterial, and an Incorporeal Spirit. Hobbs affirms God himself to be Material and Corporeal; yea, nothing else but Matter and Body, and so confounds God and the Creatures in their Essences, and denies that there is any Essential Distinction between them. These and many more the worst of Consequences are the Dictates of Hobbs's Philosophy; to which may be added that of Spinosa; for this Spinosa also confounds God and the Creatures together, and makes but one Being of both; all which are diametrically opposite to the Philosophy here delivered by us (Chap IX §2).[103]

There is significant discursive demarcation at work here: Cartesian rationalism is positioned as still compatible with Christian metaphysics (Conway's Platonic-kabbalistic Christianity is outlined in Chapters IV and V of her book), whereas the philosophies of Hobbes and Spinoza are identified as fundamental violations of central dualisms such as material/immaterial and corporeal/incorporeal. Whereas the 'grand Errour' of Cartesianism can be replaced with the vitalist principle and ultimately provide the basis for a compromise (hence Leibniz's appreciation of Conway's philosophy),[104] the 'one Substance' philosophy of Hobbes and Spinoza simply had to be refuted and positioned beyond the pale.

This demarcation became structurally consolidated in the first half of the eighteenth century, coinciding with the rise of deism, Leibniz's theodicy, and the Leibnizian-Wolffian compromise. The most anti-clerical and anti-theological currents of the 'mainstream moderate Enlightenment',[105] such as Pierre Bayle's scepticism and Voltaire's scathing satire, were ultimately palatable to the European mainstream reading public because they were grounded an adherence to Christian metaphysics and founded on a rejection of the constructed images of atheism and materialism which were represented by the infamous writings of Hobbes and Spinoza.

---

[102] Hutton (2024).

[103] Conway (1692).

[104] Hutton (2021).

[105] Israel (2001, p. 9).

10.8.1.2 Royal Society Empiricists

The English empiricist rejection of Hobbes and Spinoza was not direct or immediate, but unfolded gradually through a decades-long process of tactical distinction and discursive positioning—one that must be reconstructed from dispersed interventions across conflicting thought collectives and emerging discursive formations. It includes Hobbes and Boyle's documented conflict over the scientific method in the 1660s, as detailed in Steven Shapin and Simon Schaffer's *Leviathan and the Air-Pump* (1985), Oldenburg's correspondence with Spinoza in the late 1660s and early 1670s, where he mediated between Boyle and Spinoza, and Boyle's writings in the 1680s, which directly engaged with Hobbes and Spinoza's concepts of nature, miracles, and the deity. This rich interaction illuminates the operation of the Republic of Letters as a transnational public sphere and highlights significant conflicts between specific thought collectives.

This conflict and its strategic positioning can be briefly traced through a few key moments of communication. Firstly, in a strategy similar to that employed by Pufendorf, Boyle, in *About the Excellency and Grounds of the Mechanical Hypothesis* (1674), distinguishes his 'corpuscular or mechanical philosophy' from the atomistic view of the Epicureans and from the view of 'some modern philosophers, that supposing God have put into the whole mass of matter such an invariable quantity of motion, he needed do no more to make the world, the material parts being able by their own unguided motions to cast themselves into such a system'.[106] Boyle thereby implicitly defines his version of the mechanical philosophy as distinct from that of Hobbes and Spinoza, which he depicts as self-organizing materialism. In the recapitulation, he further differentiates his philosophy:

> [...] having first premised, once for all, that presupposing the Creation and general providence of God, I pretend to treat but of things corporeal, and do abstract in this paper from immaterial beings (which otherwise I very willingly admit) and all agents and operations miraculous or supernatural.[107]

Thus, like Conway, Boyle declares his opposition to Hobbes's conception of God as corporeal and to Spinoza's monistic conception of nature, signalling his adherence to orthodox metaphysics and his belief in miracles.

Subsequently, following the publication of Spinoza's *Theologico-Political Treatise*, Oldenburg, in his letters of 1675, beseeched Spinoza for clarification on controversial issues such as God and Nature, miracles, and the person of Jesus.[108] Boyle's *Letter on Miracles* (*Mr. Boyle's Answer to Spinoza*), which was probably circulated within the Royal Society, offers a sustained refutation of Spinoza's views in treatise form. Boyle insists that Divine Miracles had occurred, that God is a Free

---

[106] Boyle (1991, pp. 138–139).

[107] Boyle (1991, p. 153).

[108] Spinoza (2002, pp. 940, 943).

Agent capable of overruling his own laws, and that Scripture must be interpreted in this light.[109]

In *A Free Enquiry into the Vulgarly Received Notion of Nature* (1686), Boyle again sought to distance his empiricist philosophy from atheism. Here, he sets out his stall on a middle ground, attacking atheists for ascribing 'so much to nature that they think it needless to have recourse to a deity for the giving an account of the phenomena of the universe', while also criticizing 'theists' who simply invoke the 'commonly received notion of nature' as proof of the existence and providence of God'.[110]

Edward B. Davis and Michael Hunter clarify that the term 'theists' in Boyle's critique encompasses a broad range of targets, including Aristotelian scholastics, Galenism, the Cambridge Platonism of More and Cudworth, and the vitalism of William Harvey and Francis Glisson.[111] Boyle's central argument is that, despite their differences, these theistic schools all share a tendency to ascribe agency to nature, effectively elevating it to the status of a semi-deity—a conception Boyle argues aligns them more closely with Epicurean materialism. In contrast, Boyle asserts his resolute opposition to materialism by insisting on God's omnipotence and entirely stripping nature of any agency:

> I shall add that the doctrine I plead for does, much better than its rival, comply with what religion teaches us about the extraordinary and supernatural interpositions of divine providence. For when it pleases God to overrule or control the established course of things in the world by his own omnipotent hand, what is thus performed may be much easier discerned and acknowledged to be miraculous, by them that admit in the ordinary course of corporeal things nothing but matter and motion, whose powers men may well judge of, than by those who think there is besides a certain semi-deity which they call nature, whose skill and power they acknowledge to be exceeding great, and yet have no sure way of estimating how great they are and how far they may extend.[112]

God is conceived of as a clockmaker, not a puppet master; and nature is a clockwork machine, not an intelligent puppet or vicegerent.[113]

Throughout *A Free Enquiry*, Boyle frequently refers to the atheist and materialist position using terms such as 'the Epicureans' and 'corpuscularian', but in the final section, he takes a direct swipe at Hobbes. For Boyle, the principal error of heathens, idolaters, and infidels was their conception of God as corporeal—an error he attributes to the author of *Leviathan*: 'And this corporiety of God seems manifestly to be the opinion of Mr Hobbes and his genuine disciples, to divers of whose principles and dogmas it is as congruous as it is repugnant to religion'.[114]

Like Conway's refutation of Hobbesianism, the communication between Spinoza, Oldenburg, and Boyle, as well as the circulation of Boyle's papers and

---

[109] Boyle (1963, pp. 213–215).

[110] Boyle (1996, p. 3).

[111] Davis and Hunter (1996, pp. xvii-xxii).

[112] Boyle (1996, p. 14).

[113] Boyle (1996, pp. 12–13).

[114] Boyle (1996, p. 159).

publications, illustrates the fracturing and complex discursive demarcations of the period. Just as Pufendorf sought to insulate his natural law philosophy from accusations of Hobbesian atheism, Boyle worked to protect empiricist natural philosophy—developing under the auspices of the Royal Society—from similar charges.[115] Between 1650 and 1686, a critical schism emerged within mechanistic philosophy, where methodological debates were overshadowed by deeper conflicts over the nature of God and the status of nature itself.

10.8.1.3 Protestant Noncomformists

Lastly, in *The Second Part of the Nonconformists Plea for Peace* (1680), Richard Baxter, a leading Protestant nonconformist, focused on the political implications of the 'new Philosophers'. His purpose was to demonstrate that it was the principles of these 'Bruitists' that posed the real danger to the English government, rather than the benign doctrine of the Nonconformists:

> I have not yet heard of any such severe prosecutions of the Bruitists that are for Hobbes, Spinosa, Pomponatius, Vaninus, &c. as have been used against truly Loyal Nonconformists. But their principles are so pernicious, subverting humanity, morality and Government, that I will begin with the recital of them as Spinosa layeth them down, and then add the true fundamentals of Government and morality which confute them.[116]

Baxter's brutal reading of Spinoza's *Theologico-Political Treatise* casts the text as an attack on the patriarchal system, as opening the way to disobeying the father as the head of the family, and to rebelling against heads of government.[117] Baxter interprets Spinoza's conception of the state and laws of nature as allowing the individual complete freedom to break any covenant entered into.[118] Then, like Pufendorf and Boyle, Baxter associates the new philosophers with Epicureanism and atheism:

> It is the will & mercy of God to Princes and to mankind thus to permit those that will be Atheists and Rebels against him to shew the consequents of it, by their inhumane and rebellious opinions against Government: That if Princes will ever set up Epicurisme, Atheisme and Infidelity, they shall set up Rebellion with it, and expose their Lives to every man that hath but list to venture upon a secret or an open assault.[119]

Baxter concludes his section on the 'Epicureans' by asserting that 'they that hold and publish this, are such as we hold more worthy to be banished five miles from all Cities and Corporations, than our selves'.[120] The reference is to the penalties which Nonconformists were subject to following the enactment of the Five-Mile Act (1665).

---

[115] Davis Hunter (1996, p. xiv).

[116] Baxter (1680, p. 2).

[117] Colie (1963, p. 191).

[118] Baxter (1680, pp. 3–4).

[119] Baxter (1680, p. 5).

[120] Baxter (1680, p. 19).

Baxter's condemnation exemplifies a systemic discursive strategy in which unorthodox thinkers like Hobbes and Spinoza were demonized to underscore the relative orthodoxy of splintering and innovative thought collectives. By associating their ideas with rebellion, atheism, and Epicureanism, Baxter reinforces their marginalization while positioning Nonconformist doctrines as both loyal and benign. This tactic reflects a recurring effort among early modern thought collectives to delineate boundaries by casting adversaries as existential threats to the moral and political order. Baxter's attack on Spinoza also aligns with the broader campaigns of suppression and vilification discussed earlier, showing how figures like Hobbes and Spinoza were deliberately targeted as symbols of religious and political subversion.

This episode further underscores the interconnectedness of censorship and discursive conflict, with accusations of rebellion and atheism serving as mechanisms for controlling thought and delimiting the positions that could be articulated within the field of cultural production. Baxter's framing not only reinforces these dynamics but also illustrates how Nonconformist thinkers navigated a public sphere in which they were frequently targets of suppression. Thus, *The Second Part of the Nonconformists Plea for Peace* reveals Baxter's defensive posture while illuminating the complex and antagonistic interactions between competing discourses of the period.

10.8.2 Dualistic and Triangular Models of the Enlightenment

This excursus demonstrates that the multidimensional controversies ignited by the publication of Hobbes's *Leviathan* defy reduction to binary oppositions—whether between enlightened critique and the absolutist state (Koselleck), or between the public sphere and state authority (Habermas). Such frameworks overlook crucial aspects of the field of cultural production in Europe during this period. While state and religious authorities clearly sought to suppress the dissemination of Hobbesian and Spinozist thought, this effort was supported by groups and individuals often associated with the cultural phenomenon variously described as enlightened critique, the emerging bourgeois public sphere, the Early Enlightenment, and so on.

Diverse and sometimes opposing groups and networks converged in constructing Hobbes and Spinoza as outcasts, emblematic of the dangers of abandoning the core tenets of theistic metaphysics. In England, this intellectual banishment was carried out publicly by Anglican bishops, university theologians, legal scholars, Baconian empiricists at the Royal Society, the Cambridge Platonists, deists, and Protestant Nonconformists. On the continent, similar roles were played by Bayle's scepticism, Pufendorf's natural law philosophy, and Leibniz's theodicy. The exclusion of Hobbes and Spinoza from the public sphere was therefore enacted not only by the most orthodox defenders of tradition but also by figures at the cutting edge of critique and philosophy, operating within state institutions and universities, or from positions of religious heterodoxy and political exile.

These diverse individuals, groups and networks defined their positions antagonistically, primarily identifying their thought styles through their opposition to the constructed image of Hobbesian-Spinozist materialism, and only secondarily defined their positions in opposition to other thought collectives, which were attacked as mistaken but were nevertheless deemed entitled to communicate in the Republic of Letters.

Several conclusions can be drawn at this point. First, in contrast to Koselleck and Habermas's dualistic and homogenizing reconstructions of the English-French-German Enlightenment, which largely exclude developments in the Dutch Republic, an analysis of texts circulating between England, the Dutch Republic, and German universities such as Leipzig and Jena, alongside the social practices associated with these texts (e.g., censorship, clandestine publication and distribution), confirms that the public sphere was fractured and heterogeneous from the outset. Through Fleck's framework, this intense intellectual unrest and the rapid circulation of ideas among diverse thought collectives can be understood as a key catalyst for the sweeping cultural transformations of the eighteenth century.

Instead of a dualistic conception of the Enlightenment, Israel proposes a triangular model, with three vertices: the moderate Enlightenment, the conservative opposition, and the radical fringe:

> Hence Europe's war of philosophies during the Early Enlightenment down to 1750 was never confined to the intellectual sphere and was never anywhere a straightforward two-way contest between traditionalists and *moderni*. Rather, the rivalry between moderate mainstream and radical fringe was always as much an integral part of the drama as that between the moderate Enlightenment and conservative opposition. In this triangular battle of ideas what was ultimately at stake was what kind of belief-system should prevail in Europe's politics, social order, and institutions, as well as in high culture and, no less, in popular attitudes.[121]

In this framing, the moderate wing was represented by Newton and Locke in England, and Thomasius and Wolff in Germany, aiming to effect a 'viable synthesis of old and new, and of reason and faith'; whereas the radical fringe was represented by atheists and deists, such as Spinoza, Toland, and many other now-forgotten Dutch thinkers, who 'sought to sweep away existing structures entirely'.[122] Israel's analysis of the complex and extensive networks with which Spinoza was connected—English and Dutch natural philosophers, Cartesians, radical democrats, Collegiants, Socinians, radical Protestants, and others—sheds light on the rich complexity of the Early Enlightenment and the external determinants of Spinoza's thought.

However, Israel's persistent emphasis on the conflict between a moderate mainstream and a radical fringe ultimately imposes a rigid and reductive framework on the rich and intricate phenomena his research uncovers.[123] His portrayal of Spinoza

---

[121] Israel (2001, p. 11).

[122] Israel (2001, p. 11).

[123] This point was made by Talbot and North (2010).

as single-handedly transforming 'the whole of Western thought and culture'[124]—a view exemplifying what Lilti critiques as Israel's tendency to project Spinoza into the phenomena[125]—also leads to a significant underestimation of Hobbes's influence in both England and on the Continent.[126] In this way, Israel minimizes the systematic pairing of Hobbes and Spinoza enacted by a spectrum of hostile discourses, a pairing that served to construct a shared image of atheistic materialism. While he highlights Spinoza's divergences from Hobbes, such as on the possibility of miracles and censorship, Israel overlooks the extent to which Spinoza followed the key tenets of Hobbes's philosophy, only expressing them with greater clarity and precision.

10.8.3 A Fleckian Perspective

Treating the writings of Hobbes and Spinoza as expressions of related but distinct thought styles allows their philosophies to be seen as pivotal cultural phenomena driving processes of cultural change—without resorting to reductive dichotomies or attributing decisive transformational agency to individual thinkers. From Fleck's perspective, the thought styles of Hobbes and Spinoza emerge as products of, and participants in, complex networks of thought collectives that interacted in varying degrees of cooperation and antagonism.

In Hobbes's case, the key and predominantly cooperative thought collectives would include:

- **Scientific circles** encountered in England, Italy and France, through his employment with the Cavendish family and later during his exile in Paris. These connections brought him into direct contact with Francis Bacon, Marin Mersenne, Pierre Gassendi and, according to Aubrey, Galileo Galilei. Additionally, Hobbes engaged in a famous correspondence with Descartes in the 1640s.[127] These individuals and networks sparked Hobbes's lifelong interest in geometry, optics, physics, and scientific method, culminating in his adoption and radical development of the mechanistic philosophy. Yet within this cooperative context, Hobbes's antagonistic relationship with Descartes' 'two-substance' mechanical philosophy was of paramount importance, since this rejection grounded his 'one-substance' materialism and hence what came to be referred to as his Epicureanism and atheism.

[124] Israel (2001, p. 166).
[125] Lilti (2009).
[126] Israel (2001, p. 160).
[127] Mintz (1996, pp. 4–11), Popkin (1987, p. 45).

- **Radical Bible criticism**, exemplified by his association with Isaac La Peyrère in Paris, whose mix of biblical exegesis and anthropological speculation supported the controversial pre-Adamite hypothesis.[128]
- **Anglican Protestantism**—Hobbes's stance on religious doctrine reveals a complex interplay between loyalty to the Church of England and a scathing anticlericalism.[129] While vehemently opposing Catholicism and Presbyterianism, his Erastian arguments for the supremacy of the state over ecclesiastical power and religious matters align with the principles outlined in Richard Hooker's *Of the Lawes of Ecclesiastical Politie* (1597), particularly in its critique of Puritan and Presbyterian doctrines. This alignment underscores Hobbes's vision of religious authority as firmly subordinated to civil sovereignty.

Samuel I. Mintz categorizes Hobbes's opponents into three classes,[130] which can be treated as specific and general thought collectives:

- **The clergy and sectarians** (e.g., Presbyterians, Papists, Independents), whom Hobbes accused of undermining sovereign authority, with divisive doctrines blamed for the English Civil War.
- **University teachers:** In *Behemoth or the Long Parliament* (1682), Hobbes remarked that 'an university is an excellent servant to the clergy',[131] thereby pinpointing what he saw as the social function of the University. By indoctrinating students with the worst classical authors and training them in the art of scholastic logic-chopping, universities, in Hobbes's view, 'planted the seeds of rebellion and sedition'. His extensive critique of 'Vain Philosophy' in *Leviathan* Part 4, Chapter XLVI, has already been mentioned; this critique aligns with Bacon's earlier attack on the University as an institution. Like Spinoza and Kant after him, Hobbes scorned the subservient role of 'handmaid' assigned to philosophy in the University (*Leviathan*, XLVII). His assertion of philosophy's independence from religious control must be regarded as a central element of his thought style.
- **Lawyers:** Hobbes's radical doctrine of positive law—holding that law consists solely of what is legislated by the sovereign—brought him into conflict with eminent lawyers such as Sir Edward Coke. Coke, in stark contrast, argued that English law was 'based upon the primacy of the common law'.[132]

Mintz succinctly summarizes Hobbes's overarching critique:

> It will thus be seen that Hobbes's attacks on the clergy, the universities, and the lawyers have a common basis. All three classes contributed to the decline of sovereign power so essential to the stability of the commonwealth: the clergy by asserting that the Church is either independent of the state or superior to it; the lawyers by upholding the view that the

---

[128] Popkin (1987, pp. 42–60).

[129] Springborg (1996).

[130] Mintz (1996, pp. 46–48).

[131] Hobbes (1990, p. 159).

[132] Goldsmith (1996, p. 291).

> common law is an independent entity exempt from the royal prerogative; and the universities by fostering the opinions of the other two classes. If a commonwealth is to avoid civil strife it must curb the power of these three groups.[133]

Hobbes's philosophy, then, was a thought style that primarily and explicitly attacked the thought collectives in control of the key institutions responsible for shaping how and what English people thought: the Church, the Universities, and the Law. Other conflicts, e.g., with Boyle and the Royal Society over the scientific method, or with Cartesians over the mind vs. matter dualism, should be viewed as secondary.

At the same time, while representatives of the religious authorities, the Universities, and the Law immediately directed their criticism and suppression tactics at Hobbes's writings, it was Spinoza's clarification and intensification of Hobbes's materialist-mechanical thought style that fully crystallized the perceived threat of this New Philosophy to existing power relations and institutions. This development prompted a diverse spectrum of thought collectives across Europe to align with traditional authorities in the demonization of Hobbes-Spinoza as a single, discursively constructed atheistic entity.

This alignment of thought collectives became a structural determinant of the positions articulated in the writings of Leibniz, Wolff, Hume, and Kant, as well as in the institutional strategies adopted by—and directed toward—the German Universities. The multidimensional conflicts and fractures that defined the Early Enlightenment and the emergence of the public sphere reverberated throughout the eighteenth century and are still very much evident in the pages of Kant's *Critique of Pure Reason*, *Religion within the Bounds of Mere Reason*, and *The Conflict of the Faculties*. With this context in mind, the next section examines Spinoza's *Theologico-Political Treatise*, with particular focus on the issue of censorship.

10.9 Spinoza's *Theologico-Political Treatise* (1670)

In his anonymously published *TTP*, Spinoza went further—and was far more explicit—than Hobbes in stating the case for reason and philosophy, and in attacking the claims and status of theology, as is evident in the following coruscating passage:

> We have established it as absolutely certain that theology should not be subordinate to reason, nor reason to theology, but rather that each has its own domain. For reason, as we said, reigns over the domain of truth and wisdom, theology over that of piety and obedience [*ratio regnum veritatis et sapientiae, theologia autem pietatis et obedientiae*]. For the power of reason, as we have shown, cannot extend to ensuring that people may be happy by obedience alone without understanding things, while theology tells us nothing other than this and decrees nothing but obedience [*Theologia vero nihil praeter hoc dictat nihilque praeter obedientiam imperat*]. Theology has no designs against reason, and cannot have any. For the dogmas of faith (as we showed in the previous chapter) determine only what is neces-

[133] Mintz (1996, p. 48).

> sary for obedience, and leave it to reason to determine how precisely they are to be understood in relation to truth. Reason is the true light of the mind without which it discerns nothing but dreams and fantasies. (TTP 15.6)[134]

Hobbes's utilitarian analysis reduced religion to the function of providing the basis for 'Obedience, Lawes, Peace, Charity, and civill Society' (*Leviathan* Ch. XXXIV), thereby retaining a potentially positive role for theology ('the doctors of the Church') insofar as these pastors are subordinate to 'the chief pastor'—the Sovereign—and contribute to stability (*Leviathan* XXXIX, §5). In contrast to this rather cynical evaluation, Spinoza's more principled democratic republican perspective assigns theology entirely negative functions. On the one hand, it is identified as corrupting the simple morality of true religion—rooted in justice and charity—by turning it into a source of prejudice, conflict, and hatred (TTP 7), while on the other, theology and Scripture are analysed in functional terms and reduced to promoting obedience, a function that oppressive governments exploit in their efforts to 'control people's minds' (TTP 20.1).

Spinoza's attempt to emancipate reason from theological control was inseparable from his unique Biblical hermeneutics and his democratic republicanism. Since Spinoza's radical monism posits that all things are natural and that all events follow the laws of nature, supernatural phenomena, events, and agency are excluded from history. Consequently, Spinoza argued that the Bible, as a natural and historical phenomenon, should be interpreted using the same methods applied to natural phenomena:

> To formulate the matter succinctly, I hold that the method of interpreting Scripture, does not differ from the [correct] method of interpreting nature, but rather is wholly consonant with it. The [correct] method of interpreting nature consists above all in constructing a natural history, from which we derive the definitions of natural things, as from certain data. Likewise, to interpret Scripture, we need to assemble a genuine history of it and to deduce the thinking of the Bible's authors by valid inferences from this history, as from certain data and principles. (*TTP* 7.2).

The immediate consequence of this 'completely secular reading of the Bible'[135] is that miracles, conceived as events contrary to the laws of nature, simply cannot occur: the laws of nature are God's decrees and 'follow from the necessity and perfection of the divine nature', and a miracle would entail God acting contrary to his own nature (TTP 6.3). Miracles in the Holy Scripture are thus reinterpreted as unusual or complex natural phenomena that surpass human understanding.

Spinoza's method of Biblical criticism approaches Biblical events in two primary ways: either as phenomena explicable by natural causes ('It was by the same command of God that the sea opened up a path for the Jews (see Exodus 14.1), namely because of an east wind that blew very strongly for a whole night' (TTP 6.14)), or as figures of speech or visions intended to influence the imagination of the

---

[134] All quotations from Spinoza's *Theological-Political Treatise* are taken from M. Silverthorne and J Israel's 2007 translation—Spinoza (2007).

[135] Popkin (2006).

common people. While Alan Donagan contends that Spinoza's position on miracles falls short of Hume's later (1748) blanket dismissal of reports of miracles as fabrications, since Spinoza allows that non-customary natural phenomena do in fact occur,[136] Israel emphasizes Spinoza's distinctive break from his contemporaries. Unlike Hobbes, who doubted miracles but allowed that God could perform them,[137] and unlike natural philosophers such as Boyle, Locke, and Newton, who clung to the possibility of divine intervention,[138] Spinoza's consistent naturalism marked a radical departure from both theological orthodoxy and the hesitant compromises of early modern natural philosophy.

Another consequence of Spinoza's method of biblical criticism is a ruthlessly systematic downgrading of sacred text. The Bible is reinterpreted not as the pure Word of God but as a collection of imperfect communications tailored to the limited understanding of common people. Likewise, prophets and prophecy are stripped of their privileged status: anyone, Spinoza contends, can access the mind of God through natural knowledge and reason (TTP 2.25–26). Spinoza does not shy away from the political ramifications of this treatment of the Bible and theology: he asserts that the positive moral philosophy communicated by the Bible—the principles of justice and charity, and the role of Christ as a teacher and corrector of minds rather than performer of miracles (TTP 7.7)—have been distorted, obscured and suppressed by theology and the Church authorities in the service of sovereign powers seeking to exert social control.

For Spinoza, asserting the primacy of natural reason and the new philosophy is inextricable from redefining the true purpose of the state: freedom. He argues that the ultimate aim of the state is liberty (*Finis ergo reipublicae revera libertas est*), which entails ensuring that individuals can develop their 'minds and bodies in their own ways in security and enjoy the free use of reason' (TTP 20.6). This principle culminates in Spinoza's uncompromising defence of freedom of thought and speech, with which he concludes the *TTP*:

> Hence, a government which denies each person freedom to speak and to communicate what they think, will be a very violent government whereas a state where everyone is conceded this freedom will be moderate [...] Thus no one can act against the sovereign's decisions without prejudicing his authority, but they can think and judge and consequently also speak without any restriction, provided they merely speak or teach by way of reason alone, not by trickery or in anger or from hatred or with the intention of introducing some alteration in the state on their own initiative. (TTP 20.4, 7)

Spinoza's origin story of the state echoes Hobbes's, positing that it was founded when individuals surrendered their freedom to act according to their own decisions and transferred this authority to a sovereign power, which then became the sole arbiter of decisions and actions. However, Spinoza departs radically from Hobbes by asserting that it is impossible for individuals to relinquish their freedom to think

[136] Donagan (2006, p. 364).

[137] Israel (2001, p. 218).

[138] Israel (2007, p. xvi).

and judge: 'the right to private judgment is non-transferable'. Building on Hobbes's distinction between action and thought, Spinoza argues for the individual's right to 'think what they wish and say what they think', a liberty he views as indispensable to a just and secure state (TTP 20.17).

Julie E. Cooper suggests that Spinoza's position on censorship 'blurs the distinction between speech and thought'.[139] While it is true that Spinoza's argument becomes entangled and opaque when defining and tackling the actions, thoughts, and speech that qualify as 'seditious', this ambiguity can be seen as a consequence of the radical and confrontational nature of his thesis, which necessitates a degree of textual cloaking.[140] This strategy may be conceived as both a conscious response to the risks present in his intellectual environment and an unconscious response to the discursive pressures under which his argument was formed. Spinoza's engagement with censorship pushes further into a political-philosophical territory already opened by Hobbes, a territory that Kant would later cautiously enter in *What is Enlightenment?* and *The Conflict of the Faculties*. A close analysis of Spinoza's treatment of sedition thus casts light on the contours of a contested field that continued to shape debates over censorship in the late-*Aufklärung* public sphere.

Spinoza's adoption of the Hobbesian action vs. thought dichotomy enabled him to argue that, since the stability of any state is grounded in people obeying the sovereign's decision-making power, individuals can comply with the sovereign's laws while simultaneously judging these laws to be 'contrary to sound reason' (TTP 20.7). Thus, a person can remain obedient in the sphere of action while critical in the sphere of thought, without this duality undermining the state's stability. Nevertheless, Spinoza makes it clear that sedition is not confined to the sphere of action: he unequivocally states that opinions themselves can be 'seditious' (*quaenam opiniones in republica seditiosae sint*). Seditious views are those:

> which, simply by being put forward, dissolve the agreement by which each person surrenders their right to act according to their own judgment. For example, it is seditious for anyone to hold that a sovereign power does not have an autonomous right or that one should not keep a promise or that everyone should live according to their own judgment, and other views of this kind which are directly contrary to the aforesaid agreement. It is subversive not so much because of the judgments and opinions in themselves as because of the actions which such views imply. By the very fact that someone thinks such a thing, they are tacitly or explicitly breaking the pact that they made with the sovereign (TTP 20.9)

For Spinoza, the key element of sedition lies in violating the agreement that binds individuals to the sovereign, which amounts to reasserting one's right to act according to personal judgment while disregarding, denying, or disobeying the sovereign's authority. This agreement can be breached tacitly (by holding certain views) or explicitly (by expressing them): both are deemed seditious. However, it is only

[139] Cooper (2006, p. 100).

[140] A detailed and convincing argument on the overall coherence of Spinoza's *Tractatus Theologico-Politicus* can be found in Yoram Stein's *The Coherence of Spinoza's Theological-Political Treatise* (2021).

when such opinions translate into actions that the stability of the state is directly threatened.

Although Spinoza unequivocally condemns certain seditious actions—such as promoting disobedience and conflict (TTP 14.3), introducing alterations in the state on one's own initiative, making false accusations against the magistrate, or attempting to abolish the law against the magistrate's will—as the actions of 'agitators and rebels' (TTP 20.7), he stops short of advocating for the restriction of communication associated with such actions. His anti-censorship arguments are grounded in a distinctly pragmatic realism: while he acknowledges the 'disadvantages' of allowing liberty of thought and speech, he insists that a) suppressing liberty of judgment is fundamentally impossible, and b) efforts to control thought and its communication are ultimately counterproductive: 'Trying to control everything by laws will encourage vices rather than correcting them. Things which cannot be prevented must necessarily be allowed, even though they are often harmful' (TTP 20.10).

Spinoza opposes attempts to regulate seditious thought and speech through the enactment and enforcement of law, arguing that such efforts lead to the persecution of well-intentioned individuals and ultimately pose a greater danger to the state by fostering duplicity and dishonesty. However, he offers no clear alternatives to these preventative measures, referring only obliquely to post hoc remedies: the magistrate's authority may be invoked to mitigate the harms arising from freedom of thought or to restrain the fury of the common people (TTP 20.10, 11, 13).

Spinoza's final claim is that the true advantage of allowing liberty of thought and speech is that it is essential for the advancement of the arts and sciences (TTP 20.10). Spinoza contends that (a) the works of philosophers, scientists, and artists are categorically distinct from genuinely seditious texts, and (b) the potential risks posed by seditious speech and actions are outweighed by the intellectual and cultural advancements gained by society when thinkers and creators are free to communicate their ideas.

In the concluding paragraphs of the *TTP*, Spinoza puts forward the most radical argument of his treatise, advancing the striking claim that it is those who attempt to curtail liberty of thought and speech through religious decrees who are truly guilty of sedition and responsible for political instability. This reversal is grounded in his earlier demonstration of the pernicious influence of religious authorities on the state and its laws (TTP 18.2, 6), his endorsement of democratic republicanism, and his framing of sedition not as dissent but as actions that threaten the state's stability and cohesion.

Since, for Spinoza (following Hobbes), the sovereign power has complete authority over civil and sacred matters, and is thus the sole interpreter of religion and source of religious decree, 'any body which attempts to remove this authority from the sovereign power, is attempting to divide the government' (TTP 19.16). According to Spinoza, 'ministers of the word of God' are private individuals who teach piety by the authority of the sovereign powers, and even if the sovereign is impious, no private individual can claim the right to champion the divine law or right against the sovereign: such an attempt would be 'seditious' (TTP 19.19).

These assertions ground Spinoza's provocative account of the Church and the clergy within Christian states: the first Christian teachers were private individuals who opposed political power, and Spinoza suggests this is a defining, ineradicable feature of Christianity. Thus, in contrast to the Hebrew state, where 'the entire practice of religion and the sacred ministry ensued from the commands of kings' (TTP 19.22), Christian states are defined by conflicts between the sovereign and individuals who exploit religion to gain power and control the sovereign. In this framing, the Christian religion harbours inherently seditious tendencies with regard to the secular sovereign (whether a monarch, the nobility, or a democratic government) and has been a persistent source of destabilizing schisms. If the sovereign becomes influenced by the *ecclesia* to the extent that the creation of law is controlled by the Church, the sovereign has in effect been 'forced to surrender to sedition' (TTP 20.14).

The seditious nature of religious decrees and edicts becomes even more apparent in a democratic state—'the one most in harmony with human nature' (TTP 20.14). Because a democratic government is one 'where all the people, or a large part of them, hold power collectively' (TTP 20.1), and where it is 'agreed that the view which gains the most votes should acquire the force of a decision' (TTP 20.14), any *actions* undertaken by individuals on the basis of their own judgment, particularly those aimed at circumventing or capturing the democratic government, are inherently undemocratic and threaten stability: 'they have turned the sovereign powers into adherents of their dogmas of which they are recognized as the interpreters' (TTP 20.16). Spinoza refrains from explicitly naming those responsible for such manipulations:

> It is thus plainer than the noonday sun that the real schismatics are those who condemn other men's books and subversively instigate the insolent mob against their authors, rather than the authors themselves, who for the most part write only for the learned and consider reason alone as their ally. Hence, the real agitators are those who attempt to do away with freedom of judgment in a free republic – a freedom which cannot be suppressed. (TTP 20.16)

Thus, in a free republic, religious edicts that prohibit books and stifle freedom of thought constitute truly seditious actions. The unmistakable implication is that the true enemies of a democratic republic are theologians, preachers, and ecclesiastical authorities.

Letters and biographical facts confirm that Spinoza's immediate target was the preachers, theologians, and church officials that exerted power in his local circumstances—who issued condemnations from the pulpit, published refutations, leaned on the authority of the courts, and in some cases destroyed the lives of his friends. In his famous letter to Henry Oldenburg, probably from 1665, Spinoza gave three reasons for putting aside his *Ethics* and writing the *TTP*: to remove 'the prejudices of theologians' from the minds of sensible people, to defend himself from the charge of atheism, and to vindicate the 'freedom to philosophise and say what we think [...] for here it is in every way suppressed by the excessive authority and egotism of preachers' (Letter 30).[141]

[141] Spinoza (2002, p. 843).

The complex networks of Dutch natural philosophers, Scriptural exegetes, and democratic republicans in which Spinoza was embedded experienced this ecclesiastical-inspired suppression acutely. It is suggested that the uncompromising arguments for the freedom of thought and publication in Spinoza's *Theological-Political Treatise* were written in response to the trial of the Koerbagh brothers in 1668.[142] Johannes and Adriaen Koerbagh had attempted to popularize the rationalist-philosophical critique of Christianity, drawing on the works of Hobbes, Lodewijk Meyer, Spinoza, and Van den Enden. Following the questioning and imprisonment of Johannes, the Amsterdam magistrates fined and sentenced Adriaen to 10 years in Rasphuis prison, where he died after 1 year due to the appalling conditions. Adriaen's *Een ligt* (A Light Shining in Dark Places, To Shed Light on Matters Of Theology and Religion) (1668), rejected the doctrine of the Trinity, denied Christ's divine nature, described the Bible as confused, and denied 'the existence of Hell, Satan, demons, angels, magic, divination, and witchcraft' while proclaiming miracles 'completely impossible'.[143]

In the unfinished and posthumously published *Tractatus Politicus* (*TP—Political Treatise*, 1675–76), Spinoza envisages a reversal of roles for theologians and ecclesiastical authorities in his discussion of religion within the ideal aristocratic state. Rather than advocating a separation of church and state, Spinoza proposes a simple, national religion wholly subordinate to the political sovereign. Such a religion would serve to prevent sectarianism among the ruling class and, more importantly, to prevent them from depriving their subjects of the freedom to say what they think (TP 8.46). While other religions would be tolerated, they would be subject to strict regulation—for instance, through limitations on church size and mandated spatial separation. The ideal aristocratic state would thus exercise firm control over religion in order to curb its destabilizing potential and safeguard freedom of thought and communication. It is likely that analogous provisions would have appeared in the unfinished section on democracy.

From the above, it is evident that Spinoza's position on the role of the state with regard to religion is more aligned with Hobbesian control than with the Lockean separation of church and state. As Yoram Stein astutely points out, the distinction between internal and external religion is crucial for the coherence of Spinoza's conception of the state. Internal religion is none of the state's business, since it concerns what people believe and think. In contrast, external religion concerns *actions* to be taken in response to doctrinal messages, and therefore people *behaving* in accordance with justice and piety. Since it pertains to the sphere of action, external religion falls under the remit of the state, and is actually crucial for political stability: it is indispensable for teaching obedience and averting the need for the state to resort to coercion and violence (Stein 2021, pp. 8–10). The thought/action dichotomy thus runs through Spinoza's conception of religion, the state, sedition, and censorship, and entails that his political philosophy advocates Hobbesian control of religion

[142] Klever (1995, pp. 38–39).

[143] Israel (2001, p. 194).

both to maintain stability and to protect the individual's freedom to say what they think. Since the most grievous form of sedition is the ecclesiastical attempt to manipulate the sovereign and restrict freedom of thought, Spinoza suggests that state control of religion is necessary to shield individuals from such abuses.

As Mogen Lærke points out, Spinoza's contemporaries largely ignored his political philosophy and focused obsessively on other elements of the *TTP*, such as the refutation of Moses' authorship of the Pentateuch and the theory of miracles. Lærke tracks Leibniz's readings of the *TTP* to argue—rigorously and convincingly—that Spinoza's political philosophy was just too extreme to be processed by Leibniz's 'conciliatory eclecticism'. As a result, Leibniz treated Spinoza's political philosophy as a 'particularly dangerous form of Hobbesianism', preferring to avoid engaging with it altogether.[144]

10.10 Conclusion: Returning to Kant's *Conflict of the Faculties*—Philosophy and the Regulation of Thought

The case for reason and philosophy advanced in Kant's *The Conflict of the Faculties* (1798) stands in stark contrast to the attempts by Hobbes and Spinoza to free philosophy from the control of various authorities and institutions. Both seventeenth-century thinkers sought to delegitimize the dominance of ecclesiastical authorities and university theology faculties, insisting on complete freedom in the sphere of thought. While Hobbes advocated for the civil sovereign's sole control over religious doctrine and the texts permitted in the public sphere, Spinoza argued that the civil sovereign should limit its authority to the state religion, leaving the public sphere—conceived as a realm of thought rather than action—free from such oversight.

As Laursen (1996) argues, *The Conflict of the Faculties* represents a significant shift from the more radical position Kant advanced in *What is Enlightenment?* (1784), where he effectively advocated 'full freedom of the press'.[145] In the heyday of *Aufklärung* optimism, amid an explosion of publishing activities and debating societies, Kant was able to argue that while individuals' speech could be restricted in accordance with their positions and duties (e.g., as *Beamten*, or civil servants), no such restrictions should apply when they assumed the role of *Gelehrte* (scholars or men of learning): 'the public use of one's reason must be free at all times, and this alone can bring about enlightenment among humans'.[146]

However, Kant substantially reformulated his conception of freedom of thought and communication in response to shifting political and cultural realities. These

[144] Lærke (2010, p. 124).

[145] Laursen (1996, p. 588).

[146] Kant (2008, p. 19).

included Frederick William II's accession to the Prussian throne in 1786, Wöllner's *Edict Concerning Religion of 1788* (cited in 10.3), which sought to rein in Neological preachers and others who 'misled the people in the "misused name of Enlightenment"', the royal reprimand issued in response to his unauthorized publication of *Religion within the Bounds of Mere Reason* (1793), and the turbulent backdrop of the French Revolution descending into the Terror. Within this new framework, Kant articulated a more cautious role for philosophy, which now amounted to a timid assertion of special privileges within the confines of the institutional structure.

The Conflict of the Faculties was written in 1794, but only published in 1798, because, as Kant revealed in a letter to Frederick William II included in the Preface, he had promised to refrain 'altogether from discoursing publicly, in lectures or writings, on religion, whether natural or revealed'.[147] True to his word, Kant delayed publication until after the King's death. As Paulsen wryly observed, the 70-year old Kant 'was not of the stuff of which martyrs are made'.[148]

The theme of control runs throughout Kant's text. In the *Introduction*, he identifies the government's primary interest as 'securing the strongest and most lasting influence on the people', with the subjects taught by the higher faculties serving as the means to this end.[149] In the *First Section*, Kant elaborates further: the theology faculty controls 'the inmost thoughts and most secret intentions' of the government's subjects, the faculty of law controls their 'external conduct', and the faculty of medicine controls health to ensure the government has enough people.[150] Since the higher faculties are directly involved in controlling people, the government reserves the right to sanction their teachings: as instruments of control, they are in turn subject to control.

The higher faculties teach on the basis of writings—the Bible, the code of laws, and medical regulations—and their scholars (*Gelehrte*) communicate this content to the people through government-appointed intermediaries: clergymen, magistrates, and physicians. Crucially, Kant argues that the content of these writings must not be questioned 'in public discourses'.[151] He also identifies the external authorities governing the higher faculties: the Scriptures for theology, the legislator for law, and the board of public health for medicine.

In contrast, the philosophy faculty is defined as falling outside of government control: its teachings are left to the scholar's reason: 'It is absolutely essential that the learned community at the university also contain a faculty that is independent of

---

[147] Kant (1979, p. 19).

[148] Paulsen (1902, p. 50).

[149] Kant (1979, p. 27). The original German: 'Die Regierung aber interessirt das am allermeisten, wodurch sie sich den stärksten und daurendsten Einfluß aufs Volk verschafft, und dergleichen sind die Gegenstände der oberen Facultäten', accessible at: https://www.projekt-gutenberg.org/kant/streit/streit.html

[150] Kant (1979, p. 33).

[151] Kant (1979, p. 35).

the government's command with regard to its teachings'.[152] Kant grounds his argument in his conception of reason—'the power to judge autonomously', and it is this that frees the philosophy faculty from government control, assigns it a higher function, and establishes its power to control the higher faculties:

> So the philosophy faculty, because it must answer for the truth of the teachings it is to adopt or even allow, must be conceived as free and subject only to laws given by reason, not by the government. But a department of this kind, too, must be established at a university; in other words, a university must have a faculty of philosophy. Its function in relation to the three higher faculties is to control them and, in this way, be useful to them, since truth (the essential and first condition of learning in general) is the main thing, whereas the utility the higher faculties promise the government is of secondary importance.[153]

Kant adheres to the name 'the lower faculty (die untere Facultät)' to describe philosophy, referring to the faculty's traditional propaedeutic function in the German university system (as outlined in Chap. 9), but he also contests this designation, making ironic reference to the philosophy faculty's historical role as theology's handmaid—'though the question remains, whether the servant is the mistress's torchbearer or trainbearer'.[154]

Due to its higher function—the pursuit of truth, rather than the control of the people—the philosophy faculty can 'lay claim to any teaching, in order to test its truth', whether this pertains to historical cognition (e.g., history, geography, philology, and the humanities) or pure rational cognition (e.g., pure mathematics, metaphysics or nature).[155] In addition to this unique truth-testing role within the university, Kant also assigns the philosophy faculty a special role with regard to the public: while the scholars of higher faculties can only express their doubts to one another within the university,[156] the philosophy faculty is uniquely empowered to examine any teachings transmitted by the higher faculties in public. Since the sanctioned teachings of the higher faculties are based on the government's human wisdom, and hence are fallible, the philosophy faculty's task is to ensure that '*everything* put forward in public is true'—even teachings based on revelation.[157]

The Conflict of the Faculties articulates a dim view of the public. Gone are the *Bürger* and *Beamten* addressed in the early 1780s, who were envisioned as fulfilling their duties while participating in the public sphere as *Gelehrte*. By 1794, Kant had

---

[152] Kant (1979, p. 27).

[153] Kant (1979, pp. 43–45). 'Also wird die philosophische Facultät darum, weil sie für die Wahrheit der Lehren, die sie aufnehmen oder auch nur einräumen soll, stehen muß, in so fern als frei und nur unter der Gesetzgebung der Vernunft, nicht der der Regierung stehend gedacht werden müssen. Auf einer Universität muß aber auch ein solches Departement gestiftet, d.i. es muß eine philosophische Facultät sein. In Ansehung der drei obern dient sie dazu, sie zu controlliren und ihnen eben dadurch nützlich zu werden, weil auf Wahrheit (die wesentliche und erste Bedingung der Gelehrsamkeit überhaupt) alles ankommt; die Nützlichkeit aber, welche die oberen Facultäten zum Behuf der Regierung versprechen, nur ein Moment vom zweiten Range ist'.

[154] Kant (1979, p. 45).

[155] Kant (1979, pp. 45–46).

[156] Kant (1979, p. 47).

[157] Kant (1979, p. 53).

come to view the public as largely indifferent to scholarly issues, motivated by pleasure and simple enjoyment, prone to rebellion, and deeply gullible.[158] In this new context, the philosophy faculty is required to mediate between the government and the public. Owing to the public's incapacity for autonomous judgment, the philosophy faculty also has to assume the role of judge: if the clergymen, legal officials and doctors (the 'businesspeople/agents of practical affairs' of the faculties—*Die Geschäftsleute*) bring scholarly debates into the public sphere, when the people are not competent to judge in such matters, 'the seeds of insurrection and factions are sown, and the government is thereby endangered'.[159] In such cases, the philosophy faculty is obliged to step in, to protect both the public and the government—thus fulfilling its critical function publicly and issuing verdicts.

From the perspective of Fleck's theory, the claims that Kant makes on behalf of the philosophy faculty can be construed as the expression of a thought collective attempting to redefine its position within a state institution and thus exert power over other thought collectives within the institution and over the public. The university is explicitly recognized as an instrument of governmental control over the people, with education primarily conceived as a mechanism for regulating thought, conduct, and health.[160] Within this envisioned framework, Kant carves out a space of complete autonomy for his own thought collective, asserting its right to control the controllers. Having been silenced by theologians for 4 years, Kant exacts a form of intellectual retribution: philosophers now have a duty to supervise the theologians. Philosophers are finally free to pursue the truth in public, but only within a tightly demarcated context—firmly ensconced within the university, as monitors of communication between the government and the people, and as critical judges in the public sphere.

Like Plato—preoccupied with regulating cultural and educational production—and like Hegel—who revived Platonic exclusion to police disciplinary boundaries—Kant exemplifies a recurring feature of philosophy: the drive to control other forms of knowledge and cultural practice. *The Conflict of the Faculties* shows that his thought style was deeply aligned with the repressive tendencies of the German university system. His institutional conception of philosophy, while formally advocating the autonomy of the philosophy faculty, reinforced mechanisms of state control. This alignment is clearest in his explicit rejection of the unregulated public sphere and the liberty of thought defended by Spinoza.

---

158 Kant (1979, pp. 45–53).

159 Kant (1979, p. 57). The original German: '[…] und der Same des Aufruhrs und der Factionen ausgestreut, die Regierung aber dadurch in Gefahr gebracht wird'. The quotation appears in a footnote in which Kant addresses the political danger posed by *Neologie* (theological innovation). He implies that doctrinal novelties, when disseminated beyond the learned public, risk undermining civil order by destabilizing the moral consensus upon which political authority depends.

160 Bill Readings's *The University in Ruins* (1996, pp. 54–61) offers a powerful reading of Kant's *The Conflict of the Faculties*, framing the philosophy faculty as a fictional guarantor of reason within a state-aligned institution. Though I encountered his work after completing the main text, its interpretation closely parallels my own.

A more comprehensive analysis of Kant's thought style would need to examine Leibniz's theodicy and its complex relation to Spinoza's monism, as well as Wolff's efforts to resist accusations of Spinozism while opposing the Pietist theology faculty at Halle. Thomas S. Paine aptly summarizes Wolff's contribution:

> [...] unlike most lecturers on philosophy at that time, he treated philosophy as an independent system of knowledge. Up to that time philosophy had functioned primarily as a propaedeutic to the study of theology, and as a result Wolff's predecessors and opponents had no attractive system to offer as an alternative to his. They also had attained no solid European reputation, and above all they demonstrated no facility for writing clear German prose of the kind that Christian Wolf developed for expounding his system. It was he, practically alone who created the German philosophical language [...] It was not Wolff's intention simply to disguise Latin works by making them appear to be German: he wished rather to find a German terminology that was adequate to the purpose of writing philosophy, without doing violence to either philosophy or the German language in the process. He was determined, as he puts it, to write "as pure German speech would demand" (§16). Wolff was doing for philosophy what Luther had done two centuries earlier with his translation of the Bible.[161]

Kant acknowledges his debt to Wolff's methodological clarity in the second preface to the *Critique of Pure Reason* (1788), before criticizing him for failing to prepare the field for metaphysics 'by a critique of the organ, namely pure reason itself' (Bxxxvi).[162] Nevertheless, Wolff's system-building ambition, his insistence on philosophy's independence from theology, and his development of a technical German prose for philosophical exposition all helped to define the conditions of possibility for Kant's own project. This methodological inheritance formed part of the institutional and historical determinants that shaped Kant's philosophical thought style.

Unlike Spinoza, who advocated an unregulated public sphere and defended the freedom of thought and speech for all individuals, Kant confines such freedom to the philosophy faculty within the university. By the 1790s, the public—whom he increasingly described in dismissive terms—was to be managed and controlled, with access to knowledge carefully regulated. While the critique of reason may have originated as an effort to claim a space for universal thought beyond theological authority, it ultimately came to focus on shielding the public from the destabilizing effects of atheistic, materialist, and sceptical philosophies. As Kant writes in the Second Preface to the *Critique of Pure Reason*:

> Through criticism alone can we sever the very root of materialism, fatalism, atheism, of freethinking unbelief, of enthusiasm and superstition, which can become generally injurious, and finally also of idealism and skepticism, which are more dangerous to the schools and can hardly be transmitted to the public.[163]

In this respect, Kant continues the repressive tradition of the German universities, which vilified philosophers like Hobbes and Spinoza, censored their works, and claimed exclusive authority over the regulation of thought. While Spinoza's *TTP* challenged these mechanisms by defending an open and unregulated public sphere,

---

[161] Paine (1997, p. 123).

[162] Kant (1998a, p. 120).

[163] Kant (1998a, p. 119)

Kant's thought style sought to contain and neutralize precisely this kind of liberty. His institutional philosophy denied legitimacy to forms of free-thinking that operated outside the university, and aligned—implicitly but unmistakably—with the state's efforts to suppress disruptive ideas in both the academic and public realms.

Returning to the treatment of Hobbes and Spinoza, Kant's institutional critique replicates the same strategies used to delegitimize them. By associating their thought with atheism and scepticism, both state and university authorities justified their suppression as necessary to preserve social order. Kant, while claiming to secure philosophy's autonomy, adopts the very same exclusionary logic.

Ultimately, an extended critique of Kant's *pure reason* would have to begin by recognizing that the *Critique* itself was an act of cognition historically situated, institutionally mediated, and shaped by a specific thought style within the Prussian university system during a period of rapacious imperial expansion and tumultuous political unrest. In Fleckian terms, Kant did not simply theorize the conditions of experience or formulate the moral law; he cognized them—through a process shaped by the collective and normative structures of his time. In his later work, this cognitive engagement expanded to encompass first religion and the church, then the university itself, whose function as a regulator of public discourse he explicitly affirmed, and finally the wider normative order of European statehood. In this sense, Kant's critical project did not speak from a position of disinterested reason, but from within a system of interactive cognition mediated by institutional authority. Against this background, his silence on the destruction of the Polish-Lithuanian Commonwealth—unfolding in real time as Kant composed and delivered the Critiques—may be read either as a posture of philosophical detachment or as tacit compliance with a state complicit in cultural and political erasure.[164]

References

Arendt H (1992) Lectures on Kant's political philosophy. University of Chigaco Press, Chicago

Baxter R (1680) The Second part of the nonconformists plea for peace. Text Creation Partnership, 2021. http://name.umdl.umich.edu/A97353.0001.001

Begley B (2018) Naturalism and its political dangers: Jakob Thomasius against Spinoza's theological-political treatise. A study and the translation of Thomasius' text. Seventeenth Century 34(2018):649–670

[164] For a recent and strongly revisionist reassessment of Kant's political thought, see William F. Drischler's *Kant's Political Testament* (2018). According to Drischler, Kant's late political writings are best understood not in response to the French Revolution, but in the context of the partitions of Poland—*Toward Perpetual Peace: A Philosophical Sketch* (1795) appeared in the very year of the Third and final Partition, the Kościuszko Uprising, and Kant's 1794 petition to Catherine II for admission to the Petersburg Academy of Sciences. Drischler portrays Kant as actively legitimating the de-statification of Poland and opposing the inclusion of pre-state peoples—such as the Poles—within the normative bounds of republican statehood. This thesis aligns with my own interpretation of Kant's institutional and geopolitical entanglements, and, in my view, warrants further scholarly investigation. See also Śliwa (2018).

Blanning T (1981) The englightenment in Catholic Germany. In: Porter R, Teich M (eds) The enlightenment in national context. CUP, Cambridge, pp 106–117
Boyle R (1963) Letter on miracles ("Mr. Boyle's answer to Spinoza"). In: Colie RL (ed) Boyle papers Volume 3 (Proceedings of the American Philosophical Society, Vol. 107, No. 3). Royal Society Archives, London
Boyle R (1991) In: Stewart MA (ed) Selected philosophical papers of Robert Boyle. Hacket, Indianapolis
Boyle R (1996) In: Davis EB, Hunter M (eds) Robert Boyle: a free enquiry into the vulgarly received notion of nature. CUP, Cambridge
Colie RL (1963) Spinoza in England, 1665-1730. Proc Am Philos Soc 107(3):183–219
Conway A (1692) The principles of the most ancient and modern philosophy. https://digital.library.upenn.edu/women/conway/principles/principles.html
Cooper J (2006) Freedom of speech and philosophical citizenship in Spinoza's Theologico-Political Treatise. Law Cult Humanit 2:91–114
Davis EB, Hunter M (1996) Introduction. In: Boyle R (ed) A free enquiry into the vulgarly received notion of nature. CUP, Cambridge, pp ix–xxvii
Deijl L v d (2020) The Dutch translation and circulation of Spinoza's tractatus theologico-politicus in manuscript and print (1670-1694). Quærendo 50(1–2):207
Donagan A (2006) Spinoza's theology. In: Garrett D (ed) The Cambridge companion to Spinoza. CUP, Cambridge, pp 343–382
Downie A (2005) Public and private: the myth of the Bourgeois Public Sphere. In: Wall C (ed) A concise companion to the restoration and the eighteenth century. Blackwell, Oxford, pp 58–79
Drischler WF (2018) Kant's political testament: Russo-Prussian state oppression of the Polish People. CreateSpace Publishers, Columbia
Edgar A (2006) Habermas. The key concepts. Routledge, Abingdon
Epstein K (1966) The genesis of German conservatism. Princeton University Press, Princeton
Fleck L (1986) The problem of epistemology [1936]. In: Cognition and fact, Boston studies in the philosophy of science, vol 87. Springer, Dordrecht. https://doi.org/10.1007/978-94-009-4498-5_5
Fraser N (1990) Rethinking the public sphere: A contribution to the critique of actually existing democracy. Social Text 25/26(1990):56–80
Friedrich K (2012) Brandenburg-Prussia, 1466–1806: The rise of a composite state. Palgrave, Houndmills
Goldsmith M (1996) Hobbes on law. In: Sorell T (ed) The Cambridge companion to Hobbes. CUP, Cambridge, pp 274–304
Gottlieb A (2017) The dream of enlightenment. Penguin
Gregor MJ (1979) Translator's introduction. In: Kant I (ed) The conflict of the faculties. Anaris Books, New York, pp vii–xxxiv
Habermas J (1973) Kultur und Kritik: Verstreute Aufsätze. Suhrkamp, Frankfurt
Habermas J (1992) The structural transformation of the public sphere: an inquiry into a category of Bourgeois Society [1962] (trans: Burger T, Kert L). Polity Press, Oxford
Hellmuth E (1998) Enlightenment and freedom of the press: The debate in the Berlin Mittwochsgesellschaft, 1783-1784. History 83(271):420–444
Hobbes T (1986) Leviathan. Penguin, Harmondsworth
Hobbes T (1990) In: Tönnies EB (ed) Behemoth or the long parliament. The University of Chicago Press, Chicago and London
Hutton S (2021) Lady Anne Conway. In: Zalta EN (ed) The Stanford encyclopedia of philosophy (Spring 2021 Edition). https://plato.stanford.edu/archives/spr2021/entries/conway/
Hutton S (2024) The Cambridge platonists. In: Zalta EN, Nodelman U (eds) The Stanford encyclopedia of philosophy (Summer 2024 Edition). https://plato.stanford.edu/archives/sum2024/entries/cambridge-platonists/
Israel JI (2001) Radical enlightenment: philosophy and the making of modernity 1650–1750. OUP, Oxford

Israel JI (2007) Introduction. In: Spinoza B (ed) Theological-political treatise (trans: Silverthorne M, Israel J). CUP, Cambridge, pp viii–xxxiv
Kant I (1979) The conflict of the faculties (trans: Gregor MJ). Abaris, New York
Kant I (1998a) Critique of pure reason (trans: Guyer P). CUP, Cambridge
Kant I (1998b) Religion within the boundaries of mere reason (trans: Wood A, Di Giovanni G). CUP, Cambridge
Kant I (2008) An answer to the question: what is enlightenment? In: Kleingeld P (ed) Toward perpetual peace and other writings on politics, peace, and history. Yale University Press, New Haven, pp 17–23
Klever W (1995) Spinoza's life and works. In: Garrett D (ed) The Cambridge companion to Spinoza (Cambridge companions to philosophy). CUP, Cambridge, pp 13–60
Koselleck R (1988) Critique and crisis, Enlightenment and the pathogenesis of modern society (1957). MIT Press, Cambridge
Lærke M (2010) G. W. Leibniz's two readings of the tractatus theologico-politicus. In: Melamed YY, Rosenthal M (eds) Spinoza's 'theological-political treatise': a critical guide. CUP, Cambridge, pp 101–127
Laursen JC (1996) The subversive Kant: the vocabulary of "public" and "publicity". In: Schmidt J (ed) What is enlightenment? University of California Press, Berkeley, pp 253–269
Lilti A (2009) Comment écrit-on l'histoire intellectuelle des Lumières ? Spinozisme, radicalisme et philosophie. Ann Hist Sci Soc 64e année(1):171–206
Mintz SI (1996) The hunting of leviathan. Thoemmes Press, Bristol
Mittelstraß J (2005) Der Streit der Fakultäten und die Philosophie. In: Gerhardt V (ed) Kant im Streit der Fakultäten. Walter de Gruyte, Berlin, pp 40–60
Palladini F (2020) Samuel Pufendorf Disciple of Hobbes (trans: Saunders D). Brill, Leiden
Parkin J (2007) The reception of Hobbes's Leviathan. In: Springborg P (ed) The Cambridge companion to Hobbes's Leviathan. CUP, Cambridge, pp 441–459
Paulsen F (1902) Immanuel Kant, his life and doctrine (trans: Creighton JE, Lefevre AC). Scribner, London
Popkin RH (1987) Isaac la Peyrère (1596–1676). His life, work, and influence. Brill, Leiden
Popkin RH (2006) Spinoza and Bible scholarship. In: Garrett D (ed) The Cambridge companion to Spinoza. CUP, Cambridge, pp 383–407
Porter R (1981) The enlightenment in England. In: Porter R, Teich M (eds) The enlightenment in national context. CUP, Cambridge, pp 1–18
Pufendorf S (2009) In: Oldfather WA, Behme T (eds) Two books of the elements of universal jurisprudence. Liberty Fund Inc, Indianapolis
Readings B (1996) The university in ruins. Harvard University Press, Cambridge MA
Rice LC, Pastijn F (2005) Introfuction. In: Meyer L (ed) Philosophy as the interpreter of Holy Scripture (1666) (trans: Shirley S). Marquette university Press, Milwaukee, pp 1–19
Robertson R (2020) The enlightenment, the pursuit of happiness from 1680 to 1790. Penguin, London
Saine TP (1997) The problem of being modern or the German Pursuit of enlightenment from Leibniz to the French Revolution. Wayne State University Press, Detroit
Sauter MJ (2009) Visions of the enlightenment: the Edict on Religion of 1788 and the politics of the public sphere in eighteenth-century Prussia. Brill, Boston
Śliwa M (2018) William F. Drischler's study on Immanuel Kant's political philosophy. Studia z Historii Filozofii 11(2018):233–235. https://doi.org/10.12775/szhf.2018.040
Spinoza B (2002) Complete works (trans: Shirley S). Hackett, Indianapolis
Spinoza B (2007) Theological-political treatise (trans: Silverthorne M, Israel J). CUP, Cambridge
Springborg P (1996) Hobbes on religion. In: Sorell T (ed) The Cambridge companion to Hobbes. CUP, Cambridge, pp 346–380
Stein Y (2021) The coherence of Spinoza's theological-political treatise. Philosophies 2021(6):20
Styrdom P (2000) Discourse and knowledge the making of enlightenment sociology. Liverpool University Press, Liverpool

Talbot A, North D (2010) The nation, Jonathan Israel and the enlightenment. World Socialits Web Site. https://www.wsws.org/en/articles/2010/06/enli-j09.html

Vernant JP (1988) Myth and society in Ancient Greece. Zone Books, New York

Wakefield A (2009) The disordered police state. German cameralism as science and practice. University of Chicago Press, Chicago

Waligore J (2012) The piety of the English Deists: their personal relationship with an active god. Intellect Hist Rev 22(2):181–197

Whaley J (1981) The protestant enlightenment in Germany. In: Porter R, Teich M (eds) The enlightenment in national context. CUP, Cambridge, pp 106–117

Chapter 11
Conclusions

Abstract This concluding chapter brings the study full circle by returning to the questions raised in its opening discussion of Plato's *Laws*: how can cultural change be understood, and what forms of knowledge seek to control or resist it? Synthesizing the study's findings, the chapter reflects on how Fleck's theory has been applied to shed light on the emergence and contestation of thought styles across diverse historical settings. Revisiting Plato's vision of cultural supervision, it contrasts the top-down model of reason institutionalized in the *Laws* with the empirical, collaborative ethos of Hippocratic medicine—introduced here as a counter-tradition that anticipates Fleck's epistemology. It also offers a broader contextualization of Fleck's own work, situating it within neglected traditions of scientific self-reflection and noting the philosophical and political conditions that limited its reception. It concludes by affirming reading itself as an act of interactive cognition—an historically situated engagement that reanimates texts as interventions rather than dead museum pieces.

11.1 Back to Plato's *Laws*

This book began by considering Plato's vision in the *Laws*[1] of how artistic innovation and cultural change might be prevented. The Athenian Stranger outlines how artistic production could be tightly regulated by law (*nomōi*) to prevent the ideal anti-Athens of Magnesia from descending into corruption, lawlessness, and moral decay—consequences that, he argues, inevitably follow when artists are allowed to pander to the tastes and demands of their audiences.

Chapter 6 argued that in the *Republic*, Plato's Socrates focuses on the control of cultural production as a means for the oligarchic thought collective to regain and exert power. Following the failures of the oligarchic coups of 411–410 BC and 404–403 BC—which involved direct seizures of power—and in the wake of the

[1] Plato (1980).

S. Dersley, *Thought Collectives and Cultural Change*, Living Signs of Law 1,
https://doi.org/10.1007/978-3-031-97431-1_11

trauma caused by Athens' loss of hegemony in the Peloponnesian War, Plato reimagined Socrates imagining how philosophers might wield power without resorting to a coup. The solution lies in a reconceived *paideia*—a new method of educating a generation of elite thinkers capable of controlling all forms of material, craft, and artistic production.

The *Republic* looks back to a time of prestige and greatness, when Socrates, a critical yet obedient Athenian citizen, engaged actively with aristocrats, metics, and itinerant thinkers who advised the elite on how to navigate relations with the *dēmos*. The *Laws* looks forward to a possible future in which the combined arts of the lawgiver (*nomothetēs*) and the statesman (*politikos*) are given the opportunity to establish a new society from scratch—a self-contained, agrarian polity insulated from cultural change, designed for peace, permanence, and harmony, secured through unwavering adherence to ancestral laws.

The conception of law in the *Laws* is bound up with a reconceptualization of the philosopher's role. The figure of the lawgiver can be compared to the dream of the temperate man who supervises all crafts and sciences (*Charmides*), the unlikely philosopher-king produced by a revolutionized education (*Republic*), and the more feasible *politikos* with true knowledge of ruling (*Statesman*). The *Laws* provides an answer to the question raised in the *Charmides*: What does the supervisor of knowledge actually produce, apart from knowledge of knowledge? In other words, what is his craft? Plato's final answer would seem to be that the supervisor becomes a craftsman when he produces laws. The founder-lawgiver of the *Laws* is thus a master-craftsman who governs all aspects of the political community in advance, drawing it towards virtue through the ultimately nonconsensual discourse of law.

Crucially, the Athenian Stranger imagines a philosophical supervisory body—the secretive Nocturnal Council—tasked with guarding the laws and ensuring compliance. In Chap. 6, I suggested that, when read through a Fleckian lens, Plato's dialogues must be seen as representing numerous competing thought collectives. The Nocturnal Council is the last thought collective to be imagined in Plato's complex inter- and extra-referential corpus, and it is perhaps the most Fleckian of them all: a highly trained esoteric collective that supervises and exerts total control over the exoteric thought collective, primarily through its oversight of the moral and intellectual education of the ruling class (951d–952d).

This represents a key shift—from Socrates' dialogical engagement with fellow citizens in the accessible spaces of Athens to a model of secretive supervision and top-down control by old men dispensing expert wisdom. The Nocturnal Council embodies the institutionalization of philosophy—a dream of remote control over the masses and their irrational appetites for unsuitable cultural forms.

The 'nomocracy' envisaged in the *Laws*—the rule of law anchored in the ultimate principle of *nous*/*theos*/god/reason[2]—can be read as targeting two main discursive enemies. First, in 714b-d, Plato returns to the position articulated by Thrasymachus in the *Republic*—that justice serves the interests of the stronger. In

[2] Laks (2022, p. 4).

the *Republic*, Thrasymachus was effectively silenced, his assertions challenged but not fully resolved. By grounding human law in divine reason accessed via *nous*, Plato aligns the laws of Magnesia with the universal order of reason.[3] This can be read as Plato's final riposte to the Protagorean proposition that 'man is the measure of all things', including the political order. *Nous* is presented as the antidote to the destabilizing effects of arbitrary and factional rule (715 b–d), which the Platonic corpus associates with relativism, the disaster of the Peloponnesian War, and Athens' moral collapse.

Second, the Athenian Stranger's attack on atheism in the *Laws* (885b–907d) can be read as a broader polemic against naturalist science and its perceived consequences for society. The proposed death penalty for the recalcitrant articulation of atheistic claims suggests that, with the sophists long gone, Plato had identified a new threat to moral and legal order. The central thrust of the argument is that natural processes cannot arise from random material causes, but must instead be governed by rational, purposeful, and benevolent oversight—understood here as *Nous*.

By the mid-fourth century BC, with the discursive practices of the sophists successfully suppressed and the influence of tragedy on the Athenian elite much diminished, Plato's *Laws* can be seen as targeting naturalist philosophies such as those associated with Democritus. While the specifics of Plato's critique are obscured by the loss of Democritus' works, the Hippocratic corpus—with its emphasis on empirical inquiry and natural causation—exemplifies tendencies within naturalist thought that probably aligned with the intellectual practices Plato sought to undermine. As such, the Hippocratic texts serve as a valuable proxy for analysing the broader dynamics of the thought styles Plato attempted to suppress.

The top-down control of thought and production envisioned in Plato's *Laws* thus stands in stark contrast to the alternative model of cognition exemplified by Hippocratic medicine. While Plato sought to centralize and institutionalize reason under *Nous*, which functioned as a smokescreen for the authority of the founder-lawgiver and the Nocturnal Council, the Hippocratic tradition emphasized empirical observation and collective, trial-and-error methods of inquiry.

11.2 A Rival Thought Style, Other Knowledge Practices

The emergence of Hippocratic medicine in the fifth century BC exemplifies an alternative conception of rationality—one grounded not in abstract theorization but in empirical observation, cumulative practice, and trial-and-error experimentation. Texts such as *On Ancient Medicine* and *On the Sacred Disease* explicitly polemicize against the speculative abstractions of magico-religious healers, 'philosophers' like Empedocles, and opportunistic charlatans, depicting medicine as a practical, empirical *technē*. The author of *On Ancient Medicine*, for instance, traces the origins of

[3] Laks (2022, p. 3). See also Morrow (1993, pp. 564–572).

medicine to the discovery of food preparation, presenting its foundational logic as an adaptive response to necessity and rooted in the survival-driven ingenuity of early humans. By emphasizing its slow development and communicability to non-literate audiences, Hippocratic medicine positioned itself as both a cornerstone of civilization and a counterpoint to the speculative tendencies of philosophy.[4]

This contrast between the empirical reasoning of Hippocratic medicine and the abstract, generalizing approaches of early philosophy highlights a broader cultural struggle over the nature of knowledge and its transmission. While Hippocratic authors rejected the reductive hypotheses and sweeping generalizations of figures like Empedocles, they nonetheless shared key intellectual tools with their philosophical counterparts—concepts such as causation, balance, and harmony. These overlaps reveal the porous and contested boundaries between disciplines in classical Greece, where rival thought styles vied for legitimacy. In this context, *On Ancient Medicine* challenges the dominant Athenian narrative of philosophy's primacy in the genealogy of reason, arguing instead that systematic rationality emerged from the practical, cumulative inquiries of crafts like medicine. This alternative genealogy affirms the enduring value of empirical and collaborative methods of knowledge production—a point Fleck also emphasizes in *On the Crisis of 'Reality'*.[5]

The Hippocratic text *On the Sacred Disease* further exemplifies this shift toward rational medicine by rejecting divine causality as an explanation for epilepsy and instead emphasizing natural causes. This marked a pivotal moment in the history of ideas, as the text explicitly opposes religious and magical healing with empirical observation and practical treatments such as diet and regimen.[6] As Jacques Jouanna notes, this was the first instance in which rational medicine was directly positioned against magico-religious practices.[7] Yet, as both Geoffrey Lloyd and Jouanna argue, the divide between these traditions was far from absolute; both drew upon a shared fund of diagnostic knowledge and treatment methods refined over centuries.[8] The dietary and therapeutic practices of temple-based medicine at sanctuaries like Epidaurus, for instance, combined magical rituals with pragmatic remedies, reflecting the deeply intertwined nature of rationalist and traditional approaches in fifth-century Greece. The tensions and interactions between these thought styles shed light on the evolution of knowledge as a contested and collaborative process shaped by diverse intellectual and cultural forces.

In fifth-century Greece, the intellectual landscape was characterized by overlapping practices and blurred disciplinary lines. Hippocratic physicians operated alongside herbalists, midwives, gymnastic trainers, and temple healers, all drawing on a shared repertoire of diagnostic knowledge, therapeutic techniques, and explanatory concepts. Even as texts like On Ancient Medicine and On the Sacred Disease

[4] Hippocrates (1868).

[5] Fleck (1986, p. 50).

[6] Hankinson (2018, p. 91).

[7] Jouanna (1999, p. 184).

[8] Lloyd (1979, pp. 39–40).

began to formulate distinct doctrines—such as the sufficiency of natural causality—they did so within a cultural field still shaped by magico-religious traditions and speculative philosophy. The shift toward rational medicine thus marked not a sudden rupture but a process of differentiation, in which empirically grounded reasoning slowly distinguished itself from other modes of explanation. This dynamic of convergence and divergence set the stage for more explicit demarcation in the decades to follow.

Scholars like Lloyd and André Laks have argued that this period witnessed a gradual differentiation of disciplines, with philosophy increasingly defining itself as a theoretical, agonistic practice distinct from the pragmatic methodologies of medicine and other crafts.[9] This differentiation reflects a broader cultural process of rationalization, one that traversed domains as varied as law, politics, and education. Plato's *Laws*, I suggested in the previous section, exemplifies the culmination of this drive: a supervisory philosophy committed to defining and overseeing the legitimacy of competing thought styles and cultural practices.

The participatory ethos of Hippocratic medicine—with its emphasis on collaborative discovery, cumulative practice, and communication with patients—offers a compelling counterpoint to the supervisory ambitions of institutionalized philosophy. Fleck can be situated within this alternative tradition. His reflections on the democratic origins of the natural scientific thought style—rooted, as he wrote, in the practices of artisans, barber-surgeons, gardeners, and even children at play[10]—link his epistemology to forms of collective work in which knowledge emerges through shared experience, trial and error, and repeated interaction. His laboratory experience and postwar university research, his intellectual debt to the Polish philosophy of medicine, and his open, historically sensitive conception of thought styles can all be aligned with this lineage. By challenging top-down and elitist models of knowledge control, Fleck's theory provides a means of exploring and engaging in collaborative, autonomous, and productive thinking that escapes institutional control.

11.3 What the Application of Fleck's Theory Brought to Light

This study has extended and adapted Ludwik Fleck's theory of thought collectives and thought styles as a methodological framework for exploring how thought and culture can be mutually transformative in specific contexts. It fulfilled the aim stated in Chap. 1: to demonstrate the explanatory power of Fleck's theory by uncovering new cultural facts—or aspects of facts—that had been overlooked or suppressed by other frameworks. As noted then, Leszek Nowak's idealizational theory of science offers a pertinent criterion. Let us recall: Nowak defines explanatory power as 'the

[9] Laks (2018).

[10] Fleck (1986, p. 50).

proportion of facts explained by the theory to the facts in a given domain'.[11] While this study adopted a less quantitative approach, its application of Fleck's comparative epistemology has shed light on aspects of cultural transformation and historical phenomena that other frameworks failed to capture, thus demonstrating the theory's capacity to produce nuanced and sensitive reconstructions—when combined with other compatible theoretical tools.

By focusing on examples ranging from the emergence of Plato's *philosophia* to the institutional conflicts of the Enlightenment, this work has shown how the articulatory practices associated with knowledge production both shape and are shaped by intersecting economic, technological, and institutional forces. From Athens' transformation into a thalassocracy to the rise of the early modern book trade, and from intra-university disputes to tensions between state institutions and thinkers asserting autonomy, these material conditions were not simply external to thought but actively co-constituted its formation, transmission, and contestation. While Fleck's model of dynamic cognitive interaction provides the conceptual foundation, this study has extended it—showing how competing thought collectives, whether oligarchic clubs, sophistic circles, or faculties within early modern universities, created concepts and deployed discursive strategies in struggles over cultural authority, intellectual legitimacy, and the shaping of society.

The application of Fleck's framework has yielded new insights into particular historical formations. This study outlined how the oligarchic thought style in Athens between 432 and 403 BC responded to structural changes in the Athenian economy and the trauma of political instability; how Plato's *philosophia* operated as a thought style aimed at supervising and subordinating rival forms of cultural production; how and why the Socratic caesura was reinterpreted and transmitted by Cicero in the Late Roman Republic; how the concept of *Bildung* was developed through cross-cultural communication and deployed in a class struggle; and how distinct thought styles in modern philosophy—associated with Hobbes, Spinoza, Kant, and Hegel—emerged through communicative interaction shaped by the circulation of ideas between intellectual hubs and institutional frameworks. These reconstructions show that thought does not evolve through abstract oppositions or linear unfolding, but arises from communicative distortions, from obstacles produced by distance and linguistic difference, and from competition over different forms of capital.

Chapter 2 contextualized Fleck's theory and attempted to account for his marginalization. But the process of applying his framework has also clarified the historical pressures and philosophical currents that contributed to its exclusion. Here I can only sketch a broader positioning that would require fuller historical and theoretical elaboration. Fleck belongs to at least two neglected lineages. In addition to his connection to the Polish School of the philosophy of medicine, discussed earlier, his work can also be situated alongside the self-reflexive theorizing of nineteenth- and early twentieth-century scientists such as Mach, Poincaré, and Duhem. This tradition treated science not as a route to ultimate reality but as a means of organizing

[11] Nowak (2012, p. 38).

experience—anticipating conclusions later echoed by Quine, including the underdetermination of theory by data and the role of consensus in shaping knowledge.[12] These perspectives, however, were marginalized as postwar philosophies of science—logical positivism, Popperian falsificationism—reasserted philosophy's supervisory role and the ideal of scientific objectivity. Fleck's marginalization reflects a broader epistemological and political trend. His work stood at odds with both the correspondence theory upheld by the Lwów–Warsaw School and the Marxist-Leninist orthodoxy that dominated postwar Poland. These conditions constrained the reception of his ideas and contributed to his exclusion from canonical accounts of scientific rationality. His fate is comparable to that of Alexander Bogdanov, another Mach-inspired theorizing scientist who fell foul of Lenin's campaign to enforce realist epistemological orthodoxy in Soviet science.

By foregrounding the heterogeneity and interaction of thought collectives, this study has sought to reactivate Fleck's comparative epistemology as a tool for analyzing situated cognition. His concept of thought style—where 'facts' emerge through the interaction between cognizer and cognized—offers a way of understanding how epistemic frameworks are shaped by material, cultural, and institutional forces, and how our own reconstructions are conditioned not only by inherited layers of interpretation, but also by the mood and preoccupations of our own time.

Fleck's insights prompt a critical reassessment of philosophy's supervisory ambitions, particularly its tendency to impose top-down frameworks on cultural production. By emphasizing the epistemic value of collaborative inquiry and the open-ended nature of knowledge formation, Fleck challenged institutional philosophy's claim to arbitrate intellectual boundaries.

One line of investigation would trace the trajectory of supervisory reason through the history of law, beginning with Plato's *Laws* and its attempt to institutionalize divine reason as *nomos*. This would follow the transformation of *nomos* from its contested presence in Greek tragedy, through Plato's juridico-theological vision, and onward to Kant's *Metaphysics of Morals* and Hegel's *Philosophy of Right*. Kant and Hegel, despite their differences, both inherit and reconfigure the ambition to bind legal obligation to rational insight, each under distinct historical and institutional conditions. Examining these trajectories through a Fleckian lens could illuminate how supervisory thought styles evolve and adapt to changing social formations—and how reason itself has been mobilized to consolidate cultural control.

This study has shown how recent and contemporary analyses—depending on the thought styles they inhabit—can either flatten cultural change into simplified narratives or open it to deeper heterogeneity and contestation. My hope is that this book might encourage others to approach cherished philosophical texts not as dead museum pieces, but as historically situated interventions, shaped by their own epistemic conflicts, and capable of being reactivated through acts of interactive cognition. Reading, in this sense, is not passive reception but a situated engagement—one that continually brings a work back to life.

[12] Szlachcic (2006).

References

Fleck L (1986) On the crisis of 'reality' [1929]. In: Cognition and fact, Boston studies in the philosophy of science, vol 87. Springer, Dordrecht. https://doi.org/10.1007/978-94-009-4498-5_3

Hankinson J (2018) Aetiology. In: Pormann P (ed) The Cambridge companion to Hippocrates. CUP, Cambridge, pp 89–118

Hippocrates (1868) Collected works I (trans: Jones WHS). Harvard University Press, Cambridge

Jouanna J (1999) Hippocrates (trans: DeBevoise MB). John Hopkins Press, Baltimore

Laks A (2018) The concept of presocratic philosophy: its origin, development, and significance. Princeton University Press, Princeton

Laks A (2022) Plato's second republic: an essay on the laws. Princeton University Press, Princeton

Lloyd GE (1979) Magic, reason and experience: studies in the origin and development of greek science. CUP, Cambridge

Morrow GR (1993) Plato's Cretan city: A historical interpretation of the Laws. Princeton University Press, Princeton

Nowak L (2012) On the hidden unity of social and natural sciences. In: Brzechczyn K, Paprzycka K (eds) Thinking about provincialism in thinking (Poznań studies in the philosophy of the sciences and the humanities), vol 100. Rodopi, Amsterdam and New York, pp 15–50

Plato (1980) The laws of Plato (trans: Pangle TL). The University of Chicago Press, Chicago and London

Szlachcic K (2006) Konwencje, style myslenia i relatywizm. Kilka uwag o sporze I. Dambska – L. Fleck. Studia Philosophica Wratislaviensia vol. I, fasc. 1

The manufacturer's authorised representative in the EU is Springer Nature Customer Service Centre GmbH, Europaplatz 3, 69115 Heidelberg, Germany. If you have any concerns regarding our products, please contact ProductSafety@springernature.com

Printed and bound by CPI Group (UK) Ltd, Croydon, CR0 4YY
01/10/2026
02225968-0016